SNOWBLIND

SNOWBLIND

a brief career in the cocaine trade

ROBERT SABBAG

introduced by Howard Marks

CANONGATE

Edinburgh · New York · Melbourne

First published in the United States in 1976 by
the Bobs-Merrill company, Inc.

Published in 1998 and 2002 by Canongate Books Ltd,
14 High Street, Edinburgh EH1 1TE

This edition first published in 2007

1

The publisher would like to say a big thanks to Chris Sullivan who
first recommended this book. Here's to that session in The Wag.

British Library Cataloguing-in-Publication Data
A catalogue record for this book is available upon
request from the British Library

978 1 84195 820 0 (13-digit ISBN)
1 84195 820 4 (10-digit ISBN)

Typeset in Sabon by Palimpsest Book Production Limited,
Grangemouth, Stirlingshire

Printed and bound in Great Britain by Clays Ltd, St Ives plc

www.canongate.net

For Thomas J. Butler
Forsan et haec olim meminisse iuvabit . . .

CONTENTS

INTRODUCTION   xi

BREAKAWAY

1. INDIAN SUMMER   3
2. TALKING TO BOSWELL   21
3. BROWNSVILLE BREAKDOWN   41
4. AFTER MATH   58
5. AESTHETICS AND ANAESTHETICS   72

GOING SOUTH

6. A RAINY DAY IN SANTA MARTA   97
7. A WAY WITH THE SPOON   117
8. SNOWBOUND IN CARTHAGE   135
9. THE CARPENTER SAID NOTHING BUT . . .   150
10. ALKALOID ANNIE /
    POWER OF THE PRESS   174
11. HORSE LATITUDES   182
12. WHY DID YOU WRITE MY
    NAME IN THE SNOW?   196

RUNNING BLIND

13. BACK TO THE BORDER   223
14. JOURNEY OF THE MAGI   241
15. BLUES IN THE BOTTLE   260
16. THE HAWK AND THE HIRED MAN   273
17. AFTER THE FOX   289

EPILOGUE

I. NEW YORK   305
II. SOUTH AMERICA   308

APPENDICES

I. QUĀĀLUDES   313
II. CREDIT CARDS AND TRAVELER'S CHECKS   316
III. MEXICAN BROWN   319
IV. SPEED   320
V. MARIJUANA ABROAD   325
VI. A SWAN LEXICON   326
VII. COLOMBIA AND BIG BUSINESS   327
VIII. AIRLINE SECURITY   329
IX. DAY OF JUDGMENT   330

AUTHOR'S NOTE   331
AFTERWORD   335
INDEX   345

INTRODUCTION
HOWARD MARKS

Snowblind made me and a million other scammers feel totally at one with our profession, and I am greatly honoured to be asked to write an introduction to this re-issue.

I obviously wanted to re-read it. My copy had long disappeared in one of many busts, so I called a host of friends, libraries, and bookshops in what became an increasingly difficult search. Eventually, Olaf Tyaransen of Dublin's Hot Press temporarily parted with his copy, and I determined to discover just how much, if any, Robert Sabbag's book had dated in almost two decades.

I was travelling by train to London after a mad one in Manchester and I fished out *Snowblind*. In no time, I was wondering why I hadn't made a point of re-reading it years sooner. I blamed availability. There was so much I'd forgotten (an occupational hazard): the insightful articulation of how scamming is no more than a combination of waiting and winging it, preceded by the most labyrinthine of plans, fall backs, and security procedures, all somehow executed by personnel well off their trolleys; the explanation of how cocaine use was probably the most important factor in enabling America to understand the metric system; and most of all, the definition of dope, "Nature's way of saying high".

I was in the only carriage that allowed smoking. Dope-heads were bonding with yellow-haired old ladies, pipe-smoking gentry, and stressed-out executives. Lights and skins were shared with grace and pleasure. I smoked a joint.

A million centuries ago, plants said "High" to animals. Roots and seeds seduced tongues and stomachs. Vine, leaf, and resin interplayed with hand, heart, and mind. Drinking, smelling, and sucking were the order, but not the regulation, of the day.

And Nature said, "Higher".

A pyramid here and a pyramid there.

Gargling, sniffing, smoking, puking, and starving for God, Siva, and the Sun. Who'll have the booze? Who'll have the blow? Who'll have a line? Who gets the fun?

"I've got the dope. But stick to my brand. Use any other dope, and I'll kill you. Don't do this. Don't do that. That fruity stuff is verboten."

Nature asked, "Why?"

So fuck you, and let's smuggle cider into the Garden of Eden? Adam's apples are shite. Eve's cool. She calls it a SCAM. Smuggling Cocaine, Alcohol and Marijuana. But is the Snake a grass?

A legacy of murderous priests, psychopathic megalomaniacs, bloodthirsty colonialist rapists, sadistic puritans, non-inhalers, and other manifestations of sinister evil have ensured that chemically induced changes of states of mind are rewarded by imprisonment and other socially acceptable forms of torture. The Society of Satanic Spoilsports feel comforted by our suffering. Our happiness disturbs them. Congratulations to alcohol. It's done well in the rat race for the survival of the fittest psychoactive. But not without God's creative efforts in blood transfusion: the wine of Christ: 'Do this and forget your short-term memory problem.'

Murdering Spanish bullies fronted up as God's servants and discovered that Indians from the Andes had been chewing coca leaves for three thousand years, getting high, and not getting come-down hangovers. Were Catholic priests really convinced that the effects of the leaf resulted from a pact between the devil and the Indians? Not really, but nothing haunts fraudulent missionaries more than heathens getting high. The Indians worked harder when stoned, so coca didn't bother purveyors of the Protestant work ethic as Nature said, "High. But it's a lie."

The Satanic Spoilsports saw the workers were in too good a groove. They didn't lose their breath, didn't feel tired, didn't feel hungry, and felt very sexy. And what was worse, they shared their highs with Blacks. Bang them away. Lock them up. Call them murderers, rapists, and friends, except Uncle Tom. Nature said, 'Try.'

So how can we get the leaves we want, the herbs we want, the grapes we want. Nature said, 'Lie.'

And it came to pass that the world became full of scammers. Never before have so many laws been broken without a single pang of conscience. False names, forged passports, phoney driving licences, money laundering, tax evasion, customs dodging, stolen vehicles, illegal planes, false documents, lies, lies, and lots more new lies. Who cares? It's all for the cause. It's not our fault they won't let people get high. Anyway, the world of international dope dealing is fun. It's fucking great!

I began my dope smuggling career in the late '60s. Twenty years later, I was busted by the United States Drug Enforcement Administration (DEA) and was looking at life in prison. Had I not been busted until 1993, the same quantity of dope would have guaranteed me the federal death penalty by lethal injection. Zachary Swan, the paradigm of dope dealers and central character of *Snowblind*, would have also been sentenced to death had he performed his scams today rather than in the seventies.

An early copy of *Snowblind* was personally delivered to me by a New York dope dealer on December 31st, 1979. It could have been Zachary Swan. It wasn't. He was called Billy Bronx. But Billy Bronx and I had just landed fifteen tons of Colombia's finest weed on a remote Scottish island. Shortwave radios, walkie-talkies, scanners, nightscopes, Zodiacs, pulleys, anoraks, thermals, jeeps, ropes, formed a new tidemark as a mountain of marijuana heaved out of the sea near Holy Loch, the bastion of British/American defence. The Loch Ness monster had turned into the marijuana Messiah from the Highlands. The '90s will be cool. Carter's compassion will take care of Thatcher's brass. 'We'd better start the next scam before they legalise the shit,' said Billy Bronx. "Read this when you're chilling out, Man. It's on toot, not reefer, but it's really about us kind of guys. It's the only book that has ever been written about scamming. It will always be the best one."

Within months, I could not meet a dealer of any dope who was not reading (or had not already read) *Snowblind*. It became the scammer's Bible. Hunter S. Thompson and the book's reviewers have said the rest.

Then came the Satanic Years, the rule of Reagan, Major Thatcher, and the inappropriately named Bush. 'Don't smoke. Don't sniff. Don't swallow. Just say 'No', followed by, "Don't even read about it. Don't say 'Know'." It's no longer literature if it's about scamming.'

Consequently, many English language libraries and bookshelves have had glaring omissions. Primarily through the extraordinarily talented writing of Irvine Welsh, true tales of drug culture are now occasionally permitted by the mainstream. There's a long way to go: people are still being incarcerated for writing informative books on the horticulture of naturally occurring therapeutic herbs, and all kinds of scammers are writing their accounts. As predicted by Billy Bronx, *Snowblind* has stood the test of time. It's still the best.

BREAKAWAY

1
INDIAN SUMMER

Zachary Swan is not a superstitious man, but he is a very careful one. Like any professional gambler, he has survived by taking only calculated risks. So, in October of 1972, when he decided to throw a party to celebrate his most recent return to New York, he decided to throw a small one, and his caution was inspired less by the fact that it was Friday the thirteenth than by the compelling reality that on the mantelpiece above his suitcase there were three and a half kilograms of 89-percent-pure cocaine.

The cocaine had entered the United States that morning in the hollows of three Colombian souvenirs fashioned out of Madeira wood. They included a long, colorfully painted rolling pin, the symbol of marital bliss in Colombia; one rough-hewn statue, twenty inches high, of the Blessed Virgin; and a hand-wrought effigy of an obscure tribal head, about the size of a coconut. The fill had been made a week earlier in Bogotá. The load had passed U.S. Customs at Kennedy Airport, New York. It was carried through and declared: "Souvenirs."

The arrival of these artifacts at Zachary Swan's beach house in East Hampton, Long Island, launched a celebration which would not end until the following morning. It began at eight p.m. when the Madeira head was cleaved top-dead-center across the parietal lobe with the cold end of a chisel. Within minutes of this exotic lobotomy — a procedure reminiscent in equal measure of desperation combat surgery and a second-rate burglary attempt — the skull yielded up 500 grams of high-grade uncut cocaine, double-wrapped in clear plastic.

By the time the skull, which looked like that of a shrapnel victim, was reduced to ashes around the andirons of the fireplace, the celebration had assumed ceremony and the coke was performing fabulous and outlawed miracles in the heads for which it had been ultimately intended. They belonged to Swan himself; his girlfriend Alice Haskell, twenty-four, a children's fashion designer; Charles Kendricks, thirty, an Australian national and sometime employee of Swan; and Kendricks's girlfriend Lillian Giles, twenty-three, also an Australian. The Bolivian brain food they had ingested was only one course in a sublime international feast which featured French wine, English gin, Lebanese hashish, Colombian cannabis, and a popular American synthetic known pharmacologically as methaqualone.

It is difficult to verify at exactly what point in the proceedings (possibly over dessert) Swan's originally calculated risk became a long shot. The party went out of control somewhere in the early hours before dawn, and the steps he had taken in the beginning to minimize his losses were eventually undermined by the immutable laws of chemistry — his mind, simply, had turned to soup. He was up against the law of averages with a head full of coke. The smart money pulled out, and the odds mounted steadily. By sunrise, Swan was beaten by the spread.

Amagansett, New York, is situated 120 miles due east of Manhattan on the coastal underbelly of Long Island. One of several oceanfront resorts on the fringes of Long Island's potato belt, it owes its maritime climate to the temperate waters in the leeward drift of the Gulf Stream. The region was abandoned by Algonquins in the wake of colonial sprawl, a mounting overture to Manifest Destiny which brought New England to the outer reaches of the Empire State, and Amagansett, a tribute to the Indians in name only, is the custodian of a Puritan heritage. The whales are gone but the weathervanes remain. An occasional widow's walk acknowledges the debt to the sea. Anchors and eagles abound. George Washington would have been proud to sleep here.

In the off-season, order prevails. Time struggles to stand still. But when the weather breaks and the trade winds come in, the elders of Amagansett, like their colonial predecessors and the Algonquins before them, find themselves volunteers in a counterassault on cultural blight — minutemen knee-deep in the onslaught of souvenirs, fast-food and ersatz antiques. A kind of thug capitalism asserts itself. The tourists who come screeching down upon the town and the local retail sharks who surface to feed on them provoke an embarrassing display of provincial paranoia; and every summer, the town fathers, helpless, unhinged, watch their community move one irreversible step closer to the dark maw of the twentieth century, visibly shaken by what they consider to be a pronounced threat to Amagansett's Puritan soul.

Their dread has taken an inevitable turn. Amagansett has

become a working model for an aggression/response approach to municipal government. Symptomatic of such an approach is a curious brand of frontier law enforcement, characterized by an allegiance to the principle that ". . . we got a nice quiet community here, son . . .," dialogue resonant of hanging judges, pistol whippings, and the application of rifle butts to the dental work. You've got until sundown, as it were. In Amagansett the Wyatt Earp spirit runs especially high between the months of May and September, but a residual strain lingers through late autumn, tapering off appropriately around Thanksgiving, after which only the locals have an opportunity to break the law.

This is what Zachary Swan, forty-six, a pioneer whose embrace of the Puritan ethic had never been an all-encompassing one, would come up against on the morning of October 14. He and his friends would be arrested on the beach at sunrise and charged with public intoxication. And out of this circumstantial confrontation between the energetic bounty hunters of Amagansett, still juiced on adrenalin generated in the summer tourist-hunts, and a man who in six months had spent more money on cocaine alone than he had paid in state and local income taxes in twenty years — out of this head-on collision would grow a Federal investigation spanning at least two continents, twice as many international boundaries, and criminal jurisdictions as diverse as those covered by the United States Department of the Treasury and the traffic division of the East Hampton, Long Island, Police Department.

At five a.m. Zachary Swan, surrounded by $100,000 worth of cocaine, was smiling. He was smiling at the Madonna over his fireplace and dreaming of an island off the coast of Ceylon. Sprawled on the floor athwart three sleeping dogs, struggling to stay conscious, he looked like a besotted country squire out of the pages of an eighteenth-century novel.

Dawn was approaching. The room was quiet. The party had downshifted dramatically. All motor activity not essential to life had been suspended in the interest of the cardiac muscles. The body, in the grip of the downs, was making sacrifices.

Somebody had an idea (remarkable under the circumstances).

"Let's go to the beach and watch the sunrise."

A response, identifiable only in the deepest methaqualone funk, struggled to solitary life somewhere across the room. It contained many vowels. It was affirmative. Call it a sentence. A phrase. Someone had answered.

(We are on the threshold of human interchange here, speech, verbal commerce along the barren avenues of Quāālude. City. Communication at this level, although sophisticated in its own way, can best be described as haphazard. It is a kind of space-age remodeling of traditional counterintelligence techniques — scrambled messages, predistorted transmissions, sympathetically programmed transceivers — a kind of mojo cryptography which contains no universal cipher and is efficient only when two people are doing the same kind of dope.)*

Out of the chance marriage between this one remarkably conceived idea and the crypto-response which followed, there blossomed, like a flower in time-lapse motion, what was soon to be a legitimate conversation. It was force-bloomed according to the principle governing the first law

* See Appendix I.

of psychogravitational dynamics: *The quickest way to come off* downs *is to do some* ups. Follow the Quāāludes with two or three lines of coke and you can throw even the most desultory dialogue into high gear. There is order in the Universe.

Monosyllables became murmurs:

"The . . . sun."

An odds-on favorite to rise.

Murmurs became phrases:

"See . . . the . . . sun."

But nothing was taken for granted.

That the sun would not rise was a remote possibility, but one which nevertheless marshalled a certain amount of attention. Unnecessary risks, such as standing up, were postponed while an analysis of the odds for and against the sun's coming up at all was made. This delay was characteristic of severe psychochemical shock, but surprisingly it provided the first hard evidence of progress. (It marked the appearance of key polysyllabic words — participles, certain adjectives, an occasional predicate nominative — and diphthongs. A subordinate clause was pending.) The Quāāludes were still throwing their weight around, but it was a futile display of power; their defeat was imminent, and signaled moments later:

"We haven't got much time," someone said.

A clear, audible statement. The cocaine was closing in. A decision, the final factor in the psychogravitational equation, was inevitable now. It would lead to activity and thus certify the successful application of Newton's first law to the infinite possibilities of drug abuse. In fact the decision came almost immediately, a tribute to the quality of this particular blow of coke:

"Let's go," someone decided.

And so, at the zenith of the cocaine ecliptic, activity was resumed. Status quo. What goes up must come down; what goes down must come up. Q.E.D. Physics, man. But now, with four people behind some heavy coke (one of them a certified Frank Sinatra fan), anything was possible.

Phase II . . . Overdrive. Out-and-out mobilization. Tide tables were checked. Weather information from around the world gathered. Analyzed. Data was collated and patterns were charted. An expeditionary force was provisioned.

"We'll need plenty of drugs."

Yes. Of course. Consider the possibilities. Imagine the appropriateness of it. Standing in the Atlantic tide, welcoming the sun back to the United States of America. We, the people, bent, holding enough dope to fix three Kentucky Derbies. Enough to capture the imagination of . . . yes . . . even the Miami Dolphins. How fitting. How just. (How dangerous.)

They chose the Volkswagen because it was aimed at the beach, not unanimously unaware, certainly, that they were also choosing the only car in the driveway that could float. With their ranks bolstered, and their oxygen supply severely depleted, by the added company of three hyperventilating Labrador retrievers, a total, then, of twenty legs, each jockeying for position, any two feet at the ends of which might have been operating the accelerator and the clutch (the brake, reportedly, was used rarely, if at all), Swan and his friends reached the ocean through the combined application of dead reckoning and the gratuitous hand of God. (It is whispered in the cloakrooms of America's drug underground that *He* looks out for the heavy user.)

A joint, eighty-dollar Colombian, passing clockwise

around the cockpit, outlined their efforts in a surreal, purple haze, and acting as a sort of gyroscope it provided slight, but presumably adequate, stabilization. It also pushed everyone's carboxy-hemoglobin level to the red line, bringing on that shameful and subversive Reefer Madness (manifest only in the Labradors, however) hinted at in arcane government manuscripts. It was quality dope, and its sharers were suffused with the magnificence and intergalactic splendor of star travelers. But at their energy/output ratio, given the specific gravity of their load and the negligible horsepower of the Volkswagen, they looked more like the Joads leaving Oklahoma.

> Hark, hark,
> The dogs do bark,
> The beggars are coming to town;
> Some in rags,
> And some in jags,
> And one in a velvet gown.
>
> "Hark, Hark,"
> from *Mother Goose*

They erupted like circus clowns out of the overstuffed automobile and onto the beach, a tumbling agglomeration of weird, multicolored ragamuffins. For a moment it was hard to tell the humans from the quadrupeds. And then the dogs hit the water. It was not long before the idea caught on, and within minutes they were all stripped down, ready to celebrate the Rites of Spring — late.

The sun was on the horizon and all seven were bobbing in the surf when in the distance an intruder appeared. A jogger.

He approached, moving at an even pace along the water-line, his face flushed, his breathing steady, his body drenched with sweat and glory, radiating that all-American, infinite faith in the cardiovascular benefits of discomfort. He was about fifty-five and well-fed. Swan recognized him as the owner of a local nursery. It looked as if he were going to pass by, until he saw the strange variety of clothing, like a forbidden invitation, leading to the water. He stopped. And then he looked. When his eyes met Swan's, chivalry was dead. He did not return the smile — admittedly a bizarre one, glassy at best, but everything Swan could muster — he simply stared, squinting against the sun, saying nothing. He was still, and he remained that way, in mute confrontation.

And now Swan, forsaking the smile, staring back in mute defiance, returning the look ... *yes, we're out here swimming ... stoned ... Immaculate ... spawning on the current ... all of us ... breeding tiny and rebellious monsters ... the Enemy ... us ... go on, ... lock up your daughters ... scream ... you sad and friendless man ... you'll dream of us tonight ... I know you're going to turn us in, you son of a bitch.*

Without a word, the man left. He continued along the beach and out of sight.

"He's going to turn us in," Swan said.

And he was right.

Somewhere in the accumulated misspending of what was someday to become known as his youth, Zachary Swan was taken aside by a man much older than he and confronted with what, at the time, was quaintly referred to as the cold truth about life. "Son," he was told, "there's no free lunch." He did not believe it then, and now, for the first time in forty-six years, Zachary Swan had hard evidence to show in support of his opinion.

"Mine was rare without the pickles," he said, "and give me a side of fries with that . . ."

The chow wagon moved rapidly along the cell block, and Swan was left with Suffolk County's answer to winning the hearts and minds of the people.

". . . hold the ketchup," he mumbled.

Three days in Riverhead and he was as close as he had ever come in his life to an overdose . . . *another jailbird, DOA/ HAMBURGERS, poor bastard didn't even get the tourniquet off, cover him up, nurse* . . . the mayor must be from Texas, Swan thought, cow country; a Hindu would starve here . . . *Hare Krishna, pardner.*

Swan washed the dry lump down with a calculated intake of jail coffee, a 70-percent solution of refined sugar, viscous, the consistency of syrup. A diabetic would not last an hour in the slammer — one shot of this coffee in the right place and you could throw an eight-cylinder Chevy onto the scrap heap forever. Swan swallowed the slush and felt the soft embolus of the hamburger suzette skidding down his esophagus into that vast wasteland once remembered as his stomach.

On Saturday afternoon, just prior to its second ration of ground beef, that same stomach had taken the punch that was to slow it down for the next two years. It was delivered by a police officer in plain clothes. He was looking at Swan:

"We found drugs in your house," he said.

Swan's established digestive patterns changed radically and forever at that moment. It was the beginning of a progress report. One that would grow tedious. He would become indignant at what the same detective delivered in the way of an uppercut:

"The word is out that you carry a gun."

The word is out? This cop either watches a lot of television or he reads *The Daily News*. I'm an executive, for Christ's sake. I belong to the Westchester Country Club. Charlie, I own stock in some of the largest corporations in the world. My wife was on the Dick Cavett Show. What is this guy talking about? The air duct, Charlie, drop it down the fucking air duct.

While Zachary Swan was parting with his stomach, Charles Kendricks, code name the Hungarian, was parting with a sterling silver coke spoon of great sentimental value. He dropped it through the grill of the air shaft that ventilated his cell on the second floor of the Suffolk County courthouse. His nose twitched goodbye. Where had he gone wrong, he wondered.

They had been busted on the beach. Two patrol cars. That was understandable. It was a slow night and the thought of two young women swimming in the nude must have appealed to the boys on the night shift. Kendricks tried to imagine them spilling their coffee when the carburetors kicked in. They got there fast, but not before the Volkswagen was under way . . . *the Volkswagen, the latest reincarnation of the Dachau boxcar, the unimpeachable symbol of the Fatherland's relentless effort to demonstrate that the Devil himself prefers canned food.* Lillian, at the wheel, had just lost the game of musical laps that began when the four shivering getaways paused in their escape to fight over the three warm-blooded dogs, a regrettable delay under the circumstances, he thought, but then, too, it had taken them a while to get into their clothes. At the time Kendricks blamed it on the earth — spinning so fast, while at the same time . . . *if you can believe it, revolving around the bloody sun.* He remembered Swan trying to get both feet into his pants at once — cutting corners this way, he supposed . . . *but not standing up, man*! He recalled that Swan mumbled a lot . . . *yes, officer, the Kendrickses here, our friends from down under, are members of the Australian Olympic Team, swimmers, you see, and they have just crawled in from Sydney . . . my wife and I were not expecting them until tomorrow, of course . . . but then the Gulf Stream and what not . . . Gibraltar tomorrow, isn't it, Charles* . . . then, "Follow us . . . public intoxication . . . stick around . . ." and now the gun . . . all that dope . . . it all came back to Kendricks, whose nose had started running. The spoon disappeared with a forlorn rattle.

Fingerprints and photographs. More hamburgers. Then the handcuffs. At one a.m. the four prisoners were reunited before a judge and arraigned. The men and women were then driven separately to Riverhead, home of the Suffolk County Jail. They were disinfected and wardrobed. And then they were confined. The Ides of October. Sunday mornin', comin' down.

On the night of the party, Swan had loaned Kendricks some clothes, clearly a mistake, for when they were discovered to be wearing matching briefs, the processing officer ordered the guard on duty to "put these guys on different floors." They saw each other only once in the four days that Swan was there. On that occasion Swan learned his first lesson in prison discipline. Kendricks was standing four places ahead of him in the physical examination lineup, and Swan, who had been out of boot camp for at least thirty years, started forward to talk to him. He was rescued by his fellow inmates . . . *where you goin', man, they're gonna smack you* . . . who were obliged to demonstrate the series of casual pirouettes by which forward and backward progress along a supervised line is correctly achieved ... *see, man, you're just talkin' to me for a minute here, and we're just shufflin' our feet, right? and then just like magic you're lookin' that way and I'm lookin' this way, and there you are, and your friend's comin' this way, see that.* And you've both got all your teeth. It took them about three minutes to get together.

"How are you holding up, Charlie?"

"The coffee sucks."

"What did they tell you about phone calls?"

"I reckon they're going to let me make one after lunch. Jesus, if it's another bloody hamburger I'll shit."

"Call Seymour," Swan said.

"Where's your beard gone?" Charlie asked him.

"They made me shave it."

"The bastards."

"There's something wrong with these people, Charlie. They take a mug shot of me with a full beard. And then they shave it off. Can you figure that out? I can't figure it out."

"You're near fifty. You've brought the average age in here up to approximately twenty-two. You tell me why they have to play Frank Sinatra and Tony Bennett on the fucking Muzak."

"You call Seymour. Give him Sandy's name. I'll get us a lawyer."

Kendricks yawned. He nodded and turned around.

"Charlie, watch out for this guy, I hear he goes for fellas your age. Keep an eye on him. Don't let the stethoscope fool you; if he smiles, you're in trouble. I'll write soon."

Charlie made the call. Sandy never came through.

*   *   *

Swan opened his eyes. Another bad night. The man in the cell next to his had been masturbating again. Late. Their beds were each part of the same bunk, one elongated bedspring built into and passing through the concrete wall that separated them — the man had been at it again, and with every stroke Swan's bed shook. Jail, he decided, was miserable.

The library boys came around. They preceded the hamburger by about an hour.

"Bookmobile."

"Terrific."

"What are you in for?" they wanted to know.

Swan told them. They looked at one another.

"Don't stand trial here," was all they could say.

A black prisoner who occupied the cell opposite Swan's overheard the conversation with the library boys and felt obliged to say something to Swan. It amounted to:

"Hey, man, you didn't happen to get any of that stuff in here, did you?"

The hamburger came.

While Zachary Swan was washing his hamburger suzette down in the Riverhead Jail, a young Canadian man with blond hair and a horse-latitudes tan was stepping from a jet onto the runway at Kennedy Airport. He was traveling alone and traveling light. And he was traveling on a false passport. And in addition to his expense money, the young man was carrying $5,000 in cold American cash. Within an hour, Swan, by way of his Constitutional rights, would have a lawyer and have his bail reduced. Within two hours, by way of a noble gesture, Swan would have $1,000 in cash in his hand, and the young Canadian, who had come from nowhere, would be booking a flight south.

* * *

"Who was that?" his lawyer asked when the four prisoners were released and eating their first lunch together in five days.

"A friend of mine," Swan said.

"He must be a very good friend."

"He is. We're in the same business. We've known each other for about two years now."

"What's his name?"

"Canadian Jack."

"What's his real name?"

"Your guess is as good as mine. I've known him pretty well for about two years, and for two years I've known him only as Canadian Jack. In my business you don't ask your friends a lot of questions. And you especially don't ask them, 'What's your real name?'"

Swan's lawyer smiled.

Ernie Peace, of Peace, Lehrman & Gullo, Mineola, Long Island, had been recommended to Swan by a personal friend. It was only a coincidence, according to Swan, that the friend was, by profession, a narcotics detective. Swan had had to assume that there was no one better qualified to rate a lawyer than a cop, and he was right. Ernie Peace was one of the best. A lot of narcotics detectives thought so, and many of them had found out the hard way. Peace sat across from Swan dressed in an unimpressive double-knit suit, a white shirt and a blue tie. He was a shorter man than Swan, about the same age. His build was average, his hair was short, and all in all he was a very unprepossessing fellow. He was one of those people who seemed always to be thinking about anything but what you were saying, looking here, looking there, taking it easy, preoccupied with everything else but you — he was also one of those people who five minutes later would quote verbatim what you had just said. He was smiling now, a kind of smile Swan had seen many times. Swan was pleased. It was a gambler's smile, pleasant, shy, and not a few parts lethal. Ernie Peace was measuring his man.

What Ernie Peace had on his hands was a middle-aged cloak-and-dagger freak, a man who betrayed a wealth of information on bugging devices, police technique, international drug traffic, Customs procedure, organized crime, pseudo-tribal FBI newspeak, and every other contingency covering his work; Zachary Swan was a man who possessed an encyclopedic knowledge of every conceivable high-level money transaction in the world. He even knew how to beat the phone company out of a dime.

Zachary Swan was tall and trim. His posture would have embarrassed his father. He had a strong handshake, an engaging smile, and a gentle voice an octave below middle C. He had liar's eyes. They were bright blue, cool, and very hard to ignore. He had a small birthmark on his left cheekbone. His hair was short — prison-length — and thick, going from brown to gray. He looked his age. It was because he did not act his age that he was here today. He was wearing about $600 worth of clothes; he was drinking a Martini and chain-smoking Kools. He handled himself well for a man under the gun.

"O.K.," Peace said, "the way it's going to work is like this. I can get the rest of you off. The DA's not really concerned about you anyway. But I want the whole truth. Everything. And then," he said to Swan, "we'll see what we can do about getting *you* out of this mess. Now, they are going to get cooperation from the Federal authorities, so I want you to tell me what the Feds know."

"I don't think they can make a smuggling charge stick. I covered myself pretty well."

"How?"

"Well," he said, "smuggling's easy." He lit a cigarette. "Anybody can do it, and a lot of people do, believe me. They do it a million ways. Some are smart, some are very stupid — for instance there are people who still get busted with false-bottom suitcases, which I want to say right now is something I never used. It is absolutely the worst way to smuggle anything. It's a sucker move. It's the first thing a Customs agent looks for — before he even takes anything out. He puts one finger inside and one finger outside, and if his fingers don't find each other you're in trouble. He's got a ruler and he measures. If the math goes against you, forget it.

"If you've got any brains at all, smuggling is easy. It's covering yourself every step of the way that's tough. If one of my carriers gets busted, he walks away. He's got excuses down the line. No way they can break his story. And that's the trick. You've got to prop up your carriers, because if they talk, you're both finished. My people stand up because they know they are going to walk. Is the smoke bothering you?"

"No, go ahead."

"Most smugglers use mules, usually a girl, and she gets paid $1,000 a kilo to walk the load through Customs. Now, tell me, how are you going to say it's not yours if it's strapped to your back? And when the mule gets busted, nothing she can say is going to help her. She's finished, because her man's disappeared. It's really sad, but it happens all the time. And that's the way most smugglers operate. Say you're carrying. He's paid you a thousand and given you an airline ticket. You're broke, you want to get home. One of his lieutenants follows the load through Customs — if you get tossed, it's you and the lions. He's gone. I don't operate that way. If you carry for me, you're guaranteed to walk away."

Peace sat back in his chair and looked around the table.

It was apparent that the others had heard the sales pitch before. He did not pursue the Federal question any further. He simply nodded and leaned forward.

"Now, they found a lot of cocaine in your house. And they found a gun. I'd be interested to know why you told them where the gun was buried. Apparently all they found in the house were the bullets."

"That's right. The gun was buried under the pebbles of the patio."

"And you told them that."

"Right."

"Did they threaten you?"

"No."

"What happened?"

"They said if I didn't tell them, they were going to take the house apart board by board until they found it."

"So?"

Swan looked at his friends. Then he looked back at his lawyer.

"Well, you see, they missed the load."

"What do you mean they missed the load?"

"You said they found a lot of cocaine in the house."

"They did."

"How much?"

"The police say several ounces."

"Yeah, that's what the judge said when he arraigned us. I wasn't sure."

"That's what it is. And that's how the charge reads."

Swan put his fork down. He looked at his attorney:

"Yeah, well, they missed the load, then. You see, on the mantelpiece, in the house, right now, there are three kilos of cocaine that they *didn't* find. And if the police lab is right, it's about 89 percent pure."

2

TALKING TO BOSWELL

Zachary Swan was born at the peak of the Jazz Age with a silver spoon in his mouth. That he would spend the middle years of his life with that same spoon in his nose entered the realm of possibility at about the age of sixteen. Up until that time he behaved like any other boy his age forced to deal with servants around the house and a country club around the corner.

"While all the other kids were going to the creek swimming hole, I was at the country club pool, ordering club sandwiches and milk. I was playing golf at the age of nine."

An audience with his father, known to many simply as the Colonel, was a rare event in those days, one which required a visit to the golf course, a visit which Swan made infrequently. The Colonel, by all accounts, was a man with whom Swan had only chromosomes in common. "I loved him . . . but I never liked him," Swan would say.

Swan was closer to his mother, a woman whose struggle with alcoholism ended in 1965 in a fire which destroyed the house in which she slept and in which she had lived alone since her separation from the Colonel two years earlier. "She collected antique stoves ... painted them red and planted geraniums in them. They were all over the yard. They looked nice, but it was hell if you went home at night drunk. All my life she called me Cookie. She did it once in Grand Central Station when I was home on leave. "Mother," I told her, 'you don't call a Marine Cookie.'"

Swan shares his father's estate with an older sister, who lives now in Florida and whose privacy he is determined to protect. The Colonel died two months after Swan's arrest, at the age of seventy-five.

Swan is reluctant to introduce his family into a discussion of the events which presaged his decision to take that first roundtrip excursion on Avianca Airlines in the fall of 1970. The life that led him to the Riverhead Jail shortly after his forty-sixth birthday began, as far as he sees it, when he was sixteen years old and a sophomore at the Iona Preparatory School in New Rochelle (Westchester County), New York. It was there that an inevitable synthesis of wealth and leisure, generated under the catalysis of the Catholic Church, rendered its first volatile by-product.

At Iona Prep, with the help of a classmate, Swan controlled dice games on the academy handball courts — he had a natural aptitude for math — and managed to squander the proceeds before his capture by the Christian Brothers became imminent. His aptitude for geography found an outlet in the occasional daytrips he and his friends made to New York City, where they bluffed their way into the Times Square burlesque houses. Swan discovered Ann Corio at the age of seventeen. He took up cigarette smoking in deference to his newly acquired manhood, and with the War at hand adopted the hard-edged look of an OSS agent, hardly the rage at the university-oriented Iona Prep. His diploma from that institution, awarded reluctantly, came after a sophisticated and diligent application of blackmail to his Latin professor (an unfortunate man whose career with the Christian Brothers was a brief one) and a bribe well placed with that faction of the administration responsible for supplying the graduating class with a commencement speaker. Swan's father was a personal friend of Jim Crowley, the Fordham football coach, formerly one of Notre Dame's Four Horsemen. When the best-laid plans of the Brothers went awry, Crowley was called upon at the last minute to give Iona Prep's 1944 commencement address.

Before pursuing a higher education, Swan served for three years in the United States Marine Corps, a tour of duty which took him to Japan at the end of World War II. (His only other military experience, the Colonel notwithstanding, was an unsuccessful attempt at the age of fifteen to join the Free French. He and three classmates set out for Quebec in a stolen car, financing their journey with the change taken from an unattended March of Dimes receptacle in a Connecticut movie theatre. They were stopped at the Canadian border and held until a mother of one of the boys arrived to take them home. Because they were minors, they were detained in a jail reserved for women, fated to cool their heels behind a glass partition instead of behind bars. It was the cruelest blow of all.) If his military career is significant, it is so in terms of the opportunity it gave him to measure his patriotism — after an honorable discharge, he was able to appreciate the fact that opportunity knocks but once.

His university days were not uneventful. That he chose to spend them in Coral Gables, Florida, was a tribute to his respect for formal education. On the GI Bill and more than ample subsidies from home, he became an accomplished swimmer. In Florida he learned how to squander his money on women — the Marine Corps had failed him there — and, in their company, how to drink his Martinis dry. And it was from Coral Gables, as a college student, that he made his first boat trip to Bimini. He did not know it then, but what he would learn about that island's Customs procedure, and what he had learned in four years about the Florida coastline, would someday be worth the equivalent in American dollars of at least three Ivy League educations. He earned his degree from the University of Miami through the same diligence and sophistication he had applied to the acquisition of his high school diploma. He printed it himself. His craftsmanship was so refined (his father's was a packaging business, and Swan was no stranger to industrial arts) that he managed to sell the overrun to fellow students.

But as he had been sure they would, Swan's salad days soon came to an end, and he spent the balance of his youth preparing for old age. After college he joined his father's packaging company as a sales executive, and for the next seventeen years he observed, as honestly and conscientiously as he possibly could, the timeworn rituals of New York's business community. As a salesman, he handled the accounts of some of the country's most prestigious cosmetics firms. He earned a good salary, belonged to the finest clubs in New York, and enjoyed the friendship of many prominent people.

"I handled Helena Rubinstein, Revlon, Coty, Arden, Pond's — good accounts. I designed the Heaven Scent package, the Gino Paoli logo, packages for Richard Hudnut, Eileen Ford. Some of my designs are still on the market. I was underpaid for the volume of sales I was doing — my payment was always 'someday, son, you're going to be president of the company.'" But it was lucrative. Everybody got a good living out of it, especially my uncles and my father.

They were driving Cadillacs and belonged to country clubs in Westchester. I was living in Manhattan. I was taking art directors to the opera, buyers to the football games, I'd go fishing with the fishermen. And I belonged to all the clubs that were necessary and fashionable at the time."

Swan's wedding in 1958 was not at all necessary, but it was more than fashionable. His wife, Yvonne, was Norman Norell's ace model. Norell designed the wedding gown and provided the bridesmaids. It was a lavish affair. The reception went on forever. The marriage lasted four months. In 1960 Swan married a girl from Brooklyn, an Eileen Ford fashion model who was later to become one of the founding members of the New York Radical Feminists; a few years after her separation from Swan, Holly appeared on the Dick Cavett Show, wearing a Superman T-shirt, debating *Playboy* publisher Hugh Hefner on the subject of Women's Rights. Divorced in 1966, Swan and Holly remain close friends.

"Holly and I were out six nights a week, either at a party or for dinner — El Morocco, Orsini's — we belonged to Le Club and we were swinging around with the jet set. We were invited to discotheque openings, parties in Southampton — I had all kinds of energy and drive and didn't sleep. I didn't know it then, but I was hooked on speed. In 1964 I got a prescription for diet pills from a doctor and kept refilling it — for six years. It was that plus a lot of alcohol. Holly was making $40,000 a year, so between the two of us, with my twelve-five, we were going through $52,000 a year, not counting my expense account, less twelve or thirteen thousand for taxes. We never had a nickel and we always had a bank loan. Our bills were astronomical. Our Bloomingdale's bill one year had to be $7,000. I had twenty suits. I was wearing fifty-dollar shoes. Holly never wore the same thing twice. We were spending fifty dollars a week in *tips*. More. Headwaiter ten dollars, the waiter ten dollars, maybe a hundred a week in tips alone. That's where $5,000 went. But you don't know it. You don't even feel it or see it. You're drunk and you're high and you don't know a thing."

> They dined on mince and slices of quince,
> Which they ate with a runcible spoon;
> And hand in hand, on the edge of the sand,
> They danced by the light of the moon.

> "The Owl and the Pussycat'
> EDWARD LEAR

Swan's closest friend at the time was, and always had been, Mike Riordan, his partner in the prep school dice games. Riordan, the Irish heir to a Jewish department store (his father, a vice-president of Abraham & Strauss in New York, had taken over the bankrupt Stern's Department Store in 1932, and by 1940 owned a controlling interest), had graduated from Cornell, and after experience as a mutual fund wholesaler on Wall Street established his own company in Los Angeles. Riordan was loaded, and in the habit of carrying large amounts of his money in cash. One night he threw $8,000 on the bar of the Stork Club in answer to a challenge. (It is said he did it to impress a woman.) When he was not spending money, he was giving it away to anyone who needed it. Bums loved him.

Swan and Riordan had never given up gambling — in fact, the only thing they enjoyed more was taking advantage of some other gambler's greed. Whenever they were together and an opportunity presented itself, they engineered a swindle of one kind or another — either on a bookie, on a rich friend, or on another swindler. Past-posting bookies was one of their favorites.

Riordan had access to a Minneapolis wire (he subscribed for thirty dollars a month) which was reporting local track results on a simultaneous feed — it worked on the wig-wag and was running about 95 percent accurate. He knew the name of every bartender in New York who would turn the clock back for a cut, and he and Swan — one on the phone, one buying drinks for the bookie — were running almost as well as the wire. If Riordan, waiting for a bookie, happened to mention that the Professor was coming over, it meant that the bookie was working for *him*, and the flim-flam was on whoever his and Swan's drinking companions happened to be. Swan would man the phone and flash confusing signals . . . *shit, it was my fault, I'm sorry*. The bookie would clean the conspirators out and leave — Riordan, cursing his luck, would hit his friends for a fifty-dollar charge for the wire and collect from the Professor later.

Anything worth doing was worth doing wrong, and anything worth gambling on was worth cheating at. It had become a habit. Since their prep school days they had been cheating at liar's poker. With the signals they had developed, they could communicate their respective serial numbers within two declarations. Whenever a bank note came into view, they would sandwich its owner between them, suggest a game of liar's poker, and collaborate until they had won the price of the drinks at stake. As Riordan's business expanded, so did his bankroll (by the time he was forty-one, he was worth over thirty million dollars), but even while closing a twenty-million-dollar deal with a corporate president, he was not above cheating the man out of twenty dollars in a game of liar's poker. "That's cash," he would say.

At his engagement party, Riordan grabbed Swan by the arm:

"Here's a guy you've got to meet," he said. "We can play some liar's poker with him."

"Who is he?" Swan asked.

"Thomas Dewey. The governor."

He dragged Swan over:

"Governor, this is my friend [Zachary Swan]. You probably know his uncle."

Riordan would say anything to anyone.

Swan and Riordan could beat a bookie in a bar, and they could beat him on the way to the track in the back seat of a limousine. They could beat bookies on football games, and by handing out phony business cards wherever they went they could beat them without beating them. Through Swan and a Bermuda bank account, Riordan could sell his unlisted and lettered stock, and through Riordan and a phony heart condition, Swan could beat any Park Avenue doctor out of twenty or thirty amyl nitrates. (The headwaiter at El Morocco told Swan that after closing every night he would find two or three hundred broken Vaporole capsules on the floor of the dining room, most of them under the better tables.)

"One night we were at Le Club doing poppers, and some friends of ours came in with Mickey Mantle. Mike and I bought him Scotch all night and sent him home with a woman named Fay — a real tiger we knew would keep him up all night. We bet the Red Sox the next day. Mantle hit a double in the eighth and beat us."

But beyond the law of averages, which presumes the

accuracy of a Minneapolis wire and the odds against beating a guy like Mantle, there are other inevitabilities to which working the flim-flam is subject. On one occasion, thinking that he and Riordan had lost $5,000 to a bookie, Swan discovered that he had simply lost $2,500 to Riordan. The swindle had just been carried one step further. When confronted, Riordan paid up, but the two men agreed that from then on mutual robbery was part of the game. Swan's first double-reverse was staged at one of Riordan's favorite nightspots, P.J. Clarke's, an East Side saloon with bright Tiffany lamps over the bar.

Leaving Orsini's after dinner one evening — Swan with Holly, Riordan dating a woman he could easily impress — Swan suggested they all go to Clarke's for a drink. Riordan hailed the cab. Inside his coat pocket, Swan was carrying a Tiffany box he had picked up at his office. Inside the box was a ring he had picked up at Woolworth's. Getting into the cab first, he put the box on the floor and his foot on the box. When the cab was under way, Swan tapped his foot. Riordan caught the move.

"Fifty-fifty," he said.

"Shut up," whispered Swan. He pointed in the direction of the driver.

Swan picked up the box, flashed it at Riordan, and put it in his pocket. (What Swan was engaged in here, though he did not know it, was a very famous and time-honored flim-flam — in the slang of the Victorian London rampsman, it was affectionately known as the *fawney-drop*.) Under the lights at Clarke's, he opened the box, held up the ring, and said:

"Mike, I think it's a piece of glass."

Riordan was looking over the box with the Tiffany engraving. He looked at his date.

"I'll tell you what I'll do," Swan said. "You give me two thousand. I'll sell it to you for two thousand, but anything it's worth over ten thousand dollars we split."

Riordan threw the cash on the bar.

Three hours later Swan got a phone call:

"You got me, didn't ya?"

"I got ya."

"It was really beautiful."

"Thanks."

"I owe you one."

"I'm waiting."

But Swan waited in vain. In January of 1969, Mike Riordan was buried by a mud slide that crashed into his Mandeville Canyon home in Brentwood, California, a house that had once belonged to Esther Williams ('with a swimming pool as big as the AC').* He was forty-one years old.

Swan attended the funeral.

"He had a funeral so long you couldn't even count the cars. There must have been two or three thousand of them. Everybody loved Mike. Headwaiters loved him. Bartenders loved him. Everybody. You couldn't count the limousines."

Riordan had left his wife, Jackie, with instructions to sell all of his corporate stock — by then the Equity Funding Corporation was trading on the American Stock Exchange, its reported assets approaching $200 million. She sold the stock immediately after his death for $46 million. It was not until after her second husband, George Getty, died that she discovered, along with the rest of the world, that the Equity Funding Corporation of America, of which Mike

* The New York Athletic Club.

Riordan was co-founder and chairman of the board, had perpetrated the largest stock swindle in the nation's history. The figures were reported in the *Wall Street Journal*.

"That's cash," Swan said.

To this day, the Securities and Exchange Commission has not recovered.

At about the time of Mike Riordan's death, Swan's life began to change. Up to that time he had been associating with aristocrats and celebrities, and he was known in every nightclub in town. While one of his friends (later to be known as Mean Mickey) was dating a railroad heiress, Swan was almost dating a famous network bonus baby:

"We were going to go to The Latin Quarter for dinner, but after an hour together we could both see it was going to be a rough evening. I said, 'Why don't we just go to Hamburger Heaven and call it a night?' She jumped at the suggestion. 'Excellent idea,' she said."

Swan was being invited to New York high-society parties thrown for visiting dignitaries like the Chicago Panthers and Cesar Chavez. He and Holly were chumming around with Hollywood types, and throwing parties of their own. A lot of society flotsam was collecting at his door. But at about the time of Mike's death — Swan and Holly had been divorced for three years — Swan began to slow down. He had been living with a young woman, a German named Uta, for five years; she was much crazier than he, and he was pretty near burned out by the time she left. He quit his job with his father's company and started his own packaging business: "My relatives didn't have very good business sense. My uncle saw letterpress as the wave of the future. He thought lithography was a fad."

After Uta left, there was Alice, but before meeting Alice, the long-haired, brown-eyed, free spirit of the sixties, Swan had made the acquaintance of a man named Ellery, a relative of one of his upstairs neighbors. And it was Ellery, more than anyone else, who was responsible for Swan's metamorphosis. Ellery gave Swan his first taste of dope. Mexican. Swan was ready for anything, just about now, and between Ellery's dope and Alice's politics he would get everything but what he had been getting for the past forty-two years. And he would like it. A lot.

Honest Ellery was the nearest thing New York City had to a pony express rider; every day, rain or shine, he made his rounds. If he were working a legitimate job during the day, his rounds began late in the afternoon. If he were out of work, for one reason or another, his rounds began as soon as he got out of bed — late in the afternoon. Ellery did not simply move about town, he revolved. He was that consistent. At the same time every day, he stopped at the same health-food restaurant on Broadway and ordered the same thing — carrot juice. Every night he stopped at Victor's Café on Columbus Avenue for coffee. While his customers sped around town, erratic, trying either to catch him at his last stop or head him off at his next, Ellery revolved, slowly, feeding on his own momentum. At peace. He was like a Swiss watch; the last thing in this life he would be guilty of was change.

An honest dealer, Ellery was the one immutable constant in the life of every dope smoker he knew. The eye of many storms. He was safe, reliable, well informed, but above all else he was available. A message would never fail to reach him. The only thing more consistent than Ellery himself was the flow of messages across the length and breadth of Manhattan's upper West Side that either preceded or followed him. If he did not call ahead for his messages, they were waiting for him when he arrived. His customers, if they did not all know one another, knew *of* one another; if they had not met, they would — they were in continual telephone contact. Ellery's customers — as a class, not noted for their firm connection to the world's labyrinth string — had Ellery in common. Ellery was the glue that bound them, the mucilage to which the errant particles of their lives adhered.

At the end of the day, his pockets were littered with scraps of paper, fragments of matchbooks, napkins and corners of the pages of unidentifiable telephone directories and newspapers, a miniature catalogue of the day's events, meaningful only to Ellery. A message here, a number to call there, a requisition or a promise of payment early in the evening, an excuse for not showing at night. As a dealer in dreams, Ellery was often paid in kind. And in the creases of his pockets, pouched in darkness, he carried the official correspondence of his trade.

Ellery was of medium height and medium weight. His hair and eyes were brown. He was neither dark nor fair; not striking and not unattractive. Ellery was not an extrovert, but he was not an introvert either. His temperament was even. In almost every way he was average — right there in the middle, the arithmetic American mean. Even his age was medium. Ellery could have been anywhere from twenty-five to forty — only his mother knew for certain, and eventually the police department. Alice said he was a Gemini. Perhaps. Ellery wore expensive clothes and custom-made shoes. On his left wrist he wore a gold watch and on the third finger of his right hand a gold ring in the image of a snake. He smoked imported cigarettes, whatever brand struck his fancy when he entered the tobacconist's. He always used an antique silver cigarette lighter to light them.

Ellery smoked a lot of cigarettes, and he smoked a lot more dope. And like every serious dope smoker, he would acknowledge no ill effect in marijuana, asserting that its greatest danger lay in the possibility that it could lead to cigarette smoking. In contradistinction to the abuse he inflicted upon his body in the manner of that which he inhaled was the fact that he was a proselytizing health-food and vitamin freak. Ellery's daily ration of carrot juice represented only a fraction of his involvement in the cause of organically grown vegetables. His efforts in behalf of natural dietary fiber were legion. But, ironically, as mindful as Ellery was of the health-promoting properties of Nature, it was generally agreed that fresh air would kill him. It was the one thing he carefully avoided. To no one's recollection had he ever been out of New York City.

Ellery lived in the Bronx and spent all day in Manhattan. However rich he became — and he was making good money selling dope — he would never move from his seventy-five-dollar-a-month, rent-controlled Bronx apartment, not even to move as far as Manhattan where he spent all of his time. Ellery was happy. His needs were few. He owned a color television and an impressive array of stereo equipment, and home at night he was content to watch old TV movies or listen to opera. In support of the unsyncopated rhythm of his life, he took two Valium every night before retiring. There were only two pursuits in his life which could be ascribed to indulgence: he owned thousands of dollars' worth of antiques, the acquisition of which he was passionate about; the only other thing he devoted as much time to was dope.

There was no one in the city of New York who, if he had met Ellery after whatever day it was Ellery had smoked his first joint, had ever seen Ellery straight. Ellery only got stoned once in his life, and he stayed that way for years. He is stoned right now. Zachary Swan, a gin drinker, thought Ellery was stupid when he first met him; it took Swan several weeks, and at least as many joints, to realize that Ellery was simply stoned all the time. It was Ellery's tetrahydrocannabinol level that provided him with his unique circadian rhythm, his consistency in the face of chaos; it was his psychochemical symmetry that put him at the axis of revolution of the world's eccentric. Ellery was a successful dream merchant because he was a dreamer himself. And Ellery was loved because his dreams were humble ones: he dreamed of opening a chain of laundromats in the city — and stopping once a day to pick up the quarters.

Ellery was dreaming when he rang Swan's bell. Alice answered the door.

"Hello, Ellery."

"Hi," he said. "What time is it?"

"About eight-thirty."

Ellery looked at his watch. He nodded.

"I have to make a call."

"There are two messages for you on the table," she said.

"Thanks."

Ellery made two calls, Alice went back to the sewing machine, and Swan remained at his desk, where displayed before him was the upcoming week's professional football schedule. Swan had decided, after applying a simple mathematical formula to the point spreads of the previous year's games, that if, with two exceptions, he picked the home team in every game of the current season, he could beat the bookies this fall. He was behind. His simple mathematical formula, very possibly a failure, was the product of hours of research, derived from statistics that filled an entire manila folder which occupied a place of its own in his file cabinet.

The folder was filed between Fabergé and Ford. It was labeled Football.

Ellery hung up the phone and reached for the stereo. With a twist of the dial, John Denver was swallowed by *Die Fledermaus*.

"You don't mind, do you?" Ellery asked.

Swan shook his head. No one ever minded, but Ellery always asked.

"Do you have the newspaper?" Ellery wanted to know.

"It's on the kitchen table," Swan told him.

Ellery put *The New York Times* on his lap and poured some dope onto a picture of John Mitchell's face.

"Do you have—"

Before he was able to finish what he was saying, Swan had tossed a packet of rolling papers onto the headline. Ellery never had papers. It had somehow become part of his image not to. People had given up asking why. Ellerylore called for a certain understanding of the procedure which began with his arrival: he picked up his messages, made his phone calls, changed the radio station, asked if you minded, asked for the newspaper, took out his dope, started a question about rolling papers, commented on the size of the brand you gave him, rolled a joint and passed it around. From there it was free-form until he left.

His departure was marked by the marijuana seeds and stems that remained on the daily paper when he left; it was in this way that one knew that Ellery had dropped by. Alice wondered if he carried empty cigarette packs with him — he invariably left one behind with the seeds and the stems (he never left roaches behind, always sticking them in the end of his first post-joint cigarette.)

"I've got some good stuff this time."

Ellery always had good stuff. He dealt nothing but the best.

"How much?" Swan asked.

"It's really good."

"Better than last time?"

"What was wrong with what I gave you last time?"

"It wasn't bad."

"That was very good stuff."

"It cost enough."

"This is even better stuff."

"How much?"

"Well, I'm going to give you a price."

"How much?"

"Now, I'm charging everybody else ten dollars more. I want you to know that."

"You're really good to me, Ellery."

"It's the best you can buy."

"It always is."

"I can get a lot more for this than I'm charging you."

"How much?"

"I'm going to let you try it."

He handed Swan the joint. While Swan smoked it, Ellery rolled another.

"Now, tell me, isn't that great stuff?"

"It's always great, Ellery. How much do you want?"

"Well, I'm going to give you a special price."

"How much, Ellery?"

"Forty."

"Ellery, I love you, but you're a thief."

"I can get fifty dollars an ounce for this anywhere in the city."

"That's what you told me about the last batch."

"That was good stuff."

"It was O.K."

"I'm giving you a good price."

"I know. You did last time, too."

"Panama is getting very expensive."

"You said the same thing about Michoacàn a year ago."

"How do you feel?"

"It's good stuff, Ellery."

Swan finished the joint and handed Ellery the roach.

"How long have you been smoking now, a year?" Ellery asked.

"You're the one who turned me on."

"It was good stuff, too. I was dealing Mexican then, but it was good Mexican."

"Yeah, you're like Tiffany's."

"How old were you then?"

"Forty-two. How old were you, Ellery?"

"How many people do you figure you've turned on since then?"

"I have no idea," said Swan.

"That was good Mexican."

"When was the last time you smoked Mexican?" Swan asked.

"I don't know."

"Well, I don't think you'd get off on it now."

"That depends on how good it is," said Ellery.

"Well, just think of how the grass has grown in your head. You went from Michoacàn to Acapulco Gold and then to Panama Red."

"That's right. Straight up the ladder."

"And straight down the continent."

"Is that right?"

"Sounds good."

"Where's Colombia?"

"That's even farther south."

"And it's *higher* up the ladder."

"I'm sure you'll be dealing it real soon."

"Colombian's hard to get."

"I wonder if they grow it at the South Pole . . ."

"But there's still good Mexican around."

". . . maybe Antarctica."

"I've got a friend who's got some great Mexican. Good stuff."

"Mexican?"

"Yeah."

"What kind?"

"Acapulco."

"You got a friend who's selling it?"

"Yeah."

"What's he selling it for?"

"I think he wants to sell weight. You want to talk to him about it?"

"What for?"

"If you buy pounds, you can sell ounces at a profit. Get your own free."

Swan was selling dope to his friends for what he was paying for it.

"You can even make some money," said Ellery.

"Will anybody buy Mexican?"

"They're *your* friends."

"I guess they will."

"It's great stuff."

"I'm sure it is, Ellery."

"Want to meet him?"

"Will I be buying it from you if I don't buy it from him?" Ellery nodded.

"I'll think about it."

*   *   *

A year after smoking his first joint, Swan bought his first pound. Ellery introduced him to a smuggler named Vinnie Pirata who wanted $1,000 for ten pounds of Acapulco Gold. Swan bought the dope and had no trouble selling it at $25 an ounce. He made $4,000 on the load and immediately put in another order. Within a few months he was moving two pounds a week in ounces. He was taking in eight hundred tax-free dollars a week when Pirata offered him a franchise.

The franchise consisted of a Chevrolet Bel Air station wagon (one of three Pirata owned) from which the rear seat had been removed (the well, into which the seat was designed to fold down, was covered with a sheet-metal plate machine-screwed to the floor and carpeted over), and it included the use of a villa Pirata rented on a yearly basis in Acapulco where the grass was to be delivered. The car would cost $2,000, the dope — two hundred pounds of it — the same. Swan did the math, liked the bottom line, and called his friend Charlie Kendricks, who had been helping him deal ounces. Kendricks, who needed the money, said yes. Swan paid for the car, arranged to meet Pirata in Acapulco, and before the New Year was a month old — six months short of his forty-fourth birthday — Zachary Swan, industrial engineer, had designed his first pharmaceutical package.

3

BROWNSVILLE BREAKDOWN

On a rainy Monday morning in the winter of 1970, throwing the freight-modified Bel Air into operation, Swan and Kendricks set out for Mexico. They crossed the Hudson ahead of the mail. A fog rolled in at their backs, Manhattan disappeared into the mist like the detail on a fading negative, and the prospect of the West lay before them, a sinful Kodachrome promise. They moved fast. They picked up the Interstate just south of the Bridge, and as soon as they hit the open road they went for the medicine. Between New York City and the Texas line they dropped enough Biphetamine to influence the output of two defensive tackles and a weak-side linebacker. They made Dallas in thirty hours.

Just east of Dallas, short of the used car lots and the taco stands, they separated. Swan pulled the car over and let Kendricks out:

"Don't forget to get the license number," Swan told him. "If you can get a name and address, that's even better."

Kendricks nodded. He waved Swan on:

"I'll see you in Dallas," he said.

"Call first."

"Right."

Swan pulled out into the afternoon traffic headed for the city. Kendricks looked at the sky and frowned. "Balls," he said out loud. It rained. The Bel Air was gone, and Kendricks stood alone on the shoulder of the Interstate. It came down hard. He put out his thumb.

Swan drove into Dallas. Big "D," population about 700,000, he guessed, northeast Texas' answer to the Cherry Hill Shopping Mall; a city, he had always claimed, which owed its ass to oil and football . . . *welcome to the biggest little city in the world, son, take off your boots and stay awhile* . . . the home of Braniff Airlines, H. L. Hunt, and Frito-Lay, one overindustrialized office park of concrete and bean dip cooking in the cowboy sun . . . *this here town's got a big heart, boy, we'll get you all a piece of ass before breakfast* . . . America on the threshold of the twenty-first century, the implications of which were staggering and not a little bit frightening to a man who had been doing Black Beauties for thirty hours.

He drove downtown and checked into a Holiday Inn. It was like checking into a hospital — American Antiseptic, pastels and plastic from sea to shining sea — not inappropriate, he figured, given the conditions under which his nervous system had been functioning recently . . . *send up two bottles of glucose and a bucket of ice, please . . . then void where not prohibited by law*. A germ, he supposed, would never make it out of one of these places alive. If the disinfectants didn't get him, the little bastard would croak from boredom. Swan smiled benignly at the desk clerk. He registered under an assumed name.

Waiting for his room key, he heard a call come over the house intercom; they were paging a man named McCann. He made a mental note of the call, picked up his key, then went up to his room and unpacked. He would have to hurry now: the speed was losing its edge. He was coming down fast, and coming down from the shit he was on was like getting hit by the bends. Before he passed out he made one trip to the lobby.

He walked to the bank of public telephones along the wall, choosing the phone nearest the desk, and he dialed the number of the phone nearest the door, one of the same bank of telephones. When it rang once, he wrote the number down, hung up the phone and went to bed. It was five p.m.

The following morning Swan woke early. He had coffee in his room. He dressed in a gray flannel suit, a white shirt and a blue tie. He slicked his hair down with water, put on dark glasses and went out.

"I'd like to place an ad."

"You could have called it in, sir," said the woman behind the typewriter, looking up, removing the headset she wore.

"I was in the neighborhood."

She nodded. "What kind of ad is it?"

"A classified ad."

"Yes, but where do you want it to appear?"

He frowned. "In the newspaper."

"Yes," she said, "I know that, but where? Are you selling something, buying something, giving something away? Is it a job, a cat, a car? There are all kinds of categories, you see."

What a curious old bat, he thought. She kept throwing her head around from side to side when she talked. What the hell was that all about? Maybe she was not used to the hairnet. And she was nearsighted as hell. Her eyeglasses were attached to a necklace. But she kept taking them off and putting them on, back and forth, up and down. She was making him dizzy, he realized. He liked her.

"Help wanted," he said.

"Help wanted. And when did you want that to appear?"

"As soon as possible."

"As soon as possible." (Now she was repeating him.) "We can have it in by tomorrow morning," she said.

"That's fine."

"That's fine. Now," she said, turning to the typewriter, "how do you want it to read?"

"Driver wanted—"

"You really don't need that."

"Pardon me?" He tried to focus.

She took the glasses off for this. She squinted.

"You really don't need 'wanted,' do you? I mean, it's appearing in the Help Wanted section, isn't it? All you really need to say is 'driver.' You save money that way — you pay by the word."

"Oh."

"So, do you want me to put just 'driver' and leave out the 'wanted'?"

"Please."

"Fine. And the rest?" The glasses were back on now.

"Southwest Freight Company needs a driver to cover the Southwest and Mexico. No special license required. Call Mr McCann at—"

"I'll leave out things like 'at' and 'a' and 'the,'" she enunciated rapidly, "'Southwest Freight Company' is too long even if I abbreviate 'Company,' which I will do anyway, so I'm afraid all you get in boldface is 'driver.'" She looked up.

"Terrific. I'll leave it all up to you."

"How do you spell McCann?"

"You can leave that out. Just run the phone number."

"Very good," she said, pleased, it seemed, to know that he was catching on.

He gave her the phone number, paid her in cash, told her how nice it was to deal with someone so efficient and conscientious, and disappeared. She smiled as he left.

Swan spent the day in his room. He took a call from Kendricks in the evening. He watched television until the national anthem came on, smoked some dope, and went to sleep. At eight the next morning the pay-phone in the lobby, the telephone nearest the door, rang once. Swan picked it up:

"Good morning," he said.

"Hello, I'm calling about the ad in the paper."

"Your name, please."

"Kendricks. Charles Kendricks."

"Do you have the paper?"

"Yes."

"Cut out the ad and keep it."

"I did."

"Meet me in the coffee shop. Call me Mr McCann."

"O.K.," Kendricks yawned.

It was ten o'clock when Kendricks arrived. He was wearing blue jeans and a workshirt. The coffee shop was nearly empty. Swan, the newspaper in front of him, was doing Dow Jones calculations on his napkin. He was wearing the gray flannel suit. His second cup of coffee had just arrived. He waved Kendricks over to the table. He stood up and they shook hands.

"I'm Mr McCann."

"Charles Kendricks. Glad to meet you."

"Sit down, Mr Kendricks."

"Thank you. What's that, the racing form?"

"The market."

"Who's winning?"

"Them."

Swan called the waitress over. Kendricks smiled. The waitress smiled back. She was young, about eighteen, tall and still growing. Her red hair was long, but pinned up to keep it out of the food. Her eyes were blue and her teeth were perfect. Swan, who was not partial to red hair, found her attractive. Kendricks thought she was beautiful. Her ears were pierced, and the only embellishment to her face, afforded by features with which she was not born, was provided by the shadows of the elaborate opal earrings she wore and a small scar above her right eye that looked like a knife wound.

"This is Julie," Swan said. "Julie, I'd like you to meet Mr Charles Kendricks. Julie was born in October."

"Hello, Mr Kendricks," she said.

"Call me Charlie."

"Are you English?" she asked.

"Australian," he said.

"This young man is going to work for me," Swan said, "so I want you to bring him a lot of food. Anything you want, son."

Kendricks looked at the waitress:

"I was born in—"

When Kendricks decided to turn on the charm, Swan decided to spill the coffee.

"I'm sorry," he said, standing up.

The young woman moved quickly, in time to save Swan's suit and what remained of his coffee. She told him it was quite all right, that she would bring him another cup; she took Kendricks's order and left.

"She'll never forget you," Kendricks said.

"That's the idea," Swan answered. "Where did you stay last night?"

"Same place. The Pepsi Hotel."

"The Pepsi Hotel?"

"That's what it said. No name, just a fucking Pepsi sign. A real fleabag. Five dollars a night. The Pepsi Hotel, Dallas."

"Was there anyone else there?"

"I talked to the night man. He's also the day man, but he sleeps then. I talked to him at night, inquired about jobs."

"Perfect. Who brought you in?"

Kendricks pulled out his wallet, an expensive one, made of kangaroo hide, and from it he took three small pieces of paper. One had written on it, in another man's handwriting, a name and an address in Fort Worth. The second showed an automobile registration number written in Kendricks's hand; the sevens were crossed. The third scrap of paper was the classified ad from *The Dallas Morning News*. Kendricks handed them to Swan, and Swan looked them over.

"Good work, Charlie. Well done. You'd better separate them so it doesn't look like you had any plan in mind when you put them there."

Kendricks stared:

"I have a friend in Queensland," he said, "who bought Poseidon Nickel a year ago."

"Yeah?" Swan looked up.

"He's a millionaire today."

"Sure. Who was his broker?" Swan asked, handing back the scraps of paper.

"I was," Kendricks nodded. He put the wallet away.

Swan smiled. "I'm sorry, Charlie, I know you're not stupid. You're doing fine, real fine. Keep up the good work."

"Right."

"And I'm sorry about the Pepsi Hotel. We'll fix you up real nice in Acapulco."

"Quite all right."

Swan lit a cigarette, Kendricks coughed, and the waitress returned with breakfast.

Because it was difficult to drive a car into Mexico which was registered to anyone other than the driver, it had been decided earlier that the Bel Air be registered in Kendricks's name. (Traffic was heavy across the Mexican border in cars which were rented in the United States on stolen credit cards and subsequently sold in Mexico; authorities on both sides of the border were suspicious of automobiles in general.) Swan and Kendricks discussed this in front of the waitress. When they left the coffee shop, Kendricks took the phony papers that came with the station wagon and the franchise, and he registered the car in his name. That afternoon they drove to San Antonio. In San Antonio, at a second-hand furniture store, they bought a desk, a swivel chair, a hat rack and some assorted junk, and loaded the car. Kendricks drove Swan to the airport. Swan flew to Acapulco that night.

To Zachary Swan, late of the New York cocktail circuit and international hobo collective, Acapulco de Juarez, known to most as Acapulco — Aca if you had been there — needed no introduction. This sultry port on the Pacific coast of southern Mexico, the odds-on favorite of lower-echelon European nobility and mid-Atlantic-jet-set Riviera flotsam — known now more for its dope than for anything else, a kind of crypto-Casablanca without the Casbah —

was what that sixteenth face-lift and Vidal Sassoon were all about.

Swan picked up a Carte Blanche travel brochure at the airport and read it on the way to the villa. As the cab bumped along he became even better acquainted with Acapulco's cultural heritage. It was from here, he learned, one of the finest natural harbors in the world, 272 mountainous miles from Mexico City and the halls of Montezuma, that Hernando Cortés, wit, raconteur and man of letters, after winning the hearts and minds of the Aztecs and dutifully mailing them home to Spain, shipped supplies to his pal Francisco Pizarro while the latter distinguished himself in Peru disemboweling the Incas into oblivion. All in four-color.

Vinnie Pirata's villa had been described to Swan accurately. It was an old Spanish fortress, whitewashed and wired, situated high on a hill overlooking Acapulco Bay. Behind it to the east, bathed now in moonlight, was a fertile valley stretching three miles to the mountains. The villa was surrounded by a decaying concrete wall eight feet high and inset with cut glass. Its wrought-iron gate, Swan decided, was overwrought. It would become a pet joke of his. Pirata was home when Swan arrived.

Vinnie Pirata, dressed now in lightweight khaki pants and a red cotton jersey, had picked up a tan since Swan had seen him last in New York. His blond hair was blonder. His forehead was burned. Pirata was short, about five-five, and slim; he weighed about 140, he was in good shape, and his posture was excellent. He dressed down, but wore a flashy gold watch. In New York he drove a Maserati. Pirata was about forty years old, uneducated, and had a long criminal record. He did not drink or smoke, and he never used drugs. He had blue eyes, and he was the only man Swan knew who always carried a gun. He shook Swan's hand:

"The grass is going to be late," he said.

"Terrific."

Kendricks arrived in Acapulco two days later with the car. He registered at La Condesa Hotel, under his own name, as a representative of the Southwest Freight Company. He left the car keys with the clerk at the desk, telling the man that his, Kendricks's, employer would be by soon to pick up the vehicle. He made a phone call and went to the beach. Kendricks was conspicuously absent from the hotel when Swan arrived for the station wagon. Swan chatted with the clerk, asked him when Kendricks had arrived, thanked him, overtipped him, and took the car. He parked the car behind the villa, and for the hell of it he took off the plates. He met Kendricks at the beach that afternoon.

"The grass is late."

"What do we do?"

"We wait. They're bringing the shit in from the mountains by donkey. They're supposed to give us a flashlight signal or something. Do you believe that?"

Sure he did. They both believed it, and they thought it was wonderful. Though neither would admit it, they were, if for nothing else, suckers for the cloak-and-dagger aspects of this operation.

"Do you want me to stay at the hotel?"

"Yeah, you'd better."

"Fine."

While they swam, Swan explained that because the wholesalers were not in the habit of leading mule trains into Acapulco, Pirata would pay a cab driver $100 to drive him to the rendezvous point in the foothills when the signal was given.

"Fancy that," Kendricks said.

And of course Swan did.

In the week that passed, Swan and Kendricks met daily at the beach, Swan growing weary of the wait, Kendricks growing weary of the sun, both of them making the best of each. With one exception — that they were never seen together in the vicinity of Kendricks's hotel — they behaved like tourists. At night they caught the act of the Quebrada Cliff divers; during the day they took the parachute ride, pulled by a power boat one hundred yards into the air over Acapulco Bay. Swan thought the last was a real hoot and made a point of doing it often. He got a special thrill out of the release he was required to sign, before being harnessed in, which relieved the concessionaires of any responsibility in the event of his near-death. He signed his name: *I'll Sue*.

And in that week Swan learned something, a lesson the impact of which was to hold up for the next four years: smuggling is waiting. Sitting in rooms. Waiting. Killing time. No matter how intricate the preparation, no matter how airtight the scam, smuggling is innovating, winging it, changing the operation because your boat left or your carrier ran out. In the ensuing years Swan would watch a lot of television. And when the heat was on, he would drink a lot of gin. On this trip the wait paid off: Kendricks became so sunburned that border officials could take him for nothing more than an ignorant tourist.

A pair of high-powered field glasses, Navy issue, stolen, were mounted on a tripod in one of the east windows of the villa. They faced the mountains. Just after dark Vinnie Pirata had removed the drop cloth that protected them from the sun and the dust; now he sat in a chair by the window and drank coffee. Zachary Swan sat facing him with an overcoat draped over his arm. It was late on the seventh day.

"That's all bullshit," Pirata was saying.

Swan, who was still holding on to a packaging business in the United States, was waiting for a cab to take him to the airport. He would leave for New York tonight. He was trusting Charlie Kendricks. Kendricks had come to the villa to see him off and was sitting on a stool by the door applying a variety of topical painkillers to the sunburn which had rendered him almost helpless. His face had begun to swell. Swan lit a cigarette and looked at his watch. It was ten o'clock. He did not answer Pirata.

At five past ten, as Swan was crushing his cigarette out in a pre-Columbian ashtray, the signal came. Swan saw it first. Pirata, whose back was to the window, jumped up when Swan pointed.

"Are you sure?"

Swan said nothing. He looked at his watch again. Pirata turned and looked through the binoculars. He waited. Then he whispered:

"It's here."

Pirata picked up a flashlight from the windowsill and signaled back. His signal was acknowledged. Swan watched the light come from out of the mountains; he turned from the window and picked up his luggage. Pirata checked the cartridges in his gun, called his cab driver, and as Swan was leaving for the airport, he and Kendricks left to make the pickup.

"Keep an eye out behind you," Swan told Kendricks as they parted.

Kendricks and Pirata made the pickup that night. They made the fill together. Early the next morning Pirata delivered the car to the hotel. Kendricks picked up the keys at the desk. Within an hour he was on the road.

Zachary Swan was catching up on the national news in New York when Richard Nixon's terrible shithammer came down on Charlie Kendricks. It was late on a Sunday night. Swan, relaxing at home, was reading *The New York Times*. He had just turned to a provocative article on drug smuggling, in which Customs Commissioner Myles Ambrose was quoted at length, when Charles Kendricks made the border at Matamoros and from there drove into the biggest trouble of his life. Kendricks was busted by American Customs agents at Brownsville with a ridiculous smile on his badly sunburned face and two hundred pounds of premium dope in the belly of the station wagon he was driving. The smile cost him a moment of physical agony; the rest could cost him about fifteen years in jail.

The employees of Myles Ambrose read Kendricks his rights, took away his alien registration card and told him, very politely, that there was a law in this country — 21 USC 176, to be exact. After they did that, they led him into an interrogation room and confronted him with the evidence. Stacked high on a table in the center of the room was the grass, and as he looked at it, it occurred to Kendricks quite painfully that the last time he had seen the shit was when he had helped to load it into the station wagon. Realizing that his fingerprints were all over the bricks, Charles Kendricks, who had bought his client into Poseidon Nickel at forty cents, contrived to bump into the table and knock the bricks onto the floor. He helped the government pick them up.

"Well?" they asked.

"I've never seen it before in my life," he said.

They locked him up and threw away the key.

On Monday morning, shortly after eleven a.m. Eastern Standard Time, Lillian Giles was coveting her neighbor's goods in the living room of Zachary Swan's apartment on West 88th Street in Manhattan — she wanted Swan's throat. Standing thoughtfully between her close friend and the man whose future hinged on the disposition of the property in question, Alice Haskell, a woman of integrity, was considering the merits of the transaction.

". . . you and all your bullshit . . ." Lillian shouted.

"You explain it to her, will you, Allie? Tell her it's going to be all right," Swan was saying.

"Answer the phone," Alice told him.

Swan picked up the phone on the fifth ring. It was Ellery: "Charlie's standing up," he said.

Swan sighed. He looked at Lillian.

"Jesus Christ, Ellery, that's great news," he said into the phone, "but I'd sure like to know where you got your information."

"Straight from Brownsville," said Ellery. "Billy Bad Breaks passed the word out."

"Billy?"

"Yeah, he talked to Charlie."

"He what?"

"Billy talked to Charlie."

"Wait a minute, Ellery, I don't understand. Billy Bad Breaks talked to Charlie in Brownsville?"

"That's right."

Swan hesitated. He looked at the two women, who were as confused as he was. Then he asked:

"What the fuck's going on, Ellery?"

What the fuck was going on was this: Billy Bad Breaks had tried to drive across the border at Brownsville over a week before, carrying a plump joint in his pocket. Things began to break bad, as they inevitably did for Billy, when he was pulled over and searched. When the Customs inspectors found the joint, they decided to search the car Billy was driving. The car was one of Vinnie Pirata's freight-modified Bel Airs, and Billy, who for all practical purposes was traveling empty (but not empty enough), had forgotten to bolt the plate back into position; cause for a certain amount of embarrassment as well as inconvenience, it turned out, since Billy Bad Breaks was going the other way — he was busted for smuggling marijuana *into* Mexico. What concerned Zachary Swan, however, was the fact that Billy Bad Breaks had been busted at Brownsville before Charlie Kendricks had left Acapulco. Every Customs man from Matamoros to Tijuana had been on to the Bel Air trick before Kendricks picked up the car keys in the Condesa lobby. And Pirata had known it. Swan's reluctance to take revenge on Vinnie Pirata paid off in the short run; it was not until a few years later that he would wish he had at least contracted to have the bastard's legs broken.

That Kendricks was standing up was certainly good news — it meant that so far he had not admitted anything, and more important, that he had not implicated Swan in the mess. But Swan's principal concern when he received news of the arrest, Lillian Giles's accusations to the contrary, was for Charlie. And all Swan's bullshit, that to which Lillian had made particular reference when she confronted him that day, the same bullshit to which Pirata had specifically referred on the night Swan left Acapulco, was the precise bullshit that saved Kendricks's neck. When Kendricks finally convinced the United States government to listen to him, he not only vindicated Swan; he raised the level of this unique and previously unseen brand of bullshit, *en passant*, to that of an elevated, almost rarefied, and characteristically seamy kind of canon in what was to become a smuggler's equivalent of the Revised Standard Version. It happened like this:

The generous Texan from Fort Worth who had picked Kendricks up in the rain and driven him as far as Dallas had given his correct name and address. There was no need to trace the registration number of his car. When called upon, the man corroborated Kendricks's story, even so far as to recall that Kendricks had asked about jobs in the area. The night manager of the Pepsi Hotel, questioned in the painful light of day, recalled a similar conversation. The newspaper ad held up. Julie, the waitress at the Holiday Inn, remembered the interview. And the overtipped clerk at La Condesa Hotel told investigators that the car Kendricks had driven had been out of Kendricks's hands for five days while he was in Acapulco.

The furniture Kendricks had hauled South from San Antonio was never an issue. (Swan had dumped it beside an unpaved road on the outskirts of Acapulco; the next day it was gone.) Mr McCann, who had been paged at the Holiday Inn, had given a phony name or address or both (he was probably cheating on his wife) and was never located. That he was not the same Mr McCann who had placed the classified ad or had interviewed Kendricks over breakfast was never suspected by the investigators; knowing that there was a McCann registered at the Holiday Inn was enough for them. That McCann had given a phony address made sense, they had to figure, given the fact that he had intended to smuggle two hundred pounds of dope out of Mexico. (Swan's double-blind maneuver, registering under one name, itself a phony, then assuming the name of an individual actually registered at the hotel, was probably unnecessary, but it appealed to the clinician in him. In this case, McCann, or whoever he was, had fortuitously tripled the blind by registering under an assumed name himself. Eventually Swan would refine his technique, so that in South America, when checking into hotels or traveling, he could sign his own name, proceeding upon the assumption that innocence, in fact, is the best disguise.) Kendricks's fingerprints on the dope, the only flaw in the perfect scam, had been taken care of by Kendricks himself. And so, reluctantly, less than a week after he was arrested, Kendricks was released. The Feds wept.

Kendricks took a bus to New York, where he stayed stoned for about four days. Swan kept him company. When it was all over, Swan added it up. His losses were not staggering. In hard cash, $5,000. He would have made $25,000 if the deal had gone through. He did lose Charlie Kendricks, who became border-shy after the Brownsville incident, but only temporarily. Charlie would be back. There was nothing Swan could do about Vinnie Pirata; use him if he could, but never trust him. And there was nothing he could do about his own reluctance to do anything about Pirata. If he had gained anything from the experience, it was by way of a test — he now had implicit faith in his ability to beat the government. That was enough. He knew that before long he would get his money back. How soon was up to him.

He worked the flourish on Adrian a month later.

4
AFTER MATH

Ike and Freddy were two shooters from Brooklyn who were so good they could make dice do tricks. Ike was particularly heavy — it was said that he could take any pair of legit dice, throw them in a bathtub, and get the number. How Adrian the Mogul spotted these two wizards is a mystery. Adrian, a film producer who was not producing, was making his money by cutting a poker game which he ran two or three nights a week at his apartment on Central Park West. Until he met Ike and Freddy, Adrian's was a legitimate game. When he spotted them, he expanded his operation. He went into business with the two young men, and with their help he opened a casino.

Ike and Freddy supplied the dice table, of a foam rubber variety which they sidelined in, renting them to non-profit organizations in Queens on occasions such as Las Vegas nights (they came with the franchise and inevitably walked away with the lion's share of the contributions). And they supplied the wheel — where they got this no one asked. Swan, known as a man who liked action, was steered to

Adrian's by a friend, and up against Ike one night, about six months prior to the Mexican move, he got clipped for over $2,700. When he found out it was a hustle, Swan figured Adrian owed him one. When the Mexican deal went bad, he figured it was time to collect.

Swan knew that when Adrian was not running the casino, he could be found "over by" Roosevelt Raceway in the clubhouse. One March evening Swan bumped into Adrian at the track and offered to buy him a drink. He pulled out a phony bankroll to pay for it — a Michigan, two hundreds on top and fifty ones underneath. In addition to the bankroll, he flashed a few discarded hundred-dollar pari-mutuel tickets he had picked up from the previous races. It looked as if he were loaded and betting heavy. Adrian went for it.

"What are you doing these days?" he asked.

Swan looked around, then smiled at Adrian.

"I'm moving grass out of Mexico and having a ball," he said out of the side of his mouth.

Adrian bought it, and Swan sold it to Adrian just as Pirata had sold it to him. But Swan put a flourish on it.

Swan fixed Adrian up with a Bel Air in Queens that had been retired after the second bust. "Two thousand. The grass will cost you another two thousand. I'll help you get rid of it." And he fixed Adrian up with a driver, a friend of Pirata's named Homer. Swan introduced Homer to Adrian as Billy Bad Breaks.

Adrian hired Homer, and he drove with Homer as far as San Antonio. He did not bother to set up alibis. He flew to the villa, saw the shipment — two hundred pounds that Pirata had been unable to smuggle out — and paid for it. After the fill, he drove as far as Mexico City with Homer. From there he flew to New York. Homer drove from Mexico City directly back to the villa.

Two days later Adrian got a call from Swan.

"Billy Bad Breaks has been busted," Swan told him.

Adrian would not buy it:

"You're fuckin' with me," he said.

Swan told him to call the Brownsville jail, gave Adrian the number, and hung up. Adrian was angry. He made the call. Billy Bad Breaks was in jail — Adrian never thought to ask how long he had been there. He called Swan:

"What do I do now?"

He was desperate.

"It's going to be rough on you if he talks," Swan said.

Adrian came up with another thousand dollars for a lawyer.

Swan paid Pirata $500 for the use of the villa and the grass. He paid Homer $1,000. Working the flourish on Adrian, Swan cleared about $4,000. He sold the scam eventually, and once a month, between March and July, he received $500 in the mail. Pirata made $500 each time for the use of his villa and for use of the grass he had been unable to move since the Bel Airs had gone bad. (Eventually Pirata tried to make a boat move and the captain stole the load.)

Swan made one more Mexican marijuana move using Vinnie Pirata's villa. In May 1970 he bought a second-hand camper, a converted '66 International pickup truck. It was red, with a deep well between the chassis and the living space. He paid $3,500 for it. He rented a small apartment in Chelsea simply to have somewhere to put a telephone, and placed an ad in *The Village Voice*: CAMPER FOR RENT; IDEAL FOR MEXICO. It was two and a half weeks before he got the response he was waiting for. It came from two Long Island schoolteachers.

The young schoolteachers wanted to go to Mexico City, to an artists' colony northwest of there, San Miguel de Allende in Guanajuato, and they especially wanted to go to Acapulco. Swan rented them the camper for a month — $350. (He made sure they were covered by giving them a contract to sign. The *Voice* ad was added proof of their innocence.) And Swan gave them the name of a friend who rented a villa overlooking Acapulco Bay. They could stay there while they were in Acapulco, he told them. They would, they said. They did.

When the schoolteachers arrived at the villa, Vinnie Pirata, who liked having women around, was there to greet them. Nice Mickey was also there. Nice Mickey (whose name had been given to him by Swan for no other reason than to distinguish him from a small-change hustler named Mean Mickey) was first a friend of Ellery's, now a better friend of Pirata's, and happened to be vacationing at the villa in June. An ounce-dealer on occasion, Mickey had given up smuggling Vinnie's dope when Billy Bad Breaks was busted. He was very professional, a good man who watched himself carefully. Swan had not hired him for this move, but paid him $500 to help out when he found that Mickey was going to be around.

Swan flew down from New York to pay for the grass, and he stayed out of sight. He sent Charlie Kendricks to Mexico City. Then he waited.

The schoolteachers had a good time in Acapulco; the only setback they suffered was a temporary one, an oil leak the camper developed while it was parked at Pirata's villa. Nice Mickey, who discovered the leak, offered to take the camper to a garage and have it repaired. The schoolteachers thanked him, Pirata and the two young women went to the beach that day, and when the three returned to the villa the camper was fixed. It was also two hundred pounds heavier.

Swan flew to New York that night. The schoolteachers left for the United States the next day. Mickey drove with them as far as Mexico City, where they stayed in a hotel which Pirata had recommended. Pirata had made their reservations. The schoolteachers spent one night in Mexico City, and the following morning they set out for the border. Charlie Kendricks followed them through Customs at Nogales.

Swan cleared over $20,000 on the grass. He lost $4,000 in one week betting, paid off an Irving Trust loan with $5,000 of the take, and $2,000 he invested in a hash scheme that failed. The rest went more slowly, a lot of it to bartenders in New York. He and Alice, who were living on West 88th Street in New York at the time, had taken a house on Fire Island for the summer. They lived well. By September the money was gone.

What happened next happened fast, and it began by way of an accident — one of the typically fortuitous events which distinguish Zachary Swan's life from that of the average man.

Zachary Swan is not a personally fastidious individual. In fact, if one were not struck by his almost comic absent-mindedness, his undisguised failure to acknowledge the presence of his immediate surroundings (a characteristic incongruity intimated by the meticulous nature of his work), one would be tempted to think of him as sloppy. Traveling in his wake on an average day is like following a Panzer division through Europe. Whatever he touches turns to residue. It is not unusual, for example, to find as many as three of his cigarettes burning simultaneously in various ashtrays around his house, forgotten or ignored after the first puff, not because he does not enjoy them, and not always because he is drunk or preoccupied, but more often because he is simply unable, by virtue of temperament, to collate the necessary data to streamline such a task. When he does manage to devote enough attention to a cigarette actually to smoke it, the ashes more often than not end up in his lap or on the carpet (his own or his host's) at gravity's whim. He confronts them as he would an unexpected guest; to the random evidence of his own existence he is no more than a witness.

The most elementary details elude Zachary Swan. With several thousand dollars in smuggling money one year he bought a new Porsche coupé, and before he had had it a month his and Alice's dogs had torn the interior to shreds, an outcome he had not foreseen, but one with which he was not impressed either. He drove it that way for as long as he owned it. Nor is he any more careful with his clothes; rolling around the yard in a three-hundred-dollar suit with a Labrador retriever is not something he remembers until he is confronted with a wardrobe shortage. His material survival, it seems, is purely a function of contingency. His minute-to-minute life he conducts as if it were a raffle. He leaves the caps off felt-tipped pens, mayonnaise jars and toothpaste containers. He loses phone numbers frequently and is rarely in possession of his eyeglasses. He never leaves a hotel room without leaving something behind. He misplaced his girl friend once on the beach in Cartagena (he found her in the same place a year later). When the hard money is on the line, Zachary Swan is devastatingly efficient, but under routine conditions he makes it through the day on idiot's luck.

Only for a few hours each day, the intimate early-morning hours right after he wakes and while everyone else is asleep, does Zachary Swan seem to be in possession of the rudimentary personal discipline required by daily living; only then does he exhibit the fundamental self-awareness normally associated with the higher primates and commonly thought of as critical to a successful participation in any activity which is not the exclusive province of plant life. And it was at such a time on a morning early in August, while imposing his daily ration of order upon the chaos of being alive, that he stumbled upon part of a neglected back-issue of *The New York Times*. Before stacking it with a pile of periodicals destined for recycling, he folded it neatly, exposing what newspapermen refer to as the break page, page one of the second section (*The New York Times* is a broadsheet — you know, like the *Tombstone Epitaph*, impossible to read on horseback; tabloids, like *The New York Daily News* and *Rolling Stone*, have no break page), and it was a mild shock of recognition that sat him down with it amid the unattended clutter of the previous evening. What Swan had recognized on the *Times* break page was the smuggling article he had been reading the night Charlie Kendricks was arrested, the article in which Customs Commissioner Myles Ambrose had been quoted. He read it now for the second time, and when he finished reading it he cut it out of the newspaper.

Alice awoke an hour later and found Swan sitting at his desk over a pad of legal paper and an uncapped felt-tipped pen.

"Hi," she said.

He smiled, turning to look at her. "Good morning, Allie. How'd you sleep?"

"I don't know," she mumbled, "I was asleep."

Swan stood up laughing and put his hands on her shoulders.

"Al-lie!"

He said her name as if it were two, accent on the last syllable, a song. She rubbed her eyes.

"Hey, Allie, is Uta still living with Michel Bernier?" he asked.

"Uta?" she yawned. "You're asking me?"

"I thought you'd get a kick out of it."

"I don't know. Why don't you call her?"

"I want to talk to *him*."

"I think his name's in the book."

"How do you spell it?"

"In French."

"Terrific."

Swan hunted for the phone book.

"What do you want to talk to him for?" Alice asked.

"I think he used to live in Colombia, didn't he?"

"I think he's lived everywhere," she said.

Swan found the number. When he went to the kitchen to make the call, Alice sat down at the desk. She was waking up very slowly. She took a sip of Swan's coffee and did not like it any better than she had the last time she had tried it. Though she persevered, Alice Haskell had been unable, thus far in her life, conscientiously to develop any bad habits. She put out Swan's cigarette and moved the ashtray. Propping her head up with her hand, she made a serious attempt to keep her eyes open. On the legal pad in front of her she saw a series of calculations Swan had made. The numbers looked familiar. She recognized some of them as the quantities and dollar amounts that dealt with the last Mexican move. But written beneath those were figures she did not recognize. In this second set of calculations the dollar amounts remained the same, but the weights were different — proportionately they were smaller. It became obvious that here the pounds and ounces had been converted to metric weights. Continuing down the paper were still further calculations, where the metric units were embellished with alphabetical notations. The letter "k" recurred most often — it showed up in every calculation — kilograms. The letters "m" and "c" occurred on every other line. Marijuana, possibly. And centigrams? Through sleepy eyes she followed the calculations down the page, feeling sorry for anyone with such sloppy handwriting. Numbers were multiplied, totals were divided, and arithmetical proportions were indicated. At the bottom of the page a large circle had been drawn. Across the diameter of the circle lay the felt-tipped pen. She stared at the pen for a while, then pushed it aside lazily with her index finger. Beneath it, in Swan's distinctive scrawl, she read one word. It was written in longhand, capitalized and underscored twice. It was "Cocaine."

Michel Bernier answered the phone on the first ring.

Michel Bernier embodied all those individual characteristics that Americans find distasteful in a man — he was French. Dark, lean and languid, he wore his heritage like a badge. He was heir to the loose mouth, sunken cheeks and puffy lips that enable the French to deal with their language. He had the eyes of a kept woman and the deep, sultry voice of a Boul Mich café singer. He was narrow at the hip, his wrists were limp, and he moved with the fluidity of a worm. Many women and not a few men found him handsome. Of the men, the most recent was an alcoholic artist named Gomez, who had bought Bernier from a Colombian aristocrat for an unfinished landscape he managed to paint in the gaps of a two-day stupor and who had lately been abandoned by Bernier after having burned himself out so badly he could no longer see straight — and thus, as Bernier saw it, could no longer pay the freight. One of the women was Uta Dietrische.

A German national, from Heligoland in the North Sea, Uta had come to the United States as an *au pair* in 1964. She was eighteen years old at the time and had been in the country less than a month when she met Zachary Swan on the beach at Fire Island. She moved into his apartment in New York a week later and stayed for six years. Uta was an authentic blonde with an even tan and eyes as blue as a night in jail. She had good bones, a narrow mouth that turned down at the corners, and a voice that was resonant of post-war Berlin, the kind of voice that filters well through blue cigarette smoke and the sound of a five-against-two piano playing downstairs, husky and haunted, reminiscent of rainy nights, two-dollar Scotch and black-market penicillin. Her shoulders were broad, her back erect, and she carried herself with the frightening dignity of a woman whose looks had been beaten into her. Her hair was long and straight, she stood five-feet-eight in her bare feet, and she was easily one of the most beautiful women who had ever looked north to the land of the midnight sun. Like anything that good to look at, she was fragile, and from the day she was born to the minute of her most recent drink, Uta had run up against some of the hardest luck in the world. Michel Bernier was her latest mistake.

Michel and Uta were the victims of unsynchronized disgust for each other. Mutual passion was something they worked at. Between the two of them they represented every sexual idiosyncrasy imaginable — Uta was bisexual, Michel was everything else. If Uta was not a true manic-depressive, she was not far short of it, and, as if to stave off its rapid approach, she had recently turned over all her psycho-motor responsibilities to the trusteeship of modern chemistry. While living with Swan, she had enjoyed six years of relative peace and stability — probably, although neither would admit it, because they loved each other very much. But living with Michel was another thing; it was his job to look out for her now, and he frequently took a belt to her, beating her brains around as if to remind her that she was crazy. On a cool evening in the middle of August these two creatures of God were sitting at Zachary Swan's dinner table eating his food, conversing pleasantly with their host and hostess, and wondering, not without justification, why the hell they had been invited.

The answer to that question was an involved one, and one which had a lot to do with Myles Ambrose, the Commissioner of Customs. Mr Ambrose had told *The New York Times*, in front of Zachary Swan and the rest of the world, what every drug cop in America had known for a long time about cocaine — which was pretty much nothing at all with a lot of authority behind it. He did know that cocaine was beginning to show up in increasing quantities as contraband at a lot of his ports of entry and he had the statistics to prove it. He should have quit there. It would have made a nice press release. The rest of his news was a sloppy synthesis of legend and office politics. And worse.

In an effort to illuminate his myths, Mr Ambrose embarrassed himself further by citing a case study. Using one of his recently apprehended suspects as a model, he took the reader on a trip to South America, explained how a buy was made, detailed the trip home, recommended a 50 percent hit with lactose, and offered as an example his own sucker's method of distribution. Zachary Swan did not know anything about cocaine, and he was not likely to learn much from this article, but he did know something about smuggling, and it was the math that took his larcenous soul by storm. He could not resist the numbers. Even if Ambrose had confused dollars with pesos, even if he had confused them with yen, the numbers came up strong — the truth was that a kilo of coke was worth about three station wagons full of grass; two-point-two pounds, and you could fit that into a loaf of bread. Michel Bernier, late of Colombia, was the man to see.

Before the coffee was cold, Michel and Uta had the answer to their question.

"I'm thinking of going to Colombia," Swan said.

"Business or pleasure?" Bernier asked.

"Business."

Uta was staring at Alice. She lit a cigarette.

"The coffee's delicious," she said.

"It's instant," said Alice.

"Investing in coffee?" Bernier asked.

"No." Swan smiled.

"Is Vinnie still in Mexico?" Uta asked.

"He's doing traveler's checks now," Swan answered.*

"In Acapulco?"

"He's in New York," Alice said.

"No, Michel, not coffee," Swan said.

"And not tea?"

"I'm moving up (sniff)."

"I see."

"Have you been there recently?" Swan asked.

"I have a friend in Bogotá."

"A businessman?"

"He is seventy-two. He was born in Cali with a tree outside his window. He has been (sniff) taking the medicine since then

* See Appendix II.

and has not stopped. We used to go for holidays to Santa Marta. He would put his finger on his nose as he walked along the beach, and the beach boys would know instantly what he wanted to buy. His name is Vincent. You will like him. I will be writing soon, I will give him your name."

Exit Michel Bernier.

Michel and Uta were not to disappear from Swan's life altogether, but it was to be several months before they returned — separately — to the arena of his operation. Swan's next move, before making the final decision, was to see Ellery.

"Ellery," he said, "I'm looking for a connection in South America."

As simple as that. And Ellery produced, like a magician a rabbit, a connection in South America. His name was Tito. Tito, twenty-two, was a Colombian, and he had an uncle who owned a restaurant in Peru. Swan questioned Tito on more than one occasion, corroborating through him what he had been able to learn from other sources. Most significantly, Tito knew about the mail. He corresponded often with his aunt in Lima, who sent him an occasional package. He told Swan that a large package was considered freight and therefore examinable. A package sent first class was considered mail, and legally, at the time, was not supposed to be opened. Customs did, however, try to X-ray them, he said; they had a fluoroscope, but it would take nothing larger than a loaf of bread.

Swan based his first move on this information and what little more he was able to pick up. He knew he would not need a passport. At the time Americans were allowed to travel to South America on tourist cards issued by the airlines upon presentation of a birth certificate. Avianca Airlines was the carrier of choice.

On a rainy day at the end of September, Alice came in late and found Swan at the desk.

"Hi," she said.

"Hi, Allie."

"Did you get my message?"

"I did. Thanks."

"Ellery's been trying to get a hold of you."

"I got him. You haven't heard from Lillian, have you?"

"Lillie Giles?"

"Yeah."

"No, I haven't. Why?"

"I want to talk to Charlie."

"I don't think they're coming back."

"How long have they been gone now?"

"Since June, almost four months."

"He'll be back."

"What did Ellery want?"

"He had some news for me."

"Good or bad?"

"Good news."

"What's up?"

Swan lit a cigarette.

"I'm going South."

5
AESTHETICS AND ANAESTHETICS

Cocaine is the caviar of the drug market. On the street, where an equivalent amount of premium-import marijuana can be obtained for a mere $40 (anywhere up to $80 for top-of-the-line Colombian), cocaine commands a price in excess of $1,000 an ounce. And, like high-quality caviar, it most frequently embellishes the diet of the avant-garde and the aristocratic, a leisure class — in New York, a *Who's Who* among actors, models, athletes, artists, musicians and modern businessmen, professionals, politicians and diplomats, as well as that sourceless supply of socialites and celebrities of no certifiable occupation. The common denominator is money. And it is fashionable in the high-profit purlieus of Harlem — with pimps, prostitutes and drug dealers, any neighborhood heavyweight with influence on the street. Coke is status.

Significantly overshadowed by cult-fidelity to ups, downs, acid, mescaline and hemp during the drug explosion of the late 1960s, cocaine in the mid-seventies has emerged, unequivocally, as the most popular illegal drug in America — the drug of choice. Its popularity and the attractive profit margin it guarantees have accounted for an indicative increase in its traffic on the black market over the last ten years. In 1960 the United States Bureau of Customs seized six pounds of illegal cocaine at American ports of entry. In 1974 the same agency alone seized 907 pounds. In the five-year period between 1969 and 1974, Federal statistics show a 700 percent increase in the government seizure of the drug overall.*

Because cocaine is illegal and because it leaves no lingering traces in the body, it is difficult to count the number of people who use it; because it is not physically addictive, they rarely turn up at hospitals or drug clinics. As inelegant as snorting anything seems to be, most of the people who can afford cocaine are not the kinds of people one is likely to find in public hospitals or listed on police registers. More likely they are to be found coming out of the Athletic Club or the rear door of a Rolls. To snort cocaine is to make a statement. It is like flying to Paris for breakfast. These are people who raise the pedestrian procedure of inhaling to the formality of a tea ceremony. Chop up the crystals, divide the pile into "lines," one for each nostril — call it a one and one — and with a bank note of impressive denomination rolled into a straw . . . *snort*. To skip the preliminary ritual, take a bejeweled sterling silver coke spoon, about the size of a dental tool, and scooping the coke right out of its container . . . *snort*.

It's what's happenin'. And at a thousand dollars an ounce, it is probably not *happenin'* to you.

* See Appendix III.

What goes on behind the lines, between the nose and the central nervous system, is what every coke user, regardless of his economic background, has in common. Back there, in the higher centers of the brain, something is taking place — he feels good. And that is the name of the game. Psychoactive organic chemicals are Nature's way of saying "high." And this psychoactive organic chemical, which has been saying it for centuries, may very well say it the best.

Cocaine is a white, crystalline alkaloid derived from the leaf of the coca bush, *Erythroxylon coca*, a shrub cultivated in the Andean highlands of South America. The plant grows best on the eastern slopes of the Andes, in Bolivia and Peru, between 1,500 and 6,000 feet above sea level in a cool, humid, frost-free evergreen zone with a mean annual temperature of between 65 and 68 degrees Fahrenheit that varies very little from day to day. Coca requires little attention and provides three to four harvests a year, attributes that few other crops can offer. Left unpruned, the cultivated plant may grow as tall as twelve feet; South American *campesinos*, peasant farmers, exploiting the botanical principal of apical dominance (it works as well for coleus and cactus as it does for coca), cut the tree back to three or four feet, keeping it within reach, forcing it to branch outward, thicken and produce more leaves. The green leaf, glabrous on one side, dull on the other, varies in size and shape according to the subspecies of *E. coca* to which it belongs, but is generally oval, pointed at its outer end, and marked by a prominent central vein; it grows from one to four inches in length and from half an inch to two inches in width. The leaf of the coca tree is the plant's cash crop.

The leaf's known existence and use dates back at least a

thousand years to high-plains Inca religious ceremonies. In the sixteenth century, morality-legislating Spanish conquistadores discouraged its use among the Indians slave-laboring in the King's gold mines — until they discovered its potential as an incentive to the twenty-four-hour workday. Several million Altiplano Indians still chew coca leaves today to fight fatigue and to anaesthetize themselves against the high winds and chilling temperatures of altitudes of up to ten thousand feet above sea level. And to get high. The leaves are dried carefully over a fire, or in the sun, then allowed to "sweat" for about three days until the crisp, dry leaf becomes pliable. The *coquero*, the Indian coke-chewer, chews his quid of leaves with an alkaline ash-paste or a bit of lime — these liberate the existing alkaloids, at least fourteen of which have been isolated in the laboratory from the coca leaf, and only one of which is cocaine. The natural plant contains only 0.5 to 1.5 percent cocaine, a bitter alkaloid; the Indians seem to prefer the sweeter leaves, lowest in its content. It was the coca leaf, and not, as commonly thought, cocaine itself, with which Pope Leo XIII's *Vin Coca Mariani* was infused: a tonic for which Parisian pharmacist Angelo Mariani selected only the sweetest leaves and one which was esteemed for its therapeutic value by many leaders of nineteenth-century European society.

In its natural form, coca is rather nourishing. It contains Vitamin C and many B vitamins, and as a non-habit-forming stimulant recommends itself for therapeutic use in modern medicine. It cures altitude sickness, tones the entire digestive tract and promotes the health of the oral cavity and teeth, properties which result from synergy between cocaine and the associate compounds in the leaf. According to Andrew T. Weil, M.D., formerly of the Botanical Museum of Harvard University, "If there is a cocaine problem, its essence is the confusion of the whole leaf with a single component isolated from it. That confusion is a legacy of misinformed science of the last century, which has burdened us with a troublesome white powder and deprived us of the benefits of a useful green medicine."

And that brings one to an investigation of this "troublesome white powder," this motiveless malignity called cocaine, to which is attributed the downfall of more than one poor soul, but one which, by all accounts, is much less malignant than it is maligned.

Coca arrived in Western Europe with the blood and the gold of the Incas, but it was not until 1855 that a German scientist named Gaedcke first isolated from it an alkaloid he called *Erythroxyline* after the genus name of the plant (classified by A.L. DeJussieu and listed in Lamarck's *Encyclopédie Méthodique Botanique* as *Erythroxylon coca* in 1783). The species name, *coca*, is Spanish, derived from the Quechua word *kúka*, then *cuca*, meaning tree, primal tree to the Incas; and it is from the Spanish that another German, a chemist named Niemann, who purified Gaedcke's alkaloid in 1860, derived the name cocaine.

Cocaine is an organic crystalline compound, $C_{17}H_{21}NO_4$ — benzoylmethylecgonine, an ester of ecgonine, an amino alcohol base, and benzoic acid. In its pure form it is white. Its crystals are long and prism-shaped. Its chemistry is that of the hydrocarbons. Its elements, carbon, hydrogen, nitrogen and oxygen, bond covalently — they share electrons. As an alkaloid, cocaine is, by definition, a complex, organic base. Its pH is greater than seven. In solution it turns litmus paper blue. It is water soluble, and by giving up an unshared pair of electrons it will react with an acid to form a salt. To the taste it is bitter. Loosely, it is a carbohydrate. It contains no protein. Or fat. A cocaine diet must be supplemented with food in order to sustain life. This much Niemann knew in 1860. And little more.

It was not until twenty-four years later, when a young, twenty-eight-year-old Viennese physician, never to be distinguished for his medical traditionalism, took the first close look at it, that anything new was learned about this drug. And since Sigmund Freud's *Über Coca* and five subsequent papers, issued between 1884 and 1887, were published, no official study of the drug's impact on human beings has been made. (In 1974, 114 years after cocaine's discovery, 90 years after Freud, and 60 years after the United States government in a seething righteousness-frenzy began funneling massive amounts of money into the enforcement of its statutes prohibiting the possession and sale of cocaine, Dr Robert Byck, a pharmacologist at the Yale School of Medicine, was awarded a $200,000 National Institute on Drug Abuse contract to study the acute effects of cocaine in man.) Freud's cocaine papers, delivered while various surgeons were experimenting with cocaine as a local anaesthetic, detail the results of research he performed upon himself and a colleague, and they remain the only source of empirical data available to modern scientists. What is known today about cocaine is principally hearsay. Freud's first-hand research and the clinical evidence he produced was for years interred — as Marc Antony warned us it might be — with his bones. Only the folklore lived after him.

Freud discovered cocaine to be medically beneficial as a general stimulant — toward the enhancement of a sense of well-being and the temporary suppression of lassitude — and saw in it therapeutic possibilities for the treatment of digestive disorders. He recommended it as a treatment for severe malnutrition and as a local anaesthetic. He thought it might cure neurasthenia — the condition he later called neurosis — and tried it on some of his neurasthenic patients with some success. In oral doses of from .05 to .10 grams, liquid solution, Freud announced, cocaine lifted him from depression, steadied his mind, suppressed his appetite, and strengthened his hand; it was beginning to seem to him a wonder drug:

"Long-lasting, intensive mental or physical work can be performed without fatigue," he wrote; "it is as though the need for food and sleep, which otherwise makes itself felt peremptorily at certain times of the day, were completely banished . . . The psychic effect consists of exhilaration and lasting euphoria, which does not differ in any way from the normal euphoria of a healthy person . . . one senses an increase in self-control and feels more vigorous and more capable of work . . . one is simply normal, and soon finds it difficult to believe that one is under the influence of any drug at all."

Freud was describing the moderate use of small doses of cocaine, and modern clinical research corroborates his findings — Freud was right. Where Freud went wrong, ultimately, was in expecting too much of the drug. He was sure cocaine would cure morphine addiction, and in his enthusiasm for the miracle powder he pressed it on a senior colleague, Dr Ernst von Fleischl-Marxow, a morphine addict, who took what Freud called "frightful" doses of cocaine in an attempt to relieve his pain and in the hope of curing his addiction. It was cocaine's failure to do either and von Fleischl-Marxow's disastrous reactions to the megadosage (among which he claimed hallucinations) that did so much to invalidate Freud's work in the eyes of Viennese doctors and cause Freud's other claims for the drug to be ignored. In one of the later papers Freud found it necessary to defend himself against charges made by a Viennese physician, Emil

Erlenmeyer, that he had loosed "the third scourge of the race," worse than the first two, alcohol and morphine, upon the world.

Leaving the further investigation of cocaine to his colleague, Carl Köller, who had found the drug to be an effective local anaesthetic in eye surgery, Freud eventually abandoned his research.

Eye surgeons soon discovered that Köller's anaesthetic damaged the cornea and excessively dilated the pupil of the eye. (This dilation is known as mydriasis.) They would not discover cocaine's synthetic equivalents until early in the twentieth century. (Einhorn synthesized procaine in 1905.) At the same time, however, William Halsted, of Johns Hopkins, who would become known as the father of modern surgery, was developing nerve-block anaesthesia in the United States, using cocaine as a regional anaesthetic. J. Leonard Corning, in 1885, produced spinal anaesthesia in dogs, but several years passed before the technique was used in clinical surgery. Hall, with the use of cocaine, introduced local anaesthesia into dentistry in 1884.

Between 1884 and 1906 in the United States, cocaine achieved such popularity that it glutted the marketplace, spawning an era described by some historians as that of the "great cocaine explosion." Cocaine parlors, which catered to a polite clientele, opened in many major cities; the drug was available in saloons, served in whiskey shots, and the hoi-polloi could buy cocaine preparations from any number of door-to-door salesmen. Advertising had brought it into every home in America. Patent medicine companies packaged cocaine, coca extract or coca leaves in syrups, tonics, liqueurs, capsules, tablets, hypodermic syringes, cigars, cigarettes and nasal sprays, everything from Agnew's Powder to Ryno's Hay Fever-n-Catarrh Remedy; until it was made illegal, cocaine was endorsed by the Hay Fever Foundation and touted by American doctors as a cure for everything from alcoholism to the common cold. By 1902, surveys indicated, only 3 to 8 percent of all the cocaine sold in major metropolitan areas was going to doctors and dentists; America was buying the rest off the shelves. (In 1906 it was estimated that some 50,000 patent medicines were being manufactured in the United States. U.S. Treasury Department figures for 1904 show that 4,125 pounds of cocaine, either refined or in the form of coca leaves, were imported into the country; in 1905, 4,060 pounds. In 1906, 2,600,000 pounds of coca leaves, enough to yield approximately 21,000 pounds of cocaine, reached America.)

It was during this era that soda fountains first appeared in America's drug stores (in New England, soft drinks are still called "tonic'). In 1886 an Atlanta, Georgia, company introduced a patent medicine containing coca extract, marketed, amid a lot of fanfare, as a tonic to "cure your headache" and "relieve fatigue." They called this "remarkable therapeutic agent" Coca-Cola, "the pause that refreshes." But by 1903, seventeen years after the drink's debut, a growing body of medical opinion, indicating that cocaine might be hazardous to Americans' health, and the pressure applied by fear-crazed Southern politicians to keep cocaine out of the hands of blacks, was enough to prompt the Coca-Cola Company to remove the cocaine from its soft drink. From then on the drink was flavored with de-alkaloided coca extract and hit with caffeine to give it an edge. In 1906 the Pure Food and Drug Act effectively put an end to the cocaine explosion.

It was not until 1914, however, that the drug was made

illegal. In support of its ultimate proscription was that same campaign to legislate morality which led to the Volstead Act six years later; prohibitionists were as passionate about coke as they were about alcohol. But the charge against cocaine which engendered the greatest fury and led to its classification (erroneously) as a hard narcotic — its prohibition never to be repealed — was a racist one, and it was given currency by the medical profession. Writing just before the First World War, a Philadelphia doctor named Christopher Koch warned of the dangers the country faced from cocaine-using blacks of the rural South: "Most of the attacks upon white women of the South," he said, "are the direct result of the cocaine-crazed Negro brain." In *The New York Times*, February 8, 1914, Dr Edward H. Williams, citing Koch and echoing fears firmly established by 1910, reported "Negro cocaine fiends [as] a new Southern menace." The fear spawned by these and other physicians coincided with a rise in lynchings in the South and helped speed the passage of the legislation reinforcing segregation and voting restrictions which was designed to limit the social and political power of blacks in the early years of this century. (Though there was no concrete evidence of this "cocainomania," some Southern law enforcement agencies converted from .32 to .38 calibre ammunition, convinced as they were by these medical reports that the smaller rounds would never stop a "coke-crazed nigger.")

Soon black crime in particular, and the demented and the violent in general, became so closely associated with cocaine use that most Americans welcomed its prohibition. History suggests that cocaine was condemned by the medical profession not on the basis of any evidence that the drug was dangerous, but in fact because it severely threatened the physician's traditional privilege to grant and withhold medicines. While delivering the final blow to the multi-million-dollar patent-medicine industry, the spectre of the black cocainomaniac — just what the doctor ordered — helped secure the image of the doctor as public benefactor, an image tarnished by a miracle "feel-good" drug, the prescription of which put a doctor on par with a cosmetologist or wine-merchant, who catered to whims rather than needs; and it is in keeping with the tradition of modern medical practice that shortly after the eradication of cocaine, the American medical community began touting a new "feel-good" drug — the amphetamines — synthetic, marketable, and well under the medical thumb — and probably the most dangerous piece of chemistry since Alfred Nobel gave us dynamite.*

Cocaine was finally driven underground by the Harrison Narcotic Act of 1914. (By then forty-six states had already passed legislation restricting its use and sale.) It disappeared briefly, surfacing in the twenties and thirties as the drug of choice among musicians and film people, *à la recherche du temps perdu*, and was effectively absent during World War II, not to emerge again until the rock years, when musicians picked up on it once more. With the passage of the Act and subsequent legislation (specifically the amended Narcotic Drugs Import and Export Act, 1922), cocaine was classified as a narcotic — which by any pharmacological definition it is *not* — surprising to no one today, given the ignorance and moral frenzy that surrounded the drug at the time; what is perplexing is that the mistake has not yet been officially acknowledged, let alone corrected.

* See Appendix IV.

Today, the possession or sale of cocaine carries the same penalties as that for the possession or sale of heroin — five years under the Federal statutes, fifteen years to life in New York State. The medical evidence that has come to light in defense of the use of cocaine since the drug culture gained establishment status in the late 1960s only seems to reinforce a citizen's mistrust of the government wisdom.

Cocaine, externally applied, is a vascoconstrictor — it inhibits bleeding. And it inhibits impulse conduction in the body's nerve fibers; it was in this way that it became the first local anaesthetic in modern surgery. It is still used in operations on the larynx and in certain surgical procedures on the pituitary. Ear, nose and throat specialists sometimes use it, applied in liquid solution, for nose surgery. Its synthetic relatives are benzocaine and procaine, the latter marketed (in quantity to dentists) under the trade name Novocain. The synthetics differ from the original, however, in terms of versatility and application.

Coke taken internally, either in crystalline form or in solution, acts as a peripheral nervous system stimulant. It does so in much the same way that other antidepressants do. Norepinephrine (or noradrenalin), the hormone released by sympathetic nerve endings in the human periphery whenever they are stimulated, and which causes the blood pressure to rise, is normally reabsorbed by the nerve so quickly that the reaction is imperceptible. Cocaine reinforces this stimulation by inhibiting the reabsorption of norepinephrine by the nerve. There is no clinical evidence to support that a similar process occurs in the central nervous system, but the suspicion is that it might. Because there is no evidence that cocaine increases the strength of muscular contraction, one must assume that the ability of the drug to relieve or delay fatigue results from central stimulation, which masks its sensation. While the blood pressure increases, the body temperature, due to greater muscular activity under nerve stimulation and a decrease in heat elimination under vasoconstriction, rises (cocaine is markedly pyrogenic). The heartbeat accelerates, the pupils dilate. You are high.

The body metabolizes cocaine quickly. The high is brief. Cocaine takes effect most rapidly when injected (Sherlock Holmes was fond of a 7 percent solution), slightly less rapidly when snorted (the average dose is 20–30 milligrams) or gummed (rubbed into the gums of the mouth), and least rapidly when swallowed (hydrolized in the gastrointestinal tract). The stomach begins breaking it down immediately. When taken for the suppression of appetite, essentially by way of stomach-lining anaesthetization, cocaine in oral dosage may be the best. Freud often drank his cocaine in an aqueous solution and did not enjoy what users today, most of whom snort the crystals, look for in theirs: the rush that comes when the powder, dissolving in the nose and upper throat, is rapidly assimilated into the bloodstream, and the clear, open breathing that comes when the cocaine shrinks the mucous membranes and clears the sinuses and bronchi. The "freeze" that some coke users cherish is the numbing sensation that follows the drug's anaesthetizing of the mucosa of the nose; if it is an authentic freeze, it comes from a heavy hit of Novocain or Lidocaine — Freud had the advantage of pure; hard to come by on the street.

Cocaine's rush, or flash, is most profound when the drug is taken by way of the intravenous injection of a prepared solution. Call it the mainline. But the intravenous injection of anything, especially an illegal drug, is risky at best. Even doctors muck it up sometimes. And as far as sterile equipment is concerned — well, it is something you have trouble finding even in a lot of major hospitals. Given the state of the art, and the random sampling of cuts available to every dealer through whose hands street-coke passes, shooting up is a sucker move. (Sherlock Holmes was buying pure, and he was cutting it himself, with water. And he was Sherlock Holmes.) Forget it.

The effects of cocaine upon the average individual are so subtle that many users do not recognize a reaction until one is pointed out to them. Many acid-freaks, most mushroom-types, an addict of any kind, alcoholics and some heavy marijuana smokers think cocaine is a waste of money. Serious dopers hate it. Cocaine has no edge. It is strictly a motor drug. It does not alter your perception; it will not even wire you up like the amphetamines. No pictures, no time/space warping, no danger, no fun, no edge. Any individual serious about his chemicals — a heavy hitter — would sooner take thirty No-Doz. Coke is to acid what jazz is to rock. You have to appreciate it. *It* does not come to *you*.

Street coke, if you buy it by the gram, may be cut as much as 80 percent; by then all it will do is numb your nose, and that is more likely the work of the cut than of the cocaine. At fifty to a hundred dollars a gram, it *is* a waste of money. High-grade coke (anything 80 percent pure or above) is something obtained only in quantity. And that subtle, seductive *frisson* that pre-ops you for about six hours of root-canal work on the brain is expensive. The greater the number of people who handle coke before it gets home, the more often it is going to be hit. Everybody puts a whack on it before he sells it. Lactose (milk sugar) is a common cut; dextrose is sweeter, easier to spot; various amino acids, which are tasteless, provide a high-grade cut, but are much more expensive and harder to come by than the carbo-hydrates, and thus are not often used; nor is quinine. The

Italian laxative, *Mannite*, is very popular; it is heavier than lactose (coke is sold by weight) and it takes on the coke excellently. Procaine and the other synthetics are used because they enhance the freeze. Amphetamine cuts are popular because they ensure a noticeable high — they also burn the nose.

A good coke dealer will choose his cuts according to his clientele. And what every coke dealer knows is that there are very few people out there who know anything at all about cocaine, and fewer still who have ever snorted pure. Everyone's expectations are different. Every user's standard of quality is a measure of what he snorted the last time. If a user wants speed, a good dealer gives him speed; if he is looking for a freeze, he gets Novocain. Some think lumps are a sign of purity — a dealer will wet the coke down. A dealer dealing in quantity, buying and selling kilos, will hit his product with borax, because it is extremely heavy. He not only doubles his weight, but he doubles it with less than a full hit. If he ounces out a good count to his steady customers, he peddles what is left to the sucker trade, keeping the customer satisfied. The retail sucker market in cocaine thrives on the same buyer mentality that prevails on Madison Avenue — *if he's selling it for seventy-five dollars a gram, it must be cocaine*.

Latin America supplies all of the cocaine sold in the United States, where the demand for the drug has increased so greatly that the price of coca leaves in some South American countries has risen 1,500 percent since 1973, from four dollars to sixty dollars a bale (or *tambor*). Because of the large quantity of leaves required to produce cocaine — in kilos, anywhere from 100/1 to 150/1 — the leaves are often processed by the *campesinos* themselves (most of them Indians) in stills close to the growing areas. (The cultivation of coca is carried on in small terraced plantations called *cocales*, usually hillside clearings of two or three acres with an average of seven thousand plants to the acre.) The stills required are no more than oil drums containing a solution of potash (potassium carbonate), water and kerosene in which the leaves can soak. When the alkaloids soak free, the fluid is drained off and the leaves removed, leaving behind a brown paste, which when treated with hydrochloric acid will yield an equivalent amount of cocaine. (Call it cocaine hydrochloride, which is what illegal cocaine actually is. The chemical division of Merck Sharp & Dohme, one of the principal manufacturers of official pharmaceutical cocaine in the United States, markets the alkaloid bonded to the same cation. "Merck," as it is commonly called, is cocaine hydrochloride.)

Cocaine processing does not require sophisticated chemistry; a lab can be set up with about $1,500 worth of equipment. Bolivian traffickers buy the paste from the *campesinos* and either process it themselves or export it at a 300 percent profit to laboratories in Argentina, Paraguay, Brazil and Chile. Until the 1973 Allende overthrow, Bolivia exported most of its paste to Chile, which has always been known for having the best cocaine chemists in South America; it was they who first taught the Bolivian *campesinos* how to turn the coca leaf into paste. Peru (with Bolivia, the only other Latin American country where the cultivation of coca leaves is legal — together they produce approximately 11.5 million kilograms of leaves a year, the world's largest importer being the United States, which buys 200,000 to 250,000 kilograms annually) exports chiefly to Ecuador and Colombia. And Colombia sends more cocaine to the United States than does any other country in South America.

The mathematics of the cocaine trade, from South

American soil to New York nose, in the absence of any other contingency which attends it, is enough to keep the traffic alive forever. A South American farmer makes less than $2 a kilo for his coca leaves. A trafficker will pay him around $350 for a kilo of paste. A chemist, if he buys from a paste trafficker instead of directly from the farmer, may pay up to $1,000 a kilo for paste. Delivered in Latin America, a kilo of cocaine, 90 to 98 percent pure (as pure as it gets), costs anywhere from $4,000 in Lima to $8,500 in Buenos Aires. A dealer with a mobile lab can turn a $350 raw-material investment into a $6,000 product. A good lab can process one hundred pounds of cocaine a week.

When the cocaine leaves South America, the mathematics gets heavier. In New York, a kilo of coke sells for over $30,000. That is what a smuggler charges. But the kilo which the smuggler pays $6,000 for in South America is pure. He can put a full hit on it, turn it into *two* $30,000 kilos, and sell his product 50 percent pure, converting a $6,000 invest-ment into a $60,000 product. And he can make more if he ounces it. Most smugglers, however, who will always sell their product in quantity when they can (like anything else, especially something as perishable and incriminating as cocaine, the faster you move it, the longer you stay in busi-ness), will not step on their product that hard. They will move kilos at no less than 80 percent. They will sell their ounce-dealers coke that has been stepped on a little bit more. An ounce-dealer will pay between $850 and $1,000 an ounce for 70 to 80 percent pure, then step on his ounces himself and turn them over for a few hundred more. Grams go for $50 to $100 in New York; a gram-dealer never sells better than 50 percent coke. After all, he has to pay for the tinfoil. Cocaine is a seller's market. A dealer can hit his product as hard as he wants, and the sucker trade is large enough for a gram-dealer to unload his goods fast. The only way to get pure is to buy in quantity, and even then there is no guarantee. A smuggler who snorts his own product will usually cut it slightly to mellow its passage, but what he is cutting is pure, and he is only cutting it slightly. And he is snorting it right away. And as any smuggler will tell you: There is only pure, there is nothing else; if you are not buying pure, you are not buying cocaine.

"The stuff they blow on the street is shit compared with what we're doing. That's why they're doing two and two's and three and three's. We do a one and one and we're high."

The smuggler is the man out front in the cocaine traffic. And the traffic is getting heavier. People are crossing the border every day with coke stashed in everything from vaginas to live snakes. Drugs are coming into the country in boatloads bypassing those borders. Since the day the doctor stopped making housecalls and we all learned to dose ourselves, and since the day we learned that alcohol was not the only game in town, dope has become a very big business. There manifests itself today in the United States an increasing demand for drugs of all kinds. Alcohol consumption is up, tobacco consumption is up, marijuana consumption is up, pill-popping is as popular as ever; Americans are taking a greater variety of drugs, and taking them in greater quantities, than ever. Uncle Sam calls it drug abuse.

The term *drug abuse*, as employed by the Federal government, enjoys about as much grammatic and syntactic validity as the term *self abuse*. And their own abuse of the English language is not the only thing these two expressions have in common — for example, they both refer to activities that feel good. Where they differ is on much more subtle ground. The former, *drug abuse*, lacks the theological thrust by which the latter excuses itself; that is, in the stale locker rooms of Judaeo-Christian tradition, an individual has the opportunity to abuse a body not theologically his own, a body on loan from a higher Office, say, where interest rates are low. Hence, *self abuse* evolves and is embraced by the language. But in order to participate correctly in *drug abuse*, one would be required to anthropomorphize the drug in question — impart to it human characteristics — or ultimately to abuse the drugs of another (which is done not infrequently, but usually only by agents of the Federal government). Drug *misuse*, on the other hand (also frequently practiced by agents of the Federal government), is what the laws of the United States in fact prohibit. And it is these laws that are at issue here.

One is compelled to accept the implications of a medical and legal *misuse* of drugs. It is in an attempt to rationalize the determinants of this misuse that one encounters difficulty. After all, it did not take medical science two thousand years, and this in the shadow of the Church, to prove clinically that masturbation does not lead to blindness. If it takes that long to show that a little dope is just as harmless, it is not because the biochemistry is any more complex — it is because medical science is exerting all its efforts to prove the opposite.

What medical science, under the auspices of the United States government, has been able to uncover in the way of *prima facie* evidence to support the Drug Enforcement Administration's case against chemicals on its list of Controlled Substances parallels the strides made by the Unicorn in its pilgrimage across the minefield of evolution. What at first required a mere exercise of faith on the part of the American taxpayer now, on the threshold of the twenty-first century, calls for the willing suspension of disbelief. The mound of misinformation generated unashamedly by the hulking and etherized beast of government research is dwarfed only by the stack of money it costs to feed the monster, while the bureaucratic campaign to keep the beast incumbent thrives on nothing more substantial than its own propaganda. The rewards of the system are minimal. And the Controlled Substances list is the Domino Theory of the seventies.

Government antidrug literature tells us that cocaine use results in paranoia and organic psychosis. The country's most reliable experts on cocaine have been unable, either through hospital admittance records or through evidence given by clinical psychiatrists, to uncover any case of psychosis directly attributable to the drug. The best one can gather from the data available is that psychotics who use cocaine will be psychotic. The same literature tells us that coke users experience suicidal depression when deprived of the drug. Such depression has not been reported in recent medical history, even among users who consumed coke daily for years. Cocaine is not necessarily habit-forming, nor do its users develop a physical tolerance to it. Any "craving" for cocaine will develop along the same lines as the craving for money, sex, apple pie and chewing gum. Nor is cocaine an aphrodisiac — there is nothing in the chemistry of cocaine, beyond its properties as a peripheral-nervous-system stimulant and mood elevator, to indicate that it in any way enhances human sexual response — although inhaling seventy-five dollars into your bloodstream in a matter of seconds, and that at the risk of fifteen years in jail, must do something for your libido. Most of the drug's folklore, including its ability to prolong sexual performance, is anecdotal. Some men believe in applying cocaine to the glans penis to anaesthetize it against premature ejaculation, but doing so is more an act of bravado than one of clinical merit. Solarcaine, available over the counter at a fraction of the cost, works as effectively. In terms of myth, what cocaine has done for fornication it has done ten-fold for formication — the spontaneous abnormal sensation that insects are crawling over your skin. That is one of the things they like to tell you will happen if you get on the wrong side of coke — one of the literature's favorite horror stories. It is as untrue as the rest. What *is* true is as conspicuous by its absence in the literature as is the folklore by its presence. Because the government knows nothing about drugs, it does not know that there are *good* reasons for not doing cocaine.

Long-term snorting of cocaine can irritate and possibly damage the tissue of the nose, especially the septum. The chronic vasoconstriction results in ischemia and subsequent sloughing of the mucosa, by which the avascular septum is protected; and though antihistamines will do the same thing, chronic cocaine use, after tertiary syphilis, is the second most common cause of septal perforation.

> "... *my mucous membranes is just a memory*
> *Cocaine* ..."
>
> "Cocaine Blues"*
> REV. GARY DAVIS

There is abundant proof that the local anaesthetics are destroyed chiefly by the liver. Because cocaine is broken

* Additional lyrics.

down and detoxified there, those with severe liver damage are advised to stay away from it. A few people who use cocaine may be allergic to it, as one might be allergic to bee stings or penicillin; for them the risk of anaphylactic shock is a serious one. There are certainly more deaths each year attributable to aspirin than can be attributed to cocaine throughout history; like almost anything else, however, there is a lethal dose. It can be found to vary from individual to individual, and can be found very easily: fill up a syringe and shoot a gram of pure; if it does not kill you, increase the dose until it does. (Do the same with coffee, Scotch, delta-9 tetrahydrocannabinol or lighter fluid, and you are playing the same game.) It has been demonstrated clinically that, since 1914, the greatest danger connected with the moderate use of cocaine is legal and not chemical.

Cocaine's popularity in the United States may very well be a function of the fact that it, more than any other of the recognized psychoactive drugs, reinforces all those character qualities that have come to be admired as truly American: initiative, drive, optimism, the need for achievement and the embrace of power. Wherever it comes from, that popularity is clear and present. (A recent experiment showed that rats, Pavloved to push a reward lever, did so up to 250 successive times for caffeine, 4,000 times for heroin and 10,000 times for cocaine.) Cocaine is called "nosecandy" for a reason. People like it. It makes them feel good. And it makes them feel good in a way that its substitutes, procaine and benzocaine, do not. Cocaine has a sweet and subtle second-strike capability. And it was this second-strike capability that appealed to Zachary Swan — the mind-caressing, power-infusing, psychic jolt that carried him beyond the dreams of his childhood and into the kaleidoscopic wonderland of middle age.

GOING SOUTH

6

A RAINY DAY IN SANTA MARTA

"Colombia. And that's not an Ivy League University" — Zachary Swan.

Nor is it located in Morningside Heights. Colombia, with an "o," one of the few conspicuous republics in South America, occupies 439,828 square miles of prospective real estate on the northwest coast of the world's fourth largest continent. Embellished by the umbilical Isthmus of Panama, the continent's overland route to the north, it is embraced by both the Atlantic (in the costume of the Caribbean) and the Pacific Oceans, and bordered inland by Venezuela on the east, Brazil on the south-east, and Ecuador and Peru on the southwest. Its population hovers somewhere near twenty million. At Santa Marta in the north, the Sierra Nevada rise out of the Caribbean, a prologue to the Andes which dominate the western half of the country from Venezuela to Peru. At Leticia, in the country's southeastern-most corner, the Amazon, coming out of the Peruvian Andes, begins its two-thousand-mile journey across Brazil to the Atlantic. North of Leticia, delimiting the country's lower quarter, is the equator.

Colombia's capital and largest city is Bogotá, population three million, located 8,660 feet above sea level in the Cordillera Central range of the Colombian Andes. The country's natural resources include vast tracts of arable land, a favorable climate, abundant mineral deposits and two oceans. Colombia is the world's largest exporter of emeralds — it accounts for 80 percent of the total. It is famous the world over for its coffee. Its economic and political history is the subject of more than one course of study at Georgetown University's School of Foreign Service (because its economic and political future, like that of every South American country, is the foster child of United States business interests and the CIA); its cultural history, American Indian in origin, is of interest to archaeologists and anthropologists everywhere; and, because it has the greatest variety of birds of any single country in the world, one might say it is of interest to a few ornithologists as well. But to a significant majority of the world's under-thirty population, Colombia, South America — national flower, the orchid — is best known for its dope. The finest marijuana in the world grows here. And though Colombia, itself, is not South America's largest producer of cocaine, it is, through a combination of geographical, economic and political forces, what amounts to general headquarters and central bank for worldwide cocaine traffic.

When Zachary Swan stepped off the plane in Santa Marta with his finger on his nose, neo-dynamite, high-altitude, Colombian-loco-weed marijuana had just hit the headlines back home like a debutante at a cockfight. Colombian dope, overnight, had become a growth industry. Like every fishing village along the coast, Santa Marta had come alive, and was throwing all its resources behind the national effort. At least two nights a week the local power plant would shut down while the smugglers, by cover of darkness, took their cash-crop cargoes aboard and shipped out. Police bribes were the savings bonds of the nationwide drive. Swan had flown first to Peru, but left after two days, having been advised by Tito's uncle, the restaurateur and an avid coke user, that things there were hot, there was nothing coming down, that the police in Lima, alas, were honest.

After walking around on the beach in Santa Marta for three days, coming on to all the acid-heads like a kind of shipwrecked, beat-generation Ronald Colman with a sinus condition . . . as if the sight of a middle-aged packaging executive in cut-off, tie-dyed Levis were not enough for *them* . . . Swan decided to give his index finger a rest. After all, he had charged this trip to American Express. And if Michel Bernier had been wrong about Santa Marta, it was a good bet that he had been wrong about his elderly friend in Bogotá as well; and if in the end every lead was going to dead-end on him like this, Swan figured, at least in Santa Marta he could pay some serious attention to working on his tan. On the evening of the third day, after dinner alone at his hotel, Swan spotted a campfire on the beach about a hundred yards from the hotel grounds and strolled down toward it (with his hands in his pockets) to take a look.

Here, silhouetted in the firelight, he saw many of the same faces he had been passing on the beach during the daylight hours, the faces of young people, camped out, dug in for the night about thirty yards from the tide line, waiting for the sun, the Apocalypse, Godot or the local police to move them on, killing time and themselves in the process. It was what Swan would see very much of throughout Colombia before he left the country for good, and having never seen it before in his life he was unprepared to see it now for the nightmare it would be. Here he met a young man named Blackie, whom he had not seen previously. Blackie, who spoke English and was determined someday to live where it was spoken by everyone, was pleased to have found an American to talk to. Blackie was about twenty years old, half-Indian and half-Negro. Raised as part of a tribe near Leticia, he saw Santa Marta beach life as a kind of upward mobility. His African genes governed his skin color and hair. He was lean and strong. Dressed in a bathing suit and wearing a silver Aztec medallion around his neck, he was something extraordinary to behold. He gave Swan his first hit of Santa Marta Gold, and before long the two of them were old friends.

From Blackie, Swan learned of an American in Santa Marta, a Texan named Paul who was rumored to have a cocaine connection. Blackie himself had a friend in Barranquilla with a definite link, but advised Swan to see the American first because he was local. Swan was staying at the Hotel Tamaca in Santa Marta's Rodadero district. The next morning he and Blackie walked along the beach to Tahiti Estates, a tract of low-income ocean-front housing where Paul lived. The Texan wanted $8,000 a kilo and $1,000 down, a price Swan knew was way out of line. (In questioning people around town, Swan subsequently learned that the Texan was actually supporting himself by taking advances and then disappearing on his customers, hanging out in Tobago until the heat was off.) Swan would have to go to Barranquilla.

Before he left Tahiti Estates, Swan was introduced to two American women, in their early twenties, who all of a sudden began to tax his understanding. He could not tag them. *Two*

*American girls . . . not on the track . . . in their early twenties
. . .* was all he was able to put together. They had been making
lunch when he met them, a kind of fish stew, and there were
bones and fish parts on the floor all around them. In the air
around them there was an aura of dope and mushrooms.

The older of the two was Jane, tall and big boned, whose
dark brown hair took on the appearance of a hat. It covered
her ears and almost met her eyebrows. It was thick and
curly, fluffed up into an Orphan Annie Afro, but she looked
more like Sluggo's girlfriend than Punjab's. She looked
Jewish, and Swan was sure she had spent more than an
afternoon in Brooklyn. Her friend, April, was short. Her
hair was blond and straight. She was rather plain. She played
the guitar. Both of them were dressed in long, loose blouses
and nothing else.

Jane and April had fish stew and psilocybin for lunch.
Swan asked them how they liked the stew. A half hour later,
April said:

"We like it, we're stuffed."

They removed their blouses and ran out into the ocean.
Swan asked Paul who they were.

Paul explained that a rich, middle-aged lunatic from San
Francisco, appropriately named Mad Walter, in 1968 had
chartered a plane and given fifty Haight-Ashbury street
people round-trip tickets on it to Tobago. About twenty of
them had made it back to the States. The rest, having sold
their tickets — for dope or to extend their stay — or having
been robbed of them, were now strung out all over Colombia
and Venezuela, camping, backpacking, hitchhiking, getting
beaten, robbed and raped and periodically jailed, some of
them trying to get home, some trying simply to get by, and
others, like Jane and April, just not trying at all anymore.

Swan would meet Jane and April again, in Cartagena,

and, as he had done today, he would refer to Jane as June and ask questions like, "April? May June?" But beneath it all, he knew that the joke was on him. The nightmare had begun. Because these two women (and he thought back to the campfire of the night before) were just two of the many such people he would run across (and over, and around, by and sometimes with) on this and subsequent trips to Colombia, people of no certifiable age, background, job description, socio-economic class, outlook or future, people who were just ... *there* ... young men and women with the likes of whom Swan had had absolutely no previous experience, and for whom he would be able to do little but occasionally draw bail. These people were on the edge, their presence sometimes no more than physical, anchored to a place in time only by an accident of physics, the children of Einstein, their existence relative ... *the only Universal constant known to man is the speed of light* ... each in his own accelerated frame of reference ... here they were, right out of the pages of the *Mutability Cantos*, Spenser's doubts confirmed ... all is flux ... *pass the mescaline* ... *what's that, an aspirin, I'll have one of those* ... anything ... up is down, day is night, communication is dead.

> "All that you touch
> All that you see ...
> All that you do
> All that you say ...
> ... everything under the sun is in tune
> but the sun is eclipsed by the moon."

> "Eclipse," from *Dark Side of the Moon*,
> PINK FLOYD

That evening Blackie's sidekick and dope curator, Fernando, rolled one of his special joints — an entire issue of *Time* Magazine rolled around almost half an ounce of Colombian chiba-chiba; it took three matches and a Zippo to torch it — and Swan spent the night in Never Never Land with all his new friends. He left for Barranquilla the next day.

Santa Marta is the oldest European-founded city on the South American mainland. Established in 1524, still devoted chiefly to agriculture and fishing, it stands surrounded by a string of nine bays backed by the Sierra Nevada, the highest peaks in Colombia and the present-day home of the Arhuaco Indians. Snow-capped year round, the mountains provide an awe-inspiring contrast to the tropical Caribbean — if Balboa had come this way he would never have discovered the Pacific. El Rodadero Beach, where Swan stayed when he was in Santa Marta, lies between the airport and the city itself and is rapidly becoming the country's most important resort.

Barranquilla, the second-largest city in Colombia, is located about a hundred miles southwest of Santa Marta at the mouth of the Magdalena River, eight miles upstream from the Caribbean Sea. A combination port city and industrial sewer, Barranquilla displays all the drawbacks of South American coastal life and none of its advantages. An embarrassment to most Colombians, it is a city choked and teeming with disease, a south-of-the-border Dickensian cesspool, decidely urban but in no way cosmopolitan, a kind of backwater Bogotá without the mountains that everyone wishes would disappear. They do not mention it much in the travelogues. What it amounts to, in the minds of Colombian tourists, is one vast and uncomfortable waiting room to be tolerated as briefly as possible while making international flight connections at its airport. Americans never hear about it until they get there.

Swan and Blackie, with Fernando in tow, took an express bus from Santa Marta to Barranquilla, a four-hour ride through the countryside and Swan's first exposure to the rural realities of South American Indian life. The trip also afforded Swan his first look at the Colombian Army, by way of the soldiers who manned the numerous checkpoints along the road. More of a Federal police force than an actual army, these men provided the government with a kind of internal Customs, a grass-roots privacy-invasion force designed to intimidate long-hairs and indigents in transit, enforcing the dress code, as it were, and taking advantage of young women on the lam ... *Uncle Simón Wants YOU ... good pay plus all the contraband and ass you can get.*

In Barranquilla, Swan met Blackie's friend, whose name was José. José was short and round, a lower-middle-class Colombian with an apartment of his own, who spoke a little English, and, though Swan did not know it yet, was a rank amateur. But José was trying. He went out to score a sample and was gone six hours. He was trying hard. The room was hot (as they always are ten degrees north of the equator), and by the time José returned, Swan needed the lift he had expected cocaine would give him. But Swan was something of an amateur too, at least as far as cocaine was concerned, and when he failed to get an immediate reaction, looking for a rush more on the order of that which speed is famous for, he was disappointed. He gave José $100 and took ten grams. He had come with $4,000; he would look somewhere else. Swan said thanks, Blackie said goodbye, Fernando said nothing, and they left. They missed the last bus to Santa Marta, so they took a cab.

The next morning Swan was back on Rodadero Beach. This time he met four Americans. Bill was a bookie from New Orleans. His girlfriend's name was Elaine. Mike was a bartender and was traveling with a woman named Terry. Both of the women were cocktail waitresses. All had just come from San Andrés, a Colombian island off the coast of Nicaragua. They were on vacation. They had grass and mescaline and invited Swan back to their hotel to get wrecked. Swan accepted the invitation and brought along his cocaine.

From the Americans, Swan learned that his cocaine was, in fact, excellent. They explained the subtlety of the cocaine high, and they told Swan his connection had done well by him. Swan then decided that if he did not find anything better in Santa Marta, he would go back to Barranquilla and invest the balance of his grubstake in José's product. If he did go back, however, he would not go back alone — the next morning on the beach he met René Day.

René Day was a Canadian, tall and quiet, broad-shouldered and lean in the face. He had short, curly dirty-blond hair, and eyes the color of smoke. He was twenty-eight years old, more intelligent than anyone Swan would run across in Colombia, and he was careful, or at least appeared to be. He and Swan would become close friends. Swan would learn later that René had been born into money in Quebec and did what he did for the hell of it.

What René Day did before he started smuggling cocaine was pretty much whatever he felt like doing. When Swan met him he was carrying at least three passports. He had been making money cashing his traveler's checks in at banks and casinos in cities throughout Colombia and the next day going somewhere else to report them stolen. He was a very casual fellow, a good con. He loved Colombia and had backpacked throughout South America. He would hit a city in the morning looking like a vagrant and at ten in the evening would show up at the nearest casino wearing a white linen jacket, sipping Scotch and breaking the hearts of elegant women at the blackjack tables. He was well educated, confident and mature. His father was English, his mother Québecoise. He spoke fluent French. He loved women as a class, they loved him, and René was never out of their company for long.

The woman he was traveling with when Swan met him on the beach at Santa Marta was twenty-three years old, a Canadian law student René had known for two years and who had come back to Colombia with him after his most recent trip home. Her name was Debbie. She was tall and fair, as attractive as one would expect a law student to be, with long brown hair and dark brown eyes. She was nearsighted and wore wire-rimmed glasses which she never adjusted once they were on. She was a vegetarian by inclination (which made staying alive in Colombia difficult) and a Chapstick addict by virtue of her need for at least one identifying vice. She had a mind of her own, and Swan thought she talked like a lawyer. Debbie and René had just hit town and were off to visit friends. Swan went along.

Over the next three days, as Swan and René got to know each other, they pooled their efforts in the search for a coke connection. It became a two-man operation. Swan was seeing René and Debbie every night at dinner, and he was hanging out with them on the beach during the day. Blackie was always around, though he was not allowed near the hotel, and Fernando was always somewhere nearby. Mike, Terry, Bill and Elaine had left town. One evening after dinner, Swan was sharing his coke with Debbie and René, snorting through a hundred-peso note, when René suggested that the three of them try the casino.

"Can I get in like this?" Debbie asked. She was wearing jeans.

"I doubt it," said Swan.

"No problem," said René.

René reached for his knapsack, pulled it over to the bed on which he was sitting, dug his hands into it and pulled out a cellophane bag. He handed the bag to Debbie.

"Try this," he said.

In the bag was a cocktail dress.

"Rennie!"

"My little bag of tricks," said René.

"Perfect," said Swan.

"This is a survival kit." René heaved the knapsack onto the bed. "Man does not live by bread alone. Casinos are very important to me."

René reached into the sack again and pulled out a pair of trousers to match his linen jacket.

"Do you believe this guy?" said Debbie.

"You call him Rennie?" asked Swan.

"That's his name."

"Yeah, I guess it would be," Swan said. "Rennie."

Swan loved it. He called him Rainy. The name stuck.

When Swan and his pal Rainy Day failed to come up with anything in the way of a cocaine connection in Santa Marta, they decided to see José in Barranquilla.

Swan had been advised to stay at the Del Prado Hotel when he got to Barranquilla: "Everybody stays there. Every deal that happens, happens at the Del Prado. There's no second-level hotel in Barranquilla. It's a hot, sweaty town. Spread out all over. If you tell somebody you're in Barranquilla, they just go right to the Del Prado to find you. You're either there or at the discotheque across the street. You just don't go any farther."

Swan had sent a message to José via Blackie and was waiting at the Del Prado when he bumped into Mike and Terry and their friends having dinner by the pool. (They had been asked to leave their hotel in Santa Marta when it was discovered that they had been smoking dope in their rooms. They were heading west.) Swan was planning to meet José that evening and set up a score for both himself and René. He sat down with the Americans and ordered coffee. His back was to the door. By the time his coffee arrived it was dark out. Swan was lifting his second cup of coffee to his lips when Terry said:

"There's your connection."

Swan, a bit confused, put down his cup and looked over his shoulder. He let out an audible groan, ducked his head and said:

"Uh huh."

Mike, who had decided to make a buy after talking to Swan, said:

"I've changed my mind."

José had come through the door, stopped, shifted his eyes from side to side without moving his head, pulled at his sleeve cuffs, twitched his shoulders and begun to stroll nonchalantly around the pool. He was wearing wrap-around sunglasses. He passed Swan's table without looking, paused, moved away very casually and sat down a few tables away. He took in the scenery, looking everywhere but in the direction of Swan and his companions. If one did not know him, one would think he was a cocaine dealer making a connection with five Americans . . . *at that table over there.* Swan and his friends all stood up and left the place.

Five minutes later, looking from the window of his room,

Swan saw José standing below him in front of the hotel talking to a young, well-dressed Colombian with blond hair. When the stranger left, Blackie walked up. He and José talked for a minute, until Blackie was run off the grounds by a hotel employee. Blackie called Swan at the Del Prado later that evening from José's apartment.

"What happened?" he asked.

"Meet me in an hour across the street," Swan said.

An hour later, Swan was feeding Blackie at a hamburger stand around the corner. He ordered him a milk shake and said:

"I want to jump José."

Blackie stopped chewing.

"I want to get to his supplier. I want to meet with the blond kid."

Blackie took the milk shake.

"José's my friend," Blackie said.

Swan pulled out his money.

The blond kid's name was Emilio. His father, a Frenchman, was a money changer, one of Barranquilla's chief currency dealers. During the day, Emilio worked in his father's office. At night he handled about 80 percent of the cocaine sales to Americans out of Barranquilla. Swan met him that night at the discotheque across the street from the Del Prado. Emilio wanted seven dollars a gram. He could deliver in 24 hours. Swan and René scored the following night at the hotel.

Before leaving New York, Swan had been introduced to a very heavy individual named Anthony. Anthony was a man involved in crime in a rather professional way. He was organized — from above. He was not at all what Swan had expected. He was young, literate, and among thieves honest, but he was at the same time very dangerous, and Swan was not above showing him the proper respect. Swan had been introduced to him by Ellery, who had explained to Anthony that Swan was reliable, had stood up when Charlie Kendricks was busted, and was a very good investment if he, Anthony, were looking for one. "He's going South," Ellery had said. Anthony, as it happened, was looking for a sound Southern investment, and Swan was looking for financial backing. But between the time Anthony was able to change the unmarked tens into currency streamlined for travel ('Maybe you could give me hundreds, instead, something I can carry without the briefcase') and the time Swan was ready to pick it up, Anthony had talked to Nice Mickey, Pirata's friend, who suggested that a man with techniques as Byzantine as Swan's might be a bad risk. So Swan left New York with a polite excuse from Anthony (instead of the money) a "maybe next time," and what he had been able to pick up in the way of an education. Anthony had shown him how to run cocaine purity tests.

The deal went down in a room two floors above Swan's at the Del Prado, a room near the stairway, reserved exclusively for the transaction. Swan was carrying $3,000, and under his arm he had a satchel in which to carry the coke back to his room. He was nervous. Emilio came in with a young man named Ricardo, a partner. Emilio, a professional, knew better than to walk into a room with cocaine and no backup man. René was behind Swan. The cocaine was triple-wrapped in clear polyethylene to protect it from the moisture. Swan ran two tests on it before snorting it.

A water test is done with a clear glass tumbler and cold water. Crystals of pure cocaine dropped into the water will dissolve before they reach the bottom of the glass. Impurities will slick out on the way down. A smart buyer will fill the glass himself, because a smart dealer will fill it with warm water if given the chance (which is exactly what Ricardo did when Swan let him fill this one). Swan had never seen the test done, and because he did not know exactly what he was looking for, he gave the coke a passing grade. It looked good enough to him. The second test he ran was a burn test. He placed the crystals on a piece of cigarette foil and heated them from beneath with a match. If the coke were pure it would bubble and leave a light brown film. A mix would turn black and leave lumps. In this case the film was dark brown and there was some scum, but the residue was not dark enough or lumpy enough to key Swan. Before he snorted the coke there was a knock at the door. He froze.

Emilio reached into his shirt and pulled out a revolver, pearl-handled, beautiful. Swan was impressed. Emilio stood behind the door while Ricardo opened it. Swan reached into his satchel as if he were carrying a gun, which reciprocally impressed Emilio, and he discovered then that René always traveled with a knife in his boot. It was like television. Ricardo opened the door to find a hotel maid standing outside the room. She apologized for the disturbance, handed him four towels and left. Now everyone became that much more professional. They had shown off their hardware.

Ricardo reached into the overnight bag he was carrying and pulled out a three-posted gram scale, folding model. It was worth a lot of money and of a kind rarely seen outside a pharmaceutical lab. It was very impressive. While Ricardo was setting the scale up, Swan sampled the coke. He experienced a distinct rush. He was pleased. He paid for three hundred grams, and René bought half a kilo. They said goodbye, and Swan was out of the hotel in thirty minutes, wondering what to do next. He checked into a nondescript, pay-as-you-go tourist inn, and that night, alone in his room, he made the fill.

The package Swan mailed to New York was the product of painstaking preparation, much more elaborate than necessary. The load, 300 grams, was the smallest he would ever send, and the package in which he sent it was the largest. He had spent several days in New York preparing the necessary materials and over six hours in Barranquilla making the fill.

The package measured 30 x 20 x 20 inches, too big for the fluoroscope, according to what Tito had told him. But that was not enough for Swan. In the event that it *was* somehow X-rayed, he wanted the package to be deceptive. In New York he and Alice had taken a corrugated cardboard box, ripped it open, and measured the distance between the corrugations. Alice did a piece of artwork, black on white, which simulated striped wrapping paper, the distance between the stripes corresponding to the distance between the flutes in the corrugated cardboard. Swan went to a printer he knew and had gift wrapping printed to match the artwork. The stripes he had printed in metallic ink.

In Barranquilla he took a large, corrugated box he had come up with down there, and with a coat hanger broken at both ends he enlarged the flutes along its edges. He funneled the coke into the flutes with a piece of stiff plastic he had carried from New York, not sure he would be able to find any in Colombia. He spent six hours funneling the coke into the flutes. Inside the corrugated box he placed another box, filled with infants' gifts — a large doll, various stuffed animals, rattles and the like, and two of the largest containers of Johnson's Baby Powder he could find. He punctured one of the containers with the coat hanger and spread the powder around the inner box, figuring that if the outer box broke, there was a chance that the cocaine would be taken for baby powder when the package was opened. The inner package, the package of infants' paraphernalia, was gift wrapped with the metallic-stripe paper. If the box was X-rayed, the stripes of the inner package would be picked up, and they would convincingly account for the inordinate density along the corrugations caused by the presence of the coke. Only Zachary Swan could have invented this puzzle. Ultimately confronted with the package, a Customs agent who was more than curious would have come down with a stroke. Swan double-wrapped the whole thing in supermarket gauge, plain brown paper, addressed it, tied it with heavy string, and waited for the Post Office to open.

Swan checked out of his room a few hours later, pounced on one of the tourist-hungry cab drivers hanging around the front entrance of the establishment before the cab driver had a chance to pounce on him, and said:

"*Oficina de Correo.*"

Colombia has two mail systems. One is run by the government for in-city mail as well as domestic and international surface mail, called *Correo Urbano* and *Correo Nacional* respectively. The other, air mail, or *Correo Aereo*, is run by Avianca Airlines with both a domestic and an international service. Swan used the latter. He had the cab driver mail the package for him. He said he wanted it sent first class, gave him some money, and waited by the door for his receipt, ready to run if the package were nailed. The cab driver asked what was in the package — he had to make a Customs declaration — and Swan said, "*zapatas*," leather sandals, a favorite with American tourists in Colombia. The cab driver mailed the package, handed Swan the receipt, and drove him from the Post Office to the airport. Within an hour Swan was on a plane to Cartagena.

Swan spent three days in Cartagena, working on his tan, and took a direct flight from there to New York. (Pan American was flying via Miami once a week.) He arrived home at about midnight. Alice, who had been doing everything but offering Masses in her anxiety over his absence, gave him a desperate kiss at the door and said:

"The package is at Davis's."

Swan felt like Eisenhower entering Europe.

Davis, an old college friend of Swan, owned a small wholesale cosmetics business on Broadway near 48th Street. The loaded package had been addressed, in care of Davis's offices, to Jorge Enrique Ramos, a former company stock boy who had quit the previous year and gone back to Puerto Rico. Davis had been told to expect the package. Ramos was a part of his corporate records, so in the event of a bust, Davis was covered. On each trip to Colombia, no matter how much coke he was moving, Swan would send a package to Davis as a matter of course. He quit doing so, however, the day Davis called to tell him his latest package had arrived with a new mailman. (On that occasion the pickup was never made.)

Waiting for his flight in Cartagena, Swan, from his hotel window, had spotted René and Debbie walking on the beach, and on his way down to catch up with them found Blackie being chased around the hotel pool by a groundskeeper with a machete. Blackie was captured and carted off to jail by tourist police.

(Being black or Indian — Blackie was both — or an indigent white in Colombia is bad karma, especially in a resort town. On the weekends it is particularly rough, because middle-class Colombian tourists converge on the Caribbean beaches then, and on Friday afternoons, in preparation for their arrival, the local police begin cleaning the place up. The overall effect on people like Blackie and his friends is that of a harvest, and by Friday night everybody is hiding, either in the woods or on the outer beaches like the one at Tahiti Estates. The rap — just being caught off limits — is usually worth a weekend in jail and a few beatings; for a young woman, that and the chance of rape by either the cops or the jailers or both, although she can buy her way out of a stretch with what amounts to the same thing performed with the arresting officer; and if there is a dope charge on top of the vagrancy rap, particularly if the kid is an American, there is often a four-figure release fee set by the arresting officer's immediate superior, or whoever is in a position to collect the money when the check arrives from the folks back home. When the blackmail is not applied directly by the cops, it is handled by the defendant's lawyer, who takes his blood money off the top and *then* cuts in the superior police official. The American consulates and Embassy are very good at recommending the right lawyer for the job. It is not without reason, therefore, that the cop making the collar negotiates on the scene — if he follows through with the arrest he ends up with nothing, or, at best, the smallest slice of the pie.)*

That afternoon Swan and René, who finally caught up with each other, put some money together and bailed Blackie out. Later, Swan, René and Debbie were sitting by the pool having dinner, not talking about cocaine, but not unaware of the danger represented by doing business in the company of the likes of Blackie. (Swan had not asked René if he had yet moved his coke. René would tell him later that he had

* See Appendix V.

simply stuffed it into a couple of souvenirs and mailed it from Barranquilla, addressed to himself in care of his father's business in Montreal. Maybe.) Swan said, with reference to Blackie:

"Rainy, that guy is heat."

René nodded. He thought for a minute, then turned to Debbie and said:

"We gotta shake him."

Debbie frowned, looked at René and shook her head.

"Blackie is trouble, every place you go," Swan told her.

"Do what you want," she said. She turned again to René. "I'm staying with Blackie."

The next day she and Blackie took off. Down the coast. Swan, who had not seen it coming, tried to apologize to René.

"If it's all right with her, it's all right with me," René said. "She's old enough to take care of herself and as long as she's O.K., I'm not going to worry about it."

Swan and René said goodbye. René flew to Canada to distribute his coke. He showed up in New York, three weeks later, with another woman.

7

A WAY WITH THE SPOON

Zachary Swan's first capital investment upon his return to the United States was a laboratory gram scale. It was the one precision instrument, with the possible exception of a good automatic weapon, that was demanded by the cocaine trade. Swan selected an Ohaus, three-posted, equal-arm pharmaceutical balance with stainless steel trays — it appealed to the professional in him. It cost $150. And it was metric. It did not know an ounce or a pound from a counterfeit Deutsche Mark. He was impressed.

For almost two hundred years Americans have been trying to come to grips with the metric system; refusal to adopt it, from black market conversion tables in the elementary school arithmetic classroom to bisystematic mileposts on the nation's interstate highways, has come to be regarded as one of the unimpeachable insignias of citizenship. There is pride to be found in the embrace of a system of measurement that is unique in the world, truly one's own — different even from the British Imperial System, though few are certain exactly how it is different — and an even further glory, it seems, in not actually knowing what that system of measurement is called. The U.S. Customary System, as it *is* called, officially and everywhere, is as American as shoo-fly pie: Olympic swimming pools have confounded us for years; displacement in liters we have acknowledged as having something to do with foreign automobiles and French wine; and kilometers, whatever they are, we know had something to do with extraterrestrial real estate in "The Day the Earth Stood Still" — it might as well have been cubits our alien visitor was asking for. The International System of Units — for that is what *theirs*, the one the rest of the universe uses, is called — is un-American; if it is not furlongs or fathoms it is foreign, it is something we grant chemistry teachers for their amusement. Or so one would have thought. Until recently. Only recently — and seemingly overnight — did an entire post-war generation of schoolchildren learn that the metric system was a postgraduate course.

Whatever Congress decides, and no matter how long it takes a box of Spoon Size Shredded Wheat to go from twelve ounces to 340 grams, the truth is this: the United States of America effectively converted to the metric system in, or around, 1965 — by 1970 there was not a college sophomore worth his government grant who did not know how much a gram of hash weighed. That little piece of empirical data had become a matter of pride. And, on many occasions, a matter of survival. Here was some dude, not even a chemistry major, coming on to you with mikes, grams, bricks, kilos and hundredweights; off the top of his head he could go from grams to ounces and he could tell you how many ounces he got to the kilo. He hit you with lids, caps, keys, tabs, nickel bags, blotters, buttons, spoons and everything from milligrams to boatloads. You had to protect yourself. You had to have your weights and measures down, and the metric system was where you began. Anything that came out of a pharmaceutical house or across a border . . . well, man, they just did not *know* avoirdupois weight . . . *avoir do what?* The time had come to get it together. And so today everyone over the age of twelve *knows* that there are 28.3 grams to the ounce and 35.2 ounces or 2.2 pounds to the kilogram. He may not know how many swimming pools to the standard football field, but he knows how to buy dope:

Q: *And so, Johnny, if you had a pound of apples and a pound of oranges and a fifth of a pound of cherries to sell, and you needed 600 Colombian pesos to buy a second-hand bicycle, how much would you have to sell your fruit for?*

A: *Twenty dollars a key, teach — more, of course, if I ounced it.*

There is nobody in the world, let alone at MIT or Lowell Tech, who is faster at math than a dope dealer.

When he returned to the United States, the only thing Zachary Swan knew for sure about the mathematics of the New York cocaine market was that coke was sold by weight. What he was able to learn before the distribution of his first 300 grams was minimal; what ultimately accounted for his success in distributing the load was a complementary ignorance on the part of the consumers he reached. What he began with was a guaranteed marijuana market — a broad-based, middle-class clientele that was ready for cocaine — and a small network of professional ounce-dealers who were ready to open it up.

Ellery. For all his humility, kindness, honesty and seeming sloth, and beneath the ingenuous, childlike manner which made him everyone's candidate for least-likely-to-survive given the unsavory nature of the business he was in, Ellery was a professional — no flash, no jive, nothing romantic about Ellery: he was simply one of the best dealers on the street. He had been going for years, untouched, dealing quality dope in consistently high volume, and he commanded a large slice of the market. (It is interesting to note that, apart from dealing, Ellery did nothing illegal, nor had he ever done so, in his life — he did not fool around. He did not do traveler's checks, a scam that was popular among many of Swan's friends; he did not handle credit cards or counterfeit money; he did not steal or handle stolen merchandise, and he never cheated anyone. He would drive a hard bargain with drugs and that was all. To this day he has never done anything but be an honest and dependable dealer. And, as with all of Swan's acquaintances — with the exception of Pirata, "who didn't give a fuck about anyone" — he never dealt in heroin). Something of a joke, or maybe a curiosity, to those who did not know him well, Ellery was a man who never failed to deliver the goods; and it was to him that Swan owed every connection he had ever made in New York.

Charlie Kendricks. Swan's lieutenant, the man Swan relied on more than anyone else, Kendricks rarely worked exclusively independent of Swan as did the other ounce-dealers. The least professional of Swan's men, he was valued more for his wits and courage than for his ability to read people, and Swan missed him when he was not around. Shaken by his arrest in Brownsville, he had given up handling Swan's dope and had taken a long vacation with Lillian Giles on the money he had earned shadowing the schoolteachers through Customs at Nogales; it was not until Swan had made his third trip to Colombia that Kendricks came back to work for him. As an ounce-dealer in cocaine, Kendricks would ultimately fail — he had no street sense and was repeatedly robbed of ounces Swan had fronted him — but he would remain an invaluable right-hand man in the smuggling operation; he was a close friend as well as a professional asset. He carried a knife on occasion, which he never opened, used everything but heroin and cigarettes, and was so obviously Australian that Swan felt obliged to refer to him as the Hungarian. A former stockbroker, Kendricks was born in East Africa of British parents and had lived in Australia for more than ten years. He and Lillian Giles had come to New York via London, where they had met, and they were living together on Long Island when Swan and Alice were introduced to them. The introduction was made by Roger Livingston.

Roger Livingston. Code name, Seymour; it was he whom Charlie Kendricks had been instructed to call from the Riverhead Jail. Nearly bald at thirty, bearded, nearsighted, five-ten, fair and husky, Livingston was a meticulous man, a well-organized and intelligent dealer through whom Swan moved a lot of ounces. When he and Swan met — through Ellery — Livingston had been shooting heroin, a habit he kicked shortly thereafter and one he never went back to. He had dealt a good share of Swan's Mexican marijuana load, and he was the only dealer of Swan's cocaine who mainlined the product — he still carries the scar on his right leg of a third-degree burn he received after an overdose knocked him down and unconscious against a bathroom radiator pipe in his apartment. Livingston was an excellent mechanic, a man fascinated with the world's physical equipment; he drove a jeep and owned enough tools and expensive gadgetry to open a repair shop; he knew his way around a darkroom, was comfortable in a chemistry lab, and his acquisitive mind was open to information of any kind. He wore a scuba diver's watch, and could put an elaborate pocket knife to good use. He carried a lot of keys. He had an attention span far greater than that of most of his friends, and unlike many of them, he was never idle. A biology teacher in the New York City school system, he lived with a children's clothing designer, a close friend of Alice's named Angela De Santis. He shared his apartment with her, a hundred houseplants, a vast aquarium of fish and a number of amphibians and reptiles, many of the last being snakes who often escaped their cages and had the run of the house for days. Livingston was honest, trustworthy and a good man to have around when there was trouble. He kept a cool head, knew how to take care of himself, and remained a consistent, dependable dealer on the retail end of Swan's network.

Nice Mickey. Irish, tall, thin, with blond hair, blue eyes, a deep, mellow voice and the face of a choir boy, Nice Mickey was cautious, intelligent and extremely professional, the only complete, all-around pro moving Swan's ounces on a regular basis. Though he dealt in everything from credit cards to cocaine, he had never been busted, and for as long as Swan would know him he would not be. He had the finest street sense of any man Swan had ever encountered; quick and alert, his instincts uncanny, he seemed to possess interior antennae preternaturally sensitive to danger. He could read a street in a second, and never stepped onto one without knowing right away whether or not he was being followed. He was not particularly dangerous, but he was as elusive as the wind; his timing was superb, and he could appear or disappear in an instant. Well coordinated and sharp of eye, Nice Mickey could read an opponent like a Bertillon poster — it was a mistake to gamble with him. An expert gamesman, he consistently scored 700 in Scrabble, was lethal at cards, darts, backgammon and golf, and was a nationally ranked three-cushion billiards player. As a con artist he was unsurpassed. In the summer he worked carnivals and resort city beachfront concessions. He was self-assured, well mannered and elegant; he wore expensive clothes and owned thirty pairs of seventy-five-dollar shoes. At thirty-four he lived with his mother, who had worked most of her life as a professional cook; it was in the homes of her wealthy employers that Nice Mickey had lived as a child and in addition to everything else, he was an excellent chef. He was one of Pirata's closest friends and a good friend of Ellery's. Of all Swan's ounce-dealers, Nice Mickey was the most self-reliant. His life was his own, he shared very little, and he was not as heavy a user of the product as the others. The reaction of most to Mickey was one of respect, casual trust and a certain amount of awe. He was strictly professional, and unlike the others, in the dark no-man's land where cocaine was traded, he never got beat.

Moses Wellfleet. Dr W, six-four, 220, thirty-five years old, black and married to a white woman, Moses counted among his "friends" Sly Stone, Miles Davis and Flip Wilson. Moses did not work for Swan, nor was he part of the inner circle, but he handled enough ounces to affect significantly the distribution of Swan's cocaine. He had been handling coke for several years before Swan met him, and his was the initial indication that Swan's first load was "shit'; there was no way he could move it, he said, his customers were too sophisticated. It was not until the second load came in pure that he began dealing Swan's ounces. Moses was the quintessential black dealer — weight meant nothing to him. Dealing from car windows and the back rooms of bars, a man did not tote a gram scale — he carried spoons. A "spoon," sometimes called a "quarter," is the equivalent of a level tablespoon. There are four "spoons" to a "piece," which is just over an ounce. (Sometimes the words "eighth," "quarter" and "half" are used to refer to those fractions of a kilogram.) When Moses scored from Swan, he spent hours over the deal — blowing coke, talking trash, taking a break from the street. He always came with his spoons, like a pastry chef, and because Moses was buying by volume instead of by weight, Swan had made a small investment in the interest of preserving the edge — a Waring Blender, in which he fluffed up the coke just before Moses's visits. It is significant to an understanding of Swan's position in the cocaine trade to realize that, in all the years he was smuggling, he never learned what, in the way of business, went down on the street. Nor did he want to know. He dealt in weight only and stayed as far away from the gram-dealers and the street traffic as he could. Moses, buying spoons, was probably dealing in lower quantities than those to whom Swan was ouncing, if not as a rule then at least more often, but he was turning it over fast enough to keep Swan busy with the blender. He was the manager of two bars in Manhattan, and it was probably through the clientele that he was moving a lot of it. As little as he and Swan had in common, they seemed to enjoy each other's company, and because Moses was a responsible dealer they got along well. Dr W was a pro; there was no nonsense about him.

Anthony. Young, younger than one would expect a man with so awesome a reputation to be, what this man was *not* was an ounce-dealer. In Swan's words, he was a very good friend and a very bad enemy — to Swan he was Mr Big. Introduced by Ellery, Swan had gone to Anthony for investment money, cash to finance the first Colombian trip. It was Anthony who had shown Swan how to conduct the purity tests. Initially Swan had regretted not taking the money when he had had the chance, when it was offered to him in denominations of ten — he would have turned the thousand into ten thousand — but he soon had reason to be thankful for Nice Mickey's having warned Anthony off: Swan was spared the embarrassment of offering Anthony a share of the first load — Anthony, indeed, would have had first call on it — a product which, in the end, was shown to be more cut than cocaine. It was Anthony, however, who ultimately had cause for the greater regret — when Swan began showing up regularly with pure, Anthony found himself paying top dollar for a product that would have been his own by dint of a partnership. And after the third trip he never bought less than a kilo. Anthony did not keep a scale in his house, and he did not hold on to cocaine; his was a completely different way of doing business. He simply asked, "Is it a key?" If the answer was yes, it damn well *had* to be a key. He kept his buyers waiting in one room and Swan waiting in another, and the cocaine was out of the house as fast as it was in. Anthony owned at least three guns and a radio which was always tuned to police calls. He had bodyguards who were always on duty. He subscribed to a service that laundered his money and legitimized his income. He was obviously paying his dues. Aside from Swan he had another six or seven contacts; he never smuggled himself, and he was never in the vicinity of incriminating evidence for more than a minute. Swan stood to make more money ouncing a kilo to his dealers than he did selling it outright to Anthony, and at times, when the cocaine was moving as fast as he could supply it, Swan held back; but under routine circumstances, his policy was to unload in as large a quantity as possible — it did not pay to have the product hanging around — and on those occasions Anthony was the man to do business with. Cash, immediately, no questions, no heat, and a 500 percent return on the investment.

*　　*　　*

Only rarely did Zachary Swan entertain the notion that, smuggling cocaine, he might be some brand of counterculture hero; and only a little less rarely did he amuse himself with the thought that being a smuggler made him a bold and rather dashing sort of figure. From the beginning, he saw himself principally as a businessman — a rather shrewd one. And as a businessman he was able to divine early many of the unwritten rules of the game.

A cocaine smuggler, once he has beaten the border, is a wholesaler dealing in a very marketable commodity. His success, like that of any wholesaler, depends on the *volume* of business he does, obviously, and on the speed of his *turnover*. But where turnover, for the average wholesaler, is the fundamental, commercial reality upon which volume is based — you cannot have one without the other — for a cocaine smuggler turnover is a manipulable variable, and its implications are a bit more complex.

For a cocaine smuggler, turnover seems not only to work significantly independent of volume, but it would seem, on the surface, to work in one's favor at whatever speed it is generated. A coke smuggler, for example, being his own supplier, stands to make *more* money dealing his product in ounces than he does dealing it by the kilo (he could make more, still, dealing it in grams, but unless he hit a few Miles Davis sellouts he would not be South again for a year). Though ouncing cocaine is slower than turning over a kilogram, ounce-dealing yields a better bottom line — it may take a week or two to unload the ounces, but the difference, over three kilos, say, may amount to better than $50,000, which is not bad for a few weeks" work. (Kilo price does not vary significantly with volume. While gram prices are cut in half with the purchase of an ounce, and ounce prices go down respectably with the purchase of a kilo, two or three or five kilos are likely to cost exactly two, three or five times the price of one.)

Ounce money is better than kilo money. But the fact is that a smuggler will almost never pass up the opportunity to move his product at the kilo level. He not only welcomes a rapid turnover, he depends upon it. And he depends upon it to a far greater degree than the average wholesaler. Why? In the first place, but by no means the foremost — Swan, in fact, did not learn this until later — coke is perishable. The potency of cocaine diminishes rapidly with age. The product goes bad. If the product is cut, it goes bad faster — a good cut will eat up cocaine as fast as the weather will.* For this reason alone, a cocaine smuggler cannot afford to have his inventory lying around. But there are other reasons. And to Zachary Swan these became obvious almost immediately:

If a smuggler's inventory, his stash, amounts to an ounce of cocaine, it is worth about $1,000. He can afford to lose it. If his stash is hit, he can afford the take-off; $1,000, at the level on which he is dealing, is small change. He can kiss it goodbye and forget about it. If, on the other hand, a take-off man comes at him and there are three kilos at stake — call it $150,000 — the take-off man is going to come in on the tail end of an M-16. And he is going to come in with that kind of hardware because he knows, with

---

* There is a respectable body of opinion which holds that the potency of cocaine, a very stable alkaloid, is affected neither by time nor by any of the known cuts. Perhaps borax (sodium borate) provides an exception. Most agree that pharmaceutical cocaine, when protected from the air, has a very long shelf life. Zachary Swan knew as much about pharmaceutical cocaine as he did about nuclear physics — his was the smuggler's opinion.

that kind of money at stake, that coming up against a professional, he is going to be coming up against a shotgun at least. The value of life, where dope is involved, fluctuates in inverse proportion to the value of the dope; it gets cheap fast when the dope is cocaine. If the smuggler is lucky, and instead of a take-off man he greets the Feds at the door, the difference between a one-ounce stash and a three-kilo stash is the difference between some serious heat and some life imprisonment. And that is why the Feds carry hardware. It doesn't take a genius to figure out that a man facing that kind of time has nothing to lose.

Zachary Swan was not a coward, but he was not stupid either. And it did not require any on-the-job training for him to see that bloodshed, specifically his own, or a stretch at Leavenworth, however long, would be bad for business. He could guess immediately how either eventuality would be counterproductive — in terms of public relations alone the implications were catastrophic. Though he was by no means shy, and though (as he would discover later) there was an untapped reservoir of courage stagnating somewhere inside of him, Swan, by nature, had a very low threshold of discomfort. He would give the cocaine business a try, but only on his own terms; as soon as the going appeared to be getting rough, for him or anyone for whose safety he was responsible, he would get out.

Swan was of the opinion that there was an intelligent way to do almost anything. And a justifiable way. In addition to an adverse adrenalin reaction, he suffered a philosophical flu in the company of guns. He had been a lousy Marine. He generally took his virility substitutes on the rocks, or lately, by way of his mucous membranes — firearms he found perverse. Drug running would change that eventually, and unfortunately, at least for a while, but in the beginning he was determined to play it safe. And turnover, to Swan, was where safety began. Turning over in quantity, he would deal with people who were that much more responsible. And he would deal with *fewer* people. The higher the level at which he dealt, the fewer would be the people he dealt with, and the more substantial would be that distance between himself and the street. And the street, as any smuggler knows, is where carelessness, stupidity, violence and, subsequently, risk are the greatest. Swan would deal in weight. And he would deal honestly.

After distributing the first load, Swan rarely moved cocaine out of his apartment. Out of necessity he would break it down at home, but immediately thereafter would check into a hotel — very often the St Regis, New York's most exclusive, where security was the best — and from there he would ounce it. Swan would generally begin with a twenty-two-and-six cut. Six grams of dextrose or lactose to an ounce. If the coke was good, it could take a twenty and eight. Swan never cut it more than eighteen and ten. When he discovered borax, Swan could afford to hit the coke less. Borax was heavier, and though it made his ounces look smaller, it did not hurt the trade — there was always a gram scale nearby. Borax's other advantage was that it took the coke on well. Dextrose was a bad cut — if the coke was too sweet, the price had to come down. Lactose, not nearly so sweet, did not take the coke on nearly so well — sophisticated buyers could get a percentage by pointing out the granular differences and the change in consistency. (Also, in New York, because of the heroin problem, lactose and dextrose were unavailable — they had to be bought either on the black market or out of town.) Borax added weight without volume. Swan would stay with it until he discovered *Mannite*, and he would go back to it because of its availability vis-à-vis the Italian laxative, regarded by many as the more sophisticated cut. Though he touched the ounces, Swan never stepped on the kilos he dealt Anthony.

Swan's standard procedure, once the cocaine was in town, varied little: he broke down the packages that the coke arrived in, unloaded as many kilos as he could immediately to Anthony, then moved into a hotel and cut and packaged the remaining ounces. He always had a supply of cut on hand at home — borax required a significant amount of preparation. It first had to be boiled, then the liquid placed in a baking pan to dry. After the borax crystallized, white and shiny but less flaky than before, the crystals had to be ground down with a rolling pin, pulverized until they could pass through a tea strainer, the larger chunks being discarded. The strained crystals were then ground again and run through the mesh of a nylon stocking, stretched over a bowl, and worked back and forth with a spatula until the process was complete. It was tedious work, and Swan had better things to do, but the one time he paid someone else to do it, he had trouble — customers complained about their cocaine.

When the cocaine was cut, Swan weighed it again, then wrapped each ounce in a polyethylene sandwich bag, rolled it tightly, and placed it into another bag which he then rolled and secured with three rubber bands. He cut some ounces differently from others, and color-coded them by way of the rubber bands. He knew that Roger and Ellery would take a gram or two out and put in some of their own powder, stepping on the product before they passed it on to their customers. He knew that Nice Mickey, being the pro, would not even open the package, but go directly to the customer, deliver the goods, and pick up his money. Consequently, Swan made Mickey's ounces a little short.

In the beginning, Swan sold to his dealers at $700 an ounce. Later the price went up to $850. By the time Swan returned from his third trip (after the first, he was rarely in New York for more than a month at a time), his dealers were each moving an average of three ounces a day. And it got better later on. Very often Swan fronted the ounces to Roger, Ellery and Mickey. He always fronted them to Charlie. Moses did not need the credit. There were other people, casual friends of Swan's, who occasionally handled ounces, but none who did so on the order that these men did. It was not uncommon, for example, over coffee at Victor's Café, for Ellery, Roger or Mickey, or any combination thereof, to slip Swan a couple of thousand dollars under the table. The working relationship was a good one — in the end, Swan was meeting no one new and dealing only with this select group of people. He soon moved permanently to the Hamptons, where once every two or three weeks he would call in the ounce-dealers and throw a party. On New Year's Eve, 1972, fewer than ten people went through over a thousand dollars' worth of cocaine, an entire ounce of pure which had been placed on the coffee table in a tobacco humidor.

If there were fewer women than men in the inner circle of Swan's New York network (there were none in Bogotá when that end of the operation was established), it was not something that anyone noticed; if their impact upon the business was secondary, it was ordained as such by tradition.

By smuggling standards prevalent at the time — and unchanged now — Zachary Swan's approach to women was an enlightened one; if his attitude on occasion seemed a bit Pleistocene, his behavior, more often than not, was applaudable. In dope-trading circles, as reflected in the lore, women are generally distinguished only insofar as are the men with whom they are associated. Mules, the carriers, most of them women, who when busted are often abandoned, are the hallmark of industry prejudice — a smuggler, on most occasions, laments their arrest less than he does the loss of the load. The fact that Swan never used mules — every one of his smuggles was designed with a loophole through which the carrier could walk away — is probably more a reflection of his attitude toward people in general than of his attitude toward women. And, in the end, maybe the best one can say for Swan is that he exploited women no more than he exploited most men. But if he was guilty of discrimination on the basis of sex, he was no more guilty than any man of his generation, and if his metamorphosis was slow, it was because he had that much more to learn and unlearn when he began hanging around with women of the likes of Alice Haskell.

Alice, of that newly and somewhat reluctantly emancipated breed of young woman that emerged fast in the 1970s, was by every measure a feminist; though she may not have been so successful as someone like Angela De Santis in asserting her rights — Alice was the victim of an even temperament — her politics were in the right place. She, more than anyone, taxed Swan's archaic sense of justice. Coming and going with no apparent regard for his ego, it was she, more than any counterculture contact he may have achieved by way of the dope he was smoking, who was responsible for the bearded, beaded, unbleached-cotton look he began to sport at the age of forty-two. In 1969, as she set out for Washington to march in protest against the war in Indochina, Swan, a lifelong champion of Wall Street, found himself saying, "Holler at "em for me," and it was not long before he himself was walking down Broadway with candles in his hands, chanting. From there it was only a small step to an appreciation of the fact that, as a woman, Alice possessed more than "an important set of jugs."

Of the women who significantly affected Swan's business, there were only three in New York: Angela De Santis, by way of the constant pressure she applied on everyone to get out of the business; Alice, who in the end helped provide Swan with the courage to do so; and Lillian Giles, the only one of the three who actually participated in the operation — who herself probably had more courage at the bottom line than any of the men involved — and who parlayed that participation into the ultimate removal of herself and Charlie Kendricks from the business altogether.

None of the women was ever involved in ounce-dealing, although Alice was always on hand while Swan was breaking down the coke and did involve herself in occasional pickups and deliveries by way of her unique, part-time self-employment in the neighborhood: ALICE'S HOUNDS *Professional Dog Walking Service; East Side Care, West Side Cost, Bonded, Insured, Loving.* Alice, when her aid was enlisted, was principally employed in the transaction of money — she rarely handled the cocaine. On one occasion, going directly home with the cash and the dogs — Swan was hosting a poker game — Alice lingered, and because it had been raining and the dogs were dry, she and Swan had to soak them down in the bathtub before they were returned to their owners. Swan took great delight in the charade.

But the first masquerade in which Swan participated as a cocaine smuggler was one that was engineered at his expense. His first time out he had been suckered. And he did not have to take Moses's word for it. He was in town only two weeks when René Day showed up. René had flown from Canada, and he had brought his cocaine.

"I can't sell it," he told Swan.

"Your customers are obviously more sophisticated than mine. I'm selling it with a 25 percent hit."

"Yeah, well from what I've been told that brings it down to about 15 percent coke."

Swan and René would later discover — through Ricardo, Emilio's lieutenant — that what they had paid for in Barranquilla was borax, speed, aspirin, and maybe 40 percent cocaine. The sample Swan had initially taken from José was pure, but Emilio, knowing Swan had not liked the sample, had hit what he finally sold to the two smugglers with a lot of speed, a drug with an edge and one on which they were sure to get high. The heavy speed cut would have been obvious to any experienced coke user, especially in view of the purity test results. It was because Swan's customers had had no more experience with coke than he that he was able to sell it as easily as he did.

When René showed up in New York, Swan was preparing to go South. He arranged to meet René in Santa Marta within a week, took two of René's ounces and moved them before he left — he had no trouble unloading the dope. When Swan finally arrived at the Tamaca Hotel, René, who had waited over a week, was on his way to Bogotá in search of a connection — Ricardo had given him a name. René was moving fast. If René had gotten a connection through Ricardo, Swan had to assume he had already been to Barranquilla. He had. And not only that. Rainy Day had smuggled his *cocaine* back into Colombia — having crossed two borders with it on the way — and he had returned it to Emilio. He got his money back. That is how cool *he* was.

8

SNOWBOUND IN CARTHAGE

There was nobody in the Western Hemisphere who was better for public relations than Uta Dietrische. No matter how you stretched it, there was never anything within eyeshot that was better to look at. She was a knockout — grown men wept when she walked by. The fact that she was absolutely crazy did not detract from her appearance; in fact, the supposition that she was in no control of her destiny whatsoever was somewhat provocative. She was a hymn to inconsonance, a bouquet of wounds.

On their first date together, Swan and Uta had gone to a cocktail party thrown by Mike Riordan. After the party, they went with Mike and his date to Orsini's for dinner. They were all drunk when they arrived and ordered more drinks before dinner, soon reaching the unanimous opinion that they needed some amyl nitrates. Swan rushed home and hit his stash. When he returned to Orsini's, Riordan was outside, in front of the restaurant, talking to two policemen in a squad car.

"What happened?" Swan asked.

"You won't believe it," Riordan said.

"Where's Uta?"

"They took her to Roosevelt Hospital."

"Mike?"

"You won't believe it."

"Tell me."

They had ordered dinner without Swan. Uta was hungry. She was so hungry, in fact, and so drunk, that she had started eating her fettucini with her hands. The captain came over to the table and told her to stop. Uta stood up and threw the fettucini at the captain. Mike took everybody outside. When they got outside, Uta threw a small fit — she was very excited. A woman walked over and said to Riordan, "I know how to handle her." The woman slapped Uta across the face — the sure cure — whereupon Uta reached back and threw a right cross, knocking the woman to the sidewalk. The police arrived three minutes ahead of Swan.

A week after their first date, Uta moved in with Swan. They lived together for six years. She was living with Michel Bernier when Swan made his first trip to Colombia. She was leaving him when Swan returned. For two or three years she had been the chief love interest of a young woman who worked on the desk at Lufthansa, and it was into the young woman's apartment that Uta moved when she split with Bernier.

When Swan decided to take Uta to Colombia with him on his second trip, he made his decision with three things in mind. First, there was the knowledge that it would be easier to look like a tourist if he were traveling with a woman — he and Uta would spend two weeks on San Andrés, an island off the beaten track recommended to Swan by the Americans in Santa Marta, and come home with scuba equipment and a suntan. And cocaine. Second, and more tantalizing, was the scam itself. Gabrielle, the Lufthansa clerk who was in love with Uta and who had done it before, would meet the plane and escort Uta through Customs reserved for airline personnel. A shoo-in. Uta would carry the coke. The third factor in Swan's decision was Uta herself. She was Uta. Only a fool would say no.

Swan met René Day in Santa Marta. René was on his way to Bogotá to meet Ricardo's connection. They arranged to hook up on San Andrés. If René scored, Swan would buy in; if he did not, they would both go back to Bogotá and look up Bernier's friend Vincent. They said goodbye, and Swan and Uta, changing planes in Barranquilla, flew to San Andrés.

San Andrés, as a resort, was just emerging at the time. It was unspoiled. A beautiful, tropical island with small hotels that were clean and comfortable, but not deluxe, it had excellent restaurants, beaches of crushed coral, no hot water, no crowds, and one casino. Swan and Uta stayed at the Hanser Club. Their cabin was on the water. Over dinner, their first night on the island, they were approached by a well-dressed American who asked Swan if he were a photographer — he thought Uta was a model. He had sent drinks to their table by way of introduction. Swan said no, but invited the well-dressed gentleman and the suntanned man he was seated with, another American, to join him and Uta for coffee.

The gentleman who had asked the question worked for Avianca Airlines. His name was Arnold Noel. (Uta would refer to him as Mr Christmas.) His friend was an underwater photographer. They were making a publicity film for Avianca, a skin-diving movie to be shown at American scuba clubs, which they hoped would lure tourists to Colombia and its islands. Their itinerary included all the major coastal resorts, and they had been granted the use of local boats to make the movie. They asked Swan and Uta to join the tour as models (Uta could lure a hydrophobe to the islands). It was offers like this one that suggested to Zachary Swan that God supported the legalization of cocaine. He and Uta accepted the invitation.

The next day they boarded the boat and began the filming. Uta and Swan were both excellent swimmers, and they both loved the water. Making the movie was a piece of cake. Aboard the boat that day, they met *El Commandante No Barco*, exercising his official privilege as the commanding officer of the Colombian naval station on San Andrés. *El Commandante* had a name of his own, but Swan and Uta preferred to call him *No Barco* because he had no boat. The naval station was supposed to have one, but the boat had been in for repairs for a long time now. *El Commandante* spent his time drilling his troops and going to the beach. He had command of two hundred Marines who marched a lot. He used any boat he could borrow to fool around with. It was *El Commandante* who, after the first day's shooting, introduced Swan to *aguardiente*, the Colombian anisette. After one belt, Swan went immediately for a Gelusil (probably his favorite drug of all).

With *El Commandante* aboard the next day, the crew sailed to Jonny Kay, an islet about a mile out on the coral reef, where they filmed a barbecue and shot some coral-diving footage. Uta brought back an exquisite piece of drift-wood. That day René showed up. He had scored a little over half a kilo in Bogotá. He was carrying it in his golf clubs, hidden in the shafts. There were no golf courses on San Andrés. He looked funny getting off the plane . . . *And what in heaven's name brought you to Casablanca? . . . My health. I came to Casablanca for the waters . . . What waters? We're in the desert . . . I was misinformed.* Swan wanted to stay with the tour. He told René the plan he had for getting the coke into New York via the Lufthansa desk and offered to let René in on the scam if René would go back and score for him in Bogotá. René liked the idea — he did not want to risk the confiscation of his irons — and agreed. He told Swan the coke was running $7 a gram (which meant it was running anywhere from six to six and a half). Swan gave him $5,000 and held onto the golf clubs.

A few days later, René called from Bogotá:

"I'm on the girl," he said.*

René had scored the coke, and he gave Swan his flight number and the time of his arrival. He told Swan he was worried about coming in.

"The girl's a little fat," he said.

"Don't worry about it," Swan told him, "Uta and I will meet you at the airport."

Swan and Uta met René at the airport in *El Commandante's* car. They drove right onto the field and parked thirty feet from the plane. They were accompanied by two armed Marines. René did not even go through the terminal. He went from the plane to the car, and he and the cocaine left the airport through the back gate. René joined the tour, and after two more days filming on San Andrés, they all set out for Cartagena. *El Commandante* stayed behind.

The tour was scheduled to go from San Andrés to Santa Marta. At Swan's suggestion the itinerary was changed. Santa Marta was out. Cartagena was just a nicer place. Cartagena is without question the most beautiful city in Colombia, possibly the most beautiful in the Hemisphere. It is the only walled city in South America, fortified with

* See Appendix VI.

seventeenth-century stone battlements thirty feet wide and five miles long, behind which run narrow cobblestone streets with overhanging balconies. Known as the Heroic City for having resisted a 106-day siege by the Spaniards in the days of Simón Bolívar, it was where treasure was stored in the days of the Spanish Main. It suffered continual pirate attacks then, and eventually was sacked by Sir Francis Drake. Beyond the walls of the old city, out on the peninsula, are the hotels and the lush beaches. It was there that the tour took up residence.

In Cartagena the film company was afforded the use of a fleet of boats at the Hotel Caribe marina. And just as they had met *El Commandante* aboard one of the boats at the Hanser Club, Swan and Uta met Ramón Greco aboard one of the boats at the Caribe. Ramón Greco, about twenty-one years old, educated in the United States, was one of the wealthiest young men in Colombia. His father was "in emeralds." Ramón, in addition to everything else he had going for him, was a very handsome fellow.

At about this time, Uta was beginning to show the coke, the grass, and the Johnny Walker Black. She was putting a lot of Scotch away, and she was getting a little shaky. She was doing dope before she got out of bed in the morning. Swan and René were saying, "This ain't gonna work" — Uta was losing her grip. René finally gave up. He was not going to trust her. He disappeared one day with his golf clubs and left Swan a note saying he would call from Montreal. That same night Uta disappeared with Ramón Greco and did not show up until breakfast. Swan, his ego shot, figured that was it. He made plans to go home alone.

Uta moved to Greco's ranch — she would end up on the beach at Cartagena again a year later. Swan took the 600 grams of coke, bought some twine, a chisel, glue, sandpaper and lacquer and drew a bead on the driftwood. It was all he had. He opened it up with the chisel, hollowed it out and fit it with the coke, gluing it back together using the twine as a clamp. He sanded down one end of the driftwood just to get some sawdust, and sprinkled it over the glue at the seam. He ended up lacquering it — the exquisite piece of driftage was going to be hatcheted at home anyway.

He took an El Condor flight to Barranquilla, changed there to Avianca and headed north. Wearing a white Pierre Cardin jacket, navy blue slacks and a necktie, his hair short, his temples gray and his gold-rimmed glasses fitted tightly in place, he did something he would never in his life do again. He carried the cocaine through Customs. The driftwood was over his shoulder and his scuba gear was out front. He looked legitimate. He felt like hell — like the respectable forty-three-year-old gentleman he was, he crossed the border in a daze, his body full of Bloody Marys and his head full of coke. His pulse rate was abnormal, his adrenalin was high, and he learned what it was like to face some very serious trouble. From then on he would know how to prop up his carriers. He would know their thoughts, he would know their doubts, and he would know just how much dope to give them before they went across. It was a front-lines lesson in drug running. He passed the exam.

Swan hit the 600 grams right away with 200 grams of borax. (René had recommended it.) He met Anthony at Clarke's and offered him half a key at $10,500. Anthony took the sample Swan gave him and put it in his pocket. He would look at it later. They ate hamburgers, drank Vodka, and got to know each other better, and after an hour they left. Later that day, Anthony called Swan at the St Regis.

"It's not like I thought it was," he said.

They agreed on $9,000 and Anthony met Swan in his hotel room. Swan had the scale. They blew some coke and discussed the future.

"We can make more money if you don't hit it," Anthony told him.

"I touched it a little," said Swan.

"We can do much better on the pure."

Swan thought for a minute. Then he nodded his head:

"O.K.," he said. "When the next shipment comes in, I'll make sure you see it in the original container."

Anthony pulled off $8,000 in hundreds and handed them to Swan; he gave Swan the balance in fifties. Swan reminded Anthony of the time he tried to give him a thousand dollars in tens. They laughed, shook hands, wished each other luck and said goodbye. Swan moved the remaining ten ounces through Ellery, Mickey, and Roger in three days. He made $7,000 on the ounces, bringing his total to $16,000. He went back to Colombia with $10,000.

The enforcement of the laws that Zachary Swan was breaking in the late 1960s and early 1970s in the United States was the responsibility of more than one Federal bureaucracy. Smuggling cocaine, Swan was in violation of the criminal statutes listed in Title 21 of the United States Code Annotated — 21 USC(A) — dealing with the possession, sale, transportation and importation of what the Federal government had designated Controlled Substances (by way of the Comprehensive Drug Abuse Prevention and Control Act of 1970). The power to enforce those statutes, when Swan was smuggling, was mandated to the Federal Bureau of Narcotics and Dangerous Drugs (BNDD), then an agency of the Justice Department, and to the Bureau of Customs, an agency in the Department of the Treasury. The BNDD's duties were principally domestic. Customs handled smuggling. As with all bureaucracies, the duties and responsibilities of these two agencies became less clear in time and began to overlap. When the bureaucratic rivalry came to a showdown, the Treasury Department lost. Since July 1, 1973, under Richard Nixon's Presidential Reorganization Plan Number One, all Controlled Substances investigative work has been handled by the Justice Department in the form of the Drug Enforcement Administration (DEA).

The DEA, already showing signs of decay, is the latest in a long line of White House attempts to come down on international drug traffic. In 1914 the United States Customs Bureau was assigned responsibility for enforcement of the smuggling laws. Between 1932 and 1967, however, the Treasury Department saw fit to let another of its agencies, the Federal Bureau of Narcotics (FBN), carry out the Customs Bureau assignment where drugs were involved. Bureaucratically it made sense. They were all Treasury men. It was not until 1967, when the FBN went over to the Justice Department (to become BNDD), that Customs began to emphasize its mandate to enforce the drug-smuggling statutes. And that is when the infighting began. The drug traffic was now the bureaucratic baby of two Cabinet members — the Secretary of the Treasury and the Attorney General. BNDD agents and Customs agents, not to mention the local police, were all showing up at the same grass buys, stepping on each other's joints.

While all this was going on, Richard Nixon was paying off political debts and handing out favors on Pennsylvania

Avenue. In 1970 he created the Special Action Office for Drug Abuse Prevention. It was charged with duties like "development," "treatment," and "study," and put forty friends, or friends of friends, to work pushing paper for Dr Jerome H. Jaffee. They went to a lot of cocktail parties in Washington. Then Nixon brought his Republican crony Myles Ambrose (Commissioner of Customs, 1969–1972) over from the Treasury Department and made him the Director of a new agency called the Office of Drug Abuse Law Enforcement (ODALE). Under Ambrose were gathered BNDD men, Customs agents and local police narcotics people, a true bureaucratic *mélange* and ultimately the perfect Ambrosia from which to culture the DEA.

The DEA, established in 1973, consisted of all former BNDD agents (about 1,200) and 500 former Customs agents, a staff which was beefed up to 2,200 during the first year of its operation. Into it were absorbed the functions of ODALE and Jaffee's boys. On the Justice Department's Table of Organization, the DEA is an agency administratively equivalent to the FBI. It is headed by a Director who is answerable to the Attorney General. Myles Ambrose, who would have been a natural for the job of Director when the agency was formed, was booted out of the running when he got himself into an embarrassing situation soliciting funds — apparently on Nixon's behalf — from a Texas Republican, a previous campaign contributor, the source of whose income, it turned out, happened to be under investigation at the time by Ambrose's former employees over at the Customs Bureau. Nixon's "top narc" went back to private practice.

With the formation of the DEA, the Customs Bureau's drug powers were limited to interdiction at the border; Customs inspectors have the authority to make arrests, but prisoners must be turned over to DEA agents for processing, prosecution and follow-up investigation. The DEA has between 200 and 250 agents abroad. They work under the authority of the American Ambassador to the country in which they are posted, but report directly through their own chain of command to the DEA Director in Washington. DEA agents overseas serve in an advisory and intelligence-gathering capacity and are not supposed to be operational, though some countries have invited them to be. (There are twelve DEA offices in South America.) Overseas, the DEA works with the cooperation of various other American agencies under the supervision of the President's Cabinet Committee for International Narcotics Control (CCINC), which is chaired in Washington by the Secretary of State and has among its members the Secretaries of Agriculture and Defense. Established in 1972, the CCINC has no manpower of its own, but designates a State Department official in every target country to act as its narcotics control officer, coordinating the efforts of agencies such as the CIA, AID and the DEA in coming to grips with the drug traffic. Predictably, Henry Kissinger has very little interest in his job as chairman of CCINC, and the Central Intelligence Agency insists that its agents have more important things to do than hang around with DEA types. CCINC, as well as being the coordinating force behind the nation's international drug effort, is also a funding agency. The State Department's Foreign Aid Budget for fiscal 1974 contained a $43 million budget line for CCINC, spent mostly on the equipment and education of foreign personnel. In Latin America, for example, training classes were held for local narcotics and Customs police, and communications equipment, weapons, and vehicles — such as helicopters for the Mexicans — were purchased. It was CCINC to which Egil Krogh was White

House rep when the Nixon Administration started feeling the heat.

The 800 series of 21 USC(A) is a list of Federal violations governing the domestic possession, sale and transportation of Controlled Substances. The 900 series pertains to the illegal importation of same. To *conspire* to indulge in any or all of the activities suggested by the foregoing is also a Federal crime — under 21 USC 846 and 963 — and is dealt with separately in the Code under the General Federal Conspiracy Laws (18 USC 371). The fifty States have their own laws against possession, use, sale and transportation of Controlled Substances as well as the conspiracy to break the laws that prohibit doing so, and their laws are enforced by the narcotics divisions of local police departments. (Zachary Swan was arrested in Amagansett on a State charge.) The States, however, have nothing in their statutes equivalent to series 900. Smuggling is a violation only of the Federal law. An individual charged with smuggling is tried in Federal court. An individual charged with any other drug violation may be tried in either State or Federal court or both — it usually depends on who makes the arrest and how serious the charge is. Penalties for State violations vary widely, and in many cases are more severe than those of the Federal government. In New York, for example, since what is known as the Rockefeller law went into effect (September 1973), conviction on a charge of trafficking or the attempt to traffic in any amount of heroin, morphine or cocaine carries a life sentence. Mandatory. The maximum under Federal law is fifteen years for a first offense.

As a smuggler by profession rather than by inclination, it behooved Zachary Swan to keep the area of his operation clean. He did so for his own protection. The more American college students who were killed, robbed or arrested smuggling cocaine, the greater became the heat applied in South

America to professional smugglers by United States drug-enforcement agents. The amateurs were easy enough to spot — they were begging to be killed or ripped off — and Swan and his friends, unsuccessful in their attempts to discourage them, shuttled them to safe hotels and small, safe connections, and when possible they showed them the safe way out with their loads. They put the strung-out ones on planes for home, or notified their parents in the States — they were, in essence, a second U.S. drug agency, helping young people who were going to smuggle anyway, saving them from winding up dead or possibly behind bars in a foreign jail.

Federal agents, those subsidized by the American taxpayer, will customarily wait for a bust before talking to such people. Rather than walk up to someone obviously headed for trouble — where they might flash a badge and say, "Get smart, kid, it's not going to work" — they will, as a matter of policy, allow him to risk his life with the local heavies, get a few snorts of pure, and walk into jail at the airport back home. *Why prevent smuggling when you can punish it — isn't that what jails are for?* (Federal drug-enforcement agencies, like police department narcotics divisions, work on what is called the "body count" system, where promotion is based on the number of arrests made rather than the quality of the arrest. Under the system, two junkies with glassine bags or three college kids with a joint apiece are worth two and three times more, respectively, than the diplomatic attaché with six kilos of cocaine.) When the coke traffic began to get heavy — before it was monopolized by Organized Crime — Colombia began shipping a lot of bodies back home to the States. The kids that survived the heavy trade they threw in jail.*

* See Appendix VII.

The jails in Colombia are exactly what one would expect them to be. If you survive the rats, the lice and the dysentery, you still have to go up against the guards. Fernando, Blackie's friend, who came from a wealthy Colombian family, just barely survived his fellow inmates. Asleep in his cell, doing a weekend in Santa Marta after a Friday night roundup, he had his leg slashed with a razor blade by an inmate who was going after the money in his pockets. Swan put him on a train to Bogotá, hoping to get him home before the gangrene killed him. Blackie was on hand, without his medallion and without René's girl. Debbie had gone back to Canada with the jewelry. Blackie had done some hard time in jail himself — his head had been shaved.

"He looked like a chick in the French resistance," Swan said.*

In Cartagena, with the film crew, Swan and René had looked up *El Medico*, a local doctor who Blackie had told them was moving cocaine. *El Medico* presented his coke in a cardboard container sealed with masking tape. Written on the tape, in what looked like the doctor's handwriting, were the words "factory sealed." One snort of the merchandise and Swan's nose went up like a balloon — *El Medico's* coke was hit hard with procaine. Swan and René paid him for an office visit and split.

It was *El Medico* who told Swan that Blackie turned in smugglers for "*plata*" (silver), which was all Swan needed to know to stay clear of the Indian for good. But on his third trip South, Swan would meet so many new people, and make so many new friends, that Blackie, Fernando, the

* In the wake of the Nazi occupation of France, the shaved head was not the mark of the few who had resisted, it was the mark of the collaborateur. Swan served in the Pacific theater.

doctor and the entire population of Barranquilla would fade into history. After his first trip to Bogotá, smuggling cocaine would be like running at Churchill Downs in May — nothing small-time about it.

9

THE CARPENTER SAID
NOTHING BUT . . .

Zachary Swan, his confidence and his bankroll boosted by the events which had followed his last move, returned to Colombia on the crest of two decisions. He had decided that wood held the key to his future as a smuggler; it was adaptable, it was available, but even more than that it was what had worked for him once already, and he was determined to exploit it further. He had decided also that, if again, under any circumstances, he even considered carrying the cocaine through Customs himself, his days were numbered.

He arrived in Bogotá with $10,000 and four weeks of preparation behind him. His plan was sound. Having covered the delivery of at least two packages in New York, he would mail the coke. He would use René's connection, and he would package the shipment in wood, probably in one or two of the many different souvenirs he had seen in the airport gift shop on his last trip. If there was going to be a problem, it would come on the New York end. There he had two addresses, but only one of them had been previously tested and could be considered reliable. That was Davis's. The second address belonged to a stranger. And its reliability would be determined by a man code-named the Lothario.

The Lothario was one of Swan's more conventional friends. Though an intelligent fellow, rather shrewd, and, in his own way, pretty high-powered, he was not the kind of man who would have made it in the thick of the cocaine trade. Probably spoiled as a child, he was not accustomed to long-range gratification, and coming from privilege he was somewhat above the hucksterism required by the street. He took what he wanted as it came — he lived well and he got his kicks in a way that required as little risk as possible. He liked to gamble and he was pretty good at it. But when he lost, he lost big. When he was deep in the hole he would shill at Adrian's casino on the park, earning a hundred a night to mingle and make the place look full. He was also paid to bet on the crooked shooters and turn his winnings over to the house. Swan and the Lothario gambled a lot together. Swan met him over a dice table.

It was hard to say whether the Lothario ever worked for a living. His family owned a well-established and lucrative, but hardly posh, Jewish bakery in Manhattan and the Lothario, a young man who fancied himself something of a swinger, was rather embarrassed about it. He did, however, like the money. When the Lothario's father died, a few years after his association with Swan, he was obliged to take over the corporation, but at a cocktail party he would say no more than, "I have a business here in New York."

The Lothario, a likeable man, worthwhile to many, was a man very much impressed with names. He measured himself by way of his friends and his worth by that of the people he knew. Very few of the shooters at Adrian's knew anything about the Lothario, but they all knew everything about the people whose names he dropped. He had some fringe-Hollywood connections — as Swan put it, he had a lot of secondary-lead friends. He liked to advertise that he had been out with Joey Heatherton, and he claimed a popular film star as one of his closest pals. It was not that the Lothario ever lied about these things; he just let the truth get the better of him. On a gambling junket to St Martin with Swan, the Lothario brought a friend who had a supporting role in *The Lawyers* on television. The prevailing opinion was "so what."

It was pointed out as meaningful by those who knew him that the Lothario smoked brown cigarettes, Nat Sherman's Cigarettellos, manufactured in New York and a mark of distinction especially on the East Side. But the infinite complexities of the Lothario's thinking were ultimately synthesized in an offhand observation made by Alice, a woman blessed with insight and a gift for clarity:

"He drives an MG with the steering wheel on the right-hand side," she said.

Yet, as attenuated as it was, the Lothario's was not an exclusively vicarious life. The Lothario did one thing well. And it was something everyone knew he did well without his telling them: the Lothario was one of the world's most accomplished assmen. Yes. The Lothario had a way about him. He was in his thirties, tall and pretty, and he flashed a kind of backstairs elegance. He dated high-priced fashion models three-at-a-time, and this was his idea of class. It impressed his New York friends. And it impressed Swan, who knew that the Lothario had a lot of poker debts and could use some easy money. It was not long before the two talked business:

"What's in it for me?" the Lothario wanted to know.

"You get five hundred a package."

"I don't want to touch it, now. I don't want to be anywhere near the shit."

"You have the keys to their apartments?"

"Some of them."

"Just open the door for me. I'll make the switch."

"You'll have to come when they're at work."

"No shit."

"Look, I don't want any trouble."

"Have you ever been to Colombia?"

"No."

"Then how are they going to put you with the package? No fingerprints. No return address. You don't know anything. You're clean. I'm clean. Everybody's clean."

"What about her?"

"What *about* her? Her picture's been in every magazine in the world. She must get love letters every day. What does she know? She walks away."

"What if she doesn't want it? What if she throws it away?"

"Don't take out the trash. Look, if you tell her to keep it, she'll keep it."

"And you'll do the switch."

"When she's at work. Just stay close to her at package time. Remember that. And call me when it comes in."

"How much do I get?"

"Five hundred."

Bogotá, the political, industrial, commercial, economic and cultural capital of Colombia, is located on the 74th meridian just north of the equator, 2,984 miles due south of New York and just over an ocean due west of the Liberian coast.

It lies beneath Orion on a high savanna 8,660 feet above sea level in the Cordillera Central range of the Colombian Andes — a grassy plateau officially stolen from the Chibcha Indians on August 6, 1538. In the more than four hundred years since the city's founding, its population has risen to near three million — the majority of which is Spanish in origin — and the quality of life within its boundaries has sunk immeasurably.

Bogotá is an unclean city, crawling with street urchins and unfed dogs; 1,180 square miles of polluted, deoxygenated mountain air, cooler year round than the coastal resorts farther north — Colombia's climate is vertical — its average daytime temperature 57 degrees Fahrenheit with no significant variation from season to season. The Colombian businessman here wears a *ruana* — the traditional Colombian poncho — over his business suit to keep him warm during the day. At night he stays home. Any Colombian, a Bogotano first, will warn you that the streets of the city are *muy peligroso* — very dangerous — at night. A cursory acquaintance with the history of the civil strife Colombia has known over the years would be enough to impress a member of the Weather Underground — the body count is a figure to behold. In Bogotá, life is cheap.

The streets of Bogotá, in their layout, reflect the population's regard for the terrain out of which the city grew — *carreras* run parallel to the mountains, *calles* run perpendicular (east-west) — and maps of the city reflect a consummate disregard for the cartographic traditions of the rest of the world — polar north is to the left. Eldorado International Airport is located on the western edge of the city (at the bottom of the map), about twenty minutes by cab from downtown. *El centro*, the city's core, or downtown area, is where the principal hotels are located and where most tourists get their first taste of the city's night life. Outside any hotel, one can find a number of touts offering emeralds, hookers, currency and cocaine — in fact, these sinister characters, confronted immediately upon arrival at one's hotel, serve as a kind of chamber of commerce to welcome tourists to Bogotá. Alighting from his airport cab, Zachary Swan saw the promise of an adventure begin to unfold — arriving in Bogotá spawned the preliminary excitement and base-line fear experienced only upon entering a whorehouse.

Swan checked into the Hotel Tequendama. Owned by the Colombian government and overstaffed, the Tequendama would remain the most exclusive hotel in the city until the Bogotá Hilton opened six months later, and with eight hundred rooms it was the city's largest. The Tequendama was infested with amateur dealers and narcotics agents, but it had a twenty-four-hour coffee shop, and if a man were careful enough never to do business anywhere near the hotel, it was a good place to pick up information. On his second day in town, Swan met René Day at the coffee shop.

"What have we got?" he asked.

"We've got two new agents now," René said. "We've got the one with the beard over there. And we've got one with a gold earring — he's around here somewhere, you can't miss him — if you don't make the earring, you'll notice him because he wears jeans and talks like an acid freak. Very transparent."

"It makes sense. Only the smugglers wear suits," Swan said. "Is your connection still good?"

"He was busted last week. I'm dry. I was hoping you'd have something."

"All I've got is this name, Vincent van Klee."

René leaned back in his chair: "Call him," he said.

"Why not?" Swan made the call, and returned to the table five minutes later.

"I'm having lunch with him tomorrow at noon. Hotel Continental. He has a suite there."

"Does he know who you are?"

"Only by way of Michel. All he knows is my name and that he'd like to meet me. Very polite."

"What do you know about him?"

"I know he grew up with a coca tree outside his window. I know he likes coke and I know he buys it. I'll play it by ear."

"Why don't you take enough for a few lines. I've got that much."

"Good," Swan said. "It'll make things easier."

The next morning Swan took a cab to the Hotel Continental, located downtown on Avenida Jimenez, about fifteen blocks from the Tequendama and not far from the Gold Museum. He gave his name to the desk clerk and was told to go up. He was greeted by his host at the door.

Vincent van Klee was lean and wealthy. His clothes and his manner fit him well. He was neither tall nor young but he carried himself as if he were both, and like many Colombian aristocrats he was unashamedly European. His hair was white and his irises were brown, and if Swan were to abstract the essence of the man's bearing in one well-chosen word, it would be distinguished. Vincent van Klee had presence. He was alert and erect, and he moved with the grace of a fencing instructor. He was soft-spoken. He was courteous. His smile was easy, his English fluent, and his voice was that of a man who enjoyed listening. He had emerald smugglers' eyes. Swan knew that he was a man who could be trusted.

Vincent van Klee was seventy-two years old. In his youth he had dabbled in black market emerald traffic, but he was now content to indulge himself along more discreet avenues. Insulated by old money, he confined his pleasures to the moderate use of cocaine, fine wine and liqueurs; the company of close friends, those Bogotá socialites who determined Colombia's economic and political destiny; the acquisition of pre-Columbian art and choice real estate; and the sexual companionship of handsome young men and boys. A well-educated and intelligent man, he was a gentleman always, had traveled extensively, and was fluent in at least five languages. He and Swan were to become good friends.

"I have heard so much about you," he said.

"And I you," Swan replied.

As they came to know each other better they would lie less frequently.

Vincent served filet of sole for lunch. Swan served the coke René had given him. It was a pleasant afternoon all around. Over *aguardiente* Vincent demonstrated a flair for storytelling. He talked about Aztecs and Incas, cocaine and pre-Columbian jewelry, then broke down and admitted he had been an emerald smuggler.

"I will take you to the black market some day and show you how to buy emeralds," he told Swan.

(Swan bought an emerald on a subsequent trip to Bogotá. He carried it through Customs in his mouth up to the point at which it became evident he was going to be searched. Then, in terror, but calmly, he swallowed it. To retrieve the emerald he had to employ an elaborate sling fashioned out of toilet paper, a process which ran contrary to the romantic illusions he harbored with regard to smuggling; and because he made only $150 on the ultimate transaction, he gave up smuggling emeralds after one try.)

René's coke lasted no more than an hour and a half; old Vincent's pupils peaked at about f/4, held steady for a while, and began stopping down from there. Before they hit 5.6, Swan made his move:

"I would like to buy some more *coco* for us," he said.

Vincent invited Swan to stay for dinner, informed his cook, and called his connection.

Vincent van Klee's connection was a small-time street hustler named Lallo. In the presence of Vincent he cut quite a figure. About twenty-eight, black, sporting a close-cropped Afro and an elegant goatee, Lallo was rather shady looking. He moved very slowly, said very little, and it was a good guess that he had a knife somewhere. Swan wondered how he had made it through the lobby — that he was black, in itself, was enough to get him poleaxed at the elevator. In addition to an air of the street, Lallo had brought in with him ten grams of coke. Swan paid him the sidewalk price, $100, and invited Lallo, to the dealer's surprise, to stay for a sniff. Lallo, with Vincent's tacit approval, accepted the invitation.

The coke was wrapped in a scrap of white, lined loose-leaf paper, the customary package, almost a trademark in itself, for a *muestra*, or sample, of coke on the Bogotá streets. Swan cut out six lines, did his last, and after an appropriate silence, addressed Lallo:

"I have a friend," he said.

Of course. One always has a friend. Lallo nodded.

"He might be interested in some quantity," Swan added.

Yes. Lallo nodded again. He could handle it.

Then politely, and very carefully, Swan pointed out that his friend might like to buy it directly — from the Man.

"And, of course, there would be a bonus in it for you," he concluded.

Lallo nodded, made arrangements to meet Swan the next day, bid Vincent a silent good night and left. Swan and Vincent got stoned and waited for dinner. Vincent played

Roberta Flack records and poured *aguardiente*, impressing Swan with his wit and his stamina — it was very likely that after dinner Vincent would head for the nearest discotheque. Dinner was served late, Swan left after coffee, and as Vincent dressed for the evening Swan returned to his hotel with the profound feeling that good things were beginning to happen.

The next day in the Tequendama coffee shop Swan laid out $200 and Lallo took him from there to meet the Man. The Man's name was Armando. Armando was a Cuban, about fifty years old, six-two, 225, and hard all around. His complexion was fair and his dark curly hair was on its way out. He had a potbelly and the wrists of a .400 hitter. Swan would learn later that Armando had played AAA baseball in the United States, had kicked around for a while with Philadelphia's farm team, and very possibly had pitched for a year or two with the Cubs. He had played against Charlie Keller. But now Armando was strictly a cocaine dealer, and Swan was immediately impressed with the fact that their meeting took place in his home. If they got together, it would mean an end to dealing in second-rate hotel rooms and ill-lighted bars.

Swan wanted quantity, and Armando offered it to him at six dollars a gram. It was the best price Swan had ever been quoted, but, being Zachary Swan, he figured what the hell, and said that he heard he could get it for five. Armando said five and a half, they settled on that, and Swan was sure he had now found his first honest connection — a former used car salesman from pre-Castro Cuba who had played major league ball against Charlie Keller. They shook hands and Armando said, "Next week." As a demonstration of good faith he gave Swan what Swan would later find out was a handful of the finest grass in Colombia. Swan returned to the Tequendama and gave René the news.

"Splendid," said René. "Did you get us a good price?"

Swan nodded. "Six dollars a gram."

Connections in the cocaine trade are made very much as they are made in the legitimate business world. The difference is one of direction rather than of degree. Where a legitimate businessman makes money selling his customers to a wholesaler — by way of a mailing list, for example — a cocaine smuggler makes money selling the wholesaler to the potential customer. A smuggler's connections are worth money to him — he almost never gives them away. Observing the same tradition under which René had connected for Swan — charging Swan seven dollars a gram for cocaine that might have been going for six — Swan introduced René to Armando, who, under instructions from Swan, charged René six dollars for coke offered at five and a half. The $500 overage per kilo went to Swan, and until Armando and René became friends or mutually trusted business associates, and the price was altered, Swan would collect $500 on every kilo Armando sold to René. It was an understood and accepted business practice — René *knew* he was paying more — and it was never questioned by any of the principals involved. It was a tacit agreement among professionals, one that prevailed throughout the world.

In Bogotá, waiting for Armando's cocaine, Swan and René entertained themselves independently of each other. René had friends of his own there, and Swan was chumming around with Vincent van Klee. After meeting Armando, Swan called Vincent and invited him to dinner. Vincent recommended *El Zaguán de Las Aguas* on Calle 19 when Swan suggested they go native. Prompt service was rare throughout Colombia, and *Las Aguas* was one of the few restaurants Vincent endorsed. Swan, at Vincent's suggestion, ordered *ajiaco con pollo*, a thick soup which consisted of chicken, avocado, several kinds of potatoes, corn on the cob and other heavy vegetables, embellished with capers over a dollop of sour cream. "*Muy tipico*," the waiter said. Swan smiled. The restaurant and the dish would become a favorite of Swan's, and two years later he would be eating the same thing, by the same fireplace and to the same music, while he propped up a new carrier, Lillian Giles.

Also *muy tipico* of Bogotá at the time was the after-hours club Vincent led Swan to later that night. Swan had heard stories of places thus named. In the midnight travel brochure of his mind, indexed somewhere under America, South, the copy scanned something like this ... *hookers everywhere ... for men and for women ... a coca leaf floating at the top of your drink ... getting it up your nose, taking it through your mouth and getting laid between highs ... you're smoking dope and drinking aguardiente and thinking about going home around ten in the morning ... by then everybody is falling down ... everybody is getting robbed ... the pickpockets and bandits are working overtime ...* The tourists love it. It is so very *tipico*.

The place was dark and crowded. The music was preponderantly brass. And, in the smoke-drenched atmosphere, there was the dominant aroma of sin. While Vincent sipped *aguardiente* and talked to young men, Swan disappeared with a woman. Together they relived their most boring liaisons. Swan found it nostalgic. When he returned, Vincent was still talking, but clearly growing bored. It had been a very pleasant evening — Vincent's watch had been stolen — but now it was about six a.m. — time to go home. As they headed for the door they were presented with a bill.

"Your whore," Vincent said.

Swan's glasses, which were gold-rimmed, had been stolen earlier. He handed the bill to Vincent, whose eyes were no better, in fact, but who managed to read the numbers in transit as they passed three feet from his face. The bill read 600 pesos. They were hitting Swan with a 500-peso room charge for the hooker.

"This is ridiculous," Vincent said. "We won't pay it."

Swan looked at Vincent. We won't? We won't. Vincent sat down. The police were called in to deal with this recalcitrant old faggot. They were on the payroll. They stood with the bouncers. Swan gave them a Delta-9 grin. Vincent refused to move. Swan was nervous.

"Let's just pay it and get out of here," Swan said.

Vincent said no. He threw the bill at the waiter. (Oh, Jesus, thought Swan.) The policeman in charge, experienced at this kind of work, conferred with the manager and came back with an offer.

"Two hundred and fifty," he said.

Vincent remained seated. And Swan finally became caught up in it all. He was stoned and he started to get funny.

"*Dos cientos cincuenta pesos! No es* Brigitte Bardot!"

They had to agree. They settled for a hundred and twenty. Swan paid, and he and Vincent left.

It was at about this point in his career that Swan had occasion to regret having let lapse his prescription for diet pills. That evening, having slept the day away in his hotel room, Swan attended a cocktail party. Vincent was throwing it at his suite in the Continental. Swan staggered in late. Vincent was flying.

"How nice of you to come."

"You continue to impress me, Vincent."

"Oh, don't tell me."

"You look dashing."

"I have had only my first *aguardiente*."

"Vincent, I can't wait."

"You will stay late. Many people have yet to come."

"I thought I *was* late."

"The night is just beginning."

"Perhaps I had better clear my head."

"Help yourself."

Swan, after removing his coat, made a wrong turn and ended up in the kitchen. He found a carpenter working there, a young man building cabinets, who smiled politely at Swan and wished him a good evening. In his late twenties, with a pleasant face and a cheerful smile — an ingenuous-looking lad — the carpenter was working later, it appeared, than he had planned. Swan smiled knowingly, returned the greeting, and righted his course in the direction of the living room. He spotted the cocaine on the coffee table and availed himself of a blow. Interesting, he thought. He spread himself around, let his mind wander, and after a half hour had passed, he casually drifted back into the kitchen. The carpenter was still there.

Swan said hello. The carpenter said hello. By way of a strange blend of English and Spanish, Swan complimented the young man on the excellence of his work. Bilateral communication was established when the carpenter, by way of the same linguistic blend, thanked Swan for the compliment. Swan smiled. The carpenter smiled. Progress was made. They said other pleasant things and smiled some more. Swan was pleased. The carpenter was pleased. Eventually Swan managed to point out:

"I have a friend."

* * *

The carpenter, as it turned out, had a friend too. His name was Rudolpho. Swan had met him in the living room. Rudolpho had been doing cocaine.

Rudolpho, Angel the carpenter's good friend, had been Vincent van Klee's lover as a boy. As a handsome young man he had traveled with Vincent to France and to Italy, and now, in his thirties, he was a constant companion. He was married to a young woman, a seamstress named Evelyn, and he and Evelyn had two small children, but because Evelyn made very little money and because Rudolpho was such a poor businessman, it was Vincent who supported the family. It was done in a very oblique way, of course, and typically, as it turned out, with as little efficiency as possible. Vincent would invest in a business of one kind or another, and Rudolpho would run it into the ground. Their latest venture was a ranch outside of Bogotá.

Swan did not know any of this yet, nor did he know for a fact that Rudolpho was not particularly fond of his dependence on Vincent. What he did know was that Rudolpho was a friend of Michel Bernier, another of Vincent's lovers, and it was with mention of him, their mutual acquaintance, that Swan engaged Rudolpho in conversation when he left the kitchen. Rudolpho spoke English well, he dressed like a gentleman, and Swan could see that he liked cocaine. But nothing pleased Swan more than the discovery that Rudolpho, the carpenter's friend, was passing counterfeit fifties for Michel.

"Angel, the carpenter, tells me he is also a friend of yours," Swan said.

"Yes," said Rudolpho.

"How nice," said Swan.

The impact of a carpenter upon the scope of Swan's business would be, to say the least, a profound one, especially in light of his decision to exploit the properties of wood in its behalf. But things began to break so fast that before he was able to address himself seriously to the possibilities suggested by the talents of Angel and Rudolpho, talents that would ultimately provide the core for a far-reaching Colombian operation, he was to find himself sowing the seeds of fraternity among a broad network of cocaine smugglers working out of Bogotá. And again it was Vincent who opened the door.

On his fourth day in Bogotá, waiting for Armando to come through with the cocaine, Swan, at Vincent's suggestion, checked out of the Tequendama and took a room at the Hotel Continental. Vincent was quite eloquent in explaining his reasons for recommending the move — he said he thought the Tequendama was a "dump." Swan moved out — what could he say — and was not at the Continental more than twelve hours before Michel Bernier paid him a visit. Bernier, not one of Swan's closest friends, stumbled around the room for a while, stoned, making incoherent conversation — he asked Swan about Uta, talked about his friend Vincent van Klee, and after hearing that Uta was in Cartagena and that, yes, Vincent was indeed *un homme formidable*, he came to the point. He wanted $1,000. Swan explained that he, Swan, was a little short of cash. Michel smiled and explained that he, Swan, did not understand. Oh? It was not a loan. It was extortion. Oh. Swan understood perfectly. After looking around the room and satisfying himself that there was nowhere he could reasonably stash the body without forcing a showdown with the chambermaid, Swan made a deal with Michel. He gave Michel $100 and told him to come back the next day for the rest. Michel took the hundred and said he would be back. Swan said he did not doubt it and showed Michel out. An hour later Swan checked out of the Continental. He moved across town to a place called the Oriole Hotel — he would later refer to it as moving right out of the frying pan and into the golden goose.

The Oriole was owned and operated by a handsome young Colombian named Juan Carlos Ramirez, whom Swan met within an hour of checking in, and with whose intelligence, maturity and wealth Swan could not help but be impressed. Ramirez was twenty-eight years old, had been educated in Canada, and spoke impeccable English. His was a very casual approach to the hotel business, and he and Swan became friendly almost immediately. It would not be long before Swan would introduce him to Vincent, a man with whom Ramirez had at least one thing in common, Swan noted, Roberta Flack notwithstanding — Ramirez, whose own room at the Oriole was decorated with Day-Glo posters and outdated acid art, was always throwing parties. Vincent would certainly have approved. To his parties, it happened, Ramirez invited many of the hotel's guests, his favorites among whom were the young Americans and Canadians who seemed to abound there, and at least two of whom, Swan soon discovered, were definitely cocaine smugglers. One of them was Canadian Jack.

Canadian Jack, about twenty-five years old, with blond hair, blue eyes and a passion for rock and roll, had been making regular trips to Colombia for well over a year. When he was not in Bogotá, he was hanging around in Jamaica smoking dope with the freaks at Strawberry Fields or chasing his own brand of music in one direction or another — what little cocaine was available at Woodstock in the summer of 1969 was his. Arrested on a charge of smuggling a large shipment of hashish from Turkey through the Toronto airport, he had jumped bail and was wanted in Canada. He was supporting himself in Bogotá on the steady income he derived moving small amounts of cocaine into Canada and the United States, either using mules or running it himself, getting himself in and out of North America on a false passport. He managed to get home quite often. Jack had a lot of valuable connections in Bogotá and a lot of valuable information even on those people with whom he was not connected. He was not the most professional smuggler around — he seemed to get by more on luck than on any experience he might have gained over the years — but Swan liked him right away. He thought he was a "good kid." They became friends quickly, and soon after their meeting, Swan introduced Jack to Armando. Perhaps it was because Jack was not a professional — he never had a lot of money — that Swan did not put anything on the price.

Through Canadian Jack, Swan met Black Dan, another Oriole guest, an American from San Francisco who Swan would later learn was smuggling large quantities of cocaine into the United States at a rate that was remarkable for a strictly one-man operation. He was the most professional smuggler Swan would meet in Bogotá. About thirty-three years old, laid back, Dan smuggled his coke across two borders, and he had been doing it the same way for almost two years. He traveled via Mexico with the coke strapped to his legs — a dangerous and somewhat foolhardy procedure for an ordinary man. But Dan was far from ordinary. A former heavyweight boxer, he was as strong a man as Swan had ever met — he was tall, had to weigh at least 250, and his muscles were strung like bridge cables. He did not say much and was not the kind of man you wanted to spend a lot of time with if you were looking at him over a Customs counter or an airport gate barrier. Black Dan was friendly, a good man to blow coke with and a good man to have on your side, but he was frightening to look at if you were looking for more than a smile. It would be a while before he and Swan became friends.

By the end of his first week in Bogotá, Swan had put two new smugglers in touch with Armando. He, Jack and René were now waiting to score from the Cuban. And Armando, who had promised delivery within a week, was late — the delay, Swan would learn, was characteristic. Armando had a lieutenant named Raoul who, in addition to running underlings like Lallo, was employed to handle the Indian women who walked the pure across the mountains from Ecuador. Raoul would meet the couriers on the Colombian side of the border, pay them their wages — twenty dollars a trip if they were lucky — pick up the coke and deliver it to Armando in Bogotá. As a matter of course, however, Armando was forced to keep his customers in Bogotá waiting while Raoul, on the border, went out of his mind for a few days with the two young Indians and the fresh shipment of cocaine. Deliveries were made about once a month out of Ecuador, and Raoul saw them as vacations. When Raoul was not making everyone wait, he was making everyone laugh.

Raoul was short and fat, in his middle forties; always dressed in a rumpled business suit — Swan was convinced he slept in it — he looked like a cross between a racetrack tout and a flood victim. He was a Cuban and was always referred to as such — even Armando called him a Cuban. He often made deliveries for his boss, acting as a link to the smugglers, and on these assignments he liked to meet in ice cream parlors. Whenever a smuggler went out to deal with Raoul, he went prepared to watch this one-man sideshow knock off at least two double-dip cones in a sitting. When meets were scheduled elsewhere, say in a hotel room, Raoul drew on a repertoire of other entertainments, one of which Swan became party to when Raoul delivered a kilo to Swan's room at the Continental.

Swan told Raoul the kilo was not pure. "*No es pura,*" Swan said. Raoul's eyes flashed open — they went on like Lucas lamps. "*Pura! Pura!*" he said, pointing to the cocaine. Swan shook his head solemnly. "*No es pura.*" Raoul grew indignant. He picked the coke up in his hands and began to throw it all over his face as if he were sampling an exotic aroma of some kind. He splashed it around his nose, nodded and yelled "*Pura!*" While Swan shook his head, Raoul continued to throw the cocaine lovingly into his face, then into Swan's. "*Pura! Pura!*" he sang. It was when Swan started to laugh at the suggestion that Raoul started to go a little bit crazy. Raoul bent over like an ostrich, buried his face in the cocaine as if it were a bouquet of roses, shook his head from side to side, then, inhaling the coke, jumped around the room screaming "*Pura!*" He waved his arms and jumped up and down and screamed "*Pura!*" to the world at large. Swan, who did not intend to buy the coke, was really not obliged to offer an excuse for not buying it, but he found the show exhilarating — he continued to shake his head. Raoul continued to jump, then wheeled around to face Swan with cocaine clinging to his moustache and eyelashes — he looked like he had just come in from Vermont. "*Pura!*" he screamed. Swan waited for him to catch his breath, then, timing his shot perfectly, referred to the coke as "shit." This drove Raoul almost insane. By the time the Cuban finished arguing the merits of his product, he was covered with cocaine from his head to his shoes and panting like a racehorse. He put his hand over his lungs as if he were about to collapse. Swan handed him a glass of water. He looked Raoul in the eye. With a nod of his head, Raoul picked up the kilo and put on his hat. He left with a polite goodbye and, mumbling "pura," went directly to an ice cream parlor.

It was Raoul, in a more sober moment, who told Swan that you only get two years in the trade — "You can't run for more than two," he said, "after two years, quit." Two years after he began smuggling cocaine, Swan was in the Riverhead Jail — he would not know until later that Raoul had learned the wisdom of his own words the hard way.

A week after Vincent's cocktail party, Swan kept an appointment with Rudolpho. He had been invited to visit the ranch and meet Evelyn and the children — he arrived bearing gifts. He had brought flowers for Evelyn and candy for the children — he had brought two long rolling pins for Rudolpho. He was there to talk business. The agreement that he and Rudolpho would ultimately reach was born of two complementary goals: Rudolpho wanted money; Swan wanted Angel the carpenter. Rudolpho got what he wanted. Swan got much more.

Angel was no simple carpenter. He was a master craftsman who employed four apprentices. In his shop, which was located in a large garage on the outskirts of Bogotá, he had two lathes, a table saw, electric sanders and several power drills, in addition to the manually operated tools necessary to his trade. When he and Rudolpho went to work for Swan, many of the tools were moved from the shop to the top floor of Rudolpho's house — subsequently, the entire shop was transferred. Rudolpho and Angel split $1,000 on every kilo Swan moved out of Colombia. Angel handled the woodwork, and Rudolpho handled the paperwork. It was Rudolpho's job to mail the packages. Each package had to be mailed separately and from a different Post Office. In the event of trouble, Rudolpho was always given a hundred-dollar bill with which to buy his way out. Both he and Angel would accompany Swan on the score, acting as backup men, and Rudolpho, who knew cocaine, would help judge the samples. Rudolpho spoke English, thanks to Vincent, and until Swan had been working out of Bogotá for a while, Rudolpho would also provide a necessary linguistic link, not only to Swan's suppliers, but to Angel as well.

In addition to Angel's tools, one other piece of apparatus — a monster — was evident in the packaging plant upstairs at Rudolpho's. As soon as he had cemented the deal with the two Colombians, Swan had done some shopping. He had bought a press. A hand-operated, flat-bed, job printer, it was six feet high with a metal stand and cast-iron impression levers. With two handles and a torsion screw to operate the platen, it was an archaic device, suitable only for hand embossing — and with the metal frames and adjustable jigs that Angel designed, it was perfect for cocaine compressing. Swan had seen it in a print shop — he paid eighty dollars for it. He, Rudolpho and Canadian Jack were on hand to cart it away, but without Black Dan, who happened to be walking by at the right time, they would never have managed to get it into Rudolpho's car. It was big and it was heavy — they had to remove the rear seat to load it — and only Dan was able to move it more than an inch at a time. The press was essential to the business that followed; it, more than anything else, was responsible for increasing the weight Swan was able to move through his network in New York — it cut his volume by 50 percent.

Because of the weight, density and desiccated condition of the wood involved, loading a store-bought rolling pin with cocaine was impractical. What Angel would do was fashion a duplicate out of fresh Madeira wood, saw it longitudinally down the middle, hollow it out, line it with plastic, fill it, close it with glue and clamps, then paint and finish it. In New York, Swan would find that the rolling pins Angel made were about as hard to open as they were to build. But the manufacture of any item was child's play compared with what went into the compressing and packing of the cocaine — when Armando finally came through, Swan took a *kilo y medio*, 1,500 grams, and he, Angel and Rudolpho went to work.

Working in the glass-enclosed room on Rudolpho's roof was like working in a greenhouse. Though high in the mountains, Bogotá is less than five degrees north of the equator, and when the sun was high, it was directly overhead. Compressing the *kilo y medio* took hours — in the months to come, three kilos would be the minimum load. When the sweat was running and the coke was flying off the press under the drop of the impression plate, the three bandits looked like snowmen, soaking the powder up through the pores of their skin. Wearing gloves to keep fingerprints off the merchandise, they plastic-wrapped the cocaine before filling the souvenirs. They worked stoned most of the time, and drank beer to fight the heat. The impression levers on the press were always breaking, and the three men spent a good amount of their time just sitting with the coke — under the sun, gloved and sweating and drinking beer — while they waited for the broken parts to come back from the machine shop. When the job was done and the souvenirs packed, a package was made. It had to be addressed in block lettering to disguise the handwriting — the address was often printed by all three men, one man taking every third letter — then tied with string and kept clean of prints. In the case of the Lothario's packages, love letters had to be enclosed. Rudolpho handled those. And each package had to be mailed separately to account for the odds against more than one's going through.

It would work like this on all subsequent trips but two — Angel and Rudolpho would be as essential to the South American operation as the ounce-dealers were to the New York network. And Armando would continue to deliver pure. In the months to come, Canadian Jack and Black Dan would avail themselves of Swan's equipment and imagination. Raoul would begin to offer kilos on his own and other cocaine dealers would emerge. And Vincent van Klee, a good friend, would be consulted on every sample that came Swan's way. Before a year was out, Michel Bernier would return, Juan Carlos Ramirez's parentage would yield secrets, and René Day, the prince of players, would rejoin Swan to participate in what would be known as the Boat Move. Swan had gone from 300 grams on his first move to 600 grams on his second. After the kilo and a half moved on this, his most recent trip, he would never move fewer than three keys. He left Bogotá with nowhere to go but up.

10

ALKALOID ANNIE/
POWER OF THE PRESS

Swan strolled through United States Customs in New York with three rolling pins in his luggage — red, white and black, respectively, each a duplicate of one he had mailed from Bogotá. None of them was examined. Shortly after his return home, he got a call from Davis, who phoned from a booth on the street below his office.

"I've got a visitor," he said.

The package was in. Swan took a subway to midtown, carrying a blue canvas AWOL bag folded under his arm. From the lobby of Davis's building he took an elevator to the eighth floor, then walked the fire stairs to the tenth, examining the stairwell and the hallways for a stakeout before proceeding to Davis's office on the ninth. He looked the package over for signs of a search and found nothing blatantly wrong, but conducted a trial run anyway before leaving with the load. He put a heavy catalogue into the AWOL bag, left the building with it, and took a walk around the block. Satisfied that he and the package were clean, he traded the catalogue for the cocaine and took the coke home.

Before breaking the load down, he called Anthony to say that he had just returned from "down South." Allowing himself time to collect the other two packages, he made arrangements with Anthony to deliver a sample. The next morning the Lothario called. "Why don't you come and visit me?" he said.

He gave Swan an address on West 90th Street. Swan walked it. He paid the Lothario $500 cash on the spot and switched the rolling pins — they were white.

"What did she say?" Swan asked.

"Not much. It was pretty routine. She gets presents all the time."

"I thought so."

"How much are these things worth?" the Lothario asked, taking the rolling pin from Swan.

"I'll find out soon," said Swan, taking it back.

"Yeah? Well, when you do, let me know."

"Yeah. I'll let you know."

(Later, when the Lothario learned how much the packages were worth, his fee was boosted to $650.)

With two packages at home, Swan started breaking the rolling pins down. He cut out a sample for Anthony — pure — and put the rest on a twenty-two and six, hitting it with borax, adding about 300 grams of powder to the kilo of pure and packaging the ounces in plastic. He moved into the Lincoln Square Motel with 45 ounces cut and ready to move through his ounce-dealers. He was out in a week with $31,500. (He moved the cocaine at $700 an ounce. Soon he would be asking $850. In a year it would be going for $1,000.)

The third package came in late. The Lothario called Swan

from an apartment on East 79th Street which belonged to a young woman in whose direction the Lothario channeled the greatest share of his romantic energy. The Lothario was in love. The young woman was a very famous model and a part-time actress — her worldwide exposure and the Lothario's constant company, both taken for granted, accounted for two subsequent shipments to her address. Her favorite color was red. Swan walked into her plush apartment and found the rolling pin on the radiator. Bad news.

"Jesus fucking Christ."

"Well, I didn't know," said the Lothario.

They were surveying the damage.

"Heat destroys it, man."

"I'm really sorry."

Swan tossed the souvenir onto the couch and shook his head.

"God damn it."

The rolling pin was hot. The Lothario was sincerely sorry. Swan was running out of ways to take the Lord's name in vain. When he regained his composure, he assured the Lothario that it was his, Swan's, own fault.

"Forget it, man. I'll straighten it out."

Swan paid the Lothario and went directly to Anthony with the load. They had decided on $11,000 for 500 grams of the pure Anthony had sampled. Swan explained what had happened. It was painful. He and Anthony opened the rolling pin together (in keeping with Swan's earlier promise to deliver the coke in its original container). They used a hammer and chisel, cracking the pin on the floor of Anthony's billiards room. What they found was discouraging. The cocaine had turned brown — another five hours on the radiator and it would have converted to paste. They spread it out on the floor over newspaper and put lamps on it, trying to dry it out, hoping to bring it back. When it was as dry as it was going to get, it looked somewhat improved, but was still brown and crusty. Anthony got on the phone and within twenty minutes he had a customer waiting in the living room. He went out, leaving Swan with the stash, and came back shaking his head.

"I don't know what the fuck to do with it," Swan said.

Anthony left again. He kept going and coming until the price went from $11,000 to $9,000 then finally to $7,000. Swan was glad to get it. In order to complete the deal, Anthony needed a piece of evidence — unorthodox in the extreme.

"We need the rolling pin," he said.

"What the fuck do you need the rolling pin for?" Swan wanted to know — things were getting a little bit out of hand.

"He wants to know why there is sawdust in his coke," Anthony said.

"Shit."

Swan's total take on the *kilo y medio* was $38,500. He stashed most of it in a safe deposit box. As the amounts of money he made on cocaine increased, so did the amount of time he spent devising safe ways to hide the cash — he kept safe deposit boxes in several banks around the city, but could not trust them to stand up to an investigation. What evolved was a ready-cash system which in its most extreme example owed much to Swan's love affair with wood and his disdain for the conservation of human energy. He started secreting the money in logs.

His apartment in New York and every house he rented on Long Island had one thing in common — each had a fireplace. From the woodpile in the living room, Swan would select a sympathetic-looking log and soak its bark off — the process required a good deal of work. He would float the log in the bathtub for two or three days, now and then adding a knife or spatula wedgelike to the imposing piece of flotsam, hammering the implements gently into the interface of the bark and wood, and wait for the bark to soak free in one piece. Baths and showers were shared with what ultimately resembled an anchorless underwater mine, floating at the surface with its trip devices exposed. When the bark was finally worked off, Swan would chisel a hole in the log just large enough to encase the money he was hiding. The hole, carved in the shape of the currency, looked something like a robbed grave. When the money was laid to rest, the bark was replaced with glue, clamps and ropes. Swan would sand and sawdust the ends of the log, wipe off the excess glue, then stick the log back onto the woodpile. A hearth fire would cost him $30,000. He sometimes hid dope in the same fashion.

"I had nightmares about people burning logs. I made it a point never to let anyone stay in my house and burn fires while I was away."

What it all amounted to was the Zachary Swan branch of the Chase Manhattan Bank. The hours were terrible — there were many people who were of the opinion that if he had ever run across a time-and-motion studies man, Zachary Swan would have been a millionaire.

What not a few considered to be the loose wires in Zachary Swan's head sparked him down other dubious paths. Raoul, Armando's man with the ice cream habit, had told Swan that one of the waiters at Victor's Café — the Cuban restaurant in Manhattan which was Ellery's HQ and one of Swan's favorite neighborhood hangouts — owed him, Raoul, $80,000. When Swan asked what for, Raoul assured him it was not for ice cream.

"Once I tried to talk to the man about it — to do a favor for Raoul, to see if I could get any of the money for him. From then on I got very bad tables at Victor's."

Swan's Mail Moves, as they were called, were the bread and butter of his operation. In a way he was very much like Sears Roebuck — no matter what scam he was working on to cover, say, a four-kilo move, he always had at least one package in the mail. Many times he would simply send the money to Rudolpho and let the efficient Colombian handle the South American end of the deal. In order to sustain the mail-order branch of the business, he had to keep updating his New York pickup and delivery service. Davis's was the cornerstone scam. And the Lothario was very important. But there were others.

On one occasion, Swan mailed a statue of Saint Anne to Iona Prep in New Rochelle — a donation from "an alumnus." He and Charlie Kendricks showed up at Iona to photograph this beautiful piece of Colombian craftsmanship, which they expected to find in the chapel. For some reason it had been relegated to the cafeteria — they had to wait for the lunch hour to come and go before they could get to work. The photographs never appeared anywhere, but the original statue appeared that night on the floor of Swan's living room under a chisel. The duplicate left in its place suffered only the penance of the Christian Brothers.

Less difficult than the Saint Anne switch but a bit more harrowing was an experience with one of the Lothario's lovers. She was a very superstitious woman, a fact Swan had not taken into account when he sent her, as a gift "from my country," a tribal head instead of a rolling pin. The head was so frightening she nearly threw it out the window. The Lothario was on hand to prevent the defenestration, but was even more severely taxed after the switch was made. Swan had been unable to find an exact duplicate of the souvenir — the snarling face that had prompted the woman's hysteria he had replaced with one sporting a benign smile. The Lothario had to keep *her* from going out the window when she noticed that.

Zachary Swan, in his pursuit of the perfect formula for drug running, had made enough mistakes and come up hard against enough misconceptions to mistrust intuitively the folklore surrounding cocaine. There was one bright fable in the prevalent street mythology which he learned to discount early — it offered as its moral the celebrated principle that rocks in the coke you buy guarantee the purity of the sample you sell.

Rocks, in cocaine lore, are the lumps that appear dispersed throughout the sample. They are what account for the meticulous chopping which serves as the bizarre Introit to any coke-snorting ceremony. The truth about lumps is that they are simply lumps, like the lumps in damp sugar (in a gram sample of street coke, chances are better than average that the lumps *are* damp sugar), but the lore of the street holds them to be crystals of pure cocaine. A dealer, who will chop the rocks in the cocaine he snorts, will leave them alone in the cocaine he sells, and he will always point to them, if they are there, to show the quality of his product.

Pharmaceutical cocaine, that manufactured legally (1,057 kilos in the U.S. in 1969 — twenty dollars an ounce), is sometimes sold in the form of a rock, one large, lambent crystal, like rock candy, 100 percent pure. And illegal cocaine can sometimes be found, in its pure state, to crystallize in a similar fashion, but not so completely and not nearly so often. Pure cocaine of the illegal variety, though chemically crystalline, appears as a flake (as does *most* pharmaceutical cocaine). Rocks in cocaine are more often than not due to moisture, and the moisture will lump any of its impurities and any of the ingredients with which it has been cut. Zachary Swan became aware of this early. Moses Wellfleet, on the other hand, was as devout as they come.

Moses had been dealing coke for years, and he had been dealing it on the street. No one was going to tell Dr W anything about rocks. And so when Zachary Swan began pressing his coke for shipment, he had trouble with Moses. Compressing the coke essentially pulverized it — the crystals disappeared. After his first shipment using Angel and Rudolpho, part of Swan's pressing ritual included sprinkling crystals on the top of the load for Moses. It was no more than a gesture, and it kept Moses happy. Moses was getting fluff from the blender and rocks from the top of the load, and his customers never complained. The ounce-dealers occasionally got questions from new customers, but the impact of the pressing upon their end of the business was minimal. Compressing the load hurt sales maybe 5 percent.

"Most people don't know what they're blowing anyway — they know what they've been buying. You offer them pure and they won't meet your price — they say it's shit because it doesn't look like what they're used to. So you hit it with some borax and they pay your price. But that takes time. After you unload most of it at an honest price, then you can fuck around with what's left for the sucker trade."

In the months between his first trip to Bogotá in the winter of 1971 and the Brown Gold Move which he made in the summer, Swan made two trips to Colombia. He used Angel and Rudolpho on both and mailed three kilos of cocaine to New York on each occasion.

11
HORSE LATITUDES

Brown Gold Coffee, imported and packaged by the Andes Coffee Corporation of Palisades Park, New Jersey, is, as its label points out, "100% Colombian." A unique blend of the Medellin Excelso and the Armenia Excelso coffee beans, the label adds, it is "worth its *taste* in gold." Cocaine, on the other hand, a blend of coca leaf alkaloids and neutral crystals, very often 100 percent Colombian, is worth approximately its exact *weight* in gold — and that is before it crosses the border. The mathematics of this coincidence appealed to Zachary Swan, who over his morning coffee was scanning the travel page of *The New York Times*.

"Perfect," he said.

"Find what you were looking for?" Alice asked.

"Avianca Airlines is offering a ten-day excursion. Santa Marta, Barranquilla and Cartagena. Leaves from New York. It even names the hotels."

"Lucky you."

Alice, at this point, was the only person in whom Swan had confided. But to assure the success of this, his most

Byzantine move, Swan would need the help of at least two others. He would use Davis on the New York end and Canadian Jack in Cartagena. He would contact them later. What he needed now was an office. He needed an office, a telephone number, a few jars of coffee, a handful of printed material, and a lot of luck. He moved fast.

The office was a small one near Lüchow's restaurant on 14th Street. He rented it on a month-to-month basis. Into it he moved an old desk, a new filing cabinet, a swivel chair and a coffee percolator. While he waited for a telephone, he worked on getting the printed material he needed. This was not hard. As a former packaging executive (in essence a printing salesman) he had very little trouble coming by the necessary four-color work and stationery. Most of it he ordered from the Andes Coffee people himself — labels, poster ads, and packaging paper, all stamped with the Andes logo and address: ANDES COFFEE CORP., S. A. Schonbrunn & Co., Inc., Palisades Park, N.J. 07650. What he did not get directly from Andes, he got from business associates who had access to the Andes printing buyer, and what he did not get from them, he had printed on his own. The most important piece of original printing was a miniature folded brochure stamped with his new office number.

He decorated the office in appropriate bad taste with all the trappings he had accumulated — posters on the wall, coffee cans adorning the desk, subway ads, supermarket art, labels glued to everything — bought the coffee and moved in to work. It was difficult work, but after a while and several containers of coffee, he finally managed to remove the vacuum seal from a four-ounce jar of freeze-dried instant without tearing it. He inserted his brochure, replaced the seal with rubber cement, capped the jar and drove to Queens to put the jar in a grocery store. Before he returned to his office, however, he experienced a head-on collision — running hard up against America's free-market system. The coffee in Queens was cheaper than the coffee in Manhattan. Bohack was selling it for less than D'Agostino's. The price tags were different. But Swan was undaunted. In the proud tradition of Yankee know-how and a typical consumer's respect for our nation's supermarkets, Swan switched the lids and moved his jar to the front of the shelf. It was as simple as that. He was leaving nothing to chance. He walked out, wondering who had shoplifted whom, returned to his office and waited. For days.

Mrs Vagelatos called at about 4:30 in the afternoon.
"Brown Gold Company."
"Hello."
"Hello."
"I am Mrs Vagelatos."
"Yes, Mrs Vagelatos."
"I am number 21–27–37–31–32."
"Are you calling about the contest, Mrs Vagelatos?"
"Yes. The contest. Yes, I am."
"And what is your number again, Mrs Vagelatos?"
"Number 21–27–37–31–32."
"Did I hear you correctly, Mrs Vagelatos? Will you repeat that number?"
She did. (Swan's filing system was quite simple: there was only one number — it was printed into the brochure, it came with the order. There was only one number, and only one of the brochures was in circulation. If Mrs Vagelatos had not called, Swan would have waited and tried again — he did not want too many copies of the brochure floating around.)

"Mrs Vagelatos. Mrs Vagelatos, you are a winner. You have won a prize. You have won *first* prize. You have won a free ten-day trip to Colombia."

Mrs Vagelatos said she was old and that her husband was retired. He was old too, she said. She spoke English poorly. Mrs Vagelatos had, however, lived in America for some time.

"Can I have the money, instead?" she asked.

Swan explained the rules of the contest to her — essentially, "It doesn't work that way, lady." Mrs Vagelatos said she would think it over. She called back the next day, having talked it over with her husband, and told Swan that she and Mr Vagelatos would take the trip.

"You will enjoy it, Mrs Vagelatos. Yes. What? Of course. And in addition to the vacation, there will be many gifts and souvenirs."

Of course.

Swan opened a checking account in the name of S. A. Schonbrunn & Co., Inc., and bought tickets for the Avianca tour in the Vagelatoses' name. He enclosed the tickets in a Brown Gold envelope, added a letter of congratulations and an itinerary typewritten on Brown Gold stationery, and mailed them to the couple in Queens.

The itinerary: Santa Marta, Baranquilla and Cartagena. Swan knew where the Vagelatoses would be, and when they would be there, all the time they were in Colombia. In his letter of congratulations he had informed them that a representative of the company would meet them in Cartagena to present them with their gifts. He called Armando from New York and told him he would be down in a week. He needed three bottles of Chanel.

"And no fucking around, Armando, I must have it. If you've got it there, hold it. I will definitely be down."

Two weeks later he took $22,000 cash from a safe deposit

box on the East Side and flew to Bogotá. (Whenever Swan carried large amounts of currency — and sometimes cocaine — he wore a special jacket, the lining of which had been designed specifically for that purpose by Alice. Essentially the jacket was lined with pockets. They were distributed evenly around the back and sides to prevent bulging, they were invisibly tufted so that the lining itself appeared smooth, and they were hemmed with Velcro, that miracle of the Space Age, to facilitate access and obviate the necessity for zippers or buttons. At any time, but especially when Swan traveled South, the jacket was a very expensive piece of tailoring.)

Armando delivered. He charged Swan six thousand a kilo for the three keys, a half-dollar increase per gram, partly for holding the load and partly because at the time the price of cocaine was going up all around the world. Angel and Rudolpho made the fill. Swan tracked down Canadian Jack, gave him $200, a few grams of coke, and a ticket to Cartagena. The two flew north together, Swan with the souvenirs, and Canadian Jack carrying a brand new Polaroid camera.

El Caribe Hotel, where the Vagelatoses' tour was booked, is located in Cartagena's Bocagrande district, at the tip of a peninsula which separates Cartagena Bay from the Caribbean Sea. Remote from the Old Town, decidedly distant in statute and spiritual miles from any of those things which may distinguish Cartagena from the other cities of the world — out there, across the harbor — Bocagrande, on the ocean side, is devoted almost exclusively to tourists. The Caribbean front of the peninsula is covered with neo-Miami concrete-and-Formica firetraps which go by such names as Americar, Flamingo, El Dorado and Las Vegas, every room of which offers Inquisition-in-walnut furniture, a pastel, circular sink in bas relief, and a view of the beach.

Under construction when Swan worked out of Cartagena, and now a second-thought-provoking reality, these wonders of modern architecture are designed to make South Americans feel they have come a long way and make North Americans feel at home. The principle governing their birth is the same one as that which presumes the drinking of Coca-Cola in Bordeaux. Social historians call it progress.

Tucked away out here in the trees, a lush array and ample variety of trees, on a vast expanse of protected real estate, is the Hotel Caribe. A faithful rendition of Spanish architecture, old, stately, a kind of one-man Environmental Protection Agency, El Caribe supports its own arboretum and tropical gardens as well as an animal population of modest scope. Much of the fruit served here is grown on the grounds, and most of the grounds, obviously, are devoted to nothing more than the simple pleasure of being on them. A back gate opens onto the beach. A marina fronts on a bay to the southeast. The hotel itself, if not as large as some of its treeless and sunscorched upstart neighbors, affords its clientele a greater degree of comfort, and a variety of luxury that all but disappeared with the advent of terrazzo lawns and vertical expansion. Perhaps because it is impossible for a swimmer to drown in an upright position within sight of Cartagena — the Caribbean here is just too shallow for too great a distance out — or maybe because walking the beach at night, like walking anywhere in South America, is taking your life in your hands — the Hotel Caribe was blueprinted around space for an Olympic pool, shaded by palm trees on two sides, bordered by an enclosed restaurant on one and an open-air poolside dining area on the other. It was by the pool, amid these lavish surroundings, that Swan staged his awards ceremony.

Swan and Canadian Jack took a midweek, morning flight

from Bogotá to Cartagena and checked into the Hotel Caribe. Shortly after he arrived, Swan called the Vagelatoses' room and asked the couple to meet him at the pool to receive their gifts. While Swan, sporting a full beard and dark glasses, awarded the Vagelatoses their prizes and made a big show of certifying with the waiter that the coffee they were drinking was 100 percent Colombian, laughing all the way, Canadian Jack dashed around with the camera. As usual, Swan and the Canadian were stoned, so it made no difference to either one of them that the Polaroid was empty and showed no signs of developing and ejecting the pictures it was presumably taking.

Swan loaded the Vagelatoses down with rolling pins, statues, wall hangings, hammocks, blankets, *ruanas*, straw hats, leather bags — about forty pounds of paraphernalia that cost him close to $150 and which would retail in the United States for over $500, all of it dragged out of two great, overflowing plastic bags. In his room, Swan had a duplicate of every one of the souvenirs. He asked the Vagelatoses to sign an agreement by which they were bound to be photographed again with their presents in the New York office. He made an offhand joke, unacknowledged, about Greeks bearing gifts, gave them a copy of the agreement to keep, and wished them a safe trip home.

The Vagelatoses were due back in New York two days later. Swan left a day early and made a dry run with his duplicates. They were not examined. The Vagelatoses were supposed to call Swan's office as soon as they returned. They did not. Swan waited. He worried. He had to call them. They were tired, it turned out — they had arrived on schedule. Swan groaned out loud over the phone. He dispatched a limousine, which he paid for in cash, to pick them up at their home in Queens.

Davis took the New York photos. And while Swan bought the Vagelatoses lunch at Lüchow's, Davis made the switch. The Vagelatoses returned to the office, picked up their gifts, Swan wished them health, wealth and happiness, escorted them to the limousine, and sent them home. He closed down the office the next day and never saw the couple from Queens again.

Quidquid id est, timeo Danaos et dona ferentis ...

The Customs man, obviously, had never read Virgil.

With the Brown Gold move, the supposed foundation upon which Swan had based his entry into smuggling was first called into question. His claim that he would never endanger a carrier or throw an innocent individual to the lions was challenged on the basis of his use of Mr and Mrs Vagelatos, a couple who had no idea of the trouble they might be walking into, two innocent Greek immigrants whose faith in America was reflected, for better or worse, by the faith they placed in its institutions, whether these be its supermarkets, its coffee companies or its Treasury Department, and the trust they placed in its citizens, whether they be honest Customs agents, as innocent of the facts as they, or alleged felons like Richard Nixon and Zachary Swan. The evidence in Swan's favor, however, is significant.

In the first place the Vagelatoses *were* innocent, which in itself is anyone's greatest asset to getting by a Customs check. In their favor also was the fact that they were traveling with a tour, a group of Americans who are predominantly middle-class and middle-aged and who are supervised almost every step of their way through a foreign country — their luggage is even handled differently. But it begs the question to say that the Vagelatoses had a better than average chance of making it through Customs without a search. After all, Swan's idea was to get the coke through — it was what the scam was designed for. In the event of a search, then, and assuming the even more remote possibility that the cocaine was discovered (Customs did not break open Swan's souvenirs, which were identical to those Mr and Mrs Vagelatos were carrying), one must ask how well the Vagelatoses were covered.

Swan claims they were covered well. He had insisted that they save the contest number; he could assume that they still had the coffee jar. In addition to these two items, the Vagelatoses were in possession of two Avianca tickets purchased by a check accounted to S. A. Schonbrunn & Co., Inc., whose office address was on 14th Street. On their persons at Customs they had a letter of congratulations and an itinerary typed on Brown Gold stationery. And in the same envelope they had a signed agreement to appear at the 14th Street office with their gifts upon arrival in the United States. In the absence of everything else, they had at least thirty witnesses poolside in Cartagena. The evidence of their innocence, then, was overwhelming, as Swan saw it. If the Vagelatoses suffered at all, he assumed, it would be principally by way of embarrassment and perhaps temporary detention at the airport while the evidence was examined; and he supposed that the free ten-day vacation and the unconfiscated souvenirs would be sufficient compensation for that. As it turned out, in fact, everyone but Uncle Sam made out on the deal.

Swan was moving fast now. The Brown Gold move was such an overwhelming success, and his confidence in the wake of it so buoyant, that his roiling imagination began to generate more blueprints than he could follow. He had to throw them away. One outline that was carried through to success without his knowledge was one that he threw away in the company of Canadian Jack and Black Dan on a rainy night in Bogotá, when the cocaine express was taking its curves on the high side.

Black Dan had been living at the Oriole for almost two years when Swan first met him. He loved it in Bogotá. He left only once every six weeks, and he was always back fast. His visits to San Francisco were brief. Although he did not open up to Swan until a year after their meeting, it was pretty obvious all along that he was a smuggler. It was what you were in Bogotá if you were not manifestly anything else. And Dan always had cocaine. It was Dan who told Swan about *Mannite*, the Italian laxative, the cocaine cutting agent of choice and that with which Dan always cut his own coke before snorting. He preferred it that way to pure, for reasons which were unclear to Swan, and he preferred it out of a spoon, a taste Swan attributed to hours in the back rooms of Mission District bars.

Dan's closest friend in Bogotá was Canadian Jack, a friendship, in Swan's mind, distinguished chiefly by its sharp contrasts. Beyond the obvious one (Canadian Jack was a blond) was the almost polar difference in their approaches to smuggling. Black Dan was thoroughly professional. He found no need to acknowledge that he was a smuggler, even to Swan, a smuggler himself, whose professionalism was exemplified, if in no other way, by the fact that he never questioned Dan. Black Dan was a pro, and he had been going for years. He moved in quantity, unlike Jack, whose moves were small, and he was consistent. Every six weeks he flew to Mexico City with the coke strapped to his legs. From there he would fly to Matamoros or Tijuana, or whatever border town was convenient to his needs, and walk the load across, reentering the States with the bullfight crowds on the weekends, intimidating every official in his path by his mere presence. He never wasted time, and the closest he ever came to trouble was the trouble out of which he was always bailing Jack.

It was an evening in the early summer of 1971, six months after he had helped load Swan's press into Rudolpho's car and still six months before he would open up and apprise Swan of the Mexican route, that Black Dan, Swan and Canadian Jack were doing samples in Dan's suite at the Oriole, talking about the upcoming Summer Games in Cali.

"That's going to be a smugglers' convention," said Swan.

"You think so?"

"Well, just think about it for a minute. Number one — the pickpockets. Every dipper in the country is going to pack up and leave home. The thieves will be coming out of the woodwork, and they'll all converge on Cali when the games start. There'll be a million tourists there and another million people connected with the games in one way or another. Don't even count the Colombians, and that's a hell of a lot of money floating around. This country is as famous for its pickpockets as it is for its fucking coffee, and every one of them will be in Cali next month. So a smuggler doubles his money before he starts."

"I don't get the connection," said Jack.

"Can you picture the activity at the American Express office? Everybody and his mother is going to be there replacing stolen traveler's checks — 'I just got to Cali and my traveler's checks have been stolen' — and they're not going to ask them any questions. "Of course they've been stolen, this is Colombia." So what do you do? You sign 'em, sell 'em . . . use 'em . . . and then you replace them.

You can do it every day, and the banks aren't going to pick up on it. Barclay's, Bank of America, First National City, Cook's, they're all going to be giving money away. So you double your money . . . triple it . . . before you begin."

"And with all the traffic in and out," said Dan, "Customs will be that much easier."

"Or tougher," said Jack.

"So you hire a jock. Or get a crewcut. Steal a couple of warm-up jackets with emblems on them and walk through Customs carrying your equipment. Soccer balls would be perfect. Or javelins, if they're made of wood, though they might be making those out of metal now. You name it. You know what I'd do?"

"What's that?" asked Dan.

"Starting blocks. You know, the wooden blocks they use for the dash. Perfect. Who would think of cracking a starting block? And you can get a couple of kilos in there easily. It's perfect."

"It is perfect," Dan agreed.

"Let's have another blow," said Jack.

Canadian Jack told Swan that the Brown Gold Move was the most beautiful piece of business he had ever witnessed. It inspired him to christen Swan with a nickname, one that stuck, and one which gained immediate currency among the borderline elite. From then on Swan, because Jack thought he was sly and because everyone thought he was old, was known as the Silver Fox.

"The feeling after putting one over is indescribable. In the beginning, they all laughed at me, at all my long, intricate plans, my maps, my charts — my overdevelopment, they called it — Vinnie, Mickey, all of them, they all thought

I was dumb . . . but pretty soon they all ended up working for me . . . eventually they were all either investing in me or working *for* me. After that one I had so many ideas, I couldn't use them all. I gave them away. [Some, like the flourish he worked on Adrian, he sold, but he did, in fact, give many of them away. One of these was the Duplicate Bag Switch, which he gave to Canadian Jack on his next trip to Bogotá.] I wanted to keep moving, and I wanted that boat move."

Before leaving Colombia to await the Vagelatoses in New York, Swan bumped into two old friends. Somehow having drifted down from Santa Marta, at the whim of whatever currents prevailed, Jane and April had ended up on the beach in Cartagena, and they were as loose as ever — Swan was always reminded of Halloween when they were around. Assuming that they had eaten little but mushrooms since he had last seen them, he smuggled them past the guard at the back gate of the Caribe and bought them dinner. He tried to get as much protein into them as he could.

Jane was looking particularly unwell. April's voice seemed to have dropped about an octave in the past six months, but Jane was strung out to the limit. Swan saw tombstones in her eyes. She had found a pair of old walking shoes and a broken conch shell on the beach and was carrying them around with her wherever she went. They were for her brother. For his birthday. He lived in Brooklyn, she said.

Swan offered to take her home.

"No," she said.

She wanted her brother to come down and get her.

"Tell him where I am and tell him to come down and get me."

Swan said: "Please."

"No."

She gave him a note and the old shoes and the shell. He carried them back to New York with the Vagelatoses' souvenirs. He called her brother in Brooklyn, and when her brother came to pick up his birthday presents, Swan told him he had better go down soon.

"Well," he said, "you know what kind of girl she is. She ran away when she was fifteen, doesn't give a shit. And I don't give a shit. Did you give her money?"

Swan just stared.

"She probably spent it on dope. That's what kind of girl she is."

"You're not going?"

"No."

12

WHY DID YOU WRITE MY NAME IN THE SNOW?

When Zachary Swan was introduced to Harry Morgan, he laughed out loud.

"What's so funny?" asked Sea Gull Billy.

Sea Gull Billy was a Hotel Caribe boathand. If he was needed, and he often was, he could be contacted at the hotel marina. If he was not working the marina, Billy could be found at any of several locations around the hotel, either making a connection of one kind or another or waiting for a connection to make him. Billy was a promoter, a fixer. He was the man to see at the Caribe. He knew what was happening, where, when it was happening, and who was making it happen. *I'm Sea Gull Billy. You need anything, you come to me, I'll take care of it. I'm honest. You get a good deal. You need a woman, something to smoke, you name it, esmeraldas, coca, I'll take care of it. Just ask for Sea Gull Billy.*

Swan had asked for Sea Gull Billy on several occasions. When Uta ran off with Ramón Greco, Swan gave Billy $200 before he left for New York with the driftwood: "See that she gets it when she comes through again," he told Billy. Billy did. If Swan wanted to know the whereabouts of Canadian Jack or René Day, or if he needed information — current activity, traffic in and out of Cartagena, government surveillance — or if he needed a connection he did not have, he went to Billy. Billy was the man to see.

Billy was Colombian, about forty-five. He was short and wide with a weatherbeaten face. His brown eyes were constantly working, keeping up with whatever the action happened to be, jumping from side to side behind the tinted glasses he always wore. He spoke English well, would never smoke anything but his own brand of cigarette and always wore a boatman's cap. He was dressed in khaki, wearing deck shoes, and passing the pool at a good clip when Swan stopped him. Their conversation was brief.

"Billy, I need a boat captain."

Billy nodded. He looked around. Across the pool he spotted what or whomever he was looking for. He looked back at Swan.

"Tomorrow morning. Nine. At the marina," he said. He moved on, chasing whatever it was he was chasing.

A hot breeze was blowing in off the bay. Sea Gull Billy was still waiting for an answer. The boats, their boards swelling in the heat, were rocking gently, tugging at their bowlines. The temperature was approaching 90 degrees, and Swan was standing on the pier at the marina, in his bathing suit, with a towel over his shoulder. Billy was staring at him quizzically. Harry Morgan, smoking Chesterfields, knew what was so funny.

"His name's Harry Morgan, Billy."

"That's right."

"And he's a boat captain."

"Right."

"In the Caribbean."

"Right."

"Well, you see, Billy, that's very funny. Harry Morgan is a very famous boat captain."

"Harry's not famous." Billy said.

"Not this Harry, another Harry," Swan said.

"And that's funny?"

"Not any more, Billy. Thanks."

Swan paid him, and he and Harry Morgan walked back to the hotel for a drink.

Harry Morgan, thirty-five, boat captain, was not making money working for a thief in Miami. He wondered where it was he had gone wrong. And he was interested to know what it was he could actually do to make money working for a thief from New York. He listened to Swan. Harry, an American, was from Florida, just south of Coral Gables, where Swan had gone to college. He had grown up on a number of boats, and had made a living at one time taking fishing parties from Miami to Bimini — a piece of biographical information that Swan found attractive. In Cartagena, Harry was working for an American who owned several tourist boats, which he chartered out, through Harry, to scuba divers and deep-sea fishermen. Harry's American employer was a smart operator. He owned another boat, in addition to the ones Harry managed, which he skippered himself out of Miami, an 80-

foot schooner in which he had at one time invested about forty thousand dollars and converted to use as a treasure hunter. Having converted the boat, he opened an office in New York, incorporated, sold shares in the corporation, and sailed to Colombia, where he bought gold doubloons, pieces-of-eight, salvaged pottery, anchors and various bits of recovered chandlery, which he then threw overboard and slowly re-recovered, reporting a magnificent find to the shareholders back home. He then went public with his corporation and made a killing on the common stock. Because he was doing so well, Harry's employer devoted all his resources to the salvaging scam, and Harry's paychecks in Cartagena were coming in three weeks late when they were coming in at all. Harry was looking for work.

Swan had been working toward a boat move, in one way or another, from the beginning. He wanted it to be big. When he was finally ready to engineer it, he went to Anthony for backing. The agreement was that Anthony would put up the money for one kilo, front Swan a thousand toward expenses, and guarantee the sale of Swan's first thousand grams. If the move was a success, they would parlay their money and do it again. Swan had nowhere to go but up. In the summer of 1971, he laid out the plan.

The key to the move was Harry Morgan. He not only knew the waters off Colombia, he knew Florida and the Bahamas as well. Bimini, a sportsman's paradise, would provide the cover, and the Florida coastline, somewhere north of Miami, would provide the drop. The cocaine would travel, as usual, in wood — gaffs, boat hooks, belaying pins — whatever was appropriate to the vessel they used. The trip would be a long one, but the load would be big, and if the move required a lot of preparation, that was all right too, because they would use it again if it worked.

Anthony considered the details and insisted on one change, a major one. He wanted a man of his own in on the move, a man who could follow the load all the way through. And he had the man he needed, a boatman in Miami named Jimmy. Swan could have him for free. Jimmy was Anthony's man, and he would be looking out for Anthony's interests all the way down the line. Swan accepted the deal and headed for Florida to get the operation under way.

Jimmy reminded Swan of a young, but still fat and jolly, Burl Ives — if you nail Burl Ives, you've got this guy, he would tell Harry Morgan. Jimmy must have impressed some others the same way, because in the off-season, when there were no boats to captain, he made good money playing the banjo in various clubs around Miami. Swan met Jimmy at home and went to work on him right away — Swan ran his man through a fundamental security procedure, his own brand of speed clearance, something on the order of a reverse Pinkerton investigation, an intensive, counter-FBI check. It relied heavily on instinct, experience and the remarkable insight generated by the imperatives of self-preservation. And it had to be done fast.

Jimmy's wife was a waitress. She introduced Swan to a woman she worked with named Nina, and that evening the four of them went out. It gave Swan the opportunity to observe Jimmy from several angles. Swan brought some coke, and Jimmy came across with some transplanted, home-grown, Gainesville Green from his tomato garden. Swan was beginning to like him already. He and Jimmy got stoned together, and very drunk, foraging through the neon wilderness of Miami Beach. They had a wonderful time. When the party was over, Jimmy stumbled home with his wife, Swan spent the night with Nina, and by the time he got around to his second cup of coffee the following morning, Swan was sure about his man.

"Jimmy was completely trustworthy. You know a guy right away . . . whether he's going to do you or not do you . . . and if you have any reservations about him, you'd better stick to those reservations, because if you don't you are really in trouble . . . in jail or dead. I know guys who wouldn't shoot me for ten thousand dollars, but for fifteen I wouldn't turn my back on them. I had no reservations about Jimmy."

Jimmy and Swan spent the next couple of weeks looking at boats. There were several old shrimp fishers available, but most of them needed work, and there was no way Swan could work out buying any one of them without having his or Jimmy's name appear on the papers. Swan evaluated his options, discussed the problem with Jimmy, and the decision was finally made to pick up a boat in Colombia — the original plan was going to be altered. Swan called Avianca and made reservations for two to Bogotá. With three days to go before their flight, Jimmy began thinking about *his* man.

"Do you know how to handle a piece?" he asked.

"No. Not since the Marine Corps," said Swan.

"I think we better do a little practicing."

"O.K." Swan said.

Sure.

Jimmy drove to a firing range on the Tamiami Trail that was open to the public for two dollars an hour and the price of ammunition. He was carrying four guns, three revolvers and an automatic. He wanted Swan to try them all. The clubhouse reminded Swan of a golf shop, but where he was used to seeing Slazengers and Spauldings he saw Smith & Wessons and Colts. Out on the range, in the hot late-afternoon sun, Swan shot first, firing from the hip.

"Jesus, this is ridiculous," he said when they examined the target; he had missed it completely with all six rounds.

"Like this," Jimmy said.

Jimmy went into a crouch, held his firing arm rigid, and braced one wrist with the other, sighting along the barrel before squeezing the trigger. It was what Swan had seen done often in movies made after Jimmy Cagney had retired — when the cops became the identifiable heroes.

"That's terrific, Jimmy, but by the time I get into fuckin' position, we're going to have to shoot from close range or forget it."

"Look," Jimmy said, "I know exactly what you ought to do. I've got this fine Colombian back in the car. Go to the parking lot and smoke it, and when you come back, things will be different."

Swan was never one to say no to a good hit of dope. He started for the parking lot.

"On your way back in, pick me up some more bullets," Jimmy shouted.

Swan nodded. He found the joint in one of the hubcaps of the car, stood in the shade, and took his time smoking it. He stared at the sunset. Swan liked Florida. Probably, he thought, because he associated it with the sea. He knew he could never live inland. No surprises. He thought of the island he would buy someday with the money he made — someday, he thought, if he did not get shot first. He listened to the gunfire on the breeze and watched the smoke rise over the coconut palms. It looked as though it might rain. He crushed the roach out with the heel of his shoe and headed for the clubhouse to pick up Jimmy's ammunition. At the counter he ran into four policemen. He smiled. They were buying bullets, .38 calibre service rounds. He headed for the firing range.

"Well?" Jimmy asked.

Swan just nodded. He fired more slowly this time, but still from the hip.

"Not bad," Jimmy said.

"Not bad," said Swan. "It's not bad. I can see the bullets coming out of the gun now. It happens much slower. I can see it and feel it.

"Jimmy," he said, turning to his friend, "I'm really shooting good."

"You're doing fine, baby," Jimmy said with a smile.

Swan was pretty well jammed up by now.

"Jimmy, what are those fucking cops doing over there?"

"Well, you see on the other side of the clubhouse there, that's the police firing range."

In Swan's drug-addled mind a couple of transistors failed.

"Are you kidding me?"

"No."

"Well, Jimmy, I happen to make that guy we scored coke from last night." Swan pointed. "You see, he's down over there, shooting."

Jimmy looked. "Oh, yeah," he said.

"And these two guys shooting next to us, Jimmy, they don't look like they're on the side of the law, do they?"

"Nope," said Jimmy without having to look.

"Well, I got a great idea for you, Jimmy. Let's go make a deal right now."

"What?"

"I'm going to go over and talk to the police and I'm going to tell them that if they see me, don't shoot at me because I'm not out to kill anybody — you know, it was all a big joke. And as far as I'm concerned, man, it's cool, I ain't going to shoot at them if they ain't going to shoot at me, and I want to let them know, so let's go make a deal right now."

Jimmy laughed. And then Swan laughed. And the lawmen on one side of the fence and the outlaws on the other all fired their guns into the approaching darkness.

Two days later Swan and Jimmy went South.

"Bogotá at your feet," said Swan.

Swan had taken Jimmy to the top of Monserrate, the more accessible of the twin peaks that overlook the capital. They stood on the steps of the shrine facing west. Guadalupe, a hard climb by mule train, rose on their left. Directly in front of them, two thousand feet down, beneath the eagles and the wind, was Bogotá. Jimmy sighted along the funicular cables to the *barrios* at the foot of the mountain. Beneath the funicular and to the right of it ran the tracks of the older cable car, disappearing here and there into a ravine, reappearing out of the trees, and gone again, emerging finally at the terminal below. Beyond the terminal and the *barrios* was the city. The air was clean and the sun was directly overhead.

"It sure looks different," he said. "It's really beautiful. And you can breathe up here. The smog down there is incredible, isn't it? I mean, just look at it."

"There are three million people down there," Swan said, "and every one of them thinks he's rich if he owns a '58 De Soto. They've never heard of PCV valves or smog control — you figure it out — at eight thousand feet above sea level you don't have much oxygen to start with. And we think L.A.'s bad."

"Three million?"

"And tonight I'll introduce you to a few of them."

Jimmy nodded. "You in a hurry?" he asked.

"Nope."

"I think I'll take some pictures."

"Take your time."

"Do they ever use that one?" Jimmy asked, pointing to the cable car tracks.

"When they're busy. In the off-season they alternate them." Jimmy aimed his camera.

"One's the funicu-li and one's the funicu-la," Swan said.

That night at the Oriole, Swan introduced Jimmy to Juan Carlos Ramirez and Canadian Jack. While Jimmy and Juan Carlos talked, Canadian Jack took Swan to one side. They conversed quietly for a while, and Swan nodded when they were finished. Jack sat down, and Swan motioned Jimmy away from the bar.

"Jack wants in on our move," Swan said to Jimmy.

Jimmy looked at the Canadian, who was talking to Juan Carlos now.

"He ain't gonna like it," Jimmy said, referring to Mr Big.

"He doesn't even have to know," Swan said.

Jimmy looked at Swan. He shook his head.

"No," he said, "he's a kid."

Swan shrugged. He did not feel like arguing. He motioned to Jack, and together they walked outside.

"I'm sorry," he said, shaking his head.

"Why not?" Jack wanted to know.

"I got robbed in New York. All my money's gone and I'm working for a guy, somebody else. And he hasn't got any room. I'm sorry, Jack."

Jack sighed. "Well, what am I gonna do?"

"Well, what have you got?"

"I've got a girl down here."

(Customs was knocking mules over now.)

"Well, what *were* you gonna do?"

"Stick it on her back or up her cunt."

"Does she know you?"

"Yeah, I've known her a long time."

"Will she stand up?"

"I don't know. She's getting shaky."

"Well, you're in trouble, aren't ya?"

"Yeah."

"Yeah."

Swan shook his head. He liked Jack and he felt bad about having had to lie to him about the setup.

"Look," he said, "let me do some business. I don't have anything right now, but I'll think about it, and I'll meet you here tomorrow night. O.K.?"

"O.K."

Swan nodded. He turned to go.

"Thanks," said Jack.

"Don't mention it," Swan said with a wave of his hand and walked back into the hotel.

Jimmy wanted to go on the score. Swan said no. He knew he had to keep Jimmy away from Armando. He had to assume that giving Armando to Jimmy was giving him to Anthony, and with a sizable slice of his New York operation at stake, that slice of his business which was represented by Anthony, Swan was determined to keep Jimmy away from his contacts, especially Armando, his principal supplier. But Jimmy insisted — and with Anthony behind him, there was nothing much Swan could say. So Swan took him to Luís.

Luís was a connection Swan had made on a previous trip to Bogotá, a friend of Rudolpho's from whom Swan had accepted a kilo once when Armando was short. He was a Ford auto parts dealer, trying to make it in the cocaine business, and Swan was always accepting *muestras* from him. Luís was not as reliable as Armando, and his quality was not always there, but he was usually good for a kilo in an emergency. So Swan gave him to Jimmy. Swan and Jimmy scored Anthony's kilo together, after Swan had made the deal with Luís and had put five hundred on it. Swan scored his own three keys from Armando — alone.

(Swan used several suppliers in Bogotá — after his first two moves he scored only in that city — and he accepted *muestras* from everyone. His pockets were always full of the white paper packets he picked up in the course of a day, and he and Vincent spent many evenings together, destroyed, sitting around the coffee table in Vincent's living room, snorting up the day's samples. Swan would score from Luís again, and on his last move he would score from Jago, the Hawk's man. But Armando would always be his number one connection, and the reasons for it were simple: "His weight was always there, his product was always good or superior, and he'd get me all the grass I wanted free.")

Through Armando, Swan found out that René Day was back in town. He would be at the Marguerita that night. Before going to the Marguerita, Swan dropped in on Canadian Jack.

"I got one for you," he said.

"She's coming now," said Jack, and the door opened.

Swan turned his head away, his back to the door.

"I don't want to meet anyone," he said.

But by then Susan was in the room. She was tiny, no more than an inch over five feet, and she was beautiful. She had big brown eyes. Swan was reminded of a Keane painting — he said later she should have been carrying in a cat. He shook his head.

"O.K.," he said, giving up, "bring her in."

All the things you say you're never going to do, he thought. Susan sat on the bed and kept her mouth shut. Swan looked at her, then at Jack. They were both wrecked.

"Well," he said, "I'll give you a perfect one."

Jack smiled.

"Evidently we've got to prop up the chick," Swan said, "so let's give her something she can't get scared on."

"O.K., but keep it easy," said Jack.

"You know, you're not giving me room to work," said Swan. "I've got something set up so that if she gets caught, she walks out."

"An excuse?"

Swan nodded. And then an exasperated look came over his face. He stared at Jack. Susan had jumped up — and she was prancing around the room, singing, "The Silver Fox is gonna give us an excuse . . . the Silver Fox . . . the Silver Fox . . ."

"Can you get her to cut that out?" Swan said.

Susan sat down. Jack got serious.

"Now, here is how it works . . ."

And Swan gave Canadian Jack the Duplicate Bag Switch. Like all of Swan's flim-flams, the Duplicate Bag Switch is designed not to protect the goods, but to protect the carrier. The goods are taken care of in the usual manner. The cocaine is packed in Madeira wood, chosen for its high specific gravity — a distinctive physical property of that wood which, after all is said and done, is nothing more than Nature's way of telling us: it is heavy. When a Madeira rolling pin or statue is hollowed out, it does not *feel* hollow. Neither does it feel suspiciously heavy when filled with cocaine. So whenever he could, Swan used Madeira. And he used Angel, who was more than a carpenter — Angel was an artist, and his work was flawless.

So from the time it is packed, the coke is on its own, protected as well as it can be. There is no guarantee in the smuggler's handbook that *everything* that passes through Customs will not be opened (that is why Sicilians and Corsicans dealing in hundredweights of heroin go *around* Customs). The only thing that encourages or discourages a Customs man from cracking anything he finds — apart from the fundamental consideration of the time it requires — is the carrier. And if the carrier is not a consummate actor or actress (and often even that is not enough), then he or she is going to need propping up. Propping up a carrier can be done with coke, or it can be done with a foolproof smuggle. There are other ways, but the point is that if a carrier is propped up (confident, unafraid, i.e., not suspicious looking), the chances are that the Customs agent will not be any more curious than usual. Given the odds on the coke (and when you mule it, no matter where you put it, those odds conform to nothing more profound than the law of averages) and taking for granted that *there's no way you can deny it's yours, man, if it's strapped to your back*, then the Duplicate Bag Switch is the perfect scam.

". . . you have to buy two suitcases, and they have to be exactly alike, in every way," Swan said.

"Right," said Jack.

"Have Angel and Rudolpho pack the load for you — a statue, a rolling pin, anything. It should look like a souvenir."

Jack nodded.

"Now the suitcases have to open like this' — he drew his arms inward — "at a right angle. No zippers. And it's got to stand up — she has to be able to open it away from her

— so that when it is open and the inspector is going through it, she can't see what he's doing, the top's between them. O.K.? I'm talking about a standard suitcase, very simple, nothing fancy. The other shit won't do."

"O.K."

"O.K. Now, in one of the suitcases, she puts everything she owns, all her clothes, her shoes, anything that fits, and a few things that will identify her. And *she* packs it. O.K.?"

"Got it."

"Now, the other suitcase, the duplicate, is where the load goes. And *you* have to pack it. Her fingerprints can't be anywhere near the duplicate bag. *You* pack it, and you pack it with a lot of women's clothes, all size ten . . . what size are you, Susan, about a six?"

"Six," she said.

"Good. So all the clothes in with the load are size ten. Shoes to match. Cosmetics, everything. Just as if it were a woman's suitcase like any other. Everything two sizes too big, all of it clean, no prints, and none of it hers. She never touches this particular bag. Understand?" he said to Susan.

"I understand."

"O.K. You take the same plane and you don't sit together. Both bags are checked aboard and they are exactly alike except for a scuff mark on one of them. That's the loaded one. When you get off the plane, Susan, you pick up the loaded bag — this is the first time you've touched it — and you carry it through Customs. Jack, you're delayed. Susan opens the loaded bag — away from you, Susan, you undo the clasps and pull the top up toward you — and she can't see what the Customs man is doing. The lid of the suitcase is between them. She's short, so that helps; the counters are usually high at Customs. And, while the agent is examining the contents of the bag, she's fiddling with the rest of her stuff — whatever else she's carrying. She's not looking at what he's doing. If that bag goes through, Jack, you just pick up her real bag and carry it through yourself.

"*If* the man cracks the statue, Susan, *if* they nail you, you've never seen that bag before in your life. 'This isn't my bag. That must be mine running around all alone on the conveyor belt over there.' And it is. Jack has left it there. Everything fits. You got I.D. in it. No way the loaded bag is yours, nothing in it fits. No way they can put anything in it with you, no fingerprints, no belongings, no nothing, you got the wrong bag, you moved in on somebody else's hustle, no record, no nothing, out. You walk away."

There was silence.

"What do you think?"

"Unbelievable."

"You like that one, huh?"

"I like it."

"It's a giveaway, a winger, no planning, nothing, I just thought of it last night."

"It can't fail," Jack said.

"It can't fail."

(And it did not fail. They got the load through. If they had not, they could have tried it again and again until the money ran out. The Duplicate Bag Switch, if handled correctly, is arrest-proof wherever the rules of evidence apply.)

When he left Canadian Jack, Swan picked up Jimmy and headed for the Marguerita. Like every discotheque of any standing in Colombia, the Marguerita had a neo-cave quality about it. It was loud and dark, always jammed, and a good place to plant yourself if you wanted to be either lost or found in a hurry. The acoustics, like the drinks, were bad by design. The strobe lights were out of phase by accident — or incident — the kilocycle-per-second realities of South American power not entirely blameless. It was the kind of place second-rate film directors were always looking for in the 1960s in which to shoot "now" footage. It was not the kind of place that especially impressed René Day.

René was at the far end of the bar, nursing what he thought was Scotch. He was wearing a tan suit, no tie; he looked happy, and Swan was glad to see him.

"Hey, Rainy."

"Hey, man, it's good to see you."

"Good to see *you*, Rainy."

They shook hands.

"This is Jimmy. He's a friend of mine."

"It's a pleasure."

"Glad to meet you," said Jimmy.

"When did you get in?" Swan asked.

"Last night."

"I talked to Armando."

René looked at Jimmy. He said to Swan, "Yeah, I'll see him again on Friday."

"Going North?"

René nodded.

"What are you drinking?" Jimmy asked.

"I think it's Scotch, but I wouldn't bet on it."

Jimmy bought drinks all around. "Here's to a good trip North."

Everyone drank.

Then Swan lost Jimmy for two days. He left him at the Marguerita bar and did not see him again until forty-eight hours later, when he turned up alive (no small wonder in

Bogotá) with René, stepping out of the half-light of dawn through the doorway of an after-hours club Swan was leaving. Which of them — Jimmy or René — looked worse was hard to say. Neither one of them was as stoned as Swan.

"Jimmy . . . Rainy . . . Rainy . . . Jimmy . . ."

Swan was fumbling with three hotel keys he had drawn out of three different pockets from beneath his *ruana*, trying to figure out which was which. He was living at the Tequendama, stashing his coke at the Continental, and keeping his money at the Hilton. And as an edge, he had taken the plastic identification tags off each key.

"Jesus, this is difficult," he said.

"You need a drink," René said.

"A drink will fix you right up," said Jimmy.

Swan turned around, and the three of them went inside for a drink.

"Rainy wants in on our move," said Jimmy, picking up his drink.

Swan looked at Jimmy. Then at René.

"I told him it was O.K.," Jimmy added, downing his drink.

Swan shrugged his shoulders, nodded his head, turned to René, lifted his drink and smiled:

"Anchors aweigh."

Angel bought the lumber. Rudolpho flew to Barranquilla to buy the hardware for the gaffs and boat hooks. While the coke was being packed, Swan sent Jimmy with a note to Harry Morgan in Cartagena. Harry had found a boat, a 55-foot ketch with two auxiliary diesels, the *Buccaneer*, docked at the Club de Pesca. The owner would rent it for $1,500 a month. There were legal complications, something to do with smuggled liquor aboard, but Harry knew the dock master and was well attuned to the technicalities, paper shuffling, and Customs procedures involved in getting a boat out of Cartagena — any boat. With Harry Morgan's help, Jimmy rented the boat for two months. Where required to show a reason, he wrote: *buried treasure*. When Angel finished the packing, Swan and Rudolpho carted the load — gaffs, boat hooks and the rest — from Bogotá to Cartagena in a rented pickup truck, an adventure in itself, given the numerous breakdowns that attended their journey. The truck was more than twenty years old. With René's thousand grams the load came to five kilos, and in a moment of rare pique at the technological realities visited upon the host country, Swan entertained the notion that one gaff was worth three Cadillacs. It took them two days to go the last 250 miles. When they reached the coast, the *Buccaneer* was ready to go. With René Day signed on as first mate, and two assistant seamen aboard, she sailed out of Cartagena with Jimmy at the helm. Swan and Harry Morgan flew to Miami.

In Miami, Swan stayed for a time with his sister. Harry Morgan stayed at his aunt's house just north of Matheson Hammock. Neither of the women was particularly surprised to see her prodigal relative. Swan's sister never asked questions, Harry's aunt was happy enough to see her nephew to leave him alone, and under the circumstances — not unlike those of a long-forgotten summer vacation — the days of waiting were not as hard as that kind of hard time can be. Perhaps that is why it was not until the boat was a full week overdue, with no word from anyone aboard, that Swan, at the end of his patience, finally called Anthony in New York.

"Anthony, where's the boat?"

"I haven't heard anything."

"Nothing?"

"Not a thing."

"Well, I'm worried."

"There's nothing to worry about. Jimmy can take care of himself."

"It's been three weeks. They were due in two."

"What does your captain say?"

"He says two and a half on the outside."

"Well, Jimmy has instructions to call me if there's any trouble. If he's alive, I'll hear from him."

"Oh, that's terrific."

"Jimmy's a good captain. He'll make it."

"That's a lot of water out there, Anthony."

"He can handle it."

"Can he swim?"

"Don't worry."

Five days later Jimmy called.

"Where are you?" Swan asked.

"Where do you think I am?"

Jimmy was in Bimini.

"We're on our way."

Harry's aunt's house was situated on one of the many inlets which give onto Biscayne Bay. A hundred yards from the back door of the house was a dock, and, like many of her neighbors, Harry's aunt had a boat. Hers was a ChrisCraft. According to the plan, Swan and Harry, aboard the cabin cruiser, would meet the *Buccaneer* in Bimini, transfer the load to their own boat, and bring the coke in at Matheson Hammock. And they had an ace: Harry had sailed often from Bimini to Miami, and often he had brought his fishing parties home late at night, sometimes as late as three a.m. He had been told more than once by enraged Customs officials to dock for the night, *for Christ's sake*, and come back the following morning to check in. It had become standard procedure, and on this run it would pay off. So with rods and reels aboard, Swan and Harry stopped at the fishing station, bought ice, bait and fishing hats, and set out for Bimini.

"What the hell took you so long?"

Jimmy, a little bit drunk, put up his hand and, before answering, finished his drink.

"We had some trouble," he said.

"What kind of trouble?"

And Swan finished his own drink.

"We're not out of the harbor an hour and we get stopped by a patrol boat."

Swan ordered two more Martinis.

"What did they want?"

"Well, let me tell you what happened. They held us up for six hours. They drilled the mast, ripped open a couple of life preservers, and went through the bulkheads. In fact they went through almost everything on the boat. Now, I wonder what the hell they were looking for?"

"Damned if I know," Swan said with a shrug.

The drinks came.

"Well, anyway, we took a different route than we had originally planned, hoping to avoid anymore of *that* shit. A little bit more circuitous. We had one motor breakdown and we ran into a storm. Add it up."

"Jimmy, I swear, we thought you were dead."

"Not even a cut."

"Well, I'm glad you're safe, man, it's good to see you."

Swan raised his glass. Harry Morgan looked at his watch and said:

"Jimmy, it's your turn."

Jimmy nodded, finished his drink, and went out onto the

pier to relieve René, who was guarding the load. The four men drank all night, retiring to the boats when the bar closed.

The boats were docked eight feet apart, and the following morning, their heads swelling with hangovers, Swan and Harry and René and Jimmy carted the boat hooks and the gaffs from one boat to the other, going back and forth now and then with fishing gear, trying to look as cool and casual as the anglers and boat freaks who spend their lives in ecstatic fealty to the hardware of their hobbies. If the ecstasy was not there, they had certainly drunk enough the night before to look authentic. It is not hard to look crazy, anyway, awake at six o'clock in the morning. With an occasional "ship ahoy" as they passed each other, they got the job done, not the least taxing aspect of which was removing the gaff clamps from the *Buccaneer* and attaching them to the smaller boat to accommodate the larger equipment.

"We don't want the stuff just lying around," Swan pointed out. "It has to look like it belongs on the boat."

And so Harry kissed about forty dollars' worth of equipment goodbye, and they set out for Miami.

Somewhere along the line it had escaped Jimmy that, being the only captain available, it was up to him to sail the *Buccaneer* back to Cartagena.

"Oh, shit."

"Harry's got to get us through Customs, Jimmy."

And René was going to follow his kilo.

Harry and the two smugglers left Jimmy in Bimini. By eight o'clock they were off Matheson Hammock, where Swan had spent the better part of his college career swimming, and by nightfall they had made Harry's. They all had a drink with Harry's aunt, and when she asked how the fishing in Bimini had been, Swan, with a straight face, said, "Divine." When she went to bed, they unloaded the boat. Harry borrowed her station wagon, and they took everything to the Key Motel in Coconut Grove, where Swan had a room. They broke the load down, had a sniff, then René picked up his kilo. He had a connection in Miami, he said, a Cuban.

"Be careful, man, those dudes are dangerous."

"They pay top dollar," said René.

"The price sounds too high," Swan told him, and they said goodbye.

By the time Harry Morgan made Customs in Miami, Swan was boarding a New York bound train with Nina, the waitress to whom Jimmy's wife had introduced him. The cocaine was in his luggage, broken down and double-wrapped in clear plastic bags. He handed his luggage over to a porter and followed it through to his compartment. The baggage was never out of his sight, as it would have been on a plane, and there was no weapons search to worry about, as there surely would have been at an airport. And as if the safety of this form of travel were not enough, Swan was confronted, immediately upon entering his compartment, with a wide array and variety of handles attached to the walls of the Pullman, which, when taken into account with the expansive mirror opposite the bed, brought all of his sexual fantasies home to roost. He looked at Nina and smiled. They had just entered what, in Swan's mind, amounted to a playpen. Nina smiled back.

Together they explored the train. There was a fashion show scheduled for that evening. There were cocktail parties and bingo games. Nina would win a sack of oranges with

O-63. They drank and laughed with their fellow passengers, many of them elderly and afraid to fly. And between Miami and New York, between smoking and sniffing, staying high on Colombian in one way or another, they covered every inch of their compartment, flying like beatific trapeze artists, from wall to wall to open window, where the sights and sounds and the semiprecious smells of Cupid's Circus drifted out and shared themselves among the people of America.

> "Drivin' that train, high on cocaine
> Casey Jones, you'd better watch your speed
> Trouble ahead, trouble behind
> And you know that notion just crossed my mind."
>
> "Casey Jones," from *Workingman's Dead*,
> THE GRATEFUL DEAD

Swan arrived in New York with four kilograms of cocaine, three revolvers that Anthony had ordered from Miami, and several boxes of ammunition. It was getting heavy. He said goodbye to Nina, went immediately to see Anthony and unloaded everything but two of the kilos. Anthony paid him $25,000.

"Excellent stuff," Anthony said later, after he had tested the coke.

And the Boat Move was over.

Swan distributed the remaining two kilos, with a good cut, through his ounce-dealers in New York.

Two months later, Anthony got a message from Jimmy. He passed it on to Swan.

". . . Rainy left me that night in the Key Motel. That's where we broke it down and we had a sniff. He left maybe about midnight with his stuff, and that was it, I never saw him again. Later on, Jimmy got word, when he had come back from Cartagena. I didn't even know what had happened. If I had known who it was or what it was, I would have done something, because I really liked him . . ."

René Day, three hours after leaving the Key Motel in Coconut Grove, was found shot to death on a dark street in Miami. He had been wearing his white suit, and he had found someone who had wanted his cocaine. He had taken the ammunition in the face. Rainy Day, his knife in his boot, had made his connection, and the last thing in this world he had seen was the wrong end of a gun.

RUNNING BLIND

13
BACK TO THE BORDER

The boat move, the cargo from which was distributed by the early fall of 1971, marked the end of Swan's first year as a cocaine smuggler. In that year he had been to Colombia six times, increasing his duty-free quota with every import subsequent to the first Santa Marta package, and had not been hit, either by the Federal government, by local authorities, or by people in the employ of other, civilian, thieves. None of his carriers had been endangered, nor had they been as much as incriminated by agencies of either the American or Colombian governments. He was doing well. He was making a lot of money, spending most of it, giving some of it away, investing very little and snorting the rest.

In Bogotá he had developed an apparatus for the procurement, packaging and dispatch of his cocaine, an efficient assembly line that began with the ever-dependable Armando and ended with Rudolpho, the mainstay of the Bogotá operation. Since the driftwood package, he had used nothing but wood and no one but Angel, who in addition to the boat-hook hafts and belaying pins had wrought duplicates of everything he was unable to open and close cleanly, such as the base of a bowling trophy, the shaft of an occasional wall hanging, and more than one rolling pin. Roughhewn statues, such as the Madonna and the tribal head, he cut, hollowed out and reassembled. (He once drilled a set of chessmen — it was more trouble than it was worth.) Swan had so streamlined the Bogotá operation that on occasion he would simply mail the money to Rudolpho with instructions on how and where to mail the package.

And in that year Swan had established a sound network of ounce-dealers for the distribution of his cocaine in New York. What remained after Anthony bought his kilos went directly to Ellery, Roger, Mickey, Moses and Charlie. The demand for cocaine had increased significantly in a year, and the price had climbed, both north and south of the border. Soon kilos would cost close to $7,000 in Bogotá and command $30,000 in New York. Swan was turning it over fast and spending his leisure time experimenting with new and outrageous gimmicks. Some of the experiments were costly. He invested $1,000 in the failed attempt to saturate a handkerchief with an aqueous solution of cocaine — twenty grams converted to gum on the supposition that he might do the same with his clothing, wait for it to dry, then wear the cocaine through Customs. He pictured himself crossing the border in a white suit, wearing a matching hat with a broad brim and a long, white, not unsullied plume. It had worked with salt. He experimented with cocaine's miscibility in other liquids, but with no greater success. In a room in Barranquilla he had sampled a preparation of cocaine in solution with an alcoholic beverage, the inventor of which was still experimenting with ways to extract the coke after it was smuggled and in the meantime selling exclusively to shooters and drinkers. Swan later said of the drink that it would "knock you on your ass," but was unable to track down its name or ingredients.

On his seventh trip to Colombia, Swan's plan was to get in and get out fast. He established a new mail drop, having exhausted the Lothario's supply of models, and went South to buy four kilos, two scheduled to go to Davis, two to the new address. The new address was close to home. It belonged to a young woman whom Swan had known since his grass-dealing days, to whom he had sold an occasional ounce and whom he had dated briefly. She had an across-the-hall neighbor, a young man who was often out of town and who left his keys with her when he went — she fed his cats and watered his plants. Also with a key to the young man's apartment was the doorman, who, at the tenant's request, rather than store his mail in the building lobby's package room, would deliver it to the apartment. Swan would mail the package to the young man at a time when it could be picked up by their mutual friend, the Cat Lady. If the package were followed (and for some reason delivered under those circumstances) she would be in no way suspect. Swan paid her $500.

Swan was staying at the Hotel Bacata, an upper-echelon hotel on Calle 19, avoiding the action and waiting for Armando to come across with the coke, when Uta showed up in Bogotá. The last time he had seen her she had been standing alone on the beach at Cartagena and he had been hurrying to see a boat off. The time before that had been almost a year earlier — she had been standing on the same beach with Ramón Greco, getting ready to disappear. This time she was standing in the doorway of his hotel room with her biggest surprise yet. She was with Vinnie Pirata. If Swan had been awakened in the middle of the night and asked to choose the one person in the world he would least like to see when he woke up in the morning, he would have rubbed his eyes, thought for a minute, said Vinnie Pirata, and gone back to sleep. Asked now, he would have said Pirata, standing in the doorway of my hotel room with a tour guide that looks very much like the woman I lived with for six years. Give him an hour and he would say Pirata and the woman I mentioned, in Bogotá looking for a cocaine connection.

Pirata had $6,000 which had been given to him by a small-time hood in New York named Crazy Leslie, and he was looking to score a kilo.

"Terrific."

Swan fixed Pirata up with Luís, two stuffed dolls and a seamstress. He put a thousand on Pirata's kilo, the bulk of which came out of Pirata's pocket. The seamstress overcharged him too. Armando came through with Swan's coke a day later, and by the time the fill was made it had become old-home week in Bogotá — Michel Bernier showed up. With Bernier and Pirata in town at the same time, Swan saw it as inevitable that the law of the jungle would soon assert itself. By the end of the week, Bernier was trying to steal Pirata's coke, Pirata was trying to steal Swan's, and Swan was trying to get out of town with Uta. The carnival culminated in a midnight assault on Monserrate, when Swan, Rudolpho and Uta set off in Rudolpho's DeSoto in search of Pirata's cocaine, buried somewhere on the mountain according to Uta, who had accompanied Pirata earlier that night along the same roads in the same rain to wherever, in his growing paranoia, he had stashed it. They returned six hours later, sleepless, soaking wet, and empty-handed. Swan left town, Uta left Pirata, and Pirata, not about to trust Rudolpho, was left with no one but Bernier to mail his cocaine for him. Pirata addressed the package, followed

Bernier to the Post Office, and watched him hand it to the clerk. It was over in a matter of seconds. In a matter of hours, Pirata left town.

Swan picked up his packages in New York, unloaded a clean kilo to Anthony, cut what was left and moved into the St Regis. Staying at any other hotel in New York, Swan would store his cocaine in the bathroom — perhaps disguised as bath salts in a jar on the tub — close to the plumbing, where it would have been easy to get rid of fast in the event of a bust. At the St Regis, however, the Feds would never have been able to get past the lobby. The security was excellent, there was never a hassle, never an arrest, and the bellhops and chambermaids were honest. Staying there, Swan could leave the coke in his locked suitcase in the bedroom. After a week and a half, having unloaded all but forty-five ounces of his stash, Swan moved from the St Regis to a hotel on Central Park South. From the St Regis he had been making daily visits to the Chanticleer Bar a few blocks away, where Moses was hanging out. He would call Moses at home in the morning, ask him how many ounces he needed, and make the delivery in the afternoon — they were snorting lunch together every day from the chopping block in the Chanticleer kitchen. The ounce-dealers were making regular pickups at the St Regis, and the turnover was fast, but Swan figured a week and a half was long enough to stay anywhere. He moved to the Essex House.

Swan's first afternoon at the Essex House, a Sunday, he watched the football game on television. Nice Mickey was there. After the game Swan left to meet Alice, Roger and Angela for dinner at a Chinese restaurant on Broadway, and had the cab driver drop Nice Mickey off at 79th Street on the way. He did not enjoy his dinner. He apologized. He passed up the fortune cookie, said good night and dashed back to the Essex House. He was too late. His room had been hit. The lock had been worked and his suitcase was open. Gone was $45,000 worth of cocaine.

> "Now, *here*, you see, it takes all the running *you* can do, to keep in the same place. If you want to get somewhere else, you must run at least twice as fast as that."
>
> The Red Queen in the Garden of Live Flowers,
> from *Through the Looking Glass*,
> LEWIS CARROLL

Swan sat on the bed, immobilized by his own adrenalin, drained of the power to think by fear, frustration and anger, staring for a full five minutes at the open suitcase. All he could do was shake. He had been hit. Violated. Suckered and taken off hard. The honeymoon was over. From now on things would be different. All the slick had been taken out of him. All the flash and style was history. He was vulnerable now. His territory had been invaded, his delicate manhood tampered with, and he sat amid the evidence of his frangibility like a raked and exposed mast in the wind of all the heavy dues he had never paid.

He figured Pirata for the job. And that made it worse. But as painful as was the suspicion that Pirata had hit him was the thought that it might have been Nice Mickey who had set him up. As far as Swan could figure, only Nice Mickey had known he was at the Essex House. But more incriminating than that was the hard-to-swallow certainty that Nice Mickey had known, better than anyone, exactly when he was *not* at the Essex House. Swan took it to Ellery. The only way he was going to find out was to see whether Mickey was moving ounces. If Mickey was, then Swan would know.

Ellery arranged to meet Mickey at Victor's. Swan parked his car two blocks away, watched Ellery go in and kept his eye on the door. He would give Mickey until the corner, then pick him up from behind. He waited only a half hour before Mickey hit the sidewalk. Nice Mickey stepped out of Victor's, paused for only about thirty seconds to light a cigarette, and started walking. He went, without haste, directly to the passenger door of Swan's car, opened it and stepped in.

"Look, I know how you feel," he said.

Swan should have guessed there was no way he was going to catch Mickey off guard. Mickey had made him as soon as he had hit the street — he was the best there was. Swan conjured up visions of the Scarlet Pimpernel. Mickey even looked like Leslie Howard. Swan was embarrassed.

"I know how you feel, and I wish there was some way I could convince you."

Swan liked Mickey, liked him a lot, and from the beginning had been hoping to find a piece of evidence, any evidence, however slight, that would vindicate him. He wanted to be told he was wrong about the man. But Mickey was right — there was nothing but his word, and Swan would either believe him or he would not. And there was nothing Mickey could say about Pirata — Swan knew that — he was Pirata's friend, and more than its not being his place to say, it was not Swan's place to ask. But Swan did ask him about Ellery. (Swan knew where Ellery had been every minute of that Sunday — there was no question about Ellery. There never was. There never would be.)

Mickey said: "Absolutely not."

"And Vinnie?" Swan asked, as if by way of an afterthought.

"I couldn't say," Mickey replied.

Mickey's answer was enough. Taken in light of how he had answered with regard to Ellery, combined with Swan's suspicions and added to the evidence of Vinnie's recent behavior, it was enough to convince Swan. Pirata was the man. Swan would never know for sure about Mickey, but he would always try to believe the best. He would have to be content with it as it stood.

Swan had options. He made a decision. And with his response to the robbery at the Essex House, he took his first irretrievable step into the cold, compelling nightwater which led from the Byronic banks of adventure land into the dark, adult realities of the cocaine trade. He took his problem to a friend named Pepe, one of that seemingly inexhaustible supply of maître d's at Maxwell's Plum, New York East Side saloondom's answer to Versailles. Pepe made a phone call. It was brief:

"I got a friend — he's been South — ya know? He lost a couple packages."

There was a pause. Pepe nodded and hung up. He turned to Swan, who was standing with Uta — always good for public relations.

"He's gotta come in from the Island. He'll meet us later. Not here."

An hour later they were sitting in a bar on 34th Street.

"When he comes in, talk to him," Pepe was saying.

"How will I know this guy?" Swan asked.

"You'll know him."

"Yeah?"

"Yeah."

Yeah. Swan knew him. He walked right by the table. Walt

Disney could not have created a man who looked any more evil, threatening or downright dangerous than this man — mean and rotten and a real *big* son of a bitch. He passed them without saying a word and took a table in the rear. Swan did a slow take in Pepe's direction.

Pepe said: "Okay, go back and talk to him."

Swan swallowed hard. They discussed Pepe's percentage. He and Uta went back.

"Hi," he said.

"Hi."

No names.

The man waited for them to sit down. He ignored Uta. He eyed Swan. Then slowly he spoke:

"Well, Mr Prep School, here's how it works . . ."

Awesome. Blood and raw meat.

". . . If the guy has it, I'll get it. But if he didn't do it, you'll never see him again — because I never leave anybody to come back at me."

That was all. Swan said: well, Uta and I, we'll have to talk it over. Sure, Swan, that makes sense. Idiot. He crept back to Pepe's table. No sale.

"Pepe, do you know anyone maybe a little bit *down* the ladder, someone who'll just go *beat up* the guy?"

With Pepe in the lead, they set out for Pemble's, a bar on the other side of town. There they met Mike, medium heavy, who after a few blows of pure said he and his partner, Frank, would be glad to take the job. Swan paid Pepe. He filled Mike in. Within two days, Mike and Frank knew who had made the hit and how it had been done. A creeper named Joey had gone in. He had been seen later hanging around with Pirata. They were friends. Pirata had been seen sitting in a car outside the Essex House at the time of the robbery. The money was gone, blown at the track.

"I think you need a partner," said Mike. "You wouldn't want anything like this should happen again."

Swan had heard that line before. On television. A lot.

"I'll have to talk it over with Pepe," he said, thinking fast.

You know Pepe. My partner. The one with connections from Disneyland.

Mike left. He did not come back. Swan said a few ill-remembered prayers of penance, abandoned all his contingency arrangements, the last of which would have been going to Anthony with the facts, and wrote off the robbery and its aftermath as an education, inexpensive at twice the price, a naïve man's look at the realities of his business, a breath of smoke from the back room. Welcome to the real world, Mr Prep School — the sink. In here there are only the quick and the dead — he who hesitates is lunch. Eat or be eaten. Or move to Pennsylvania. This is where Fantasyland ends.

Swan's awakening was rude and abrupt. He opened his eyes and found himself looking down the throat of a beast disguised as the American Dream. And his troubles had just begun.

Two months later, Swan would be asking Michel Bernier: "How did you do it?" And Bernier would answer: "It was simple." He had merely written his own name and address on a gummed label, carried it into the Post Office in his breast pocket, and with his back to the door withdrawn it, licked it and slapped it into place on the package. "It was very simple," he would repeat. "I did not even stop." And Swan would smile, very much impressed, and say: "Beautiful."

Vinnie Pirata had never received his package. And if that were not necessary to explain the robbery — Pirata never needed an excuse to steal — it went a long way toward explaining why a hood named Crazy Leslie had been trying for a week to locate Swan. Swan was taking a vacation of sorts, hanging out at home, contemplating a quick trip to Bogotá, staying away from everyone but Alice, who, just prior to the Essex House break-in, had returned from a prolonged trip to Europe. Swan remembered having met, on one occasion, a man introduced to him as Leslie, Crazy Leslie if one took his Christian name into account. The introduction had been made by another individual with an adjective for a first name — Mean Mickey.

Mean Mickey, anything but mean, was a something-for-nothing small-change hustler who worked hard at making money the easy way. An Ivy League graduate and a former ad man, he came from a wealthy family in New York, hard-line WASP, and at thirty-eight he was chumming around with bookies, hookers and holdup men and living on other people's credit cards. A small-time hood himself, he was proud of his record. He had started as a swindler, dealing in lettered stock under the auspices of some West Coast religion in which he was an ordained minister. He was arrested stepping off a plane from Miami in priest's garb, carrying a kilo of mix — he dealt cocaine in drag, too — and, after the lab test, sued the City of New York to get it back.

The arrest that put him away for a while was made when he tried to sell some stolen stocks that matched a bunch found on the bodies of two young women that had recently floated to the surface of a river in Florida. He would not reveal the source of the stock — in the business he was known as a stand-up guy — he got four years, did a year and three months and went on parole. At the time of his arrest, one of the local papers nicknamed him Mean Mickey. He was proud of the name. He saved the press clippings and waved them around at parties. At Moses's Feast of the

Epiphany at the Chanticleer, he would show them to all the pimps and dealers from Harlem — a big man in Crime. After his release from jail, Mean Mickey failed in an attempt to hold up Maxwell's Plum — Crazy Leslie, who was to steal the getaway car in Long Island City, got stuck in traffic on the Bridge, and they missed the payroll man — but he did ultimately manage to stick up Adrian's casino, which destroyed the myth of the Mafia protection represented by Ike and Freddy, the shooters from Brooklyn.

It was Mean Mickey who had introduced Swan to Moses. He had also introduced him to Pepe. (After leaving his job at Maxwell's, Pepe opened an office on 34th Street and started a transatlantic charter service, taking deposits and leaving people stranded all over Europe. The Civil Aeronautics Board got him.) Mickey, who made sure it was known that he was dating a prominent black jazz singer, had given marriage a try for a while — he was married to a "very big Social Register chick" who eventually divorced him to marry a Kentucky Derby trainer. Swan introduced Mean Mickey to Mike Riordan, but they never got along — Swan suspected that they were trying to rob each other and never settled it properly. Mean Mickey, during the cocaine years, was pretty much outside Swan's sphere of activity; he handled ounces now and then, but there were really only two things for which he was responsible that actually touched on Swan's business: he was directly responsible for Nice Mickey's name, and he was indirectly responsible for Crazy Leslie.

Crazy Leslie, distinguished by no special feature beyond the fact that he was several parts mad, finally located Swan. They had a talk about the package that never arrived. Swan told him all he knew. Leslie listened, and, still not satisfied, left to talk it over again with Pirata. Swan went South. He returned on November 8 at six p.m. A Monday. On Tuesday the ninth, at two p.m., he was stashing his coke in a safe deposit box in a midtown bank. Alice, at home, was putting on water for instant coffee. By the time Swan had located a phone and picked it up to call her, the water had boiled over. Alice was sitting egglike on the living room couch confronting her future — face to face — a future full of guns around the house, three of which were aimed right now at her head, and one of which was in the well-muscled hand of a man known to be crazy. The party was over. There were dues to pay.

Alice Haskell came into this world on a spring day in 1949 with nothing to recommend her to Zachary Swan but her description — she was a pretty girl. While she was struggling to see light and foraging for her first high-calcium rations, he was trading war stories with a stewardess in Coral Gables. He knew he was going to get drunk. The stewardess knew he was going to get laid. Alice did not know anything yet. The only thing she and Swan had in common at the moment was that they were both very breast-conscious. They hit paydirt at about the same time.

Swan never changed. Alice, of course, did. For twenty years she changed along the lines of most middle-class American children in the care of loving and responsible parents. Healthy, educated and not unattractive, she was quieter than most, somewhat shy, but for the most part conventional. After high school she enrolled in a junior college close to home, did not really like it much, left, decided to spend some time finding out just what it was she did like, and went about doing so in the same way many people of her age and time went about it. She split. Splitting recommends itself as a verb which does not take a direct object — it was very popular in the sixties. Alice ended up in New York at about the time Lyndon Johnson was declining the throne.

Alice met Swan through Ellery. She had met Ellery in the neighborhood — if you lived anywhere on the West Side of Manhattan between 116th Street and the Tunnel, you were bound to meet Ellery in the neighborhood sooner or later. Alice did not cheat, she did not steal, and she would never learn how to lie. When she arrived in New York, she still had nothing more to recommend her to Swan than she had ever had — she was a pretty girl. Shortly after they met, she moved in.

Alice moved in at a time when Swan's life was undergoing a gradual downshift, a life the style of which was now less influenced by gin and more by marijuana, and was more susceptible to change than ever before. He was smoking a lot of dope, and in his posh 88th Street brownstone apartment in the middle of the city he was beginning to take on the character of a country squire. He was going out less and hanging out more. Within a short time of Alice's arrival he would be sharing that apartment with several dogs. Cats would come later. And soon he would let almost anything come through the door.

"If I let Alice run things we'd be living in a zoo. We had a fifteen-pound toad living under the sink in the kitchen eating roaches. I wonder what Crazy Leslie thought when he saw *that*. Alice didn't want to use roach spray, because it was bad for the animals and for the people in the house — not to mention a roach or two here and there."

What Crazy Leslie thought of the toad and the dogs was nothing to what Alice thought when she saw Crazy Leslie and his friends. Her trip to Europe had been only one of several attempts to leave New York, a city full of crazed people, behind for good. Her experience with lower-echelon freaks was growing with every shipment of dope that passed through town. At the end of their second year together she and Swan as a unit were about as stable as Leslie's brain chemistry — they were living apart as often as they were living together, channeling their emotional energies into one casual affair after another. Alice was asserting her womanhood through the use of men, and Swan was asserting his manhood through the use of cocaine. Neither of them was going anywhere but nowhere, and when the oblivion express occasionally slowed down it was simply to wait for the sky to fall in. Crazy Leslie provided the first rent in the firmament.

Alice put water on for coffee and opened the window for the dogs (the apartment was on the ground floor — it was from the same window that Swan had run his curb service a few years earlier, passing marijuana ounces to his friends). The doorbell rang. Through the eyeglass, Alice recognized one of the three heavies who had come the day before looking for Swan. She threw the bolt and ran immediately into the living room to close the window. She was too late. Crazy Leslie was halfway in.

"The doorbell is ringing," he said, grinning. "Aren't you going to answer it?" In addition to everything else, Leslie was a notorious comedian.

Alice tried to push Leslie out. She failed. He threw her off and shoved her in the direction of the kitchen. When she screamed, he drew a gun.

"Shut up."

It was cold and blue — like the eye of a snake — in off the November streets and aimed right at her brains. She would never do acid again.

"Open the door," he said, and she began to cry.

Leslie closed the window and pulled the curtains to. Alice opened the door, and two men came in, any distinguishing features they might have possessed overshadowed by the fact that they, too, were carrying pistols. They threw Alice onto the couch and told her to stop crying. Alice continued to cry, and the dogs continued to bark. She was told to lock the dogs in the bathroom. She did. She kept crying and Crazy Leslie and his friends kept telling her to shut up. They wanted to know where Swan was.

"I don't know," she kept saying.

They searched the house and found nothing but two amyl nitrates and a small sample of coke. After an hour Crazy Leslie said, "Watch her, she keeps looking at the window," and went out. He returned five minutes later with a Patty Cake and a quart of milk. He offered Alice a bite of the cake. While Alice remained seated in one position, her knees against her chest and her face buried in a pillow, the tough guys walked around her, circling the couch, talked of killing Swan and twirled their guns, now and then resting the barrels against her head. There was always at least one gun aimed at her all the time they were there. They listened to music, and when they tired of that, they decided to watch television. They agreed on a movie. It was between commercials when the phone rang.

"Tell him to come home."

Alice answered the phone. It was Swan. He asked what was wrong. She said everything is O.K. but please come home. When he asked again, she cut him off. She said goodbye, and hung up the phone. One of Leslie's heavies waited outside in the car. The other stood by Alice in the living room. Leslie stood by the door. They waited.

Swan did not step right into the apartment. He kicked the door open and called Alice's name twice. She whimpered in reply. Leslie stepped from behind the door, showed Swan the gun, and told him to come in quietly. He pushed Swan onto the couch and waited for his partner to come in from the car. When the man arrived, Leslie asked:

"Was there anyone with him?"

"I didn't see anyone," the man replied.

"Did you close the door?"

The man nodded.

Leslie turned to Swan:

"Are you alone?"

Swan said yes. Leslie hit him with a right uppercut, gun first, in the mouth. He asked:

"Did anyone follow you here?"

Swan shook his head, and Leslie hit him again, this time above the eye. He asked the question a few more times, using the gun, and Swan kept saying no. Soon there was blood all over his face. Leslie used a rolling pin to ask where the cocaine was. Swan kept giving him the same answer — the coke would be in town in two days, they could have all they wanted — and Leslie kept calling him a liar. When they ran out of things to talk about, Leslie said:

"You're coming with us."

They were going to lock him in a garage and chain him down until the coke arrived.

"You can come if you want," he said to Alice.

Alice could not stop crying.

"Ah, you'd only be in the way, anyhow," he said.

Swan's clothes were covered with blood. He would have to change them, Leslie said, to get by the doorman. Swan leaned forward on the couch and the blood dripped onto his shoes. He would change them too.

When Swan was taken away, Alice threw herself down on the couch and cried. And she prayed. She called Trude Daniels to ask Trude to chant, but there was no answer.

As soon as Alice replaced the receiver, the phone rang. It was Swan. He had escaped.

"Get all the mix you can find, pack a bag, and go up to Jeannie's. I'll be home real soon, and we're going to split."

Alice collected the mix (half a kilo of borax) grabbed what she thought she would need in the way of clothes, and went upstairs to her neighbor's apartment. Swan showed up twenty minutes later. He explained in a hurry how he had gotten away.

When the four men had reached the car, Leslie's heavies got in ahead of Swan. Very unprofessional. Leslie had Swan by the arm and released his grip long enough for Swan to get in after them. Swan had other ideas, none of which was spending the next two days with Leslie and the boys. He had bloodied his shoes for a reason — the shoes he had worn home had leather soles, the ones he had changed into, rubber — and it was now or never. He broke free and ran, heading for Broadway and screaming for the police. (A familiar cry on the West Side — not worth much.) Leslie, in pursuit, gained on him, and when he was a foot away, Swan went into a crouch. Leslie tumbled. Swan grabbed a cab in front of the New Yorker theatre and said, "Get going." He had called Alice from a corner phone booth while the driver waited.

Swan had only a chipped tooth to show for the night's work. Within an hour of his return, Ellery showed up. Then came Charlie and Lillian. Lillian helped Alice clean the house and pack. Nice Mickey arrived. Then Roger and Angela. Suitcases were packed, and all the animals were jammed into Alice's Volkswagen. She was finally leaving New York. That night she stayed with friends. The next day, she and Swan moved to Long Island. In Amagansett, where Swan had spent so many summers, he would now set up business.

14

JOURNEY OF THE MAGI

It was finally the cats — two black and white American shorthairs, cantankerous and corpulent, neither with the benefit of a legitimate name, sometimes called "my little Babunchkas," more often referred to as just "the fat cat" and "the skinny cat," because as fat as the skinny cat was, the fat cat was fatter — these two sinfully spoiled but not unlovable brats, that finally prompted Trude Daniels to turn to Zachary Swan.

"I've got to get out," she said.

Swan had known Trude for years, her husband longer, and there were few people in the world for whom he would do more. She was the kindest person he had ever known, the gentlest and most generous, a woman who sought nothing but tranquillity, a kind of earth-mother sorcerer's apprentice who knew all her friends' sun signs and drew on an eclectic collection of prayers for everyone she met. Swan was an old friend and a friend in need when Trude's husband committed suicide, throwing Trude into the depths of depression, the embrace of heroin, and the small West

Side apartment of her mother. With an infant child, she was a broken woman at twenty-eight.

Now in her thirties, free of her heroin habit but not of unstable men, Trude, jobless, was still living with her mother, not an unpleasant woman but a mother nevertheless; her brother, whose disdain for work of any kind, especially work that might render him self-supporting, was exceeded only by his passive and passionless love for music — this week it was classical; and her daughter, Elaine, the reason for Trude's moving in with her mother in the first place and, at five years of age, the only thing that made explicit sense at this moment in Trude's young life. And there were the cats, aloof and self-indulgent, obviously ready for analysis, and Trude blamed this on the adverse living conditions which she and they had suffered for so long now. She was ready to move.

Swan was still lying low after his run-in with Crazy Leslie. He was living in Southampton and distributing his coke through Charlie Kendricks. It was Charlie's responsibility to get the coke to the ounce-dealers. Kendricks and Swan met regularly at the Red Coach Grill off Exit 57 of the Long Island Expressway. Charlie liked the roast beef there. When the transfer was not made there, it was made at the McDonald's parking lot in Riverhead. Swan liked the hamburgers. Swan would park his car next to Charlie's, leaving a sack of groceries on the front passenger seat with the cocaine packed in dairy substitute jars, and buy a hamburger while Charlie made the transfer. They never talked to each other during these meets; messages were transferred to Charlie via the grocery bag and to Swan by way of the money bundle with which Charlie replaced it. Business was taken care of over the phone. Swan would call Kendricks in New York from a pay phone, ask him to call back, and give him the Long Island number with the last two digits reversed. Kendricks would call back from a pay phone. It worked the same way if Kendricks wanted to reach Swan. Over the phone, Swan was always Jonathan, Kendricks, the Hungarian. Meets were scheduled often when the coke was moving well. On a meet early in December, Charlie showed up at the Red Coach Grill with a bundle of money and a message from Trude Daniels. She wanted to see Swan.

"I know the risks involved."
  "Are you sure?"
  "I'm sure."
  "Can you tell me why, Trude?"
  "I need the dough to get out and get my own place."
  "I can lend you some dough."
  "I can earn it."
  Swan nodded.
  "Well?"
  "Couple of weeks."

Swan did not want Trude in a hotel, near any trouble, or near any of the action. He had Juan Carlos Ramirez, owner of the Oriole, write Trude a letter, inviting her to Bogotá. It was her first piece of cover. When she arrived she would stay at Juan Carlos's girlfriend's house, out of the way. Swan would fly first on Avianca. Charlie Kendricks would follow a week later on Pan Am. Trude and Elaine would travel the third week. Swan wanted Trude and the baby to stay down there at least a week after they arrived.

*   *   *

When Swan arrived in Bogotá, as he passed through the airline gate, he saw Canadian Jack trying to get out. Jack was trying to board a flight to Kingston, Jamaica, and was being held up by two immigration officials — his papers were not in order. He looked scared. (Canadian Jack's papers were never in order. Having jumped bail in Canada following a big hash bust, he faced a ten-year sentence at home, and he was moving in and out of the country on false passports, sometimes hitchhiking in from the States on U.S. credentials. On this particular occasion he was doing what Swan called one of his triple-border routines — smuggling his coke into Jamaica, where he would hang out for a while at Strawberry Fields, crossing the U.S. border on his way home, and finally smuggling it through Canadian Customs for distribution in Toronto — according to Swan, a sucker move.) Swan walked over to see what he could do, and as soon as the immigration people averted their heads, Jack handed Swan a package. Swan moved on.

That night at the Hilton, never having made it out of the country, Jack picked the package up in Swan's room. It did not contain a lot of cocaine, but it contained enough to get him in a lot of trouble. He had the rest strapped to his legs.

"When are you going to grow up, man?"

Jack shrugged.

"It's going to come down on you, Jack. You gotta get smart."

Before trying to leave the country again, Jack sent Christmas wishes to all his friends in Canada. Using a small wooden press with a hand screw, which cut his volume by about 30 percent, he compressed a kilo and a half of cocaine into flat ounces, placed each ounce between the two halves of a folded piece of paper, and inserted one piece of paper into each of about fifty Christmas cards. The cards, which he mailed first class, more than one to a customer, earned him an average of $1,000 apiece and read, *May All Your Christmases Be White*. He signed them, *Frosty the Snowman*.

By the time Trude Daniels arrived in Bogotá, Swan had mailed a package of his own. There were two kilos of cocaine in his hotel room. He was staying at the Hilton, Charlie Kendricks was at the Tequendama, and Trude was now on her way to stay with Ramirez's girlfriend. They stayed away from one another for a week, giving Trude time to establish her cover. At the end of that week, Swan and Kendricks visited the house. Kendricks arrived first. Swan arrived soon after. Swan was wearing the cocaine, and under his arm he was carrying a large stuffed white rabbit.

Angel had compressed the coke, and now Trude stuffed the rabbit, sewing it carefully back together along its original seams when she was done. Charlie took the rabbit back to the Tequendama, where he kept it on top of the dresser in his room, innocent and evident to anyone who might enter. He, Swan, and Trude made separate reservations on a midweek, off-peak flight to New York. They arrived at the airport separately.

On uncrowded Avianca flights, passengers may sit where they want. Their seating assignments are simply a formality. Charlie Kendricks, carrying the rabbit in a shopping bag, boarded first, choosing a window seat over the wing in the coach compartment. He removed the rabbit from the bag and stuffed it under the seat, careful that it was not visible to anyone who might sit behind him. Trude Daniels, with Elaine, boarded next, sitting across the aisle from Kendricks. She and Kendricks did not speak. Swan followed close behind Trude and chose a seat behind Charlie on the aisle. A stranger, whose name and address Charlie managed to get, in writing, in the course of the flight — he was good that way — sat directly in front of Swan, in the aisle seat between Kendricks and Trude. He was a free witness.

(fore)

(port wing)   (starboard wing)

E = Cocaine Elaine
T = Trude Daniels
W = Witness
K = Kendricks
S = Silver-Haired Gent
X = White Rabbit
M = Colonel Mustard
L = Library
P = Lead Pipe

(aft)

The jet was not in the air five minutes when Charlie Kendricks, making sure the stewardess was nowhere around, "found" the bunny.

"Oh, look what I found."

He held up the bunny and called for the stewardess. The

stranger shrugged. Before Kendricks could call a second time, the silver-haired gentleman in the seat behind the stranger tapped Kendricks on the shoulder.

"Why don't you give it to the baby?"

The gentleman pointed to Elaine. The stranger nodded his agreement. Charlie smiled. He handed it over.

"Oh, thank you," said Trude.

> "Cocaine Elaine, she never complains
> She's so aware, you know, she likes to share
> It's such a shame, she's not to blame
> Let's cry for Cocaine Elaine."

> "Cocaine Elaine,"
> Isis

Kendricks, Trude and Swan walked through Customs in New York in the order they had boarded the plane. Trude preceded her witness.

When he laid out the plan, Swan had asked Trude:

"Who are they going to arrest?"

He was unable to find anyone to answer the question.*

Before he left Bogotá with Trude Daniels and the rabbit, Swan bumped into Black Dan at the Oriole, and Dan invited him up to his suite for a drink.

"I've been using your press a lot," Dan told him, "and I'd like to pay you for half of it."

The news did not come as a surprise to Swan (everybody

* See Appendix VIII.

had been using the press), but the fact that Dan had finally opened up — admitted he was a smuggler — did. Swan took it as a compliment.

"No sweat," he said. "We're both making a lot of money."

"Well, let me give you some of this, then," said Dan, reaching for a package on the coffee table in front of him, and he opened up a brick of the strangest looking marijuana Swan had ever seen. It was white.

"Where the hell did that come from?" Swan asked.

"*Rubia de la costa*, the blonde from the coast, the finest, complete dynamite 'up' grass in the world. Take a hit."

"Be glad to."

While Swan explored the wonders of *rubia*, Black Dan gave him the rundown on the Mexican route. Over a second joint, Swan outlined the Trude Daniels move and described the immense white rabbit he had found after searching all over town.

"Stick this in the bunny," Dan said, nodding in the direction of the brick.

Swan smiled, a bit confused. He figured the *rubia* must have hit Dan a little hard. Taking his own condition into consideration, he had to assume that Dan was seeing pseudo-scopic holograms where he should have been witnessing the work of the world's hardware. A typical Delta-9 problem. Incidence-and-rebound was becoming a problem. Perhaps Dan was telescoping. The brick weighed a pound — Dan could not have meant what he had said.

"I want you to have it," Dan nodded. "And I've got something else I want to give you."

Dan handed Swan a hard, white, luminescent rock,

uneven at the edges, about the size of a Slazenger 3. Swan reached out slowly and took it in his hand, which was shaking a little now, along with his other appendages and the rest of the world — a complement of nerve endings just about shot with the latest toke of high-voltage Colombian blonde — and under the cool, familiar touch of the rock, his fingers began to flicker. The rock weighed about a quarter of an ounce.

"Jesus Christ, Dan."

The rock was cocaine — through and through. As pure as it gets.

"My compliments," said Dan.

"I don't get it, Dan, what's this all about?"

Did Dan want something? Could this 250-pound black son of a bitch with the eyes of a killer and arms like mahogany trees be a bellowing lunatic pansy? Dan? My idea of the complete professional? Is this the end of the line . . . the doors locked, my mind wrenched . . . thrown to the floor by a faggot spade heavy-weight with the thighs of a Roman war horse? What will Alice think?

"The Games," said Dan.

"What games?"

"Cali. The Summer Games at Cali."

"Yeah?"

"Yeah, I used your scam."

"Yeah?"

"Yeah."

"No shit."

"It worked. Best load I ever moved."

"No shit."

"I figure I owe you."

Swan laughed (at the expense of a third "no shit').

"Thanks, Dan."

"My pleasure. Thank *you*."

"How'd you do it?"

"Like you said. Had a couple of friends come down. Short hair. Athletic. We put on warmup jackets with the U.S. patch, and we walked through with equipment."

"What did you use?"

"Baseball bats. We had a bunch of baseball bats and Angel made us a bat rack — filled that too. It was perfect. They didn't even stop us."

"Unbelievable."

"Well, you were the one who said it would work. You were right."

"And they let you right through?"

"Right through," said Dan.

"That's unbelievable, Dan. It's perfect. How absolutely beautiful."

"Nothing unbelievable about it," said Dan. "It was a perfect scam. How could it fail?"

Swan smiled.

"Dan," he said, "they didn't have baseball at the Summer Games."

Dan's eyes shot to about sixty standard candles.

"No shit!"

"No shit."

Dan rolled another joint. Swan wrapped the rock in his handkerchief.

"I know just the man to give this to," he said. "Thanks a lot, Dan."

"My pleasure," said Dan.

The rock and the *rubia* went into the rabbit with the cocaine.

*   *   *

In the United States of America, where Zachary Swan lived, worked, distributed cocaine and occasionally paid taxes in the 1970s, the term *Black Culture*, where it was acknowledged at all, was treated by most as an oxymoron; as recently as today, in fact, the word "nigger" accounts for a greater part of the national vocabulary. Before the term gained currency among journalists and advertising copywriters, who had no idea what they were talking about when they used it — they saw it as a kind of pig-knuckle-and-chitlins equivalent to whatever Little Richard had meant when he sang *Good golly, Miss Molly, sure likes to ball* — it had been grappled with by a number of America's unctuous and minimally educated politicians, who had felt it coming like shit against the fan, some odoriferous blend of all that was red, white and blue about Jesse Owens and certifiably "pink" about Eldridge Cleaver. Up until recently it was embraced to no further end by certain tenure-seeking sociologists and a few blackboard-bound Ivy League Ph.D.'s as part of an end-of-the-rainbow answer to the irrelevance of Marx — they were destined to eat crow, as it were, when Angela Davis began doing public relations for Herbert Marcuse. Persisting was the reality that somewhere out there, between first base and the foul line of the Fourth Estate, growing, was this phenomenological monster known as *Black Culture*.

In whatever way, if ever, its aesthetic and ideological validity was to be affirmed, it was certain that New York City was going to be the Florence of what was soon to be called a *black renaissance* in America; and by the time it became a recognizable force in the United States, this renaissance would have its Botticellis. Long before that day on which everything that was Black became as a consequence Beautiful, John Coltrane and Charlie Parker were legends. If it was music in which this flowering was going to be cultivated, jazz was its *disembodied line*. Stevie Wonder, it was tacitly agreed, made white man's music, so cultural elitism had already begun. About the time Lincoln Center discovered that the Alvin Ailey Dance Company was a force to be reckoned with, the Theatre, which was pretty nearly dead at the time in New York, struck up a brief romance with Melvin van Peebles. And while James Baldwin was struggling from abroad to demonstrate that he could write at least as well as any member of the New York Jewish Authors' Cabal, a young man from Harlem named Claude Brown was writing a book called *Manchild in the Promised Land* which was going to be the last word on just where this groundswell was coming from.

And where it was coming from was the only place it could come from in Harlem: the street. The street was where everything was beginning to happen. It was where money was being made. It was where respect was being gained. It was on the street, and by his influence on the street, that a man was being measured. On the street in Harlem, and only on the street, according to Brown, was a man able to come by . . . *status*. And status, the predeterminant of . . . *re-spect* . . . *man* . . . was not something you earned working for somebody else. If you were able to get a job, and coming from Harlem your chances were slim, you were not going to find one that paid for anything beyond the rent. If that. Wall Street was a long way off — it was going to take more than the Broadway Local to get you there. So you were not going to make big money legitimately. And you were not going to make it running numbers for somebody else. Or fencing — to somebody else. All that second-story jive and bag-holding was for losers and junkies; self-employment, capital gains . . . *this is a business, man* . . . is what paid for the El Dorados and the quadraphonic sound . . . *get your shit together, Jack . . . do not be a fool . . . you got to look out for your . . . self!* And if you were going to take the initiative, you had to use the tools at hand . . . *look around you, man . . . you grew up on this street . . . you know where the cash is.* And when the cash comes home, you do not put it into tax shelters . . . *brother* . . . you advertise. Clothes, cars, shoes, women, jewelry . . . power . . . and cocaine. A thousand dollars an ounce . . . *suck-er.*

And a man had something to work for in Harlem. Street status. No more steppin'-fetchit-nigger-yessuh-nossuh heroin or reform school got-to-get-out-of-the-ghetto-or-die-young blues. After all, Walt Frazier was driving a Rolls Royce, making a million dollars a day playing basketball for the Knicks. There were alternatives. Harlem was becoming a place to *be*. And be from. Downtown was O.K. if you wanted to eat at the Plaza or something — they could not throw you out anymore . . . *We Shall Overcome* was history, and they were kicking down the doors at City College to prove it — but Uptown was the place to show it all off. Everyone was coming off the tenement roofs and out of the alleys. It was as if a carnival had come to town. To stay. The prevailing mode was flamboyance. Extravagance. Why be outraged when you can be outrageous. Pimps, local policy heavies, dealers, and just plain *hustlers* were showing themselves off now, unashamed, flaunting it, every man outdoing the next, throwing the new money around. Status. Only in Harlem could you get a reading on the word "hustler" . . . *hey, baby, how is that nigger fucked up, I mean, what does he . . . do? He is a hustler . . . Fred* . . . and that could mean he was doing everything or he was doing nothing, but whatever he was doing . . . *man* . . . he had bread. He was heavy and he had influence, and . . . *baby* . . . if you did not know where his bread was coming from, that was his business. The dude's wearing eighty-dollar shoes, so he ain't working for a living, and that's all you gotta know.

> "Once I lived the life of a millionaire
> Spent all my money, I just did not care
> Took my friends out for a good time
> Bought bootleg whiskey, cocaine and wine . . ."
>
> 'Nobody Knows You When You're Down and Out';
> JIMMIE COX

And the vibrations coming out of Harlem moved south across 96th Street, and they were picked up all over the city. Now there is fascination and awe . . . *I mean, how outrageous can you get . . . take a look at that spade, Stanley* . . . because in New York City only a black man knows how to . . . *walk* . . . on the street. You *know* where he's coming from. This man has turf sense . . . an air of territoriality . . . he's got . . . *moves*. This man is fluid. There is a hydraulic principle at work here that you do not understand, and you have to call it something, so you call it . . . *funk*. Everywhere you look there is this new standard of cool. And you pick up on it. And if your man is stepping out of a Rolls Royce, you *know* he's doing something right. Add to that the fact that he's got knife wounds all over his body and in America you have got yourself a culture hero. Here is a guy so downright virile, and sure of it, he can afford to dress like a *woman*. He's wearing a mink coat, a contoured silk shirt and high-heeled crocodile shoes . . . he's got diamond rings up and down his hands . . . he's . . . *the fucker's wearin' pearls!* . . . He's got on a white felt hat with a brim as wide as the Astrodome . . . and maybe there's a feather in it . . . velvet trousers with a twenty-eight-inch flare . . . and shades . . . always shades . . . three a.m. and shades . . . he's got lace cuffs . . . and . . . *Jesus Christ . . . a cane . . . with sterling silver brightwork.* And the son of a bitch is six-four. He never bends his knees or his back . . . he folds at the waist . . . he pivots from the hips and struts like a bayou water crane. He has a tall, fragrant, fox-furred woman on either arm, calling him *baby* . . . or *sir!* And this motherfucker's wearing a sixteen-hundred-dollar, gold and ivory, emerald-encrusted coke spoon around his neck.

Step aside, suck-er.

Now, you *know* your girlfriend is going to be in bed with him tomorrow. All day. Broadway Joe has let you down. Budweiser is a thing of the past. You have been sold down the river. And all you can say is *shit . . . suck-er.*

And, brother, you have got *Black Culture.*

And you have got cocaine.

And so it was special, and it was somehow fitting, on an unseasonal night in the winter of 1972, that a white man's cocaine should bring the Uptown, street-heavy, Harlem elite from 125th Street to midtown, to the Chanticleer Bar at 57th Street and Lexington Avenue. Something was happening. And it had to be big.

"Where is it happenin' tonight?"

"At the Chanticleer."

"There's a *thing* at the Chanticleer?"

"That's where it is happenin'."

"Is that right. And *whom* is it, Fred, that is makin' it happen?"

"Moses."

"Say what?"

"Moses."

"Moses?"

"At the Chanticleer."

"Moses is the man that is makin' it happen at the Chanticleer."

"Tonight."

"And do you know what is it that is happenin'?"

"I do."

"You do?"

"I do."

"Then when are you goin' to cut the jive and tell me?"

Moses, who would never again in his life know a night like this, was having a "showing." Moses had the *rock* — one-quarter ounce of snow-white, self-evident purity, a dealer's dream and a gift from his man, Swan, who had known when he had first seen it that there was no one in the world who would appreciate the rock more than the good Dr W. The rock had belonged to Moses before it had left Bogotá. A *beau geste*, and Moses would never forget it. For one night in his life, at the Chanticleer Bar, New York City, America, Moses Wellfleet Esq., who would never be President of the United States, was God.

It started late, as it always does upstairs and in the back at the Chanticleer, an after-hours bar once the lights go down on the street floor. It is a night like other nights, with one or two Cadillacs hogging the curb out front. But tonight is different. Tonight something is happening. Tonight something . . . real . . . is in the air. Something is coming. Tonight 57th Street is holy.

They begin to assemble at around three a.m. . . . white El Dorados, two-tone Lincolns . . . with sculptured rear windows, white sidewalls, custom-cut sunroofs, TVs, telephones, blue interior lighting, leopard upholstery, ermine, chrome . . . everywhere. Everyone is double-parked. Limousines are pulling up, and stepping onto the curb are the most elegant, outrageous and flamboyant men and women that ever adorned a sidewalk . . . five, ten, a hundred street-wise birds of paradise . . . a fluid mix of all that is Harlem street status . . . a blend of flash and sparkle and slow-movin' funk . . . and East 57th Street lights up like a loose neon Christmas tree . . .

. . . *Ecce advenit Dominator Dominus: et regnum in manu Eius, et potestas et imperium* . . .

. . . the procession continues.

Past the jukebox, up the stairs, and in the back. Private. The place is coming to life. There is music. Blue light. Saxophones and silver spoons. The women smell good. There is cocaine in the air. Moses is seated at a table against the wall. He is wearing an apple-green suit with a broad-lapelled jacket and high-waisted trousers flared wide at the ankle. His yellow silk shirt is open at the neck, its collar overlapping the lapels. His coke spoon is platinum. His serpentine legs are crossed knee-over-knee to show off his two-hundred-dollar alligator shoes. He is wearing a white felt hat with a soft brim the size of a Cadillac fender. He is leaning back in his chair. He is accepting praise. On the table in front of him, for everyone to see, is the rock.

. . . Behold the Lord, the Ruler is come, and the kingdom is in His hand, and power and dominion . . .

. . . There is awe in attendance at this badass Epiphany . . . the Mass is Solemn High . . . the journey is ended. Moses was not kidding.

Seated next to Moses, on the right, is Swan, dressed in a Paul Stuart glen plaid suit, a blue silk, four-in-hand tie with foxes *courant*, and a white broadcloth shirt. Cufflinks. Folded handkerchief. Wing tips. Madison Avenue all the way. The only thing jive-ass about this freak, beyond the forty-candle-power cocaine burn in his eyes, is the bejeweled black hand on his left shoulder.

"This is mah *ma-an*," Moses is saying. "He is my ace number one *brother*. And this is my product," pointing to the rock on which he had built his church, "the purest flake on the street."

Moses sang this tune until eight in the morning, and not once, as long as the party lasted, did he or Swan come close to ego saturation. They sat there, smiling, sharing the coke, shaving it with a scalpel and passing it around, riding the crest. There were always drinks on the table, compliments of admirers, and there was always one more street-heavy admirer to outdo the last. At five o'clock a tall, lanky, ostrich-like pimp in a tapered calf-length cashmere coat — navy blue — approached the table. His hat was white. His collar was fur. He carried an elaborate cane. He wore gloves. He was accompanied by two intoxicating, statuesque women in satin evening dresses who entwined him like Paris at midnight. Each was enveloped in fox. They were good to look at. If they were hookers, they were expensive. They were not unacquainted with the imperatives of respect. The man was cool, not in a hurry. He reached into his overcoat pocket and pulled out twenty Federal Reserve notes. He placed them on the table.

"Two thousand. I want it."

Moses looked up. He glanced at the women. He leaned back in his chair and acknowledged the pimp. He turned back to Swan, and as he turned he spoke to the pimp, with a wave of his hand:

"Take a little blow. Sit down someplace."

Dr W was ridin' high.

"Now, where was I?" he asked Swan. "Oh yeah" — he straightened Swan's tie — "you don't dress bad . . . for a white man."

BLUES IN THE BOTTLE

What Alice Haskell, in her diary on November 9, 1971, referred to as "the Catastrophe" — the sudden appearance at the apartment on 88th Street of Crazy Leslie and the boys — and its concatenations marked a kind of turning point in Zachary Swan's career as a cocaine smuggler. The effect the deracinated B & E man had upon the immediate conduct of Swan's business was negligible, but his impact on Swan's psyche was nothing short of profound. An examination of that impact, even a superficial investigation, leads one across a minefield of subtleties.

Swan, by his own admission is a "classic case of immaturity." Now, the self-awareness implied by that admission does not really go very far toward proving he is any less immature than he ever was — if it does anything at all, it merely shows that his regressed development is somewhat more unusual than he gives it credit for. In fact, though he would bitterly deny it, the truth is that today he is as ethically loose as he ever was — and having come this far in his life, the chances of his ever growing up are pretty slim. Nevertheless, he has achieved a certain level of self-awareness, and he is quite candid in his evaluation of those answered impulses which accounted for his becoming a drug runner in the first place. He would be the first to admit, for example, that cocaine, like motorcycles, machine guns and White House politics, is, among many things, a virility substitute. Its mere possession imparts status — cocaine equals money, and money equals power. And, as if in mute imitation of its symbolism, cocaine's presence in the blood, like no other drug, accounts for a feeling of confidence that is rare in the behavioral sink of post-industrial America. The *sang-froid* with which Swan walked into that room up against a certifiable lunatic and a loaded revolver, when all he had to do was slam the door open into the freak's face, was no more than the residual belief in his own invincibility that came with hanging around cocaine for a year, smuggling it past everyone in sight and living to tell about it.

Curiously, it was that one poorly calculated act — he was sure he could talk his way out of any trouble he might find on the other side of that door — that set him free to explore the true potential of his manhood. Or so he claims.

"After going up against the gun with Allie, I knew I didn't have to smuggle anymore."

Whether the statement is merely a gratuitous piece of hindsight is probably something not even Swan will ever know for sure. And how much of what followed was actually attributable to Leslie, and how much to mere fatigue, is probably a question he will never entertain — in less than a month he had been hit by the news of René's murder, the theft of his kilo at the Essex House, the holding hostage of Alice and his own near-kidnapping. But the fact is that after this last brush with the realities of his trade, Swan's attitude toward smuggling became far more businesslike and significantly less cavalier. He lay low on Long Island, meeting fewer people, satisfied to move most of his cocaine by mail, flying to Bogotá alone and getting out fast. The fun never went completely out of the work, and the impulse to embroider never left him, but over the following year Swan became increasingly more professional. He was making a lot of money, and he would continue to do so for the duration.

His thinking in the beginning had been that an arrest on a first offense, especially in light of his background, his age and his record — a clean one — would cost him little. He would smuggle until they nailed him or until he had made enough money to buy his way out of ever working again. In light of the professionalism he demonstrated over two years of smuggling and the reputation he had established for being extremely shrewd and calculating, and in light of the fact that he got better at what he did with every kilo he moved, the amateurish blunder that accounted for his arrest in the fall of 1972 invites the suggestion — one he readily entertains — that he *wanted* to be caught. But the manifold subtleties of *that* psychological gem are too dizzying even to begin to ponder. And anything Swan might add to an analysis of his motivations, it seems, must be taken *cum grano salis*; his self-awareness quotient is appreciably mitigated by the very components of that self-awareness — and here the gymnastics really begin.

"You learn to lie as a smuggler. You have to if you're going to be safe. After a while, it's all you do. You don't know what you told the last person, and you don't stop."

Who is conning whom? And why? A hardened shrink would turn in his license.

Whatever one divines out of the residue of years spent

on the edge, whether they be one's own years or those passed through the prism of another's imagination, certain thematic patterns recur. A man on the run does learn to lie. There is no clearer evidence of this than the example given by a man who will lie when there is no ostensible reason to do so. Ask Zachary Swan what color his eyes are, and he will tell you they are brown. Tell him you know they are blue and he will tell you you are colorblind. When he trusts you, he will tell you the truth — maybe. It is all a matter of self-preservation. His is not a voluntary exercise at deception — it is reflex. A man with something to hide also learns to forget. He forgets names, dates and numbers. And really forgets them. He becomes skilled at autogenic amnesia. If he forgets enough, he will beat a lie-detector and a perjury conviction. It is just another part of staying alive.

And there is more. A man on the run develops an intuitive sense, the dubious merit of which separates him from the rest of us — he can always spot someone else on the run.

"I can look around a plane and tell who's doing something. It's a feeling you get. You can sense it."

Flying out of Bogotá once, he struck up a conversation with a young woman seated in the international departure lounge at Eldorado Airport. He asked her how she liked Colombia. She claimed not to have seen too much of it; she was married to a minister and taking only a brief vacation, and she had kept pretty much to herself, she said. She was wearing her only souvenir, a bright red *ruana*.

"You lie," Swan said.

The cocaine was strapped to her back.

Swan bought her a couple of Bloody Marys and learned she was a judge's daughter from Westchester, New York. She was taking the load she was muling to Buffalo. She told him she thought he was very good cover because he looked so distinguished — she generally stayed away from older men, she said, because they inevitably put an arm around her and inevitably felt the kilo. She and Swan flew to New York together.

"You're underpaid," he told her.

He explained that carrying it through was a sucker move. They exchanged addresses and made arrangements to discuss her working for him.

"You can't deny it's yours, if it's strapped to your back," he said.

In New York they separated.

"Break a leg, Ellen," he said as they parted.

He tried calling her a month later. She was away. He did not leave his name. Six months later he read she was arrested.

Whatever new sensation Crazy Leslie brought to the funhouse of Swan's mind, and whatever cumulative toll finally made itself felt after a year of running blind, there is one exhibit in evidence of Swan's altered behavior that cannot be dismissed lightly. And it is pretty much what all the preceding introspection and second-hand analysis serves to introduce — within hours of his escape from the three hoods who had abducted him, Zachary Swan bought a gun. A .32 calibre revolver. And if, indeed, everything he did afterward was mingled with a desire to be caught, it was done with a desire to be caught before he had a chance to use it.

Swan overpaid Trude Daniels for the White Rabbit Move. He gave her $2,000 a kilo, twice the going rate. When the overweight bunny (five pounds with the two keys of coke and the pound of *rubia*) was disemboweled, he made a quick call to Anthony. They arranged to meet in the backgammon room of Le Club, where Swan was a member. It was the perfect place to do business — there was no way to get in unless one was a member or a guest of one. The deal was for one kilo.

"Thirty-two thousand," Swan said.

"It better be good," said Anthony.

It was. Anthony put a full hit on the kilo, turned it into two, and sold the two keys for $20,000 apiece that night. Swan put a half on the second kilo and moved the fifty-two ounces through Charlie Kendricks and the New York dealers at $850 an ounce. His total take, before expenses, on the cocaine Trude Daniels moved was $76,200. The rock went to Moses and the *rubia* went to the wind. The kilo he mailed never made it through — it was bust number one.

Between the end of February and the first day of summer, while Alice — on the run again — was living alone in New Orleans, Swan made only two trips to Colombia; he relied on Rudolpho to handle the Bogotá end of the other spring shipments without him. In July, when Alice returned to New York, Swan planned a five-kilo move that would take the two of them to Cartagena on a busman's holiday — he was ready for a big move, and he figured a Caribbean cruise was just what his and Alice's unstable love affair needed. Among the cruise ships in town at the time was the *Leonardo da Vinci*. She was scheduled to sail on a hot Saturday morning.

Swan and Alice, carrying gift-wrapped packages with *bon voyage* cards attached, left Long Island early that day and drove into Manhattan to see the Italian liner off. Once they were aboard, they climbed to the upper passenger deck and strolled the corridor outside the starboard cabins until they encountered a steward leaving a vacant stateroom. They exchanged smiles with the steward as he passed, and as soon as he was out of sight they entered the cabin he had just prepared. There they unwrapped their packages.

Alice's gift was a plastic Clorox bottle, Swan's a Deer Park Mountain Spring Water container — each was filled with two-point-two pounds of sugar. While Swan craned his head through one porthole, Alice dropped the containers through the other. Though Newton and Galileo were nowhere around, their laws were enforced by Nature — Swan saw the bottles hit the water and disappear beneath the surface of the harbor. He did not see them emerge. Deeming it unwise to linger, he and Alice hurried out of the cabin, down to the gangway and off the ship.

From the pier below, Swan looked for the answer to the last of three questions. The first had been answered when he saw that the bottles would in fact fit through a porthole. The second question was tied to the third — would the bottles, when dropped to the sea, if necessary from the highest passenger cabin of an ocean liner, break under the impact? And if not, would they float? Swan, standing straight-backed on the pier, with a cigarette in his mouth and his car keys in his hand, turned to face the south. He looked at Alice and winked — the bottles, floating midway between the anchor chain and the stern of the *Leonardo da Vinci*, had given him his answer.

Swan would make his move in the Verrazano Narrows. As soon as the ship had cleared the Bridge, he would drop the coke. He would need two power boats, one on the Brooklyn side and one on the Staten Island side of the Narrows, and he would need enough personnel to ensure that the pickup was made smoothly. He called Ellery and Mickey.

"No," said Ellery.

"Absolutely not," said Mickey.

They wanted no part of being retrievers.

"Carry a knife," said Swan. "If you're spotted, just cut the bottles. What are they going to do? Run a lab test on the Hudson?"

"No."

"Absolutely not."

Swan needed more personnel than he had, and there were too many loose ends — one of which was the possibility of a night-time arrival and not the least of which was the boats — to tie together. Even with all contingencies met, he was reluctant to make the drop without Ellery and Mickey. He called Adrian the Mogul.

Adrian had been hounding Swan since Vinnie Pirata had squealed to him about the Billy Bad Breaks flourish. Swan, though he did not feel obliged to make amends for what he thought was a justified swindle, had set Adrian up with some people who were doing traveler's checks, and since that time Adrian had made double what he had lost to Swan. But Adrian wanted to get into some smuggling. Swan figured that now was as good a time as any for Adrian to begin.

"Adrian, I've got one for ya."

They met the next day, and Swan laid out the plan. He wanted $1,000 a kilo on a minimum five-kilo move. In advance. Beyond that, Adrian could handle it any way he wanted. Adrian said he would let Swan know. Swan knew what *that* meant. He heard from Adrian a day later.

"My backer wants to meet you," Adrian said.

That is what it meant.

"I don't want to meet him," said Swan.

Adrian whined for a while and Swan relented.

"O.K. I'll meet you at 86th Street. We can have coffee."

"That's not necessary," said Adrian. "We can meet in his limousine."

Terrific.

Adrian's backer looked exactly as Swan had expected him to look:

". . . shaded glasses . . . Jewish . . . fat . . . cigars . . . white-on-white . . . pinky ring . . . and a chauffeur that carried heat . . ."

Swan would learn later that he ran a VIP limousine service "in Jersey" and that Adrian had done TC's with him on more than one occasion. He evidently had some very good customers, because he was prepared to invest $20,000 in the five-kilo scam. Swan figured he was looking to make $100,000 on the deal. He listened as Swan laid out the plan. When Swan finished, the fat man looked at Adrian and said he thought it was "a little dramatic." Swan was on his way out of the car:

"Look, man," he said, "I don't really give a shit. You can use any method you want. What you're really paying for is the connection and the know-how — how to carry your money down there, how to get the load on board, how to do everything. You can take it or leave it."

"I've got a man I want to use."

"I know. Everybody's got a man."

But the man you use to follow the load cannot look like a gangster, Swan was thinking as he eyed the fat man. Adrian looked at Swan, then at his backer. The fat man nodded. He bought it.

Swan met with the fat man one more time. Adrian had called to tell Swan that his backer was bitching, and Swan made his final offer:

"Move the locale. I don't care. I don't want to know where or how, and I don't want to know who. I'm just going to show you how to get it on. The rest is up to you."

Swan knew then that the carrier was going to be Adrian.

*　　*　　*

Adrian booked a cruise to Colombia and other Caribbean ports of call with his wife and young son. The tour would return to New York with stops in Venezuela, the Windward Islands and Florida. Swan met the ship in Cartagena. He had paid Evelyn, Rudolpho's wife, $200 to sew the five kilograms of cocaine into a large stuffed panda which Adrian's son carried aboard. In addition to the $1,000-per-kilo charge for the scam, he had put $500 on each of the kilos he had scored for Adrian, bringing his total take on the deal up to $7,500. While he was in Bogotá, he had mailed a package of his own.

Adrian had booked passage on a ship with a scheduled daylight departure for New York from Fort Everglades, Florida. It was there that he made the drop. He had carried the five empty containers with him from New York — at Swan's suggestion — against the possibility of their being unavailable in the Caribbean, and Swan had seen to it that the cocaine was wrapped in such a way as to make the transfer from the panda to the containers simple. The cocaine cleared the porthole at the appointed time — Adrian waved a towel for the boatmen to target on. The pickup was made by water skiers.

While in Bogotá, Swan was introduced to Rudolpho's cousin, Camillo, who worked in a mobile cocaine-processing lab in Leticia. Swan had heard that paste was available in Leticia for three dollars a gram — Camillo offered to handle the chemistry for a thousand dollars a kilo. The deal would bring Swan's capital investment down to four dollars a gram while prices were going up in New York. He said he would think it over.

One of cocaine's more primitive effects upon Zachary Swan was the ego problem it gave him — after he had been at smuggling a year, there were a lot of people who knew what he did for a living. He was careless that way. He could not resist the attention. He became kind of a cult hero, a guest lecturer on the crime circuit. He was approached once on Amagansett by a casual acquaintance, a man who knew Swan as well by reputation as by personal association, and offered a typical speaking engagement.

"I've got a friend," the man said. "He needs some advice."

"Send him over," Swan said.

But the man's friend, who introduced himself to Swan as Peter Crawford, needed more than advice. He had a very big problem.

"I sent a package," he said.

So, it was like that, thought Swan:

"Yeah?"

"Well, I'm not sure about it."

"Not sure how?" asked Swan. "Did it arrive?"

"That's what I'd like to find out," he said.

"Well?"

"Well, let me tell you how I did it."

"Please do."

"You know that they don't deliver the mail out here."

"Right."

"You have to pick it up. At the Post Office."

"Right."

"Well, it's there."

"Very good."

"I think."

"In your name?" asked Swan.

"It's addressed to Peter Crawford."

"Well done."

"Thanks."

"It's a good scam," Swan said.

"That's what I thought."

"What's the problem?"

"Well, I'm afraid it's being watched."

"How did you send it?

"I don't know. However you send packages from down there."

"There is only *one* way to send packages from down there. First class."

"Yeah?"

"Yeah."

The man calling himself Peter Crawford shook his head.

"I don't think I sent it first class."

"Then you've got trouble."

"Shit."

"What did you save — a buck and a half on the postage?"

"I didn't know."

Swan nodded his head.

"Well," he said, "if it's being watched, it's easy enough to find out."

"How?"

"How do you think?"

Swan took a drive the next morning. To pick up some stamps. In front of the Post Office he saw two men tossing a Frisbee back and forth. They wore windbreakers tied around their waists. It was July. Inside, the man behind the Parcel Post window was wearing a jacket. Swan bought his stamps and left. He saw the man called Crawford that night.

"Well?"

"Well, I'll tell ya — I asked one of the Frisbee players the way to the beach. He didn't know."

"What does that mean?"

"It means he was Federal."

"Shit, it's only two blocks away."

"I know. And he looked so Ivy League."

"What should I do?"

"Hell, I don't know about you, but I'm going to go back again. I can't resist, now that I know it's there. Why don't you talk to some people? Find out where they take the packages at night. I'll find out what I can."

The next day Swan went back. The Frisbee throwers were tossing a baseball. Swan saw a car parked in the IGA lot across the street that had been there the day before. It had the same two men in it. And the same jacketed man was behind the Parcel Post window. Swan did not even bother to buy stamps.

"You're out of luck," Swan said. "It's a stakeout."

"No suggestions?"

"Where do they take the packages when the Post Office closes?"

"To the station."

"Well, then, there's only one thing you can do."

"What's that?"

"Well, I happen to know from some people I talked to that none of those guys can run seventy-five yards without collapsing — so what you do is you get yourself a track star, preferably dumb, with nothing to lose, pay him a lot and have him jump over the counter, grab the package, and then run like the Pan American games depended on it."

"I pass."

"You're smart."

Peter Crawford's package is still waiting to be claimed.

16

THE HAWK AND THE
HIRED MAN

"I can't hack it," Charlie Kendricks finally said.

He was close to tears. He was shaking, and he was ashamed of it. He was completely shot.

"I just can't make it anymore," he said.

As an ounce-dealer, Charlie Kendricks was finished, beaten, taken off once too often. His nerves were shot, and he was through. Swan should have seen it sooner. Charlie had been strung out for weeks, stoned all the time, close to the edge. If it had gone on much longer, it might have killed him.

"Look, man, it's O.K., you don't have to explain a thing," Swan said, putting a hand on Charlie's shoulder.

Charlie's head was down.

"Forget it, Charlie, it's not a problem."

Charlie had lost another five ounces, this time to a dealer from Harlem and two of his friends. *Put the money on the table and get out, motherfucker* . . . either that or get your head shot off. The five thousand dollars' worth Swan had fronted him was worth thirty thousand dollars on the street — that paid for a lot of guns.

Charlie had been losing that kind of money regularly. He had once fronted five ounces to an actor friend who was going to fly to Chicago to sell the load. The actor, smiling, chatting up the personnel, carried the coke through airline security in a handbag. In the handbag, next to the coke, was a knife. (James Bond.) It triggered the metal detector. They busted him right there in the airport. He never made it out of New York. *Break a leg, sucker.*

There were other occasions. Charlie Kendricks was always getting robbed, suckered or soft-touched by people who were just better suited to the kind of work he did than he was. It was Lillian Giles who finally pointed it out to him. Lillian had had enough — Charlie was losing his grip, and she was losing Charlie. It was time to call it off. She wanted out. If he could not pull it together, she could. And she did. She went to Swan and laid it out.

She and Charlie were going home, she said. They wanted a farm. It was now or never. She wanted $1,000 a kilo on a five-kilo move — down and back fast. Charlie would be given extra ounces to sell to his safe customers, and as soon as he had unloaded them they would split.

"We gotta go," she said. "If we don't break now, we might never make it."

If Lillian weighed an ounce over ninety-five pounds, Swan would have been amazed. She stood no more than five feet off the ground, and her blond hair was so straight it would not even curl at her shoulders — it just slid on by. Though he thought she was pretty as hell, Swan had trouble thinking of her as the nursery school teacher who had come to New York with Charlie Kendricks — the one who wrote home to mother in Brisbane every week. She chain-smoked Kents, had no threshold when it came to dope of any kind, and she had nerves that would not bend under all the stress in the world. On her own she was as serene as a sunbird, but when there was shrapnel in the air she was as cold as they come. Swan saw her as one who would easily cut your arms off for trying to get tough, then kick you in the face for bleeding on her shoes — he thought she was wonderful. He said O.K. — he could not say no — and set up the scam.

On the following Monday morning, Charlie Kendricks took a subway to West Fourth Street and put an ad in *The Village Voice*:

Help Wanted. Import/Export. Good money. Travel and Expenses. Call Mr McCann 212–361–0555. 9 a.m.

On Thursday morning at nine, a pay telephone on the corner of Madison Avenue in the fifties rang once. Zachary Swan answered it.

"Mr McCann."

"Hello, I'm inquiring about the job advertised in *The Village Voice*."

It was Lillian Giles. She had made the call through an operator — she had had trouble getting through. The operator had taken her number and made a record of the call. For billing purposes. The call and the *Voice* ad were Lillian's responsibilities. Swan's job was to see that the phone he had listed in the ad actually worked.

"Why don't you come over to the store," Swan said. "About noon."

He gave her the address of an establishment around the corner from where he stood.

"You can't miss it," he said. "It has a sign out front that says 'Things Colombian.' O.K.? About noon. See you then."

At five minutes to twelve, Swan walked into the store in shirtsleeves. He had left his jacket in his car, parked a block away. In the breast pocket of his shirt he carried an array of retractable pens and mechanical pencils, all clipped to a plastic pocket insert designed for that purpose and imprinted with the name of a defunct hardware store. Approaching the counter, he passed stacks of *ruanas* and woven baskets, leather sandals, pottery, hammocks and an assortment of other handmade Colombian artifacts with which he felt quite familiar — a lot of them were made of wood. He smiled at one of the clerks and started his routine with the other.

"I've been to Colombia . . ." he began.

He chatted about his souvenirs, and theirs, and asked if they had trouble with the Customs people. Yes, they said, our crates arrive open. I know what you mean, said Swan, who appeared as if he were going to stay for a while, chattering away, a sourceless fountain of anecdotes, quips and tasteless flattery leading to boredom. He was leaning with his elbows on the counter, quite at home, when Lillian Giles walked in.

"I'm looking for Mr McCann?" she said.

"I'm Mr McCann," said Swan.

He shook her hand.

"Look," he told her, "things are a hassle here — let's go around the corner for a cup of coffee."

He took her arm. He turned to the clerks he had been talking to.

"Take care of the place," he told them.

They nodded.

"O.K.," they said.

Swan left them to think that one over.

Swan flew first to Bogotá. He had instructed Lillian to fly a day later and check into the Tequendama when she arrived — there would be a reservation made there in her name. When her plane landed at Eldorado Airport, Swan was there to meet it, but not to meet her. There was a change in plan. He walked up behind her as she left the Customs counter, bumped into her gently, and in place of an "excuse me" said, "Go to the Hilton." He kept walking. Lillian said nothing, but continued forward in the direction of the main entrance. She handed her bags over to a cab driver and asked him to take her to the Bogotá Hilton. Swan was nowhere in sight.

The Tequendama, Swan had learned, was hot. There had been a number of arrests there in the previous month, according to Canadian Jack, and the place was crawling with agents. Stay away, Jack had told him.

"Things are getting very tight."

Things were getting very tight all around. Both Armando and Luís were keeping their inventories down. Camillo was in Leticia — Rudolpho had not seen him in over a month. After a day making the rounds, Swan found Canadian Jack at Vincent's.

"What have you got?" he asked.

"There's always the Hawk," said Jack.

Swan nodded: "There's always the Hawk."

"Tsk tsk," said Vincent.

Vincent van Klee, for over a year, had been prevailing upon his friends to go straight. He and Swan had become very close friends over that year. Always, Vincent would take Swan to gallery openings, society parties and after-hours clubs in Bogotá, and Swan, coming in from New York, would bring Vincent the modern consumer miracles unavailable to Colombians, not the least of which were the Carter's Little Liver Pills Vincent relied on for his regularity and the latest Roberta Flack L.P. — the old man was a sucker for Roberta. And Swan always brought him cocaine.

Vincent was very proud of a cosmetic skin cream he had invented, and because he looked far younger than he was, he was the product's best advertisement. He called it Vincent Dior. He would not disclose its ingredients, but he did sell it to his friends for five dollars a bottle, and they swore by it. When Vincent learned that Swan had been in the cosmetic packaging business, he asked Swan to find an American pharmaceutical company which sold chemical stabilizers — Vincent Dior had a habit of going rancid in about six weeks. He gave Swan the names and addresses of companies he had written to in the United States. Though Swan never came up with the stabilizers, he did come up with a package. He designed a box on white Kromecote which, except for the word "Vincent," would pass for a Christian Dior package. Vincent was thrilled with it — Vincent Dior had finally arrived. Swan's cosmetic dealings with Vincent — correspondence, print orders and the like — apart from everything else provided the perfect cover for his operations in Colombia.

"Vincent, may I fix you a drink?"

"I will have only a small *aguardiente*," said Vincent, pivoting his head to throw his face into profile — one of his favorite gestures.

"Vincent, you are such a faker."

"Oh, don't tell me" — one of Vincent's favorite expressions. He liked nothing better than to be told about himself. Vincent was the only man over seventy Swan had ever thought of as coy. He was a real coquette.

Swan poured the drinks, and Jack proposed a toast:

"To the Hawk."

"To the Hawk."

"Shame on you both."

The Hawk was Juan Carlos Ramirez's mother. It was she who had paid for the hotel he managed. (As good a way as any, Swan figured, to keep him off the streets.) The Hawk was in real estate — in addition to the Oriole, she owned at least ten of the largest whorehouses in Bogotá. When Swan and Canadian Jack had first met, they had figured each other out fast — smuggler, they said — but Swan had never given Jack credit for his end of the figuring: Canadian Jack had had the Hawk's number from the beginning.

"I'm telling you," he said.

Even after meeting her — as a dinner guest with Jack at Juan Carlos's home — Swan would not buy Jack's story. An immense woman, in emeralds and Incan jewelry Mrs Ramirez came on like a countess. Her husband was less than half her size, a tiny man, and he said nothing, but Swan attributed this to the man's poor command of English, nothing more. No, said Jack. The man said nothing because his wife was the Hawk. And though the nickname was apparently not so much a comment on her formidable position in the underworld as it was a comment on the formidable size of her hooked nose, the truth was this: Juan Carlos Ramirez's mother was not only the matriarch of her immediate family and of half the whores in Bogotá, but she was the matriarch of an extensive Colombian cocaine network as well. She could buy and sell Armando in a minute, and her man, Jago, would just as soon cut your lungs up as piss on the carpet. The Hawk was heavy-duty. Level-one. If you had the money, she would sell you all the cocaine in Bolivia. Swan could not help but believe the story once he had met Jago.

Swan had met Jago on more than one occasion, and though they had discussed business often they had never come together on a deal — with Armando and Luís coming through, Swan had not needed the connection. His experience with the Hawk's man, apart from the occasions on which he bought samples from Jago, was limited. Jago was not a man whose company one would seek for any reason other than a professional one. He wore a long-barreled revolver holstered to his leg, and an expression on his face that said he was not afraid to use it. He had an air of homicide about him. There was always a look in his eye which seemed to indicate that his body was metabolizing raw flesh, that it would not be long before he required feeding again. Swan could not imagine his ever throwing a dinner party. He did not smile a lot, and he was not the kind of person one would automatically be inclined to say hello to upon introduction. He inspired caution. People responded to Jago less as they would to a man and more as they would to, say, the boss's Doberman. Swan recalled that his samples were always of the highest quality. With Lillian growing old at the Hilton and the entertainment provided by the agents at the Tequendama, where he was staying, growing stale, Swan decided it was time to see the Hawk.

The Hawk and Jago together were more than Swan had the energy to make jokes about. He did notice that the Hawk looked less forbidding in Jago's presence, a conclusion which led him to a re-evaluation of his initial impression of the woman: he decided that though she did behave like a countess, she very definitely looked like a hooker (so there was a pun, if not a joke) — more like three, in fact, given the hulk out of which her nose blossomed. He would have to tell Canadian Jack, he decided. Because the pressure was on in Bogotá, the Hawk could only come up with three and a half kilos overnight. Swan would have to wait a day for the rest. Swan said that would do and made arrangements to meet Jago the day after the next.

As brief a trip as it was, Swan would always think of this one as his most enjoyable. Apart from the fact that he had learned to relax in Bogotá over the years he had been visiting it, there was Lillian Giles. He and Lillian had been getting it on since the night she arrived, performing new and wonderful gymnastics for six or seven hours at a stretch behind the cocaine they lavished upon themselves, mellowed by the expense of energy and no doubt liberated somewhat by the tacit, mutual certainty that Alice and Charlie were doing the same back home. It was how things were. Everybody had his goodbyes to make.

Swan had always harbored something — call it affection, respect, or maybe nothing more than a curious appetite — for Lillian Giles. Whatever it was, it was nothing he would have indulged easily in years past. He had been married twice, and then there was Uta, and that was pretty much the story — he did not fool around much. There had been plenty of women in his life, but his love affairs had usually been sequential, very rarely simultaneous. By inclination he was monogamous, observing a pattern of sexual exclusivity because it was in his nature to do so. Until he met Alice Haskell and the sexual revolution. In the beginning, he had not been very good at spreading himself around, but with time and smuggling he developed an ease with it — Alice, Uta, Jane's friend April in Cartagena, Nina in Miami, Trude Daniels in Bogotá, off and on around Colombia with Blackie's little fifteen-year-old Indian friend Pachita, now Lillian, and others — back and forth, up and down, here and there, us and them. It was not something he would care to talk about later on, when it was over — he and Alice both left it behind rather suddenly — not because he was ashamed of it, but because he saw it as not really genuine in terms of his character. It represented a style of life that was not his. Not really. Zachary Swan, for all his skill at playing the child, was actually rather conservative.

Nevertheless, he and Lillian Giles had a wonderful time in Bogotá. Swan made a point of introducing her to Vincent van Klee. Lillian and Vincent hit it off particularly well. She loved listening to his stories, and he loved telling them.

"Tell her about the volcano, Vincent."

Vincent shook his head.

Swan always had trouble getting Vincent to tell the volcano story. It was Swan's favorite and one that Vincent was always pushed into when Swan was around. Lillian looked at Swan and then at Vincent:

"Oh, please, Vincent," she said.

Vincent did his Venus de Milo.

"Some other time," he said. "When I am excited."

Swan threw up his hands.

Vincent's volcano story has one principal character — Vincent. He is dining *al fresco* at a nightclub on the water — Swan seems to remember its being in Acapulco. The story is twenty years old. Vincent is with a group of friends, and he is stoned. The music is enchanting, there are strolling minstrels and dancers. The floor show is delightful. As the music crescendos there is a grande finale, with everyone jumping up from his table and dancing. There is a lavish fountain display. Vincent turns to his friends to comment on the beauty of the whole production. He looks up and around and discovers the place to be empty. He is the only one sitting. The band has hung in there — the music is still glorious. What Vincent soon realizes, very slowly because he is so stoned, is that the fountain display is in fact a volcano erupting. There are rocks flying and splashing splendidly in the water. The colors are marvelous. There is lava. How wonderful, he thinks. How beautiful it is.

Everybody had run away. And there he sat. Alone. In the middle of it. He thought it was grand.

"Vincent, you should write a book," said Lillian.

"I have been in two books already."

"Really?"

Vincent posed.

"What books, Vincent? I will read them."

"One you will never read. It is a terrible book. By a Colombian. He could not write, and he made me look very bad. I do not even remember the name."

"And the other?"

"It is by an American writer," he said.

"Do you remember the writer's name?"

"Yes, his name was F. Scott Fitzgerald."

There was a moment of silence.

"Vincent, he is a very famous writer."

Vincent shrugged.

"What is the name of the book?"

"*The Night Is Blue*."

"You must mean *Tender Is the Night*."

Vincent twirled his head.

"Vincent, what is your name in the book?"

"I am the South American."

"Did Fitzgerald know you then?"

"When I was nineteen he took me to Berlin. I was living in Switzerland at the time."

"Vincent."

"I do not think we slept together," Vincent shrugged. "He kept me."

"Come on."

Vincent gave Lillian his profile.

"He found me amusing."

Nor was Fitzgerald the only one. Vincent was introduced to Douglas Fairbanks by a mutual friend and worked as Fairbanks's social secretary for a year while the actor was married to Lady Ashley. Lillian Giles ate it up. She was thrilled with Vincent, and she was thrilled with Bogotá. She was having the time of her life.

Swan made it a point never to meet Lillian in the Hilton lobby or anywhere near the Tequendama, but made it a point also never to leave her alone for too long. He would later say that much of it was for the benefit of propping her up for the border, but it is unlikely. What is more probable is that all of it had to do with the fact that, for the first time in almost a year, he was not alone in Bogotá. He was sharing all the good things with a close friend — the restaurants, the clubs, the mountains, the people he knew. Bogotá, for the first time, it seems, was a city he knew well, and he enjoyed opening it up for Lillian.

Lillian had been practicing her Spanish. At breakfast one morning she wanted eggs.

"*Huevos*," she said.

"Werewolves," said Swan. "If you ask for werewolves, you'll get eggs."

"One's as easy as the other."

"Maybe for you it is."

"Give it a try," she said.

"The waiter's coming. *You* give it a try."

"*Dos huevos,*" she said.

The waiter looked at the menu in front of her, trying to see what she was ordering.

"See," said Swan.

Lillian looked at the waiter.

"Dose werewolves," said Swan to the man.

The waiter smiled, nodded, and left to get the eggs. Lillian was astonished.

"They can't even speak their own language," she said.

"Don't tell them that."

"My accent was perfect."

"I know it was. But somehow that doesn't carry much weight down here. Our high school Spanish teachers never understood that. For instance, they don't have much truck with consonants in Colombia. All you have to say is 'weh-woh' to get eggs. Listen closely the next time someone says hello to you — it'll sound like 'weh-a ee-a.' The *buenos* and the *días* translate that way. If you want to get by, you have to translate what they say into Spanish first, then into English. It's harder the other way around — English to Spanish isn't tough, but Spanish to whatever they speak is a killer. The only words that sound the same each time I hear them are '*coca*' and '*esmeraldas.*' "

Lillian pulled a paperback out of her carryall:

"I know what *coca* is. What's *esmeraldas? Emeralds?*"

"You got it. Stick with me, kid, I'll make a smuggler out of you yet."

"I don't remember any South American in *Tender Is the Night*," she said. "Do you?"

Swan scored from Jago in a taxicab. He carried the money (more than $20,000) stuffed in his shoes, the lining of his jacket, an Abercrombie & Fitch money belt and four pockets. It was like the Keystone Kops. After the score, he went directly to Rudolpho and Angel. The entire load was packed in one night. With the cocaine safely in the wood, he moved into the Hotel San Francisco — "*¡La Capital en su mano!*" the capital in the palm of your hand, they advertised — a lower-echelon hotel on Avenida Jimenez. The Tequendama was no place to be now that he was holding. The next morning he called Lillian Giles at the Hilton.

"I'm coming over with a bag. Get out of the hotel."

The Tequendama was within walking distance of the Hilton — just up the street — but from the San Francisco Swan had to take a cab. Lillian was out when he arrived. Rudolpho was sitting in the lobby. Swan asked at the desk for Miss Giles. When told she was not in, he asked to leave a bag with the "concierge." The bell captain was summoned. Swan handed him the bag and a note, written in Spanish by Juan Carlos Ramirez, and asked that they be given to Miss Giles when she returned. Swan overtipped him enormously. The bell captain smiled. Swan thanked him and left. Rudolpho kept his eye on the bag.

When Lillian picked up the load — she was not gone long — she asked the bell captain to read the note. He began in English:

"Dear Miss Giles—"

"Wait a minute" — she reached into her purse — "I want to write it down. I have a terrible memory."

As she searched through her pocketbook, Lillian smiled at the bell captain, asked his name — got that — and told him, in general, how wonderful he was. He was pleased.

"Let me get this right," she said.

"Mr McCann . . .," he read, ". . . can't make it today . . . had to go to Brazil . . . take the samples to the New York store . . ."

With Lillian writing it all down, the bell captain knew the story as well as she did — call him a witness for the defense.

Swan and Lillian flew to Cartagena together on a nine a.m. plane out of Bogotá. There they played for a few days and bought more "samples" — baskets, rugs, beads, hammocks and such — two of everything. Before leaving for Barranquilla, they ran into Uta. She and Swan spent an evening together.

"Where'd you go?"

"Out for cigarettes."

It had been just about a year again.

Uta had not changed much. She had lately been involved with some people moving stuff North by air and had been questioned by the authorities of both governments — there was heat on her. She needed looking after, and Swan wanted to help her out, but he could not take a chance while he was working. He gave her money to get to New York — she never made it. He and Lillian took a cab to Barranquilla, were stopped only once — "Turista! Turista!" they screamed, and paid off the border patrol — they stayed at the Del Prado and left for New York a day apart, Lillian following Swan's night flight the subsequent morning.

Lillian had been instructed to make a scrupulously

complete Customs declaration. The rule was never to say "statue"; always use the Spanish name of the saint it represented, and never leave anything out. Swan went through Customs with no trouble. Lillian had less. Charlie met her flight — Swan was on hand — and the load was in Amagansett before the sun went down in Bogotá.

Three days later Swan was busted.

17

AFTER THE FOX

The Algonquin Hotel in New York is one of those curious American antiques fashioned by our vagrant culture in its passing, and left behind, like a priceless cabinet in the attic of an aging house. It is an elegant relic which has survived one Great Depression and thirteen American presidents that the dollar and the national outlook have not. An outspoken tribute to permanence, the Algonquin has somehow managed to endure the vicissitudes of a national economy heavily reliant on planned obsolescence; an economy whose principal contribution to the technology of city planning announced itself more than thirty years ago, in a typically lavish fashion, over the rooftops of Hiroshima — the A-Bomb: urban renewal the American way, a bold architectural concept introduced by the United States Army Air Forces. Predating by more than forty years that reverberating policy statement, that direct-mail piece delivered in nuclear support of our continuing Keep America Beautiful campaign, the Algonquin assumes the significance of a legacy. At one time the landmark of cultural taste in America, it is cherished now as a souvenir, a bittersweet memento of a brief encounter with *style*, a keepsake reminiscent of the pre-Niels Bohr innocence of a new century.

The Algonquin is located on West 44th Street between Fifth and Sixth Avenues in the occluded heart of midtown Manhattan. On George Washington's Birthday, in February of 1974, while Zachary Swan was confronting American history in the lobby of that venerable establishment, New York City was entering the fourth week of its annual survival drill. January's repeated attempts at snowfall had been aborted, and the atmosphere had avenged itself by coughing up a seemingly endless cycle of ice, slush, and pH-critical rain. Manhattan was in the grip of a temperature inversion. Saturated hydrocarbons choked off the air, and periodic high-velocity winds helped reproduce the conditions of a vast decompression chamber. For weeks the light had been bad, the sky, a luminous gray, etherizing the city against anything exciting or healthy, not the least of which was the sun; and day-to-day living was one continuous Act of Contrition, spiritually draining, psychologically touch and go. By Valentine's Day the mood of the people had grown dangerously ugly. Stepping outside was like entering a snakepit. Hibernation was growing fashionable.

Today the Algonquin lobby exhibited all the charm of an autopsy room. The customers were drinking heavily. The staff was wired. The electronegativity in the air oscillated precariously between category-one violence and all-out despair. Each table took on the distinct penumbra of an armed refugee camp. Swan wondered how recently any of these people had done cocaine. It was six p.m. He had ventured into this elegant literary watering hole only once before, and it had been in the evening, at night in fact, when only the foolhardy go forth, when only the volunteer goes up against New York. Now the Algonquin was occupied by the draftees, New York's victims, impressed into combat by the requirements of commerce. And there is nothing in the world more helpless and depraved than an individual impelled onto the streets of New York City by any agency other than choice. Zachary Swan stood on the perimeter, wondering if he truly cared whether the headwaiter was going to find him a vacant table, and risked his sanity in the heroic attempt truly to understand how he had arrived at that place, at that time, and in that condition on the 242nd birthday of the congenital syphilitic who had become known as the father of our country.

He was there to talk about cocaine.

Swan's initial encounter with what the New York publishing establishment was calling writers these days was not a particularly auspicious one.

"You look just like a Fed," he was saying. "They all have long hair and wear bluejeans."

"You don't look anything like a cocaine smuggler," he was told.

He was wearing a dark gray charcoal suit of worsted wool, a white French-cotton broadcloth shirt with French cuffs, and a plush, Burgundy red velvet bow tie the size of a hummingbird, all tailored by Paul Stuart on Madison Avenue. A linen handkerchief tucked neatly into the breast pocket of his jacket matched his shirt. His dark brown cordovans matched his belt. He wore ceramic cufflinks and a gold watch. One would have taken him for an advertising executive.

"That's the idea," he said.

Swan sat facing the door, nursing a Martini, chain-smoking Kools. It had been more than a year since his arrest, and he was still awaiting trial. His preliminary hearing had gone against him. He faced fifteen years in prison for possession of the cocaine and the gun, and he had already run up $10,000 in legal fees. The IRS was investigating him — they were looking for $15,000 in Federal taxes on what they had been able to unearth already in the way of supportable income. The Justice Department wanted him too.

"What have they got on you?"

"Thirteen trips to Colombia."

"Is that all?"

"They've got a guy in a Mexican jail who they say will do business with them if they get him out of there."

Vinnie Pirata.

"A friend of yours?"

"He used to be."

"Can he hurt you on the State charge?"

"No, nothing there. But the Feds and the DA are cooperating. They are feeding each other all kinds of information. The Feds say they can make it easy for me out on Long Island if I cooperate with them."

"What do they want you to do?"

"Talk. Turn in some friends. Go South again and work as a narc. You've seen it all on TV."

"Can you stand a Federal charge?"

"The Feds are always tougher. But I don't think they can make a smuggling charge stick. I covered myself pretty well."

"How?"

"You really ask a lot of questions."

"I used to get paid for it."

"They must have paid you well."

"Not well enough."

"I've got to be careful," he said.

"You can say that again."

"I've got to be careful."

Everyone laughed.

"What do you think of smugglers?" he asked.

Everyone stopped laughing.

"You ever handle smack?"

"Never. I wouldn't have anything to do with the shit, and neither would any of my people. Was that worrying you?"

"That was worrying me."

"And I don't like Nixon either. What else do you want to know?"

"You ever pull the trigger on anyone?"

"I'm a pacifist."

"What were you doing with a gun?"

"It was purely a matter of self-preservation. Somebody threatened me. That's why I moved to Long Island. I was running. I never fired the thing. I still have nightmares."

"Another friend of yours?"

"He was a small-time hood. His name's Crazy Leslie. Last year he was arrested for beating up a cop. He escaped from the hospital by jumping out the window, but he broke his leg in the jump and they picked him up again. It made the papers."

"Do you live in New York now?"

"Yes, but I'm getting out."

"Because of the nightmares?"

"No. Because Crazy Leslie's back on the street. He's got a gun and he's looking for old friends."

Somebody hit the service bell. Between that time and the waiter's arrival, there was silence. When the waiter left, the conversation returned to a discussion of Swan's health. It was pointed out that he had recently undergone cancer surgery (for basal cell epithelioma) and faced a hernia operation in the spring. He took downs (Valium) to ease the stress responsible for periodic attacks of bronchial asthma and massive doses of Gelusil to keep his stomach together. He had a detached retina. His body was like a beleaguered city, it seemed, coming apart under assault. Today it was holding out on rations of alcohol and tobacco. And it was beginning to look like Troy. Zachary Swan III, this man with the funny name, was up against some serious odds.

"Was it worth it?"

"Not if I have to spend another night in jail."

"What are your chances?"

"My lawyer says they're good."

"First offense?"

"If it comes to that. But he thinks we can get it thrown out on the illegal search. They broke into the house."

"No warrant?"

"They didn't have any evidence. There was no way they could get a search warrant. They got one after they went in."

"What were they looking for?"

"They were looking for dope."

"Just because you were stoned when they brought you in?"

"Most of us were pretty straight by then."

"They must have had some reason for wanting to go in. They can't be that hard up for work."

"They used the dogs as an excuse."

"The dogs?"

"They said they wanted to take the dogs home for us. Humanitarians, right? We said don't trouble yourself. It was one of those things — they're smiling, I'm smiling, we all know what's going on . . . *thanks, but I know you're busy, appreciate it all the same, though . . . by the way, can I see a lawyer?*"

"But they must have had a reason."

"The newspaper said they had my name from 'a previous drug investigation.'"

"Well?"

"They had my name, but it had nothing to do with any of this. Something altogether different. It was nothing I was involved in."

"What was it?"

"One of the ironic twists of the whole story is that the house I rented in East Hampton, I rented from a narcotics detective — you like that, right?"

"Just a coincidence?"

"Just a coincidence."

"Very nice."

"I thought you'd like it. Anyway, we were friendly and I happened to overhear something once. I made the mistake of repeating it in the wrong place. It was an accident, but an unfortunate one. It blew over quick enough, but somebody remembered it and picked up on it the morning I was arrested. It was totally without relevance to anything I was involved in, a complete fluke, but it came home. You might say poetic justice caught up with me."

"Had they been keeping an eye on you?"

"I don't think so."

"They just made the connection because they had you for being under the influence?"

"No. They didn't have me for anything. They busted Lillian for driving under the influence and for not having her license. They told *me* to drive the car back to the station. After I paid her bail, and we all got up to leave, the cop says, 'We're gonna lock you all up for public intoxication.' Well, shit. If I'm sober enough to drive — they *told* me to drive — how are they going to lock me up for public intoxication? Well, logic doesn't carry much weight down there, you see. It's a problem, but they're going to take care of that. The idea is to hold us until they can search the house. I demanded a blood test. A lot of good that did me. This is the part in the movie where the Fourteenth Amendment starts getting the shit kicked out of it."

"How did they 'take care of it'?"

"Are you ready for this? They lied. In court! They said a cop drove the car. Can you believe it? They lied. Now, isn't that something? I mean, that's disgusting. It's dishonest."

"You mean they broke the *law*?"

"You can't trust anybody these days."

"It's terrible, isn't it?"

"It's an insult."

"Did they feed the dogs?"

"They didn't even let them out of the car until the next day."

"So they didn't take them back to the house?"

"No."

"How did they get in?"

"Well, the Sherlock Holmes on the case was a guy named Paulsen. Detective Sergeant Paulsen. At the hearing he told the judge that he was on his way back to work that day, after lunch at home, and he just happened to be passing my house — which is like passing Anchorage on your way back from New York to Pittsburgh. Anyway, he was worried about the dogs. And I feel sorry for the guy, because it obviously ruined his lunch — he only spent about three minutes at home if his addition is correct; and then there were some typographical errors on his application for the warrant. He didn't get around to correcting them until the dogs were safe and he had had an opportunity to talk to the DA —

just prior to his testimony, in fact, five months later. So, Detective Sergeant Paulsen pulled into the driveway and drove to the back of the house to see if anyone was home."

"Why didn't he go to the front door?"

"It's hard to say. I guess he didn't want to block the driveway. He did say at first that he parked in the street and walked across the lawn. But he changed that under cross-examination. If he did cross the lawn he would have ended up at the front door. You have to remember that he was concerned about the dogs. He was an animal lover. Anyway, it was through the back door that he saw a suspicious plastic bag on the kitchen table."

"What was suspicious about it?"

"He said it contained dope."

"And he went in?"

"I think he *was* in. If he wasn't, he was trespassing anyway. He got a warrant."

"Why didn't you just pay your bail and go home that morning?"

"They told us there was no magistrate to arraign us."

"When did they finally arraign you?"

"One o'clock the next morning."

"But they had a judge there at lunchtime to sign the search warrant."

"Somewhere between noon and one p.m. That was one of the typos. Hell, we didn't even get a phone call until Sunday afternoon."

"Is that the Fourteenth Amendment again?"

"I think it's the Bill of Rights."

"Do you think that would have happened no matter where you were?"

"That's a good question. The harassment, maybe. But not the search. A New York cop would never take that kind of chance. He knows he's got to have the goods on you. New York City cops at least have a little bit of style. And they know what's going to make them look bad later."

"Do you have enough money for an appeal?"

"I hope it doesn't go that far. We're waiting for a good judge. There's one out there with a good drug record. He's also trying to get on the appellate court. My lawyer figures that if we can make a strong enough case, so that it looks like a guilty decision will be overturned on appeal, then this judge won't take any chances. He can't afford to be over-turned if he wants to make the appellate court someday."

"It looks like you've got a good lawyer."

"I don't know. Sometimes I think so. Sometimes I wonder."

"Sounds to me like your chances are good."

"Well, I'll tell you one thing."

"What's that?"

"I'm not going back to jail."

Zachary Swan, determined not to go back to jail, was at the time of his trial in possession of false papers with which to leave the country in the event of a conviction. He also had money. Most of it in cash. He had not been idle in the year and a half since his arrest. On the "Things Colombian" smuggle, Lillian Giles had walked through U.S. Customs in New York with five kilograms of cocaine. Prior to the costly celebration of that event, which took place two days later at Swan's Amagansett beach house, Swan had managed to move 1,500 grams of the load — he had met Anthony under the Maxfield Parrish painting in the King Cole Bar of the St Regis Hotel and picked up a quick $48,000. What the Amagansett police busted was most of the 500 grams Swan had withdrawn from the head he cleaved that evening. What they missed were the three kilos shared by the Madonna sitting on the mantelpiece in the living room and the rolling pin hanging over the stove in the kitchen. They confiscated Swan's gram scale, his marijuana, and an assortment of pills along with over 500 grams of mix, most of it borax. Taking the coke and the mix together (if the lab techs at headquarters were smart they used Swan's Ohaus), they estimated the bust at a kilo. Of cocaine.

What the Amagansett authorities did not do — to their credit — was waste their time dealing with newspaper people. What they might have done to help their case was take a tip from the Feds. When Federal agents make a cocaine (or marijuana or heroin) bust, they not only overestimate the load for the benefit of the press, but they quote inflated gram prices. If they bust a smuggler at Customs, for example, carrying three kilos of pure, for which the smuggler has paid a total of, say, $18,000 and on which he stands to make anywhere from $80,000 to $100,000 profit, they will estimate their haul at $2 million, as if the weirdo they have captured were going to go home, buy a truckload of Reynolds Wrap, sixty pounds of lactose and a gram scale and devote the rest of his life to putting 30,000 packages together — not one of which is any larger than a stick of chewing gum, each only 10 percent of which is cocaine — and *then* go out and sell the snow for $75 a gram. It is the same logic that presumes bituminous coal is worth $3,000 a carat because someday it will be diamonds.

What the cops in Amagansett did was merely overestimate the weight. They hit Swan with a couple of possession-one drug felonies — they were worth fifteen years apiece — and a felony charge on the gun — worth five. The judge let everyone else go, and the DA went for the limit on Swan. Charlie Kendricks and Lillian Giles left for Australia as soon as the heat was off, and Alice stuck around to help Swan through the wringer.

Swan's first move, when his bail came through, was to get the three kilos out of the beach house. He made a couple of dry runs before making his move, then carried the load out under the cover of darkness, driving it northwest to his stepmother's house in Greenwood Lake, where he stashed it in the basement behind a couple of snow tires. He then rented an apartment in the name of Zachary Swan on West 84th Street in Manhattan and laid out some money at Radio Shack on a pair of walkie-talkies. He gave one to Roger.

Roger Livingston's living room window, giving southern exposure to his apartment on West 85th Street, was visible from the bedroom window of Swan's apartment on West 84th. In the weeks that followed, Swan maintained radio contact with Roger, who was in touch with Anthony, Moses and the other ounce-dealers, and through Roger and the radios he moved the cocaine by Thanksgiving. The three kilos, which had become four and a half with the hit, he moved at $1,000 an ounce, bringing his before-expenses total on the broken load up to over $200,000. He spent the next year and a half postponing his trial.

While Ernie Peace was submitting notices of motions to reargue and hard-nosed memoranda of law to the Suffolk County Court, claiming that his client was being railroaded beyond belief, Zachary Swan was out meeting his legal fees. In the year and a half between Swan's arrest and trial, Angel the carpenter made at least two trips to New York carrying peculiarly bound books. Armando was meeting people in Bogotá who introduced themselves by saying, "I used to play for Detroit." (If anyone had used Swan's name without the code, Armando's reply would have been something like, "God, I don't know *what* you're talking about, man.") Old friends were coming and going. Moses, still in business on the West Side, was getting visits from people who knew Swan: "We're back-to-back buddies," they would say. (Swan and Moses had matching scars on their backs, Swan's as a result of his surgery — he called it a knife fight in Bogotá — Moses's as a result of a gunshot wound he received working an East Side saloon.) There were marijuana moves out of Miami and consultant's fees on two-border boat moves through Mexico. The code words were flying back and forth, and the cloak-and-dagger back-stairs forget-me-not cocaine blues carried Swan back to the border again and again. And there was always that one big move he had never made.

Two weeks after his interview at the Algonquin, Swan, walking down Broadway in the direction of a newspaper stand, felt a tap on his shoulder.

"Hey, don't I know you?" asked a voice from the fog.

Swan, whose face was buried in the collar of his trench coat and whose drenched hair covered his eyebrows, shook his head and mumbled something like "No, I don't think so" to the man. He grabbed his newspaper and walked away. Fast. When he looked back, Crazy Leslie was gone. But Swan suspected it would not be for long. A week later, he left town for good. New York City was a thing of the past.

Swan and Alice, who had been living together for a year in Alice's apartment on 87th Street, moved out of state with the permission of the court. They rented a house with a garden, and in the spring Swan took up organic gardening. Alice was pregnant. She would never go back to New York. She put down roots. Swan and Ernie Peace, having failed in repeated attempts to have their case thrown out of court, prepared for trial.

* * *

Six months after Swan's trial, Alice gave birth to a boy. Nine pounds five ounces — and five days before Christmas. Swan had said that his son — he was sure it would be a son — would never in his life do anything illegal. Old Geoffrey would live off the land. He would learn to farm and he would do his own carpentry and he would never go near New York. Swan had assured Alice that after all the years of running he was determined to go straight.

"Things are going to be different," he said.

But for all one knows Swan may still be planning the big one he never made. On June 10, 1974, Swan went to trial. On June 26 he was found innocent on all counts of possession of a dangerous drug. He was put on three years' probation for misdemeanor possession of a dangerous weapon. He was told to go home and behave himself.

Ernie Peace had said from the beginning that the gun would be the problem, and he went to great lengths to demonstrate that because the patio, where it was buried, was enclosed on two sides, the patio was a part of the house — possession of a gun in one's house in New York, he pointed out, is a misdemeanor, not a felony. The legal memos he submitted, in which he cited drug decisions that the judge's law clerk could not ignore, won the acquittal on the cocaine charge.

Choosing to go without a jury, choosing to go before a judge who could be counted on to resist pressure, and gambling on the judge's ability to respond clearly to the technical and legal merits of the case as it was presented on both sides ('He's got a damn good law man behind him," Peace said afterward), Ernie Peace had beaten the DA.[*] Swan's character witnesses, Iona Prep boys who had gone

[*] See Appendix IX.

straight, and the letters he submitted from influential friends, one of them a judge, were too much for Amagansett's finest, who came off looking bad. Swan, himself, at the trial, was 100 percent Zachary Swan. Outraged and indignant, he testified in his own defense, entertaining the judge and the DA at the same time. Posturing and appealing, he played the innocent fool, but when he appeared for sentencing two weeks later he was as frightened as hell. He thought they had lost it (particularly when the DA asked the judge to lay down the maximum). Facing the judge, all Swan could think of was jail.

The sentencing took less than five minutes. Swan was instructed to report to a probation officer. He was free to go.

As he left the courtroom he kissed Ernie Peace. And as he left the building he said:

"This is just like walking through Customs."

EPILOGUE

I NEW YORK

VINNIE PIRATA dropped out of sight sometime in 1973. He was not heard from again until DEA agents in New York threatened Swan with his testimony, which Pirata allegedly offered them in exchange for his extradition from a Mexican jail. If Pirata was there, he was never extradited. His closest friends have not heard from him in years. The best one can assume is that Pirata, if he is alive, is behind bars in Mexico. If he is in for drug running, he is in for a minimum of six years.

BILLY BAD BREAKS, sentenced to a stretch in Federal prison after his Brownsville bust, returned to New York, where the breaks got worse. In the summer of 1974 he was on the run.

ADRIAN THE MOGUL is by every account a producer who is still not producing.

IKE and FREDDY, the shooters from Brooklyn, are still renting crap tables to the local houses of worship in Queens.

NICE MICKEY lives in New York, where he shoots pool, plays backgammon and makes the best fudge Alice Haskell has ever tasted. Currently, he makes his money legitimately — in 1975, for a month, he operated a concession at a New Jersey department store stitching names on Christmas stockings. He made a bundle. Nice Mickey has never been busted.

MEAN MICKEY was last seen by Zachary Swan popping an amyl nitrate while on water skis. He is on parole in New York and still proud of his press clippings.

MOSES, who offered to have Crazy Leslie eliminated by two fifteen-year-olds who would do anything for $100 — "That's a hundred apiece, you understand" — in 1973 was shot in the back in a bar on the East Side, and lived to advertise it. The manager of a bar on Eighth Avenue in New York, his business is better than ever.

ROGER LIVINGSTON, busted on a marijuana charge, lives in New York with Angela De Santis. She is a children's clothing designer. He teaches biology in the New York City school system. Angela got the cocaine out of the house; now she is working on the snakes.

CHARLIE HENDRICKS and LILLIAN GILES are married and living on a sheep station in Australia.

DAVIS has not been near a package from South America in years, and he intends to keep it that way.

THE LOTHARIO, who has never done anything illegal outside the company of Zachary Swan, has a steady girl and "a business here in New York."

TRUDE DANIELS got her apartment. She lives in New York with her daughter, she has a steady job, and if she is not as happy as some of her friends, it is because she does not have a friend that makes her as happy as she makes them.

HONEST ELLERY, who once owned a Maserati but never a driver's license (he took it as collateral on a loan to Pirata, then rented a garage where he visited it every day for months — Ellery had always loved Maseratis but had never learned to drive), was busted in July of 1973 for selling two ounces of cocaine to New York narcotics agents. He stood up — he did not reveal the source of the coke. He beat the Rockefeller law by a few months and got probation. He lives in the Bronx and holds a legitimate job in Manhattan. He dreams of laundromats — Pirata stole the Maserati back.

ANTHONY was last heard from shortly after Swan went to trial. "He has a problem," Ellery said. Anthony's problem kept him busy for a year. He could not be reached. At the end of a year he went to Federal prison for three and a half. He can be reached there.

CRAZY LESLIE is walking the streets of New York, frightening people. Alice Haskell, who should know him as well as anyone, thinks of him only rarely: "I wonder if his mother knows what he does for a living?" she asks.

II SOUTH AMERICA

UTA DIETRISCHE was never seen again after her final appearance in Cartagena. Swan continued to get word of her, however, and continued to send her money. The last he heard was that she was living in the Canary Islands. It was Alice who suggested: "Why don't we have her come and stay with us for a while?"

VINCENT VAN KLEE, having moved out of his suite at the Continental, lives in a posh apartment complex at the foot of Monserrate. As of the spring of 1975 he had given up liquor and cocaine, deeming them detrimental to a lifestyle that has changed no more since his seventy-second birthday than it has since his nineteenth. He makes occasional visits to New York, where he monitors his investments and keeps in touch with old friends, and when Swan last saw him, in Bogotá in May of last year, he had just returned from Cartagena, where, Vincent said, he had taken the part of "a faggot ballet instructor" in a big-budget Italian movie.

MICHEL BERNIER is selling himself to the highest bidder in Brazil.

RUDOLPHO is keeping his nose clean in Bogotá, where he spends money for Vincent van Klee.

ANGEL was last heard to be doing honest carpentry in Bucaramanga.

ARMANDO began feeling the heat in Bogotá shortly after Swan's arrest. As of May 1975 he was not answering his telephone.

RAOUL, who told Zachary Swan that a smuggler's luck is good for only two years, is doing a life sentence in Florida for running cocaine. He gets ice cream once a week.

HARRY MORGAN and JIMMY the boat captain are in the Caribbean, doing what they do best.

SEE GULL BILLY can be contacted at the Hotel Caribe marina.

BLACKIE and the beach people in Santa Marta and Mad Walter's Haight-Ashbury transplants are still playing hide-and-seek with the local police around the coastal resorts of Colombia.

THE HAWK is playing hide-and-seek with the authorities of more than one South American government. It was Vincent van Klee who said: "She has a problem."

JAGO, the Hawk's man, who had fronted Swan the fifth kilo on the "Things Colombian" move, a year and a half later was looking for Canadian Jack, who had disappeared with a fronted five. In May 1975 the pistol-packing flesh eater was on the run himself. Having double-crossed the wrong people on his own end of the business, he was last seen heading in the general direction of Ecuador.

CANADIAN JACK was last in touch with Zachary Swan in the summer of 1974. In the year between Swan's arrest and Jack's last letter, the young smuggler had been in and out of the United States and had stepped across into Canada at least once. He was known to have been in Jamaica and eventually in Mexico, where his lieutenant, a twenty-four-year-old Canadian named Roy, was arrested and imprisoned on a cocaine charge. In May 1975 Juan Carlos Ramirez told Zachary Swan that Jack was married to a young Indian woman and living in Cartagena, where he owned a leather shop. Swan was unable to find him. Jack is still wanted in Canada, where he faces ten years on his hash bust. Said Swan, shortly after he stopped hearing from the young Canadian: "He knows how to run."

BLACK DAN, known for being a professional, was not seen in Bogotá after the heat came on. Last seen at the Oriole, he just disappeared one day, and was never heard from again. Everyone's guess is that he is alive and well and semi-retired, living either in San Francisco or somewhere in Colombia. Zachary Swan suspects that wherever he is, he is in touch with Canadian Jack.

RAINY DAY — R.I.P.

ZACHARY SWAN and ALICE HASKELL, married a week after Swan's acquittal, are living under their own names on a half-acre of land on the East Coast of the United States. The growing season is a long one there, and Swan raises organic vegetables, the surplus of which he sells to the local health food store. He also deals in antiques, he and Alice making weekly roundups of available merchandise at local auctions and selling them on the flea market circuit. (Swan occasionally raids the neighborhood Good Will depository, faking a drop-off to pick up choice items.) While Swan monitors the New York Stock Exchange and the National Football League, Alice cans and sews and devotes the best hours of her time to hanging out with their year-and-a-half-old son, Geoffrey. The three dogs have rooms of their own,

and they like the country just fine. They treat the towheaded
Geoffrey as if he were one of the family — a very remarkable golden retriever. Swan, in the two years since his trial,
has been on probation. He has a perfect record and a year
to go. He likes his probation officer, and his probation officer
likes him. He is a family man and a model of industry, and
as far as the probation people are concerned he has been
rehabilitated. Recently they have pointed out, and particularly applauded, his growing interest in carpentry.

APPENDICES

I QUĀĀLUDES

In the late 1960s, at about the time Richard Nixon was taking over, downs became the most popular drug on the American pill-popping market. Acid was on its way out, and speed was killing everyone in sight — it was natural that under a Republican administration young dopers would turn to the favorite drug of their parents. Just as meprobamate (Miltown) had been the drug of choice in the Eisenhower years, so barbiturates would assert themselves in the years of the "silenced majority." The most popular barbiturates at the time were Seconal (sodium secobarbital — *reds*), Nembutal (sodium pentobarbital — *yellows*), and Amytal (sodium amobarbital — *blues*), the second manufactured by Abbot, the other two manufactured by Lilly. The newer, and far milder, sedatives, Librium and Valium — Roche Laboratories' bid to take the sweepstakes — were still in their infancy.

Barbiturates, known to be habit-forming, hit the college

campus with a reputation. Though marketed chiefly to domestic addicts and made available by the drug companies to the occasional thoroughbred, it was known that they were manufactured principally for suicides. Toying with them ensured status ... *if they were good enough for Jimi Hendrix, they are good enough for me.* The pharmaceutical houses worked overtime — reds put Lilly on the map and, by themselves, could be counted on to take up the corporate slack for a long time after the Darvon patents ran out.

"What in the world ever became of sweet Jane
She lost her sparkle, you know she isn't the same
Livin' on reds, Vitamin C and cocaine
All a friend can say is, 'Ain't it a shame.'"

"Truckin," from *American Beauty;*
THE GRATEFUL DEAD

A couple of years later, while Nixon's back was turned — call it Ziegler's mistake — the newspapers managed to get hold of some truly electrifying national news. A new drug had hit the campus. (Yawn.) All they had to do was call it an aphrodisiac, and their advertising revenues would triple. *Great Caesar's ghost!* It was a celibate city editor's dream. It, too, was a down, this pill, but not only would they attribute deaths to it, they would attribute WILD HIPPIE ORGIES IN FLORIDA and BARE-ASSED RUTTING IN THE STREETS to this miracle drug. Get ready, Mom and Dad. (Do you know what your children are doing tonight?)
Quääludes.

*   *   *

Quāālude is the brand name given by William H. Rorer, Inc., to a sedative and hypnotic agent known pharmacologically as methaqualone — 2-methyl-3-o-tolyl-4(3H)-quinazolinone — a new, non-barbiturate hypnotic, useful, according to the Physician's Desk Reference, in the treatment of insomnia, and designed for those cases in which barbiturates are contraindicated or where other hypnotics have failed. Because of its side-effects, or absence thereof — methaqualone is not physically addictive, though psychological addiction is almost guaranteed to the heavy user — methaqualone is in many ways preferable to the barbiturates.

Adverse neuropsychiatric reactions include headache, hangover, fatigue, dizziness and torpor. Of course, it is these reactions and others that the serious doper looks for — an absence of side-effects altogether would throw the drug off the market. Two things which make methaqualone as popular as it is are its availability over the barbiturates and its ability to knock you down without knocking you out. It goes right to the central nervous system and turns you to jelly — you are loose in about twenty minutes. The exact mode of its action is unknown (of course), but methaqualone apparently acts on a different CNS site than that of the barbiturates. The tactile sensitivity it promotes makes lovemaking preferable to baseball for a good eight hours — that is what the newspapers mean by an aphrodisiac — but after the first hour, nothing is preferable to sleep. And if you happen to play baseball the next day, you might slouch a little, off and on, at second base, as the bends come and go. It is that kind of dope.

The prescribed dosage for sleep is usually 150–300 mg at bedtime. The maximum will set you up for anything you have in mind. An overdose — a very important factor, without which its popularity would slide significantly — can get you off on anything from spontaneous vomiting, delirium and convulsions to something as far out as cutaneous or pulmonary edema, hepatic damage, renal insufficiency and bleeding, shock, respiratory arrest, coma and death. Dig it. Two-point-four grams will throw you into a coma. Eight grams will kill you — reds are faster — and most fatal cases have followed ingestion of overdoses accompanied by alcohol.

Quäälude comes in a scored white tablet in two sizes, one containing 150mg methaqualone, the other containing 300mg — the famous "714." Both bear the manufacturer's name.

Sopor, manufactured by Arnar-Stone Laboratories, Inc., is the other popular source of methaqualone. Sopors come in green, yellow and orange, 75mg, 150mg and 300mg respectively.

Parke-Davis (Parest) and Cooper Laboratories (Somnafac), as did Wallace (Optimil), market methaqualone bonded to a cation — methaqualone hydrochloride. A rose by any other name . . .

II CREDIT CARDS AND TRAVELER'S CHECKS

In New York City, as in any major city in the country or around the world, there is a lucrative traffic in bad traveler's checks and stolen credit cards. Credit cards are marketable because the mechanism for listing the card number of any account against which theft or loss is reported is a very slow one, and it is made slower by the reluctance of many people, especially the businessman whose cards have been lifted by a hooker in a hotel room in the Tenderloin, to report the theft immediately. Traveler's checks are marketable on the same basis, but with traveler's checks there is a bonus.

The traveler's check scam (if someone is doing TCs, he is dealing in traveler's checks) works off the guarantee given by American Express and the respective banks that a customer's checks will be replaced immediately in the event of loss or theft — the no-liability clause, which makes the checks preferable to cash, streamlines crime in this area because it eliminates the weakest link in the chain, the thief. While credit cards have to be stolen, traveler's checks can be bought.

If a man like Adrian the Mogul wants some fast money, he can buy $5,000 worth of traveler's checks from First National City Bank, and Swan will give him the name of someone downtown who will pay him $2,500 for them. Adrian will pick up the $2,500, then redeem the $5,000 from FNCB. The trick with the traveler's checks is that a customer has to report them lost or stolen immediately to cover himself. New York cops know the swindle:

"Officer, I want to report stolen traveler's checks."

"Sure. You owe me a new hat or I'll misspell your name."

"Thieves! Thieves!"

The success with which the traffic flourishes is amplified by the scope across which traveler's checks and credit cards are honored — if a credit card stolen at the Americana in New York shows up the next morning in San Francisco, the odds against its having been listed, which are slim to begin with, are slimmer still over the distance. Not only does the listing mechanism, which is heavily computerized, function poorly, but chances are very small that a clerk on the West Coast is going to question a well-dressed tourist who can duplicate the signature on the card, especially if the out-of-towner is carrying corroborating identification.

The man who makes the traffic go controls two networks. He operates a centrally located headquarters where he buys credit cards from thieves, and traveler's checks from either their owners or the same thieves, and he operates an apparatus by which he can get the cards and checks out of town fast with teams of professional penmen. A good penman, man or woman, dresses well, speaks well, and can forge a signature as blatantly not his as John Hancock's without raising suspicion.

At 2:30 a.m. in one of Manhattan's larger pool halls, Nice Mickey will be shooting nine-ball. At three a.m. they will start coming in — hookers, pimps and cab drivers; the creepers and second-story men who work the hotels with the help of the desk clerks; the pickpockets, the stickup men, and all the thieves who have called it a night. They get $100 a card. Traveler's checks — half the face value.

"Now, God forbid a guy should give him a card that's three weeks old and is on the list. The guy never does any business again, ever, and it takes a while for his arm to get straightened. So it's got to be fresh, and it is fresh — no more than a day or two old."

From the poolroom the cards and the traveler's checks go to a man named George — he owns several flower shops in New York. In one of his offices, George has electric typewriters and blank social security cards, automobile registration forms and driver's licenses from every state in the Union. He calls in the teams. They get two or three cards apiece, and by the following morning they are all leaving town in different directions. They go to banks first, then to the retail stores. George takes 50 percent on whatever the teams bring in. He gives his man at the pool hall a percentage on every card, a flat fee for the checks.

And *that* is what Mean Mickey and Vinnie Pirata were doing.

III MEXICAN BROWN

In 1973, for the first time on record, the New York City Police Department's Narcotics Division reported making more cocaine than heroin "buys" through its agents on the street. Though the statistic attests to the current availability of cocaine, it is much more an indication of the heroin shortage that was brought on in 1972 by the American-instigated foreclosure by Turkey on her poppy fields. (The Turkish government prohibited its farmers from cultivating the poppy in return for $35.7 million in U.S. aid.) The Turkish ban was a temporary one, lifted in 1975, and one which more than any single factor accounted for the popular emergence of Mexican Brown on the streets of New York and other large American cities. The Mexicans, who learned to cultivate the opium poppy during World War II, were encouraged to do so by the United States government, whose legal stockpiles were threatened by the fighting in Europe. The brown heroin coming up from Mexico, though not as pretty to look at, is sold on a shorter cut than the white imported from Turkey and Southeast Asia. An addict shooting white runs the risk of an overdose if he mainlines an equivalent quantity of brown; of course, if you are spiking anything called heroin, your days are numbered to begin with — the scag may as well be blue for all the difference it makes.

IV SPEED

Speed, in the counterculture, is affectionately known as that which kills. Misused correctly, it can burn you out faster than smack. It was the methedrine shooters who were dying all over the Haight in San Francisco and up on the corner of Hazelton Avenue in Toronto in the late 1960s: speed, a kind of white man's scag, the young middle-class loser's own hat full of rain, coming off the street cut with anything that would melt in a spoon, bleach, rat poison ... *anything, man, just give me the spike.* The speed freak was a culture hero, the last daredevil cowboy — guaranteed to vanish. He had an air of death about him.

A good, hard-line methedrine habit is the electromotor Grand Prix of suicide drug use — out of the needle, speed will throw your insides into overdrive and take you out on the high side. It is the ultimate challenge to tolerance, dying with your boots on the American way, vital organs pumping the limit, synapses firing — you redline. In the death house of modern chemistry, where barbiturates are the gas chamber, speed is the chair — one high-voltage electro-orgasmic jolt and the lights go out. Overload. Oblivion express.

It was methedrine that was responsible for all those strange autopsies coming out of the drug underground in the Leary years — sixteen-year-olds with the insides of eighty-year-old men. The pathologists had never seen anything like it. It was this new and hideous phenomenon that subsequently spawned all the public service announcements coming over the underground FM stations made by people like Grace Slick and Frank Zappa ... *look, man, smoke all the grass you want, and do acid, if it's Owsley, but for your own good stay away from speed — it'll fry*

your brains and ruin your liver and, in general, it'll make
you about as fucked up as your parents ... speed kills.

Amphetamines were first synthesized by L. Edeleano in 1887.
It was not until 1920, however, while searching for a
synthetic substitute for ephedrine — an herbal central-
nervous-system stimulant used in the treatment of asthma
— that Gordon Alles discovered that Edeleano's original
compound, amphetamine sulfate, and its even more active
dextro isomer, dextroamphetamine sulfate, exhibited the
properties that make them so popular today — Smith Kline
& French, the pharmaceutical house which acquired Alles's
patents, wasted no time convincing the American medical
establishment that Benzedrine and Dexedrine were modern
chemistry's answer to the Crusades. Immediately, things
began to look ... *up*. Reports of attrition — Smith Kline
& French never bothered to record the side-effects of the
amphetamines — did not start coming in until 1939, but by
then speed was an institution, and every doctor's practice
depended on it.

The amount of Benzedrine supplied to American soldiers
stationed in Britain during the World War II has been estimated at 180 million pills. Between 1966 and 1969 the
American Army consumed more amphetamines than the
combined British and American armies of World War II. In
1970 over 225,000 pounds — ten billion tablets — of
amphetamines and amphetamine substitutes were manufactured legally. In 1971, when production was allegedly being
cut back, twelve billion pills — sixty 10mg tablets for every
person in the United States — were manufactured. The
profits derived by the pharmaceutical companies from
amphetamine sales, and the revenues derived by the

American Medical Association from advertisements for the drugs in medical journals, account for heavy lobbying by the industry among legislators, FDA officials and the physicians themselves (many of whom make money on every speed prescription they write).

Though amphetamines may be defended as the drug of choice for such rare conditions as narcolepsy, their prescribed use for anything else — other than speeding, of course — is usually no more than an excuse to lay an up on a good customer. A lot of doctors prescribe amphetamines as diet pills — anorexiants, appetite suppressants — but they rarely hand out prescriptions to overweight people. (Speed's anorectic effect is short-term — tolerance is a big problem.) Speed is for people who like to speed, not for people who like to eat. And if you like to speed, far be it from the drug companies or the doctor to stop you . . . *speed is good for America*. Cocaine is to speed what the Bolivian blow gun is to the *Enola Gay*. In the doper's paradise of 427-horsepower freak behavior, speed, not coke, is the real thing.

Speed, the word itself, is America's nickname for the amphetamines — those sympathomimetic amines of the amphetamine group with CNS stimulant activity. The amines are a group of organic compounds of nitrogen that may be considered ammonia (NH_3) derivatives — the word amine is a derivative of the word ammonia just as the word amino (as in amino acid) is a derivative of the word amine — and amphetamine is only one of them. Amphetamine, $C_9H_{13}N$, is *alpha*-methylphenethylamine — or *a(lpha)* m(ethyl) ph(enyl) et(hyl) . . . amine. Sympathomimetic simply refers to its agency as a sympathetic nervous system stimulant. The amphetamines come in many varieties, but they all have one thing in common — they are all called speed.

Smith Kline & French markets Benzedrine and Dexedrine,

and it markets another very popular form of speed called Dexamyl, which is a combination of dextroamphetamine sulfate and amobarbital, a barbiturate. Abbot Laboratories markets methamphetamine hydrochloride (the most famous of the grade one amphetamines, known generically as methedrine, once a brand name) under the trademark Desoxyn. Abbot also markets Desbutal, a combination of methamphetamine hydrochloride and the barbiturate sodium pentobarbital. The famous "Black Beauty," Biphetamine, a resin complex of amphetamine and dextroamphetamine sulfate, is marketed by Strasenburgh.

All of the above are marketed in easy-to-pop form. Benzedrine comes in 15mg capsules and in tablets of 5mg and 10mg. Dexedrine comes in 5mg, 10mg and 15mg capsules and in 5mg tablets, and it also comes in the form of an elixir — by the pint. Dexamyl comes in capsules containing 10mg and 15mg and in tablets containing 5mg respectively of dextroamphetamine sulfate. It too is available in the form of an elixir. Desoxyn comes in tablets of 2.5mg (white), 5mg (white), 10mg (orange) and 15mg (yellow). Desbutal comes in a green capsule containing 5mg and in tablets containing 10mg (orange and blue) and 15mg (yellow and blue) respectively of methamphetamine hydrochloride. Biphetamine is supplied in three strengths, a white capsule containing 3.75mg each, a black and white capsule containing 6.25mg each, and the Black Beauty itself, containing 10mg each of amphetamine and dextroamphetamine sulfate. Biphetamine is also available as Biphetamine-T in two strengths — the T stands for Tuazole, Strasenburgh's brand name for methaqualone.

Commercial speed is available through any physician in the country and through any reputable dope dealer on the street. Illegally manufactured speed, though not as popular as it once was, is still available on the street and comes in many forms. Bathroom variety — as it is called — is very easy to manufacture and was manufactured in quantity in the sixties. Called crystal by those on the spike, illegal methedrine is what most shooters mainline. The few crazies left over from the dope years who still use speed — and of serious dopers they are very few — usually pop commercial speed when they can. When they cannot, they generally buy whites, the most popular current variety of which is called "crossroads." Some MDA (methyl di-amphetamine) is still available. White is the color most often attributed to speed today — the most popular word is *ups*. Brain ticklers, browns, cartwheels, chalk, Christmas trees, coast-to-coasts, dominoes, footballs, greenies, hearts, leapers and truck drivers are words of the sixties and are out of use now. What is more important is that speed in any form is pretty much out of use now by people who paid their dues in the sixties. Serious dopers know better.

The copy lavished on every amphetamine listed in the Physician's Desk Reference is preceded by a brief warning which cautions against prolonged use — "short-term anorectic effect and rapid development of tolerance" are the token negatives required by the publisher. What the warning actually points out, then, but not so clearly that it might be interpreted correctly by anyone interested, is that as a diet pill speed is pretty worthless — it might work for a month. (Zachary Swan had a prescription for diet pills for six years.) None of the drug companies lists for any of its amphetamines an LD 50, the industry-standard average lethal dose (that dose measured in milligrams per kilograms of lean body mass which will kill one-half of the sample of subjects tested), nor do they spend a lot of time outlining the side-effects of a drug that in many cases is marketed for no other purpose than as an aid to dieting (which one has already been warned is not a very good reason for taking it). The fact is that not only is tolerance inevitable, but psychological addiction is guaranteed. The depression that follows speed's use is deadly. Once you have been up, everything else is down. And it takes more to get you up every time you take it. What the drug companies call the manifestations of overdose are merely the extreme side-effects of overuse — confusion, assaultiveness, hallucinations and panic; arrhythmias, hypertension and circulatory collapse. With fatal overdose, life terminates in convulsions and coma.

It does not take a cardiologist to figure out that if your heart is pumping twice as fast today as it was yesterday, then today you are one day closer to dead than you would have been under normal circumstances. Think of your body as an automobile with only so many miles on the warranty — speeding puts the mileage on faster than cruising. After all, speed is called speed for a reason. The faster you go, the sooner you are going to get where you are going — the faster you force your body to age, the faster it is going to get old and get where every aging body is headed — dead. And when you speed, whether you are an automobile or a soft machine, the chances of your throwing a connecting rod are always greater. Frank Zappa was right — speed kills. If not today, tomorrow. Sooner than you think. However you cut it, you come up short.

V MARIJUANA ABROAD

Contrary to the prevailing folklore, there is just as much heat smoking dope in Colombia as there is in the United States; more, in fact, given the likelihood that anyone, old or young, who spots you doing it will call the law. As strapped for liberty as U.S. heads claim they are, the fact is that a marijuana charge in the United States is easier to beat than it is anywhere in the world, and that is accounted for more by American justice's emphasis on individual liberty and human rights — manifest, if nowhere else, in its strict rules of evidence — than any liberal marijuana statutes it may engender. Only a failed intellectual with a grudge, a third-rate subversive or a fool would come back from a place like Marrakesh, Istanbul, Port-au-Prince or Rome, or even a place as allegedly enlightened as Amsterdam, and try to make a case for its drug laws. (A zoo like Capetown is so surreal as to defy intelligent consideration; compared to the South Africans, Indian elephants are an enlightened race. And if the Iron Curtain countries, such as Czechoslovakia, escape mention, it is because the issue here is marijuana, and, so far, as far as anyone has been able to gather anyway, the cops there have never heard of it.) Where the laws exist, there is heat, and in the whorehouses of civilized society, like Colombia and the Mediterranean poppy republics, the heat is worse, because high-level corruption thrives on the corruptibility of the thug element empowered to enforce those laws. The image of a young tourist walking the streets of Casablanca or Mazatlán with a joint in his hand is a myth perpetrated by college-campus travel agents. The only place you can get away with that is in New York.

VI A SWAN LEXICON

Zachary Swan's personal undercover lexicon evolved as an aid to telephone communication; it appeared in written transmissions where necessary, though instances of such contact were rare, and was almost never used in up-front conversation. It grew out of the need for secrecy. There are countless synonyms for the proper name of every illegal drug, and every drug dealer's vocabulary is replete with the argot of his trade, as well as that of the underworld in general and that of whatever subculture or counterculture to which he might pay his dues. The glossary which follows is no more than a very particular list of the words Swan used over the phone to protect himself.

1. *Chanel* — Cocaine; by way of Coco Chanel, the cosmetic and fashion designer. Cocoa (coco) and coca were interchangeable in Swan's vocabulary.

2. *Dust* — Cocaine.

3. *A Duster* — The same thing.

4. *Lady or Girl* — A specific reference to cocaine; as in "on the girl," or "the girl is fat."

5. *United Parcel Service/U.P.S.* — Amphetamines; ups.

6. *A Johnson* — A pound of marijuana; by way of L.B.J., or Lb./J — a pound of joints.

7. *A Pamphlet* — An ounce.

8. *A Book* — A pound.

9. *Two Books* — A kilo.

Heroin was always smack.

VII COLOMBIA AND BIG BUSINESS

Though it is in fact one of the more inhospitable nations in the world, Colombia, for reasons which are economically understandable, places a premium on tourism. Nor is the government's faith ill-placed — resorts are luxurious, beaches are beautiful, and money goes farther here than it does in any of the major Caribbean resorts. The government's official flag-carrier, Avianca Airlines, the oldest airline in the Western Hemisphere, has promoted Colombia increasingly around the world over the past ten years, spawning an attractive cash flow, and as a growth industry tourism in the country is today unsurpassed. If Avianca's efforts have been undermined in any way, it is by virtue of the fact that the people and the government of Colombia have failed in a corporate way to conceal what manifests itself as an outright hatred for foreigners; but be that as it may, one gets what one pays for, and one can expect that the tourists will continue to converge, like the penny-wise consumers they are, on this bargain basement of the world's black market.

Avianca, of course, sells Bogotá, the capital and cultural core of the nation, but no Yankee worth his tan can resist the copy lavished on the country's two principal seaside resorts, Cartagena and Santa Marta. (The offshore islands, Providencia and San Andrés, are slowly achieving similar stature.) Both share the same attributes — sun, sea and indoor plumbing. Each has a casino (American-operated) at its leading hotel, and both resorts are long-established enough to handle in a streamlined fashion what the Colombian government owes its future to — the acquisition of American dollars. And if these tourist dollars account for national stability to any great degree, it must be said that individual stability and political longevity, for any man near the top, rest with the even more streamlined flow of illegal dollars that float at every level.

When Zachary Swan, in the early 1970s, exploited Colombia's natural resources, he did so in the company of many other independent businessmen, most of them younger than he, from North America. Now, however, his and their enterprise has been co-opted by an organized criminal element with training in the French heroin markets and influence at the upper levels of government in South America. Officially condemning the drug traffic, South American governments, especially that of Colombia, encourage it unofficially. The reasons are simple and chiefly economic: cocaine is traded worldwide in American dollars; whether those dollars come into the country legally or illegally is of little importance when given the scope of the trading. And so the independent smuggler is a thing of the past in Colombia. The low-level dealer, the college student, and the housewife from the Texas panhandle, as well as the middle-level smuggler on the order of Zachary Swan, can expect to be thrown in jail and make the headlines in Bogotá while the Corsican heavy and the diplomatic attaché who pay their dues are encouraged for helping the balance of payments.

VIII AIRLINE SECURITY

In Colombia, metal detectors notwithstanding, the airline frisk has become a matter of policy. Because of stepped-up airline security checks and the opportunity they afford the Colombian government to conduct a contraband search of every passenger boarding any domestic or international flight, it is effectively impossible today for anyone to get anything like a large white rabbit aboard the cabin of an aircraft without its being at least seen and very likely examined.*

* Zachary Swan: "Oh, yeah?"

IX DAY OF JUDGMENT

In Peace's own words, he had chosen to "go without a jury, because of the technical, legal deficiencies in the prosecutor's case" and go "forward before a firm but fair judge who could be counted on to give the defendant the benefits of the Law as it applied to this case and to resist pressure from prosecutors and Federal Authorities who would attempt to ensure a jail term for [Swan] regardless of the insufficiency of the evidence. The pressure by Federal authorities," he said, "was impelled more by pique at the failure to induce [Swan] to give up his friends than by what they believed he had done."

Peace said, "The judge rejected the prosecutor's request, refusing to consider what amounted in his mind to innuendos and unconfirmed rumors about [Swan]. Reciting and recalling the minimum of legally proper evidence against [Swan], his clean record and the overwhelming testimonials paid to [Swan] by those who had attested to his good character, the judge stated that jail was not a proper sentence." Peace, citing the "character, integrity [and] ability" of the presiding judge in particular, suggesting that "this was one hell of a fair judge who rendered a fair and proper decision despite the obvious pressure upon him," extended his comments to apply to the Suffolk County Court in general.

AUTHOR'S NOTE

Work on this book began in the winter of 1974 in New York City and did not end until the finished manuscript was delivered in the spring of 1976. Much of the intervening time was spent in a process of distillation: the separation of truth from information designed either to cover it up or to glamorize it. The facts, as they emerged, were pieced together en route between New York City, a vegetable farm southwest of there, the Inner Sunset district of San Francisco, the outer reaches of Long Island and the capital and coastal cities of Colombia. The story that evolved owes its internal validity to the author's initial skepticism and to the ultimate faith placed in him by those whose story it is. Because they offered what they offered in confidence, it is impossible for the author to acknowledge many of them, or, for similar reasons, to thank the many others who helped him stay alive and out of jail when occasionally taking the assignment to the edge. There are also those whose efforts, if less hazardous, were no less essential to the book as it stands.

For their help in the preparation of the manuscript, or for the research material they provided, the author wishes to thank: *Richard Collier; James Pappas: Walter Peek; Michael Sabbag; Michael Sallette; Gwen M. Vallely; Joseph Vallely; Stephen Wheatley;* and *Oklahoma Nancy Wright.* For their invaluable personal and professional contributions: *James E. Bradof, M.D.* and *Mary A. Ryan, BSc, R.N.* For the faith they demonstrated awaiting the outcome of their professional gamble: *Dorothy L. Pittman* and *Tom Gervasi.* For the use of her diaries and hours of corroborative research: *Alyce Hans.* And for the countless hours of informative conversation, the many recorded hours of audio tape, the firsthand research and the primary-source material, painstakingly secured, without which the book could not have been written; who after everything else and at the risk of his own personal safety unlocked the back doors of Bogotá: *Charles Forsman.*

The author wishes to thank his parents and family for their encouragement and personal support, and to acknowledge the following for their contributions not to the book itself but to its successful writing: *Deborah Meltzer,* who, when the prevailing opinion was that it could never be done, said do it; who more than anyone, in the years of his literary apprenticeship, helped the author pay his dues and finally generated the energy that made writing the book possible. *Carol Doerrer Bradof,* who, lending grace to the simplest of endeavors, took it upon herself to inject humanity into the author's back-street journalism. *Robert L. Billingsley,* a good friend, a great American, ". . . the one fixed point in a changing age," who picked up the bar bill in the hard years. Always there when the going was rough, he never passed the dice when the hard money was on the line. And, with love, *Mary A. Ryan,* whose efforts in behalf of this book are innumerable and whose efforts in its author's behalf are better rewarded elsewhere than in its pages. The last word will always be hers.

New York, May 1976

AFTERWORD

It was a Smith & Wesson, the Model 10, with a six-inch barrel and walnut grips, and when it hit the floor and turned my way I could see that he was loading hollow-point.

I had wondered why he was wiggling his leg.

The revolver had begun snaking its way along the inseam of his trousers when he reached into his waistband to take out the dope. Making contact with the ceramic of the hotel-room tile, it had come to rest, a source of only mild embarrassment, in the space that separated his feet.

"What is a man to do?" or so his grin seemed to say.

I did not volunteer that in my part of the world, plainclothes policemen wore holsters.

If you factored out the Disneyland, it was a classic South American shakedown. Zachary Swan had been set up on the beach, busted there in possession of a ten-dollar bag of some of the best smoke in Cartagena. Federal heat, the cop wanted a hundred U.S. Swan brought him up to my room. Swan's room was where the bankroll was stashed, and the last thing he figured he wanted *this* guy to see was *that*.

Following through on an impromptu charade that presumed the existence of an absent associate, I excused myself, broke into Swan's room, uncovered the cash, grabbed the hundred, returned and had just made the payoff when the pistol hit the floor.

The dope was immediately returned. I think Ricardo, for that was his name, actually shook hands before retrieving the gun. It had been a pleasure, he said, doing business with us.

The pleasure, I assured him, was all his.

I was not out of my twenties when I walked into the lobby of New York's Algonquin Hotel to be introduced to the man who would one day be celebrated as Zachary Swan, an alias distinguished not by its novelty — it was by no means his first — but by the undeniable reality that it was provided by me. Not included in the details of that encounter as they are reported in this book is that, being invited to tell Zachary Swan's story, my initial response was no.

That I knew nothing about cocaine at the time, and very little about drugs, had negligible influence on my decision; in an abbreviated career as a newspaper reporter I had been trained to navigate the earth's darker precincts on a half-assed combination of dead reckoning and beginner's luck. My misgivings ran deeper than that. Luxuriating in an exaggerated sense of my own importance, which had convinced me that the subject was hardly worthy of my attention, I was that much more readily discouraged by the fact that, of the principals in the project, I was the only one breathing oxygen that day who was interested in telling the truth.

Humility inevitably prevailed, however, and eventually a deal was struck. Zachary Swan agreed to essay an honest account of the activities in question, I agreed to write the book, and for the next fifteen months we together went about establishing its singularly delirious architecture: I took notes, and he consistently and unashamedly lied about those activities.

And so did everybody else.

It was more fun than a barrel of monkeys.

Not until well over a year after I met him did Zachary Swan come across. Not until he and I went up against Ricardo together in that hotel room in Cartagena did Swan — who had met me coming into the Algonquin lobby and frisked me before introducing himself — trust me enough to start telling me the truth.

The story, as it was finally revealed, was a story very much of its time.

America has always suffered a fondness for outlaws. Her romances, however, are characteristically brief. Her flirtation ten years ago with Zachary Swan is typical of the inconstancy of her attachments. And as revealing as it may be about her changeable nature, it is an utterly naked reminder of the modern velocity of change.

Like ballplayers before the Black Sox scandal, the characters who animate *Snowblind* flourished at the end of an era. Theirs is an America the spiritual coordinates of which swiftly and irrevocably shifted.

While no one, with the exception, perhaps, of a few Colombian visionaries — call them the founders of the modern Medellín Cartel — could have foreseen the magnitude of the changes the cocaine business would undergo, it is pleasing to think that *Snowblind* went as far as to anticipate the direction those changes would take. The dramatic structure of the story, itself, parallels the course of the industry's metastasis.

Zachary Swan's was a naive man's journey through the labyrinth delineated by cocaine. Seduced by coke's prelusory glitter, he followed its promise to an epiphany as horrifying as the contemporary mythology could provoke. Few things have changed since Swan began looking for trouble, but those that have changed have changed oceanically. One of them is the money.

None of the rewards cocaine has to offer is as contaminating as the illegal cash. The darkness of Zachary Swan's darkest hours can be measured by cocaine's equivalence in currency. And Swan's experience, in a day which saw the *contrabandista* as the paradigm of the independent entrepreneur — a day as dead now as the Latin Mass — predates cocaine's equivalence in billions. It is money that begets the corruption and violence, and the corruption and violence the cocaine trade is famous for have waxed in direct proportion to its rapid advance as a growth industry.

No less conspicuous is the change in the product's availability. Before the market for cocaine expanded, before the merchandise became cheap, much of what had been written by Freud, the only clinical source-material extant in Swan's time, continued to hold true. There was no evidence to suggest that Swan's clientele was self-destructing by agency of the drug. Those who could afford cocaine were relatively few, and they were not doing it routinely by the quarter-ounce. If the implications of megadosage remained a secret to anyone, Pandora's box was opened in liberation of the alkaloid.

Snowblind's publication antedates the breathtaking manifestation of freebase. When the book appeared in North America, the dark chemistry that would be crack had yet to come ashore. The book on freebase cocaine and her evil stepsister is a book yet to be written; a genuine watershed in the literature of revenge, it will put *The Count of Monte Cristo* in the shade.

To seek further to update that material in *Snowblind* which was designed to be educational a decade ago is to overlook the fact that, if the book, indeed, were to be written today, inclusion of the material would be unnecessary in the first place. When *Snowblind* was written an overwhelming majority of the nation's lay population had never even heard of cocaine. At best, many confused it with the principal constituent of cough medicine. If you do not know now that the stateside kilo-price of cocaine, which was $30,000 in Zachary Swan's time, went to $52,000 in 1980 and hovers today at about $15,000 — if you do not know now that cocaine, alone, has inspired the creation of an entire sub-cabinet level law-enforcement bureaucracy — the restraint you bring to bear upon your enjoyment of television is not something I am prepared to tamper with.

Personally, I find it more fascinating, in reviewing the material, that in Zachary Swan's time fifty-dollar shoes were considered expensive.

When *Snowblind* was finally delivered, its subject matter was considered a handicap to its success by the very people who had commissioned it. Not without good reason. Nor were they entirely wrong. The early fan mail engendered by the book, that which did not originate on the nation's university campuses, can be divided into two general categories: that bearing the return addresses of the nation's penitentiaries, and that posted from Caribbean islands whose governments have no extradition treaties with ours.

Never in the history of American literature, I would

venture to guess, has a book been purchased by so many people who had never before purchased a book in their lives. Out there, hammered clearly, was a closet literati, and it was the power of that renegade following that brought the book to the attention of the public at large.

The greatest champion the book ever had, though, a man to whom it owes much of its early success and to whom its author will long be in debt, is a man in the American literary mainstream, Hunter S. Thompson, as fine a writer as the country has ever produced, who came out of nowhere, a total stranger, to give *Snowblind* all the respectability any book ever needed.

Having conjured Dr Thompson — a vision as comforting to entertain as that of Oedipus with his eyes bleeding as he emerges screaming from the palace at Thebes — I am drawn to the words of one of his spiritual forebears, Joseph Conrad, from the author's note to *The Arrow of Gold*:

"In plucking the fruit of memory one runs the risk of spoiling its bloom."

Which is pretty much where I came in — Ricardo, Zachary Swan and I, and the Smith & Wesson as it hit the floor of that Cartagena hotel room.

Zachary Swan, married and the father of three, lives today in suburban Pennsylvania. He pays his taxes and he is active in the PTA. That he votes Republican would come as no surprise to me.

Tempora mutantur et nos mutamur in illis.

Times change, it is said, and we change with them. Well, some of us do. When I called him on the occasion of *Snowblind*'s recent reissue, Swan, a pillar of the community, remarked:

"Who says crime doesn't pay?"

If, when he and I met, anything about Zachary Swan impressed me at all, it was his constitutional inability to take anything too seriously. Perhaps therein lies a lesson for all of us.

Reviewing the progress of the past half-century, we watch time rapidly contract. We no longer measure the velocity of change, we measure its acceleration. Precession of the equinoxes — an extravagant expression for the simple, sublunary truism that "torque never sleeps" — makes it a cinch that the Southern Cross, in twelve thousand years, will be visible in the northern hemisphere.

My guess is we can learn to live with it.

Zachary Swan, a man who was clearly ahead of his time, so profoundly so, in fact, that he is now an anachronism, stands in dramatic illustration of the changing nature of what is acceptable in this country.

Cocaine is merely the metaphor.

Wellfleet
Fall 1989

Zachary Swan in the late 1970s

INDEX

Abott Laboratories, 313, 323

Acid *see* LSD

Adrian the Mogul, 58–60, 152, 194, 234, 269–269, 305, 317
casino, 58–60

Agency for International Development (AID), 145

Airline security, 329

Alcohol, 79, 81, 89, 316

Alcoholics, 85

Algonquin Hotel (New York), 289–290

Alice's Hounds (dog-walking service), 133

Allergy, 93

Alles, Gordon, 321

Altiplano Indians, 75

Alvin Ailey Dance Company, 252

Amagansett (Long Island), 5, 146, 240, 270, 288, 298–299

Ambrose, Myles, 53, 64, 68–69, 144–145

American Medical Association, 322

Amino acids, 85

Amphetamines (speed), 82, 85, 86, 134, 313, 320 –325

Amytal (sodium amobarbital), 313

Anaphylactic shock, 93

Andes Coffee Corp. (New Jersey), 182, 183

Angel (the carpenter), employee of van Klee, 163–164
craftsman, 170–172, 208
epilogue, 308
Swan's aide in smuggling, 181, 186, 208, 209, 213, 214, 223, 245, 286

trips to New York, 300
Anthony, 232
  in Boat Move, 190–200,
    214–215
  dealer in Swan's network,
    124–125, 130, 142,
    175–177, 206–207,
    219, 224, 227, 265,
    298, 300
  epilogue, 307
  introduced to Swan,
    109–110
Aphrodisiac, 91
April (friend of Jane),
  101–102, 194, 280
Argentina, 87
Armando (the Man)
  cocaine dealer in
    Colombia, 159–160,
    165, 172, 173, 186,
    206–207, 212, 223,
    226, 277–280, 300
  epilogue, 308
  meets other smugglers,
    167, 168, 206
  meets Swan, 159
Arnar-Stone Laboratories,
  Inc., 316
Aspirin, 93, 134
Attorney-General (US), 143
Avianca Airlines, 70, 113,
  137, 141, 201, 245
  promotion of tourism,
    328
  used in Brown Gold
    Coffee Move, 182, 185,
    190

Bacata Hotel (Bogotá), 225
Baldwin, James, 252
Barbiturates, 313–315, 323
Barranquilla (Colombia)
  Swan in, 103–105,
    107–109, 112, 115,
    134, 137, 141, 149,
    213, 224, 287
  Brown Gold Move
    from, 182, 185–186
Benzedrine, 321, 322
Benzocaine, 83, 93
Bernier, Michel, 99, 136,
  156, 173, 308
  attempted extortion, 165
  description, 66–67
  first contact with Swan,
    65–70
  friend of Rudolpho, 164
  Post Office switch,
    226–227, 232
  Uta and, 136
Bill (New Orleans bookie),
  105, 106
Billy Bad Breaks, 54–55,
  59–60, 61, 267, 305
Bimini Island, 215–216
Biphetamine (Black Beauty),
  41, 323
Black cocainomania (Negro
  cocaine users), 71, 81,
  123–124, 252, 259
Black culture, 251–256
Black Dan, 167–168, 171,
  191–193, 247–250
  Colombian blonde and
    Cali Summer Games,
    249–250

epilogue, 310
Blackie, 148
  epilogue, 309
  friend in Colombia,
    108–109
  in jail, 114–116
  Swan meets, 100, 104
Boat Move, 173, 196–207,
  211–220, 223
Bogotá (Colombia), 131,
  134, 137, 139, 149, 150,
  265, 301
  description, 98, 154–155,
    328
  the Hawk in, 279
  Swan in, 150, 155–173,
    186, 188, 191, 201,
    204–213, 223–227,
    244–250, 260, 262–263,
    269, 277–288, 308
Bogotá Hilton, 155, 213,
  244, 277, 280, 284, 286
Bolivia, 74, 87–88, 280
Borax (sodium borate), 86,
  129, 130, 134, 141, 175,
  181, 240, 299
Brazil, 87, 97
Brown, Claude, 252
Brown Gold Move, 181,
  182–189, 193
Buccaneer (boat), 214–218
Burn test on cocaine, 111
Byck, Dr Robert, 77

Caffeine, 93
Cali (Colombia), Summer
  Games in, 192–193,
  249–250

Camillo (Rudolpho's cousin),
  269, 277
Campesinos (peasant
  farmers), 74, 86
Canadian Jack, 197, 280
  in Brown Gold Move,
    183, 186, 187–188,
    193
  cocaine smuggler,
    166–167, 171, 173,
    244
  epilogue, 309–310
  friendship with Swan,
    191–192
  meeting with the Hawk,
    279
  to Swan's rescue, 17
  used Duplicate Bag
    Switch, 194, 205–211
  warning to Swan, 277
Cartagena (Colombia)
  Boat Move, 198, 199,
    213–214, 217, 219
  Brown Gold Move, 182,
    183, 186–189, 190
  Swan in, 114, 140, 148,
    194, 225, 265, 269,
    287, 308, 310, 328
Cat Lady, 225
Central Intelligence Agency
  (CIA), 98, 145
Chanticleer Bar (New York),
  227, 234, 255–256
Chile, 87
Civil Aeronautics Board, 234
Clarke's (New York), 141
Cleaver, Eldridge, 251
Coca-Cola, 80

Cocaine
  Boat Move, 199,
    214–220, 223
  business operation,
    125–131, 160
  classed as narcotic, 82
  dealers, 86–89
  Duplicate Bag Switch,
    208–209
  effects of, 7–9, 76–78,
    83–84, 91–92
  explosion in US, 79–80
  folklore regarding,
    180–181
  gimmick experiments, 224
  government moves
    against, 90–92
  history and description,
    74–89
  made illegal, 81–82
  methods of taking, 84–85
  most popular illegal drug,
    74, 319
  New York State law
    against, 146
  non-habit-forming drug,
    91
  now big business, 329
  perishability of, 127
  pharmaceutical uses, 180
  price and value, 72–74,
    87–88, 175–177,
    223–224, 299–300
  processing, 87, 130, 172,
    180–181, 245, 269
  rock, 248–250, 256–259,
    265
  smuggling operations,
    126–130, 146–149,
    191–192, 208–209
  Swan's initial move with,
    66, 68–71
  Swan's lexicon, 326–7
  synthetics, 83
  trade from South America,
    86–89
  use in patent medicines,
    79–80
  used in anaesthesia, 77,
    83
  users, 73–74
  water and burn purity
    tests, 110–111, 134
  White Rabbit Move,
    245–248, 264
Cocales, 87
Coffee Move, 181, 182–189,
  193
Colombia
  Boat Move, 196–207, 211
    –220, 223
  Brown Gold Coffee Move,
    181, 182–189
  cocaine from, 3–4, 65, 69,
    72, 87, 97, 124, 134,
    223
  description of, 97–98,
    103–104
  jails in, 148
  later trips by Swan,
    137–141, 148–151,
    155–173, 181,
    223–224, 225, 277,
    292
  Summer Games in Cali,
    192–193, 249–250

Swan's first trip to,
97–116, 149
Swan's third trip to, 120
tourism and big business,
327–8
Coltrane, John, 251
Comprehensive Drug Abuse
Prevention and Control
Act, 142
Continental Hotel (Bogotá),
156, 162, 165 –166, 169,
213
Controlled Substances, 91,
142–143, 146
Cooper Laboratories, 316
Coquero, 75
Corning, J. Leonard, 79
Counterfeit money, 164
Cox, Jimmie, 254
Crawford, Peter, 270 –272
Crazy Leslie, 226, 233–240,
242, 260, 264, 293, 301,
306, 307
Credit cards, stolen, 48, 122,
233, 316–319, 1020
Crowley, Jim, 23
Customs, Bureau of (US),
73, 143–144
Customs checks, 3, 55, 62,
174, 189–190, 193, 205,
209, 210, 214–218, 224,
244, 247, 277, 288, 299
Czechoslovakia, 326

Daniels, Trude, 239–240,
241–248, 264, 280, 307
Darvon, 314
Davis, 151

in Brown Gold Move,
183, 189
epilogue, 306
old friend of Swan, 114
receives mail drops, 114,
174, 179, 225
Davis, Angela, 251
Davis, Miles, 123, 126
Davis, Reverend Gary, 92
Day, René (Rainy), 197, 310
in Boat Move, 173, 207,
212 –218
buys cocaine, 110, 111,
160
friendship with Swan,
105–109, 114,
115–116, 134,
137–140, 148,
155–157, 168
killed, 220, 261
De Jussieu, A. L., 76
De Santis, Angela, 122, 132,
133, 227, 240, 306
Debbie (Canadian law
student), 106–107, 114,
115, 148
Del Prado Hotel
(Barranquilla), 107–109
Desbutal, 323
Desoxyn, 323
Dewey, Governor Thomas,
28
Dexamyl, 323
Dexedrine, 321, 322
Dextrose, 85, 129
Diet pills, 324
Dietrische, Uta, 230–231,
280, 287

with Bernier, 65, 66–70, 136, 165
description, 67, 135
epilogue, 308
with Pirata, 226
with Ramón Greco, 140, 197
trip to Colombia with Swan, 136–140
Downs, 72, 293, 313–316
Drake, Sir Francis, 140
Drug companies, 314, 324
Drug Enforcement Administration (DEA), 90, 143–145
Drugs, weights and measures, 117–119, 123–124, 127, 129
legislation against misuse, 82–83, 89–91, 142–143, 326, 330
Duplicate Bag Switch, 208–211

East Hampton (Long Island), 4, 6, 131
Ecuador, 87, 97, 162
Edeleano, L., 321
Einhorn, Albert, 79
El Caribe Hotel (Cartagena), 186–188, 196
El Commandante No Barco, 138–140
El Medico (Cartagena doctor), 148
Elaine (friend of Bill), 105, 106
Eldorado International

Airport (Bogotá), 154, 277
Ellery, 54, 70, 119–120, 123, 240, 266–267
Alice meets, 236
buys drugs from Swan, 130, 142, 224
epilogue, 307
gives South American connection to Swan, 70
information on Essex House history, 229
introduces Swan to Anthony, 110, 124
New York drug dealer, 32–40, 119–120, 178
Emerald smuggling, 157
Emilio (Barranquilla drug seller), 109, 110–111, 134
Ephedrine, 321
Equity Funding Corporation, 30
Erlenmeyer, Emil, 78–79
Erythroxylon coca, 74, 76
Essex House (New York), 227–229, 233, 261
Evelyn (Rudolpho's wife), 164, 170, 269

Fairbanks, Douglas, 284
Federal Bureau of Narcotics and Dangerous Drugs (BNDD), 143–144
Federal Bureau of Narcotics (FBN), 143
Fernando (Blackie's friend), 104, 106, 148
Film tour, 138–140, 148

Fireplace logs, cocaine in, 177–178
Fitzgerald, F. Scott, 283–284
Flack, Roberta, 159, 166, 278
Fleischl-Marxow, Ernst von, 78
Folklore of cocaine, 180–181
Frank (New York heavy), 231
Frazier, Walt, 253
Freddy (Brooklyn gambler), 58, 234, 306
Freud, Sigmund, 77–79, 84

Gabrielle (Lufthansa clerk), 136–137
Gaedcke (German scientist), 76
Gelusil, 138
General Federal Conspiracy Laws (US), 146
Geoffrey, 302, 310
George (credit card dealer), 318
Getty, George, 30
Giles, Lillian, 13, 54–55, 240, 295
  carrier for Swan, 133, 161, 298
  epilogue, 306
  Kendricks's girl friend, 4, 54–55, 71, 121, 274, 299
  with Swan in Bogotá, 275–288
The Grateful Dead, 219, 314

Greco, Ramón, 140, 197, 225
Gun smuggling, 219

Hall (used cocaine in dentistry), 79
Hallucinations, 78
Halsted, William, 79
Harlem, 234
  cocaine and street life, 72, 251–256
  Dr W gets rock from Swan, 256–259
Harrison Narcotic Act (1914), 82
Haskell, Alice, 122, 152, 227, 306
  helps in drug deals, 112, 186
  marriage to Swan, 301, 310
  Swan's girl friend, 4, 64–66, 69, 71, 114, 132–133, 182, 233, 235–36, 265–266, 280, 281–303
  threatened by Crazy Leslie, 237–238, 261, 307
Hay Fever Foundation, 80
Heatherton, Joey, 152
Hefner, Hugh, 25
Hemp, 72
Hendrix, Jimi, 314
Heroin, 93, 121, 129, 209, 241, 293, 299, 329
  legislation against, 82, 146

Mexican Brown, 319
in New York City, 319
Holly, 25, 29, 31
Homer (friend of Pirata), 59
Hydrochloric acid, 87

Ike (Brooklyn gambler), 58,
234, 306
Internal Revenue Service,
292
International attitudes and
laws, 326
Iona Prep, 179
Ischemia, 92
Isis, 247

Jaffee, Dr Jerome H., 144
Jago (Hawk's man), 207,
280–281, 286, 309
Jane (friend of April),
101–102, 194
Jazz music, 252
Jimmy the boat captain,
200–207, 211 –220, 309
Joey (friend of Pirata), 231
Jonny Kay islet, 138
José (Blackie's friend in
Colombia), 105, 108–109,
134
Justice Department (US),
143, 292

Kendricks, Charles, 4,
13–15, 64, 240, 281, 288
arrested, 53–57, 110
epilogue, 299, 306
gets out of drug business,
133, 273–274

involved in smuggling
deals with Swan, 62,
71, 120–121, 131, 179,
242–247, 265, 273–274
trip to Mexico, 40–57
Key Motel (Florida),
218–220
Kissinger, Henry, 145
Klee, Vincent van, 137,
155–159, 160–165, 171,
173, 207, 277–278
epilogue, 308
Vincent Dior skin cream,
277–278
volcano story, 281–282
Koch, Christopher, 81
Köller, Carl, 79
Krogh, Egil, 145

Lactose (milk sugar), 85,
129
Lallo (Colombia street
hustler), 158, 168
Legislation, anti-drug, 82–83,
90–91, 142–149, 326,
330
Leo XIII, Pope, 75
Leticia (Colombia), mobile
processing lab in, 269
Librium, 313
Lidocaine, 84
Lilly (drug company), 313
Lincoln Square Motel (New
York), 175
Liver damage, 93
Livingston, Roger (Seymour),
15, 121–122, 131, 142,
227, 240, 300–306

'The Lothario,' 151–153, 173, 175–176, 179–180, 225, 307
LSD (lysergic acid diethylamide), 72, 85, 313
Lufthansa Airlines, 136
Luís (Bogotá connection), 207, 226, 277, 280

Mad Walter, 101
Mail Moves (drops), 150, 170–179, 223–227, 244–245
  at Davis's, 114, 174, 179, 225
Mannite (Italian laxative), 86, 129, 191
Mantle, Mickey, 28–29
Marcuse, Herbert, 251
Marguerita bar (Bogotá), 207, 211 –212
Mariani, Angelo, 75
Marijuana, 4, 85, 89, 105, 236, 299, 301
  abroad, 325–326
  from Colombia, 98, 160, 202, 207, 249, 325–326
  Colombian blonde, 249
  compared to cocaine, 69, 72, 119
  Ellery as dealer, 32–40
  Swan smuggles from Mexico, 40–57, 59–62, 121
Matheson Hammock, 214–215, 217
Maxwell's Plum (New York), 230, 234

McDonald's (Riverhead), 242
Mean Mickey, 61, 233–234, 306, 319
Merck Sharp & Dohme, 87
Mescaline, 72, 105
Methaqualone, 4
Methedrine (methamphetamine hydrochloride), 320, 323
Methyl di-amphetamine (MDA), 324
Metric system, 117–119
Mexican Brown, 319
Mexico, 301, 309
  Pirata in jail in, 292, 305
  smuggling from, 40–57, 59–62, 121, 167
Mike (New York heavy), 231
Mike (the bartender), 105, 106, 108
Miltown (meprobamate), 313
Money laundering, 125
Morgan, Harry, 196–200, 214–218, 309
Morphine addiction, 78, 145
Muestras, 207
Mules (carriers), 132, 167, 168, 205, 263
Musicians and cocaine, 82
Mydriasis, 79

Narcolepsy, 322
Narcotic, cocaine classified as, 82
Narcotic Drugs Import and Export Act (1922), 82

Nembutal (sodium pentobarbital), 313
Neurosis (neurasthenia), 78
New York State anti-drug laws, 83, 146
New York Times, 64, 68, 81, 182
Nice Mickey, 240, 266–267
  cocaine dealer, 130–131, 142
  epilogue, 306
  gambler, 122
  name, 234
  Pirata's friend, 110–123, 122–123
  and theft from Swan, 228–229
Niemann, Albert, 76–77
Nina (the waitress), 200, 218–219, 280
Nixon, Richard M., 53, 143–146, 189, 313, 314
Noel, Arnold (Mr Christmas), 137
Norell, Norman, 25
Norepinephrine (noradrenalin), 83
Novocain, 83–84

Office of Drug Abuse Law Enforcement (ODALE), 144
Optimil, 316
Organic psychosis, 91
Oriole Hotel (Bogotá), 166, 167, 191, 192, 205, 243, 247, 279
Owens, Jesse, 251

Pachita (Blackie's friend), 280
Paraguay, 87
Paranoia, 91
Parest, 316
Parke-Davis (drug company), 316
Parker, Charlie, 251
Patent medicines, 80
Paul (Texan in Santa Marta), 100
Paulsen, Detective Sgt., 296–297
Peace, Ernie, 17–19, 300–303, 330
Peebles, Melvin van, 252
Pemble's (New York), 231
Pepe (of Maxwell's Plum), 230, 234
Peru, 74, 86–88, 97–99
Pharmaceutical cocaine, 180
Physician's Desk Reference, 315, 324
Pill-popping, 89
Pink Floyd, 102
Pirata, Vinnie, 110, 120, 123, 267, 305, 319
  drug deals from Acapulco, 49, 52, 55, 57, 59–62
  in jail in Mexico, 292, 305
  lost package, 228, 232, 235
  Swan meets, 40
  theft from Swan, 228–232
Pirata, Vinnie Uta and, 225–226
President's Cabinet

Committee for International Narcotics Control (CCINC), 145
Procaine, 79, 83, 86, 93, 148
Pure Food and Drug Act (1906), 80

Quāālude (methaqualone), 6–7, 313–316
Quinine, 85

Rabbit, cocaine in, 245–248, 250, 264
Ramirez, Juan Carlos, 166, 173, 205, 243, 245, 279, 286, 310
Ramirez, Mrs (the Hawk), 277–281, 309
Ramos, Jorge Enrique, 114
Raoul (Armando's lieutenant), 168–170, 173, 178–179, 309
Red Coach Grill, 242
Ricardo (Emilio's partner), 110–111, 134, 137
Riordan, Mike, 26–31, 135–136, 234
Roche Laboratories, 313
Rolling pins, cocaine in, 3, 170–171, 174–177, 208, 209, 224, 299
Roosevelt Raceway, 59
Rorer, William H., Inc., 315
Roy (Canadian Jack's lieutenant), 310
Rubia, 248–250, 265
Rudolpho, 206, 277

in cocaine deals, 170–173, 179, 181, 186, 192, 209, 213, 214, 223, 226, 265, 286
epilogue, 308
friend of van Klee, 164–165

San André's (Colombia), 137–139
San Francisco Hotel (Bogotá), 286
Sandy, 15
Santa Marta (Colombia), 97–100, 106, 108, 134, 137, 148, 194, 328
Brown Gold Move, 181, 182–189, 193
Schonbrunn, S. A. & Co., Inc., 183, 185
Sea Gull Billy, 196–197, 309
Seconal (sodium secobarbital), 313
Septal perforation, 92
Slick, Grace, 320
Smith Kline & French, 321, 322
Solarcaine, 92
Somnafac, 316
Sopors, 316
South Africa, 326
South America, 57, 68, 70
See also names of countries
cocaine from, 74, 87
international narcotics control, 145
Southampton (Long Island), 242

Souvenirs, cocaine in, 3,
   170–179
Special Action Office for
   Drug Abuse Prevention,
   144
Speed (amphetamines), 72,
   82, 85, 86, 134, 320 –325
Spoons, 123–124, 191
St Regis Hotel (New York),
   129, 142, 227, 298
State anti-drug laws, 82,
   146
State Department (US), 145
Statues, cocaine in, 179,
   208, 211, 224, 288
Strasenburgh, 323
Suicide, drugs and, 91, 314,
   320
Susan (with Canadian Jack),
   207–211
Swan, Zachary
   arrest, 6, 13–15, 146,
      294–298
   attitude towards women,
      132–133, 281
   Boat Move, 196–207, 211
      –220, 223
   Brown Gold Coffee Move,
      181, 182–189
   cocaine move with
      Bernier's help, 65–71
   cocaine stolen from,
      228–232
   conversation with writer,
      291–298
   description and habits, 18,
      62–64, 128–129
   drug dealing as a business,

   125–131, 160,
      160–172, 328
   early life, 21–24
   early marriages, 25–26
   education in Coral Gables,
      23–24
   first trip to Colombia for
      cocaine, 97–116
   gambling, 26–30, 35,
      58–60
   getting started with drugs,
      32–40
   gimmick experiments, 224
   health, 293, 301
   hooked on speed, 25
   in jail, 16–7
   later trips to Colombia,
      137–141, 148–151,
      155–173, 181,
      223–224, 265
   leaned on by Crazy Leslie,
      233–240
   lexicon, 326–7
   in Marine Corps, 24
   marriage and epilogue,
      301, 310–311
   move to Long Island, 240,
      262, 293
   named 'the Silver Fox', 193
   New York cocaine dealer,
      117–134, 142,
      175–181, 224,
      227–228, 241–244,
      264–269, 273, 298–301
   New York connections,
      119–125, 130–131
   packaging business, 31,
      278

relations with family,
21–25, 214
smuggles marijuana from
Mexico, 40–62
on smuggling, 19–20
trial, 302–303, 330
with Uta, 135–140
Syphilis, 92

Tahiti Estates (Santa Marta),
100, 115
Take-off man, 127
Tamaca Hotel (Santa Marta),
100
Tequendama Hotel (Bogotá),
155–156, 159, 165, 213,
245, 277, 280, 284, 286
Terry (waitress friend of
Mike), 105, 106, 108
Tito (Ellery's connection in
Colombia), 70, 112
Tobacco, 89
Travelers' checks, 120,
192–193, 267, 316–319
Treasury Department (US),
119, 192–193, 268,
316–319
Tuazole, 323
Turkey, 319

United States Government,
legislation and anti-smug-
gling actions, 82, 90–91,
142–149, 292, 298–300,
319, 326, 330
Ups see Speed (ampheta-
mines)

Vagelatos, Mr and Mrs,
184–185, 188 –190, 194
Valium, 293, 313
Venezuela, 97
Victor's Café (New York),
32, 178
Village Voice, 60–61, 275
Vincent Dior (cosmetic
cream), 277–278
Volstead Act (1920), 81

Wallace (drug company), 316
Water test on cocaine,
110–111
Weil, Andrew T., 75
Wellfleet, Moses (Dr W),
133, 234
drug dealer, 123–124,
131, 181, 227,
300–301
epilogue, 306
gets rock from Swan,
256–259, 265
White Rabbit Move,
245–248, 250, 264
Williams, Edward H., 81
Williams, Esther, 30
Women, 132–133
Wonder Stevie, 252
Wood, use in cocaine smuggling, 3–4, 165, 170–172,
193, 223–224, 286

Yvonne, 25

Zappa, Frank, 320, 325
Ziegler, Ronald, 314

"[*Smokescreen*] will undoubte[...] adrenaline pumping." *The Tim[...]*

"Mr Sabbag is a first-rate writ[...] piece of reporting." *New York[...]*

"*Smokescreen* looks set to become a classic of the genre. A pacy and stylishly written account of the exploits of charismatic American pot smuggler, Allen Long, this is several cuts about the run-of-the-mill, cut-and-paste true crime . . . it reads like a brilliantly conceived thriller." *Bookseller*

"It's blistering reportage with a matchless line-up of renegades. The narrative zips along. Sabbag writes like one of his breathless fugitives, hungry for the next hit and high." *Observer*

"This guy Sabbag is a whip-song writer." *Hunter S. Thompson*

"There is much drinking and snorting. More deals are done and everyone gets filthy rich." *Daily Mail*

"One can't deny that *Smokescreen* is a funny, stylish, entertaining book, and that the traffickers, even at their most addled and odious, prove strangely congenial company."
Financial Times

"Long and his buddies got high any time, any place. Except when their DC-3 failed to get high enough to clear the coconut palms at the end of the highway." *GQ Magazine*

"Told with Chandler-esque verve, *Smokescreen* is part-thriller, part-nostalgia trip, and, surprisingly, part-morality tale by its end." *Sunday Herald*

"Sabbag has a wonderful ear for dialogue and Long has some wonderfully outlandish yarns to spin . . . extremely entertaining."
Observer

"A truly remarkable tale." *Publishing News*

"Sabbag turns the true story of a dope-smuggling operation in the 1970s into a full-blown adventure story." *Metro*

"It reads more like a pacy thriller than a biography. And that may prove to be to *Smokescreen's* advantage, drawing in the more general reader than just those in awe of cannabis culture."
Daily Express

"[This] nail-biting foray into the seedy Columbian underworld, is shocking, irreverent and impossible to put down." *Scotsman*

"Sabbag's ability to conjure up the characters and stories behind the events make this a superb and enthralling read . . . Stories full of larger-than-life characters and equally larger-than-life plots, make this a book you'll definitely want to read."
What's On in London

"A good story brilliantly told." *Irish Independent*

"Whatever you think about the ethics of Mr Long's exploits, there's no doubt that, thanks to Mr Sabbag, his is a wild and wooly adventure story – and the sort of book you gobble up in a night." *Sunday Tribune* (USA)

"Sabbag keeps the narrative racing along in an account which would put most thrillers to shame. A celebration of the dangers, delights, and disasters of dope dealing, this is a must, even for anyone who's never appreciated the demon weed." *BBM*

"This high-octane thriller looks set to become a classic."
Vivid Magazine

"One for all you dopers out there. If you're a fan of Howards Marks' *Mr Nice* you'll snap up *Smokescreen* . . . a tremendous story." *Straight No Chaser*

"Sabbag sure has an ear for good storytelling and there are elements of a good thriller tossed in here. This isn't your typical true-crime book." *Tyrone Times*

SMOKESCREEN

Also by Robert Sabbag

Snowblind
Too Tough to Die

SMOKESCREEN

a true adventure

ROBERT
SABBAG

introduced by Robert Sabbag

CANONGATE

Edinburgh · New York · Melbourne

First published in the United States of America
under the title *Loaded*
in 2002 by Little, Brown and Company

Published in 2002 and 2003 by Canongate Books Ltd,
14 High Street, Edinburgh EH1 1TE

This edition first published in 2007

1

British Library Cataloguing-in-Publication Data
A catalogue record for this book is available
on request from the British Library

978 1 84195 820 0 (13-digit ISBN)
1 84195 820 4 (10-digit ISBN)

Typeset in Sabon by Palimpsest Book Production Limited,
Grangemouth, Stirlingshire

Printed and bound in Great Britain by Clays Ltd, St Ives plc

www.canongate.net.

To the memory of my father

CONTENTS

GLAMOUR PROFESSION

1. EMERALD COAST   3

2. EL NIÑO PERDIDO   23

3. AZTEC TWO-STEP   41

4. CADILLAC MOON   71

5. GIVE A MAN ENOUGH
   ROPE AND HE'LL SMOKE IT   87

6. SMOKE OF A DISTANT FIRE   110

ELDORADO

7. RED, WHITE AND BLOND   135

8. PICKUP AT PERICO   167

9. AUTOMATIC PILOT   192

10. SMOKE AND MIRRORS   214

11. FIRE IS THE TEST OF GOLD   236

THE LORDS AND
THE NEW CREATURES

12. DISPOSABLE BIRDS   253

13. SMOKE ON THE WATER   281

14. VIOLETS FOR YOUR FURS   302

15. CEILING ZERO   319

16. MUCH HAVE I TRAVELED
IN THE REALMS OF GOLD   348

     EPILOGUE   379

     ACKNOWLEDGMENTS   392

     INDEX   399

N

Caribbean Sea

Punta Gallinas

Riohacha
Camarones
Perico
Río Palomino
Santa Marta

Guajira

Barranquilla

SIERRA NEVADA
Villanueva

Maracaibo

Cartagena

SABANA RUBIA
Valledupar

SIERRA DE PERIJA

Lake Maracaibo

VENEZUELA

PANAMA

Río Magdalena

Map by Jeffrey L. Ward

Medellín

Pacific Ocean

COLOMBIA

Bogotá ★

Buenaventura

Cali

0 Miles   100   200
0 Kilometers   200

© 2001 Little, Brown & Company

Richmond

UNITED STATES
OF AMERICA

Atlantic Ocean

Miami

Caribbean Sea

Area of detail

Pacific Ocean

★ Caracas

VENEZUELA

★ Bogotá
COLOMBIA

INTRODUCTION

I met Allen Long in New York in the late spring of 1978. Maybe it was the early summer. It was the night I saw *Dog Soldiers*. I had been invited to a press screening of the movie — based on the novel by Robert Stone, and released under the title "Who'll Stop the Rain" — by a magazine editor who knew me to be a great admirer of Stone's. It was a year and a half since the publication of my first book, *Snowblind*, of which Hunter Thompson, another writer I greatly admired, had written the following:

> The only other two books I've read in the past five years (or maybe ten) that can even breathe at this altitude are *Dog Soldiers* and *Fear And Loathing in Las Vegas*.

When that was written — by the author of *Fear and Loathing in Las Vegas* — I had met neither Stone nor Thompson, but had read everything each had ever published. I was twenty-nine years old. Try to imagine being me at that moment.

I do all the time.

And now a guy named Allen Long, who introduced himself over the phone as a movie producer, wanted me to drop by.

Mr Long, as I addressed him until I laid eyes on him, lived on the Upper East Side of Manhattan. His apartment, situated high above Second Avenue, exposed on the south and west by walls of tinted glass, was aromatic of perfect taste and money. Spacious, irredeemably contemporary, it was sparsely but expensively furnished and hung with one or two large works of art. Its most striking personal touch was an original one, a 1972 Triumph Bonneville parked on the parquet in the southeast corner of the living room — a small patch of cloth had been placed below the motorcycle's crankcase to catch the oil it dripped.

Long did have a financial interest in at least one movie at the time, but he was actually working in the music business, employed by CBS Records. Within half an hour of our shaking hands, I learned that he had recently retired from the marijuana business. (Or so he thought. The marijuana business was still paying him more than the music business and the hours were a lot better, so his days in the music business were numbered.) His nest egg at the time amounted to about $8 million, all of it in cash, most of it in hundreds, a briefcase full of which he wanted to give me for the film rights to *Snowblind*.

What would Jesus do?

The film rights to *Snowblind* had already been sold. I was building a house with the money. Selling them again didn't seem the Christian thing. And was probably a felony.

But nice meeting you all the same.

With Allen Long, there was always a Plan B. How, he wanted to know, would I like to write a book about *him*? It took me more time than maybe it should have to realize that this was probably Plan A. In any case, my answer was immediate.

"I've already written that book."

As much as Long's adventures might differ from those recounted in *Snowblind*, I saw no percentage in writing another book about drug smuggling out of Colombia.

And then twenty years went by. It was now the spring of 1998. Allen Long and I were on the phone, I sitting on the deck of that house I had built, Long calling from Charlottesville,

Virginia, where he had recently reunited with his wife and children after being released from prison.

He and I had remained in touch over the years. Indeed, we had been friends. On one occasion I had traveled with him to Colombia, entertaining the possibility of writing an original screenplay based on his adventures. Soon thereafter, however, he was back smuggling pot, eventually to become a federal fugitive, and like many of his acquaintances, I would then hear from him only rarely, usually in the middle of the night, over the phone from a hotel room that might be anywhere in the Western Hemisphere.

Taking that call from Virginia — it could have been exactly twenty years from the night of our initial meeting — I was polite with Long, but distracted, having just hung up the phone after talking to my literary agent. She was growing impatient with me. She had been pushing me to come up with a nonfiction project, and I had yet to find a story worthy of my time.

It took a few minutes, but only a few . . .

I was back on the phone to Long.

"Hey, you still interested in doing that book . . . ?"

Three years later — an adventure in itself — the legal department of my New York publisher received the final draft of the story that follows.

In the twenty years between my first hearing the story and my retelling it, *Smokescreen* became a very different book. Any danger that it might recapitulate *Snowblind* had vanished with time and shifting circumstance. I had never thought of either as a drug book, anyway. Each, as I approached it, was simply a good yarn. And a good yarn is hard to find. Twenty-five years passed, almost to the day, between publication of the two stories — I wrote other books over that time — and I do not dismiss the possibility that after the passage of another twenty-five, I might again take an outlaw up on the offer to tell his tale.

While you're waiting, give this one a try.

GLAMOUR
PROFESSION

EMERALD COAST

Allen Long descended from a short line of American aviators. He in effect was the first. One morning off the coast of South America, as his DC-3, with the break of dawn, violated Colombian airspace, there rose before him, as palpable as the peaks of the Sierra Nevada hovering on the horizon, the probability that he might be the last.

"Red to white, red to white, I have bad news for you, sir."

Bad news in Allen Long's business, of which aviation was only a part, was typically very bad news, and transmitted on an air-to-air frequency from a clandestine Colombian landing strip, the news had to be that much worse.

"Sir, I am sorry, but you cannot land," squawked the voice over the cockpit radio. "You must go back, you cannot land. Repeat, you must go back."

Long and his crew, who had been airborne for fifteen hours, stared stupefied at the source of this advisory, the three of them gazing at the instrument panel as if the radio itself were crazy.

Long's transmission was blunt. He keyed the microphone, and said: "We can't go back."

Nor could they put the aircraft down in nearby Barranquilla or over the border in Venezuela. To say that the plane was not "cleared" for that was an understatement at best, but Long said it anyway, and short of announcing the choices they faced, that was about all he said.

"We have to land and take on fuel, or we're going to crash this airplane."

As it happened, they did both.

The Sierra Nevada de Santa Marta rise out of the Caribbean in a sheer, almost vertical ascent to an altitude of 20,000 feet, the highest coastal range in the world, its perennial snowcaps dominating the tropical beaches of Colombia's oldest city. From the fertile forests of Santa Marta the mountains run parallel to the shoreline and reach one hundred miles to the east. Here their north face terminates on a hot, semiarid peninsula, a flatland of hardscrabble and stunted vegetation that stretches to the northernmost point of the continent.

This inhospitable region into which the mountains decline, settled by Indians who survived the Spanish conquest and home to their descendants today, subsists outside the mainstream of Colombian life, sparsely populated, underdeveloped, historically bereaved of economic opportunity, and largely neglected by the federal government. Here in the northeastern desert is a Colombia untouched by the magical realism evoked by its finest literature, unenriched by the supernatural, a Colombia drained of its mystery, where the metaphysical happens only at night.

These are the Colombian badlands. This is the land

beyond the Río Palomino. Independent, if not autonomous, unregulated, virtually lawless . . .

This is the Guajira.

This is where Allen Long conducted business in Colombia, trading on what the region's inhabitants extol as its principal natural resource: that "the Guajira is ruled by the gun."

In the fall of 1976, that morning as his cargo plane came within view of the mountains, Allen Long's business was booming. Up there, high in the foothills, waiting, lay the treasure of the Sierra Nevada. Up there, unburied, proliferating, was the Santa Marta Gold of legend. The finest marijuana in the world. And from there to the docks and the Mayday strips that were strung out along the Guajira, mule trains moved, by day, by night, in seemingly endless procession, under the weight of the find.

The gold rush was underway. Back home, 30 million American heads luxuriated in notions of getting twisted on nothing less than prime Colombian, and for almost a year now Long and his partners had been delivering it to them by the ton.

Among those partners were the pilots of the DC-3, Frank Hatfield and Will McBride. Allen Long American Flyer was really just a state of mind, his rating as an aviator being — well, call it unofficial. As architect of the criminal conspiracy and operational leader of the enterprise, Long was more than just along for the ride, but even in a mind as rich with fantasy as his, there abided no doubt that his taking control of the aircraft unsupervised was the functional equivalent of suicide.

McBride, an erstwhile musician, had known Long for about five years, and like Long, whose own pursuit of a career in the record industry was presently being ignored, he had been operating on the fringes of the marijuana

business for much of that time. It was not in support of his musical ambitions that McBride had decided to take flying lessons. McBride was co-pilot of the DC-3. It was Hatfield who ran the air show, and it was Hatfield, the professional, to whom the other two smugglers looked when the radio message came in.

They were flying with the surf, following the shore break, having descended to about 2,000 feet on making landfall at Punta Gallinas. Banking southwest from there and running along the coast at a speed of 110 knots, they had begun picking up omens one by one as day was breaking behind them. Everything was different this time. The air was not crisp, but humid and heavy, the sunlight murky not bright. The underbrush below them was green, not brown. Clouds obscured the mountains. And just northeast of Riohacha, as the aircraft descended to a thousand feet, raindrops hit the windshield.

The precipitation merely suggested itself, a grace note, nothing more. Still, it was something new.

Breaking clear of it almost instantly, the smugglers started searching for smoke. A billowing column of thick, black smoke would bring them in to the runway. Spiraling from the flames of a burning tire, the plume could be seen on a normal flight to rise 200 feet in the air. Long, this time, was the first to spot it, and this time it hit the ceiling at fifty. At Camarones, they made radio contact. Only then did the omens add up.

"Sir, it has been raining here."

It had rained half the night. Torrentially. The downpour had ended only an hour before. Effectively, there *was* no runway.

The low drone of the radial engines, resonating through the cockpit, was the only sound for an instant. The ever-present

hypnotic hum, the theme song of the operation, rising now on their collective silence, gave weight to the realization that they had seriously pushed the season.

The color drained from Long's face. He turned to Hatfield, the man in whose hands their fortunes rested — their lives and their fortunes literally, their sacred honor only if you stretched it — for something in the way of instructions. Hatfield, five years older than his partners, at thirty-three the oldest of three would-be millionaires whose lives were now up for grabs, differed from them most significantly in that he was not a smuggler by vocation. Marijuana, as far as he was concerned, was just a really good reason to fly. A professional pilot, Hatfield had been recruited the year before, and in a matter of months he had demonstrated an aptitude for crime that most pilots could only aspire to. But Hatfield remained true to his roots. His instructions were in keeping with conventions established by aviators throughout history, and characteristically brief.

He said: "Buckle up and hang on."

A flyover of the airstrip, under favorable landing conditions, revealed what could be called a runway only in the most optimistic interpretation of the term. Unidentifiable as such from the air, it was clearly discernible as a landing strip from only one point of reference. To see it you had to walk it, and trace for yourself the unmistakable tread marks of the various landing gear that had touched down there. The airstrip was invisible by design. Its engineering, or lack thereof, owed less to limitations of the local technology than to the threat of observation by government aircraft, which flew the coast routinely on drug-interdiction runs.

The strip began a couple of yards from the beach, which sloped up from the Caribbean to a rise of three or four feet. It extended eighteen hundred feet into the bush, a stretch

of uneven ground, partially overgrown, the grass knee-deep in places. And today it was more than invisible. Today it was nonexistent, a third of a mile of fine, red clay that overnight had turned to mud. The field stood abandoned now, and crossing the strip, coursing the hardpan like rushing creeks, rivulets of rainwater ran so deep you could fish them.

Long's experience was limited, but what lay below him did not even approximate conditions as he had tried to imagine them when he had first heard a veteran flyer use the expression "soft-field landing." Just below the radar of his awareness, there was a sudden sense of his being in serious danger. The terror was stark and immediate. Catching sight of the airfield, he was overcome by a surge of adrenaline. His heart raced, his pulse quickened, his breathing grew rapid, and his palms began to sweat. It was a total and absolute physiological immersion in fear. And it was plain that he was not alone. The cockpit was filled with the smell of it.

Hatfield banked the airplane to starboard, circling north to make his final approach. He came in off the sea. With a wingspan of more than ninety-five feet, and standing almost two stories high, the airplane was more than sixty feet long and weighed 26,000 pounds. Buffeted by drafts and thermals, the wings of the aircraft seesawed as Hatfield nursed it down. He ordered McBride to lower the gear, and everything started to shudder.

The plane hit the runway at 80 knots, the gear throwing up mud, the trees visible through the cockpit glass speeding by in a blur. The instrument panel shook as the airplane thundered down the strip, the landing gear rumbling irresistibly through the depressions of the washed-out airfield. Struts thudding, fuselage rattling, the plane felt as if it were

coming apart. Then the tail wheel hit. Momentum diminished dramatically. Shoulder belts and cargo nets strained under the shifting equilibrium of everything on board.

Hatfield's effort to slow the plane down was balanced now by an equally urgent need to keep it rolling. He had to circle the aircraft. He had to position it for takeoff, or no amount of fuel would get them home again. When the plane hit the end of the runway, the mud inevitably took hold, pinning it down as effectively as the arresting gear on a carrier deck.

Hatfield throttled up. He took all the power he could get out of the props. Engines roaring, tail wheel dragging, he slowly brought it about, inching the plane through the quagmire until the deep blue of the Caribbean filled the frame of the windshield. Moving just as sluggishly then, he taxied back up the strip, bouncing in the direction of the beach. Finally achieving the water's edge, he circled the plane again, pushing the revs to the redline to bring the tail wheel around. When he cut the power, the airplane sank, settling hub-deep in the mud, the cargo doors flew open, and the airstrip came alive.

Two trucks and twenty-five men broke cover. They bolted out of the brush from twenty yards off the runway, and they all converged on the airplane. The Colombians were in action now. Now there would be very few variables.

And there would be no testimonials. This was the Guajira. It was round-the-clock combat ops. Out-at-the-extreme, balls-to-the-wall flying was what it took to get business done here. It was the minimum required of aviators. The stunts typically associated with close air support on the battlefield were very cheap theatrics. Hatfield's would go unnoticed.

It was a routine pickup on the Guajira. A thousand gallons of flight fuel would be hand-pumped into the airplane's tanks

from 55-gallon drums mounted on one of the farm trucks, as more than two tons of high-grade marijuana, nothing but gold and the finest Colombian red, were unloaded from the other. A well-ordered, methodical cargo operation, it would differ from the standard commercial procedure only insofar as it was conducted with unusual dispatch and almost exclusively by people wearing guns. Revolvers, semiautomatic pistols, shotguns, submachine guns, automatic rifles . . . It was a real festival of lethal hardware, a classic Latin American get-together, one in which the three gringos always took part unarmed.

Long threw back the cargo doors and stepped down into the mud. He embraced the two men he did business with, the younger of whom, named Miguel, the one who had manned the radio, inevitably addressed him as "sir." Long took care of business with them, shook hands with a rugged character named Ernesto, the operational chief of the airstrip, and while Hatfield and McBride busied themselves shutting the airplane down, he set about inspecting the pot. Once approved for loading, each forty-pound bale would be hoisted aboard.

The first few bales had no sooner passed through the doors of the plane than they started flying back out. Long, bewildered, looked up to see Frank Hatfield standing on the cargo deck. Hatfield, at five-feet-ten, was about three inches shorter than Long, his military-cut, straight brown hair maybe that many inches shorter than Long's thick mane of blond. The lean but heavily muscled Hatfield was the beneficiary of quiet good looks, an easygoing manner, and an almost tangible good humor, the last of which appeared to have gone missing-in-action as he glared down at Long from the cargo doorway of the plane.

"What the fuck are you doing?" he said.

Granted, this was not the first use of the word "fuck," not by any of the three smugglers, and certainly not since the initial shock of the radio announcement had hit. But Hatfield's use of it here was like the overture now to an entirely new symphony of invective. In the next two minutes, replicated, mutated, compounded, and prodigiously exchanged by Hatfield and Long, the word would be traded so fast that its movement would be utterly impossible to clock. It would run through their altercation like gonorrhea through the crew of a merchant vessel on liberty in the Philippines.

"If you load this airplane," Hatfield said, schooling Long in the dynamics of flight, "we're not going to make it out of here."

Lifting off the runway in its current condition, even lifting off empty, was going to be a crapshoot at best, as any fool could see. Long, of course, was not any fool. Long was a fool of such sterling distinction that he was immediately willing to ignore the fact, even as he stood in ankle-deep mud, that having survived the landing just minutes before, he had already beaten the odds.

"I didn't come down here to go back empty," he said.

"We're not going back loaded," said Hatfield, and that should have been the end of it.

Long owned the franchise, it was he who ran the trip, but when it came to flying the airplane, and, yes, Long owned that, too, the chain of command started with Hatfield. The safety and ultimate success of the flight were Hatfield's responsibility. In the air Long always deferred to him. But right now Long was unable to think beyond a quarter-of-a-million-dollar payday, and for the first time in the months they had been flying together he challenged his pilot's authority. He started by taking a reckless position and elevating it to the arrantly ridiculous.

"Nobody said this was going to be easy," he said, challenging Hatfield's manhood.

Neither Hatfield's ability nor his courage, of course, was open to any question, but Long was not going to get very far by criticizing him for sound judgment. Hatfield, for his part, understood that in a beef as demented as this the last place to look for mileage was in an appeal to common sense. And so he fell back on simple intransigence. He just kept saying no, hoping that if the two of them screamed at each other loud enough, Long's delirium would burn itself out.

Long tried pulling rank.

"If we go back empty," he warned Hatfield, "you're not coming back on the next trip."

Not an entirely idle threat, but one Long was unlikely to act on, the remark was Long's way of telling Hatfield that he was nothing more than hired help.

To the Colombians watching, the shouting match was strictly a gringo thing, the fair hair, the flashing eyes — the very blue of the irises, so out of place in a place like this. There were six of them now, eyes as limpid as the surface of the ocean, as Will McBride was inevitably drawn into the argument.

As tall as Long, as blond, his impression upon the Colombians manifestly Nordic, McBride was clearly averse to jumping into the dispute. In what might be construed as the operation's table of organization, his authority outweighed Hatfield's, but he knew better than to think he knew better than Hatfield when it came to flying an airplane. When dragged into the fighting by Long, McBride, a man impatient with incompetence, ill-inclined to suffer clowns, shrugged his shoulders, threw up his hands, and voiced an opinion as brief as it was unequivocal: "Frank says no."

"If he doesn't want to go, that's fine," said Long. "I'll fly it out of here." He pointed a finger at Hatfield. "And I'll put a bale in your seat."

Maybe Hatfield really believed that Long was crazy enough to try it. If so, it was the pilot in him, his sense of responsibility for the lives of his partners, that made his continuing the argument with any conviction impossible. Maybe Hatfield was just exhausted. In any event, he finally gave up. In the end, the sheer force of Long's personality prevailed. The same insubmissive strength of will that had brought them all this far, that had enriched them each and fattened the bank of so many others, predominated once again in the face of conventional wisdom. In the end, every smuggler's story comes down to the triumph of greed over good judgment, and it would be no different here.

"You'll probably get us all killed," said Hatfield.

Long said, "I'd rather die rich."

It took every man on hand, and more, summoned from the local village, to push the airplane out of the ruts into which it had settled. The field was soft but firming up. The earth had begun to dry. Heaving on the undercarriage, muscling the struts, rolling the wheels up out of the eighteen inches of mud into which they had sunk, the Colombians inched the airplane forward, stepping away as Hatfield built up the speed of the engines. Props roaring, brakes on full, Hatfield pushed the revs, giving the airplane, standing still, more power than Long had seen him do in the months that he had been flying it. The airplane began to vibrate. The headphones crackled with static. Hatfield signaled the other two men to tighten up the straps on their seat belts.

"If we don't get airborne before we hit the end of the

runway," he shouted, "we're gonna take the trees head-on. Just hope the cargo nets hold."

"It's not too late to unload," yelled McBride.

"No," said Long. "Let's go. Let's do it now."

He flashed the Colombians a thumbs-up through the cockpit window, and Hatfield released the brakes. Slowly the plane started to roll.

As the plane lumbered down the runway, the Colombians fired their guns, urging the gringos on. The Colombians applauded machismo in all its manifestations, no matter how ill advised. The expression of manhood exhibited here was all the more highly prized for being so poorly considered. Not lost on the Colombians, either, was the fact that if the Americans went home empty, nobody was going to get paid.

When the plane hit 35 knots, the tail came off the ground. The plane leveled off and picked up speed. At 65 knots it would fly. When Hatfield ran out of runway, the plane was doing no better than 60.

"Raise the gear!" he shouted.

To Will McBride, flying right-seat, this particular order was miles off the intuitive grid. Raising the landing gear of an airplane, he knew, while the airplane was on the ground would lead to rudimentary, aerodynamic instability of a kind covered in every textbook. A classic loss of equilibrium known to every pilot, it was one that was subject to quite specific, technical interpretation in the science of flight. It was called crashing.

"Raise the gear!"

They were skimming the brush now, and suddenly McBride saw the danger; he understood the urgency behind Hatfield's command. The mesquite, if it entangled the under-carriage, was going to flip the airplane. With visions of a massive fireball cartwheeling down the field, he raised the

landing gear. The smugglers could feel the fuselage drop as the undercarriage came up. Long was sure he was going to die, and McBride gave voice to the certainty.

"Shit, we're going down," he said.

With that the plane caught air. Gear up, it achieved rotation speed, and lifted ten feet off the deck.

And stayed there.

They hit the high brush, and started churning it up, the beveled edges of the propeller blades slicing shallow troughs in the undergrowth. The rpm's dropped abruptly, the high-pitched whine of the engines backing off to a roar. Two perfectly manicured parallel tracks sculpted in the high mesquite, interrupted only intermittently as the plane, struggling, managed to catch air, would follow their passage for several miles. They gained a couple of feet, and then a few more. They disappeared from view of the airstrip. The Caribbean was just off to their left, but the salvation it promised was way out of reach. With the mesquite growing more than twelve feet high, Hatfield was unable to drop the port wing to bank in the direction of the sea. He was forced to maintain a straight flight path.

They were fourteen feet off the deck, moving at 75 knots, unable to get higher or go any faster. Periodically a tall patch of brush would drop them back down a foot. And then, in all its majesty, the Caribbean circled their way. As the coastline curved to the south, the ocean rose up to meet them. Once over the water, they were safe, they knew, and all three were now sure they would make it. The panorama, in stunning color, opened up gradually before them. Ahead of them, they could see the breakers. And then they could see the shoals. And then, finally, they saw the beach. And lining the beach, a row of coconut palms. An unbroken row of tall coconut palms.

"Shit!"

"Hold on! . . . Hold on!" said Hatfield.

"Ahh . . ."

They hit the palm trees.

". . . SHIT."

They actually uprooted one of the palm trees. They caught it full in the starboard engine. It remained hanging there as they flew. Smaller palms drove holes in both wings. Flight fuel poured from the starboard tank. Miraculously they were still flying.

They were about twenty-five feet off the water, gaining altitude now as they dumped fuel. Hatfield, studying the instruments, performed some rapid calculations.

"What do you think?" said Long.

"We can make it maybe four hundred miles. Which will put us maybe a hundred off the southern coast of Haiti."

Proceeding, therefore, was not an option.

One of the distinguishing features of the marijuana business, as pursued by Americans like Allen Long — one of the attributes that distinguished the marijuana business from other fields of criminal endeavor — was a conspicuous and, to those who thought about it, rather consoling absence of gunplay. This can be explained by the fact that, for many of the industry's pioneers, the marijuana came first, in both time as well as importance. The industry was created by pot smokers, a casual brotherhood of aficionados, loosely associated, relatively young, usually stoned, united around little more than a near-religious passion for the noble weed. A characteristically (and understandably) merry band of outlaws, who pledged at least passing allegiance to the values of the counterculture to which they and their customers

belonged — "Peace and Love" being prominent among them — these people were accomplished pot smokers long before they were professional criminals. Prohibition would have gone down pretty much the same way if alcohol had been new in the Roaring Twenties and Al Capone had been one of a loose affiliation of drunks who had discovered bootleg whiskey in college.

Guns were a big fixture of the business south of the border and in American cities like Miami, where the money had begun to attract gangsters for whom dope was just one more commodity. Like a large majority of Colombians, whose disinclination was cultural, these were people who never smoked pot. But raise the issue of guns with smugglers like Allen Long, and it was axiomatic that you better bring lunch. It brought forth dissertations. It invited an immersion in metaphysics, in a kind of mojo eschatology, with discourse on things like destiny and the implications of karma. In the end, what you came away with was . . . Well, there just seemed to be no place for guns.

Unless you were Frank Hatfield.

Frank Hatfield never embarked for the Guajira without a .45 caliber pistol within his immediate reach in the cockpit. The Colombians, who paid attention to such things, would recognize the handgun as a Model 1911 Government Colt. This single-action semiautomatic with the seven-shot magazine was at the time the official service pistol of the United States armed forces. And had been for sixty-five years. American pilots had been carrying the weapon into combat for generations. But it was not out of any sense of kinship with, or aspiration to the heroic stature of, the nation's military aces that Frank Hatfield always flew armed. He carried the sidearm not to use on the enemy. He carried it to use on himself.

Frank Hatfield sported an idiosyncrasy, a quirk that had become as definitive of his character as his brevity of speech, his winning smile, and his proficiency with airplanes and women. Frank Hatfield had a pathological fear of being eaten alive by sharks. It was the terror that alone haunted him. As brave as he was, as bold in the eye of danger, as brassbound as his aviator's balls had proved to be, it was the one manifestation of death's many faces into which Hatfield was unable to spit.

Haiti lay upon the island of Hispaniola, which, as islands will do, lay surrounded by a lot of water. And one hundred miles off the coast thereof, sharing a kitchen with the local marine life, was not where Frank Hatfield wanted to be.

Hatfield circled the airplane and headed back to the strip. The starboard engine was laboring, ill-equipped as it was to function with a tree choking the air intake of the cooling system. The temperature was rising, the oil pressure was dropping, and the engine was calling it quits. Then it went up.

"Fire in the starboard engine!" McBride yelled.

Flames licked along the cowling as the red-hot engine ignited. In fascination and horror, the smugglers watched the flames creep closer to the leaking fuel. If Hatfield shut the engine down, the airplane would explode. He had to keep her moving, had to keep the propeller turning, he had to hope the prop wash would blow the fire out.

The tongues of flame receded, and finally the fire died. Hatfield feathered the engine, and made for the airstrip on a single prop. As the starboard propeller went dead, he could see that the blades were warped — bent back at severe angles and twisted, violently and instantly made junk upon impact

with the trees — and he had to assume the same to be true of the port-side prop as well. They never would have seen Haiti. They would be lucky now to make it back to the beach.

It was no place for endorsements, but not lost on any of the three smugglers aboard was the miracle of engineering being exhibited for their aeronautic enjoyment: The wings of the airplane were perforated by trees. The landing lights had been ripped entirely out of them, further deforming the airfoil. There was a palm tree hanging from the starboard engine. That engine was dead, and the propeller blades of the other, the one operational engine, were presumably warped to resemble the tines of a garden rake. The plane was dumping fuel. Soon the oil would be history . . .

And still the airplane was flying. And flying with a heavy load.

It flew that way for six miles.

Closing in on the beach, coming in dangerously low, the plane did not project any undercarriage. Deploying the landing gear was a luxury Hatfield could not afford. He could not risk adding a degree of resistance to the drag he was already up against. He had to make the runway. And he had to hope that what remained of the mud that had so effectively fouled his takeoff would now give him the skid he needed to land the plane in one piece.

With a smoking engine on the starboard side, with flight fuel pouring from the tanks, with hot steel glowing every-where — with the likelihood of an explosion now came the added thrill of the bales. Some two and a half tons of lethal cargo would come crashing through the cockpit bulkhead if Hatfield came up short on the landing.

Hatfield skimmed the sloping beach, and put the plane belly-down on the runway. Sheet metal screaming, fuselage buckling on collision with the ground, the disabled craft

crashed down the strip, slamming in with all the excitement of a freight train leaving the rails. The cargo nets held, the mud did its job, the plane slewed at an angle of about 30 degrees, nosed to a stop, and the smugglers bailed out.

Long obliged the starboard engine with a blast from the cockpit fire extinguisher, and backed away to wait for the explosion. The engine smoldered but failed to ignite. A column of smoke rose from the starboard wing, and would do so for better than an hour. The airplane refused to surrender.

Long offered a silent prayer for the well-being of the good people of the old Douglas Aircraft Company who forty years before had engineered the plane — this, the DC-3, the venerable commercial airliner in service since 1936, which as the C-47 Skytrain had become the most widely used military troop-and-cargo transport in history.

And now, more than just a part of history, the airplane literally *was* history. It was finished. It was the latest in a line of similar losses that stood as the hallmark of a new industry. In the multibillion-dollar enterprise that drug smuggling had become, such expenditures were a routine write-off, a line item in the operating budget under the heading "disposable birds." One preferred to write them off empty, however, on landing strips back home.

The Colombians had departed the airstrip. They had left after the airplane vanished from sight, assuming the takeoff had been successful. The smugglers were now on their own. Soon, a small group of Indians who had witnessed the crash assembled. No, they told Long, there was no phone in the village, they had no car, there was no way to reach Ernesto.

"Do you know what we need to do?" Long said. "We need to get rid of that airplane. We need to get the marijuana out of that airplane."

The villagers knew what to do. This was not the first plane that had crashed here, they said. A simple, familiar gesture of the hand served as the DC-3's epitaph.

"Fine, chop it up now," Long said.

"We can't just leave it like this," said Hatfield.

And he and McBride began removing from the airplane anything that might identify it, anything bearing its registration number, anything that might lead back to them. They destroyed all the documentation, then went to work on the hardware. The transponder, the radio transceivers — all the plane's avionics had to go. While the pilots, using screwdrivers, worked on the instrument panel, the villagers unloaded the pot. And once the starboard wing stopped smoking, the Indians started butchering the plane.

It was noon, and Long was sitting on the beach, the sun directly overhead. The air temperature was pushing 110, the humidity skyrocketing in the wake of the rain. With the local Indians to his back, cannibalizing the smoking aircraft, he stared out over the Caribbean like a man who had not only lost his dog, but had just seen its name on a witness list in a divorce proceeding against him.

"Look, man," McBride said, walking up behind him, "you told me and you told Frank, if anything like this ever happened down here, these guys would take care of it. You said the Colombians would get us out of it."

"I know."

"Well . . ."

"What?" said Long.

"Get us out of it."

"I'm working on it."

"Okay."

There were no arguments now about who was in charge. Their lives and freedom were in jeopardy. The responsibility for their escape rested with Long.

And Long was working on it.

Okay.

2
EL NIÑO PERDIDO

Allen Long was born the year Harry S. Truman was elected
to the American presidency, and was first arrested for marijuana possession the year Bob Dylan released *Blonde on
Blonde*. The year before, the year he took his first hit, Long
dropped out of school. Dylan went electric. Not necessarily
for that reason, nor even in that order. By 1966, when Long
was arrested, certain cultural patterns were well established.
By the end of the year more Americans would own the Dylan
album than would even be aware of Leslie Bassett's
Variations for Orchestra, winner of the Pulitzer Prize for
Music. By the end of the decade more Americans would be
in possession of marijuana than had voted for Truman.

When he was dragged off to jail by sheriff's deputies,
Allen Long, seventeen, was living on Queen Street in
Arlington, Virginia, a minute over the Potomac from the
nation's capital, sharing an apartment with two other
teenagers. The three misfits were students at the nearby
Hawthorne School, a very exclusive, very expensive school
for the deranged — or so Long liked to describe it. More

accurately characterized, it was a school for those whose aspirations deranged the orderly function of others, an experimental, free-form academy for bright kids who marched to the beat of a different educational drum.

Several months earlier, Long, a senior, had dropped out of the private school he had been attending in Richmond. Not merely a Catholic school, it was a Catholic military school, and more than merely military, it was run by Benedictines. Long's father, who had enrolled him, was leaving nothing to chance in addressing the discipline problem his son had become. Long jumped scholastic ship to travel with a rock and roll band. Its members, older than Long, all of them in their twenties, had needed a singer with looks to front their new act. Tall, blond, and blue-eyed, passable as a teenage heartthrob in a kind of second-lead B-movie way, Long had the looks, but he had no musical talent. That, of course, deterred no one. He could jump and shout — a virtuoso at both, he had been proving it since infancy — and like others of his species with opposable thumbs, he could bang a mean tambourine. That was enough. With that and a record contract, the group, the Counts Four, picked up regular gigs in Georgetown, and just months before graduation, Long dropped out of high school to go on the road.

The tour ended in Los Angeles at the Whisky A Go-Go, where the band opened for the Byrds, an act whose cover of Dylan's "Mr. Tambourine Man" had recently hit the top of the charts. And there the band immediately dissolved, when the musicians, the real ones, were exposed to the chops of Byrds lead guitarist Jim McGuinn, and realized to their utter dismay that they would never be that good, nor equal to the achievement of even middling success in the music business.

Long persevered. To join the band, after all, he had

dropped out of school, which carried with it significant consequences. And these he had risked for reasons that transcended the music. They were reasons anyone could appreciate, but none more readily than his classmates. As Long explained to them, being in a band was "the best way to get pussy," which to a seventeen-year-old was a quest that compared favorably with that of Percival for the Grail.

At that age, in those days, the only thing as cool, or seemingly so, as being affiliated with a band was being associated in some way with marijuana. Pot was forbidden fruit, the flesh of which was naturally suffused with the juice of romance and glamour. Shot through with totemic significance, it grew from the tree of knowledge around which Long's generation gathered, the talisman of a new age, the drug that would power the following year's Summer of Love and Woodstock two years after that. Marijuana, emblematic of the outlaw, was the badge of the burgeoning counterculture. As Long saw it, smoking dope — more importantly, having it, and thus being able to provide it — made you attractive to girls.

Having smoked his first joint as a member of the band, Long in 1966 returned to the D.C. area a man with experience to spare. He enrolled in the Hawthorne School, joined a new band, and moved with two of its members into the apartment on Queen Street. There, in that earthly paradise, nourished by the food-giving trees of the new Eden — sex, drugs, and rock and roll — he luxuriated. And in that idyllic garden he lasted about as long as Adam.

The music, the dope, they both played a part, but as Adam might have told him, had the two men shared a cell, you really had to hand it to the girls.

*   *   *

One of the young women who frequented the Queen Street apartment left there one night with a couple of joints she had been given by the members of the band. Busted by her father, who called the police, she made a subsequent visit to the apartment accompanied by a "friend." That he, the friend, was maybe twice her age and sported what was known at the time as "a Beatles haircut" provoked in Long and his roommates no second thoughts. These were the days of "harmony and understanding, sympathy and trust abounding." Everyone trusted everyone. To be mistrustful was just not cool.

"Do you know where I can get some grass?" asked the long-haired friend.

Police undercover work is a cycle of constants. Only the barbers change.

In exchange for a ride to their gig that night, the musicians scored a dime bag of weed, which they split with the undercover cop. Four days later, following a raid on their apartment, Long and his roommates were taken to jail. The parents of the other two boys intervened on behalf of their sons, whose cases were eventually adjudicated the way such cases usually are, much the way Long's was adjudicated four months later: the suspects released on probation to their parents' custody, the criminal record to be expunged after a year of good behavior. Long's parents, however, whose understanding of such things led them to suppose that their son was injecting marijuana into a brachial vein, thought jail was just what he needed. Rather than put up bail, they let the state lock him up until the case came up for a hearing.

To escape the predation of older, more dangerous inmates, Long, on the advice of a second-rate lawyer, applied to the court for a psychiatric evaluation, that he might end his pretrial detention in the safety of a hospital. The judge ruled

in his favor — having smoked marijuana, the judicial thinking went, Long had to be nuts — and ordered him shipped off to Southwestern State Hospital, a mental health facility, where he was incarcerated in the wing set aside for the criminally insane. Not a bad approximation of his idea of hell, the curative bedlam served as his sanctuary for a full ten weeks. Long celebrated his eighteenth birthday in the custody of the state, and by the time of his release he had developed a grudge, a contempt for the legal system that would last his entire life.

Allen Long, born in Richmond, was six years old when his parents divorced, and he moved with his mother, a schoolteacher, and his infant brother to the small town of South Hill on Virginia's southern border. As a boy, he spent many days in the local auction barns there, lying atop bales of tobacco, lulled by the drone of the auctioneers, moving to Charlottesville at the age of eleven, when his mother married a psychology professor at the University of Virginia. Seeking the approval of his father, a prominent Richmond businessman, Long exhibited the values of the Virginia gentleman through his sophomore year in high school. At fifteen he spearheaded Virginia Youth for Goldwater, intending one day himself to be elected President of the United States. It was not his father but his grandfather from whom Long took his guidance, the elder man from whom he inherited his sense of risk and spirit of adventure, the very spirit in which, as a high school junior, he eventually twisted off.

Long's paternal grandfather, after whom he was named, lost his parents at the age of eight, and was taken in by relatives. He had been sent from Ireland by his family to work for a distant relative in Tennessee. At eleven, he escaped

what amounted to indentured servitude, stealing a mule and riding it a hundred miles to Louisville, Kentucky, where for the next three years he worked as a slop boy, cleaning the vats in a brewery. At fourteen he apprenticed as a factory tool-and-die maker, eventually moving to New Jersey to work for a lock-making company. Securing a patent on a suitcase lock he developed, he moved to Petersburg, Virginia, where in 1919 he founded the Long Manufacturing Company, which would become the world's largest manufacturer of trunk locks. Among the company's customers for the Long T46 — the trunk lock whose classic design would continue to be widely copied long after the patent expired and the company lost its dominance — was the United States Army.

It was into the fountain of money generated by this company, and eventually into the proprietorship of the company itself, that Long's father, John, fell by accident of birth. Long felt that his father fell into everything he did, navigating life with no purpose, a failing Long came to blame on the grandfather he so admired, who, holding out the promise of independence, tethered his son to a family enterprise whose control he never intended to cede. Long's low opinion of his father was not an opinion shared by everyone. John Long, in his own student years, had dropped out of Notre Dame to fight the Second World War. Achieving the rank of captain, he fought Rommel in the desert of North Africa and was part of the Allied beachhead at Anzio. He was awarded the Silver Star not for aimlessness but for gallantry in action. The Junior Chamber of Commerce named him Virginia's Man of the Year before, not after, his eldest son was arrested for pot possession.

It was into his father's custody that Long was released on probation in 1966. He moved to Richmond and earned

his high school equivalency diploma while working at a lumber mill, a silk screen shop, and at a succession of other, low-paying jobs. Eighteen months later he returned to Charlottesville and entered the University of Virginia as a psychology major. While a student, he landed a job at a television network affiliate in Richmond. Rising to the position of night news cameraman, he was eventually promoted to head the news-film department. Convinced by then that his only competition for work was Federico Fellini, he put together a reel of film, quit the job, dropped out of college, and in the summer of 1970 departed for New York in a '57 pickup, determined to make waves in the film industry.

Choosing not to direct *Satyricon* — Fellini took that gig — Long accepted a job as a production assistant at a commercial production house, Motion Associates, on Madison Avenue. There he worked as a gofer on commercials for, among other clients, Eastman Kodak, Esso, Chanel, and Rival dog food. Capitalizing on the experience he gained, and exploiting the contacts he developed, he went on to secure backing for a documentary movie he wanted to shoot. A cutting-edge exposé, it was a project he sincerely believed would lead to an enduring and lucrative career in the entertainment business.

He was right. It was a movie about marijuana smuggling.

The trouble started with a guy named El Coyote.

A Mexican-American, born on the Texas border, the self-styled El Coyote was a thirty-year-old pot smuggler who lived in a penthouse apartment on the Upper West Side of Manhattan. He was the first of various characters Long would come to know whom he would remember as larger than life. Six feet tall, built less like a coyote than a

greyhound (he weighed 140 pounds), El Coyote projected the image of a man of the world, a man as wily as the fabled creature from which he took his name: the legendary trickster of Southwest myth. Like that of almost any man whose Christian name is a definite article, El Coyote's image was simply that — nobody really bought it. But he projected it with magnificent enthusiasm, and the exhibition was always worth the price of overlooking the obvious.

A textbook of antic behavior, as high-strung as is stereotypical of a man proportioned in such a way that his photograph could be confused with his X ray, El Coyote transcended the manic in aspiring to the maniacal. A random urine sample from the excitable Chicano would screen positive for every recreational drug ever written about in the 1960s. They would show up all at once, all of them in the same test.

Long was living in the Village at the corner of Bleecker Street and Seventh Avenue, supporting himself on his production assistant's salary, when he met El Coyote. A West Village shop owner who distributed pot, knowing that Long owned a pickup truck, had offered him a chance to earn some extra money making deliveries. Long was driving his half-ton GMC around town delivering pot to the shop owner's customers or picking it up from his supplier, ten to twenty pounds of Mexican or Jamaican at a time.

The supplier was El Coyote. One of the customers was a guy named Crosby, who would gain notoriety several years later when he opened one of the more famous drug bars in New York. A downtown establishment with a video camera at the elevator and a bouncer at the door, it featured, where the back bar would ordinarily be, a blackboard on which were listed the various strains of dope available for purchase that day. Police eventually shut the place down, but failed

to eliminate the concept, which later would be raised to an art form by the Dutch when such places became legal in the Netherlands.

One evening Long and Crosby — by now the Village shop owner had been bypassed as a middleman by all concerned — sat smoking in El Coyote's apartment, playing audience to the demented smuggler, while the latter regaled them with fascinating and largely hilarious tales of misadventure along the Mexican border.

El Coyote was all over the place, slipping in and out of coherence. There was something Long wanted to say, but before he could really get a handle on things the subject had shifted from dope to another equally urgent topic of the day: the vexing political reality that ten of the nation's larger corporations controlled the world. No attempt was made to identify them, but it was agreed that the fix was in.

"And they did it without controlling magnetism, that's the amazing thing," said Long.

This particular observation brought the colloquy to a stop. The other two men looked at him not with fear and pity at the terrible pharmacological mess he was in, but with anticipation of some germ of wisdom.

"Dick Tracy," Long explained. "'He who controls magnetism will control the universe.' Sundays. It was a recurring theme in the Crimestoppers Textbook."

Crosby ventured that if he remembered correctly it was also an essential element in the Revelation of Saint John.

Long made use of the hiatus to lead El Coyote back to the original subject of his oratory. He was eager to hear more smuggling yarns. El Coyote was happy to oblige, and as his performance began picking up steam, Long remembered what had been on his mind.

"You know . . ."

Politely brooking the interruption, El Coyote paused. Observing what a rhetorician would identify as the aposiopesis, he and Crosby once more turned their attention to Long and patiently waited for him to continue.

"You know, this would make a great movie," he said.

Stoned.

He was thinking of a documentary movie. And he was confident that its financing would prove to be no problem. Among Long's many friends in New York was the owner of an uptown saloon, a fellow by the name of Ives. Ives was El Coyote's age, and standing five-feet-six, weighing some 260 pounds, he was El Coyote's morphologic reciprocal — not simply obese, but morbidly so, he was as overfed as El Coyote was undernourished. The two men looked, in each other's company, like some horrible livestock experiment. Bringing them together for the purposes of a movie, as Long was about to do, was certain to succeed if the movie were a cartoon and the two of them were cast in the leads. In default of that proposition, Long's project ran a very strong second.

With a contemporary soundtrack, a strong narrative line, and an audience base of some 25 million pot smokers to build from, Long's documentary was well positioned to make money, he believed, and that was how he presented it to Ives, a man whose ample waistline was dwarfed by the girth of his wallet. Ives's saloon was a mere indulgence. Ives was heir to one of the nation's older and larger industrial fortunes, one of the real ones, one of those corporations whose combined performance accounted for the Dow. Excited by Long's idea for the film, he readily agreed to be its producer.

Long, by way of research, planned to accompany El Coyote on his next trip to Mexico to pick up a load. Their friend Crosby would make the trip with them.

"He's going to finance the move."

"I thought I was financing the movie," said Ives.

"You *are* financing the movie," Long said. "Crosby's financing the move."

"The move."

"The move," said Long. "He's the guy who's paying for the pot."

"Oh," said Ives. "The 'move.'"

"The move."

They left New York for Guadalajara in August 1971 on an AeroMexico flight from JFK. Before they left, El Coyote, the professional, had given Long instructions on how he was to act: appear conservative in the extreme, cool in every respect, draw no attention to himself. El Coyote would dispatch a limousine to pick him up for the flight. The limo arrived at six A.M., and at six-thirty the car, with Long in back, was idling quietly curbside below El Coyote's apartment. Long was dressed as staidly as a stockbroker, everything on the up-and-up from the haircut to the briefcase to the jacket and tie. When El Coyote finally appeared the production values shifted. The tone of the masquerade went from Dun & Bradstreet to Barnum & Bailey.

El Coyote's suit, which had just come back from the cleaners, had been washed rather than dry-cleaned. The explanation for this travesty was rendered so incoherently by its victim that it was to be lost to history forever. As time went by, Long would learn not to seek answers to certain questions, his experience teaching him that with guys like El Coyote these things were just God's way. The suit was about eight inches short in the inseam, about five inches short in the sleeves. From his footwear to his fedora — yes, he was wearing a hat — El Coyote was as inconspicuous as a school bus. He wore black Carnaby Street boots, zipped

up to his lower shin. And then his pants began. As if it redeemed respectability in the midst of this terrible fall from sartorial grace, El Coyote was wearing a necktie. And if the fashion statement itself were not sufficiently frantic, he had been up all night on cocaine.

His panic, however, arose from an altogether different disaster. El Coyote, a federal fugitive, had been unable to memorize the information on the false identification he was about to use to purchase his airline ticket. According to the birth certificate he had recently bought, his name was Kyle something, and he was desperate to get it right.

"Ask me my name," he said to Long. "Go ahead, ask me my name."

"What?"

"Go ahead. Just ask me my name."

"What's your name?"

"What?"

"What's your *name?*"

"I can't remember."

It was like that all the way to the airport.

Once inside the terminal, Long found a place to hide as El Coyote made his assault on the AeroMexico ticket counter. In calculating the odds on serious trouble, Long read the setup this way: El Coyote was wanted for smuggling. He was about to present fraudulent identification for the purpose of leaving the country. And as Long had just discovered minutes before in the limousine, these were only two of three conspicuous felonies for which the madman might be arrested. Around his waist, beneath his miserably shrunken suit, El Coyote was strapped with a money belt. In it he carried the cocaine, mescaline, opium, and hashish that, in addition to the variety of other drugs available there, he would need in Mexico for personal use. A maintenance

stash, carried against the risk of any severe, psychochemical imbalance that his body might find itself running — against the possibility of his waking up straight — the bindle was necessarily hefty. There was no room in the belt for money.

El Coyote, issued a ticket, swaggered through the gate, and Long, nursing misgivings, joined him on board the plane. Crosby sat by himself. The flight was uneventful until they were about two hours out of Guadalajara, at which point El Coyote turned to Long and said, "Okay, now you have to put on the money belt."

"What?"

The possibility of a search was remote, virtually non-existent. Customs officials were not thoroughly stupid. Nobody brought drugs *into* Mexico. Nobody who was in his right mind.

"Okay, I'll do it," said Long, realizing that El Coyote was not somebody who fit that description.

Upon arrival in Guadalajara, El Coyote rented a car, a Volkswagen painted a bilious, general-issue green. The three Americans climbed aboard, El Coyote behind the wheel, and stopping only long enough to sign into a hotel and deposit their luggage, drove directly to the Plazuela de los Mariachis and started drinking.

Guadalajara, located 300 miles northwest of Mexico City, is the country's second-largest city and considered one of its more beautiful. Situated a mile high in the Sierra Madre, the capital of Jalisco state, it is a city of narrow streets and intimate plazas, a city awash in bougainvillea, poinciana, orange blossoms, orchids, palms, lemon trees, and water, spilling everywhere, the water of 146 public fountains. Allen Long saw fountains everywhere he looked. The Plazuela de

los Mariachis, just off the city's central square, was surrounded by cantinas and open-air cafés and resplendent with several groups of the street musicians for which the plaza was named, no fewer than five mariachi bands, all strolling the cobblestones, simultaneously playing requests.

Allen Long, moviemaker, sitting there in a cantina in the company of smugglers, was just where he wanted to be, alive to the magic and the promise of adventure, breathing the fragrant air of the Torrid Zone just below the Tropic of Cancer. Drinking tequila, chasing it with beer and chasing both with the stash of inebriants concealed in the recesses of the money belt, he and Crosby, after a couple of hours, were very severely bent, but not nearly so severely as their chauffeur. El Coyote's necktie was gone, his shirt was open — his pants were still way too short — his eyeglasses were off, and he had commandeered the entire cantina. The tables were pushed together, the patrons seated as if all of them were members of the same party, and urged on by El Coyote, all were toasting one another, drinking to America, drinking to Mexico . . . "*Viva la*" this . . . ! "*Viva la*" that . . . !

The sun fell, and the stars rose. It was a clear, balmy, late-summer night on the Plazuela de los Mariachis, and for a moment Long was overcome with what he would remember as a heavenly glow. Shortly thereafter he woke up lying face-down on the floor of the men's room in two or three inches of wet sawdust. That was when he remembered it, the heavenly glow. How long he had been passed out was a mystery. Why the sawdust was wet was not, but it made no impression on him, or on anybody else for that matter. He woke up, brushed himself off, and returned to the table, where his disappearance was remarked by no one.

In Long's absence El Coyote had organized a battle of

the bands. There was $100 in prize money for the mariachis who impressed him most. There were three bands surrounding the table, musicians in full regalia — silver-studded *charro* suits, trimmed with piping, tricked out in braid, sombreros rimmed with pom-poms. One band was outfitted in pale baby blue, one lime green, the other yellow . . . There were guitars, violins, *vihuelas,* trumpets, and maybe a hundred spectators crowded around the table. The Americans had plenty of friends now. El Coyote, living large, was laying out the cake. The cash was moving fast. He was buying drinks for everybody.

A hush came over the cantina when one of the bands played "El Niño Perdido," the lost child, a mariachi standard. It climaxed in a mournful trumpet solo, calling out into the night. When the music, echoing in the darkness, stopped, and the song drifted off into silence, the trumpet called out again, its music more forlorn. And once again it was met by silence. Then in the stillness, playing somewhere in the distance, a second trumpet could be heard. The first trumpet player responded. Again came the sound of the second horn. And now it was moving closer. A sigh went up from the crowd. The music of the trumpets, seeking each other, steadily converged, and by the time father and son were reunited, everyone in the cantina was crying, the sobbing mixed with cheers as the approaching horn found its way into the plaza, the second trumpeter suddenly visible, standing across the square. The two musicians, playing counterpoint solos, advanced across the cobblestones, and the trumpeters, standing side by side, rejoicing, began playing as one. The drunks in the cantina went crazy. And then the band kicked in.

And it just did not get any better than this, especially if you were wasted.

These mariachis took the grand prize.

Within minutes of proclaiming their victory, El Coyote, the toast of all Guadalajara, managed to work his way into a verbal pissing match with one of the locals seated at the table. A dispute over some asinine point of pride, it was one of those beefs that tend to make sense only when two people are equally drunk, one of those altercations that tend to resolve themselves in the throes of equally asinine, slobbering expressions of love. And more drinks. This particular quarrel, however, escalated beyond hope of resolution when El Coyote, enraged, jumped up onto the table, dropped his pants, and mooned his new drinking companion.

Long and Crosby instantly grabbed him and hustled him out of the joint, half carrying him to the Volkswagen.

Which El Coyote insisted upon driving.

El Coyote was thoroughly drunk — his pants were still down around his ankles — but he was El Coyote, and nobody but he was driving that car. Long and Crosby were drunk themselves, and the argument they put up, taking no probative value from the fact that they at least were wearing their trousers, was aimless, nonsensical, and ultimately of no effect. Long climbed into the back of the car, Crosby climbed onto the front passenger seat, and with El Coyote behind the wheel, the three witless pilgrims sped off. With predictable results. Turning down a one-way street, heading in the wrong direction, El Coyote ran the Volkswagen into the front bumper of a double-parked sedan idling just off the corner in front of an ice cream shop. The collision, which brought the Volkswagen thudding to a sudden stop, lit the other car up like the scoreboard on a pinball machine.

They had actually hit a police car.

The flashing red of the squad car's roof light instantly drew a crowd, and Long's thoughts instantly shifted from

vehicular misdemeanors to the felonies stashed in the money belt. Prison came to mind. The police alighted, called the Americans out of the Volkswagen, and ushered them into the rear of the squad car. There, the prisoners were presently joined by a pair of Good Samaritans, a couple of civilian bystanders who managed to squeeze in with them. These self-appointed interpreters took seats on the prisoners' laps.

"Don't worry gringo, no problem . . ."

As the squad car followed the Volkswagen, driven by a third policeman, through the streets of Guadalajara, making its way to the station, Long tried to reason with the arresting officers. He took his cash out of his pocket and waved it in their direction. The interpreter sitting on Long's lap, making clear that he was there to assist — specifically to assist the Mexican police in relieving the Americans of their money — snatched the bills as they passed in front of him.

"One for you, one for you, and one for me," he said, sharing the cash with the cops. "Don't worry, gringo, no problem . . ."

This was Mexico, and because it was Mexico, events had a way of escalating beyond the narrative threshold at which they merely taxed credulity. Because it was Mexico, it was necessary that events, in their inevitable recounting, proved not merely hard to believe, but atmospheric of the supernatural. What happened next would have to be sufficiently strange, something implausibly operatic, something like a flat tire on the squad car. Yes. And it was while the policemen were changing the tire that El Coyote started working on them.

"We're brothers . . ." And that kind of stuff.

About fifteen hundred dollars later, the police decided that they and El Coyote were brothers, and that if Long drove the Volkswagen, and drove straight to the hotel, the

gringos were free to go. With Crosby on his right, and El Coyote in the back, Long aimed the Volkswagen in the direction of the hotel, La Posada Guadalajara. "That way," the police had told them. And "that way" was the way Long drove. But El Coyote had descended so far into the affliction of drugs and alcohol that he saw chicanery and treachery in everything — El Coyote had really lost it now — and he was certain they were being directed to jail.

"It's a trick," he insisted. "A trick. Go the other way."

Long, dismissing him with a wave of his hand, told him he was imagining things. El Coyote lunged forward, and snarling with a ferocity worthy of his namesake, snapped Long's ear between his teeth.

"Grrr . . ."

"Arrrghh . . . !"

He bit down until Long obeyed.

Throwing the car into a quick U-turn, Long sped in the opposite direction.

Until he sped past the police.

When the police caught up to the Volkswagen, one of the officers stepped into the car, and *he* drove the Americans to the hotel. El Coyote by then had passed out in the back.

"What . . . ? What happened?" he grumbled, patting himself down for a joint while Long was hauling him into the building.

"Man, you shouldn't smoke," said Long, snatching the drugs. "It stunts your clothes."

3

AZTEC TWO-STEP

It was six A.M. and Long had been in town maybe three days when he was rousted from sleep by a knock on the door of his Guadalajara hotel room. Sunlight streamed through the window. He groaned when it hit his eyes. Half awake, he crawled out of bed and crossed the room, and standing in the frame when he pulled open the door was a tall, dark-haired gringo. He wore faded blue jeans, leather sandals, a white T-shirt and Ray-Bans, and carried a leather jacket slung over his shoulder. He removed the sunglasses when he saw Long.

He said, "Goddamn it, you're not them."

His eyes were dark, his complexion was fair, and when he opened his mouth to express his dismay he exposed teeth as bright and perfect as an octave on a Steinway.

"I guess I'm not," said Long.

"I'm sorry, buddy," the stranger continued, in a deep but pleasant baritone. "I asked the lady at the front desk where the Americans with long hair were staying. I guess my friends have checked out."

"I guess they have," said Long, whose hair, while in conformance with nonconformist counterculture standards, was positively short when measured against his intruder's dark halo of curls.

"Sorry," said the stranger again.

Long shut the door and went back to sleep.

The trip had become a complete downer. Two days earlier, El Coyote had made his connection. The meet had been set for two P.M. at the site of pre-Columbian ruins outside the city. The machinery of the marijuana-trafficking conspiracy had slipped smoothly into gear. At the appointed time Long and Crosby were standing with El Coyote at the top of a small pyramid at the site, when a truck arrived, and out stepped a Mexican in a cowboy hat. He climbed the steps, shook hands all around, and shared with El Coyote the obligatory *abrazo* — very masculine, very forceful, the signature embrace of the dope industry's brothers-in-arms.

"*Mi amigo.*"

"My friend."

"My good friend."

"*Amigo.*"

Crooks are always hugging each other. In the dope business such hugs are typically vigorous and the greetings accompanying them cheerful. They lack the ecclesiastical reserve of those hugs one associates with the mob, and they serve their purpose without the kissing, or other solemn affectations of piety. They are especially outlandish in those cases where the parties involved understand that in the course of business they will be trying to steal money from each other.

"I need two hundred pounds of your *best* merchandise," El Coyote declared. He needed it across the border, in Texas or Arizona.

The Mexican said, "Consider it done."

El Coyote, pleased, and playing it large for the benefit of his cinema-biographer, asked when he could take delivery — El Coyote, the consummate professional.

"I will be happy," the Mexican answered, "to do that for you in six months."

El Coyote was struck momentarily dumb. What kind of response was that? In El Coyote's facial expression you could actually read his accent. It was an expression that seemed to ask the question: "What you doing, *cholo*, you sticking some hot poker up my skinny Chicano ass?" El Coyote shook off his disbelief the way a dog shakes off water, and said, "What do you mean?"

"This is not the time of the harvest, my friend, you know that," answered the Mexican.

There was never pot in August. Not in North America. Of course not. El Coyote had forgotten that.

"What do you mean, you forgot?" Long gasped. "Are you absolutely out of your mind?"

Crosby, who had financed the trip, was that much more incredulous. He ordered the expedition back to the hotel, and started packing his suitcase. He and a chastened El Coyote left Guadalajara the next day.

Exeunt. They were gone, stepping not simply into the wings, but completely out of the theater of operations into which Long was now making an entrance.

Long, hoping to salvage the trip, had decided to stay in town. He had a movie to make, and would try, in the sudden absence of sources, to develop some contacts, scare up some

leads. He knew no one in Guadalajara, but it was as good a place as any to start. That evening he drank alone in the Plazuela de los Mariachis.

On the morning he was awakened by the knock on his door, Long was heading back to the plaza when about halfway there he instructed his cab driver to pull over and stop the car.

"Hey," he called out the window, "remember me?"

Walking in the dust on the side of the road was the American who had interrupted his sleep.

"Yeah."

"You want a ride downtown?"

"Well, yeah, okay, I guess, sure," he said.

Stepping into the cab, the American introduced himself as Lee.

"Let me buy you a drink," said Long.

They made their way to La Copa de Leche, "the best bar on the Plazuela de los Mariachis," Long told him, sharing the weight of an opinion that had been in the family for, hell, almost fifty-six hours, and there he and his new acquaintance sat down and ordered lunch.

"What brings you to Mexico," asked Lee.

Long explained that he was a filmmaker, that he was researching a documentary. "It's about pot smuggling," he said. "I'm down here from New York."

He asked Lee where he was from.

"California," said Lee.

"What brings you to Guadalajara?"

"I'm a pot smuggler," he said.

Lee Carlyle, twenty-four, was a man of classically American enthusiasms, and characteristically Carlyle allowed those

enthusiasms to run away with him. As a teenager in Escondido, California, indulging a youthful passion for hot rods, he had succeeded in building a low-rider so low that he could not get it out of his driveway. Adulthood did not temper his spirit. Later, when he was moving tons of marijuana out of Miami, Carlyle would purchase for his personal consumption the entire South Florida allotment of Château Lafite-Rothschild's 1972 Carruades de Lafite. It would take him — and his friends, and their various girlfriends, and all the hookers and coke dealers in Miami — a year and a half to drink it.

Carlyle got into the dope business the way most otherwise law-abiding Americans got into it: as a consumer, a pothead who bought weight and sold off the surplus to cover the cost of the pot he smoked. Carlyle began dealing as a teenager, selling nickels out of ounces, then ounces out of pounds. Soon, he and a couple of friends were smuggling pot out of Mexico and selling it by the brick.

Pot coming out of Mexico at the time was molded and packaged in rectangular blocks that mimicked the shape of the standard building or paving brick. A brick of Mexican marijuana tipped the scale at about two pounds, as its weight was expressed in standard English. Scientifically, it weighed a kilogram, or two-point-two pounds, which is how a kilo of anything is technically expressed in the U.S. Customary System of measurement.

In the 1970s, before that and ever thereafter, dope, worldwide, licit and illicit, was sold by metric weight. Cocaine, heroin, hashish, Bordeaux, aspirin, Valium, reds, Quaaludes, prescription speed . . . They were sold by the kilogram or liter, or fraction thereof, in keeping with the International System of Units, as the metric system is formally known. Mexican weed was no exception. Only after it crossed the

border to be sold by Americans was commercial Mexican sold by avoirdupois weight.

And while that piece of cultural trivia might prove useless to a contestant on all but the hippest of television game shows, it serves as an illustration of the contraband-marketing skills of Allen Long's Colombian friends, whose merchandising genius would later change the world. For when Colombia entered the dope-dealing sweepstakes, traffickers there, right from the start, made marijuana available to smugglers priced by the pound.

When Lee Carlyle was twenty-one, he and his partners were running loads of pot out of Culiacán, moving maybe one hundred pounds of Mexican per trip to a group of buyers in Chicago. Carlyle was married to an aspiring actress, driving a new Camaro, and living in an apartment in Los Angeles. He was living the American dream, or the Lee Carlyle version of it anyway. As Allen Long would come to view it, Carlyle's was not a complicated horizon. On the last run he made before meeting Long, Carlyle was headed for the border with the dope in the trunk of a convertible, when he crashed the car, the trunk popped open, he was arrested for smuggling, and thrown into a Mexican jail. By the time he was released his wife had run out on him, taking with her everything he owned — the Camaro, the furniture — and all the cosmetic surgery he had paid for, the complete, marijuana-subsidized makeover, which had been instrumental in nailing her a gig on *As the World Turns*.

When Long and Carlyle met in Mexico, Carlyle was just getting back into the game. And to an observer unfamiliar with the rules under which it was played, chances appeared remote that Carlyle would ever cover the spread. His buyers in Chicago, running up against the seasonal drought suffered

by pot smokers every year, would have done better than to take his call when Carlyle was released from jail.

"No pot," they told him.

"No problem," said Carlyle. "I have a friend in Guadalajara."

The friend and putative savior of all the pot-smoking faithful of Chicago's Near North Side was a Mexican named Jesús, with whom Carlyle had served time in jail, a connection who could load Carlyle up, he said, with all the weight he could handle. The Chicago distributors chartered a plane and flew down to Guadalajara. They had a forty-foot boat in Mazatlán, 300 miles away, which had been sailed down from San Francisco, ready to pick up half a ton of weed. They had sent a lot of people, moved a lot of equipment thousands of miles, and they had spent a lot of money — on a boat captain, a crew, on pilots, on marine and aviation fuel, not to mention the hotel rooms and other, exorbitant incidental expenses necessary to fund the move out of Mexico. Additional cash had been eaten up by logistics and personnel at the site of the scheduled off-load in Southern California. They had done all that only to discover that, yes, Jesús could load them up, but not that time of year.

They had cleared out overnight, leaving Carlyle behind.

That an operator as experienced as Carlyle could have miscalculated so seriously, or more to the point in his case, thrown the dice so recklessly, opened a line of questioning into the workings of the marijuana business that Long would have been smart to pursue. How the ambitious Carlyle had made the same mistake as the majestically confused El Coyote, a smuggler who had actually brought into Mexico more drugs than he had taken out, was worthy of investigation. But Long knew nothing about Carlyle yet. All he

knew was that Carlyle was a marijuana smuggler, another American scammer coming off a deal gone bad in Mexico.

"What are you going to do now?" he asked him over drinks at the Copa de Leche.

Carlyle reached into his pocket. "You see this?" he said, and pulled out a dime. "This is what I have left. I'm going to take this dime," he said, holding it up, "and I'm going to turn it into a million bucks."

Sitting at the Copa de Leche, Long made two decisions. He decided, first, that this guy Lee was "off his rocker." And he decided that Carlyle's attempt to turn the dime into a million dollars was just the dramatic element that his documentary needed, the narrative thread that would pull the movie together. After listening to Carlyle's story, and hearing his plan, he said: "I want to use you as the subject of my film."

Carlyle said fine, undoubtedly thinking that if nothing else he would get room and board out of the deal. Long gave him $500, which was enough to rent a villa in Guadalajara for a month (Carlyle was now one two-thousandth of the way to his goal), and returned to New York to pick up money to finance the continuing research.

It would be two months before pot was available, and Long spent that time at the villa. Carlyle introduced him to Jesús and his partners, and a variety of other troublemakers in or on the periphery of the marijuana business in Guadalajara. While in residence at the villa, Long gathered a wealth of valuable material. And he had a lot of fun. Pot, unavailable commercially, was readily obtainable for personal use, as were cocaine and a variety of women. The region was abundant in visiting American art students, and

a flock of young gringas, attracted by the drugs and the endless amenities of the villa, fell prey, not entirely unwillingly, to the ne'er-do-wells in residence. The swimming pool was always full.

Jesús came through with the pot on schedule, but the deal instantly went south when Carlyle's airplane failed to make the pickup. The pot had been waiting on a dry lakebed outside Guadalajara, and Carlyle's partner, Elwood, flying in from Arizona, had landed at the wrong location. When Carlyle dashed to Tucson to straighten things out, Long followed. The trip was memorable on two scores. Well, only one was actually a score: the amiable desk clerk who checked Long into his motel.

"Say, where'd you get those boots?" she asked.

"New York."

"Are they snakeskin, or what?"

"I don't know, I forget," said Long. "Gila monster or something. Some kind of poisonous lizard."

"Not too many poisonous lizards," she said. "Gila monster's about it."

"You a biology major?"

"Name's Rita."

With hair a shade darker than workingman's whiskey and eyes a shade darker than that, she sported the innocent, feverish gaze of the libidinous and congenitally nearsighted, and her wise-ass manner was punctuated by prominent lips that had supposed a perpetual pout. She was loose and in her twenties, she had nothing to hide, and which of them, she or Long, charmed the other into bed was unclear.

The trip was memorable on a second count for the speed at which the marijuana waiting in Guadalajara was sold. Long and Rita's romance was just one more one-night stand. Carlyle and his buddy Elwood, getting their act together

fast, got the airplane down to Mexico before another night had passed. But by then the dope was gone.

A classic pot-smuggling clusterfuck, the deal represented Long's first foray into what Hollywood calls creative financing. With money earmarked for research, obtained from Ives in New York, Long had backed a part of Carlyle's load. He had invested the money in logistical support, intending to take a cut of Carlyle's profit and use the cash to subsidize the movie. The pot had been sold out from under the partnership in what amounted to two installments. The first half of the load was already gone by the time Elwood was set to make the follow-up flight. Carlyle's suggestion that the half in question was Long's half of the load raised an understandable dispute. Failing to move Carlyle with logic, Long threatened to call the police. Carlyle's response was the only response that was reasonable under the circumstances. Carlyle just hauled off and hit him.

"You can't go to the police!" he screamed. "Are you crazy? You *never* go to the police. No matter *what*, you don't go to the police."

Of course not. The first thing an outlaw, by definition, gives up is recourse to the law. In desperado school, it is a lesson you learn in kindergarten.

Rubbing blood from his lower lip, which had opened up with the fanfare of a circus coming to town, Long said, "I guess you're right," realizing the eminent sense of it. And then he hit Carlyle back.

What was notable about the altercation — the two men traded punches, put the fight behind them, and both got screwed on the deal — was that Long at this point did not think of himself as anything more or less than an honest filmmaker.

Optimistic in spite of the deal's failure, Long returned to New York ready to move the project forward. He figured that sooner or later Carlyle would get a load through, and until then there was plenty to work with. He would rendezvous in Mexico with a smuggler named Alejandro, a contact he had made at the villa, who had offered to introduce him to farmers in the mountains above Mazatlán. In the flowering marijuana fields Long would shoot footage of the harvesting and processing of the crop in preparation for its shipment north.

He leased $20,000 in equipment from General Camera in New York, choosing a state-of-the-art Eclair, the 16mm handheld camera that recently had made a name for itself as employed by director Michael Wadleigh in shooting the feature-length documentary against which all others were being measured: *Woodstock*. Hiring a soundman and an assistant cameraman, Long headed back to Mexico, traveling by way of Tucson. In Tucson he and his crew rented a station wagon — from Hertz, brand-new, a couple of miles on the clock — and planning to head for the border the next day, they checked into the motel at which Long had stayed on his previous trip to town, where Long checked in on Rita.

"Lee's at my place," she said.

This was the first sign of action in a developing pattern of behavior whereby Long and Carlyle, under the flag of the doobie brotherhood, would troll the waters of each other's casual romances, catch and release the castaways, and continue to steam onward, leaving women to drift like jetsam in the wake of the ongoing campaign.

Lee was at Rita's place, sitting in front of the kitchen stove, drying out brick by brick some 200 pounds of marijuana he had succeeded in moving across the border. The pot had been delivered to Arizona in the middle of the night,

a night on which it had snowed in Tucson for the first time in any heavy smoker's admittedly questionable memory. The Mexican smugglers had stashed the marijuana in an arroyo that did what arroyos do — it filled with water — after a snowmelt. The dope was soaking wet.

Sitting there on the kitchen floor, speaking into the lens of a camera, Carlyle, drunk on 7-and-7s, expounded on his circumstances, the how and why of his becoming a smuggler. He was part of a revolution, part of a movement, he said, a cause. This was nothing less than a crusade. He was contributing, he declared, to the "positive change the earth needs to go through." And, he said, besides that, he wanted to make a lot of money. And he wanted a Playboy Bunny for a girlfriend.

The cannabis leaf: the Cross of the new Evangel. And here, enunciated by Lee Carlyle, were the essential tenets of the smuggler's Gospel. Motor whirring, machinery fluttering with the sound of film snaking through the camera aperture, Long's assistant cameraman, cross-legged on the floor, held the lens of the Eclair on Carlyle while Long conducted the interview.

"See this two hundred pounds of marijuana," Carlyle said. "I'm going to turn this into a million dollars."

An echo of his remark at the Copa de Leche, it was a dramatic expression of the smuggler's dream, just the kind of bullshit that Long as a filmmaker was looking for. And like the first time Carlyle had expressed it, its realization struck Long as being just about as remote as Alpha Centauri.

"How," asked Long, "are you planning to get it to Chicago?"

"Greyhound."

"Come again?"

Carlyle directed the camera's attention to the ten-dollar

footlocker — red-white-and-blue, still sporting its Sears Roebuck price tag — on the edge of which Long was sitting.

"I'm going to put the marijuana in it, get on a bus, and take it to Chicago," he said.

The guy *was* off his rocker. Long wished him luck, and the next day departed for Mexico.

Crossing into Mexico with $20,000 in camera equipment raised a predictable sea of bureaucracy on both sides of the international border. But invariably, Long discovered, when one ran into officialdom, however entrenched, and one happened to be in the movie business, the waters tended to part. The holy aura of Hollywood put the power of Moses in the shade.

Everybody, everywhere, wanted to help you make a movie.

High in the mountains above Mazatlán, with the help of his contact Alejandro, Long and his crew shot film of marijuana being harvested, gathered, dried, and processed. From Mazatlán, he and the crew drove to Guadalajara, where Alejandro promised them access to footage at a second location.

The day things came together, Long paid Alejandro $500, agreeing to meet him the following morning to make the run up into the mountains. Alejandro, spending the money in a whorehouse, which kept him up all night, showed up drunk at Long's hotel on a local rum and vanilla cream concoction commercially known as Ronpope. He and an associate, equally drunk, arrived in a rented Volkswagen, the same one the company rented to all the drunks in Mexico, as far as Long could tell — there it was again, that same bilious green. And naturally, being drunk, Alejandro insisted upon driving.

Long's assistant cameraman was a Puerto Rican named Joey Martínez. Long had hired him for his talent, for the fact that he spoke Spanish, and for his willingness to take the risk that the assignment in Mexico entailed. Long and Martínez were in the back of the Volkswagen, Alejandro and his partner up front. Space being severely limited, Long's soundman had stayed behind.

Careering — and then, as he continued to drink, careening — down the highway, Alejandro blustered incessantly, talking over his shoulder as he drove. The straight-away over which they were flying ended in a high face of rock, visible in the distance, a cliff on which the local highway department had painted a bright yellow arrow, and Long took it upon himself to alert the bragging Mexican to its approach.

"Alejandro, better slow down, there's a turn coming up ahead."

"You want to see me make a turn? Motherfucker, I'll show you how to make a turn!"

Long would look back upon moments like this to explain why it took another twenty-five years, a full quarter century — and that spent under the day-to-day tutelage of criminals in Colombia, the most sophisticated criminals in the world — before Mexico became a really significant player in the international dope trade.

Taking the turn at seventy, Alejandro put the Volkswagen into a 180 degree spin. Long was looking out the rear window as the car went backward through the guardrail and pitched over the cliff. It tumbled downhill, rolling several times before coming to a stop, and when it did, it looked like a hard-boiled egg after you beat it with a spoon. All the windows were busted out, and through one of them Long escaped, miraculously unhurt. He pulled Joey Martínez

out of the wreck. The big, handsome Puerto Rican, whose ribs were broken, had suffered a head injury that was to put him in the hospital. Alejandro's inebriated partner was uninjured, but his sunglasses were broken and he was really pissed off.

"*Mis lentes! Cabrón!*" my glasses, he screamed.

That was all he could say. And, drunkenly, he was saying it to Alejandro, who was dead. Well, he was nearly dead. "He'll be dead in a minute," Long remembered thinking at the time. When Long pulled him out of the car, and placed him on the ground, flies started buzzing around Alejandro's head. He was not breathing, not obviously, but he was still alive. He was *trying* to breathe. Blood overflowed his face, and Long placed a bandanna over it to keep the flies away. His partner did not get the picture, and was standing over Alejandro, yelling at him, bemoaning the condition of his sunglasses. "*Chinga tu madre! Mis lentes . . . !*"

Which cracked Joey Martínez up. Joey, his body flirting with the inevitable onset of shock, busted out laughing, and not even the pain of his broken ribs was enough to make him stop.

Alejandro's body had begun shuddering, and his partner, shouting down at him, was still casting aspersions upon Alejandro's parentage, when a police cruiser rolled up. An officer stepped out and approached down the hill with a notebook in his hand. With all the composure and dispassion of the typical U.S. highway patrolman, he asked who the driver of the car was. Long pointed to the body on the ground. The cop, dismissing Alejandro's partner, took over the conversation the latter was having with Alejandro, who by then had silently departed the cool sequester'd vale of life. While the partner rooted around the wreck for his bottle of Ronpope, grumbling because the sunlight was bothering

his eyes, and while Joey Martínez continued uncontrollably to laugh, the cop questioned the late Alejandro, whose face beneath the blood-soaked bandanna was invisible to him.

And each time the cop asked a question, Alejandro said nothing.

"Your name, sir?"

Alejandro said nothing.

"How fast were you traveling?"

Alejandro said nothing.

"May I see your license, please?"

Tar-baby ain't sayin' nuthin', en Brer Fox, he lay low.

Joey Martínez was about to crack another rib, and Long, fighting the contagion of Joey's laughter, struggled to stifle his own.

"*Muerto,*" Long finally said.

The cop looked up from his notebook.

"*Muerto?*"

Alejandro's body had gone still. Long studied it for a second or two, then nodded in affirmation.

"*Muerto,*" he told the cop.

"*Oh,*" the cop said. "*Muerto!*"

He flipped his notebook closed, walked back up the hill, and radioed for an ambulance.

The medics arrived, removed Joey and the body, and the cop drove Long and the other man to the hotel.

Long's soundman packed it in, and with Joey Martínez recovering in a Guadalajara hospital, Long returned alone to Mazatlán.

The first and most reliable pot connection Allen Long made south of the border he had made through a fifteen-year-old Mexican kid on the street outside a Mazatlán restaurant

who offered to wash his car. The kid's name was Tomás, and Long, after paying him for a job well done, asked if Tomás could score him some pot.

To smoke. Long had run out of personal stash.

Tomás earned his money hustling tourists, and like every hustler Long would run into everywhere in Latin America, he operated on the fringes of the dope trade. Long was looking for an ounce of pot, and Tomás could handle that with no problem; in fact, he came up with a brick. It was his way of showing off. Like most hustlers on the periphery of the market, Tomás saw himself as a player. But Tomás was young yet. It would be a while before he moved up to the big show. The brick was supplied by his uncle, and was grown about 200 miles southeast of Mazatlán in the vicinity of Tepic, the capital of Nayarit state, where the first Mexican sinsemilla, the seedless cannabis prized for the potency of its flowering tops, would later be cultivated.

Long had first run across Tomás on a trip he had made to Mazatlán while living at the villa in Guadalajara waiting for Carlyle's deal to go down. Returning now to Mazatlán, upon Alejandro's rather theatrical drop from the payroll, Long sought out Tomás, the only lead he had, looking to score the additional footage he needed of marijuana cultivation in the mountains. Tomás reached out to his uncle, who eventually consented to a meeting with Long, an uncharacteristic move for an established criminal, attributable perhaps to the thrill of the movies, that and $500 in cash.

The meeting took place in a tiny cantina in the mountains surrounding Tepic. Long arrived with his camera, and no sooner had he stepped through the door than he suddenly stepped back in time. Within minutes of his taking a seat, gunshots rang out nearby. He swiveled his head in

the direction of the noise. A figure raced past the open window. Long made ready to move.

"Just two men shooting at each other . . ."

The sepulchral voice from across the table, droning words of assurance, drew Long's attention its way. There was a near-imaginary, frontier quality to this stretch of Mexico's coastal mountains, and its essence was expressed in high relief in the visage of the man sitting opposite him. Tomás's Uncle Francisco embodied all the visual attributes, as gringos tended to interpret them, of the classic Mexican *bandido*. About forty-five years old, he had the broad face and prominent mustache that jumped forth from familiar, archival photographs of the legendary Pancho Villa, the revolutionary leader with whose countenance that of the stereotypical Mexican outlaw was commonly identified. Of medium height and heavyset, heavy in more ways than one, Francisco was outfitted to play the part. The tooled-leather boots were not for show, serving a preference for travel by horseback for which he was very well known, just as the twin revolvers in tooled-leather holsters served his local self-employment as the Man: the *traficante* who controlled the flow of marijuana out of Tepic. Many of the other outlaws Long would meet in the mountains that day would look as if they had stepped unblushing out of the same photo archive.

From Tepic, situated about 3,000 feet above sea level, it was a steady climb to Long's destination. Francisco and his men, staging from a ranch not far from the cantina, progressed from there on horseback, leading the earnest American up through the dry chaparral into the high reaches of the desert. Hidden there in the mountains, on the cleared slopes of shallow ravines that cleaved the rugged landscape, flared the rich green of cultivated marijuana planted row

upon row. Hundreds of ravines were being worked, three or four to a farmer, and every ravine was productive. Long was struck by the industry that enabled the crop to prosper, by the primitive yet effective technique by which irrigation was engineered. A large stone placed at the head of a ravine diverted spring water to the uppermost row of plants. The crop rows traversed the canyon at a slight angle downhill, left to right, then right to left, and as the water ran down the hillside every plant received its share. Both sides of the canyon, alternately, were irrigated in this fashion.

Long got the footage he needed, and returned to Tepic with the promise of a second trip, sometime later, higher into the mountains — there, Francisco would show him the airstrip from which the pot was dispatched. Meanwhile, Long checked on Joey Martínez, recovering in Guadalajara.

"No way," said Joey, from his hospital bed.

"Forget it, Joey," said Long.

"I'm not letting you go without me."

"Joey, you can't go."

There was no need to point out the obvious. Joey, in his condition, would have a hard time making it to the door of his room, let alone making the difficult climb, much of it on foot, to the airstrip.

"You could get killed up there," Joey said. "You're a stupid American."

Joey, being Puerto Rican, reasoned that he himself in this situation was somehow not an American — well, not to the Mexicans, anyway — that his speaking Spanish would in some way mitigate any perception of stupidity in Long that the outlaws happened to harbor.

"They'll kill you," he maintained.

"You can't go with me on this one, Joey."

"I'm going."

"You can't go," Long insisted. "When I'm finished, I'll come back and get you."

The airstrip was located on a barely accessible escarpment high above the marijuana fields, at the upper reaches of the mountains' deciduous growth. When the trail became too steep for the horses and burros, Long and the smugglers walked, occasionally forced to secure handholds on the rock face overhanging the footpath. When delivering pot to the runway, Long was astonished to find, the smugglers, from the point at which the pack animals were abandoned, would have to carry the cargo on their backs.

Making the arduous climb, Long had good reason to be thankful for having selected the smaller, lighter, more expensive Eclair over the industry-standard Arriflex when he had rented his equipment in New York. Unaccustomed to the altitude, he had difficulty keeping up with the Mexicans. He fell behind. Then hurried forward. Then fell behind again. He fell behind rather rhythmically, in fact — he was running on a manual fuel pump.

Allen Long's romance with cocaine was like the worst of marriages. It was passionate and eager, but stormy. It was an arena for the indulgence of every tendency toward self-destruction, and it went on for years, infinitely lingering, doomed to everything but failure. It was a veritable circus for the expression of twisted behavior, and the big top never left town. From the moment he first encountered cocaine, Long was seldom without it. Buying it was like filling a prescription. He would carry it with him the way diabetics carry insulin. In the early years of his infatuation, the drug in debilitating amounts remained an affliction chiefly of the wealthy, and so the worst of it came later, the level of his engagement a kind of barometer of his rising fortunes. Time and the ravages of addiction would soon bleed the performance of its charm,

but in the beginning, before things got way out of hand, there was an almost comic quality to his appetite. In the beginning, at a time when dope use in general was new — when dope was first insinuating itself into the collective identity of a generation — getting stoned, as a spectator sport, was not entirely unrewarding.

In scaling the mountains that day, as Long fell behind, he would pause to inhale a couple of thumbnails of flake from a stash he had purchased the night before. It had worked for the Incas for 2,000 years, and it worked just as well for him. It helped him overcome the effects of altitude and fatigue, and eventually to overcome the lead of the Mexicans rearmost in the line of ascent. Long would speed up the trail until the influence of the drug waned, the Mexicans overtook him, and he fell behind again. And did cocaine again. Acting out the fable of the tortoise and the hare, he found himself testing its hypothesis, and the result, he was dismayed to discover, was just as Aesop had reported it.

Ascending through stands of oak and maple, passing beneath the same foliage that flourished in his backyard in Charlottesville, Long followed Francisco and his men to the site of a high, cloud-free mesa, a narrow elevation with drop-offs of up to 2,000 feet on a side. The setting was surreal, of a kind that had existed up to then only in his imagination. Running out over the face of the cliff, like an optical illusion, stretched the landing strip, a phantom of a runway no longer than 1,200 feet.

"No margin for error," one pilot later told Long. "You're perfect or you're dead."

It was like hitting the deck of a carrier. Overshooting the landing meant instantly picking up sufficient speed to achieve lift before falling off the front of the mesa. It was the only

correctable miscalculation, and correctable only within a window of seconds. Any other miscalculation and there was no coming around for a second pass.

Entering a small hut in which a fire was going and coffee was brewing, Long settled in with the Mexicans and waited for operations to begin. Activity picked up the next day with the delivery of pot to the runway, and the appearance overhead soon after that of a single-engine Beech. Scaling the peaks, the plane circled the airstrip, nosed in at an acute, almost acrobatic angle and dropped onto the runway. Out of the plane stepped a smuggler from Tucson named Bobby, who generously consented to Long's shooting footage of the load-up and takeoff.

"But don't shoot the tail numbers," he said.

The Mexicans threw 600 pounds of reefer aboard, and Bobby — no time to chat — jumped back in the cockpit, threw up a thumb, and took off. The Beech, before catching air, dropped precipitously off the edge of the cliff, tail dipping, just like a Navy F4. It picked up altitude, banked to the left, leveled off and disappeared, heading for the border.

Another load, off to market. There would be joy in Tucson tonight.

When he returned to Guadalajara to pick up Joey Martínez, Long received a call from the States. It was Ives, his producer, phoning from New York. Long, since leaving town with the camera equipment, had spent a couple of months in Mexico, and Ives was calling now to remind him that all the money was spent.

"I hope you've finished the movie," he said.

Long had footage of Carlyle, he had all the footage from

the fields, and now he had the footage he had shot on the escarpment above Tepic. But he still lacked the narrative element, the simple story value, that would raise the movie above the level of those documentaries typically found on public television. What he had right now, at best, might secure his movie a slot there, but he wanted more than that. If he went back to New York, it was over, he would have to start raising money again. Figuring he could stretch things for a couple of days, he decided to hold on to the equipment. Joey Martínez, a stand-up guy, told Long he would stick it out with him.

Long called Rita's number in Tucson to see what Carlyle was up to. It had been a while since the crazy Californian had voiced his determination to take the pot-filled footlocker and turn it into a million dollars.

Rita said, "Lee doesn't live here."

Of course not, Long concluded. That ship would have sailed a long time ago. Captain Carlyle, circling the party boat, passing the SS *Rita* in the night.

"But he left a phone number," Rita continued, "and said to give it to you if you called."

Long reached him at an apartment in Chicago.

"Come on up, buddy," Carlyle said. "Get up here, man, I did it."

"Did what?"

"Just come," he said, "you'll see."

Long dumped the station wagon at the airport in Guadalajara, and he and a heavily bandaged Joey Martínez headed for Chicago. Carlyle met them at O'Hare. He arrived in a blue Maserati convertible. Long hopped in, and with Joey and the equipment following in a limousine, the three men sped into town. They dropped off the gear at Carlyle's place, and Carlyle took the filmmakers to lunch. Carlyle,

whom they had last seen squatting on the kitchen linoleum of a half-duplex in Tucson, was now renting an Oak Street penthouse with a panoramic view of Lake Michigan and a good stretch of Chicago skyline. Over lunch at a three-star restaurant, Carlyle, last seen draining a bottle of Seagram's, squatted now behind three longnecks of Dom Pérignon and told the two filmmakers his story.

Taking the money he had made selling the 200 pounds, he had returned to Mexico and paid his suppliers, who then fronted him another 400. When he sold that, the Mexicans sent him a thousand pounds. He bought a truck, hired a driver, and doubled up again, after which his Chicago buyers offered to put a fleet of trucks on the road. All this time the Mexicans had supplied the pot on-the-arm, and because the pot was fronted, Carlyle's margin was necessarily thin. He was making somewhere between $5 and $10 a pound. He had been operating only a couple months, but, now, with enough of his own money, he was in a position to pay for the pot in advance, to buy it from the Mexicans himself. He was in the process of moving serious weight, somewhere in the vicinity of a ton, and on it he stood to make as much as $100 a pound. He was investing everything he had in this truckload, and Long and Joey Martínez were just in time to see him celebrate his success.

Joey Martínez turned to Long and said, "Now you've got a story."

Carlyle was about to turn his original dime into a cool quarter million. And he had done it in a matter of six months. In two months he had gone from traveling by Greyhound to driving a new Maserati. At his penthouse later that afternoon, he introduced Long to his new girlfriend. Valerie, who had been featured in *Playboy,* was employed in customer service at the magazine's flagship Chicago club — yes,

Carlyle had landed a Bunny. In the apartment, Long and Joey set up their gear and committed the smuggler's story to film.

It was magic hour in the movie business. The sun was setting on the black anodized aluminum and tinted bronze glass of the Hancock Tower, which rose like a whale spout on a windless ocean just beyond the window. Its lights and all the lights in Chicago were just beginning to show. With Long conducting the interview, Carlyle paced the penthouse, moving between the window glass and a black leather executive chair that appeared to have been upholstered by the same guy who had fitted out the interior of the Maserati. Expansive, uninhibited, no longer the picture of failure and resignation that had become familiar to Long, Carlyle shared his wisdom with the people, the big-time smuggler high on cocaine, Quaaludes, and champagne.

Staring into the camera, falling into silhouette, Lee Carlyle enlightened the world. He explained how things were done. He told how he had pulled off the move, talked about his plans for the future. He edified his fellow Americans. He revealed the true meaning of life. As only a twenty-four-year-old could do it. Lee Carlyle was in possession of the secret. He held the key to the Kingdom of Heaven. And Allen Long had the story he needed. With a little fleshing out in the middle — footage of the smugglers loading trucks in Mexico, transporting the dope to Chicago — Long had his documentary.

The telephone rang, and Carlyle uncradled the receiver, taking the call, being the executive that he was, even as he spoke into the camera. His side of the phone conversation went something like this: "Hey, man . . . Oh . . . What? . . . Yeah . . ." He turned away from his audience. "Oh, shit, they did? . . . Oh, God . . . Oh . . ." And then he said, ". . . No."

Carlyle sat down, hung up the phone, held his head, and started to cry.

"They caught him."

The guy driving Carlyle's truckload of pot. A six-foot-three-inch bar bouncer posing as a minister, right down to the clerical collar and the phony driver's license. They caught him in Arizona. They busted the load. It was gone. Carlyle was broke.

"It's a rags-to-riches story."

"No."

"It's the American dream personified. Rags to riches, back to rags, and back to riches, as far as I know."

"You've spent a hundred and forty thousand dollars, and you have nothing to show for it. If you want to finish the movie," said Ives, "you'll have to raise the money yourself."

According to the professionals for whom Long had run the footage, he needed an additional hundred thousand to finish the film. His mentor, a cinematographer at Motion Associates, the production house at which he had worked, told him the story was there, but that he would have to go back and rebuild it. And to do that he needed more footage. Included in the overall estimate was $60,000 for processing and editing.

"And," said Ives, still hemorrhaging money, "I want you to go get the car."

The car?

The station wagon, rented brand-new from Hertz, which had been driven into Mexico from Tucson, and was still sitting there after two and a half months. The car parked at the airport in Guadalajara with several thousand miles on the clock. *That* car.

Long, retrieving the station wagon, turned it in at El Paso, about 200 miles closer than Tucson to where the car was parked. He made the trip in a hurry, traveling virtually nonstop, fueled on pharmaceutical speed, high on a handful of Black Beauties he bought from a Guadalajara filling station attendant. He traveled as well with an ounce of very good pot, every leaf of which he was determined to smoke rather than give up before he arrived at the border. About fifteen miles short of the Rio Grande, where the landscape was desolate and the mountains were as black as the pills he was popping, he pulled off the highway to smoke a joint that was big enough to stop a door and emptied the car of all the drugs he could find. A half-hour later, with his body racing on amphetamines and reefer, he made the bridge at Juárez.

He pulled up at U.S. Customs, and with the car having been out of the country so long, was ordered as a matter of form into the inspection lane.

Run up and down the mountains for a couple of months, carrying people who just maybe smoked a joint once in a while, the car looked like it had been through some protracted and possibly psychedelic guerrilla insurgency. A careful examination was almost certain to show its interior to be littered with shake. When Customs inspectors approached the car with a German shepherd on a leash, Long knew he had some fast talking to do. In his condition, under the influence of a blood chemistry that could honestly be called festive, the talking was going to be fast whether he liked it or not.

"Look," he told the woman heeling the dog, as the other agent lowered the tailgate, "I smoked pot in that car . . ."

Just around the edge of her aviator shades, the inspector's eyes shifted his way. There he stood, yellow-eyed, sallow-skinned, and reeking of the skunk weed he had smoked

moments before, going on as if the same aroma, currently choking the vehicle, might prove to be the source of some mystery to officers of the United States Customs Service working the Mexican border. Just around the edge of her aviator shades, her eyes seemed to say: No shit?

"There's no marijuana in it," Long continued, "but . . ."

"Then why worry?" she said, and released the dog into the car. She glanced back at Long and confided, "That dog's never caught anybody."

The dog sniffed around, executed a quick pirouette, sat down on its haunches, and stared out over the tailgate, panting, as if waiting for a ride into town.

"Go," the agent told Long.

The Hertz agent in El Paso was not similarly unruffled. Freaked out but faced with no other choice — after pathetically failing to intimidate Long with a fifty-dollar drop-off charge — he took possession of the marijuanamobile. The damage, billed to Ives's credit card, amounted to more than $6,000.

Long, in Mexico, had struck up a friendship with an American he ran into in Mazatlán, a troublemaker by the name of Pomeroy. A California biker, Pomeroy was a member in good standing of the Oakland chapter of an organization he reverently called the Angels and official law enforcement documents called the Hell's Angels Motorcycle Club. Having recently wiped out on his bike, he had ridden into Mazatlán with his girlfriend on the back of his Harley and plaster casts on both of his feet. Long met them at the same tourist trap outside of which he had encountered Tomás. Maybe fifteen years older than Long, with dark brown hair that was going gray and the body language of

a rodeo cowboy, Pomeroy, a lovable rascal to Long's way of thinking, had been smuggling marijuana for years, and the two took to each other immediately.

Intrigued by Long's idea for a movie, Pomeroy had given him the name of a friend, a concert promoter in New York who had just been given a record label, suggesting that Long might be interested in talking to the man at some point. Pomeroy, convinced like most smugglers that his life story was worthy of immortalizing, offered to help the would-be filmmaker any way he could, and invited Long to look him up at a Marin County address if he ever got out to the Bay Area.

Returning to New York from El Paso, Long put in a call to Pomeroy, figuring that maybe Pomeroy's promoter friend could help him get the movie going again. The project was hopelessly stalled now, and Long was running out of options.

"My friend wants to meet you," Pomeroy said, before Long got around to asking.

There are character traits, both personal and collective, for which the Hell's Angels are notorious. Inefficiency is not among them.

Pomeroy's friend had an office in New York's Gulf & Western Building, and Long, when he stepped through the door, knew that he had come to the right place. The promoter sat at his desk gripping a bone-handled knife, and centered on the desk pad below the blade was a rock of cocaine the size of a lab rat. Long, to be gracious, helped Pomeroy's friend snort it. Their conversation opened where conversations in such circumstances invariably do, with casual but predictably earnest expressions of their appreciation for the agriculture of Peru. It was agreed — for etiquette in such circumstances always demanded it — that this particular sample was excellent, as pure as either had ever seen his

life, and by inference significantly better than that which somebody else might be willing to share. With that rap meandering to a conclusion, the meeting turned to a more pointed and professional discussion of their common interest in documentary filmmaking. Pomeroy's friend saw in Long's movie an excellent vehicle for a soundtrack album. Long concurred with the view. Both men knew that the right album would generate more revenue than the film itself. Pomeroy's friend said he would very much like to work with Long.

"How much do you need to finish the movie?" he asked.

Long, elated, answered that he could get the job done for a hundred thousand dollars.

"All right," the friend said, wiping his nose. "Call me when you get the money."

And that was the end of the meeting.

Long had a good mind to grab the guy by the shirt and tell him his cocaine sucked.

Failing to raise financing for the film in New York, Long refused to give up. Determined to keep the project alive, he did what any filmmaker in similar circumstances would do. "Hell, I can do this," he said, and did what all the great filmmakers before him had done . . . Ford, Truffaut, Fellini, the giants of the art, Orson Welles . . . He did what all of them had done in establishing their careers in the cinema.

"I can go back and do a load."

Sure.

He became a marijuana smuggler.

CADILLAC MOON

Marin County, California, lay at the confluence of every cultural stream of any importance to a man of Allen Long's ambitions in 1972. In Marin the values of the youth movement that had flowered down the road in the sociological greenhouse of San Francisco's Haight-Ashbury district were being expressed in the backwash of their inevitable commercialization. In Marin, on the Sausalito side of the Golden Gate Bridge, free love, dope, and music, five years after the Summer of Love, were being celebrated in the hearts and hormones of the steadily employed.

Having tapped every source of potential financing for his documentary and come up dry, Long had called Pomeroy again.

"How'd the meeting go?"

"I need to raise some money," said Long.

"Come out here," said Pomeroy. "I got a job for you."

And Long, if not on the next, was on the next best flight.

He spent his first evening in California with Pomeroy and his girlfriend, Justine, hanging out with Quicksilver

Messenger Service between the band's sets at Winterland. After the gig they all went to the Trident in Sausalito, one of the more popular joints in a town where hospitality demanded that smoking dope be something you do without leaving your table. Sitting with Pomeroy and the easy-going Justine, the blonde who had ridden into Mazatlán on the back of his Harley-Davidson, Long, stoned to the point of embracing religion, was made to feel instantly at home. Little was there at home, however, to compare with the wait-ress who was serving him drinks. A redhead named Fleurette, she so exceeded Long's aspirations for a waitress that to order his first shot of tequila he was forced to adjust his breathing. The first time she asked if he wanted another he had to adjust his clothes.

In Marin that night and those that followed, under the dutiful ministration of Pomeroy, Long was received like a visiting dignitary. Call it a sales pitch. Long was sold. The breathtaking Fleurette would seal the deal, Fleurette, an authentic redhead, whose pubic hair, he would later discover, was trimmed in the shape of a heart. Long fell in love — with both — and in the fragrant blush of her topiary he languished for the next six months. He moved into Pomeroy's Mill Valley house and swiftly got down to busi-ness. He had a movie to make. There was a cinematic muse to satisfy. It was time to try some professional smuggling.

Pomeroy had been moving marijuana in loads of between fifty and one hundred pounds, and was getting ready to step things up when he brought Long on board. He had just taken on a partner, a small-time hustler by the name of Big Jim, a San Francisco bus driver who had been augmenting his income dealing herb. Big Jim was eager to move weight. He had a growing clientele and money to invest, and needed a dependable source of dope at a decent price. Pomeroy,

who had been supplying him, had the personnel and equipment and the organizational skills necessary to get marijuana into the country. What Pomeroy did not have was a connection in Mexico sufficiently reliable to supply the necessary weight on a regular basis. That was where Long came in. Long impressed Pomeroy as a guy quick enough on his feet to be an asset to any operation. He was a guy who knew his way around Mexico, and Pomeroy believed him to be the guy who could help him establish the connection he needed.

Long, proving to be as quick with his hands as Pomeroy believed him to be on his feet, reached into his hat and pulled out a rabbit. A mustachioed bunny in tooled-leather boots wearing six shooters on both hips. Long had Francisco in Tepic.

"*Olé!*"

Long went to Mexico to set up the deal, and once it was made, was joined in Tepic by a fellow named Tex. Tex was there to check out the airstrip. Hangared in a barn on his ranch in El Paso, Tex had a surplus T-6 trainer unregistered with the FAA. Tex, a man of few words, as if honoring the stereotype of characters so named, was the more matter-of-fact of the aerial cowboys riding for the Pomeroy brand. There were two pilots on the payroll. The other was Pomeroy's hairdresser, Decidedly Effeminate Frederick, as he was known to the Mill Valley crew. Thanks to the flamboyant Frederick, Pomeroy was one of the more fashionably coiffed outlaws ever to wear Angels colors. Frederick owned a single-engine Cessna.

With all the players in place, and a 600-pound load sitting on the runway in Tepic, the team went operational with the approach of the first full moon.

Long awoke early that day, and he and Pomeroy

descended to the garage. The house in Marin was a four-bedroom, two-story rental on a half-acre north of Mill Valley. A second-floor balcony overlooked an in-ground pool, which was one of two main attractions of the gray-clapboard hillside property. The other was the large, below-grade garage on which the house was built and in which one could park three cars end-to-end and close the door behind them. Parked there were two Cadillac limousines.

The rear panel as well as the passenger seats of each car had been removed. Everything behind the driver was cargo space, all the way through to the trunk. The rear suspension of each limousine was outfitted with air shocks. Pumping them up raised the tail of the car, which when loaded with cargo would then level out, and appear as if it were traveling empty.

The impact of what Long was about to do gave him a moment of pause. It was one thing to be in Mexico — *bandido* country to him, where no law applied, where you could buy your way out of trouble — and quite another to be here, he decided, here in the USA, getting ready to drive off and pick up a planeload of dope. Having set up the deal was nothing. This was inescapably hands-on. This was narcotics trafficking.

"Are you going to back out?" he asked himself. "Or are you going to grab your balls and get in the car?"

He got in the car. And they drove.

With the fog lifting off the redwoods, they drove up through Northern California, following Interstate 5. They wound through the Sacramento Valley, and swung north-east at Redding. They followed Highway 299 across the Cascade Range, skirting the Shasta National Forest, and a couple of hours after midday, at about 6,000 feet above sea level, they hit Cedar Pass and descended to the alkali lakes.

Maybe eight hours out of San Francisco, Pomeroy pulled into a filling station, and drew Long's attention to a narrow dirt road.

"You see that bypass? That little track that goes past those houses up there and into the woods? That's the road we're going to take on the way back."

It would allow them, he said, to circumvent California agricultural inspection.

In Cedarville they ate, drank a couple of beers, smoked a joint, and waited till dark, then pumped up the air shocks and made for the border, heading south on Highway 447. As they ran down the hills on the eastern slope of the mountains, the scenery changed dramatically. They dropped from the lush, four-color world of the California foothills to the floor of the Nevada desert, which greeted them like a postcard from the surface of the moon. The highway undulated through a series of valleys in which huge irrigation systems gave rise to everything that was green. The road seemed to disappear into infinity, to run endlessly in places between one change of elevation and another. South of Lower Alkali Lake, for mile upon mile, as the two-lane blacktop entered the Smoke Creek Desert, the valleys were flat and the road was straight.

On that highway, that night, Pomeroy received a radio transmission telling him the flight was delayed. Smuggling was waiting. It was axiomatic. Nothing about the trip would prove more characteristic of the work Long had chosen than the fact that the load was late.

They would have to put up for the night. The nearest place to do that with two Cadillac limousines, without drawing too much attention, was Reno, some 160 miles south. They arrived there early in the morning, checked into a motel, and slept. When Long awoke, which was sometime after one P.M., Pomeroy was gone.

The next several hours, Long's first stretch alone as a federal offender, bordered on the existential. Before turning in, on the chance that Long might wake up before him, Pomeroy had given orders: "We leave at six. Until then, don't go out. Don't go anywhere. Stay here."

Now Pomeroy had disappeared. And Long labored for hours under a restriction he was too inexperienced to break. Pomeroy had made it clear that Long was a link in the chain of responsibility upon which the success of the operation hung. Others had placed their faith in him. And others were at risk. If Long slipped up in the slightest, others might go to jail.

Not far beyond the door flashed the neon lights of Reno. They flashed around the clock. The desert town was one large caravansary in which casinos were the water. And Long was exceedingly thirsty to be anywhere but by himself. "Stay here," Pomeroy had told him, and "here" was a cheap motel room somewhere on the outskirts of town, with two beds, a telephone, and a color TV. The telephone was bolted to a table. The television was bolted to a dresser. The dresser was bolted to the floor. The walls were painted white, and all were free of artwork. The only colors, and there were all of them — all those dazzling, artificial colors one imagines when one imagines Reno — jumped from the bedspread and the carpet, their design, which was enough to make any guest vomit, having been engineered intentionally to be unaffected when he or she did.

Long paced the room like a zoo animal, compulsively studying the checkout notice posted on the door. He wondered what he was supposed to do if Pomeroy did not come back. He had been gone for four or five hours. Right about now, Tex, the T-6 cowboy, would be refueling south of Nogales, and sometime after midnight he would be on

the radio to Frederick the hairdresser, making contact 5,000 feet over the valley Long had driven through the night before. And Long had better be there.

At six P.M., Pomeroy returned.

"Okay," he said, "let's go."

"Jesus, where the hell were you?"

"Calm down," said Pomeroy. "Relax."

"Where'd you go?" Long wanted to know.

"Relax," repeated Pomeroy.

"I've been here, man, I've been ready."

"Just get in the car and follow me."

Where Pomeroy had gone is where Long would go, systematically, later in his career, doing to a hundred other people what Pomeroy had done to him.

"You gotta stay here, and you gotta stay straight," Long would tell the people who worked for him. "Don't go out and get wasted. Don't go anywhere. I don't want you to move."

And then, in the same way that Pomeroy had gone out to kill some time at the blackjack tables, Long would go out to play — in his case probably pick up a woman and all the drugs he could find — to return just before the load was due, and tell everybody, "Okay, let's go."

They revved up the limos and headed east, hitting a service station outside Sparks and pulling up to the air compressor, where they pumped up the Cadillacs' shocks before turning into the desert. They traveled north through the Nightingale Mountains with the cars riding high in the rear. Long's fear conspired with the moon and the night to throw the land's features into stark relief, altering his perception of everything. As the road rose to meet the mountain range, the peaks, like distant pyramids, ascended as if on elevators into his line of sight. Wheeled carriages, supporting the pipes of

vast irrigation systems, dominated the flat terrain, the pipes themselves, traversing the landscape, stretching to opposite horizons.

Just southeast of the alkali lakes, the smugglers pulled to a stop and backed the limousines off the road, edging into the brush bordering the blacktop. Removing eight portable strobe light assemblies from the trunk of his limo, Long positioned but did not activate them, four on either side of the highway, delimiting a run of about 700 feet. He returned to the car. And they waited.

The cars were parked three feet apart. The broken white line of the highway dashed off into infinity. The night was still, and every second seemed like an hour to Long, scared to the point of shivering, sweating in the cool night air. Pomeroy fired up a joint. He laid out a few lines of cocaine. He handed Long a beer. The moon, suspended over the left-front quarter panel of Long's black limousine, full-blown, ostentatious, was doing what it could to wash the heavens clear of stars. Every now and then there was a sound. A mule deer on the move. Jackrabbits rustling. A coyote.

"What was that?"

"It's a jackrabbit, man, relax."

Long would get cool later.

High above the desert, Frederick circled. The valley floor stretched below him, revealed in the glow of the moon. From the cockpit he could read the highway, able to pick up oncoming headlights almost an hour away. In air-to-air contact with Tex, coming up from the south, and ground-to-air contact with Pomeroy, he could call off the rendezvous at the sign of any activity. Only then would Pomeroy hear his voice. In the absence of danger, Frederick would maintain radio silence. To signal a landing, he would simply key the microphone twice.

The windows of both Cadillacs were down. Pomeroy was smoking a cigarette. The desert was silent, the breeze was light. Long was staring over his sideview mirror, watching a jackrabbit change its mind. And then on the night, in the stillness of it, came the sound of radio static.

Click. Click.

Pomeroy fired his engine, Long did the same, and using only their running lights, they powered the Cadillacs up onto the highway. They pulled side by side, facing north. Long jumped out and set the strobes, then jumped back into his car.

Seconds passed. The strobe lights pulsed.

Silence again.

Click. Click.

The smugglers hit the headlamps. An explosion of incandescent light, as the eight sealed beams fired simultaneously, illuminated the highway for a mile. And then, in the silence, Long felt a shiver in his neck. As though a bat had just flown through his hair. There was no sound but the flutter of a feathered prop, and the airplane was there over the hood of the car, lurching down out of nowhere, flared out to catch ground effect with its forty-two-foot wingspan. Wheels down, accessing the highway at an angle of maybe 25 degrees, it glided in on the beam of the headlights to touch down on the asphalt in front of him. With a single squeak of the gear as the rubber hit the blacktop, it made a perfect three-point landing and rolled north at about 65 knots.

Throwing the Cadillacs into drive, the smugglers hit the accelerators, and chased the airplane down the highway, catching up as it braked to a stop and 300 bricks of Mexican weed in burlap hit the asphalt. They executed rapid three-point turns, backed the Cadillacs up to the plane, popped

the trunks, and loaded the dope. Before Long could pick up the strobes, Tex and the T-6 were airborne. From the moment Frederick had first keyed the microphone, maybe 130 seconds had passed.

They drove through the night. And as Long followed Pomeroy through the wilderness, his body running with sweat, it occurred to him that he was a criminal now. In the eyes of a beer-swilling, pill-popping nation, Allen Long was a felon. He was driving a car in which 300 pounds of dope were stashed. And there was no way to pretend that he was somehow unaware of it. Pulled over by the police, for any reason, he was busted.

A few hours after sunrise, they pulled into a service station off Interstate 5, driving the limousines up to the pump on opposite sides of the same island. It was 1972, and America had yet to realize the vision of an Interstate highway system entirely free of the scourge of human assistance. The self-serve island, in glorious ubiquity, from sea to shining sea, was just a gleam in the nation's eye. It was a *service* station into which they had driven — always an exciting stop for a smuggler.

"Hey, what's that hangin' out the back of your car?"

It was the guy pumping gas, he was talking to Long, and he might just as well have been asking him, hey, what is that gushin' out your aorta? What was hangin' out the back of Long's car was reefer, an extrusion of weed, projected from a kilo onto which the trunk had been slammed in Long's haste to gather up the strobe lights. And it had been hangin' out the back all morning, all the way from Nevada.

"Oh," said Long, "that's lespedeza."

"What?"

"Yeah," said Long, retreating to the cover of mono-syllables.

"What's that?"

"It's a special kind of clover," he said. "We're carrying it down to the horse farms in Marin."

"Huh," said the attendant, who nodded his head. "I'll tell my uncle about that."

His uncle had some horses, he said.

When the attendant stepped away from the pump, Long stood there paralyzed, certain that the California Highway Patrol, after taking the man's call, would soon be asking the same question. Pomeroy walked over and, gauging the weight of Long's apoplexy, engaged him in what seemed from a distance to be a conversation about the weather.

"After we leave here," he said quietly, "pull over, push the brick back in the trunk and close it."

Sure. That is what Long had intended to do.

"Lespedeza?" Pomeroy said. "What the fuck is that?"

"A kind of hay, you feed it to horses."

"You made it up?"

"No," said Long. "It's real. It's green and it comes in bales."

Pomeroy smiled. He nodded his head.

"You're going to do just fine," he said.

From the beginning, Pomeroy had been telling him that.

"You can do this," he had said, when Long signed on. "I know you're the guy for this. When I met you, I knew I could trust you."

Pomeroy had really laid it on, and as Long would discover later, using the same technique on others, when you lay it on them, they *have* to do it. It was a man thing. It was a characteristic, Long believed, that lived somewhere in the American spirit. A Frenchman, for example, would back

out. Any good *parisien,* he theorized, would say, "What? You have to be kidding." But Pomeroy had told him that he was the guy, and as downright terrified as he was, he had to *be* that guy, because Pomeroy was counting on him.

Long would look back on this point in his life and see Pomeroy as something of a surrogate father. He would see Pomeroy as the man who had given him the chance to be great, the chance to be great in his own way. Pomeroy said, "You can do it," and he never went back on it, never reneged. Not once did he ever look at Long and say, "I'm not sure you can handle this."

When Long left Marin, he would leave having learned something about himself, and having discovered something at which he was good. If he had not discovered his destiny, he had discovered something that looked a lot like it. To his mind, he had taken something from start to finish, risked it all and won. It would be a defining moment in his life.

Once a month for the next five months, he and Pomeroy landed 600 pounds of Mexican pot in the desert southeast of Lower Alkalai Lake. And they did it with the efficiency and reliability of a very expensive Swiss watch. Long made $5,000 a load, which would not have been enough to finish his movie, even if he had saved the money. But the prospect of saving it reflected a flaw in his logic that had not been apparent to Long when he decided to finance the movie smuggling dope.

"If you have money and a Harley in Sausalito," he reported to Lee Carlyle at the height of it all, "it's amazing how much pussy you can get."

The silence on Carlyle's end of the phone line was a clue to how ridiculous that sounded. Not the revelation itself, but the fact that Long had felt the need to announce it. He was talking to Carlyle, after all, he was proselytizing before

the converted. Hell, he was preaching to the mission's Apostle.

Long had the Harley. He had Fleurette. And numerous other young women. He was twenty-four and living in Marin. What more could any man ask for? On a typical day on top of the world, he would roll out of bed about three P.M., smoke his first joint, drift over to Sausalito for coffee, and kill time in no particular way before heading for the Trident at night. From the Trident, it was off to wherever the party happened to be: Winterland, some club, some musician's house in the hills. And he did it all with a buzz on, just one more pot-smoking outlaw in what seemed to be an entire generation of them.

"It's true, I have a lot of friends in politics, but they wouldn't be friendly very long if they knew my business was drugs instead of gambling . . ."

"You gonna Bogart that thing, or pass it on?"

"Shhh . . . !"

"Drugs is a dirty business . . ."

"Sorry, man."

"Don Corleone . . ."

Long was sitting through a movie about real gangsters, attending a late showing of *The Godfather,* and a joint was making its way down the aisle from his left.

"Here, man," whispered the guy behind him.

Another joint came over Long's shoulder.

"Very righteous shit," the guy told him.

"I think that's mine," said Long.

He took a hit, and passed it on, handing it to the woman in front of him.

"Delicious," she said, and thanked him.

Counterculture ritual, as he and his contemporaries celebrated it, was ripe with a feeling of ease, and Long himself took pride in his share of the responsibility for fueling it. Stoned on one drug or another, doing whatever they did — student-athletes at schools back east were playing intercollegiate hockey on acid — an entire generation was tripping to the same popular, four-color fantasia. It was hard to imagine that a time would come when America did not know what it was like for a good chunk of the population to be completely fucked up all the time.

"... Ups, downs, acid, mescaline, cocaine, Salk vaccine, what do you need, aspirin, I got that, too ..."

Everybody was doing everything, all the time, with the possible exception of smack (at least among Long's acquaintances), the really effortless purchase of which probably meant a trip to the city. There was always someplace to hook up, plenty of places in the Bay Area, but if you lived outside New York, the best and by far the easiest places to score heroin were Vietnam and prison, the latter being the place where most marijuana smokers were exposed to it.

Estimates out of Washington that year were running as high as 25 million for the number of pot smokers nationwide, and Marin County, with a significant share of them, was ground zero for all that was cool. And all was going along splendidly for Long as well as his associates. Pomeroy and Big Jim, who owned the franchise, were each probably pulling in about $20,000 a load. On Pomeroy, the veteran scammer, the money had little discernible impact. With a lifestyle that cycled through alternating periods of wealth and relative poverty, Pomeroy was accustomed to being rich whenever he was not broke. For Big Jim things were a little bit different. It was not only his first taste of big money, but his first taste of the outlaw life. He fancied himself

something of a drug kingpin now, and in a man of largely middle-class aspirations, the metamorphosis was amusing to watch. His living out the image of a crime lord expressed itself in such goofy ambitions as stealing other men's girlfriends.

Greed, megalomania, and paranoia were just around the corner for Jim. He and Pomeroy shared the combination to a large safe in the Mill Valley house, and in it they deposited the money generated by each shipment of marijuana. Once the balance of a shipment was sold, the two men divided the profit. For all the time they were smuggling pot, money never came between them. The operation from the outset was as gratifying as a Japanese tea ceremony and as predictable as a Catholic Mass. Until they started messing with karma. And in the good-old-boy-herb-smoking-and-smuggling brotherhood, karma, of the negative variety, when not brought to bear on the subject of guns, usually meant cocaine.

Not far down the fat-and-happy trail to success, with the plane bringing in loads every month, the partners decided to have the Mexicans throw some cocaine on board with the pot. They landed ten keys, put the cocaine in the safe, and three days later, Long walked into the house to find Jim holding Pomeroy by the throat, trying to throw him off the second-floor balcony.

"I'm going to kill this motherfucker!" he shouted, accusing Pomeroy of stealing cocaine.

"Motherfucker, you're the one stealing the shit!"

Long jumped in to separate them.

Both of them and neither of them were stealing the shit — they were not stealing it, they were simply doing it. Had Long known the safe's combination, he would have been doing it, too. All of them had a taste for it.

Up to that time, as Long viewed it, the safe had represented the honor and trust of the partnership. But they had put twenty-two pounds of cocaine in the safe, and three days later, by his count, they were trying to kill each other, literally.

Men must endure their going hence even as their coming hither, and in the immediate aftermath of the episode, seeing ripeness in the moment, Pomeroy took Long aside and told him: "This is probably a good time for you to get out."

The Marin County adventure was over. A mere six months had passed, and Long was on his way home.

New York. Where the deer and the antelope play.

With the documentary footage in hock to the film-processing lab — by now, Ives, his producer, had written off the investment — it was hard for Long to know what he was going to do next. Or maybe it was just hard for him to say. Maybe it came to him smoking a joint at 37,000 feet. He left Marin with what he told himself was no great sense of criminal purpose, but he had not been home more than a New York minute before it became pretty obvious to him that a movie camera was the last thing he needed.

GIVE A MAN ENOUGH ROPE
AND HE'LL SMOKE IT

Aspen, Colorado, American folklore's answer to such exotic
wonderlands as Sodom and Gomorrah — in the contemporary mythology a kind of drugs-and-deep-powder, post-
alphabet Babylon without the agriculture — was singularly
appropriate to Allen Long's launch into the rarefied air of
big-time smuggling. Situated just west of the Continental
Divide in the valley of the Roaring Fork River, 8,000 feet
above sea level and about 4.3 light-years removed from the
nearest star with an apparent magnitude greater than that
of any one of its resident celebrities, the big-ticket ski resort
and upmarket-bohemian hideaway owed its reputation to a
brand of renegade income that only the glamour professions
could provide. Arriving in December 1975, Long walked
through an airport in which even the innocent passengers
fit the federal drug profile: the gold Rolex, the hand-stitched
lizard skin boots — a DEA shakedown every minute at any
other port of entry. Long, of course, was not among the

innocent. Since leaving California some three years earlier he had been earning his money moving dope, and in doing so had been preparing for just such a meeting as the one he was in Aspen to attend.

Returning to New York from Marin in the fall of 1972, Long had rented an apartment downtown at the corner of Prince and Wooster Streets. Sporting his new California threads and displaying a newly acquired swagger — pursuant to his success as an outlaw, having pretty much redecorated his life — he made a big point of making the uptown scene, made a lot of new friends, and burned through what remained of the money he had made smuggling. In the course of going broke, he looked up a guy by the name of Little Eddie.

The world of the marijuana smuggler, in many ways, was a small one. While the traffic in cannabis stretched across three oceans, several continents, and numerous national borders, its flow was restricted by narrow channels of affiliation. The search for sources and outlets was conducted by word of mouth. Owing to the rigors of an illicit market, in which neither buyer nor sellers advertised, reliability and trust came at a higher premium than in the legitimate business world. Solid connections were seldom abandoned, and the same was true of one's customers. It was not unusual for numerous reasons for a pot wholesaler in Denver, say, to be buying his weight from a smuggler who lived in Boston. Just as Lee Carlyle had traveled from Los Angeles to market his product in Chicago, a New Jersey dealer like Little Eddie might quite naturally travel to Mill Valley to investigate the possibility of doing business with someone like Pomeroy. That is how Long and Little Eddie had met.

Despite the dope-smoking, the dark mustache, and the hair that fell to the middle of his back, Little Eddie, seemingly anchored in the counterculture, was the nearest thing Allen Long had ever run across to an early-talkies mobster. A short, tough, street-smart operator, who had been hustling since his teens, Eddie followed all the old rules. In a business where squealing came with the turf, where state's evidence was the lingua franca, Eddie was a stand-up guy, proudly observing the code of silence adhered to by the gangsters he and his New Jersey friends looked up to. In addition to being a man of his word, Eddie was meticulous. He seldom made mistakes. He and Long would remain friends for years, well beyond the point at which Eddie was eventually busted and, refusing to cooperate with the government, followed the old rules right into jail.

When Long looked him up, Little Eddie was doing a big hash trip, part of a crew that was moving some 5,000 pounds of hashish out of Morocco.

"If you know somebody who can buy this hash," he said — he had access to 1,000 pounds of it — "we can both make some money on it."

Long thought he did know somebody. Through a series of random associations that started with the various pot and cocaine dealers he patronized, Long had begun moving, if only socially, in pretty fast company in New York. Among the people with whom he was running were members of the Howie Fuchs organization.

Howie Fuchs, twenty-seven, a former city welfare investigator, soon to be dubbed "a Horatio Alger of crime" by a New York district attorney, would querulously claim a Bronx beer distributorship as the source of his wealth. That he would protest his innocence in a press conference was an indication of the level of celebrity the Yeshiva University

graduate would eventually come to enjoy. In addition to whatever amount of beer Fuchs might have been distributing, he was, when Allen Long knew him, distributing cocaine by the key, along with a variety of other drugs. (Conspiracy to distribute sixty kilos of coke was the crime of which he would be convicted in federal court. Later he pleaded guilty in state court to smuggling some 270 kilos of cocaine and 4,000 pounds of hashish.)

Howie Fuchs was a guy who could move a lot of hash, and Long's approach to him, proposing that Fuchs take a share of Little Eddie's Moroccan load, led to an immediate change in Long's standing with him. In the spring of 1973 Long was invited to participate in a high-stakes poker game hosted by the flamboyant crime lord in a suite at Manhattan's Essex House hotel, a nonstop, no-sleep, three-day coke-and-hooker binge at which only the anointed were welcome.

Of such moments were memories made. Long felt warm all over.

The Moroccan arrived a couple of months later. There was, however, so little room in the deal that Fuchs declined to take it. "There's not enough room in this deal for your dime," was how such things were traditionally explained, the dime being a figurative reference to whatever "your" take on the transaction happened to be.

In short, the hash was priced a little high for Fuchs and his boys, one of whom, a friend of Long's by the name of Danny, volunteered the following: "That guy Jeff, he'll probably buy it."

"Jeff . . ." said Long, shaking his head.

"You played poker with him," said Danny.

Like all gatherings of its kind, in the corporate as well as the criminal world, the card-game-cum-bacchanalia had

been underwritten by Howie Fuchs in support of business as well as pleasure. People came and went, and among those present was a severe, rather secretive, tight-lipped character with an oddly studious air and an accent straight out of the Bronx. Aloof, in his early thirties, introduced as Jeff, he and some guy named José from Detroit were among the few men who attended the gathering who remained unknown to Long. Jeff made it pretty clear that he was not interested in getting to know anyone, or more to the point, in anyone getting to know him. The name was almost certainly a phony. It was a good bet that "Jeff" was somebody significant in the dope business, as was everyone else at the party. José was definitely a player.

"What do you know about Jeff?" asked Long

Jeff, according to Danny, was the biggest marijuana dealer in the Midwest.

"How do I get to him?" Long asked.

Danny could not help him there. He knew Fuchs was selling hash to Jeff. The two had been dealing through another buyer whom they recently had managed to jump. (Not enough room in the deal for *his* dime anymore.) Danny said he would ask around.

He got back to Long a few days later.

"Physics?" said Long.

"Maybe engineering. Someone thinks he heard him say the guy once taught at Harvard."

The name Danny had come up with was no name at all, but a description he had pieced together from bits of conversation picked up by various players the night of the game. Long could get to Jeff through a certain college professor, Danny told him.

"He's here in New York?" asked Long.

"That's what I assume."

And with little more than that to go on, Long eventually tracked him down. He reached him by phone.

"Hi, I'm Allen Long. I met a fellow named Jeff . . ." he began, and kept it vague.

"Mm-hmm."

"I've got something he might be interested in."

"Give me your number."

Twenty minutes later the professor called back from a pay phone.

"Jeff," he said, "is very security-conscious. He doesn't want to talk to you. I, however, would be interested in hearing what you have to say."

A college professor? No kidding. Could this be for real? Long figured what the hell. He said he had a load of hash.

"The only way Jeff would be interested would be if he were to see some," the professor responded.

Howie Fuchs would have put it differently — Howie Fuchs *had* put it differently — but the sentiment was the same; notwithstanding the mobilization of a conditional clause that featured elegant employment of the subjunctive, the professor's response was the appropriate one. Wondering what academia was coming to, Long said fine.

He met the professor, whose name was Abe, a few days later at Teterboro Airport in New Jersey. Long had assumed that, flying out of Teterboro, Abe was traveling on a private flight rather than a commercial carrier. But when he spotted the professor standing beside a single-engine Cessna, he was surprised to find him unaccompanied by a pilot.

Hairdressers, science professors . . . all God's creatures had private tickets. Misery had nothing on dope when it came to acquainting a man with strange bedfellows.

Abe, who held a doctorate in physics, was very much the scholar, sporting the acquired slouch of the academician —

he had the slouch down cold — and the affected, pseudo-tribal stammer that betrayed an undergraduate degree from Harvard. With the deliberative speech and deferential manner that when necessary could be deployed in a back-handed show of superiority, he gave the appearance of being unfocused, which stood him in stark contrast to the anything-but-absentminded, blunt-spoken Jeff. Tall and slim, his hair a laboratory study in arranged disarray, he was wearing a houndstooth jacket, a bow tie, and desert boots, and carrying $4,600 in cash, which he gave to Long for a four-pound brick of blond Moroccan hash. He said he would be back in touch.

The call came two days later.

"This is John."

"John?"

"We met in New Jersey . . ."

Of course.

". . . His name's Jeff, my name's John."

His name's cloak, your name's dagger.

"Okay, " said Long.

"You understand?"

Long understood.

"Call me from a pay phone."

Instructing Long, from then on, to call him only from pay phones, the professor gave him a number. Long hit the street.

"Here's what you do . . ." said Abe, when Long called him back.

Long and Little Eddie, in a rental car with 150 pounds of hash in the trunk, drove to Ann Arbor, Michigan, and checked into Weber's Inn, located on Jackson Road. There, the following morning, Long received a phone call and was instructed to proceed to the Paul Bunyan restaurant.

"You can't miss it," Long was told. "You'll see a big statue on the highway of Paul Bunyan and his ox."

"Babe."

"What?"

"Babe," said Long. "Paul Bunyan's ox. Babe the Blue Ox."

"Babe the Blue Ox. Yeah. Be there at eleven."

Long entered the restaurant alone, caught sight of Jeff sitting at a table with a view of the door, and pulled up a chair.

Tall and trim, no more physically imposing than the average long-distance runner, Jeff was dark-haired, fair-complexioned, well-groomed, and dressed for croquet. He wore loose khaki trousers over white canvas shoes, a plain sweep-face wristwatch with a simple leather strap, and his tortoiseshell sunglasses were tucked neatly into the collar of a blue, short-sleeved knit shirt free of ornamentation but for an embroidered trademark crocodile. He shook hands with the enthusiasm of a man surrendering his wallet.

If he remembered Long from the poker game, he gave no indication of it.

The pleasantries were kept to a minimum. Jeff passed Long a briefcase. Long found his way to the men's room, locked himself in a stall, and counted the $172,500 the briefcase contained. He returned to the table and passed Jeff the keys to the rental car. Jeff left the restaurant, returned an hour later, handed the car keys back to Long, and slipped him a piece of paper.

He said, "Here's a number you can reach me at if you can ever do this again."

And left.

*   *   *

Long and Little Eddie made $15,000 apiece on the hash (their collective "dime" being $200 a pound). About a week after they got back to New York, Howie Fuchs, already facing trial on drug-trafficking charges in state court, was arrested on a federal complaint. Long's name came up in the latter investigation, and rather than talk to an assistant U.S. attorney who asked him to drop in for a visit, Long packed up and left town.

Long moved back to Richmond, and for the next year or so he behaved himself. Or tried to. He went to work for a friend, a building contractor, but not before blowing six months on a failed Jamaican ganja trip — a Lee Carlyle extravaganza, horribly conceived — in the course of which he managed to burn through the $15,000 he made on the hash. Eventually, he and his builder friend went into the contracting business together. And did no better financially than he and Carlyle had done on the Jamaican deal.

It was while living the straight life in Richmond in the fall of 1973 that Long met a young woman who, in her ability to piss him off and play fast and loose with his ego, drove him slightly crazier than other women he had known, and with whom in consideration of which he necessarily fell in love.

Cherie Harris, all energy, longing, and imagination, aspired to a career in literature or "something in the arts," but at the age of twenty-one the only thing she knew how to be was a movie star. A student at Virginia Commonwealth University, where she majored in being cool, she found an outlet for her creativity in the invention of herself. Cherie was five-feet-seven, her dark brown hair was long, her eyes were brown, as big as doughnuts, and a good old boy would tell you she was pretty as a crocheted afghan. But when history was written, Cherie would be remembered

for something other than her looks: Cherie, as the cultural record showed, and as she herself acknowledged, was "the first girl in Richmond with platform shoes."

In creating a place for herself in the world, Cherie, a thrifty shopper, paid special attention to her clothes. The look that she was going for, which she explained to her contemporaries as "a glam-hippie thing," was only half in evidence on the cool blustery day in November when Long first saw her on the street. She was bundled up in a long, black, imitation-fur coat that she had purchased from the Salvation Army, her feet were clad in construction boots, and she was carrying a big umbrella. A day later, when Long picked her up for a date — they were off to a club to hear music — he did not recognize her at first. Over an evening dress and platforms, she wore a big, white, loop-stranded wig, a contraption that played out somewhere between Afro and astrakhan, which she had sprayed with football grip and sprinkled with sparkle and glitter. It was a look Long associated with New York streetwalkers and entertainers like Mozart. Noting his disappointment, she changed in the club's ladies' room.

Upon first spotting Cherie on the street that day, Long unleashed what Cherie and her friends — and many of his friends — came to refer to as "that Allen thing." That Allen thing was charm. Affability and plenty of it. Observable in the stereotypical Southern gentleman and a certain variety of sociopath, it was a gift Allen Long possessed in abundance, and one he cultivated assiduously. His expression of it was state-of-the-art. It worked on everybody, not just women, and was notable for remaining seductive well after Long had demonstrated that there were risks attached in getting to know him. To say Allen Long had personality was like saying Secretariat had legs.

Cherie thought Long was cool — so, right from the beginning of the relationship the two had something in common — but played unimpressed, at the same time trying to figure out how she could take things further. Cherie did not possess a wealth of sexual experience, but knew enough to realize that Long was going slow, and she found herself having to push a little to get him to pay attention. Eventually Long would come around, and the sum of their years together would outnumber those of Long's earlier love affairs combined. But by the summer of 1974 Long had other things on his mind. Returning home from work one day — he was renting a room from a friend — Long received a message that a guy by the name of JD had called, leaving the phone number of a local motel. Long returned the call wondering who he might be.

"Lee gave me your number," said JD, over the phone.

Carlyle's friend JD. Long remembered meeting him in Florida, briefly, on that failed Jamaican trip.

"Can you come out here?" he wanted to know.

Long made his way to the motel.

"You remember me?" JD asked, when Long showed up at the door.

It was like asking him if he remembered Mount Rushmore.

JD Reed, twenty-three, stood six-feet-five-inches tall. The 220 pounds he weighed looked to consist entirely of muscle and cartilage. The overall physical impression he made smacked of the landscape that gave rise to his clothes — the blue jeans, white T-shirt, and Tony Lama boots, the Stetson hanging on the door hook — the gene pool on which he drew seemingly financed in the closing of the American frontier. He had arms the size of railroad ties, long brown hair, combed like that of a renegade cavalryman, and eyes as

resolute as Manifest Destiny. Meeting him was like crossing paths with Crazy Horse — lighting upon the venerable Sioux at the close of business that day in the valley of the Little Big Horn River.

Reed introduced Long to the other man in the room, a skinny guy by the name of Speed, who when not traveling with Reed held down a lucrative gig as a valet parking attendant at one of the larger Las Vegas hotels. The two had just driven in from Tucson in the Chevy Suburban parked outside loaded with 1,200 pounds of Mexican pot. Reed's buyer in Richmond had failed to come up with the money he owed for the load Reed had fronted him on his last trip to Virginia. Reed needed to unload the 1,200 pounds and get paid before he went home.

"Lee said maybe you could help me."

In the biographical scheme of things, it was like Mrs. Wright saying to her son Wilbur: "Maybe your brother Orville could help."

(And maybe someday, when things worked out, there would be room in the deal for her dime.)

JD Reed, born in West Virginia, raised in Las Vegas from the day he could walk, took his first toke on a joint in high school. After dropping out of college in Southern California, he started growing pot in the mountains of Ranchita, about fifty miles north of the Mexican border. Self-possessed and soft-spoken, in those instances where he spoke at all, Reed was imperturbable, cool in a way that he was happy to let strangers misunderstand as cold-blooded. He emanated what on first encounter seemed to be an air of menace. One got the feeling he could be very dangerous. It was his habit, even at his happiest, to tear in half the telephone directory of every American metropolis it was ever his pleasure to visit. He looked upon Manhattan the way Agamemnon

looked upon Troy. His instinct was to cut fence. It was his nature to think of everything west of the Divide as his own.

Reed's appetite was huge. If he wanted a drink of water, he drank a gallon of water. When he wanted something to smoke, he rolled a joint that outweighed his hat and smoked it all by himself. He was neither rude nor stingy. "If you want to smoke some, help yourself, it's over there," he would say. "This one here's for me." And he was never without something to smoke. Upon checking into a hotel room, everyone who knew him would tell you, the first thing he did, before halving the phone book, was remove a drawer from the dresser and use it to clean his pot. Separating the buds, crumbling up enough of the weed to fill a decent smoke, he sifted out the seeds, shaking the drawer side to side like a miner screening gold. It was what he was doing that day in Richmond when, sizing up his new acquaintance, he said, "Lee said maybe you could help me."

And Long said, "I believe I can."

In moving Reed's 1,200 pounds, Long's first call was to a casual acquaintance, a local business owner and R&B bass player by the name of Will McBride, who had been dealing pot by the pound. McBride took half the load. Another friend put Long in touch with a dealer he knew in D.C., who "could probably move a lot of this." In fact, as Long discovered, he could have moved it all.

Easy Matthews, a Washington-area contractor, was one of the more coolheaded pot distributors Long would ever meet. A big-boned, bearded redhead with hands as broad as banjos, he was self-reliant, self-assured, endlessly unruffled, and had excellent instincts for the work. A dealer in significant weight, Matthews was a major player. As large

as JD Reed, with a resounding laugh and expansive gestures —
"I want it all," he would sing, when offered a piece of the
latest load — he had a wife, four children, and a partner, a
fellow motorcycle enthusiast named Myles, a soft-spoken,
skinny character who played serious basketball, always wore
coveralls, and never did drugs. Together Myles and
Matthews managed an apartment building in which all the
units were occupied by dealers, drivers, money handlers, and
others employed as part of their distribution network.

Matthews paid half the cash up front for the balance of
Reed's 1,200 pounds and the other half two days later, which
was all the time it took him to sell it. Long put a nickel-a-
pound on the pot. In three days, without leaving town, he
made $6,000 on the load.

"When I was a little boy," said Long, reporting his success
to Carlyle, "my grandfather told me it's better to make a
fast nickel than a slow dime."

"Yeah, I remember your telling me," Carlyle said.

"Often enough that today it remains imprinted upon my
consciousness."

"And mine."

"Volume is everything, man. The way to riches is to sell
volume. Quick turnover, low overhead. Whether it's the drug
business . . ."

"Or the car business," said Carlyle.

"Yeah."

"I remember," Carlyle said.

The drug business differs from the car business, however,
in at least one way that jumps to mind, and a fast nickel
selling weed conveys certain advantages not necessarily
apparent to the typical Oldsmobile salesman. Selling dope,
alas, is illegal. Getting the contraband out of your possession as fast as possible (removing the evidence) and dealing

with as few people as possible (reducing your exposure) substantially minimizes your risk of arrest.

Within ten days, Long had rented a new apartment, opened a bank account, and made the down payment on a BMW sedan. And Reed was back with another load. Two hundred pounds went to McBride. Matthews was clearly the man now. Waiting in Richmond when the pot arrived, he took the bulk of the shipment, a thousand pounds, and turned it over in two days. From then on, no matter how much weight he was moving, Long would always manage to keep Matthews supplied with a piece of the load. He would never limit himself to one buyer: Sell to a single buyer, he knew, and soon *he* will be telling *you* what the price is.

JD Reed, by this time, working with a partner in Tucson, had moved thousands of pounds of "lime green," as he described the commercial Mexican he was selling, but had yet to progress beyond "ground smuggling," picking up his pot in the American Southwest and driving it cross-country to sell. Now, with Long moving 1,200 pounds of the product every couple of weeks, it was time for him to step things up. To do so, Reed partnered with a hillbilly in Tucson by the name of Cactus Jack. Toothless, Tennessee-born-and-reared — "He'd be the guy drivin' them mules," said Reed — Cactus Jack was sixty-five and just about as cool as they come. A flat-out American original, he was a married to a Mexican national who had family in Sonora, and working with him, Reed went on to establish an operation south of the border.

Using a Piper Navajo Chieftain, Reed did two trips a week out of Mexico. He brought the first load into the country using a whorehouse airstrip near Las Vegas. To off-load subsequent flights he used a series of dry lakebeds in the desert. Everything after the landing — unloading the pot,

driving it east, and selling it — Reed handled by himself. On the first trip, he went to Mexico and loaded the airplane as well. He moved 3,600 pounds a week, most of it to Long. So busy did he become that often he would just drop off the pot and immediately turn around, leaving collection of the money to Cactus Jack and a peg-legged partner named Arlo. Long, when they first showed up to collect, had to ask neither of these guys for ID. When he turned over the cash the only problem he had was picturing the pair — the halting Arlo trailing behind the toothless Jack, who was carrying a knapsack with nothing but money in it — trying to board a plane at National Airport.

Long had been doing business with Reed for just about a year when Reed found a DC-3, and Long saw the opportunity to walk his own operation upstairs. His plan was to take an entire shipment, 4,000 pounds, and move it all at once. Knowing only one man who could move that much weight in a hurry — knowing that Easy Matthews, as good as he was, did not have the cash to handle it — he told Reed to get the pot to Ann Arbor.

"This guy up there has a lot of money, he'll pay right away," he said.

The pot had to be moved in a hurry, and it had to be moved at Reed's price. On the line was Reed's credibility with his suppliers. Long, therefore, was taking a risk when he guaranteed the deal without ever talking to Jeff.

It was the first of many times that Long would take such a flyer, gambling everything on intuition. He knew if he tried to negotiate over the phone, the deal would probably never go down. But could Jeff say no to a load-in-hand? Long's gut told him no. And he had to take the chance. Nailing down quality and price was always contingent upon speed, upon rapid turnover of the product, and just as importantly,

rapid turnover of the money. Few were the people who could buy drugs in volume, and they were not known to more than a few others. This was Long's opportunity to exploit his access to Jeff, and in a way that, if all went well, would allow him to continue to do so.

Assured of a *reasonably* rapid turnover, "right away" being a relative term, Reed loaded up in Las Vegas, and drove the pot to Ann Arbor. Only after meeting him and taking the truck did Long put in a call to Jeff, not even knowing whether Jeff was in town.

He was. And soon Long had him looking at a sample.

"You know," said Jeff, with a put-upon air, "I got a whole barn full of the same kind of weed." Here we go, thought Long. "And your price is not that much different."

This was to be Long's first taste of a new, hybrid style of negotiating, a tough but eminently polite brand of bargaining transplanted to the upper Midwest from the busy streets of the Bronx. In one way he was reassured. He had made the right decision in coming. But he had also put himself in a serious squeeze. He had told Reed the deal was done. He had to close the deal, he had to do it now, and he had to get Reed his price.

"I'll do it for you . . ." sighed Jeff.

Long knew what was coming next.

". . . but I can't pay right away."

Meaning Jeff would have to sell it first. That was not good.

"How soon?" Long asked.

He had promised Reed a rapid turnaround.

"I don't know," said Jeff. "Tomorrow? I can probably get it done by tomorrow."

Long looked like a dummy who had been hit by a quiz, like a kid in the last row who had been instructed by his

teacher to, maybe, name the nine Muses in alphabetical order. His mouth was hanging open, but he had nothing to say. Looking at Jeff, he thought, here is a guy who can move two tons of pot overnight. And get paid for it. Overnight. Reduced to a complete nonplus, he gave Jeff the keys to the truck. The following day, when he and Reed left town, he was $20,000 richer, and Reed was paid in full.

The gamble paid off big.

"Bring me all the pot you can at this price," Jeff told him. "I'll take it all."

It was like Willy Loman landing the Macy's account.

Long, with money in his pocket, driving a BMW that was now paid for, moved out of his apartment, rented a house just south of Charlottesville, and flush with success in the marijuana business, reinvigorated his pursuit of simultaneous failure in the music business.

For all the years he smuggled pot, Long would maintain a presence in the legitimate world by way of a half-assed career in the record industry. He did not consciously intend it to be half-assed — though a fear of success was almost certainly embedded somewhere in his character — but his subordination of it to a criminal career presupposed an outcome that even he could not fail to predict. It was as an aspiring cameraman, while working at Motion Associates, that Long had first approached executives at CBS Records in New York to propose the idea of his filming rock concerts. His promoting the concerts himself was a natural follow-up to the idea. Never having done so before did not prevent him from trying, and while his efforts met with little success, they were courteously received, solidifying a relationship with one industry executive that would last for many years.

Over the course of that time Long demonstrated an aptitude for the music business that might have been amply rewarded had he followed through on any of his projects beyond the point of initial enthusiasm. His indulgence in the charade served various purposes.

First, of course, it provided a cover for his criminal activities. It made questions about what he did for a living — how he earned his money — all that much easier to answer. But more than that it served a necessary self-delusion. Long, clearly proud of what he was able to achieve as a smuggler, and understandably so, given the enormous challenges it presented, was not secure in that pride of achievement. Notwithstanding all his justifications — the victimless nature of his crimes, his alleged membership in a brotherhood of pioneers and cultural evangelists — Allen Long, given his upbringing and education, was unable by virtue of both to ignore the reality that he was a criminal. If he was not ashamed of what he did for a living (and in some deep subconscious place he was loath to dredge he might have discovered that to be true), neither could he brag about it with impunity. The only people he could trust to show what he saw as appropriate respect and admiration for his accomplishments as a smuggler were other smugglers. The music business gave him something to brag about. And more than that, it allowed him the opportunity to tell himself that being a smuggler was merely a temporary diversion from his more laudable aspirations in life.

Had he actually pursued those aspirations wholeheartedly, chances are he would have been successful. The entrepreneurial aspects of the music business, the development and management of talent, came naturally to Allen Long. The necessary instincts were there. He proved to be very good at it. But that would come as no surprise. Anybody

who could go up against the odds he was about to go up against, and not only survive but prevail, anybody who could succeed as a smuggler, doing business with the kinds of people he was about to do business with, was perfectly suited to an industry controlled by even bigger criminals.

The music business dovetailed rather naturally with the pot business. Rock and roll and marijuana, music and dope in general, if not actually born under the same sign, came together at so many crossroads as to insure that Long, so deeply involved in the latter industry, would make numerous friends in the former. He would develop those friendships and the sundry professional contacts that followed — CBS being a good example — very early in New York. By the time he had left for Richmond, he could easily claim as many friends in the music business as in the dope business. The industries fed each other. Each was home to operators who had segued from one to the next. Some were involved in both.

Long, who had first smoked dope as the member of a rock and roll band, had remained as enthusiastic about music as pot, and impressed by the talent of singer-songwriter Steve Bassett, whose performance he caught at a club in Richmond, signed him to a management contract. Over the next three years he would invest a substantial amount of money in the act. (Eventually signed by John Hammond to Columbia Records, Bassett recorded an album produced by Jerry Wexler. Yielding a single that hit the R&B charts, the LP suffered commercially when, as Long understood it, the soul stations discovered that Bassett was white.) Long later managed songwriter Robbin Thompson, whose first album in a three-record deal with Atlantic made the *Billboard* charts. (Thompson, who later collaborated with Bassett on the song "Sweet Virginia Breeze," was dropped

by the label when he failed to follow the LP up with material its executives liked.)

For years Long would remain energetic in his support of these acts — he paid for the national tour to promote Thompson's album — but he was far more energetic in escalation of his own activities as a smuggler. The decision by now had been made. Smuggling pot was not some dubious adjunct to filmmaking, and it had risen well beyond the level of an experiment. He was in it. All the way. It was what he did for a living. More than what he did, it was a large part of who he was. And it was time to take control of it. He wanted to be the biggest scammer he could possibly be.

JD Reed and his partners had been bringing pot into the desert at Lake of Wells, Nevada. Nearby, supposedly unknown to the world, stretched the vast nuclear test site at Indian Springs. When the DC-3 pilots, low on fuel, had landed within the boundaries of the installation, bringing down not only government heat, but national security heat, Reed bowed out of the deal. (The airplane was busted on the next load.) With Reed in temporary retirement, it was time for Long to underwrite an operation of his own. And he was not the only one making a change.

Will McBride had learned to fly.

"I want to do something big," said Long.

It would be a while before McBride checked out in multi-engine aircraft, but he knew a guy with a lot of hours who might be interested, he said.

"You set it up," said Long. "I'll talk to him."

Long called Reed in Las Vegas, and told him what he had in mind.

"What kind of airplane we gonna use?"

"Haven't decided," said Long.

"What does your pilot say?"

"I haven't talked to him yet."

"What about the money?"

"I figure maybe two hundred and fifty thousand to get it going."

"Where do you figure to get it?"

"We get it from my friend in Detroit."

"Talked to him yet?"

"No."

No plane. No pilot. No money.

No problem, not for Reed.

"If you're waitin' on me," he said, "you're backin' up."

And two weeks later, Long was stepping off an airplane in Aspen, Colorado.

Aspen, the playground of choice to a high-scale hobo collective of American celebrities and the lower echelon nobility that journalist Hillary Johnson in 1982 would be the first to describe as Eurotrash, was esteemed for already having a coke problem as early as 1975. A mile and a half high in the Rockies, a resort in the throes of giving birth to a solar-heated airport piped with music by Steely Dan, it was a town sanctified by the passage of every major dope smuggler of the day, and Long, had he been aware of it, would have been proud to be joining their number.

Walking through the airport, he and JD Reed stepped directly into a taxi and headed for a house on Red Mountain. Night had fallen and it had been snowing for a couple of hours when they entered on the lower level of the modified, multilevel A-frame. Removing their boots, they were ushered into a wood-paneled den, the windows of which, with an

unimpeded view of the ski trails snaking their way into the valley, overlooked the flickering lights of a town jumping at the height of the season.

Jeff had arrived in Aspen a week before with his family. Long had not discussed his purpose with Jeff when he called Ann Arbor to schedule a meeting, nor had he told him, when Jeff suggested they meet in Aspen, that he would be arriving in town with Reed. Jeff knew better than to think that this was a social visit, however, and showing his guests to red leather armchairs warmed by the heat of the fireplace, he was quite happy to get down to business, interested to hear what Long had to say. Long, after all, had proved he could deliver good Mexican pot at a price. Jeff had put $25 a pound on the 4,000 Long had sold him, and turned it over in twenty-four hours. He was that much more interested when Long told him: "We're not going to Mexico."

SMOKE OF A DISTANT FIRE

Ann Arbor, Michigan, in 1975 was not the cannabis capital of the world. On a given day there would be more dope on hand in, say, maybe, Morocco. But for per capita consumption of pot, the university town forty-one miles west of Detroit was pretty tough to beat. The annual Ann Arbor Hash Festival, the on-campus "hash bash" held every April, was known to attract thousands, and the city's "$5 herb law" was counterculture legend.

The youth vote in Ann Arbor in 1974 constituted a full one third of the city's population. That electoral bloc drew substantially from some 40,000 students at the University of Michigan. A charter amendment enacted that year (voted initially into law in 1972, voted down the next, and reinstated in the more recent election) made possession of marijuana, even in amounts exceeding a pound, a misdemeanor subject to no greater penalty than a $5 fine. The amendment carried the added force of restricting Ann Arbor police to enforcement of the local ordinance, the state law being more punitive. That summer the Michigan Court of

Appeals upheld a similar marijuana law in Ypsilanti, home to Eastern Michigan University, ten miles down the road. Pot was interwoven so naturally into the fabric of the two cities that when the *Ann Arbor Sun,* a nonprofit community newspaper, ran its "Win a Pound of Colombian" contest in January 1975, the winning entry was drawn by a county commissioner in a ceremony conducted at Ann Arbor City Hall.

Announcing the winner, the newspaper cited the "limited supply" of Colombian, and acknowledged paying "the hefty price of $350" for the weed. The best Mexican pot was worth maybe half that.

To pot smokers nationwide, Colombian marijuana was not the stuff of myth. It was certainly available, but came around infrequently and in relatively small amounts. And characteristically what came around was Colombian marijuana of the commercial variety. Only a few smugglers were bringing pot up from Colombia, and of those going down to get it, fewer still were connoisseurs. The pilots flying it up, one could readily assume, were pilots first and smokers second; the boat traffic was dominated by Cuban-Americans organized in South Florida who did not smoke marijuana. Insensitive to any subtleties, neither pilots nor boat captains knew what they were getting when they loaded on the Guajira. By the same measure, neither did Colombian traffickers, nonsmokers themselves, really know what they were selling. Between the Sierra Nevada Indian and the dedicated American smoker, who both identified differences among varying strains of Colombian, stood businessmen who did not.

Into this quality-control vacuum, Allen Long was about to step.

To connoisseurs like Long and legions of American heads, there were only three kinds of Colombian pot. There was

gold, there was red, and there was everything else. *Punta roja,* the red, compared favorably with Thai weed, the gourmet grass of Southeast Asia. JD Reed said that it was when he tasted his "first little *punta roja* bud" that he knew he would one day go to Colombia. In the Western Hemisphere, it was generally agreed, there was only one thing better (with the possible exception of Hawaiian, which was cultivated so near the International Dateline as to be considered oriental, and was for the most part unavailable). That one thing better came from the pale leaf of the plant that the Indians of the Sierra Nevada identified as *mona,* or *rubia,* the blonde. The Americans called it gold. This was the legendary gold of Santa Marta.

Everything else, everything other than gold and red, was commercial Colombian, and everything else was what typically turned up in the United States. Commercial Colombian was what the *Ann Arbor Sun* gave away. And commercial Colombian was as good as anything on the everyday market.

The best Colombian, by contrast, was as good as anything in the world.

Allen Long knew this. Long had tasted connoisseur Colombian, but had never seen it in great supply, and he had never seen evidence that it existed in great supply. But Long had heard the stories. It was out there, he was told. Everyone spoke in awe of the bounty of Santa Marta. The tales of it lived on and had grown into legend. The Sierra Nevada held forth the promise of a mythical land of gold, and like the conquistadors who centuries earlier had gone deep into Colombia in epic search of El Dorado, Long, in dreams of smuggler's glory, had come to believe in this land of plenty. He imagined entire mountain valleys carpeted in leaves of gold, there for the taking in fabulous abundance. He nurtured a vision of Colombian treasure awaiting

discovery, and for him, bringing it home presented an adventure that by the fall of 1975 had assumed the heroic character of a quest. When he raised the notion of an expedition, Reed had been quick to sign on, and the two explorers had set out for Aspen seeking an audience, paying a call on a Michigan businessman who, for the purposes at hand, looked to them very much like the King of Spain.

Jeff had company in Aspen. Visiting that week was Abe, who proved a source of entertainment when, wandering into the den, he sat in on the conversation. Excited perhaps by the intrigue to which he was suddenly a party, Abe made the innocent mistake of addressing Jeff as Jake. A spirited argument between them followed, conducted at the level of a whisper, in which "Jeff" rebuked "John," an argument that appeared, in one form or another, to have been in progress for years.

Jeff's name was not Jeff, and he was not, as Danny in New York had asserted, the biggest marijuana dealer in the Midwest. He was not even the biggest in Ann Arbor, which in 1975 was probably home to as many pot dealers as Guadalajara, Mazatlán, and Tijuana combined. In Ann Arbor you could always tell when a load was in town — that night, Whiffletree, a popular dining establishment on West Huron, would be overflowing with counterculture capitalists, their number divisible by the busful, ordering champagne.

The marijuana market in Ann Arbor, a town defined by its concentration of university students, mirrored the national market as a whole in 1975 in that the typical pot smoker was — or certainly saw himself as — part of an American counterculture that even then displayed the characteristics of a discernible movement. It has been argued

that not until April of that year, with the fall of Saigon, did the 1960s as they are commonly appreciated really come to an end. But while the typical consumer might have reflected a certain, even if only vestigial, opposition to the establishment, the typical dealer did not. Dope dealers, like dealers of almost any commodity, while paying lip service to their customers' cultural values, were firmly anchored in the mainstream of American commerce.

Jake, aka Jeff, was no exception.

Jake Myerson had arrived in Michigan as a college student. As a young businessman in the late 1960s, several years after graduation, he started selling pot because he liked to smoke it — an ounce here, an ounce there, just to keep himself in personal stash. By 1970 he was getting loads from Mexico. By 1975 he was buying pot by the ton. More than ten years older than the oldest undergraduate, Myerson probably had more in common with the university's administrators than he had with its students. Serious-minded, highly organized, and almost avuncular in his dealings with the people who worked moving his pot, he was in many ways a generation behind the customers he served. By temperament, he differed not only from his clientele, but from many of his competitors as well. Easy Matthews, for instance, was an outlaw who acted like one, fun-loving, flamboyant, anything but uptight — he had the personality of a pirate. Jake Myerson was an outlaw with the disposition of a grocer.

Not so much disobedient as dyspeptic, Myerson was neither voluble nor particularly expansive. He spoke in a nasal, almost metrical monotone, and played a rich array of interpersonal cards close to a heaving chest. He seldom raised his voice, even in disagreement, choosing instead to meet antagonism with a show of injured dignity, retreating from confrontation to the cover of a conversational style

that had its parallels in jujitsu and its antecedents in the ancient marketplace. Talking to him was like talking to a guy who was talking to a cop. But while the hangdog demeanor masked a forceful will, it was incapable of disguising the attributes that inevitably defined him: generosity, loyalty, and a hopelessly kind heart. Eminently responsible, reliable, and utterly efficient, Jake Myerson was a man whose measure could be taken from the value of his phone number. If you ever found yourself in a jam, he was the first guy you called.

All the time he was in the pot business, Myerson, a discriminating smoker, remained as devoted an epicure as he was a merchant. In Allen Long's opinion, Jake Myerson was "a true head." Paying for the two tons of Reed's Mexican weed that Long had delivered to Ann Arbor, he had told Long to bring more, saying he would take all he could get. "But if you can bring me this," he had said, furnishing Long with a fistful of Santa Marta Gold, "we can make a lot more money."

Long figured he said it to everyone who supplied him with product.

Where a pound of Mexican pot was worth about $100 wholesale, Colombian pot, at the same level in the market, was worth about $300. Where a "single" of commercial Colombian, like the pound given away by the *Ann Arbor Sun,* was worth $350, the same pound of Santa Marta Gold, sold individually, was worth in excess of $500. The gold was that much better, and it was what everyone wanted to smoke. Including Myerson himself.

What was immediately obvious to the businessman in Long would be obvious to almost anyone, but few were the businessmen who could truly appreciate what was so readily apparent to the pothead in him. Or so irresistible to his ego.

If Long could get gold — as a true head like Myerson need not remind him — not simply could they make more money, they could lay claim to a small stake of counterculture stardom.

The meeting, then, in Aspen between Long and Jake Myerson bore witness to the wedding in each man's personality of the shopkeeper and the swashbuckler. Neither man, however, came to the matter of marijuana smoking with more authority than JD Reed, one swashbuckler in whose nature the shopkeeper did not abide. At the meeting in Aspen, there was no truer head than he.

Reed was a head who, at length and unapologetically, could provide poetic discourse on "the energy, the magic, the beauty of the herb." And mean it. He was a smoker who had started smuggling pot because he got tired of looking for it. Feeling quite emphatically that "it should be in hand when you need it," he was religious on the subject. Literally. Marijuana was not an article of faith, it was the Faith itself, and Reed was its Defender. All the money he made smuggling herb he reinvested in smuggling more. The millions never caught up with him, he was always working. Reed, like other smugglers, lavished disposable income on cars and boats, but only on those in which he could haul marijuana. Where another scammer might seek joy in the extravagance of a platinum Rolex, an indigo blue Maserati, or a house with eight bathrooms on the rim of Red Mountain, Reed would be quite happy, he argued, "if I could keep enough smoke around me."

> "Dope will get you through times of no money better
> than money will get you through times of no dope."
> Freewheelin' Franklin
> Fabulous Furry Freak Brothers

It was smoke, no doubt, that had led JD Reed to his appreciation of the transmigration of souls. Reed believed that he had been a great warrior in a previous life. "Many lifetimes I had to be a warrior," he reasoned — "I got the build for it, I got the instincts" — and he took pride in the fact that, after coming of age in his present life, he had never inflicted harm on anyone. "With my body strength and knowledge," he explained to Long, "I manipulate 'em, I don't hurt 'em. That's what marijuana did for me. It turned my warrior-ness into peace."

Reed was a warlord who had established his kingdom securely in the realm of the ethereal, and to achieve the celestial precincts thereof, he followed his very own *camino real*. The journey began with his laying hands on the highest grade ganja any man could possibly score, and rolling a joint the size of a prairie dog. He would soak the joint in Afghani hash oil, a bottle of which he always kept handy, and hang it in the sun to dry — he would clothespin the oiler to the laundry line outside the kitchen of his Las Vegas ranch. Picking it at just the right moment, Reed would fire it up and smoke it until nothing but ash remained. That was how he started his day.

For anyone smoking with him, it signaled the end of the day.

Hash oil is chemically extracted from the cannabis plant and purified through repetition, and good hash oil can be up to four times as potent as the resin itself. In 1975 it sold for about $20 a gram. A pound was worth a little over $5,000, and Reed was known to buy all he could get. A big deal on the dope market, it was a hot item in Las Vegas, especially among show folk. Carrying an ounce or so in a medicine bottle, and removing it with an eyedropper, the typical smoker — that is, a smoker other than Reed —

would paint a line of oil on the side of a cigarette, take a couple of hits, and get instantly stupefied, as high as he or she could ever hope to get on a bowl of hash. A sidereal sort of high, the sort of "mental medication" that Reed enjoyed, it held no appeal for smokers like Allen Long, who preferred the "up" high of good grass.

The meeting in Aspen, if for nothing else, would be memorable for the union of opposites to which it ultimately gave rise, for the bonding in eternal brotherhood of the pothead and the egghead. For no more unlikely a friendship would come out of the meeting than that which developed between Reed, practicing noble savage and sagebrush philosopher, and the earthbound, empirical man of hard science, intellectual Abe, Ph.D., "Q.E.D.," theoretical physics. Within a few months of the meeting in Aspen, back on the East Coast, these two characters, in holy communion, would be scouting landing strips, stoned, in the cockpit fumatorium of a single-engine Cessna. Abe, manning the stick, would be smoking an oiler as plump as Schrödinger's cat, while metaphysician Reed, mystic of the Mojave, theorized on the way of the warrior:

"If I was a general, my army'd be cannibals, we wouldn't carry no food . . ."

"Interesting, I can dig that . . ."

Abe's effortless drift from the halls of the academy to the ranks of the American felonry, his full gainer from the ivory tower, prompted no questions in Allen Long. Long, because it was true of him, believed that the glory of big-time drugs was irresistible to everyone. Learjets, cocaine, reckless young women — it was like being a pop star, only better, to Long's way of thinking, because you were not on the road so much.

The academic life has its own rewards, and many of them

in their own way are probably just as tawdry. But in the end the glory of intellectual endeavor would seem to feed at its hungriest on provender more rarefied than the gruel available to the average criminal. Or so one would assume. Well, forget it. Long was right. Notwithstanding the academic accomplishments both admirable and enviable from which Abe could proudly take sustenance, the intrigue and excitement of pot smuggling, the lure of the scammer's life, were just too much for him to resist. His hanging with Reed gave new meaning to the notion of extracurricular activity.

The meeting in Aspen was relatively brief. On the surface it was quite straightforward. Long was proposing a partnership, a merger of sorts. Admittedly ill-defined, it was met by Jake Myerson with understandable misgiving. But Myerson's well-tempered skepticism was rapidly displaced, superseded by his undisguised annoyance with Abe — presumably in Aspen to get some skiing done — and the latter's sudden intrusion into discussion of the deal.

"I've got two expert pilots," Long was saying. "And I have JD here, who has done more than twenty airplane trips this year."

"Would you say five thousand pounds, Allen?" interrupted Abe, who was running calculations on a yellow legal pad.

Myerson swiveled his head and hosed Abe down with a menacing glare of which the latter was joyously oblivious.

"Say forty-eight hundred," Long answered.

"How much do you need, Allen?" Myerson asked, refocusing his attention on Long.

"I figure one hundred and fifty thousand to buy the plane . . ."

Myerson, in the naked face of the number, looked like a man who had taken a bullet.

"Forty-eight hundred," mumbled Abe, calculating the

return on a planeload of Colombian, "at three hundred a pound . . ."

Myerson said, "That's a lot of money."

"That's one point four four million," said Abe, impressed with his own figures.

Myerson, turning to face him, said, "Abe, you can put that thing away."

"Gross," said Abe, defensively.

"You're not being asked to put up anything now," said Long. "We're going to go to Colombia and firm up the connection before we spend any money on the plane."

"I thought you had the connection in Colombia . . ."

"Excuse me, gentlemen . . ." said Abe.

Myerson, like a prizefighter clearing blood clots, heaved a chestful of air through his nostrils, and fixed his eyes on Abe. "Forget the one point four four million," he muttered, pointing a finger at the legal pad. "You can put that aside."

"I'm sorry . . ." said Abe.

"That's okay," Myerson said.

". . . but I'm about to agree with you," said Abe. "Allen, you said one hundred and fifty thousand dollars. That might be enough to outfit the airplane, but what about paying for the pot. You've forgotten the pot. Add forty-eight hundred pounds to the cost of the plane, and you're looking at a quarter of a million dollars."

"Let me see that," said Myerson, reaching for the pad.

"Actually," Long said, "I figure the down payment on the pot at maybe fifty to sixty thousand. The Colombians will front the rest. Say thirty-five to forty thousand dollars in expenses between now and the time we do the first load . . ."

"Wait a minute," said Myerson.

"I need two hundred and fifty thousand, cash, to do this," Long concluded.

"Allen," said Myerson, stopping him before the number went any higher, "you're asking me to invest in something brand-new — something brand-new even to you."

"JD has been doing airplanes for over a year now," said Long.

"From Mexico," said Myerson.

"Allen, I think Jake's main concern —"

"Please, Abe," said Myerson, raising a hand to silence him. The professor as crime lord. Just what he needed. He said, "A quarter of a million, Allen, is a hell of a lot of money to bet on an operation with no track —"

Reed got to his feet.

It was bad enough for Myerson that he had Abe to deal with. Bad enough that he had Long, who as trustworthy as he seemed to be, was essentially running a con: no connection, no plane, he probably had no pilots. That was bad enough. But now the beleaguered Myerson had JD Reed to deal with. Up to now, Reed had been silent. Up to now, he had been motionless, albeit having chosen somewhat disconcertingly to sit on the floor rather than take a chair. To people like Myerson an impassive JD Reed was the human equivalent of a hand grenade with the pin securely in place. It was not Reed's habit to explain to strangers that standing before them, blocking the sun, looming in their path like some heavy-equipment breakdown, was a 220-pound Man of Peace. It was not Reed's habit to say much of anything. One's immediate response to greeting him was reflexively to ask oneself whether there were women and children in the house.

Reed stood up and said, "Come on, let's go, Allen, it's time to get out of here. We'll get what we need somewhere else. I know five people in Vegas who'll give you the money to do this. Shit, I got that much cash at home. If this man don't see it, fine. We don't need his money. Let's go."

"Hold on," said Myerson.

Jake Myerson, misgivings aside, had every reason to welcome the partnership that Long and Reed were proposing. Here was the opportunity to set up his own line of supply, to get product at his own price, the opportunity to dig that much more deeply into the financial structure of the deal: his opportunity to control the load. Such a setup was worth a substantial amount of money to Myerson as a distributor. In the face of a solidified Mexican market, pricing had become a pivotal issue. And the Colombian market was wide open. No one knew the true value of cultivation in Colombia — four million pounds in a single valley, some said. It was known that in both quantity and quality the Colombian crop dwarfed that of Mexico. And the product sold at a higher margin.

But Long did not need to explain any of that to Myerson. It was Myerson who had explained it to him. The advantages of the proposition were self-evident, and would be so to any distributor. Myerson was not the only major distributor accessible to Long. There was Matthews in Washington. But Matthews did not have the necessary cash; he could not move and pay for two tons of pot overnight as Myerson had proved capable of doing. Long was therefore gratified, if not especially surprised, when Myerson very politely waved Reed back to his seat — or floor, as it were, in his case — and advanced the discussion.

"You said you have pilots."

Long said he had pilots, and assured Myerson that there were none better.

"So, who is this guy?"

"He's my flight instructor," McBride responded.

Long said, "You're kidding."

When a few days later, Long caught his first look at Frank Hatfield, he turned to McBride with a dubious look, and said: "You really *are* kidding."

Chest out, shoulders back, all squared away, the haircut apparently unchanged since the day he asked for his first "regular boy's," Hatfield impressed Long as very much the stereotype of the kid next door. You could put him on a cereal box. Well built and classically handsome, with the cool, unstudied confidence that eluded men like Long, he introduced himself with a smile, speaking in an unhurried drawl the geographical source of which was difficult to nail down. He was wearing khaki chinos and a navy blue nylon windbreaker, and in service of some functional utility beyond Long's understanding he wore below the jacket both a sweater and a short-sleeved shirt. His handshake met the specifications of good adjustable locking pliers. Long's instinctive reaction to seeing him was: This is not going to do it.

It was a brisk December day, and McBride, by way of setting Long up to lay out the proposition, had booked him a flying lesson. But Long's characteristic impatience, coupled with his gut response to Hatfield, prompted him to forgo the charade.

"Let's just get right to it," he said.

McBride explained to Hatfield that he, McBride, would be going up also, and the three men climbed aboard a Cessna 172.

Frank Hatfield had taken up flying upon his discharge from the Army, using the GI Bill to cover his advanced training after picking up a private license. In the early 1970s, after bouncing around the country, Hatfield moved to Virginia, divorced and out of a job, and went to work as

an instructor and charter pilot for a general aviation outfit in Richmond. He had about 2,500 hours when he was introduced to Long.

"Frank, do you know what I do for a living?" Long asked, once the plane was airborne.

Long was wearing a jacket, no tie, a French-cotton shirt of the collarless sort, seventy-five-dollar blue jeans, and smooth lizard-skin boots. The jacket was silk and he had paid more for his wristwatch than Hatfield had paid for his car.

"I think I have a pretty good idea," Hatfield said.

"Well, before I tell you" — it was not in Long's character not to presume that Hatfield gave a damn whether he told him — "I want to ask you something. Do you think you have the balls it would take to risk your life for a million dollars?"

"What do you have in mind?"

Long told him.

Hatfield smiled, and said, "I thought you'd never ask."

Long cast a glance behind him, eyeing McBride.

"What kind of airplane are you planning to use?" asked Hatfield.

Long said he was not sure, that he hoped to discuss it with the pilot, but knew he wanted a large cargo plane. Hatfield told Long he was type-rated to fly a DC-3.

"Where would I get something like that?" asked Long.

"Well, Will and I were looking at *Trade-A-Plane* . . ."

Long glanced at McBride again. The latter simply threw him a smile.

"I've been waiting for you to ask me to do this," said Hatfield, "since Will first told me about it."

Long said, "You want in?"

"I have some questions I want to ask first."

He wanted to know what Long was offering in the way of guarantees. He wanted to know what would happen if he got arrested, who would get him out of jail. Long, conceding that the questions were reasonable, assured Hatfield that the proposition on the table was not.

"First," he said, "there are no guarantees."

And, he continued, going to jail was in fact a very real possibility. Smuggling, conspiracy to smuggle, possession with intent to sell — on a first offense they were looking at maybe five to ten years. Hatfield, he warned, had better understand that up front. That was the deal he was buying into.

Hatfield wanted money placed in escrow to cover his legal fees.

Long said, "That's not gonna happen. I don't know," he concluded, shaking his head, "I'm not sure you have the balls for this."

Hatfield nodded, shrugged his shoulders, put the Cessna into a dive, and cut the airplane's engine. Nose down, in free fall, the aircraft plummeted.

"How do you feel now?" he asked, folding his arms, turning to study Long's face, his evaluation quietly clinical. "How are your balls?"

"In my mouth," Long, who admired the tactic, admitted.

Hatfield fired the engine, pulled the plane out of its dive, and without looking at Long, said he was in.

Long still had his doubts. And in the car, leaving the airport, he shared them with McBride.

"I'm worried about that guy," he said.

"What are you worried about?"

"Will he be there? Will he do it when the time comes?"

"He'll do it."

And that was just about everything Will McBride needed

to say. To know McBride was to know why.

Will McBride, a native Virginian, grew up amid the peanut farms just west of the Great Dismal Swamp. Attending college in Richmond, he dropped out to play bass guitar in a series of rhythm & blues bands. He met Long, then a college student, at a party at which he was performing. Setting off to travel the country in 1971 with the pit crew of a racing team, McBride returned to Richmond at about the same time Long returned from New York, and the two remained casual acquaintances until JD Reed showed up in town.

McBride, by then, was running his own company, a small service agency in Richmond to which he had turned his talent for selling ideas, and one of two ambitious endeavors to which he had turned his entrepreneurial skills, the other being a small but thriving marijuana distributorship in town. He and Long had been doing business for a little over a year, and Long had come to know McBride as a guy who got the job done. McBride did not tolerate improficiency or a willingness on the part of anybody to yield to failure without a fight. McBride's confidence in Hatfield sealed it for Long — if McBride believed in the pilot, that was enough. Long was being asked to believe in McBride, which made things pretty simple.

Had Long asked Cherie, things would have been simpler still. Her opinion of McBride was uncomplicated. She adored him. In judging Long's friends, Cherie took a narrow focus. It was a point of view she had refined working high school summers as a lifeguard, a role she later resumed out of necessity as Long's girlfriend, evaluating a large cast of reckless characters. And McBride measured up to the standard that mattered: He was trustworthy. Beyond that she admired his attitude. In the no-bullshit department he ranked in her

opinion right up there with JD Reed. He would tell you when he was not going to go a step further.

McBride and Hatfield were in.

Allen Long, like other scammers, evinced an abiding faith in human corruptibility, and he discerned in Frank Hatfield the workingman's approach to crime. He believed that any red-blooded American male, when offered the chance to make close to a million dollars for doing thirty hours of work four times a year — for flying an airplane, for doing anything thirty hours straight — was going to say yes. In Long's estimation, jail as a deterrent carried very little weight. A criminal who really believed he would end up in jail would never break the law in the first place. Sure, in his mind the possibility existed, but until the cuffs were biting his wrists, until that door slammed shut, jail was just not a reality. At the outset of any criminal enterprise jail was no more than a hypothesis. And once the gig paid off, once a man got a taste of the money? In Allen Long's view of the world, it was all over, pal.

Hatfield's saying yes was the first move in getting air operations underway, and the last encouraging move for quite a while when it came to the airplane. The airplane itself was the problem, as airplanes always were. Airplanes, boats — the vehicles were always the problem, as Long would discover time and again. They were what kept you from doing the deals. And the Drug Enforcement Administration knew it. The DEA knew where to look for people looking to register an airplane for no immediately evident, practical purpose. The agency knew where to find people looking to establish an airline, or to buy any craft that could conceivably be put to the purpose of carrying cargo. They were the

ones who had the ads in *Trade-A-Plane* saying "DC-3 For Sale."

Trade-A-Plane magazine, "the aviation marketplace," is a color tabloid published three times a month out of Crossville, Tennessee. Promoting itself as the "world's largest general aviation resource," the magazine is distributed in a hundred countries, and has been bringing together buyers and sellers of airplanes since 1937. In its pages, through contemporary display ads and an enormous classified ad section, those in the general aviation market can find virtually any type of new or used aircraft. The first place an aviator would look if he wished to buy a used airplane — the place Hatfield and McBride would have gone under any other circumstances — the magazine was the first place the DEA would look for someone wishing to do so. And consequently the last place someone in Long's position would go. Long's best bet in escaping the scrutiny of the government was to buy an unregistered airplane. The best way to do that was to buy the airplane in parts. And the best way to buy an airplane in parts was to go to Tucson, Arizona — to go to Davis-Monthan Air Force Base — and buy the airplane from the government.

At Davis-Monthan sit some 5,000 decommissioned planes, "retired military inventory," 80 percent of which can be returned to flyable condition. Most of the mothballed aircraft are maintained to be sold for parts, chiefly to those overseas governments in whose military arsenals the models are still in service. In 1975 the C-47 Skytrain was still in military service in the United States and in more than ninety other countries. Twenty-five years later, its civilian equivalent, the DC-3, would still be in commercial service with small airlines throughout the world. Unlike the fighter jets and other serious combat hardware in the government graveyard

at Davis-Monthan, the C-47s were available for civilian purchase through airplane brokers around the country. Hatfield and McBride managed to find a broker in Long Beach, California, who specialized in locating and reassembling surplus aircraft, and who was willing to accept a contract to do so without asking too many questions.

The DC-3 would cost $110,000. On the contract the buyer was listed as ALL Air, Inc. (A.L.L. for Allen L. Long). The incorporation of ALL Air, which was necessary to the advancement of the smuggling enterprise, broadened the criminal conspiracy in the customary way; expanded it in the time-honored manner predictable in such cases. For no drug-smuggling conspiracy of any significance was complete without the participation of a member of the bar.

By the standards of the legal profession Buddy Blanchard was pretty young. Long put him in his mid-thirties. By any standard, Blanchard was a pretty slick individual, and in Virginia vernacular that made him "a smart old scoofer." A connoisseur of fine wine, food, and antiques, Blanchard, with a home and practice in Richmond, held fast to a position in the upper echelon of Virginia society and was highly regarded as one of the better lawyers in the state. Blanchard was six-feet-five-inches tall, and had a face like a gargoyle on the Cathedral of Notre Dame. His ears were big, his nose was long, and his lips looked like they had been laid on lovingly with a trowel. He was one of the more ill-favored men it had ever been Allen Long's pleasure to meet, and Long could not have been more pleased to meet him. He had been recommended to Long by a satisfied client, whose referral carried with it all the unrestrained faith and outspoken assurance that women bring to the sharing of

their gynecologists. "He'll do anything for money," is how such lawyers come advertised.

Long presented Blanchard with an entirely hypothetical question on a matter of law. Suppose, he said, someone wanted to buy an airplane for some undefined illegal purpose. How would one go about backstopping the purchase to protect himself, Long asked.

"Hypothetically?"

"In theory," said Long.

"Strictly hypothetically," Blanchard said, "not that I would ever advise someone to do this . . ."

The someone in question, Blanchard said, would ascertain a fictitious address, say a vacant lot, get a Post Office box attached to that address, and use it as a mail drop for a party who existed in name only. One would then write a letter to an attorney in the name of that party, enclosing a $5,000 money order and a guarantee of available funds for the purchase of the aircraft. One would retain the attorney to establish a corporation, to act as business agent for that corporation, and acting in that capacity to purchase the aircraft in the name of the corporation for said party.

". . . should anyone want to do that," Blanchard concluded.

Neither Long nor Blanchard, of course, knew anyone who might want to do something like that. Pursuant to their conversation, however, Frank Hatfield flew out west, and using the address of an empty lot, opened a Post Office box in the name of a fictitious leasing company. Long typed a letter to Blanchard from the fictitious owner of the company, retaining the lawyer to incorporate ALL Air for the purpose of flying cargo throughout the Western Hemisphere. He enclosed a $5,000 cashier's check, and stated that upon receiving correspondence from Blanchard in care of the PO

box he would arrange delivery of $110,000 for the purchase of a DC-3.

A few days later Long was back in Blanchard's office.

"Funny thing," Blanchard said. "You know that question you asked me the other day? I got a letter right here . . ."

Jake Myerson gave Long $110,000 in cash, which was placed in an escrow account opened by Blanchard to be paid out to the airplane broker in Long Beach. ALL Air, Inc., seeking to hire ferry pilots to supervise reassembly of a DC-3 and fly it from Long Beach to Richmond, placed a help-wanted ad in the Richmond classifieds. Two local pilots, looking for work, responded to the ad and were quickly hired.

Dispatched to Southern California, the pilots — Frank Hatfield and Will McBride — would not return to Richmond for some time. Getting the airplane up and running would drag on seemingly forever. But that was yet unknown to Long.

With the pilots taking the sun out west, he and Reed headed south.

Booking passage on Avianca Airlines, Long and Reed, poster boys for pot smoking in the land of the free, for the first time since hearing its name, for the first time since having located it like some dreamscape on the map of the world — for the first time since learning to spell it correctly — flew to the Republic of Colombia.

ELDORADO

RED, WHITE, AND BLOND

Barranquilla, Colombia, some 1,600 nautical miles due south of Richmond, sits about ten miles upstream of the Caribbean on the west bank of the Magdalena River. An industrial city, fifty-eight miles southwest of Santa Marta, it is Colombia's principal port of entry from the north. Long and Reed arrived on a nonstop Avianca flight from Miami, and when they stepped out onto the airport tarmac, the heat hit them like a shovel. When they stepped inside the terminal, they were hit by knowing smiles from customs and immigration inspectors, whose experience had taught them that few gringos like Long and Reed traveled to Colombia for any reason other than the reason for which Long and Reed were there.

Of those Americans who did visit Colombia, fewer still lingered in Barranquilla — they remained no longer than the time required to catch a connecting flight. Barranquilla was that kind of place. As described in the travel literature, it was "a lively, happy city," and tourists, for whom it held "little interest," were quite happy to take that for granted.

As far as the typical traveler was concerned, the city's 700,000 inhabitants could have it.

The two smugglers took a cab downtown and checked into the Del Prado, the city's only hotel of consequence. Everything that happened in Barranquilla happened at the Del Prado, every deal that went down went down there. As every gringo knew, you simply did not go any farther. The two checked into a poolside room, Reed turned on the air conditioner, and said, "I need something to smoke."

Long had arrived in Barranquilla with the typical Colombian connection, which was no connection to speak of. His friend Little Eddie knew a guy in New York who knew a guy in Miami who worked for Avianca named Felipe who had a cousin in Barranquilla. Or something like that. As often as not, the cousin, a cab driver whose name was Benito, could be found parked outside the Del Prado. (At one time or another throughout the day every cab driver in Barranquilla could be found parked outside the Del Prado.) After a couple of drinks at the hotel bar, Long and Reed stepped outside. Slammed once more by the punishing heat of the day, they walked the curb in front of the hotel, and found Benito at the wheel of one of several cabs stationed there, snoozing in the shade of a tree.

Long, introducing himself as an acquaintance of Benito's cousin Felipe in Miami, came right out and told Benito, a small, fast-talking fellow in his thirties, "I'm here to buy marijuana." Had Long not been hooked into Benito, he would have said pretty much the same thing to the driver of the first taxi he hailed. It was the natural place to shop.

Benito smiled, and as expected, assured Long: "I am the man."

U.S. currency went a long way in Colombia, and a hell of a long way in the dope market. The difference between

a five-dollar and a ten-dollar buy was the difference between an ounce and two ounces of street-level marijuana. When Benito asked Long how much he wanted, Long figured what the hell, might as well get down to it.

"*Yo quiero cinco mil libras,*" he said.

Long had picked up some Spanish in Mexico, and like many Americans who had spent time there, unable as they might be to converse fluently, he did know how to buy dope. Benito understood what he said — in the matter at hand Long's limited vocabulary presented no problem, and his grammar, syntax, and pronunciation bordered on excellent.

He wanted to buy 5,000 pounds.

With an audible intake of breath, Benito exclaimed, "I am the *man!*"

Long said, "Benito, my friend, I don't think you're the man. But I think you can help me find the man."

Both Long and Reed, in operating south of the Rio Grande, had learned what to look for in "the man." If you needed a runway, the man was someone, no questions asked, who could see that you had a runway. If you needed fuel, he could pick up the phone and within minutes get you a truckload — any of three grades of gasoline, kerosene if you were landing jets. The man was not a taxi driver. Nor was he a bartender, or your local dealer in the city. The man was a guy with clout. The typical profile of a guy like this was a man in his early to mid-fifties, maybe as old as sixty. He lived in a compound surrounded by servants. He owned a Mercedes or two, he had been to Miami, or at least he had been around. He traveled with a retinue of yes-men, lieutenants, and bodyguards, a variety of people whose job description was to do nothing but his bidding, much like the assortment of citizens and slaves who traversed the Forum behind Roman senators in the years of the Republic.

Benito was not the man. But of course, he knew the man — in Latin America everybody on the hustle knew a guy who knew a guy who knew a guy who knew the man. Everybody knew where to score dope.

"I know where to get it," Benito said.

"Yes," said Long, "you know where to get it, but I need to talk to the man who's got it."

Benito said, "I'll take you."

And so began the predictable climb up the chain of associations leading to a marijuana connection, each Colombian along the way assuring Long that he was "the man."

Through Barranquilla's crowded streets, the yellow taxi made its way to the outskirts of town, pulling into a neighborhood that was home to little prosperity and the dope dealer with whom Benito did business. About ten years younger than Benito, more on the slick side, more in the style typical of the nightclub trade, a Latin American street hustler in the Hollywood mode, he leaned through the window of Benito's cab, and told Long he was the man. He could get him all the marijuana he needed.

"Okay," said Long. "Tomorrow, I need to go see a three-thousand-foot runway, a thousand gallons of flight fuel, and five thousands pounds of pot."

"Oh, I can't do that," he said.

"Well, you're not the guy I'm looking for, then. But if you have some marijuana, I'll buy some for my friend."

Ten dollars bought Long all he needed for now. He and Reed returned to the hotel, and fired up a couple of joints. Long agreed with Reed that the pot was not especially good.

Doing big business with gringos was every gangster's Golden Fleece, everywhere south of the border. Neither monsters nor magicians would deter the serious small-time dealer in quest of that particular prize, and never would a

simple "No, thank you." So it came as no surprise when the next morning Long answered a knock on the door, and standing there when he unlatched it were Benito and his dope-dealing friend. They had someone waiting outside, they said, whom they wanted the Americans to meet. Long and Reed made their way to the street, where they were introduced to a man named Moisés. Moisés was slender, with sleek, brown hair and an earnest, honest, ovoid face that came to a point like the face of a flying squirrel. Moisés was a taxi dispatcher, and looked to be in his early thirties. He said, "I am the man you are looking for." He knew someone who could show Long the things he wanted to see, but meeting this person, Moisés confided, meant going to Santa Marta.

Well, thought Long, if only mildly encouraged, that would be the right direction.

Moisés had to work that day, but that night, as soon as he finished work, all five men — he, his friends, Long and Reed, the last two carrying their luggage — squeezed themselves into the dispatcher's cab, a tiny yellow Fiat, and sped up the coast to Santa Marta. They hit several government checkpoints on the way.

Highway 2 along the Caribbean coast was a bracelet of security checkpoints manned by soldiers and federal police. Part of an internal customs system designed to interdict traffic in contraband, including the time-honored domestic smuggling of merchandise like whiskey and cigarettes, such checkpoints were a fixture of Third World life, providing a federally sanctioned form of local extortion. In Colombia, a country in which violent civil insurgency was rooted as deeply as coffee and homicide enjoyed popular endorsement as a form of political expression, such installations served the government further as a means of gun control, keeping weapons

from the interior. And they took on added significance when it came to the traffic in dope. East of Santa Marta armed guerrillas of Colombia's assorted leftist insurgencies improvised numerous checkpoints of their own, stepping out onto the highway to shake down people in transit. Between Santa Marta and Riohacha a motorist might hit as many as twenty.

At each government checkpoint the taxi was stopped, and once the gringos were spotted all five men were ordered out of the car and they and the taxi were searched. At nine p.m. the smugglers reached Santa Marta. Long and Reed checked into the Irotama, a first-class hotel just north of the airport. Moisés told the Americans to wait, and he and his friends disappeared. An hour later two strangers appeared.

The older of the two men was a few years older than Long and a good eight inches shorter. He was lean and balding, wore gold, wire-rimmed spectacles, and was dressed the way Americans of Long's generation had dressed in high school. He wore a white cotton shirt with a button-down collar, casual slacks, and dress shoes. He was introduced as Dr. Cepeda. A manifestly emotional, high-strung man, clearly working to suppress his intensity, Dr. Cepeda vibrated beneath the casual clothes with the undifferentiated energy of a Chihuahua, which worked to exaggerate the physical contrast between him and the man introduced as his associate. The latter's name was Miguel. He was all poise and self-possession. He was even-tempered, tall and plump, a credible human analog of the North American harbor seal, his body on a longitudinal plane perfectly elliptic. He had a broad, tranquil, good-humored face and skin the color of honey, unlike his friend the doctor, who had no Indian blood in his background. Miguel spoke English well. He explained that he was a medical student and was present to serve as a translator for Dr. Cepeda, who did not.

"My name is Pablo Cepeda," Miguel said, as the doctor spoke, "and I am the man you are looking for. I can do whatever you want. It is my business to sell what you want. This is my associate, he is helping me."

Long said he was expecting an older man.

Miguel, translating, said, "Dr. Cepeda wants you to know that he is the man for you to do business with. He says he has what you need."

What Long needed had been outlined for him by Reed, who had worked with DC-3s in the past, and Hatfield, who adding to what Reed knew, had schooled Long in the specifics of the particular aircraft they would be using. The standard DC-3, which carried 800 gallons of fuel, had a range of a little more than a thousand miles. The airplane being assembled in Long Beach had auxiliary tanks in the wings, each with a capacity of 400 gallons, effectively doubling its range. More than a thousand gallons of fuel would be needed to fill the tanks when the airplane reached Colombia. The flight fuel Long was looking for, Hatfield told him, was green. It was gasoline, not kerosene. The latter, with a lower octane rating, was used as jet fuel; it was colorless. The extra fuel carried in the wing tanks — amounting to some two and a half tons if the tanks were filled to capacity — reduced the plane's military-maximum payload to about 5,000 pounds on a decent runway. Hatfield would need a half a mile of hard-packed earth to take off. There were other things to look into — did the Colombians have ground-to-air radios, for example — but Long would look into them later.

"What I need," Long responded, "is to see five thousand pounds of the very best marijuana."

"*Mercancía.*"

"Merchandise. Yes. The best."

Miguel communicated this to the doctor, who answered in the affirmative.

"Dr. Cepeda says to you, if you want him to show you the merchandise, he can show you the merchandise," said Miguel.

"I need to see a runway."

"*La pista?*" Miguel said, consulting his associate.

"*Sí,*" replied Dr. Cepeda.

"Dr. Cepeda says you can see a runway."

"Flight fuel," Long continued. "I need to see eleven hundred gallons of high-octane gasoline."

"*Gasolina,*" replied Cepeda. "*Sí. También.*"

"That Dr. Cepeda can show you also."

"And I need to speak to the man."

When the latter remark was translated for him, the good doctor exploded. The accumulating energy with which he had been oscillating finally achieved critical mass. Clearly outraged that his credibility was in question, he sputtered unintelligibly, as if he were possessed by a demon, frantically waving his arms to punctuate his remarks.

Miguel just nodded in reply.

"Dr. Cepeda says he is the man. He tells you, do not ask that question anymore. Dr. Cepeda says that tonight he will bring you something. If you like that, he will show you much more tomorrow, when he takes you to see the runway."

Reed did not say a word.

Dr. Cepeda, Miguel explained, wanted to know if Long had brought money.

"No," said Long, "but once you show me that you have what you say, I will come back and bring you the money."

It's not a setup, they're not cops, it doesn't feel that way . . .

Yet, still, as he found himself thinking this, Long could

not help wondering whether these two Colombians were for real. Were these the people he was looking for? Are these the guys? he asked himself. Could this demoniacal doctor really be the man?

An hour after the two men departed, Dr. Cepeda returned, handed the Americans a folded newspaper, and said he would see them in the morning. Wrapped in the folds of the newspaper was a half-pound of Santa Marta Gold.

Santa Marta Gold, a product that ranges in hue from a deep, varnished oak to a pale, buff manila, owes the lightness of its leaf color to the nitrate content of the soil in certain stretches of Colombia's coastal mountains. Described accurately as blond, *rubia,* or *mona,* and identified by some Colombians as *la rubia de la costa,* "the blond from the coast," it was known to connoisseurs like Long not only for its color but its unmistakable aroma: pungent, spicy, a single note. There was nothing that smelled quite like it.

It was doubtful that Dr. Cepeda and his associate, nonsmokers as were most middle-class Colombians, instinctively appreciated the unique quality of the pot the doctor had provided. The Indians who had given it to them probably said: "This is what the Americans like." The storied gold of Santa Marta, the legendary blond — Long had seen it before, but never anything so fresh. The pot had just been cured. Reed took one look at the stuff and said: "Allen, these are the guys."

Rolling a couple of joints, the two smugglers strolled down to the beach.

It was a clear, cloud-free Caribbean night, the kind of night on which rank amateurs were inclined miraculously to fathom the mysteries of celestial navigation. The air was cool, the heavens were clear, the ambient starlight was uncontaminated. It was a night that summoned images of snipers and Phoenicians. They sat on a log that had washed

ashore, and there in the darkness they smoked. They fired up the dope — "delicate, flavorful, and smooth-smoking," in the description of the experienced pot smoker, unequaled when it came to inspiring mirth — and soon the marijuana had them laughing, philosophizing, and carrying on. Long, doing nothing more than looking at Reed, who sat there scouring the coastline as if he held a lease on the place, became dangerously entangled in the throes of his own merriment. His glee ran out of control. Eyelids fluttering, mouth stretching across the occlusion of cheerfully buzzing teeth, he snorted paroxysmally, laughing without benefit of his vocal cords, his outburst entirely sibilant, his facial musculature drooping like the jowls of a Virginia bloodhound, his grin so idiotic it was sublime.

"I got stoned that time," he said.

Reed was studying the joint in his hand, twirling it between his fingers, as if searching for a set of instructions. A man who embraced the cannabis plant as the gift of a benevolent God, JD Reed viewed every leaf as if it had his name on it.

"I can go anywhere in the world, and I'll find a connection," he said. "They'll come to me. I don't care where it is. I can go anywhere, and get the best deal."

They had been in Colombia not even thirty-six hours. And what they had was what everyone wanted. Everyone wanted Colombian Gold, and very few people could get it. There on a beach in Santa Marta, they howled at a starlit sky, convulsed with belly laughter, Allen Long and JD Reed high on grade-A dope and on the consequences of their score.

To Long the prospects were thrilling.

"If these people have access to thousands of pounds of pot like this? And we pull this thing off? Man, we're going to be rich," he said.

And at least within a small circle of American renegades, more.

"We're going to be heroes."

As expected, the Americans never saw Moisés, the taxi dispatcher, or his two friends, again. They were gone, cut out of the picture. They had been paid off and told to go home.

The next morning Miguel appeared at the hotel with discouraging news.

"I'm sorry, sir," he said to Long, "Dr. Cepeda wishes me to tell you that he cannot take you today. The army is patrolling in the area, searching for the *guerrilleros*, and traveling will not be possible."

Reed spent most of the rest of the day burning Santa Marta Gold. Long went for a run on the beach. Wearing emerald green nylon, split-sided jogging shorts — as goofy an outfit on any hombre as the locals were likely to see — he hit the beach in front of the hotel and ran toward Rodadero, sun-worshiping central in Santa Marta, by far the most popular beach resort in Colombia. Approaching along the waterline, he was brought up short by the presence of a group of teenage girls gathered at the edge of the surf. One in particular captured his attention, striking him in such a way as to throw him awkwardly off-stride. A Colombian, not yet twenty, with dark hair, green eyes, and almost nothing in the way of a bathing suit, she caught sight of him and smiled. She whispered something to her girl-friends, who checked Long out and giggled. Long smiled back, recovered his stride, and ran on without its ever occurring to him that they might be making fun of his outfit.

"Man," he told Reed, when he returned to the hotel, "I

saw the most beautiful girl in the world today. And I think she liked me."

"Far out, man. Here, have a hit."

So much for love in the time of gold.

The following morning Long and Reed set off along the coast with Dr. Cepeda and his young associate in the doctor's Toyota Land Cruiser. Their destination, the village of Camarones, lay ninety-three miles to the east. Fifty miles into the journey they hit the Río Palomino. A large billboard greeted them there. It carried a U.S. State Department advisory notifying American citizens that the area beyond the river was considered extremely dangerous. U.S. passport holders were not prohibited from entering the badlands, the billboard merely served to warn them that once they crossed the river they were on their own.

Crossing the Río Palomino, the smugglers entered the Guajira.

Dr. Cepeda raised an imaginary pistol. "Boom, boom, boom," he said, turning to smile at the gringos. "La Guajira. It is . . . ruled . . . by the gun!"

At Camarones they left the paved surface of the highway, and followed a dirt track into the village. There they abandoned the Toyota. Joined by several more Colombians, all of whom carried handguns, they climbed aboard a pickup truck driven by a man introduced as Ernesto, who seemed to be in charge. Appearing to be about forty years old, wearing a straw cattleman's hat and stockyard boots, Ernesto would say little that day, and when he did speak, would speak only to the medical student, who translated for the Americans.

The truck, following near-invisible dirt tracks and bouncing through arroyos, penetrated the backland on a journey of a type with which Long would become familiar,

a bone-jarring ride over washboard trails at speeds generally reserved for highway travel. Colombians, he would learn, did not slow down simply because the road ended. In the future, as now, whenever Long infiltrated such terrain, he would do so as part of a crowd. There would always be about fifteen guys, invariably armed, tagging along for the ride, none of whom spoke English. He did not know what to expect of them. Fifteen weapons, fifteen strange, indecipherable smiles — he did not know which way these characters were going to jump. Eventually he would come to understand that they were there to protect him.

After twenty-five minutes the truck came to a stop, the smugglers bailed out, and the expedition proceeded on foot. They were deep in the brush now, and every quarter of a mile or so an armed Indian wearing nothing more than a loincloth — "a guy in his underwear with a .45 pistol," as Reed later described it to the pilots — popped up out of the scrub, smiled, and dropped back down. About a mile in they came to what could loosely be called a clearing. There, under military tarp and camouflage netting suspended from trees, stacked ten feet high and twenty feet square, stood about 30,000 pounds of marijuana.

This was a classic Colombian *caleta*.

The word *caleta*, literally a hole, or hiding place, could be applied to a stash of any kind, including certain large caches of money, and was used to describe those mobile camps or staging areas where large supplies of marijuana were held in preparation for shipment.

As Long and Reed entered the *caleta* from one end, a burro train, kicking up dust, was entering from the other. The burros were slung, about seventy pounds on either side, with farm sacks containing loose marijuana, cured in the mountains and ready for market. On the edge of the

clearing, mounted on sawhorses, stood large, square, steel mesh screens in wooden braces, and onto these screens the sacks were emptied. Two workers shook the screens until loose seeds, small stems, powder, and dirt fell through. Removing the larger sticks by hand, they then dumped the culled pot onto a canvas tarp spread over a table. From the canvas, the pot was scooped into a burlap bag that hung from the hook of a farm scale. In measured loads the pot was poured from the bag onto the bed of a screw-driven baling press, where it was compacted into rectangular bundles before being wrapped.

The smell of the place was overwhelming.

"This is it, Allen. These are the guys. Give 'em the money."

Reed spoke as if he had been there before, if only in his dreams.

"These are the guys," Long said.

Back in the truck, bouncing down more, barely discernible trails, the smugglers traveled to a tapering neck of shoreline that hooked out into the Caribbean like the acuminate beak of a parakeet, a topographical congruity from which the place took its name: Perico. The truck pulled into a clearing, and everyone aboard jumped out. Long hiked up his jeans, stretched his legs, and, brushing dust from his hair, stood waiting for whatever came next. Reed directed his attention to the tracks in the dirt at their feet.

Long looked up, incredulous.

"This is it?" he said.

The soil ran rough with tread marks.

"This is the strip? They're landing airplanes here?"

As fossil evidence the traces were incontrovertible: the unmistakable tracks put down by aircraft rolling in. The tires that had left the largest tread impression were easily as large as those of Reed's DC-3.

Walking the strip from the touchdown point, just above the tideline, and following it to the trees, Long paced it off. He estimated the length of the runway at about 1,800 feet, substantially shorter than Hatfield had told him was necessary.

Reed said, "It'll do."

Miguel, taking his lead from Dr. Cepeda, assured Long that large aircraft of every kind had safely landed on and lifted off the strip.

"Come with me," he said.

He led Long and Reed into the brush. There, under a tarp, in 55-gallon drums, were more than a thousand gallons of flight fuel. The fuel was green — gasoline, not kerosene — and as determined by Reed, who checked it for rust and found none, it was fresh and uncontaminated by water.

Long found himself thinking, okay, now I'm impressed.

Everyone boarded the pickup, and Ernesto pushed through the sandy backcountry to a tiny fishing village on the coast just north of Perico. There, Long and Reed, parched, overheated, and covered with dust, were ushered into a one-room adobe, the door and windows of which were nothing more than openings in the brickwork. They were followed through the doorway by Dr. Cepeda, Miguel, and Ernesto and as many of Ernesto's subordinates as could fit, no doubt in descending order of authority. Children from the village gathered and hung on the sills, leaning in from outside the windows, remarking on the presence of the gringos. Apart from a few stools and a couple of crates upon which the men took seats, the interior was empty of furniture but for a pale blue, propane-fired Kelvinator refrigerator. Opening the refrigerator door, Ernesto asked the medical student to ask if the gringos would like drinks. Long and Reed saw that the refrigerator was filled with nothing but cans of

Heineken beer. They exchanged glances, said yes with no hesitation, and one more time it crossed the minds, if not the lips, of the two Americans: "These are the guys."

Convinced that others before them had been entertained here, Long and Reed were nonetheless curious. Plainly, this was more than a pit stop. It was apparent that the Colombians were waiting for something. Before the second can of beer, Miguel cleared up the matter.

"You are satisfied with what you have seen, sir?" he asked.

Long said yes, he was.

Miguel nodded his head, conveying reciprocal satisfaction on the part of Dr. Cepeda. Taking his lead from the doctor, he said: "Now, you will meet the man."

A smile commenced its journey across the surface of Long's face, lighting it up like morning sunshine bleeding across a blanket with the opening of a bedroom blind.

Don Julio was maybe sixty years old. He had a full head of white hair and a heart condition. He was overweight by about thirty pounds, carried in a paunch appropriate to his stature, and he fit Long's preconception of "the man" perfectly.

He arrived in a cloud of dust at the wheel of a new Ford Ranger. Bouncing around in the bed of the pickup were two armed men on his payroll, and riding with him up front in the cab were two eighteen-year-old prostitutes. The young women remained outside, and his two henchmen followed him into the hut.

He wore blue jeans and a new pair of ostrich-skin boots. The brim of a tall white Stetson shaded his weathered face from the sun, and holstered to his gunbelt were two pearl-handled six-shooters. Every Colombian present stood and offered Don Julio his seat. Selecting a packing crate opposite

Long, he sat, removed his hat, ran a hand through his hair, popped a nitroglycerin pill, and smiled.

"So, you are Allen," he said. He unholstered one of the revolvers, and placed it on his knee. "I am Don Julio."

Long nodded his deference.

"You have seen the runway?"

"Yes."

"The merchandise, the marimba. You are happy?" Don Julio asked.

"Yes. I am very happy."

Marimba, a slang reference to marijuana, was in common use among Colombian traffickers, but never really caught on with Americans. It was taken from the name of the resonating xylophone popular with Caribbean musicians — its etymology unclear to Long — and those who played the marijuana game, like those who played the instrument, were known as *marimberos*. As a veiled reference to pot, like the Spanish words for merchandise and material, the expression was abandoned by Long and his Colombian associates, along with other formalities, as soon as trust was established. They just called it marijuana and left it at that.

"I am glad you are such a happy man. Now I will tell you," Don Julio said, "about another happy man who came here."

With Miguel translating, Don Julio proceeded to tell Long the story of another American who had recently visited the village. The American had looked very much like Long, and had asked to see all the same things.

"He asked to see the *mercancía*, the strip, the gas . . ."

Don Julio threw up his arms, and with genuine laughter explained to Long that they had shown the American these things only to discover that he was a policeman, and had come there intending to arrrest them. The other Colombians

nodded as one, and laughed with Don Julio at the memory. It was very sad, Don Julio declared, shaking his head, smiling at the folly of it all. At any rate, he continued, it had been necessary to kill him. Here Don Julio raised his eyes, and looked directly into Long's.

"You look like a nice man, Allen," he said. "I hope we do not have to kill you."

Long granted Don Julio the concession he sought: an acknowledgment of his understanding that he was now in very deep. Staring into the wise and matter-of-fact gaze of the old man, he said: "I am not a policeman, I am a *contrabandista*."

Don Julio jumped to his feet and smiled.

"*Bueno!* I am glad," he said, explaining that he would greatly lament the need to cut off Long's head.

Don Julio holstered the revolver, shook Long's hand, and left. He disappeared in the pickup with his henchmen and his whores, and Long never saw him again.

The deal Long struck with the Colombians represented something of a first on the Guajira. He wanted nothing but Santa Marta Gold, he said, and made it clear that he was willing to pay for it. And he wanted to pay the Colombians enough per pound to guarantee its availability on subsequent trips. The difference in price made little difference to him — what were a few dollars more, he figured, if he were going to sell the product with a 650 percent markup. Ernesto told him that the marijuana he wanted grew only in select parts of the Sierra Nevada, and further, that the region produced only a limited amount every year.

"But I will get it all," promised Ernesto, when the deal was finally struck.

Long would pay the Colombians $50 a pound for the pot, a total of $250,000 for a first load of 5,000 pounds.

He would accept a few bales of *punta roja,* if the Colombians ran short on weight. He would pay the Colombians in three installments. He would return immediately with the first installment, a $60,000 down payment. That would be sufficient to cover the cost of holding the load.

(The Colombians would be paying the farmers between $10 and $12 a pound for the pot. And the farmers had to be paid. The difference between the $12 the Colombians paid for the merchandise and the $50 for which they sold it covered, in addition to profit, such things as security, the cost of the airstrip, and the price of fuel. The budget line for security included bribes paid to police and military officials. A fee of, say, $10,000 might buy a four-day window in which to operate; delays, typically due to weather, and more commonly associated with the arrival of boats, could therefore be costly.)

The Americans would deliver another $65,000 when the airplane arrived in Colombia, bringing the total paid out before distribution to $125,000, or one half the value of the deal. The other half would be paid to the Colombians, in a third installment, after the pot was sold. That money would be delivered within a couple of weeks of the load's arrival in Ann Arbor, optimally on a second flight down, along with a $125,000 down payment for a second load. And so on.

Santa Marta's newest hotel was Puerto Galeón. Situated on a private beach about five minutes from the airport, the resort was celebrated for its first-class suites and conspicuous for its restaurant, which was housed aboard the replica of a sixteenth-century Spanish galleon. Adjoining the ship was a casino, and that night before he left for the States, Long hit the blackjack tables, accompanied by Miguel.

Reed remained at the Irotama, kicking back with a stash of dope, having suffered his share of gambling joints as a resident of Las Vegas.

It was in the nightclub attached to the casino at Puerto Galeón that Long's Caribbean expedition was temporarily blown off course, driven from the predictable sea of a Herman Melville novel and fetching up on the uncharted shoals of something by the Brontë sisters.

On the patio outside the club Long was struck by the sight of a young woman in white. She was tall, about five-feet-nine, with bright eyes, full lips, and hair the color of mahogany. She was becoming in a way that was almost electrifying, and it was clear as she stood there in the darkness, surrounded by friends both male and female, that she had long since arrived at a level of comfort with the fact that others were naturally drawn to her. Radiating sophistication and at the same time an angelic innocence, she held special appeal for someone like Long. Here in a vessel of physical beauty was the promise of that treasured attribute so highly prized by American men, the attribute they find so alluring in the plainest of Latin American women, so elusive in women at home: subservience.

Like Saint Paul on the road to Damascus, Long was blind to everything but her light. Unable to take his eyes off her, he inevitably drew her attention his way, and reading in her glance what he took for an invitation, he made a pointedly casual approach, coming on to her with a pickup line that was as unimaginative as it was disingenuous.

"Do I know you?" he asked.

Not until she smiled at him did he realize that the answer was yes.

And she remembered him. She had seen him the day

before. He was the gringo running along the beach, she said, in the "sexy" green *pantalonitas.*

They danced the night away.

Her name was María, she was nineteen years old, and according to Miguel, everyone in Santa Marta knew her as "a flower ready to be picked."

"Be very careful with María," he said.

In one way it was a little bit late for that. The young woman had stolen Long's heart.

"Qué sueñes con los angelitos," she whispered, when she and Long said good night, "May you sleep with the little angels." She addressed him as *lindo,* pretty boy, invited him to give her a call, then lightly touching his face with her fingers, she left.

With or without the angels, he would be unable to sleep that night.

Miguel, a true romantic, could not have been happier for his new friend. But he told him again to be careful. And then he told him why.

"She is the niece of Raúl Gaviria," he said.

The name was unfamiliar to Long, but it would not remain that way. Raúl Gaviria was one of the more famous smugglers on the Guajira. He moved his loads by boat, shipping tons of commercial Colombian out of Bahía Profundo. He would make headlines in Miami three years later as part of a smuggling ring whose flamboyant U.S. component styled itself the Black Tuna gang. His brother would figure prominently in a U.S. magazine feature in 1978, exercising his power to close down the Santa Marta airport, mobilizing the local military to land and load large smuggling aircraft at night.

Long, quite prepared to be careful, looked forward to his next trip to Colombia.

On the Guajira, Pablo Cepeda had asked how soon the

Americans would return with the airplane. Long replied through Miguel.

"Tell the doctor I will call next week, and arrange with him to deliver the money. After that, the airplane will come. We have done it this way many times. And he has done it, too. Tell him the airplane is ready."

"I don't care what it takes! You have to get down there and see to it! I want you down there now!"

Long, standing at a pay phone in Richmond, Virginia, had reached out to touch Will McBride, who was encamped in a hotel room for which Long was paying in Marina Del Rey, California. And the news that Long received was not the news he had called to hear — the DC-3, for which the Colombians were waiting, was currently lying in pieces on the floor of a hangar in Long Beach.

A delay at this point in getting the operation airborne could blow the entire deal, and Long believed that given that prospect, McBride and Hatfield, assigned to move the job along, were having too much fun. Long envisioned their lounging poolside, fishing for flight attendants, a large, transient population of which bathed the city of Marina Del Rey in its singular brand of cultural sunshine. Long wanted his pilots off the party circuit and on the scene in Long Beach, where he expected them to make life as miserable for the airplane broker as Long was prepared to make theirs in the face of any further delay.

McBride and Hatfield assured Long that assembly of the airplane was on schedule. Promising that it would be in Richmond, ready to go, in a month, they departed for Long Beach to pressure the broker, and Long, in Virginia, turned his attention to putting together a ground crew.

There are over 10,000 airports, from large metropolitan airfields to small grass strips, within the borders of the United States. All of them are listed, detailed, and diagrammed in the *Jeppesen Airport and Information Directory* — from O'Hare International in Chicago to all the triangle strips, most of them county airports, built as part of the nation's civil defense at the time of the Second World War. Hatfield and McBride, to make the pickup in Colombia, could take off from almost anywhere. (They chose Fayetteville, North Carolina.) Where to land the load upon their return was a decision that required some research. Using the *J-AID,* they selected a municipal airport at West Point, King William County, Virginia, about thirty-five miles east of Richmond. McBride spent a couple of nights observing the field, and saw that nothing happened there after dark. He and Hatfield would be bringing the plane in under a full moon at midnight, when the airport was deserted.

On the night of the flight Long would be on the beach in Colombia manning a ground-to-air radio. He could not leave communications to chance. Everything depended on the use of codes and the fallback to special frequencies; any confusion caused by the language barrier, and the entire operation could go sour. From the beach he would be in contact with Reed, who would be aboard the DC-3, the one man aboard the airplane who knew the exact location of the strip. Reed would have been the logical choice to serve as chief of the off-loading crew at West Point. With him in the air and unavailable, however, the open position had to be filled.

Orchestrating routine ground operations — the off-load, conducted by cover of darkness, as the airplane came in heavy from Colombia — eventually, and somehow inexplicably, took on the proportions of staging a grand opera. To

run the job, Long came up with a guy named Hathaway, who owned a storage facility in Virginia. Long had used him in the past, paying him a dollar a pound to warehouse pot that came in from Nevada. Long admired his organizational skills and deliberative turn of mind, but not even Long was prepared for the professionalism that Hathaway eventually brought to the task.

Hathaway actually prepared and issued a ground operations manual. The ring-bound booklet was indexed with tab dividers in three colors. Instructions and contingencies were covered under separate headings for each phase of the operation: "Pre-Flight," "Off-Load," and "Post-Delivery," respectively. The booklet provided maps showing how to get into the area, how to get out, what lay to the east, what lay to the west, where to find a gas station, and the location of the nearest pay phone. It stipulated what to wear, what not to wear, and when to be there wearing (or not wearing) it. It contained instructions on how to proceed in the event of a breakdown, and detailed various ways to exit the area in the event of a bust. It included a checklist.

In addition to Hathaway, the pickup team would consist of three men recruited out of Virginia by Long and two of Reed's men from Las Vegas. There would be six men, two trucks, and a car. They would use a fourteen-foot U-Haul, a pickup with a snap-top camper over the back, and a sedan. The U-Haul would accommodate the entire load, but Long had made the decision to throw the first 1,000 pounds into a pickup, enabling him to get a half-ton off the scene while the larger truck was being loaded. In the event of a bust, he figured, he would have a thousand pounds on the road. The sedan would be used as a scout car. Hathaway allowed twelve hours for the drive from West Point to Ann Arbor.

* * *

"Hey, buddy, can I give you a hand?"

Allen Long was walking the street, shopping for a pay phone in midtown Manhattan, when he ran across a comedian. The guy was in his forties, well dressed and drunk. He was standing in front of a church with a credit card in his hand.

"Says 'Jesus Saves,'" the guy told Long. "I thought it was a bank." Stepping back several feet to take in the building's architecture, he reached into his pocket for a handkerchief, wiped his nose, and said he should have known. "Bank doesn't have that kind of money."

Long wished him luck before moving on and told him to go easy on the blow.

Long had arrived in the city that morning and was leaving the following day, but not before suffering a certain nostalgia for the kinds of things a man runs into only on the streets of New York.

The phone booth on Lexington Avenue had been decorated to rival a subway car, its translucent panels rendered festively opaque. Aerosol spray paint in primary colors had been applied to give it the visual flavor of something as funky as the No. 4 train — brushed aluminum and corrugated steel, sealed windows of newly stained glass, rolling into the gray air beneath Grand Central like a floral bouquet from Latin America. Long loaded the phone with quarters, and called Myerson in Ann Arbor.

"Hey," he said, "let's talk."

"Where are you calling from?" said Myerson.

"I'm at my mother's house."

"Where's that?"

"Let me spell it."

"Go."

"T-O-T-E-C-E-O-F-O-F."

"I'll call you back."

Allen Long, like everyone who violated the conspiracy statutes at a professional level, adhered to a security protocol governing the use of the telephone. Communication was conducted over public phones, never private lines.

Call it the American way.

Authorities in various other parts of the world seldom concern themselves with evidence, circumstantial or direct. They lock you up or waste you in accordance with the prevailing folk wisdom, maybe the direction of the wind. The American system of justice is more sinister. In the United States the government, in quaint deference to due process of law, subpoenas your telephone records, then cracks you for collusion, for conspiring to get away with what you easily have gotten away with, or simply intend to get away with. Outlaws, gangsters, racketeers, pirates, bandits, their respective lawyers, and desperadoes in general are by nature cloak-and-dagger freaks, and the domestic conspiracy laws impart a certain legitimacy to that aspect of their collective behavior which very often appears foolish to the weird minority of the population that can safely be called law-abiding.

Everybody has his communications procedure, and Long's was one he and Reed had developed over the course of their moving Mexican loads. Receiving a call at home, the conspirator would be given a code containing the number of the pay phone to which the call was to be returned, then go to a pay phone himself and return the call from there. Various codes had been established by Reed, and each consisted of a ten-letter word in which none of the letters was repeated, the letters corresponding in sequence to the ten telephone digits. The words presently in use were "cornbasket" and "motherfuck," and a caller would signal the code by saying

something like, "I'm sending a cornbasket," or "Call me at my mother's house." (Using "cornbasket," where C is zero and T is nine, the area code for Manhattan, 212, would be given as R-O-R.) Later, the smugglers would add an alternate procedure, signaled by use of the word "Roger." If a phone number was given accompanied by any variation on the commonly used radio phrase — the expression "Roger that," for instance — one knew to transpose the number's area code and prefix.

Since leaving Barranquilla, Long had been on the phone to Colombia several times. He would call Miguel at home from a public booth in Virginia, telling the young medical student that he was sending a cornbasket. He would end the conversation with a series of letters corresponding to the number of a second public phone, where, at a specified time, Miguel, with Dr. Cepeda at his side, could reach him from a secure phone in Barranquilla.

A nighttime station-to-station call to Barranquilla from the United States cost $9.75. Long would always resist explaining this to the overseas operator who was handling the call, patiently allowing the operator to look up the charges.

Long's side of the subsequent exchange generally went something like this: "No, ma'am, it's not a credit card call . . . I see, well I have some change here, let me look . . . Why, yes, I just happen to have it . . ."

Long, holding a roll of quarters, would then interrupt the operator's calculations.

"It's thirty-nine," he would say. "I'll start now."

By the time he started doing business in Colombia, Long had achieved a level of proficiency whereby he could fire thirty-nine quarters into a pay phone in approximately thirty seconds, and that included pausing three times, as the coins,

maxing out the telephone's capacity, were collected in three-dollar increments. Long would continue to better his record, achieving a per-quarter personal best in good weather in 1978 on a call from New York to Caracas.

On those occasions when getting through to Colombia proved virtually impossible, which was often enough, owing to an antiquated phone system and a limited number of lines, Long would present himself to the overseas operator as a pediatric cardiologist, a volunteer with Save the Children. Fabricating a medical emergency and an unfortunate Colombian infant, he would ask that the call be expedited to his colleague in Barranquilla.

"How is the little girl," he would ask when put through to Miguel.

"She is stable, sir, but she must be transported to your country very soon. Do you know when this can happen?"

Alexander Graham Bell, patron saint of conspirators everywhere.

Over the course of numerous phone calls, a meeting was scheduled with the Colombians. Long would fly to Venezuela to hand over the $60,000 down payment. He would deliver the cash in Maracaibo, about a hundred miles southeast of Riohacha, the capital of Guajira department. At the meeting the smugglers would also work out details of the flight — the date and time of arrival, and any other contingencies that needed attention. In Maracaibo, Dr. Cepeda would be waiting to meet Long at the Del Lago hotel.

Standing on Lexington Avenue, taking his callback from Myerson, Long asked if Myerson had confirmed his flight.

"I'll meet you tomorrow," said Myerson.

"Pan American."

"JFK. I got it."

"Caracas."

"Yeah, Caracas. I'll see you tomorrow."

Long did not travel to Maracaibo alone. Jake Myerson, whose money was scheduled to change hands, went along for the ride. But it was more than the money that prompted his doing so. The trip represented Myerson's share in the adventure. Action, excitement, X-rated entertainment in exotic locales — getting out of the house and getting down with the boys was a large part of the attraction of being an outlaw. It was very much like golf in that way.

Long and Myerson, flying into Caracas on Pan American, hopped a domestic flight the following day from there to Maracaibo. They checked into the Del Lago hotel wearing aviator shades and dark business suits, each man carrying a briefcase containing $30,000 in cash.

It was a bright, beautiful, hot afternoon on the Gulf of Venezuela, and within minutes of their arrival the two Americans were hopelessly stoned on the dope they had brought along with them. Myerson's observable universe, a motion picture projected in Technicolor at an equable twenty-four frames per second, had commenced to reveal itself to him intermittently, like a 35 millimeter slide presentation: (snap) . . . (snap) . . . (snap). It was a psychedelic entertainment Myerson was condemned to enjoy in the privacy of his own head. Long was slipping slowly into something like stage-three anesthesia. His voluntary muscles had seized almost entirely, and in another few minutes, if he did not consciously exercise it, he would lose the power of speech.

The two quickly changed into their bathing suits and headed poolside for some piña coladas. They navigated the beach chairs, convinced that they blended nicely with the tourists lounging there, each wearing nothing but a bathing suit, each of them having demonstrated the presence of

mind — and the simultaneous absence of any connection to reality — to carry with him a large, black leather briefcase. Not until they were sufficiently drunk did they realize how stoned they were, and not until the *federales* showed up did their condition, the nature of their mission, or their idiotic appearance engender in them any measure of paranoia.

The first military helicopter touched down about sixty feet away. The soldiers aboard hit the ground running, armed with automatic weapons, and quickly secured a perimeter within the boundaries of which the two Americans sat. The effect on the smugglers' cocktail hour was predictably dramatic — like some pleasant Atlantic crossing interrupted at that moment at which the stowaways run out of Dramamine.

Myerson's search for excitement seemed to be paying off. His face turned a cadaverous white, the blood supply to the tissue there suddenly draining away, abruptly reversing itself like a man accidentally swinging into an autopsy room.

A second Sikorsky touched down. The soldiers aboard were accompanied by personnel armed only with what appeared to be a red carpet. It was from the third and last helicopter that Venezuelan President Carlos Andrés Pérez emerged, stepping out onto the aforementioned carpet and following it and a plainclothes security detail into the hotel.

El Presidente was there to attend a meeting. The smugglers' briefcases, so conspicuously and laughably out of place, escaped examination. Andrés Pérez did manage, however, to send all American businessmen a message. Within a year he nationalized twenty-one oil companies, mostly U.S. subsidiaries.

Long would attend his meeting with the Colombians alone. Myerson's meeting them was not even discussed. Injection of a stranger into the transaction would serve to

unnerve the Colombians, but that was only a part of it. Just as Myerson would never introduce Long to his buyers, neither would Long be expected to introduce Myerson to his suppliers. The dope business was no different from any other business that way. One's connections, whether sources or markets, were like intelligence assets in the business of espionage — one did not readily share them if one wanted to *stay* in business.

Long's phone rang at seven P.M.

"Hello, sir, this is Miguel."

The young medical student invited Long to his room. He was alone when Long arrived.

"Where's Dr. Cepeda?"

"Pablo could not be here," answered Miguel.

And now, suddenly, Long, who was carrying $60,000 in cash, was unnerved.

"Maybe you need to call him."

"That will not be necessary, sir."

"I have money for him, Miguel. I don't know if it's right to give it to you."

"It is all right."

"I need to talk to Dr. Cepeda."

"Sir, maybe I should tell you —"

"I think you should get Dr. Cepeda on the phone."

Miguel, assured that Long would not part with the money until he spoke to Cepeda, dialed up the excitable doctor in Santa Marta and put him on the phone with Long.

"*Sí! Sí!* Yes, it is okay," Dr. Cepeda finally told Long, after the two had waded through a blend of broken English and Spanish.

"Okay," Long said, and hung up the phone. But before handing Miguel the money, he pointedly asked the young medical student, "Do you want to explain this to me?"

"Yes, sir," said Miguel politely. "I should tell you, it is I, not Pablo, with whom you are doing business . . ."

Long did not have to hear what came next to know what was going on. But he did hear Miguel say it — and this time it was true.

". . . You see, Allen, *I* am the man."

PICKUP AT PERICO

Long's outburst of laughter was infectious. Miguel laughed along with him. Once Long got himself under control, Miguel told him a story.

Miguel was not a medical student. His degree was in engineering, a degree he had received in the United States. All Miguel's life Pablo Cepeda had been his friend. Pablo was indeed a doctor — a doctor of veterinary medicine. When Long and Reed were in Barranquilla, Pablo had received a call from his cousin Moisés the taxi dispatcher. Pablo had then come to Miguel, mentioned the Americans Moisés had found, and asked if he thought Miguel's father would agree to do business with them.

Miguel explained to Long that his father was a man of great importance on the coast. Miguel Sr., a native of Santa Marta, was the first man ever to send marijuana from Colombia to the United States; that is, the first ever to do so commercially. A legend on the Guajira, he had pioneered the growth of the industry there.

"And I am the one," Miguel said, "who knows Ernesto

and Don Julio and all the people in the villages. I used to go always with my father when he was doing his business there, and now it is my business."

It had been a year, Miguel explained, since his father had started doing so much cocaine that he had become unable to function.

"He thinks only about women and his *pinga* now."

Long said he was familiar with the syndrome.

Long had been witness to a charade orchestrated for his benefit. The deception was Miguel's way of throwing off suspicion in the event that Long was not who he claimed to be. If Long and Reed were DEA, Miguel was not "the man." Impressed by Miguel's cleverness, Long would see him demonstrate it repeatedly over time. The young Colombian would prove to be an invaluable resource, he and his good friend Pablo — they were equal partners, and between them could get anything done that needed doing in Colombia.

Miguel and Long, in the months to follow, would talk a lot about Miguel's father, a man who personified the origin of what would one day become the most lucrative black market in criminal history. In the story of Miguel Sr. was the story of the creation of Colombia's narcoeconomy. It did not start with marijuana, and it did not start with cocaine, nor did it start with the emeralds for which Colombia was equally famous, the country's geographical borders delimiting a natural repository of 80 percent of the world's supply of the gem. In Colombia it started with coffee, and it came about by accident, not by design.

Some ninety miles off the coast of the Guajira lay the island of Aruba, a Dutch free port where Colombian coffee fetched a far higher price than the impoverished Colombian farmer could realize selling his crop to the national cartel,

the Colombian Coffee Federation. Outlaws like Miguel's father made their living trafficking in contraband between Aruba and the South American coast, shipping coffee in one direction, moving black-market Scotch and American cigarettes in the other.

Of course, smuggling was not new to coastal Colombia. *Costeños* had been trafficking in black-market goods since the imposition of government there, since the moment there were trade restrictions to violate. Marijuana cultivation on a limited basis began in the 1930s. Cocaine had been around much longer. On a smaller scale than in Bolivia and Peru, indigenous Colombian Indians had been growing and chewing coca for 2,000 years. But neither marijuana nor cocaine in Colombia enjoyed a significant market outside the country until the mid-1960s, when citizens of the United States started getting high on dope on a regular basis.

When the 1960s rolled around, and a boat captain with whom he worked told him that American merchant sailors in Aruba were in the market for marijuana, Miguel's father moved his first pound of pot. As Miguel explained it to Long, it was soon thereafter that the first commercial shipment of Colombian marijuana left the country bound directly for the States. The load, five pounds of pot in a suitcase, was delivered in a skiff by Miguel's father; he raised it to the porthole of an American merchant vessel anchored in the harbor in Santa Marta as the freighter took on a load of coffee destined for New York. The seaman who took delivery was one of several who inevitably followed. Soon a boat arrived that was there to pick up neither coffee nor anything other than that which had been stashed in the suitcase. Miguel's father sent the boat back loaded with 500 pounds of weed. And the face of the Western Hemisphere changed.

* * *

As April approached, there was a lot of worry in Ann Arbor. It had been two weeks since Miguel had been paid and still the airplane was not ready. How strict would the Colombians be? How much longer would they wait? How long would they honor the agreement, Jake Myerson wanted to know. Long had told Miguel he would be ready in a couple of weeks, and now it looked as though he would be lucky to be ready in a couple of months.

"Don't worry, sir, your money is safe," Miguel said, when Long finally put in the call. "You can come in two weeks or four weeks, but two weeks would be better."

Three weeks after that call, some five weeks after the meeting in Maracaibo, Hatfield and McBride ferried the DC-3 to Richmond.

The final briefing took place in a motel room in northern Virginia about ten miles from CIA headquarters. While Hathaway handed out copies of his booklet, Long read aloud from a list he had prepared. It had been decided that public relations would be well served if the Americans landed in Colombia not only carrying the money they owed, but also bearing gifts. Loaded onto the plane with the $65,000 in cash, he announced, would be Levi jeans, Nik Nik brand polyester shirts, Adidas running shoes (in what seemed to Myerson to be sufficient supply to outfit the entire Indian population of the Guajira), four cases of Heineken, a case of Marlboros, and a gross of Swiss Army knives.

This variation on the American CARE package, which seemed like a good idea at the time, would set a regrettable precedent, leading to ever longer lists of requests on the part of its Colombian recipients. Subsequent flights would carry patent medicines, tape players, and Seiko wristwatches. On one flight down, Long carried a twenty-three-hundred-dollar gold Pulsar watch to be presented to the commander of the

local military garrison. A later flight arrived in Colombia carrying a seventeen-foot inflatable Zodiac with a 70 horse-power Johnson outboard and a brace of pedigreed German shepherd puppies.

It was flights such as these and those of other smugglers that accounted for the proliferation on the Guajira of the Sony Trinitron as a status symbol — in homes that received no television signal and many of which enjoyed no elec-tricity. Within three years of Long's arrival, one could visit the most humble adobe in the smallest of villages there, cut off from power and running water, and find the latest in high-end audio equipment stacked steep against a wall inside and a late-model four-by-four, its high-gloss paint reflecting the sunshine, parked on the hardscrabble outside. Within that time, impoverished local Indians would come to occupy dwellings assembled with parts salvaged from out-of-commission airplanes — a wing here, part of a fuselage there, a tail number over the door. (On a trip to Perico in 1979, an elder of the nearby village reintroduced Long to his DC-3, the nose cone, complete with windshield glass, serving as a makeshift solarium on his humble sheet metal home.) By then, with America's appetite for dope as well established as its appetite for coffee, Colombia would account for more than 70 percent of the marijuana reaching the United States from abroad, and between 30,000 and 50,000 farmers along the coast would have come to depend directly on its culti-vation for their livelihood. Another 50,000 Colombians would make a living from it. Local food production would decline as tens of thousands of hectares were converted to marijuana farming, producing unprecedented prosperity and a degree of economic stability never before enjoyed on the Guajira.

"Bullshit!" said JD Reed.

Reed's legendary cool evaporated when he beheld the ground operations manual that Hathaway had prepared. Leafing through the printed matter as a citizen would a mug file, Reed grew red in the face.

"This is bullshit!" he said, slamming it down. "Lose this fucking thing!"

Reed's argument was persuasive. If the document fell into the wrong hands, police would be waiting for the plane when it landed. If the publication were to come to light later, even several years down the road, it would win a contest, hands down, for Exhibit A in a conspiracy prosecution. But more than that it was just bullshit.

"I've done this twenty times," Reed said, "and I've never had a book like this."

"This is professional," countered Long, holding the document aloft, extending his evaluation to apply to the operation in general.

Reed grabbed the booklet, and got to his feet. He looked Hathaway in the eye, scrutinizing him as he would a phone book, as if Hathaway were some manner of urban directory that wanted tearing in half.

"There's only one thing I want to know," he said. "I want to know are you gonna *be* there. I don't care if you have this book with you or not. You better fucking *be* there. That's what's important — you're *there,* man."

Reed, who on more than twenty occasions had met planeloads of pot from Mexico, had only one rule when it came to off-loading: Stay there until the plane shows up. Do not set a time. Too many things could go wrong. Just *be* there. You sit there until you hear something. It had once taken one of his pilots three days in Jalisco to fix a flat tire. Reed, with no means of communication, had just stayed where he was, waiting right there where he said he would be. The

airplane showed up on the fourth day. He had once sat alone in the middle of the desert, he and five trucks, waiting for his DC-3. He sent everyone else on the crew home. The plane, scheduled to show up at midnight, arrived at three P.M. the following day carrying 5,000 pounds of pot. "No communications," he said, and he had managed to get the job done. "Just tell 'em what you're gonna do and stick with it. A basic warrior tactic." He had never lost a load.

"Be there, motherfucker," he said to Hathaway, and yielded the floor to Frank Hatfield.

Hatfield said, "We leave Fayetteville at five P.M., fat with fuel, we fly low over the Piedmont and head south until we hit Jacksonville. We enter the normal flow of air traffic, and bear about thirty degrees southeast making for the Bahamas. No lights, no radio contact, no radar transponder. At Great Inagua we turn south, which will take us over the Windward Passage, around Cuban airspace, and up over the Haitian mountains. The Maracaibo beacon will bring us in just east of Riohacha. We fly southwest from there, and follow the coast. JD will bring us into the airstrip. We arrive at eight in the morning, and we're about two hours on the ground. With the manpower they have down there, it'll take only about thirty minutes to load the plane, but we have to pump a lot of fuel, which is going to take a couple of hours using the equipment they've got. Coming back, our airspeed's cut. Over the Bahamas we fly low, we drop down to lose radar, maybe fifty feet off the water, then pick up an airway, joining the weekend traffic coming out of the islands into the States. We rendezvous at midnight. We kick out the load at West Point, take the plane and park it somewhere. Round-trip, we're looking at over thirty hours of work, nonstop."

He asked if there were questions. There were none. The briefing ended. Long and Reed worked out the radio codes

and frequencies for the rendezvous at Perico. One week later, Long was in Colombia, and the DC-3 took off.

"Once you've been a smuggler, you know it's not Murphy's Law, it's Murphy's Law times ten. When you talk about contingencies, you don't know what you're talking about, until you've done a smuggling trip. Because not only anything that *can* go wrong *will* go wrong, things that *can't* go wrong will go wrong. If there ever was a true story about, 'How I was captured by aliens and forced to submit to torture,' it's the story of some smuggling pilot, who it really happened to. And nobody will ever believe him. And they took all the dope."

It was just after seven A.M. Allen Long was crouched in the morning light, hugging a low dune that sloped away from the Caribbean to the edge of what passed for a runway on the northeast coast of Colombia. And his heart was racing. With him, hidden in various places in the vicinity of the airstrip, were about twenty-five people — Miguel, Pablo, Ernesto, and others — a ragtag assemblage of personnel whose faces had filtered in and out of his consciousness over the preceding several weeks and whom he had come to view collectively as "the Colombians." Long was the only gringo on the scene and the only man not carrying a gun. Even the mild-mannered Miguel was strapped. He was armed with a .45.

In the bush, about twenty yards off the runway, hidden, stood a truck stacked with two and a half tons of high-grade Colombian weed. Delivery of the marijuana had been handled by the Colombians without any help from Long. Whether coffee going out or cigarettes coming in, it was something that had been done on this coast for a hundred

years. It was what they knew how to do — being mustered at two o'clock in the morning, or noon, or eight at night, to jump in the truck or jump on the donkey and go off and do this stuff.

The Colombians, ready for anything, were in a sufficiently serious mood, and Long was in a condition that boiled down to barely repressed hysteria. Counter to his confident self-portrayal — the assurances he had given the Colombians that he knew what he was doing, that he had done it numerous times before, that he was a capable, experienced professional — the truth was that he really had no way of knowing whether the plane would ever make it. This was all new to him. He was ripe with anxiety over the possibility that his partners might not show up. He knew that they had *left*. He had called the States at midnight, and no one there had heard from them. The plane, he had to assume, had taken off on schedule.

All he had now by way of control over the flight was a hermetically sealed, hard-sided case about six inches deep, sixteen inches wide, and twenty-two inches tall. Crouched on the beach, he checked his watch, and releasing the clamps on either side of the case, removed its cover to expose the workings of a ground-to-air radio. Manufactured by Narco Avionics and purchased by Reed, the radio came recommended as the latest in high-end aviation equipment, engineered specifically for ground-to-air communications. Long tuned it in to monitor an air-to-air frequency.

Hatfield, once within range, would be transmitting on a frequency designated to carry air-to-air traffic. The smugglers did not want their voices picked up on a frequency that was used, by international standard, for transmissions between control towers and incoming craft: a pretty dead giveaway that a man on the ground was nursing an airplane

into a strip. On the radio frequency the smugglers were using, they would be taken for a couple of pilots conversing cockpit-to-cockpit, like interstate truckers discussing highway conditions over their dashboard citizens band radios.

With the pilots coming down the coast, the first move was to burn a tire and bring them in with smoke. If still unable to locate the runway, the pilots would use the plane's direction finder to home in on a radio signal transmitted by Long. Popping on headphones, they would tune to his frequency, pick up the transmission — the simple repetition by Long of a monotonous syllable, *bah, bah, bah* — and the unit's receiver would bring them in on his position.

But none of that should be necessary. The pilots had the strip's coordinates, they had maps and charts, and more than that they had JD Reed aboard. Estimating a fifteen-hour flight, they had timed their takeoff to insure that they not arrive before daybreak, when they could pick up the runway visually. Whatever happened, Long's job now was simple: monitor the frequency to which the radio was tuned and await their first transmission.

An hour earlier, side by side, Long and the Colombians, all of them, had walked the dry, hard-packed clay of the runway, moving from one end to the other, clearing it of the burrs of a local thorn that flourished near the strip. The burr, about four inches in diameter and spiked in such a way as to resemble the head of a medieval mace, exhibited spines up to an inch and a half long, which could very easily puncture a tire.

It was just after seven A.M., and even at seven the air temperature on the coast of Colombia will make you think twice about building your dream house there. Long, in a knit, short-sleeved shirt, was dressed pretty much the same as the Colombians — some wore chinos, some wore jeans,

as he did — the difference being that where he wore sneakers, they wore shoes or sandals. Some of the Indians were barefoot. The heat had not yet reached the point where it might typically induce perspiration, but Long was sweating nevertheless. He had a planeload of grass, and it was ready to go. He was excited, expectant, he was apprehensive. He was out to beat the government. His adrenaline was pumping at the redline. He was sweating like a movie cop defusing a bomb. He was even sweating the small stuff.

Everything looked different to him all of a sudden. The colors were richer, the textures more diverse. It was like looking at the world with a new set of senses. And so, like the protagonist of a popular novel, at the appropriate and perfectly predictable point in a particular brand of narrative, Long chose that moment to inventory his natural surroundings, to conduct a personal inspection of earth's physical plant: soil stratification, atmospheric phenomena, botany. He gave the world a good going-over. Angles of incidence of visible light, the presence of wildlife, the absence thereof — he noted things like that.

Crouched five or six feet from the water, he had a chance to look at the Caribbean through different eyes. He noticed the interesting mix of aquas and cobalt blues, all the different species of jellyfish that floated on the surface, the color of the sand. And the color of the clay bank reminded him of Albermarle County, where he had grown up in Virginia, the same red clay, which sent him off on another thought . . .

Which one is behooved to let him entertain alone.

And now it was eight o'clock.

Long that morning had been awakened at five A.M. by loose fragments of thatch falling upon his face. Asleep in a

hammock that was strung between two of the poles of an open-sided hut, he had passed the night in the tiny village down the trail from the runway. A crescendo of jungle sounds had risen with the moon. "Love talk between the animals," Miguel had observed, drifting off to sleep nearby. Between the hammock and the moon, unknown to Long, hidden in the thatch above his head, were the cables, batteries, hoses, and pumps that would be used to fuel the airplane. As Ernesto's men were retrieving them, the thatch was disturbed, and the pieces spilling on Long's face awakened him.

Easing back into sleep, Long was startled by the sensation of something crawling through his hair. He bolted upright, slapping his head furiously, fearing the presence of a scorpion. Opening his eyes, he heard giggling, and turned to see two five-year-old girls standing behind the hammock. They had sneaked up to feel his hair. He laughed and started carrying on with the curious pair, encouraging them to resume running their fingers through his curls, of a color the Colombian children had never seen before.

It was not until ten o'clock that morning that Miguel expressed concern.

"Sir, do you think you should call them on the radio?" he said.

"No, Miguel, I'm listening for them. There's no reason to call," said Long. "It could only attract attention to us. They're only on one frequency."

Beyond that, he had nothing to say.

Periodically, individually, the Colombians, over the following hour, approached and asked him what was happening. What they did not do is point out the obvious: There was a truck over there loaded with two and a half tons of marijuana. The pot was good to go. There was another mounted with drums holding more than three tons of fuel. They had

mobilized a couple of dozen people who had to be paid for the morning's work. They simply wanted to know what was happening.

It was a question to which Long had no answer.

At eleven-thirty the plane was more than three hours late. There were few things that could have accounted for that, none of which Long cared to imagine. The flight was not the typical shakedown cruise. It was a long haul over blue ocean, and it was inconceivable to him that the crew had put the plane down anywhere. The only reasonable answer to the questions he was getting was that the pilots had crashed it. Of all the plans the smugglers had, they did not have a plan for that.

Long vacillated between anger and serious worry. Pablo Cepeda appeared to vacillate between a nervous breakdown and whatever came next. It was hard to tell with Pablo. Dysphoria was a condition the high-strung Colombian constantly walked the verge of.

"Where's the plane?" he wanted to know.

And he was asking the question with increasing frequency. He approached now, and he stood there as though under a cloud, his eyeglasses so uncompromisingly thick that his countenance favored that of an albacore, the melancholy he embodied so eminently turbid as to be observable even to Long, and asked the question one more time. It was one time too many.

"Okay, that's it, they're not coming," said Long. "Let's wrap it up."

Not a decision JD Reed would look upon as "a basic warrior tactic."

With little complaining the Colombians demobilized. Long headed to Santa Marta with Miguel and Pablo, and from there he called the States.

"You hear from JD?"

"Not yet," said Myerson.

"Neither have I."

"You're kidding."

"No," Long said. "Did they leave on time?"

"As far as I know. They'd have called if they didn't, right?"

"I guess. Yeah, they should have," said Long.

But he was not really sure of that.

At about four P.M. Long and the Colombians stepped through the door of Miguel's house in Barranquilla, and they were inside no more than a matter of minutes when the call came from Riohacha.

"Sir," said Miguel, hanging up the phone. "Sir," he said, his eyes receptacles of resignation and wonder, "the airplane has come."

"What?"

"It is there. In Riohacha."

Well, not exactly. It was not there any longer. It had *been* there. It had been there, loaded up and left. Slowly, as though on a rheostat, Long's eyes brightened. The corners of his mouth inched upward, and his face opened like a chrysanthemum. It took him a second to shake off his confusion, throw up his fists and cheer. Wavering between elation and incredulity, he was not sure what to think. He felt shameful for not having been there, but as terrible as he felt, he felt a hell of a lot better than he had a few minutes before, under the weight of his responsibility for the lives of the crew, when the plane had not come at all. But how the hell had they done it? No radio, no pot, no fuel, nobody there on the ground. And why were they running so late?

* * *

The installation of auxiliary fuel tanks in the wings of the DC-3 was referred to by Hatfield as the Pan Am conversion, initially performed by Douglas, as he explained it, to increase the aircraft's range for Pan American World Airways' commercial operations in the Pacific. The adaptation was a feature of various military configurations of the plane. The tanks, however, while legally installed, had been officially decommissioned. Rigging them for use, as the smugglers had, without securing a waiver, was against the law.

So what else was new?

As JD Reed had it figured, the fuel gaskets in the auxiliary tanks had dried out in the desert, in the government graveyard at Davis-Monthan. Not having needed the tanks until now, the pilots had never tested them. According to McBride, the tanks *had* been tested. And having been tested, they failed. And the problem had been corrected. With fuel found leaking through a dumping valve, the bladder tanks had been drained, and the plane had been flown on its main tanks from Long Beach to Virginia, where the leak had been repaired.

Or so it had been assumed.

When the airplane was being fueled for the flight to Colombia, gasoline poured out of the tanks. The problem was traced to a feeder line. But diagnosing it meant replacing the fuel gaskets, and in the time it took to remove and replace them you could have undergone brain surgery. It required disassembly of the wings. The wing rivets had to be removed, and once the new gaskets were finally installed, all those rivets had to be replaced. And then the fire department had to be called in to wash down the runway.

"Puttin' heat on us," Reed maintained.

The DC-3 left the States five hours late.

When the pilots reached the Guajira, they failed to pick

up radio contact. There was no smoke in the vicinity of Perico. Reed, standing in the cockpit, leaning over Hatfield, directed him to the location of the strip. When the airplane came in over the beach, the runway was deserted. The stillness, the emptiness — they were something you could feel. Words were absolutely unnecessary. Nothing that passed through anyone's mind was as memorable as what happened in his stomach.

When it came to the conduct of business, JD Reed would have been the first to admit that he was not much of a talker. He left the back-and-forth to others, to people like Allen Long. He let others do the talking, let others negotiate the deals, and let others worry, usually unnecessarily, in advance of what transpired. He was a worker. He liked getting out in the middle of it. Working with people who knew what they were doing, he exercised his right to remain silent. But at those moments when he saw that nobody else knew what to do, a change came over Reed, a change that was physically measurable. At those moments Reed took charge. At those moments, Reed was suddenly the one who knew exactly what to do. Forced by circumstances to act, he did. And nobody challenged his authority. It was not his imposing stature, but something in his tone of voice, his absolute, unequivocal certainty at those moments that made questioning his decision unthinkable.

Reed contemplated the jungle.

"That way," he said.

He directed Hatfield over the treetops.

A mile and a half inland, he said, "There. Back there."

He had sighted the camouflage netting. Beneath it, the last time he had looked, had been 30,000 pounds of pot.

Hatfield buzzed the *caleta*.

Activity in the staging area came to a halt as the DC-3,

dipping its wings, roared in over the trees. Hatfield circled the plane. He made a second pass. He dropped in so low the mules shied and the flyers could read the astonishment on the faces of the Indians processing the merchandise. When the DC-3 turned and made for the airstrip, Ernesto was chasing its shadow, speeding below in a jeep. Pulling up at the runway, he waved the smugglers in, and Hatfield landed the airplane.

"Espera aquí!" wait here, shouted the Colombian, when he saw Reed emerge through the cargo door.

Jumping back into the jeep, Ernesto sped off, and re-appeared moments later at the head of a rushing motorcade carrying pot, fuel, and personnel.

The first bale of marijuana had not yet been hoisted aboard the plane, when Reed turned to Ernesto and asked him, "Where's the stuff for the pilot?"

Reed had been on the ground not much more than a minute, and he was looking to roll a fat one. And Ernesto, who instantly provided the dope, wanted to know why. Which, in turn, astonished Reed. Here, thought Reed, was Colombian marijuana's very own Juan Valdez, and he could not understand why Reed wanted to light up?

Not smoking marijuana never even suggested itself to JD Reed. It was not something that ever would. Not even haphazardly. Reed needed his energy, as he was quite willing to tell you, and coming from Reed, it was something even a Colombian could try to understand.

In Latin America, to the native speaker, the adjective "macho" simply means male. "Machismo," a noun derived from it, is a modern social-sciences construct, and it enjoys little currency south of the border, especially among those alleged

to exhibit the behavior specified by the term, which is defined in American dictionaries as "strong or assertive masculinity, characterized by virility, courage, aggressiveness, etc."

Commonly ascribed to Latin American men, almost always pejoratively, machismo is used rather conveniently to bootstrap a variety of qualities that have less to do with gender than they do with human circumstance. In parts of Colombia, those parts where life is cheap, acquaintance with danger comes with the turf; acceptance of violence and violent death is neither masculine nor particularly Latin. On the Guajira, where life is *really* cheap, risking your life, as often as not, is part of earning your daily bread: eking out a hardscrabble existence, taking bare subsistence from the land, straining literally to put bread on the table.

On the Guajira, in the time of the Americans, "courage and aggressiveness" were what it took to get by. Machismo, if you want to call it that, was born out of desperation, the way of the desperado in all its nuances of meaning. These were the badlands. And carrying a gun, when it actually came to doing so — illegal everywhere in Colombia — came with understandable indifference to everything but the money it cost to buy it.

With large quantities of merchandise and money lying about, possession of a weapon was mandatory among marijuana traffickers in Colombia, serving them in a way not intuitively obvious to the average American.

"It is not to protect the money, Allen," a young *guajiro* explained to Long. Nor, he added, were guns necessary to fend off the police. "In Colombia, when a man takes from you, yes . . . ?"

"Yes, if he steals."

"If he steals from you, he must also kill you. If he does not kill you, he will walk forever with *culebras* in his back."

"*Culebras.* Snakes?"

"*Sí.* He knows that you will find him, that some day you will kill him."

"In English we call it revenge."

"In English and Spanish the words, I think, are the same. In Colombia we call it *justicia.*"

"Justice."

"Justice. Yes. It is what must be done."

Carrying a gun on the streets of Riohacha was like carrying a gun on the streets of Tombstone, up in Deadwood, or maybe Dodge, there and in other mining towns and cow towns of nineteenth-century America. Nor were the names of these places unknown to the smugglers of the Guajira. The image of the American West was as familiar to the average Colombian as to any moviegoer anywhere in the world. It held a special place in the heart of the *guajiro.*

And JD Reed was its embodiment.

Reed was the receptacle of every Colombian Spaghetti Western fantasy of the American frontier, nothing less in the eyes of the typical *guajiro* than a personification of gun-fighting myth. He was Wyatt Earp on steroids, the inner outlaw in Wild Bill.

And so it came as a big surprise to Ernesto when the first thing Reed did was fire up a joint.

Ernesto said, "You are a burro?"

"A burro? You mean like a donkey?" said Reed.

In Colombia, Ernesto explained, a man who smokes marijuana is referred to as a burro. "The Colombian people," he said, "they do not smoke this, only the lazy ones." Acting the part of such a man, Ernesto rolled his eyes, dropped his head, and rocked forward in imitation of a junkie on the nod. "He smokes, and he is like the donkey."

Earlier, Allen Long had been told this by Miguel. Long

had laughed when he heard it, and nodding enthusiastically, explained to the Colombians gathered, *"Todos los gringos son burros,"* all gringos are burros. And lucky for him they were. Lighting up, he sucked in smoke, showed his teeth and waved his head, and he cracked the Colombians up, braying: "Hee-haw, hee-haw . . ."

There was another drug the Colombians associated with animal behavior. They called cocaine *perico*. It made a man chatter like a parakeet. Long did not have to do any acting to pull that imitation off. The Colombians got it without the clowning.

When Reed handed Ernesto the suitcase containing the $65,000 in cash, refueling was underway and the Colombians were overloading the airplane.

"Colombians, same as the Mexicans," Reed later told Long. "The more they put in, the more they get paid for."

The standing rule for smugglers — "You always over-load" — held for almost any decent military aircraft on a decent runway. On a marginal field, such as the strip at Perico, pretty rugged and too short to start with, one had to consider the fact that the DC-3, carrying an added two and a half tons of fuel, was pushing the military-maximum overload hauling any significant amount of cargo.

"Let's try it," Hatfield said.

The plane never got off the strip. On takeoff it hit the high brush at the end of the runway and stayed there.

Hatfield, knowing he would never catch air, chopped the throttles and hit the brakes about a thousand feet down-field. The wings took the worst of it. The crash ripped the aluminum and tore away the petcocks fitted to drain water from the fuel.

For the second time in twenty-four hours gasoline was leaking from the airplane.

Reed, the first man off the plane, stepped through the cargo door carrying his survival gear, prepared, pending assessment of the damage, to take up residence in Colombia. He circled the plane, inspecting the wings. It was McBride who stepped up and stuck a finger in the hole from which most of the fuel was leaking. Reed pulled out his Swiss Army knife. He cut branches from the standing brush, whittled them into shape, and with fuel pouring down over his Stetson, he plugged the holes where the petcocks had been. Ordering the Colombians to commandeer a tractor, he and the pilots set to work applying duct tape to the torn aluminum.

By the time a tractor arrived, it was no longer needed. The twenty-five men on hand had muscled the 26,000-pound airplane out of the trees. Reed ordered the unloading of almost half the pot aboard. The fuel that had been lost was replaced.

"Okay. Once more, with feeling."

And now the operation was running another two hours late, a total of seven.

Once the DC-3 had cleared the trees, Reed left the cockpit, climbed up onto the bales in the back of the plane, and started smoking. The pilots had assumed that Reed, who had flown a number of airplane trips, would be a relatively competent, interim pilot, that once the plane was in the air they would be able to take a break. Both of them. But as soon as the plane took off, Reed rolled himself a large spliff. And he sat there on top of the bales, smoking and talking to God, all the way back to Virginia. On the one attempt they made to hand the plane over to him, "it did things in the air that planes aren't designed to do," said McBride,

who blamed it on the pot, informing Long that, "we had to relieve JD of command."

The plane did not fly up the Chesapeake Bay under cover of darkness. With the seven-hour delay, it flew up the Chesapeake Bay in broad daylight, roaring over the heads of fishermen who had been working on the water since dawn. Over the Oceana Naval Air Station at Virginia Beach, over Portsmouth and Newport News, over the nuclear fleet at Norfolk, it came in over the express lane to, if not on the doorstep of, the Pentagon.

"The Distant Early Warning system and all that stuff, forget about it," Hatfield said. "If you come in low enough and slow enough . . ."

A hundred feet off the water, a large military aircraft with no markings except indecipherable, three-inch tail numbers, came roaring in over the trees. The loggers on the James River had never seen anything like it. At West Point crop dusters were landing and taking off. Private aircraft were being fueled. The runway the smugglers were using, one of three 5,000-foot runways, represented the leg of the triangle farthest from all the activity. It was partially obscured by trees. Observers on the ground, while unlikely to be alarmed, were nevertheless sufficiently mystified to take note of what they saw. They saw a big cargo plane touch down, and disappear behind the trees for only a few minutes before taking off.

Equally mystifying in that moment was what the smugglers saw.

". . . the curious incident of the dog in the night-time."

"The dog did nothing in the night-time."

"That was the curious incident," remarked Sherlock Holmes.

Hatfield brought the airplane about. McBride handled the talking.

"Where the fuck are they?" he shouted.

By "they" he meant the ground crew.

"Stay where you are," said Reed. "I'll unload it."

The pilots shouted questions as Reed retreated to the cargo deck. Reed shouted back, yelling over the roar of the engines.

"Forget about the pot," he said. "We've got to save the airplane."

The pot was easily replaceable, the airplane was not.

"I'll unload it," he shouted, "you get out of here."

He threw open the cargo doors, and started throwing out the marijuana. There were more than fifty bales aboard at around eighty pounds apiece, and in six minutes Reed had the airplane empty. He jumped to the ground, McBride slammed the doors, and Hatfield released the brakes.

"Motherfuckers!" Reed said.

There was no one to hear him say it, he stood on the tarmac alone, but to say that Reed said it "to no one in particular" would be to overlook the six particular people Reed had in mind when he said it.

The marijuana stood in a small mountain, stacked as close to the tree line as Reed had been able to throw it from the cargo deck of the plane. He opened one of the bales, grabbed about three pounds of dope, which was as much as would fit in his knapsack, stashed it, and started walking. He hiked through the woods away from the airport until he hit blacktop, and hitched a ride into town.

Passing a roadside diner, Reed spotted a familiar assortment of vehicles parked out front, and instructed the driver to pull over.

"I'll get out here."

Inside the diner, seated at the counter with their backs to the door, members of the ground crew were enjoying

breakfast. Reed, entering, walked up behind them, started throwing them off the counter stools onto the floor, and, calling them worthless shitheads, told them they had work to do. He sent them scrambling out the door, took a seat at the counter, ordered bacon and eggs, and ate his first meal in forty hours.

"Excuse me, ma'am. Nurse. Excuse me. Your royal highness. I asked for a *quart* of water. Thank you."

Long had started celebrating within minutes of his learning that the plane had made the pickup at Perico. He and the Colombians spent the night drinking, and early the next morning he caught a flight out of Barranquilla.

In Miami, standing at a pay phone in the airport, Long heard what happened in Virginia. That was where he heard everything these days: standing at a pay phone in some airport, or standing at a pay phone somewhere. And all the pay phones and kiosks eventually became one. There were retail clerks in various cities who knew Long rather well, but did not really understand him — all he ever wanted from them, as he came strolling into their shops off the street, was a roll of quarters. "I'll pay you eleven dollars for a ten-dollar roll of quarters . . ."

What happened in Virginia was this:

After finishing his breakfast, JD Reed headed for West Point. And so did the county sheriff.

The sheriff got there first.

Nearing the airport, Reed, on foot, was intercepted by a member of the ground crew, and was informed that numerous police cruisers had arrived at the airfield in advance of the trucks.

The load was busted.

At that moment the sheriff of King William County was having his photograph snapped, sharing the frame with the impressive stack of contraband he had seized. Posing before the bales of pot that Reed had off-loaded, he told reporters he had no suspects, and speculated quite matter-of-factly that what he had was probably the result of a "flubbed pickup."

The next day it took him and his deputies six hours to burn the load and bury the ashes.

Not even Reed could have smoked it that fast.

AUTOMATIC PILOT

All the planning, all the training, all the checklists and charts — all that, and the crew had ignored the only instructions that mattered: Do not leave, no matter what. Stay where you are. "Just *be* there," as Reed had said. Had they waited, the newspaper accounts confirmed, they could have easily unloaded the pot and nobody would have seen them. The sheriff did not get the call until an hour and a half after the drop.

"Strange planes have been seen there numerous times," the sheriff said. "Really, no one pays a lot of attention to them. Anything or anybody could have come in there at night and nobody would know the difference."

Had they been there, even had they been seen, they could have been out of there before anybody had been able to stop them.

"Nobody lives down there," explained the sheriff. "It's strictly a wide-open area."

And had Long called from Colombia — to say the plane had come and gone, that it was running seven hours late —

the ground crew in all likelihood would have been there. But no contingency plan existed for his doing so. No phone or radio contacts, no channels of communication, had been established for that purpose. Similarly, neither the pilots nor Reed had a number to call to announce that they were leaving late. Nor should that have been necessary. Not according to Reed. Long's one move from Colombia would have been to try to call a member of the ground crew, try to get lucky and catch him at home. He had had about six hours in which to do it, but like Reed he had believed it unnecessary.

"Somebody's gonna have to pay for it in one way or another," the sheriff speculated. "I'm reading the papers and keeping my eyes peeled. We'll probably have a body come out of the James River with no identification one of these days, something like that."

Something like that.

From the phone booth at which he heard the news, Long instantly called Ann Arbor. He told Myerson what had happened, told him not to expect the trucks, and said he would be back in touch in a couple of days. Arriving in Virginia, he sent Reed's crew back to Las Vegas, and immediately jumped aboard Reed's hobbyhorse to join him in blaming the failure of the operation on Hathaway.

A lot of people were pissed off. *Everybody* was pissed off. The pilots were pissed off at the ground guys, the ground guys were pissed off at Long. The Colombians were happy, but the Colombians had yet to learn what had happened. Long owed them a hundred and twenty-five grand. He owed Myerson two hundred and fifty. And he had to lay it on somebody, so he laid it on Hathaway. He was out, that was it, Hathaway was done. They were looking for a scapegoat. Long did not like owning up to the fact that he had made a mistake. But the truth was he had neglected to call from

Colombia to say that the plane was running late, or anyway had neglected to try. It was *his* fault. His trip, his fault. Now *he* was the man.

And there was only one move to make. Double-up the bet. He broke the news to the pilots, told them there would be no payoff on the load.

"All we did, we did for nothing," he told them, "unless we go down and do it again."

Pushing the proposition, he said, was the only way to go.

"I'll fix it," he promised the pilots.

They agreed to fly a second trip, and he told them to prep the plane.

Reed needed no such assurances. His faith in Long and the operation was exceeded only by his belief in the crusade.

"Call me when you're ready," he said, before he headed home.

To get ready Long needed money. There were airplane maintenance and fuel to pay for. There were payoffs he had to make. Reed's crew would have to be flown back in, everyone's expenses covered.

He flew to Detroit with a pound of the pot that Reed had salvaged from the load, and said, "This is what we could have had," knowing it was a pound of the best marijuana Myerson had ever seen. "All we have now is the airplane," he said, by which he meant to say they should use it. Everything was up and ready, he reported. Reed would be on the ground this time supervising the off-load. And the pot was all set to go.

"The Colombians will front us the next load."

Long expected Myerson to say no. But his business partner surprised him, agreeing that they should try it again.

"Why pull back now?" was his answer. "I have faith in you, I believe you can do this." Before Long had a chance

to dance out the sales pitch he had prepared, Myerson went into his pocket. "I'm in, do it," he said, and coughed up the necessary cash.

Three weeks after talking to Myerson, Allen Long was standing on the tarmac at a general aviation facility in North Carolina, and Will McBride was telling him that the airplane "occasionally fires up. It catches fire when you turn it over. So you stand here with the fire extinguisher, and when we start it up, you spray it real good . . ."

It catches fire. Terrific.

Long was undergoing this drill in response to a simple arithmetic problem. Flight operations required a third man in the DC-3, and with Reed now running the ground crew (in the arithmetic problem, call him the subtrahend), the flight crew was reduced, by process of simple subtraction, to a remainder of two. Someone (yes, an addend of one) was needed to make up the difference. Allen Long, for the first time in his smuggling career, was about to go seriously airborne. Long, on the threshold of a deepening romance, was about to consummate an affair with the DC-3, and his palms, like those of any young suitor, were sweating.

Long was scared to death of the airplane. First of all, he knew the wing rivets had been put in by hand, and he fully expected to see them come popping out while the plane was in the air. The reassembled plane was thirty-four years old, commissioned in 1942, and some of its parts came from aircraft that were — God knew how old they were or what condition they were in.

In fact, the airplane, as part of a class, was as safe as airplanes get. Douglas manufactured more than 14,000 of them, in one variation or another, both civilian and military — it

had undergone more conversions in forty years than the government of Italy — and there was no greater testament to its safety record than the fact that so many of them were still flying. Everywhere. Douglas shipped them all over the world. The DC-3 was ubiquitous in the sky during World War II, over Burma, over Normandy. The U.S. government was still flying them during the war in Southeast Asia. The DC-3 ushered in modern, economical air transportation in 1936, and civilian airlines would still be flying them after the turn of the century.

The plane was more than an antique. It had a personality and a presence of its own. It was a tail dragger, and everywhere it showed up, pilots came out to admire it. It was not something you could hide. Long, despite his misgivings, took great pride of ownership in it. The plane had now become his close friend. But as with all close friends under pressure, he was waiting for it to break. He was looking for the chinks in the armor.

Planting season in North Carolina is never uncomfortably warm, but seldom is it especially cool. Tobacco country enjoys a temperate climate. Spring weather tends to be mild. And so Long, confronting the terror of flight, had all the more reason to sweat, laboring as he was under the weight of three layers of clothing.

Long and the pilots had shown up at the airport dressed the way pilots dress: in the navy blue trousers, visored caps, and crisp white shirts with epaulettes favored by commercial aviators, the doormen of pretentious nightclubs, and bell captains of the world's finer hotels. In any position short of parade rest, they looked the part they were playing, flyers ferrying short-haul cargo. Once aboard the airplane, however, the smugglers had stripped off the uniforms, and geared up for the flight they were making. Beneath military-surplus

flight fatigues, they wore warm civilian clothes, and beneath the civvies thermal underwear. At 14,000 feet, which was the altitude the plane would have to exploit to make the long haul to the coast of Colombia, the air temperature in the DC-3 would drop by almost 50 degrees Fahrenheit.

In the thin air above 10,000 feet the crew would have to suck oxygen (after dark they would do so above 5,000 feet, the altitude at which hypoxia begins to devitalize one's night vision). McBride, familiarizing Long with the aircraft, directed his attention to the location of the O_2 supply in the cockpit. One of the lengths of rubber tubing running from the tank would serve the purpose of an oxygen mask. Long was to place it in his mouth and breathe through it if he wished to remain conscious at high altitude.

Mandatory only if he were flying the plane. The guy in the back could pass out, he would learn — and soon be happy to demonstrate — he did not need to stay awake.

In the cockpit, behind the captain, the smugglers had installed a first-class cabin seat salvaged from a Braniff Airways jet. A stretched-canvas cot on a collapsible frame was set up in the cargo bay behind the flyers. Separating the cockpit from the cargo bay was a firewall, and running from the firewall the length of the plane were tracks rigged for cargo netting. Long would spend the first few hours of the flight lining the cargo bay with Visqueen, using duct tape to attach the edges of the green plastic tarp to the bulkheads, elevating the vertical face of the liner three or four feet off the floor. The tarp would keep the airplane clean, preventing seeds and stems — or evidence, as the latter were viewed forensically — from collecting in the cargo area.

Once Long was instructed in how to accomplish the various tasks assigned to him, which included opening and

closing the cargo doors on the port side of the aircraft, the pilots went through their pre-start check.

You do not start a DC-3, it has been said. Instead, you wake it up. Hatfield, manually, pumped up the brake and hydraulic pressure, before he cracked the throttles. With his left hand on the magneto switch, using his right to operate the primer, the booster coil, and the starter switches, he watched the left prop turn six blades, and then he fired the magneto. The engine yawned and snorted, and erupting in a distinctive blend of sounds, smells, and vibrations, the airplane started its day. Hatfield then fired the starboard engine. Long jumped aboard carrying the fire extinguisher, strapped himself in, the plane received clearance from the tower, and before the admiring eyes of those pilots who had come out to watch the takeoff, the old DC-3 lumbered down the runway.

The plane's tail wheel came off the ground. The plane leveled off — it felt more like an airplane now — and Long, unable to help himself, unstrapped his belt, stood with his hands on the shoulders of the pilots, and watched. At just over sixty-five knots the plane achieved flight. Catching the air, steady and slow, it lifted off, and with a couple of hurrahs from the flight controllers, sailed away, as smoothly and as slowly as only a DC-3 can.

Long would remember experiencing a rush of exhilaration unlike anything he had ever felt. There he was, truly embarking on a life-or-death enterprise. He was doing it for the money, yes, but no amount of money would replicate the experience. They were off, on their way to Colombia, searching for some clandestine runway, there to meet a bunch of machine-gun-toting desperadoes who would load them up with contraband. And Long and his partners, manning the cockpit, would fly it back against all odds. It was *Treasure Island* and he was Jim.

Over the Carolinas they flew relatively low, maintaining an altitude of under 10,000 feet. Overflying Savannah, Georgia, they came up on Jacksonville, Florida, and banking southeast from there, they joined the normal flow of air traffic headed for the Bahamas. Under FAA regulations an aircraft leaving the United States must file an international flight plan. The smugglers left the country illegally. Being required by the same and other regulations to report to Customs upon reentering, they would render that particular infraction inconsequential some thirty hours later.

With the sun setting behind them, they made for the dark blue of the night, rumbling out over the Atlantic. They picked up the twinkling lights of Freeport. And soon they were flying by moonlight. Hatfield took a break. While Long, taking left seat, flew the airplane, McBride acquainted him with the navigational instruments, various radio frequencies, and other things they were not using. The radar transponder was disengaged. They maintained radio silence. They were flying with no lights.

The plane settled into a rhythm. There was the steady, hypnotic hum of the engines pitching against each other, running in sync for a moment or two, then slipping out, like a pair of joggers whose strides fall apart, then come together again. The course the smugglers followed took them south from Great Inagua over the Windward Passage, circumnavigating Cuban airspace. They were sucking oxygen when the mountains of Haiti passed below the fuselage of the aircraft. As they broke through the clouds hovering about the peaks, the incandescent glow of Port-au-Prince came into view on their right. Before them, invisible, lay the Caribbean. Below them everything was black. In the distance, through scattered clouds, they could see fast-moving formations of thunderheads drifting away.

High above blinked the lights of commercial airliners, their pilots talking to Houston, Caracas, Nassau, Miami, one of them advising that his radar had picked up an aircraft but he could see no lights.

Long was really enjoying himself now.

There was a beauty to flying an airplane at night. He instantly came to appreciate why pilots so quickly grew addicted to flying. There was a solitary beauty up there. At one point, up in the cockpit, flying all alone, he took a few, long, lazy S-turns just to have some fun, canted the airplane to starboard and back to port, just like a kid on his bicycle.

Hatfield was unable to sleep. He took to the cot, but with every shift of the plane, he would ask if everything was all right. Long and McBride were having a good old time, yakking away and flying the airplane. And then McBride took a break. Hatfield returned, and Long, taking the right seat, flew with Hatfield for a while.

They had picked up the Maracaibo navigational station and were following a VOR radial that would lead them in on a magnetic course over the easternmost tip of Colombia. At five-thirty the sky brightened. The breaking dawn vaguely illuminated the South American coastline. Streams of sunlight, penetrating the clouds, hit the glaciers high in the Sierra Nevada. You could almost hear the explosion of light. Spiring in the sky, reflecting the sun, the mountains shone like a beacon in the morning, burning with the intensity of a star. As the sun ascended the heavens, the daylight broadened and flattened out. The diffusion of light diminished, and the geography came into higher relief. The foothills became clearly discernible. The shore and the plain came into focus. The smugglers could see coastal freighters plying the waters below. Picking up a visual of the coast, Hatfield banked the airplane. He tuned the VOR receiver to the

Barranquilla frequency, and activated the plane's DME unit to get a fix on their position.

They were flying southwest along the coast, maybe a hundred miles from Riohacha, and it was starting to warm up. Off came the flight suits. The three men were a bit haggard, but at the same time they were excited, and none more excited than Long, for only he had serious reason to wonder what the next couple of hours would bring.

At 2,000 feet off the water, Long was no longer worried about the plane. He had another, more unstable variable to confront. Long, that morning, was the one man aboard the DC-3 who knew that, contrary to what Myerson and the pilots believed, not everything had been taken care of. He knew he had not worked things out with the Colombians.

The Colombians knew nothing about the seizure at West Point. They were expecting Long to return with their money. He owed them $125,000. And here he was coming back empty-handed, bluffing it out, assuming that they would be satisfied with less, with something else entirely, guessing that maybe instead of the money, these guys would go for the smoke he was going to blow up their ass.

The possibility at this point that the airplane would crash paled by statistical comparison with the probability that the three men aboard would be shot.

The pilots did not have a clue.

McBride and Hatfield were flying to the Guajira expecting the second load of pot on the arm — fronted by the Colombians, pending distribution in the States — putting the Americans in position to pay for the load and also pay for the load that had been lost. The pilots would not have agreed to the trip had they thought the load was a "maybe."

The Colombians expected the plane to land carrying not only the money the Americans owed, but a down payment on the pot the Americans were there to pick up. From the Colombian point of view, the plane, when it landed, would be — to the penny — a quarter of a million dollars short.

The thought that the Colombians might kill them right there as they stood on the beach for showing up empty-handed would have been that much more discouraging to the pilots.

All three men were playing light, but only one of them knew it.

By unofficial agreement in the dope business, the impact of a seizure like the one at West Point is absorbed evenly by buyer and seller. By tradition, if a smuggler can show the loss to be legitimate — providing a police evidence sheet, for instance, to prove that he is not actually stealing — the loss is split down the line, usually at the farmer's price. The farmer gets paid in full, and the traffickers share the hit. Long assumed the protocol to be standard, but never having worked with the Colombians, was not sure they observed the convention.

One way or another, by raising the issue beforehand, he jeopardized his shot at a second load, or so had been his reasoning. He was presenting the Colombians with a fait accompli, judging it a way to improve his odds. Apart from Long himself, only Reed knew he was running a con.

"You'll do it," said Reed, when Long laid out the plan. "You can talk 'em into it, Al."

But even now, a hundred miles from touchdown, Long wondered what to say. He wondered how he was going to handle it. He knew only one thing for certain. For whatever it happened to be worth, he knew he could count on

Reed. He knew he could trust JD to be there, waiting for the airplane, no matter when it got back.

If it got back.

"White to red. White to red."

"Red to white. This is red, sir. I read you five-by-five."

Loud and clear. No static. No interference.

They flew in over Riohacha at 1,500 feet. Below them, a fishing boat tied to the pier was tossing in the waves. Indian dugouts were motoring up the coast, powered by the small Volvo gasoline engines ubiquitous on the Guajira. At 1,000 feet the temperature in the cockpit reached 90 degrees. It was probably 95 on the ground. The mist had burned off the jungle. At the mouth of the Río Camarones, children played in the tide.

"Red to white. Red to white. We have you. We can see you."

Hatfield did a flyby of the airstrip, circled north, and brought her in. Banking in on the northeasterly sea breeze, he put the airplane down.

Boom, they were on the ground.

Soon it was *abrazos* all around. The tail wheel was hanging on the edge of the ocean, the pilots were shutting the airplane down, and Long was exchanging hugs with the Colombians, when the truck hauling gasoline pulled up. While greetings were still underway, the Colombian crew pumped fuel. On one wing they used a hand pump, on the other an electric unit hooked up to a 12-volt battery. Behind the fuel truck came the reefer.

Long had not seen these bales. They had been selected by the Colombians. And so he spent the next hour and a half, the time required to refuel the plane, inspecting the load for

quality. He borrowed a knife, cut two sides of a triangle in the face of each bale, peeled the wrapper back and removed a bud. He crushed and smelled a sample taken from every bale that went aboard the airplane. He rejected fifteen bales. The remainder of the load was strapped down, and the refueling was just about done, when Miguel reminded Long of the money.

"Sir, we forgot something," he said with a laugh.

"No, Miguel, I didn't forget," said Long, walking his Colombian friend away from the airplane. "And I think now you need to call Ernesto."

"Ernesto?"

"Yes, call Ernesto over here. And Pablo, too."

Long told Miguel what had happened.

"Oh, sir," Miguel said, shaking his head.

"It was the seven-hour delay," Long explained.

"You do not have any money?"

"No."

"This is a big problem. This is a very big problem, and I don't know what is going to happen. I don't know what we can do."

"You have to tell Ernesto," said Long. "And he has to make this decision."

It was Miguel's deal. To Miguel the setup owed its existence. It was he, as his father's son, whose word had been good, he to whom everyone finally deferred. But while it may have been Miguel's deal, it was Ernesto's operation. He ran the camp where the pot was processed. All the men on hand worked for him. The logistical work, the organization, Ernesto controlled the show. In every way that mattered, it was Ernesto's marijuana. A former employee of Miguel's father, it was he who had to answer for the pot. Long knew that no matter what Miguel thought, it was Ernesto who

would make the call. However reasonable the young engineer might be in the face of the "problem" before them, its resolution rested with the man who approached them now toting a submachine gun.

Long and Miguel were standing about sixty feet from the aircraft, where no one else could hear them, when Ernesto and Pablo walked over. Long took from his pocket a newspaper clipping that he had cut from a page of the *Richmond Times-Dispatch*. He opened it up, and he showed Ernesto the photograph that had been snapped the day of the bust, the picture of the county sheriff posing with the confiscated bales. Ernesto studied it for a moment, pushed back the brim of his hat, and placed his finger on the photo.

"*Mis bultos,*" he said, identifying the bales. He recognized them as his own.

Confounding to many a casual observer of the international traffic in dope is why anyone involved in the trade, why any *contrabandista* in his right mind, would do something so incriminating as to personally brand his product. Yet it is done all the time, just as ranchers brand their cattle — or rather, in Ernesto's case, brand someone else's cattle. What Ernesto identified in the photograph were markings that he himself had affixed to the burlap in which the bales had been sewn up. Marijuana sent to a runway might originate with three individual farmers. The bales are labeled to indicate which farmer's merchandise constitutes which bale. Each farmer is compensated according to how many bales of his product make it aboard the plane. (In certain cases, depending on how a particular operation is structured, the brands are affixed by farmers, who sometimes bale the pot themselves.)

Examining the photo, Ernesto grew indignant, remarking that it was clearly a policeman standing with his foot on the bales.

"Quién es este hombre?" he wanted to know.

Long told him who the man was.

"Hijo de la gran puta!" he said.

He asked what happened, and Long told him.

"Yo no tengo dinero," I have no money, said Long.

Ernesto squared his shoulders, looked at Long and narrowed his eyes.

"No dinero?" he said.

Life on the Guajira was tough, Ernesto was a very tough character, and eye to eye with him now, Long suspected he was younger than he looked. He was a short, rawboned, rope-muscled man. His features were sharp and weather-beaten. His sunburned skin was like leather. The devil-may-care smile of the adventurer had just disappeared from his face, and his eyes looked like jacketed nine-millimeter rounds that had just been chambered.

"Sí," said Long, shaking his head. *"No dinero."*

Yes, we have no bananas.

Ernesto inhaled deeply. He had to think this over. This was a grave situation, and one he had never had to grapple with — not using anything more than his trigger finger, or so it appeared to Long, who wondered how many others, having lost a load, had ever had the temerity to return.

"I'm here," Long said, "because I intend to come back and pay you. *Yo regreso aquí con dinero.* Not just for this one, but for the first one that we lost. *If* you will give me this one. But I have nothing to pay you now."

He told Ernesto he would come back with the money or die trying. He had planned to say that. It was the extent to which he had come up with anything to say in rehearsing for the showdown — it was as far as he had gotten. From here on, he would be winging it.

"Nada?" Ernesto said. Nothing? Not even a piece of it?

He wanted to know what Long had. Long gave him the entire inventory.

"I have . . ."

He paused, and continued in labored Spanish.

". . . *Yo tengo solamente mi avión* . . ." he said, gesturing to the airplane. And then grabbing them, he said, ". . . *y mis cojones.*"

I have only my airplane and my balls.

Ernesto stepped back when he heard this. It took a moment for the words to sink in. For just an instant, as he locked eyes with Long, it seemed that almost anything could happen. His pupils appeared to close down about the equivalent of four F-stops. The barrel of his submachine gun rose. Long's temperature dropped like the price of bad livestock. And slowly the corners of Ernesto's mouth turned up. He raised the weapon into the air, screamed and started firing.

"Okay!" he cried. "Okay, *ándale!* Go, Allen! Go!"

He grabbed Long's hand and wrapped him up in a vigorous embrace.

He said, "*Adiós!* Go. Good luck, my friend. Go, *bandido!* We will wait for you."

Miguel released the breath he had been holding, and heaving a sigh, broke into uncontrolled laughter. So touched by the whole thing was the unpredictable Pablo that he broke into tears.

Long would look back on the moment as consecrating the birth of a brotherhood. These were men with deep wells of sensitivity, who at the same time could kill you without breaking a sweat. They would do so with sincere regret — "I'm sorry, my friend, but we have to kill you" — then bury you where you fell. It was a joyous moment for Long, and his spirits were visibly elevated as he leaped aboard the airplane.

Hatfield, revving it up, asked him, "What was that all about?"

"I told them we didn't have the money, and they agreed to give us the pot."

The silence rolled in like thunder.

"You didn't straighten that out?" McBride said. "You told me you straightened that out."

"If I didn't, would you have come?"

"No fucking way," said Hatfield, spinning around to face Long.

"Well, now we're on our way. Let's go. No need to worry."

But Hatfield was breathing fire.

"I trusted you, man!" he said.

"Well, Frank, your faith has been validated."

"Bullshit! We could have been killed."

"I asked you if you had the balls."

"Don't give me that shit. Coming down here, we could have crashed. Anything could have happened. On a trip that wasn't worth the risk."

"Yeah, but it worked out okay."

"Motherfucker, no, it is not okay. This is not okay with me. I'm pissed."

McBride said, "Let's get her out of here."

The revs were up, the brakes were on full, and the propellers were straining. Hatfield let her go, and as the airplane bounced down the runway, the Colombians waved their guns in the air, following alongside in their trucks. The plane cleared the trees, banked out to sea, and dropped to forty feet over the water. There was no more to be had out of the engines.

"What do you think," said McBride, "should we throw a couple of bales over?"

"No!" said Long, "we're not throwing anything out."

An hour later they were flying at 400 feet.

*   *   *

At 400 feet they were not shark bait. The plane was running like a young thoroughbred, they had forty-eight hundred pounds of the world's best marijuana aboard, and Long had just been imbued with a rainstorm of faith by a guy named Ernesto for whom he would ever maintain admiration. He had stood eye to eye with this man who was from a culture very different from his, and the only thing they had understood at that moment was that they had to place faith in each other. Otherwise, there was no future to their enterprise. It was going to end right there. Long could not go home empty-handed and come back and try it again. And if Ernesto did not give Long the pot, he could not get paid for the first load. A lot of people would have cut their losses right there.

"But I looked at him," Long told Reed, "and it was one of those moments in my life, JD. I discovered I have this ability: I can get people to believe in me. I can lead people. And that's what happened. I promised him I would die trying to do this rather than fail."

And so Allen Long, leader of men, the General George S. Patton of pot, breathed a sigh of relief, climbed back into the cargo bay, opened a bale, and rolled himself a bone.

"Oh, no," said McBride, "not you."

"Hey," said Long, "I'm not JD. I can still fly the plane. But I'm smokin' some of this stuff. Don't worry, bro', I ain't gonna roll one no bigger than a donkey dick."

Long's adrenaline had been pumping for hours. As it dissipated, he proceeded to get buzzed on the variety of ingestibles aboard the plane. Near the airstrip at Perico was a processing lab, and there, just off the runway, stood several 55-gallon drums of cocaine. Long, seeing a lid being removed

from one of the drums, had said, "Hey, can I have some of that?" Ernesto emptied out a Marlboro pack, scooped it into the drum, filled it with flake, and handed the pack to Long, who tucked it into the pocket of his flight suit. Halfway to Haiti, Long opened the pack, removed a rock about the circumference of a dime, chopped it up and shared it with the pilots. And then he broke out the beer.

There was no head aboard the aircraft, not even a relief tube, just a bucket containing blue toilet liquid and lime. Whether it was alleviation of a lot of the anxieties of the trip, or all the beer and cocaine with which the Americans celebrated their safe departure from Colombia, the bucket, which they called the honey pot, got a good workout on the way home.

Drinking Heineken, sucking oxygen, snorting coke and smoking pot, and flying back to the USA with some two and a half tons of blond — this for Allen Long was perhaps the finest moment of the trip. Pulling the trip off was not *all* about money. It was also about the achievement. It might have been the *only* good moment had there not been money waiting at the end of it. But right now nothing else seemed to matter except what he had just done. Getting the load into the country, getting the pot to market, and finally getting paid for it did not seem like much of an obstacle compared with what he had already accomplished.

Long, fast in reverie, was flying right seat when he spotted below him, rising out of the blue of the Caribbean, an island that did not exist. Or had not existed until that moment. No more than a strip of sea floor, ringed by coral, it was probably listed on the charts as a shoal. A sandbar. But for now, for one instant, it was an island, a piece of the Caribbean upon which no soul had ever set foot. And Long let his imagination put him there. Nothing could change the

inevitable now. They would touch down safely, or maybe not. Maybe upon landing they would be busted, but in a way, that was out of their hands, too. He was overcome by a feeling of calm. He had faith in the airplane — he was no longer waiting for the rivets to come popping out of the wings. The plane was on time, flying just fine. And JD was on the ground waiting. There was no worry about anyone's not being there.

The plan was to land in northeastern South Carolina, on the dragstrip at Darlington International Raceway. Lookouts were posted at all access points within five miles of the track. Reed was equipped with wire cutters, and nothing short of a buffalo gun was going to stop him from going through the fences. Darlington was one of three potential landing sites, a triangle of strips within fifty miles of one another. They were coded A, B, and C. The pilots would communicate with the ground crew within an hour of the plane's arrival — a good hour out they would be in radio range — and if the rendezvous were compromised in any way, the crew would have a decent head start in getting from A to B.

Reed had used a chartered plane to ferry his men into the region. Flown in from Las Vegas and Virginia, they had not known where they were going, and even now did not know exactly where they were. Reed had them bivouacked in a hotel somewhere near the state line, waiting for night to fall, waiting to begin the slow, steady progression to Darlington. There were eight men on the crew, two look-outs, three loaders, and three drivers, one of whom was Reed's father.

Reed would use two pickups fitted with snap-top campers to haul the load to Ann Arbor. At Darlington there would be a third such truck, a backup to be used in the event of a breakdown. The trucks were not new, but in perfect

running condition, and were made less conspicuous by the exterior-mounted tool boxes and aluminum extension ladders they carried. They looked like the trucks of working men, whose vehicles were an established presence on the nation's byroads early in the morning.

As he did on every airplane trip, Reed had scouted the landing strip exhaustively in advance. Once Reed had located a strip on a map, it was his practice to park far away, walk to the location, and securing a nearby vantage point, sit there and watch it all night, using an infrared scope, and all the following day. After the off-load, he would assign a lookout to remain at the site, parked nearby in a motor home. The lookout would wait twenty-four hours, staying to see if anyone came to investigate the night's activities. In that way Reed would know if he could use the strip again. A nightwatchman's appearance would not scuttle a trip — Reed would already have selected a tree branch to cut to break the telephone line.

The same motor home that would remain at the strip that night would be serving another purpose as the DC-3 came in for a landing. Reed's father, at the wheel of the vehicle, would be parked some distance away with an open bottle of whiskey.

"His job is to run people off the road, a cop or whatever," Reed said, assuring Long that from the time the DC-3's wheels hit the ground to the time it was airborne again, it would take only six minutes to off-load it. "For those six minutes, I need somebody I can trust, and that's my dad, the only man I know who has the nuts to drive over and ram into a cop."

Long had reacted with amusement to the notion that Reed would be bringing his dad along as a member of the ground team. He found it rather quaint. But that was before Long

knew much about the elder Reed. Once he finally met him, his amusement would evaporate, to be replaced at least temporarily by something like stone horror. Only later would he appreciate just how much of JD Reed, how much of who he was, had been inherited from his father, and given what his father had to offer, how lucky it was for Reed that he had not inherited it all.

The DC-3 crossed Haiti at mid-afternoon. After passing over Great Inagua, as the plane approached Eleuthera, Frank Hatfield initiated a series of evasive maneuvers. At that point the plane had come within range of mobile radar stations along the Florida coast, and was showing up as a blip on the screens of U.S. Coast Guard vessels patrolling the Straits. Appearing north of Haiti, it could be taken for almost any aircraft, a passenger plane, for instance, flying from Port-au-Prince to the Bahamas. At the southern tip of Eleuthera, as though bringing her into the airport there, Hatfield took the airplane down to forty feet off the deck, hugging the ocean for about fifty miles, taking cover of the island's land mass. At the northwest tip of the island he climbed, bringing the airplane up from below radar as though it were taking off, one of countless aircraft leaving the Bahamas for the States. He ascended to 5,000 feet, headed to Freeport, Grand Bahama, and beyond it to Florida, setting a course for Palm Beach.

10
SMOKE AND MIRRORS

The plane entered the United States in daylight, at about five in the afternoon, with all the air traffic from the Bahamas. On radar screens that were lit up like the Milky Way, it showed up as just one more aircraft, an unidentified blip. It entered U.S. airspace not at 25,000 feet, not at 300 feet, but at 5,000 like all the others. It came in at Palm Beach, Florida, but its crew, unlike those of other flights, would not report to Customs upon landing.

Coming out of the Bahamas, homing in on the Palm Beach directional beacon, Hatfield had known that within fifty miles of the Florida coast he was going to get a call from air-traffic control instructing him to switch on his radar transponder.

They had been calling for half an hour when Hatfield flew directly *over* the airport. He could not have been more conspicuous had he come in upside down.

"Unidentified aircraft, you are requested . . ."

The smugglers maintained radio silence.

"Please turn on your transponder and switch to . . ."

They did none of it. The tower ordered them to land.

". . . execute a turn to the south, descend to twenty-one hundred feet and prepare to . . ."

They just kept flying.

"Please announce your intentions . . ."

They were overloaded, fighting a slight headwind, and Long, who spent no measurable stretch of the trip not stoned, had become fascinated by the movement of automobile traffic below. The cocaine, acting chiefly as a motor drug, did not interfere with the immaculate marijuana buzz he managed to maintain. He took note of the fact that many motorists were in fact traveling faster than he. The plane had been holding even with one red car that continued to occupy his attention until, finally overtaking the DC-3, it disappeared out of sight.

Hatfield climbed to 12,000 feet, picked up an airway, and headed northwest, pushing through central Florida. They were sucking oxygen again, and the cockpit was cold, when over Lake Okeechobee, Long took the left seat, relieving Hatfield, who needed to rest up for the landing later that night. Exhausted now by twenty-four hours of flying, Hatfield, unlike his second officer, had not been shoveling cocaine for the past eight.

The plane was on a heading for north Georgia, where the Blue Ridge and the Great Smoky Mountains converge. The smugglers planned to disappear from radar for a while, running in and out of the valleys there, and check to see if anyone was following, before swinging around to Darlington. They were about fifty air miles north of the Everglades when in the top left quadrant of the windshield they picked up a massive storm front coming their way.

"What do you think?" said Long.

"Hey, Frank?"

"Where are we?" said Hatfield, leaning into the cockpit. McBride said, "I think I saw Sebring back there."

"Give me the map."

Moving southeast, and moving fast, the thunderstorm presented the DC-3 with fewer options than enjoyed by other aircraft. The storm was too heavy, it was carrying too much turbulence, to go through or attempt to go under, and the DC-3, with a service ceiling of about 20,000 feet, was unable by design to achieve the necessary altitude to go over it. Going east would get the smugglers safely around the formation, but constituted a collateral risk Hatfield was unwilling to take. Advancing in that direction, the storm could very well push them back out over the Atlantic.

"We can't gamble that kind of fuel," he said.

And there, even with sufficient fuel, they would have to beat the U.S. border a second time. The odds on doing so were not prohibitive, but considering that and considering what the move might cost them in fuel, Hatfield figured why go up against the percentages. To circumnavigate the storm, the smugglers took the better odds, choosing the only course left to them. They went west, into the clear sky over Tampa. And into the restricted military airspace surrounding MacDill Air Force Base.

"Cool," said Long.

"Wake me when it's over."

Allen Long's equanimity at this point in the trip could be explained quite conveniently by the parts-per-milliliter of dope in his blood. But viewing it that way would ignore the very elements of his personality that accounted for his being where he was in the first place. The trip was far from over, the deal was far from done. With Reed in charge of the ground crew, there was reason to be confident that the off-load would go smoothly, but as a source of potential danger

it still could not be ignored. All that lay between Darlington and Ann Arbor, not to mention what still lay between Florida and Darlington, could be evaluated quite rationally in the light of how much could go wrong. And yet, as he sailed around the thunderstorm, Allen Long was way past worrying about anything. Whatever is gonna happen is gonna happen, he reasoned. Now he was just having fun.

If one examines the overworked principle that cops and criminals are flip sides of the same constitutional coin, one might arrive at an appreciation, if only superficial, of Long's nonchalance. The average well-adjusted individual is programmed by nature to recoil from danger, to avoid it, and, failing that, to flee. Cops are trained to run in its direction. Their fitness reports, like those of firemen and military officers, measure their ability and their eagerness to do so. Their careers thrive on confrontation and their willingness to initiate it. Allen Long and other outlaws come by this trait not by formal training, but by a combination of natural temperament and experience. Crime's rewards reinforce their antisocial behavior. The syndrome sometimes expresses itself as an addiction to action. JD Reed described himself as an "an adrenaline junkie," and readily admitted that in the absence of confrontation, he felt the need to scare it up.

"I got to go wrestle a mule or have somethin' thrown at me to keep that life going."

There is nothing particularly profound in this. It is nothing new, or even strikingly novel, and it is not unique to outlaws. The same character trait can be found in a variety of law-abiding soldiers of fortune and, to one degree or another, in the typical downhill skier. It is a quality that propels certain people to become cops and firemen in the first place. Indeed, in Allen Long's case it was one of the more innocent

manifestations of a psychological profile the darker side of which revealed itself in other ways. But it helps explain why in the air over Florida, facing a constellation of negative prospects, probably the least of which was a prison stretch, Long could ignore everything but the upside of the proposition and all the fun he was having. He was high on reefer and luxuriating in an almost unlimited supply of coke, he had an oxygen hose stuck in the left side of his mouth, a cigarette stuck in the other, he was holding a Heineken between his legs, he was flying that airplane, and he was having the time of his life.

That is what makes guys like Allen Long different from you.

"Hey, what do you think those are?" he said, turning to McBride.

He directed the co-pilot's attention to four black dots, appearing like pencil points in the distance, forming a diamond in the sunlight off to the west. In the time it took Long to turn his head back, the fighter jets had closed the gap, coming in on the smugglers at about 200 knots. They made a deafening pass over the DC-3, roughing it up. Air Force F-4 Phantom jets. The cockpit shook as the tactical fighters roared by, the explosion of jet wash, hitting the fuselage, rocking in with the shock of a breaking wave.

"Hmm," said McBride, "were you speeding?"

The fighters came back around, and the formation pulled alongside.

"License and registration."

A traffic stop in the wild blue yonder.

Throwing on all the brakes — gear down, flaps down, flying at a high angle of attack — the Air Force pilots were unable to slow their craft sufficiently to pace the DC-3 for more than seconds at a time. One of the flyers, hanging on

the edge of the stall envelope, holding for as long as he could on the smugglers' left wing, looked Long and McBride over and checked out the cockpit. The weapons system officer, flying rear seat, tapped the edge of his helmet, over his ear, signaling Long to get on the radio.

Long raised his mike with a shrug and a series of idiotic gestures understood by international standard to mean: "Radio's busted."

Total platform kill. Sorry, man.

Over the cockpit radio the smugglers heard MacDill tower trying to raise them on the override frequency.

". . . Douglas eight-six-four . . . ordered to exit military . . ."

The tower eventually gave up. And then, over their UHF receiver, the smugglers heard the F-4 reporting to MacDill.

"Probably just another weed smuggler. And that is not our business. Tango flight is departing the area."

No threat to national security, just some dumb, severely stoned citizens flying a planeload of drugs. The F-4 pilots raised their gear, hit the burners, and were gone.

Long raised his Heineken in a farewell salute.

"God bless America."

"The arsenal of democracy," McBride volunteered.

"Let's have some more of that coke."

Just before sunset, as the shadows below were lengthening and house lights were switching on, Hatfield took over. Running up the Smoky Mountain valleys, he dropped the aircraft to 1,000 feet, and disappeared from radar for a while. They were about five hours from touchdown when darkness fell, and the plane came out of the mountains flying with no lights. All three men were exhausted. It was time to shave and clean up. At some point the pilots would have to step off the plane to face the personnel of some general

aviation facility. By then the plane itself would have to be cleaned up. There was still a lot of work to do.

The DC-3's extended range, thanks to the auxiliary tanks, was of significant advantage to the smugglers, enabling them as it did to land as far north as Virginia and the Carolinas. The distance between Colombia and the U.S. border was a good piece of what put so much heat on Florida. And made Darlington such a good bet.

They were a hundred miles out when they raised JD Reed on the radio. He and Long, over an air-to-air frequency, gave the impression of two pilots shooting the breeze, Long transmitting not from Douglas 86459, but Cessna 4603 Zulu, on a putative flight from Hilton Head to Spartanburg.

"Yeah we can see you over there, what are you flying?" said Long.

"This is Piper Cherokee four-six-seven-three India," responded Reed, transmitting from the dragstrip. "I see your lights. You at about eight thousand?"

"I'm at eighty-six hundred, descending into Spartanburg now. Golfing was great at Hilton Head. Are you the guy that operates the fleet of planes out of Middleburg, Virginia?"

"Affirmative," said Reed.

"What was the weather like over Spartanburg?"

"Everything was just fine, you're going to have a fine landing, shouldn't be any problems."

"Fine. That's an A on that then?"

"Yes," Reed said. "That's an A. I'd give conditions there an A."

Meaning Darlington, coded Landing Site A, was secure.

Hatfield navigated visually, carefully studying the landmarks below. As he closed in on the dragstrip, he started looking for a signal.

"I hear you. Yeah, I see your lights," said Reed. "I sure can. I see your lights. Can you see mine?"

The headlights on the pickup trucks flashed at the end of the dragstrip. Hatfield in response flashed the landing lights of the DC-3. Hatfield buzzed the runway, came back around to land, and Long was working the cargo doors when the airplane hit the ground.

The trucks pulled up, Reed secured the hatches, and Long started throwing bales. McBride, eager to be airborne, stepped back into the cargo bay and heaved bales along the fuselage, throwing them in the direction of the door. It was then, as the rhythm picked up, that one of Reed's crew, a guy named Billy, took a bale in the side of the head, momentarily knocking him cold. Reed, without missing a beat, picked the unconscious crewman up, and threw him into the back of the truck along with the cargo as if he were one of the bales.

"Don't say it."

"I wasn't going to say it."

"Yes you were," said Reed. "I could tell."

"I wasn't," said Long.

"Yes you were."

"Can I say it later?"

"I'll think about it."

After a quick consultation with the pilots, in which McBride confirmed that he could clear up the Visqueen by himself, Long decided that there was no need for him to go on with the airplane. The DC-3 took off without him. The plane lifted off in one direction and the trucks took off in the other. Before jumping aboard the blue Chevy Suburban in which they would follow the pot to Ann Arbor, Long and Reed, both patting themselves down for a match, looked at each other and simultaneously asked:

"Got a joint?"

The smugglers, facing each other, turned like the two halves of a French door swinging closed, and watched the trucks disappear into the distance with 4,800 pounds of weed.

The pot was aboard two covered pickups, one driven by Reed's father, the other by the crewman Billy, who had been knocked unconscious for only a minute. Long and Reed, using a CB radio to stay in touch with the drivers, followed a half-mile behind in what they were prepared to use as a crash car. If a truck were pulled over by police, the driver would report it over the CB. Long and Reed would slow down, allow the trooper to advance toward the truck on foot, then rear-end the police cruiser at about sixty miles an hour, just take it right off the road. The cop was not going to care what happened to the truck at that point, he was going to bust Long and Reed for reckless driving.

Long had been up now for almost two full days. Awake at six A.M. the day of the flight, he had not slept in forty-two hours. His system had been subjected to a lot of heavy sensory input — a significant share of emotional and psychological stress — and a lot of psychotropic substances, without benefit of solid food. He had been forcing fluids, but his liquid intake consisted exclusively of Heineken. He was a bit removed from the situation. He had ceded control of things to Reed.

They ran due north, avoiding the Interstate, up through Asheboro and Greensboro, North Carolina, to Roanoke, Virginia, cutting northwest from there, taking to the backcountry, and circling through the hills around Beckley, West Virginia, where Reed had been born and his father had been reared. It was somewhere in the West Virginia hills that Long and Reed lost radio contact with the trucks. And Long, in

his compromised spiritual condition, found himself wondering just how terrible it would be if he never saw them again. It occurred to him that he did not know how to reach Billy in Las Vegas, and he had never laid eyes on Reed's father. Reed was his only contact with these guys. What if they just decided to dump him, wondered Long, who had been doing drugs for two days now. When they broke out of West Virginia and still were unable to raise the trucks on the radio, he turned to Reed and casually asked him, "What does your dad do for a living?"

"Oh, he's a hit man," Reed said.

Long laughed. "No, really," he said, "what does he do?"

"Oh, no, I'm not kidding," Reed said. "He's a hit man. I can't tell you the number of times I've gone with my dad to throw a gun out somewhere in the desert. Police have been to my house plenty of times with warrants for my dad's arrest."

Still, Long did not get it.

"For what?"

"Murder for hire, mostly. But he's never been convicted."

Indictments by the dozen. No convictions.

"Really," said Long.

"No witnesses." Reed's dad was old-school. "Yeah, he's not allowed in any of the casinos in Vegas. But he does a lot of work for them."

"Like a collector?"

"He does jobs — dirty jobs for the mob and people like that — an independent contractor."

Luther Reed, a confidence man, rip-off artist, and killer for hire, had been doing contract murders all of JD Reed's life. The seventh son of a seventh son, Luther had gone to war against Hitler as a teenager, and killed his first civilian for the operator of a Biloxi casino. He was a cornucopia of

sound advice — "Don't carry a gun" — and bad example. He had turned his son on to cocaine as early as 1967, when the latter was sixteen years old. Instructing his family to rent a motor home and meet him in Death Valley, the elder Reed alighted from an airplane there carrying two suitcases filled with coke he had picked up in Ecuador. A few years after Long met him, Luther Reed's latest indictment would result in his first conviction, on charges of operating a bootleg Quaalude factory outside Las Vegas. Under surveillance by drug agents, he was convicted, he explained to his son, only because "you can't kill a video."

And this guy now had a truckload of Allen Long's pot.

"JD, I hate to ask you this, but what happens if your dad decides he's gonna keep the weed?"

"My dad wouldn't do that. No, he'd have to talk to me about that."

Which Long found only marginally consoling.

They found Luther and Billy waiting, as instructed, at a motel off Interstate 94 in Ann Arbor. The trucks were parked outside. The two men had checked in about an hour before. It was Long's first look at the elder Reed, a robust man with bone-white hair, shorter than his son. Looking into the eyes of an animal that evinces no response to seeing you is precisely what it was like for Long to meet and look at Luther. He had dead eyes, Long decided, eyes Long would never forget.

Long and Reed took the trucks from the motel, and not far away they met Myerson.

"Follow me," he told them.

They followed him to a farm he owned, where they backed the trucks into a large, brightly lit Quonset hut. Champagne, cocaine, and caviar awaited the two smugglers when they pulled in. After a brief celebration, five men wearing gloves and dust masks started unwrapping the pot.

The industry-standard wrap for bales of marijuana is three-fold. The bales are first wrapped in brown paper, which is sealed with masking tape. The layer of paper is necessary because the merchandise sweats. Much like a haystack gets moist and hot in the middle, this too is organic material. And even well cured, the product needs to hold moisture if it is to maintain any level of quality. If it were wrapped in plastic alone, it would decompose as its natural juice heated up and tried to evaporate. It is wrapped in paper to absorb the moisture, then wrapped in plastic to make the bale water-proof, to protect it not only from rain and seawater, but from contamination by crude oil and bilge. The plastic is taped, and then the bale is wrapped in a burlap bag that is sewn up on the open end, making the bale easy to handle — smugglers can grab the burlap by the corners and throw the bale around.

While the bales from the first truck were being unpacked, Long and Reed drove the second truck out of the building and dumped its load in an open field. Wearing burlap bags over their heads, they posed arm-over-shoulder in front of the mountain of Santa Marta Gold while somebody snapped a couple of photographs.

"Powerful stuff . . ." said Long, from inside the burlap.

"You're going to say it, aren't you," said Reed, speaking in the direction of the camera.

Long said, ". . . It goes right to your head."

Myerson gave Long the cash necessary to pay off the ground crew, and Long and Reed returned to the motel. Handing Luther Reed $25,000, Long detected the hint of a smile, but saw no change in the hit man's eyes. With his forefinger and thumb, Luther Reed pantomimed a gun, pointed it at Long,

and said, "Al, you're a good guy to work for. You know, if you ever need anything done . . ." he let his thumb fall ". . . give me a call." He walked out the door, stepped into his truck, and drove away.

The $25,000 that Long paid each member of the ground crew was more than the going rate. In many cases, half that would have been sufficient to cover the cost of the job. Throughout the industry, off-loading, driving, and similar activities were very often handled by otherwise law-abiding citizens, working men with mortgages to pay and families to support. Many of the workers Long recruited fell within that category, and he paid them well, believing they deserved it. It changed the lives of some of them, and not always for the better — once they got a taste of that kind of dough, they decided they wanted to be scammers.

With the drivers on their way back to Las Vegas, Long and Reed celebrated late at Mr. Flood's Party, the bar on West Liberty being a mandatory stop for any visiting trouble-maker, and that night they settled into Weber's Inn to await the payoff on distribution of the product. The 4,800 pounds of dope that arrived in Ann Arbor was by far the best available there, and Myerson found himself able to sell it for an average of $325 a pound. But before any profit could be taken on this, the first successful load, the loss on the previous trip had to be swallowed. Myerson had about a quarter of a million in start-up costs to recoup, most of which had gone into the purchase and outfitting of the airplane, and the smugglers were in arrears to the Colombians for $79,000 on the busted load.

Paying the Colombians for the busted load, which Long had promised to do on the airstrip, was unnecessary and highly unusual, according to Myerson, but even had Long not promised to do so, Myerson would have insisted on it.

It achieved its intended effect, substantially raising Long's stock with the Colombians. With an unspecified number of bales being thrown off the overloaded airplane at Perico, the first flight had left the airstrip in Colombia carrying only 4,080 pounds — according to the sheriff of King William County, who weighed the load — hence the balance of $79,000.

Once all the numbers were crunched — an additional $240,000 had to be deducted to pay the Colombians for the pot that had just been distributed — the load generated over $900,000 in profit. Under the original terms of the deal, this was to be shared by the principals according to a formula that left the pilots with about 30 percent less than Long. If the trip was anomalous to begin with, considering all the necessary deductions, the decision to change the formula, once the money was finally counted, made it that much more irregular.

McBride and Hatfield had flown two trips, they had seen no money at all, and right now the pilots were probably asking themselves whether they ever would. They had risked their lives, invested their faith, and they had done it all on a maybe. McBride knew what it was like to make money on pot but had never done so on so large a scale. Hatfield, for his part, a man who had never before earned an unlawful dollar, had no idea what to expect.

To minimize carelessness and the influence of greed, Long had led everyone including the pilots to believe that they were doing business with the mob — the "boys in Detroit" is how he referred to Myerson and his pot-smoking pals in Ann Arbor. On one occasion Myerson had even been cast to play the heavy in person. Long put him in a trench coat, handed him a cigar, and had him mug it up for the benefit of Buddy Blanchard, using Myerson to impress upon the

Richmond lawyer the importance of discretion. Jake Myerson: Murder Incorporated.

Long had shown on the second flight down that he was willing to let the pilots believe anything. The pilots, when it came to their end of the deal, could be excused for thinking, "I'll believe it when I see it." And so once the Ann Arbor money came in, the second thing Long had to do was get back to Richmond to take care of them. The first was to talk to the others involved and propose a juggling of the arithmetic, a one-time deviation from the formula governing the split. They agreed it was the right thing to do — the pilots this time would take a share equal to Long's.

"A plague upon it when thieves cannot be true one to another!"

This is as close as Falstaff comes to the subject of honor among thieves. And while thievery may not be entirely accurate in defining the smuggling operation in question, its correlative can probably be found there if one ransacks the conspiracy's ethical character.

Criminal endeavor, in general, flourishes in a behavioral no-man's-land between questionable ethics and no ethics at all. Smuggling as a criminal subcategory boasts situation ethics, at best. In any case, when you stop following the established rules, you have to make up your own. Seldom in any criminal conspiracy do the rules undergo codification, and almost never over the long haul do one man's rules remain consistent with those of his fellow conspirators. The greed of the typical capitalist manifests itself earlier in the outlaw simply because the ethical train has been running without brakes from the start. Greed and self-preservation — turning on your accomplices when your conduct gets you in trouble with the law — inevitably afflict even the most collegial conspiracies. Until that time, you just do the best

you can. And call it honor if it makes you feel good.

This conspiracy would be no different. But in the beginning it sported attributes that reflected a surprising measure of sophistication on the part of Long and his partners. And it featured a strain of goodwill that was unique to its place and time. It was not honor so much as enthusiasm that gave the enterprise its special quality. In the early days of the marijuana trade there was so much money to go around — the numbers just came up so big — that Long and his partners were in a position to discover that generosity was good for business. Overpaying the Colombians for the merchandise, paying members of the ground crew higher than the going rate, kicking in as they did for the pilots — cutting the pilots in for a percentage in the first place — all of this promoted the success of an enterprise that would soon generate so much cash that eventually, rather than count it, the smugglers would simply weigh it.

Long delivered the money to the pilots in two $400 leather briefcases that he purchased for the occasion. Neither man knew exactly what his cut was going to be, but imagined it was going to come in at around $100,000. Long took great pleasure in toying with their expectations, and was exuberant in his willingness to take credit for the benefaction when he handed them $150,000 each. Giving them a handwritten record of accounts showing all the operation's expenditures, he did everything but take a bow.

The pilots should have been speechless. Instead, Hatfield hit Long with a question, Hatfield, for whom everything up to that point had been a maybe.

He said, "When are we going to do it again?"

Frank Hatfield was now a believer.

* * *

Long's biggest one-time score up to that point was the $25,000 he had earned on the Mexican load he and Reed had sold Myerson the previous fall. Now, on the Colombian trip, he hit for $150,000. And the next flight would be worth almost twice that. "He now starts havin' money," as Cherie Harris would later explain to a friend, introducing an attribute that would be colorfast in the character of the man others came to know. From then on, no one who met him would mention meeting him without mentioning the money; failing mention of the money, Long's character was inexpressible.

Long was not alone in flashing his newly acquired wealth and undergoing the numerous changes that came with it. McBride bought a house. Hatfield bought a plane, a cabin-class, twin-engine Cessna Titan. And Reed — "I never been extravagant" — moved onto a small ranch in Las Vegas that he "got cheap, four acres on a corner, $54,000," next door to singer Wayne Newton. (History does not record what "Mr. Las Vegas" made of the camouflage gear, the shotgun, and the dogs with which Reed routinely patrolled the grounds, nor the fatties laced with hash oil hanging from the laundry line outside the kitchen.) Jake Myerson's fortunes were largely unaffected. The money he earned was insufficient thus far to alter a lifestyle already influenced by what might be called very tall bank. Soon, however, at least for a while, Ann Arbor would become known as the place to score the best Colombian pot in the country, and as Myerson's reputation as a distributor of it grew, his business would grow along with it.

Long and Cherie had been together on and off for several months when he told her he was going to "do this other thing." It was no different from running liquor, he told her. In a few years marijuana would be legal, and he would be

in the forefront of the industry. Because she did not want to appear unsophisticated, also because she wanted to appear somewhat aloof — reinforcing the notion that they were keeping the relationship casual — Cherie acted cool, as if what he was proposing were no big deal. Now, with another year or so having passed, the relationship was more than casual, and the pot business was a big deal in ways that Long had merely dreamed of.

Wealth's effects on Long were nothing if not predictable. The money and the cosmopolitan air it encouraged him to adopt made him attractive, he found, to a much greater range and variety of women, and he adapted to the change accordingly. Dating Cherie, whom he had fallen for when he did not have money, he started to see a lot of other women who were available to him now that he did. It was getting complicated. At least for him. Cherie was beginning to find his infatuation with himself a little bit stifling anyway. When he gave her the I-need-my-space routine, she was neither surprised nor especially chagrined. When he announced his intention to return to New York, she looked forward to having her own space back. Or so she told herself. When he subsequently asked her to go with him, she readily quit her job and made arrangements to go. Only after she had cut her ties did he announce that he had changed his mind, that he wanted to go without her. Cherie's response to the breach of promise — "Send me to Europe and I'll forgive you" — was a measure of her current commitment to the relationship. Long bought her off with a two-month trip.

If and when Long moved to New York, Cherie would not be the only one he was leaving behind. Tom, his twenty-one-year-old brother, estranged from both sides of the family, and finding himself pretty much adrift, had needed a place to be,

and Long, who had not been there for him for the past ten years, had taken him in. Having no real direction at that point in his life, Tom, benefiting from his brother's prosperity, decided that what he wanted to do was work with him in the marijuana business. Long turned him down. That he himself might end up in prison Long relegated to the realm of the metaphysical. The prospect of his little brother's landing in jail was a hypothesis he found unbearable.

The same prosperity that enabled Long to look after his brother, had other, less salutary effects on his behavior. It was more than the money itself that made him difficult to deal with. He was loaded in more ways than one. Through his friends in Colombia he could buy cocaine for two dollars a gram. Which was just about for free. Street cocaine in the United States sold for exactly fifty times that. Long could pick up pure in Colombia, and at that price he could pick up weight. And with all the money he was making, he could easily pick up what he needed at U.S. retail when he ran out. In Richmond he started spreading so much blow around, and doing so much of it himself, that his wealth had come to be attributed to it. The misperception was part of the reason he considered leaving town. "I'm not a coke dealer, I'm a marijuana smuggler," was not the kind of protestation of innocence a judge was inclined to look upon favorably.

By now Long had a cocaine jones that was the envy of every junkie in America. If, as has often been said, a cocaine habit is God's way of telling you that you make too much money, Allen Long was the word made flesh. And he was way ahead of the curve. It would be a couple of years before the rest of the country caught up.

"Most I could do," JD Reed would say, "was three days. Third day I was done, I couldn't do it again for a month.

I knew guys who went weeks without sleeping. Yeah, guys like Allen."

Of gringos in the marijuana business virtually all were marijuana smokers, and many were on the cutting edge of cocaine use. The dope smugglers of Long's acquaintance, like dope smugglers and dealers in general, tended to be prodigious in their use of a variety of drugs, but few matched Long's appetite for cocaine. More interesting, however, is that none of them, Long included, mixed business with obsession, at least in the early days.

As Lee Carlyle understood: "The two don't go together, coke and pot, you can't mix the two in business." Pomeroy and his partner had proved it in Marin when they stashed twenty-two pounds of cocaine in the safe in the Mill Valley house. Pot smugglers like JD Reed explained cocaine as a different vibe, "a different business altogether, out of harmony with what we do."

"Try explaining *that* to the Colombians," Long told him.

It was on the third flight to the Guajira that Ernesto approached Long with what seemed to be a very reasonable question. Why come with such a big plane, when he could come with a small one, load it with cocaine, and make more money? As Long well knew, Ernesto had plenty of coke. Moreover, Ernesto said, he knew people in the States who would buy it, Long would not have to find a way to distribute it.

"My nose says yes, but my mind says no," answered Long.

This of course made no sense to Ernesto. It required an explanation. And so Long, whom the Colombians had come affectionately to refer to as "El Piloto Loco," favored Ernesto with a tutorial on karma.

The two men were squatting in the shadow of the airplane

just above the beach, and Long fell back on the use of a visual aid. He picked up a rock and drew two stick figures in the sand. "If I take cocaine and give it to this man," he said, drawing an arc in the sand between the two figures, inscribing a vector from left to right, "this is not a good thing for this man. This is bad for him. And karma will come back," he said, inscribing a reverse arc, "and hurt me. Something very bad will happen to me."

Ernesto pondered this for a moment. Cutting to the heart of the problem, he jumped up and pushed Long aside. Long tumbled to the dirt, and his ears rang with the sudden report of Ernesto's submachine gun as the Colombian emptied a short burst of nine-millimeter rounds into the sand, obliterating the hieroglyphic.

"Allen, if this Karma comes back to hurt you, I will kill him for you," Ernesto declared, smoke rising from the barrel of his Ingram.

Allen Long sincerely loved the Colombians, and this was one of the reasons why.

It was a pot smuggler named Tom Forcade, founder of *High Times* magazine, who was credited with saying, "There are only two kinds of dealers, those who need fork lifts and those who don't," and it would be a few years yet before a proposition such as Ernesto's held any appeal for the former. In 1978 Lee Carlyle would still be able to say with authority, "Coke does not generate the flow of cash that pot does." He would look upon the days when pot smugglers made millions as "the days when coke smugglers were making peanuts." There was just not a market for cocaine in the United States that came anywhere close to the market for pot. It took muscle to sit on a hundred kilos of coke for the month and a half required to move it. It was a dangerous game. The only people with that kind of muscle were guys

like Vito Genovese and other heavies in the rackets. When the market for cocaine did open up, which it did shortly thereafter — with the suddenness of an artery hit with the blade of a knife — it would not be Americans who benefited most substantially from it.

FIRE IS THE TEST OF GOLD

In advance of the third flight, Long paid a visit to his Colombian partners. He traveled alone to Barranquilla as a houseguest of Miguel's. But he was there to do more than pay the Colombians the money they were owed. It was apparent that if, before each flight, he did not select the marijuana personally, he would not get loads consisting exclusively of Santa Marta Gold. If half the load were of even slightly lower quality, it could mean a difference of at least a hundred thousand dollars in Ann Arbor.

Miguel had married his childhood sweetheart, and they and their two children lived in a large house in suburban Barranquilla, with his mother, his mother-in-law, and two female servants. The house was surrounded by a seven-foot concrete wall topped with fragments of broken glass. As an architectural statement, the security feature, a deterrent to the common criminal, was pretty typical of upper-middle-class residential construction in Colombia. With all the women in the house waiting on them, Long and Miguel were served lunch, a typical *almuerzo*, or noonday meal, of

rice, chicken, and salad, followed by flan and immediately thereafter a siesta, during which all the residents of the house slept off the meal and the midday heat.

Long's first order of business after paying Miguel was to select pot and oversee its packaging. The size and weight of marijuana bales were anything but standardized; every farmer and trafficker baled the product differently. Long would instruct the Colombians to limit the bales to between thirty-five and fifty pounds of what he referred to as semipress. If the pot was compressed too tightly, if the buds were crushed, the quality of the product suffered. In addition to affecting the pot's cosmetics, crushing the buds crushed the seeds, the oil from which permeated the pot, imparting a bitter taste. Long was carrying $50,000 in hundreds against unforeseen expenses, portions of which he intended to pass around when necessary to whet someone's appetite for the rest of it. In four packages, each of which was less than half an inch thick, the cash was stashed in his boots on either side of each leg.

Nailing down a load of high-quality pot was his first priority. The other was to see María. "Sometimes love is a matter of the special chemistry between your skin and hers," he had been advised by an Italian fashion photographer to whom he had confessed his infatuation with the beautiful young Colombian woman. But it was the memory of María's eyes that Long could not get out of his mind, the look she had given him, her parting touch when she whispered *"lindo"* that night at Puerto Galeón and told him to call. The closer he got to Santa Marta, the more irresistible the memory became.

Before making their way inland to the town of Aracataca in the Sierra Nevada foothills, where 5,000 pounds of *mona* were being held for Long's inspection, he and Miguel would stop in Santa Marta, but not to see María.

"We must go there," Miguel said, "to get Armando."

Long knew Armando well. Rarely did he see Miguel, in fact, without seeing the reticent, soft-spoken mestizo lingering somewhere nearby. Short, dark, and thick-bodied, loyal, fearless, and efficient, Armando, about forty, former bodyguard to the younger man's father, now worked for Miguel. And really worked for him. Armando was ever-present on the smuggling side of Miguel's life. When something needed handling, Armando was the guy who handled it. Traveling deep into the foothills carrying $50,000 in cash, Miguel and Long would travel with Armando, who would travel with a gun.

Arriving in Santa Marta late in the afternoon, the smugglers pulled up before a modest house where a woman in her late twenties, holding one naked child in her arms and dragging another along behind her, responded with a shake of her head when Miguel inquired after Armando. Miguel thanked her and drove off.

"We must go to the home of his wife," he said.

"That was not his wife?" said Long.

"Yes."

"Yes, that was *not* his wife?"

"No."

It was like an Abbott and Costello routine.

"Armando has many wives," Miguel pointed out.

Many wives, and he had children with each of them.

Long's limited experience in-country had shown monogamy, or more precisely marital fidelity, to be the exception not the rule among Colombian men. Of the Colombians Long had met, most were married men, and most of them had girlfriends, many had more than one, and as often as not their girlfriends bore them children. But where monogamy was unusual, polygamy was rare. Armando, in that way, was

eccentric, compelled as he was by honor to marry every woman he fell in love with.

"He is called the hardest working man in Santa Marta," Miguel said, smiling. "We say that you can always find Armando on the road to his house."

They found him that day speeding by in his truck.

"Observe," said the young engineer.

Hitting the brakes when he saw Miguel's car, Armando turned the truck around and pulled it up alongside.

Miguel asked, "Where are you going?"

"Home to my family," Armando replied.

Miguel nodded his head, then turned to smile at Long. "Q.E.D."

They followed Armando "home," and from there, an hour later, the three set off for Aracataca.

"Do you know the book *Cien Años de Soledad,* Allen, written by Mr. García Márquez?"

Long told Miguel that he had read it.

"This is his home, sir, Aracataca. This is where he was born."

Gabriel García Márquez and his masterpiece, *One Hundred Years of Solitude,* were a source of understandable pride to Miguel and his countrymen. And the citizens of Aracataca took equal pride, Miguel explained, in the eccentricity ascribed to them by the author.

"Where we are going is Macondo," he said.

Macondo, the fictional village in which the book is set, is not imaginary, it is Aracataca. It was a town, Miguel said, where everything ran contrary to nature, where yes meant no, where bad fortune was cause for celebration, and the rivers ran uphill.

The tropical foothills of the Sierra Nevada, emerging out of the sea, rose toward Aracataca curving like the prop roots

supporting the trunk of a bald cypress. They ran rich with banana trees and fast with the rivers and streams that irrigated the marijuana that Long had come to see. Aracataca lay hidden in the hills a hundred miles from the coast. The smugglers arrived at nightfall. Buses were still running, and the central plaza was busy, the marketplace alive with local people doing their shopping. Miguel, skirting the activity downtown, made for the old section of the city, site of the original village.

There on a cobblestone street, awash in the glow of lanterns, the smugglers entered a small house illuminated by candles. They were greeted by an elderly woman whose skin was wrinkled by age and weather. She wore a peasant dress and sandals. She ushered them to a table, and sat them down in the shadows. Filling a clay bowl with a loose handful of yellow buds, she set them afire. She leaned into the curling smoke, and cupping her creased hands, swept the fumes into her nostrils. She inhaled deeply, opened her eyes, favored Long with a smile that featured no more than three teeth, sighed and said, *"Buena."* With outstretched fingers she urged the smoke in his direction and invited him to do the same.

Long, moved to poetry by the color of the buds alone, did so eagerly, discovering to his satisfaction that *"buena"* did not come close.

"You are happy?" said Miguel.

"I am happy," Long said.

"You have a question?"

"I have a question about something else."

The walls of the room, reflecting the light of the candles, had galvanized Long's attention. They were papered with U.S. currency, decked in a splendid array of one-dollar bills.

"These, Miguel, where did they come from?"

Miguel inquired.

After conferring with the old woman, he turned to Long and said, "Years ago an American paid her this money for marijuana. One suitcaseful, she says."

Miguel did not translate the obvious follow-up question. Asked by Long *why* she had used the money to paper the walls, he simply smiled at his American friend.

He said: "Because it is Aracataca."

Before leaving the old village, Miguel walked Long across an ancient stone bridge.

"Look," he said, "see the river? This is that river, sir."

And viewed from the bridge the river appeared to be flowing uphill.

"In Aracataca," Miguel said, "the people think everything goes the opposite way. We call them the yes-no people. When they say yes, they mean no, and when they say no they mean yes. All Colombian people know this to be so. It is one of the things that we love about our country, one of the many things that make my country so interesting."

The next day Long and the Colombians drove high into the hills to meet the farmers who had grown the pot he had sampled that night. The fields Long visited were blond — acre upon acre, nothing but pale yellow covering the side of a hill. The plants were eight to ten feet high, all female, packed with buds. It was what Ernesto in Riohacha had wanted Long to see. Ernesto was not going to move the pot unless it met with Long's approval.

The farmer who owned the crop led Long to a small outbuilding and showed him thirty-five bales ready to go.

"I need five thousand pounds," Long told the farmer, and said he needed it right away.

"Bueno," the farmer said.

If Long paid now, $10 a pound, the farmer would guarantee its delivery.

Long instructed him not to pack the rest of the pot so tightly. He pulled out the $50,000 he was carrying and handed over the cash to the young farmer.

Back in Santa Marta, with Miguel's help, Long found and was once more bewitched — willingly and that much more helplessly — by the headstrong, eager María. They swam at Bahía Profundo, ending the day in a coconut grove, where for what might have been the first time in his life, even as her bathing suit came off, Long denied himself indulgence in the exercise of immediate gratification. It was the first time he was able to recall, and it would be the last time for a while, that his racing libido was impeded by common sense. He feared that in taking what he assumed to be her virginity he would be taking an irretrievable step. This was Latin America, where casual behavior carried ceremonial freight, and he was unwilling to make the promise inherent in what she proposed. She was Raúl Gaviria's niece, and he was not yet prepared for the consequences of summarily breaking it.

Before leaving Colombia, Long received a visitor at the Irotama. A stranger, he appeared at the hotel unannounced with an endorsement of the soundness of Long's instincts. The man was tall and slim, easily as tall as Long, with fine European features. His hair was black, recently barbered, thick and apparently oiled, exhibiting the bright reflective properties of a carefully Simonized fender. He wore cotton slacks, a fitted silk shirt, no smile, a platinum wristwatch, and made-to-measure shoes. Just under forty, elegantly mannered, he struck Long as a cross between a classic matinee idol and a member of the recruitment arm of some Ivy League business school. Around his neck, he wore a thin gold chain, suspended from which was a piece of black coral carved in the image of a fish.

He said, "I am Raúl Gaviria."

His English was perfect and the black coral fish was a tuna.

The visit was extremely cordial, the conversation for the most part casual, and where formal, pleasantly so. Asked what kind of smuggling he did, Long described the airplane. Gaviria talked about boats. His visit lasted about twenty minutes, and then it was time to go.

"María is my favorite niece," he told Long. "I would hate to see anything happen to her." To see her heart broken, her sanctity violated, "This would be bad," he said.

Long was left nodding his head as Gaviria turned and let himself out.

"You fellas are lucky sons of bitches," the old-timer at the airport said. "I'm gonna help you this time, then I want you to go. And I don't ever want to see you back here again."

The sun was high in Georgia when Frank Hatfield and Will McBride returned to the small municipal airport west of Atlanta to discover that the DC-3 had been moved. The fixed-base operation was a one-man facility, and the seasoned FBO operator who was staring them down had a piece of advice for the pair.

"Next time you set down," he said, looking around, and seeing no need to lower his voice, "you clean up that plane."

Running a hand through his crew cut, he pulled a bent cigarette from his pocket, patted himself down for a match, and with the tip of his ring finger removed a trace of particulate matter from the corner of his brown, or left, eye. Batting his lids, he huffed air through his nose, evacuating his sinuses in passable imitation of a steam locomotive, massaged the side of his face, aimed his blue eye at the pilots, and said: "Bird's a mess."

They had landed the plane at about two-thirty that morning after dropping a load at Darlington, called a cab from the pay phone, and, exhausted, had checked into a nearby motel. They did not wake until noon. The FBO operator, an ex-military mechanic, had come upon the airplane when he showed up for work. He found palm fronds hanging from the air intake, opened the plane up, saw seeds and stems all over the cargo deck, towed the plane behind the hangar and vacuumed it out.

"You get yourself some more gaffer's tape, and do a better job of sealing the tarp. She'll fly another forty years, you boys keep her out of the trees."

And with that they were dismissed. Just one more good old boy with a hustle, they figured. But even in the absence of a scam of his own, which explained his not calling the law, his reluctance to turn them in would have come as no surprise. They had seen it happen before. After landing the busted load at West Point the previous spring, a friendly FBO operator in Virginia had obliged them, no questions asked, when they said, "You got to put her in a hangar." He did pose a rhetorical question: "So, I wonder what you guys are up to." As expected, the feds showed up inquiring about a cargo plane like the one seen landing at West Point. "I seen a plane like that," the FBO operator told them, "a couple of months ago. Never seen it since." As he spoke, the DC-3 was parked right there, behind the locked door of an aviation hangar no more than a few yards away.

Long attributed such acts of defiance to a protective instinct, a feeling of brotherhood among pilots that extended in varying degrees to the aviation community in general. He believed that all pilots had a similar streak. To say that all might do something similar is definitely stretching the point when the something in question is smuggling dope. That all

pilots might be able to see themselves doing it is probably true. What every pilot can probably imagine himself doing is manning a cockpit with his life on the line in support of some wild adventure, going up against the odds with the success of the operation riding on him. Or her.

Nobody has ever tried to fly who does not know how to dream.

On the third flight of the DC-3, moving the blond buds he bought in Aracataca, Long earned some $300,000. After that trip, he moved back to New York. He sold his two-year-old BMW, bought a new one for cash — a 3-liter sedan, top of the line, loaded, $17,000 — and rented a two-bedroom, corner apartment, facing southwest, on the twenty-seventh floor of a luxury building on East 68th Street in Manhattan. Convinced that he was smarter, sexier, and better-looking now than when he was the same guy without a half a million bucks, he was a lot of fun to be with. Women, he decided, loved him — he had a bag full of coke, a pocketful of money, and he had plenty of time to spare, time to sit there and listen to their life stories.

But Long, for all his erotic adventuring, was nonetheless susceptible to the seduction of true love. Because neither was likely, any time soon, to find anyone quite so trouble-some to be with, it was only a matter of months before he and Cherie were back together. Long's pot was selling in Ann Arbor for $350 a pound, and as Cherie discovered when she moved in with him, he had really learned how to spend money.

"I could just point to stuff in the window, and he'd get it for me," she would recall.

And sometimes for everybody else.

Long's visits to Tourneau on Madison Avenue had taken on the flavor of religious duty. He dropped in with regularity, the way other Catholics dropped into church. One trip was memorable for its piety. He was there to buy Cherie a Rolex, a Lady Day-Date President in 18-karat gold, an elegant product of what might be thought of as the school of applied jewelry, a variety of ladies activewear that addressed the simultaneous physics of precious metals and explosive decompression, tasteful, endlessly feminine, and certified accurate at up to something like thirty atmospheres. While Long was pondering the purchase, another Oyster Perpetual caught his eye, a Datejust for men with a rotating bezel in gold and stainless steel.

"And I'll take a dozen of those," he told the jeweler, picking up a thirty-eight-hundred-dollar watch for every member of his team.

The loss of the load — call it physical evidence — on the DC-3's maiden voyage was more than an inauspicious beginning in the operational life of the airplane. It was the beginning of the end. People at West Point remembered what they thought to be a DC-3 landing that day. There was nothing to tie it to the pot that had been found, but as an investigative lead it was sufficient to go on: a DC-3, no name and a tail number too small to read. (The registration number of an airplane, which might appear among other places on the tail of the aircraft, is sometimes called its N-number, the N designating an airplane of U.S. registry. At three inches high, the digits of the DC-3's tail number satisfied FAA regulations for aircraft operated at speeds within its limit.) Over the ensuing weeks FAA investigators and federal drug agents visited airports in the vicinity of West Point. The plane came under suspicion when they pulled its N-number off a refueling receipt that had been issued at one of them.

Shortly after their run-in with the FBO operator in Georgia, Hatfield and McBride were practicing touch-and-go's on a deserted airstrip in Florida, when the airplane was surrounded by squad cars, bringing it to a halt. Calling the pilots out of the plane, police threw them to the ground, put shotguns to their heads, and told them not to move. They opened the plane up and found nothing. Neither pilot had drugs on him, not a joint, not a gram. The two men were clean. They were thrown into the back of a patrol car, and sitting there, unattended, they listened to the radio — the police radio — over which the officer in charge, seated in another car, was querying the feds. Patched through to the government, he described the behavior that had raised his department's suspicions — an old cargo plane, a deserted runway — and reported the DC-3's N-number.

"Yeah, well they're suspected of smuggling," came the official reply, "but if there's nothing in the airplane, there's nothing we're interested in. You're free to let them go."

The DC-3 went on the FAA hot list.

The pilots, on purpose, had been bouncing the plane around the country. Georgia, Tennessee, Florida — it was based no place in particular, and rarely did it show up at the same place twice. The cover story everywhere was pretty much the same: ferry pilots working under one contract or another. It was in Knoxville, Tennessee, after the Florida incident, just before their fourth trip south, in the fall of 1976, that Allen Long discovered what it meant to be on the FAA hot list.

With a load waiting in Colombia, Long traveled to Knoxville to rendezvous with the plane. When he arrived at the general aviation terminal at Knoxville Metropolitan Airport, wearing a uniform that smacked convincingly of commercial aviation, the DC-3 was parked there, cargo door

open, chocks up under the wheels, gassed and ready to go. He stepped inside the office, where McBride and Hatfield were waiting, dressed exactly as he. Also waiting, ostensibly for the arrival of some private flight, were three men in civilian clothes, outfitted as concordantly as the smugglers. All had military haircuts, all wore black shoes, dark pants, and white, short-sleeved shirts.

"Will, what do you think?"

McBride said, "They're narcs."

"Frank," Long said, "those are feds."

"No question," said Hatfield.

And they could not have been friendlier.

"Nice little airplane," said one of them. "What are you fellows doing?"

Long gave the man the cover story McBride had come up with. They were ferrying rebuilt mining machinery parts between Knoxville and West Virginia.

"How long have you been doing that?" the man asked.

We know what you're fucking doing, pal.

"Oh, about six months."

"Interesting," the man said.

We're on to you.

He wished Long luck.

The atmosphere at the airport that day was pregnant with legal authority. At the end of the runway stood two non-descript Dodge sedans, idling with the doors open, and the two guys who stood beside the cars snapped photos of the smugglers' takeoff.

"Very nice," came word from the Knoxville tower as the DC-3 caught air. "A lot of people are interested in you guys today."

There it was again, the aviation fraternity.

"You're looking fine. High, wide, and handsome."

The airplane was running beautifully.

"Best of luck."

Before boarding the plane, Long had called Ann Arbor to tell Myerson the feds were watching them. They would have to abandon the plane after this flight, he said, bring it back, land it, unload it, and find somewhere to blow it up, maybe set fire to it, claim it was stolen.

That was the plan when the smugglers hit Colombian airspace the following morning. And Miguel said: "Sir, it has been raining here."

THE LORDS
AND THE NEW
CREATURES

12
DISPOSABLE BIRDS

By the end of 1976 smuggling aircraft were beginning to stack up over the Guajira like commercial flights over JFK. In the 130 miles between the Palomino River and Portete Bay, northeast of Riohacha, there was always an airplane somewhere. (Within a couple of years, traffic in the skies east of Santa Marta would take on the scope of the Berlin Airlift.) Vessels of all kinds, from oceangoing sailboats to heavy freighters, were being loaded every day at docks along the coast. And every day the Colombian government sent air patrols aloft to spend the drug-interdiction money it received from the United States on something that looked like drug interdiction. In its endeavor to cooperate with traffickers, the government expected at least a modicum of effort on the part of smugglers. Leeway was not unlimited.

Allen Long, sitting on the beach at Perico with the DC-3 undergoing cannibalization behind him, had a couple of hours at most to get his ass out of there. He and the pilots. And with any luck, the pot. On the beach, so that Long would have somewhere to put the ass in question, the Indians

had placed the first-class cabin seat ripped from the cockpit of the plane. But Long was not going to be comfortable no matter how much legroom he had. At that point, not even a complimentary cocktail would help. The humidity, holding in the wake of the rain, along with the escalating heat of the day — the same atmospheric conditions that had deprived the DC-3 of the lift necessary to clear the trees — conspired to make sitting in the sun just about unbearable. Looking out to sea now, Long was not studying the interesting mix of aquas and cobalt blues; he was not marveling at the rich variety of jellyfish. Not this time. Right now, he was wondering.

"What the hell am I going to do?"

The question, echoed by McBride, had gone without an answer for more than an hour, and Long's assertion that he was "working on it" was growing impoverished of the force of persuasion.

Well. Time to get classical.

Deus ex machina, literally translated, means "god from a machine," small *d* in *deus,* small *g* in god. The term is defined as: 1. *A deity in Greek or Roman drama who was brought in by stage machinery to intervene in a difficult situation. 2. Any unexpected, artificial, or improbable character, device, or event suddenly introduced to resolve a situation or untangle a plot.* Or, some dictionaries add: 3. *Anyone who unexpectedly intervenes to change the course of events.* As a dramatic technique the device was employed sparingly by Greek playwrights Aeschylus and Sophocles, but came into common use with Euripides. A purely mechanical contrivance, judged an unnatural stage convention, it invited criticism soon after its appearance on the theatrical scene in ancient Athens. Aristotle was particularly penetrating in his argument against its use. Some modern scholars maintain that its employment in classical

drama, rather than a sign of poor workmanship, was often deliberate and achieved striking effects. Contemporary writers are granted no such license. Its use today is unanimously deplored as a cheap, artificial trick or coincidence for conveniently resolving a story's action.

If Allen Long were a fictional character, that is how one would size up the fifty-foot bay shrimper that hove into view that morning while he was sitting on the beach. The boat came to a stop in front of him a few hundred yards offshore. As Long was trying to make sense of the vessel's appearance, over the side went a twelve-foot Zodiac, and into it a single crew member, who motored ashore, heading straight for the beach where Long was sitting. The man at the throttle was in his late thirties. He had black hair flecked with gray. Long took him for a Colombian fisherman. He came ashore, stepping out of the inflatable clad only in cutoff blue jeans, walked directly up to Long, stuck out his hand, and said, "You must be Allen. I'm Tony. I'm from Miami."

Out of nowhere, completely improbable — like the Virgin Mary utterly misused in a medieval mystery play.

"I buy this shit from the same guys you do," Tony explained, his pronunciation of English influenced by the phonetic habits of a Latin American Spanish that was different from that of the Colombians, abbreviated, more rapid, less self-consciously deliberate. His was the Spanish of the native Cuban. "They told me about you. You get all the good stuff. I ask them for the good pot, they say you have it all locked up. All the best marijuana, Allen gets that."

"Yeah, well, that's me," said Long.

Always nice to have a fan, he thought. But really, could this be happening?

Tony, anchored off Perico, had been waiting to load 20,000 pounds of commercial weed when the call came from the

Colombians telling him to lie offshore for a while. The DC-3 was coming in. Waiting for his own pot to be delivered to the beach, he had seen the plane return with smoke rising from the starboard engine. He had been watching when it crashed.

"So, look," he said, consulting his watch, nodding his head in the direction of the wreckage, "you want a ride home?"

"Well . . ." This could *not* be happening. "Man," said Long, "I don't know. Let me get . . . I have to talk to my guys."

He did have to talk to his guys. His instinct was to say no. The trip was well over a thousand miles by sea. But by whatever means available, he could not deny his partners the chance to escape. He laid it out for the pilots, who were understandably skeptical. Seven days at sea in the vessel Tony was sailing, a carvel-built shitbox of wood plank and questionable vintage, was duty not even the heartiest mariner would readily volunteer for. Hatfield and McBride waited for Long to weigh in.

"This is what I think," he said. "That guy has a radio. He can call the Colombians to come and get us out of here." Long felt the best odds on their getting back to the States still lay with the Colombians. "Hitching a ride with this guy," he said, "we run the risk of dying at sea." In Colombia, he argued, they were not facing the prospect of being killed.

"Not immediately anyway," McBride observed.

To which theory Hatfield applied the wisdom of the tax accountant.

"Defer."

They voted no on the boat, agreeing that the better bet was giving Miguel and Pablo the opportunity to make good on their word.

"What I *am* going to do," Long said, "is I'm going to

give him the pot. I'll pay him a hundred a pound to deliver it to Miami. If he makes it, it's a good arrangement. We can make two hundred a pound on it."

A comfort, no doubt, to the pilots. Never could it be said of Allen Long that he let life-and-death decisions distract him from the deal.

Tony, waiting for his own pot to show up on the beach, happily took aboard the bales removed from the DC-3. Running Long's pot out to his boat in the Zodiac took him several trips. Writing his phone number on the palm of Long's hand, he said he would see him in Miami. Long wished him bon voyage.

Two dugouts manned by Indians had motored into sight, dispatched by Ernesto's people in response to Tony's radio call. The Indians picked the smugglers up off the beach and ferried them to a tiny coastal village just east of the airstrip, one of numerous fishing communities on the Guajira given over to the marijuana trade.

"Where do you think they're taking us?" asked a nervous Will McBride.

Long, who was just as nervous, felt compelled to assume the image of confidence. These were Ernesto's people, he answered. Ernesto would call Miguel. Once Miguel was notified, he and Pablo would take it from there.

"Are you sure they can get us out?"

"Absolutely," Long lied.

The boats pulled into a tidal creek. The Indians tied them down in the grass. It was only fifty yards from there to the village, which comprised no more than a dozen huts and might as well have been deserted. In the early afternoon heat, nobody was moving. An adobe hut had been cleared for the smugglers. The Indians put up hammocks, brought the Americans food, and asked what else they wanted.

"Cigarettes . . ."

They got a carton of Marlboro: a product of Virginia.

"Beer . . ."

A case of Heineken: brewed in Holland.

"Marijuana . . ."

A bag of it: grown in Colombia.

"Cocaine . . ."

Two bags: extracted in Peru.

"Women . . ."

The Colombians drew the line.

"Can't have any of our women."

The smugglers were settled in, and Tony was on his way back to Florida, when on the beach at Perico the DC-3, undergoing disassembly, was spotted during a routine government overflight of the area. The Americans were instructed to stay in the hut. They were not to step outside for any reason, they were told. There were military patrols in the air. There were soldiers in the surrounding villages asking questions. What had happened, the army wanted to know, to the people who had been flying the plane that went down? Where were the pilots?

"What now?" McBride said.

And as meaningless as Long's answer might be, the question did not surprise him. Ambitious, aggressive, a guy who kicked ass to get things done, McBride was very much like Long that way. He took poorly to having no control over his fate. The revelation was Hatfield. Long cast a glance his way. He had been entirely wrong about Hatfield. Of the three of them, he was the coolest. He had asked only one question since the plane went down. On the beach, reporting to Long on the progress the locals were making in their demolition of the airplane — "I think they're going to bury it right here," he observed — he had simply asked, "What's

next?" When there were no instructions forthcoming, he had just kicked back and waited. He had asked no questions since then. Now he reclined, if not wholly relaxed, as fearless as one could be in the sinister circumstances, stretched out in a hammock, less like a pilot than an airline passenger.

As the day wore on, and collective anxiety turned inward, McBride gave voice to a question that had already passed through everyone's mind, a question that had taken up residence in the neighborhood earlier that day: Why, having come so far, had they been so stupid as to push their luck?

"We're rich, already, all of us," he said.

Hatfield just burst out laughing.

Long admitted his culpability, saying, "It was stupid to load the plane."

"It was stupid to come down here in the first place," said Hatfield. "If you hadn't been that stupid, we never would have done any of this. None of us would be rich. It takes balls to be that stupid. I got no regrets. I'm glad we did it. I'm happy."

And by now he was also drunk.

"I guess we learned a lesson," said Long.

McBride said, "You're right about that."

Hatfield nodded his head. The lesson was pretty clear.

He and Long said it together:

"What we need is a bigger *plane*."

While the fugitives were exercising bravado, their Colombian partners were doing everything necessary to get them out of the country. The plan was to hold them in the village until nightfall, then move them someplace safe, someplace where the Colombians could deploy more muscle, where they could throw some more men and some more guns on the job.

By sunset the three men were strung pretty tight, the fear

of capture exacerbated now by growing physical discomfort. They had been drinking and smoking, they had been snorting cocaine, and they had been unable to relieve themselves for a period of several hours, forbidden as they were to leave the adobe in the light of day.

They waited for darkness.

It came late.

"There's a man in the doorway," McBride said.

It was just before the sun went down that the Colombian soldier appeared. Neither particularly tall nor especially young, he was armed and impeccably tailored. His uniform was immaculate, his combat boots were shined, he wore a holstered semiautomatic pistol and the visored cap of a commissioned officer.

"Do you think he's grinning 'cause he's glad to see us?"

Overseas jails are not what popular fiction would lead most Americans to believe. They are significantly worse. The writer who has come closest to describing incarceration therein is probably Dante, who did it as early as the fourteenth century with *Inferno*. None of the three smugglers was conversant with the writings of the Italian poet, so each was entertaining his own particular vision of the hell he was facing when the soldier walked through the door.

He walked in carrying a battle rifle, and reached for Long with his left hand. His lips parted. His teeth flashed. And so did the jewelry on his wrist: a twenty-three-hundred-dollar gold Pulsar watch with a red screen and a push-button LED readout.

"*Gracias para el reloj,*" he said, thank you for the watch.

Which Long had bought in New York and had delivered on the second flight down. The watch identified him as the commander of the local military garrison. From every flight of the DC-3 this officer and his soldiers had reaped benefits

far in excess of the value of the timepiece. There in the half-light of their one-room quarters, their hammocks suspended over the dirt floor of the thatch-roofed hut, the *comandante* sized up the smugglers. It did not take combat infantry training for him to identify the fragrance fouling the atmosphere. He picked it up instantly. Adrenaline. The smell of it was thick in the air. The adobe walls ran wet with it.

"Don't be afraid," he said. "Everything will be good."

Soon Ernesto arrived, then Miguel and Pablo. Armando pulled up to the hut at the wheel of a jeep. The Americans climbed into the back of it, and were driven out of the village. At the Río Camarones highway bridge, a roadblock had been thrown up by the army. As the jeep approached, McBride, seated in the shadows behind Armando, saw the bodyguard's hand reach down below the driver's seat and grasp a .45 automatic. Standing at the checkpoint when the truck pulled up, in charge of the soldiers assigned to it, was the unit's commander, who inspected the truck himself, checking a twenty-three-hundred-dollar wristwatch as he passed the vehicle through.

Some forty-five miles west of the village the truck pulled onto a secluded piece of rural property on the banks of the Río Palomino.

"My *finca*," Pablo said.

Underutilized and overgrown, Pablo's *finca,* his country estate, was hardly magnificent. The property flourished on the edge of disrepair. But being isolated as well as unoccupied, it came highly recommended for safety. Hammocks were strung up for sleeping. The Americans were not to be alarmed, they were told, if they saw armed men walking by the windows. In the morning they could wash up in the river. They were warned against going near the Palomino at night, when local traffickers would be using the

waterway to ferry marijuana down from the mountains.

Once the Americans were settled in, Miguel and Armando departed for Barranquilla. Long gave Miguel a phone number to call in the States — in the absence of notification Reed would never leave the strip. The smugglers turned in early. Pablo told them to check their shoes for scorpions before putting them on in the morning, then climbed into his own hammock and bid them good night. He told them to ignore the bats.

Against the eventuality of a problem, the Americans always carried their passports when flying to Colombia. Under any circumstances, it would have been insane for them not to do so. They were flying over maybe five sovereign nations. To put it in Long's words, and to say the least, it would "raise a lot of eyebrows" if a cargo plane with three Americans aboard landed, say, in the Dominican Republic, and the pilots were found to be without passports: *Imagine our surprise! We were flying to Texas and somehow we ended up here!*

So the Americans were carrying passports, but the documents displayed no immigration stamps showing that the three men had entered Colombia, or more to the point, that they had entered Colombia legally. To exit the country, they first had to acquire the necessary entry stamps. Their passports, ex post facto, had to be officially stamped to show their arrival in order for them to leave. An international traveler with any experience would have told them that getting it done loomed as an undertaking of epic proportions, that pulling off something like that, even if it were legal, presented a bureaucratic mountain all but unclimbable anywhere in the world.

In Colombia it was like buying a pack of cigarettes. It just cost more.

A lot more. And it took some political juice. Miguel, of course, had money, and his money bought him plenty of influence, but neither would be sufficient to enable the government official in his pocket to pull off the trick more than twice, not without running the danger of exposing the trick altogether. Things were very tight right now, Miguel had been told. The DEA was pressuring the Colombians. U.S. drug agents were adamant — they wanted the pilots of that DC-3.

(A photo of the downed aircraft would show up in local newspapers two days after the crash. A couple of months later the surveillance photo would run in *High Times* magazine.)

"I can get only two," Miguel said of the stamps.

"What about me?" said Long.

It went without question that the pilots would be the first to reap the fruits of the bribery. Their passports would be stamped. They would go immediately. Of the operational ship that was going down, Long was clearly the captain.

"Soon," answered Miguel, assuring Long that once a couple of days had passed, and the heat had died down, getting the third stamp would present no problem.

In the morning food was supplied by women from the nearby village, which was located about half a mile away. The Americans ate well, bathed in the river, and spent the rest of the day drinking *aguardiente* and twelve-year-old Scotch and wallowing in the endless supply of drugs available on the Guajira. They had been given something to wear while one of the local women washed their clothes in the river. Among the clothing delivered to them were souvenir T-shirts, in limited circulation, imprinted with a smoking gun and the legend: SOY GUAJIRO, Y QUE!

Roughly translated, it meant "I am from the Guajira, you want to make something of it?"

They spent the next three days at the *finca*, McBride being the only one among them to show any impatience. One morning he watched a boy with a stick in his hand walking a small donkey in the direction of the sea. When the boy returned about three hours later the animal was covered with thirty-pound snook, to McBride's mind an excellent game fish, and the only tackle the smuggler saw was the sharp stick the youngster carried.

He said: "Next time I'll bring my gear."

The night Miguel returned with the passports, everyone at the ranch was wasted. They were sitting on the poured-concrete patio of the house with a campfire burning in the dirt nearby. Hatfield was so gone on coke, Johnnie Walker, and *aguardiente* that he was sitting on the edge of his chair leaning into a conversation Long and Pablo were having, serving in the capacity of a translator. Long spoke passable Spanish, Pablo slightly less passable English, and both of them were so loaded that they sat there nodding in agreement with Hatfield, grateful for the intervention of a translator who spoke no Spanish at all. McBride, staring at the fire as if in its flames there were dreams going up, was so drunk that had it not been for the coke he would certainly, and quite mercifully, have passed out by now. His condition was laboratory proof of the hypothesis held by many that cocaine's most pernicious effect on man is in promoting the effects of alcohol.

Miguel, handing their passports back, told the pilots: "You leave tomorrow."

It was late in the evening when Long, his natural bonhomie and volubility amplified, his rheumy gaze intensified, by the collective good cheer and his massive intake

of dope, smiled at Miguel and said, "I have to tell you something."

Miguel's eyes were glassing over as he drank to catch up with the others.

"When we met," Long said, "I told you I had been doing DC-3s for years."

"I remember," Miguel said.

"I had never done one," Long admitted. "Ever. I was lying."

Miguel laughed. They all did.

"That's okay," he said.

Long smiled and said, "I'm sorry." And then he told the truth. "No, I'm not," he said, and laughed again. And everyone else laughed that much louder. Long was really stoned now. Miguel poured another drink.

He said, "You asked the same of me and Pablo. How many airplanes. No?"

"Yes," said Long, "I did." And now his smile began to fade. "'So many I cannot count,' you said."

Miguel looked at Pablo: *"Sí?"*

"Sí," said Pablo.

Pablo, so buzzed on flake that he was grinding his teeth, had to close his eyes to make room for his grin.

Miguel turned to Long, and said, "We did not do even one."

"What?"

Pablo was in stitches, he was snorting with laughter, tickled with pride.

"Not one," said Miguel.

Long was incensed that Miguel had lied. The others found it hilarious.

Encouraged by their laughter and a nod from the beaming Pablo, Miguel carried his confession to its high-spirited

conclusion. It was not simply airplanes that had been new to him, he said. Before Long and Reed showed up in Barranquilla, Miguel now revealed, he and Pablo had never smuggled marijuana at all. "My father can't do this, but we can," Miguel had answered, when Pablo approached him that day about working with the Americans. "I know all the people my father knows. I will do it." And he did. He did it never having done it before. And he had carried the charade a step further, engineering the appearance of Don Julio, a friend of his father's, who fit what he knew to be Long's profile of "the man."

"I don't believe it," Long said, his outrage giving way to admiration. "Don Julio?"

Yes, admitted Miguel. They had even fabricated the gringo policeman whom Don Julio had claimed to have killed.

"You made him up!" said Long.

Yes, Miguel said. He was as bogus as Don Julio himself.

Long, the object of everyone's laughter, surrendered to the beauty of it all.

"*Et tu*, Pablo?" he said.

Everyone was having a great time now. Perhaps it was in the spirit of brotherhood, or maybe it was the *aguardiente*, but Hatfield had something to say. He stared at his feet, a picture of penitence, everything but sackcloth and ashes.

"I said I'd flown 3s all over the West. I told you I had thousands of hours in 3s . . ."

"Don't . . ."

"When we left Long Beach, I had eight."

At midnight the pilots were smuggled off the ranch.

The immigration official on Miguel's payroll had warned him not to move the Americans through the airport at Barranquilla. In Santa Marta the following morning they boarded a domestic flight to Bogotá. They flew from there

to Caracas and then on to Paris, before eventually catching a flight home. Unlike Long, McBride and Hatfield both enjoyed relatively stable relationships with the women in their lives. Before the two left France, they were joined in Europe by their girlfriends, and spent some of their money as tourists, returning to the States at the speed of sound aboard the Concorde.

It was in one of his more serene moments that the excitable Pablo Cepeda, who had come to be known affectionately as El Demonio to his pot-smuggling partners, tipped Long off to the fact that María wanted to see him. The two men were sitting in the darkness with a campfire going, twisted on Scotch and the latest delivery of uncut cocaine, when Pablo broke the news.

"She asks for you, she wants to be with you."

Long could not resist allowing the thought of it to carry him away. Here, at the heart of a true adventure, danger and romance had just converged. All of a sudden he was more than a smuggler, more than a pirate, he was a leading man.

"María loves you," Pablo said.

All of a sudden he was the handsome hero of some swashbuckling, bodice-ripping tale of derring-do.

"She has told everyone she is going to marry you."

All of a sudden . . . Hmm. Marriage was a prospect Long had not entertained. He did not remember bringing it up. This was the first he had heard of it. Could he have mentioned something like that? He did love María. He loved her, in a way. But what could he have said to her that she might have taken for a proposal?

Yeah. What was there in the longing of a young Latin

American woman, the trusting, treasured daughter in a traditional Roman Catholic family, with whom a man had lain naked, whispering under the stars, that could possibly lead her to believe that a wedding was in the works?

"She looks for you," said Pablo.

When María had come to Pablo to ask where her lover was being hidden, Pablo had remained silent. Mindful of security, Pablo was also a realist in matters of the heart. The demon in Pablo Cepeda, the turmoil that had earned him his nickname, owed much of its intensity to the suffering that romance had inflicted upon him. Pablo was in love with his wife, a medical doctor, a career woman, whom he admired as much as he adored. More than anything he wanted her respect. And it was the one thing she was unwilling to give him. Pablo's wife was a *cachaca,* a native of interior Colombia, her conservative manner, her mode of dress, and her overall sophistication standing her in visible contrast to the typical *costeña.* She was unhappy and intellectually unfulfilled living on the coast. And with Pablo resisting repeated pleas that they relocate to the city, she had moved back to Bogotá without him. It had left him a broken man. Traveling to Bogotá regularly, he spent time with her and their children, but he could not, as a man, move in with her. They could not be seen to be living under *her* roof, his masculinity would not allow it. As it was, he had become a laughingstock among his friends in Santa Marta, ridiculed on the coast as a man who could not control his wife.

It was Miguel, the romantic, who eventually gave Long up.

Armando was behind the wheel of the stake-bodied truck that pulled up to the ranch the last night Long was in residence. Miguel stepped out through the passenger door, and María stepped out after him. She was wearing a hat with the brim turned down and matching shirt and trousers of

the kind associated with the stalking of missionaries, a beau monde rendition of the field khakis in evidence when Stanley presumed to meet Livingstone. Walking into the light of the fire, immaculate, beatific, like some fashion-forward vision of the Virgin, she removed the hat, her hair dropping like syrup poured from a jar and funneling in the region of her seventh cervical vertebra, and she threw herself into the arms of her intended. Long's excitement at seeing her was exceeded only by his incredulity, which was evident in the look he cast Miguel's way.

Miguel shrugged, spread his arms, and raised his hands palms-forward like a man submitting to arrest.

"She has asked her uncle to help us get you out of the country," he said.

And the look Long was giving him suddenly changed, Long's face assuming the expression known to speakers of every language to mean: Whoa, dude, back up.

He said, "I thought that was taken care of."

Miguel shook his head. "The situation is growing dangerous." They would not be waiting for the immigration stamp. "We leave tonight," he said.

María, the warmth of her eyes softening the urgency in her voice, said, "You will go through Sabana Rubia."

Again Long looked to Miguel.

There was a place in the mountains, Miguel said, where no gringo had ever been. Few Colombians dared go there. Not even he himself had been there. A valley in the Sierra de Perija in the Eastern Cordillera, it was known as Sabana Rubia. It was southeast of Villanueva at the southern tip of the Guajira. More marijuana was cultivated there than anywhere in Colombia. Long would be smuggled out of the country by way of the valley, up through the high pass, and into Sabana Rubia following routes controlled by traffickers.

"Raúl Gaviria," said Miguel, "has offered his help. He said, 'I will help Allen because I love María.'"

And now it was time to leave. Pablo's cousin Ricardo, who lived in Caracas, would have people waiting to meet Long at the Venezuelan border. They would lead him to Maracaibo. Ricardo would obtain the necessary documentation, the stamps and visas required for Long to fly home from there.

"It is far and the way is dangerous," Miguel said. "But Raúl Gaviria has sent his man ahead to Villanueva to meet us. He will know María."

"María? She can't go with us."

"Without me . . ." said María.

"You're not going. I won't allow it."

"Without me, Del Río will not take you through the pass."

Del Río: her uncle's man in Villanueva, said Miguel. It was he who would insure their safety.

"And now we must go."

He instructed Armando to collect any evidence of Long's stay at the ranch. Long and María were hustled into the back of the truck, where they lay on a blanket over a bed of banana fronds, under more of which they were hidden. For the next eight hours they remained there under the leaves, as the truck with Miguel and Armando up front wound along the coast and up through the backcountry, making for Villanueva, 170 miles away. They arrived at Del Río's house just before dawn.

Like Raúl Gaviria himself, his lieutenant Del Río was a man of Spanish blood, his complexion fair, his bearing aristocratic. His wife was Indian, his household alive with children, and staffed with men of indeterminate age who under indigenous costume carried nine-millimeter submachine guns. Long and the others spent the day at the house, setting

out for Sabana Rubia just before midnight escorted by Del Río and two of the bodyguards in his employ. Following a dry riverbed, they drove up into the foothills of the Sierra de Perija. They abandoned the truck at three A.M., and leaving Armando behind, proceeded on foot for another two hours, until they reached the mule station from where they would stage their two-day journey across the mountains to Venezuela.

Like a stagecoach stop or similar outpost conjured up intact off the American frontier, the mule station marked the foot of a trail snaking out of the mountains, the first sign of life as one descended out of the clouds at the end of a day-long journey. Still hours from civilization, it was overseen by a man named Augusto, home to him and his family.

Augusto was in his late thirties, thickset and swarthy, his hair waved close to his head, his hands showing the calluses of a man who worked hard for a living. Under his wool *ruana*, the traditional Colombian poncho, he wore the off-white cotton pants of the native and a bright orange T-shirt old enough to qualify as one of those CIA giveaways that continued to haunt the Third World. His sandals had been fashioned from rubber tire treads and leather, and his smile was so big you could park in it.

"Five mules," Del Río told him. "Hurry."

But before leaving, the guests would meet the children, and there would be *arepas* and coffee served by Augusto's wife. Ordinarily there would be little sense of urgency at this point, but after leaving Villanueva, as they drove through the night, the smugglers had hit a roadblock. A four-thousand-dollar bribe had bought them passage, but was unlikely to buy silence. They had to assume that government troops would be on their trail soon. The mules were

saddled, and the party set off, Augusto in the lead, followed in order of ascent by Miguel, María, Long, and Del Río. The Indian bodyguards made the climb on foot.

The distance from Villanueva, which they had departed six hours before, to the headwaters of the Guasare River, which rose on the Venezuelan side of the cordillera, was approximately fifteen miles as the crow flies — after the crow's altimeter started pushing 10,000 feet. Long asked how many hours they must ride before they reached Sabana Rubia.

"*Cuántas horas,* Augusto?"

Augusto raised an index finger, then pointed to the rising sun, and describing an arc from east to west, threw out a number in Spanish.

Long was confused, laughing more at himself than at Augusto when he told Miguel, "I thought he said seventeen hours."

"Pay no attention," said Miguel, smiling. "He does not own a watch."

The journey to the mule station at the southeastern foot of the trail would take exactly seventeen hours. And that would bring an end to the first day's ride. It would be almost sunset on the second day before they reached the border.

For seventeen hours they zigzagged up the mountain, moving from microclimate to microclimate, from the dry brush of the foothills into a lush, tropical rain forest, where monkeys and parrots flourished. Up from there through the high desert, they ascended into the coniferous range, where the path was strewn with pine needles and the air was thin. Across rock, snow, and boulder, they inched through canyons overlooking glass-blue lakes, in the still, icy waters of which were reflected the distant glaciers of the Sierra Nevada.

The trail in places was no more than eighteen inches wide, marked by a switchback every few feet. The mules moved two feet left, then two feet right, inching their way up the cliffs, turning to face back down the mountain even as they climbed it. Within inches of the mules' hooves were drop-offs of a thousand feet.

Periodically there would be the tinkling of a bell, and the ascending party would be forced to find a cutout and pull off the trail as a burro train loaded with marijuana descended toward them. The burros, each one packed with more than a hundred pounds of pot, as much as the creature could carry, crab-stepped down the trail, heading for the mule station at Villanueva. Around the ridge would come the first burro, then the next, and the next, hopping, sidling down the slope, lashed together, the animals stacking up behind each other as the trail narrowed and reversed itself. Long tried counting the burros of the first train he encountered. He stopped counting at eighty, estimating there to be at least half as many more again. Well over a hundred burros — maybe 15,000 pounds of pot — all driven down the mountain by one small boy with a switch.

Shortly before midday, the bodyguards detoured. Turning down the mountain at a point where the trail divided, the Indians descended into a river valley, leaving the other members of the party to continue straight up.

Long asked, "Where are they going?"

"They are going where we are, sir," Miguel said.

"They're going the long way," said Long, watching them take off downhill.

"They will meet us later."

The heavy weapons and ammunition necessary to defend the pass were hidden somewhere below, and the bodyguards had set off to retrieve the hardware, Miguel explained.

Following an alternate route, they would rejoin the party farther up the trail.

"They are going the long way," Miguel said, "but they will be there first."

"How's that?" Long wanted to know.

"Because," Miguel answered, "they are much faster than the mules. The mules have to rest, sir," he reminded Long, laughing. "The Indians do not."

They rested the mules at noon. The temperature had reached 90 degrees on the high, arid plateau. They dismounted at the site of a dry wash where mesquite, desert grass, palms, and other vegetation sprouted in the absence of any evidence of water. And here for the next two hours they would wait out the midday sun.

Augusto began digging a hole. He crouched on his knees, and using only his hands, he dug about two feet down, creating a depression in the arroyo that measured maybe a yard in diameter. He lined the hole with leaves from a banana tree growing in the creek bed. The indentation resembled the head of a drum in a Caribbean steel band. He stood up, clapped his hands clean, and walked off to take a nap in the shade.

About forty-five minutes later Long was roused from his siesta by the sound of the mules lapping water. The humans, as thirsty as the animals, joined the mules at the edge of the pool that Augusto had created. The water percolating into it was neither cool nor sweet. But it was pure and it was water, and everybody drank.

It was late in the afternoon when Augusto, leading the way up the mountain, stopped the mules again. He raised his hand, turned in his saddle to face the others, and pointed to the cliffs below. Long alone was surprised. An army patrol was climbing the mountain four or five hours behind them.

Clearly, word had been passed that an American was on the trail.

"What will they do if they see us?" he said.

Augusto essayed a smile, exposing a wide and crooked array of gold teeth.

Del Río answered for him.

"They will make sure they do not catch us," he said.

And Augusto told Long why.

"Because," he said, when Long inquired, "we have more guns than they have."

"The army," Del Río confided, "has never come through the pass."

Long was unsure of what Augusto said next. Assuming it to be a statement of corroboration, he looked to Miguel for a translation.

"Augusto says if they entered it, they would never leave it," Miguel explained.

Perhaps more than Long needed to hear.

"We will kill them, they know that," Del Río confirmed.

Yeah. Thanks for spelling it out.

Long was unfailingly fascinated by what he heard and saw in the course of the journey. Finding Augusto to be a boundless source of information and entertainment, he was gratified by the chance to reciprocate, to reward Augusto's fascination, when Augusto rode up beside him to get a better look at his watch.

"*Es oro?*" Augusto asked.

"*Sí,*" said Long, happy to confirm for Augusto that the Rolex was indeed gold.

"*Puro?*"

Yes, Long said, pure gold.

Augusto raised his eyebrows, favorably impressed.

"*Cuánto vale ese reloj?*" he asked, how much did it cost.

"*Diez mil,*" ten thousand, said Long.

"*Diez mil pesos,*" Augusto said, with a whistle.

"Dollars," Long told him.

"*Dolares!*"

"Yes, my friend."

This inspired an animated soliloquy on Augusto's part. Delivered in rapid Spanish, it had Miguel and Del Río laughing and Long entirely confused.

"Why is he so excited?" Long asked. "What did he just say?"

Augusto could not take his eyes of the watch, and now he was talking to himself.

"He is calculating," said Miguel. "He thinks perhaps it is worth more money to kill you and take the watch, than to take you over the mountain."

Now and then, in the course of the journey, Augusto, for Long's amusement, cast a surreptitious glance at the watch and narrowed his eyes, playing the part of a man doing arithmetic in his head.

At sunset they reached the pass, and to Long it was immediately clear why the army had never attempted to breach it. The trail passed through a canyon that ran for about half a mile, ten feet wide at its widest point, walled in by hundred-foot cliffs. From the far side of the canyon as few as three men armed with rifles could hold off a well-equipped military patrol, the ultimate body count limited by nothing more than the defenders' ammunition supply. Only by way of some high-performance, high-altitude parachute drop could an army penetrate such a stronghold. But marijuana trafficking would never be enough to justify trying, even if doing so were within the capacity of the Colombian military. Beyond a fundamental survival mentality on the part of the typical soldier, a characteristic reluctance would reveal itself.

The Colombian soldiers on the trail were men from the villages. A guerrilla incursion was one thing — they would do what they had to do — but to pursue a difficult, determined mission that required their eradicating the sole source of income of people just like them was not what they had signed up for. They climbed the mountain. They did not enter the canyon.

Augusto, emerging from the pass, was greeted by an Indian holding an automatic rifle. Draped in a woolen *ruana* with a *mochila* slung over his shoulder — in the woven pouch indigenous to the region, he was probably carrying ammo — the gunman embodied a rather effective tourist office advertisement for the country's native handicrafts. The M-16 was imported. Standing with him, protecting the pass, were the two Del Río bodyguards who had detoured off the trail with submachine guns earlier in the day. Now, in addition to their Ingrams, they had six automatic rifles and enough ammunition to slow down the cast of a Cecil B. DeMille movie. Under the weight of the weapons and cartridges, the Indians, going the long way, and traveling there by foot, had beaten the mules to the pass by three hours.

As darkness fell, the party descended into the valley, a high, tropical grassland in which, Long had been told, farmers produced between four and five million pounds of marijuana a season. From the cliffs he could see, flickering below, the distant light of campfires spread out for miles. Still hours away, these were the home fires burning outside the huts of the pot farmers of Sabana Rubia. The party traveled until midnight. The air was cool when Augusto led the others into a clearing in the forest on the eastern slope of the range, to a small stand of thatch-roofed huts where several men sat surrounding a fire, drinking *aguardiente* and cooking a goat. Here the party would spend the night.

Long, dismounting after seventeen hours on a mule, had difficulty walking upright, and was far too tired to do anything but sleep. He and María were handed blankets, a lean-to was cleared for them, and the weary couple expended the last of their energy trying to shake the blankets free of fleas. Walking off to relieve himself before turning in, Long, looking out over the valley, urinating into the clouds, was startled to hear coughing behind him, and turned to find his safety assured — it was Colombia, after all — by the presence of a bodyguard standing in the moonlight with an assault rifle cradled in his arms. Known as El Tigre, he was Del Río's man, and Long had a question for him.

"I am told there is marijuana everywhere," he said, zipping his jeans. "Can you show me where it is?"

"*Aquí,*" said El Tigre, waving to indicate the forest. "It is here. There is marijuana everywhere."

"Yes, but I don't see it," said Long. "All I see is the trees. Where is the marijuana?"

"My friend," said Del Río, stepping out of the darkness, "it is all around you, the marijuana, everywhere you look. In the morning you will see."

And in the morning he did see.

The forest itself was marijuana, the jungle in which he stood. It grew to the height of trees, ten, fourteen, sixteen feet high, rising on stalks that were five inches thick. Everywhere he looked he saw it, choking the hillside, growing wild. He stood in the very shade of it. Flowering from the seeds that had been spilled over a decade as marijuana passed through the camp, shooting up coarse and fibrous, it grew undisturbed, a thriving profusion of *Cannabis sativa*. Visible beyond the camp, here in its natural habitat, the weed, propagating as part of the region's native vegetation, had been overgrowing the mountain for ages. The fact that

it was all but unsmokable — growing untended, it was suitable only for hemp — made the sight of it nonetheless breathtaking.

"You've got to be kidding," he said.

"Come with me," said Miguel.

He led Long out of the clearing, walked him to the edge of the cliff, and waited for the clouds to move. Through the mist, as the clouds scattered, the valley rose into view.

"Look," he said.

And there it was.

Long had never seen anything like it. He had never dreamed it even existed. There in the valley, on terraced hillsides, as far as the eye could see, the red and gold of cultivated marijuana carpeted Sabana Rubia, from horizon to horizon. In every direction, the crop undulated, seemingly into infinity, its colors coming alive as it absorbed the light of the early morning sun.

"Yes, the other ridge, too," said Miguel.

The other ridge, five miles away — cultivation ran as far as the river, Del Río had told him.

Allen Long was gazing upon the largest marijuana field in the hemisphere, possibly the largest on the planet. And for just a fleeting instant, perhaps, in his own much smaller world, in a small pocket of civilization living on Jimmy Buffett time — a dazed population of freak-disciples whose gospel was spread by Cheech & Chong, a flock of wasted acolytes who were "waiting for Dave" — for just a fleeting instant, perhaps, Allen Long felt what Vasco Balboa must have felt when he ascended that final mountain peak and was met by the sight of the Pacific.

"More marijuana than you will ever need, sir."

Long was at a loss for words — as hard as that is to believe, as hard as that was for *him* to believe. For a full

moment he could think of nothing to say. And finally it came to him.

He said, "I want it all."

Later that morning he entered the valley. As far as he knew, he was the first American to do so. This was impenetrable Colombia. The farmers of Sabana Rubia had never seen a gringo before. They were poor people, typically barefoot. Probably the most expensive, single material good a family owned here was an automatic weapon. They wanted to show Long their marijuana, and as he traversed the valley, they did.

Passing slowly through the fields, the party pressed on, four of them now, Augusto, Miguel, María, and Long, escorted by the Indian bodyguards. Del Río had turned back that morning, heading home on foot. They reached the Río Guasare at about four that afternoon. Long and María drifted off. As he was bathing in the river, Long heard Miguel call his name.

"Allen, Ricardo's man is here."

"Vaya con dios, lindo."

María turned back at the river, returning home with Miguel.

Long traveled for another two days, making the journey through Venezuela on a mule supplied by Ricardo's people. Augusto, in protection of Raúl Gaviria's interests, which were invested in the protection of Long, made the trip with him, seeing him all the way to Maracaibo. By the time he reached Caracas, it had been exactly seven days since Tony's boat had left the beach.

13
SMOKE ON THE WATER

Tony A., that capital letter being the surname by which everyone knew him best, was a rogue in the Golden-Age-of-Hollywood mode, "a throwback to another age," in the words of those who worked with him. A modern-day buccaneer, he gave new life to the term debonair. Tony was an authentic lady-killer with a perpetual, irresistible sparkle in his eye and a charm about him few could resist. He could just as effortlessly knock you off as sweep you off your feet — you and maybe six guys at the bar — and do it without losing the smile. Married to a highly regarded Miami lawyer, Tony, with eight children at home and as many girlfriends on the side, was as cavalier with his marriage vows as he was nonchalant in the conduct of business. Assuring his wife that he would never allow another woman to come between them, he promised her that when he fooled around, it would always be with several. Similarly, on every financial deal, he played both ends against the middle, unable really to help himself and unabashed in the face of discovery: "Hey this is the way we do business here. This is the Cuban way."

Like other Cuban-Americans in the upper echelon of the South Florida dope trade, Tony had honed his prodigious smuggling skills with the support of the Central Intelligence Agency, which had provided his covert operations training and continued to back his activities. The son of a lawyer, Tony had been a university student in Havana in the late 1950s when he, like many young, middle-class Cubans, took to the country's Escambray Mountains, later to be joined there by Fidel Castro's guerrilla forces, and fought to overthrow the dictatorship of Fulgencio Batista. Along with numerous other revolutionary officers, he was dispatched by Castro to a reeducation camp when the insurgency succeeded and the cigar-smoking dictator-in-waiting stepped out of the Communist closet. Escaping to the States upon his release, Tony was one of some 2,000 exiles recruited, trained, and outfitted by the CIA as part of the expeditionary force whose dream of retaking the island died an ignominious death at the Bay of Pigs in 1961.

With the failure of the invasion, this cadre of Cuban exiles continued to carry out covert operations for the agency, not only in Cuba but around the world (and not only internationally but domestically, as when they burglarized offices at Washington's Watergate complex in 1972), and they comprised the operational vanguard of the numerous anti-Castro groups that would control the political thermostat in Miami for the next forty years. Their unique brand of government service presupposed a lot of specialized, paramilitary training, and brought with it a significant layer of insulation against criminal investigation.

The drug business was a natural place for their talents.

Acting on behalf of the government and carrying no identification to prove it, they lived undercover in Florida, constantly training and hauling equipment. Discharging

their duties would have been virtually impossible without official cooperation within the Miami police department. Tony's CIA liaison there was a politically powerful lieutenant named Jack, who, when he retired to practice law, continued to oversee and coordinate not only the exiles' government-sanctioned work but their criminal activities as well.

Of the Cuban-born drug traffickers who worked with Tony, many were CIA-trained; of the gringos who worked with him, most were former cops. (Some were still on the job.) Allen Long's arrival on the scene in Miami would result in a kind of weird, dope-dealing dialectic, a synthesis marked by the coming together of ex-cops and ex-hippies in a marriage of contradictions brokered by government-sponsored anti-Communists. It was a dialectic driven by a materialism free of all philosophical freight. What brought the counterculture, the cops, and anti-Communists to the same conjugal bed was nothing inherent in the mind-altering chemistry of the drugs. It was the money. Forget the antiwar movement, the war on crime, forget Castro. These boys had a business to run.

Long arrived at Kennedy Airport in New York on a direct flight from Caracas, and the first thing he did, from the first public phone he hit after clearing Customs, was call Tony at the Miami phone number that the Cuban a week earlier had written on the palm of his hand.

"Tony, this is Allen."

"Who?"

"Allen. You know, the guy you met on the beach."

"Hey, brother! How are you? I was kind of hoping you weren't coming back." Tony broke into a laugh, and said, "No, man, I'm just kidding. Good to hear from you. Where are you?"

Long said, "I'm in New York."

"Well, I was getting ready to sell this stuff. You better come down here."

Long flew to Michigan, arranged for transshipment of the pot to Ann Arbor, and flew from there to Miami with the cash necessary to secure it. He checked into a room at the Coconut Grove hotel, called Tony, who met him there, and before getting down to business, listened to Tony describe the adventure he and the pilots had missed on the boat trip back.

Tony had set sail for Colombia with two crewmen, one of whom, a kid named Nick, had never been to sea before; Nick, a relative of Tony's partner, had come along for the money and a taste of the outlaw life. The other crew member, Dwight, was a marine mechanic whose responsibility was to keep the boat running. The fun began after the boat, steaming home from the Guajira, had cleared the Mona Passage. (The Windward Passage offered the more direct route home, but would have put Tony too close to Cuban waters, where if the boat were stopped for any reason, his arrest would have led to almost certain execution.) Just below the Tropic of Cancer the boat hit a tropical depression. The wind was blowing maybe 55 knots, and the boat, pitching and heeling in thirty-foot seas, started taking on water. The engine quit. And so had Dwight — having overdosed on Quaaludes the day before, the mechanic lay unconscious. The boat, with no power, was unable to make headway, and fell victim to the storm that much more perilously. The storm was so furious and the turbulence it caused so disorienting that young Nick found himself doing what mariners throughout history have done when hit by inescapable seasickness sufficiently virulent to deprive them of reason. He jumped overboard. Or tried to. Tony caught him, grabbed him before he went over the rail,

hit him hard enough to knock him out, and lashed him to the anchor winch on the bow.

Tony fought the storm alone.

With passage of the storm Tony finally got the engine running, but the bay shrimper by then had undergone irreparable damage, and was taking on water faster than the bilge pumps could empty it. With the boat slowly sinking beneath him, he finally established radio contact with the smaller vessels scheduled to meet him off the Florida coast. He managed to off-load all but a few of the bales before the boat went down. He had a bale in his arms when he stepped off the tip of the bow onto the deck of a Bertram, and the bay shrimper went under.

Long, straight from Sabana Rubia, had no trouble buying the story. Not that there was any reason to doubt it beyond the sheer hair-raising nature of it — years later, he would come to appreciate that his own tales sounded just as wild. Tony, as it happened, was a wellspring of fantastic stories. They always proved to be true, and always taxed the imagination, as did those of the other Cuban exiles Long eventually met through him. One, an underwater demolition expert named Hector, told Long of swimming alone one night from the hatch of a U.S. submarine into Havana Harbor, where, before swimming back, he blew up a Soviet PT boat. A curious collection of characters, Tony and his friends, at one time or another, all seemed obliged for some reason to volunteer alibis for the day of the Kennedy assassination in Dallas, and all appeared to know at least two other guys whose alibis did not stand up.

These were the people with whom Allen Long was about to do business.

"So what about the pot?" Long said, after listening to Tony's story.

"It's here."

"Then let's go get it."

"It's here," said Tony, "but I don't have it."

"Well, okay," Long said, "who's got it?"

"One of my partners has it," Tony said. "We have to make arrangements with him. That's how you're going to get it."

Long said he was prepared to pay for half the pot in front. Tony said it was up to his partners whether Long, in that case, got more than half the load. A meeting was set for noon the following day at a crab house in Fort Lauderdale. When Long arrived, two of Tony's partners were with him. One, a guy named Lonnie, was a former Miami police officer. The other was a character named Virgil.

"So, you're the guy with the airplane," Virgil said.

Virgil was a native of one of those small Bahamian islands where all the locals of English ancestry make do with the same last name. His family had immigrated to the Florida Keys, settling there, impoverished, with their rural roots intact. He had gone barefoot for most of his youth, and as a citizen now of the Conch Republic, he managed to get by without wearing shoes except on formal occasions. This, apparently, was not one of them. At the meeting in Fort Lauderdale, it was he who did the talking, and the temper of his remarks signaled a significant atmosphere shift — a forecast of the heavy weather that would overhang any business Long conducted in Miami.

Allen Long's appearance in Florida coincided with a cultural sea change, and in the swift and turbulent race of things its measure was hard to read. He arrived on the waters of a rising tide in the marijuana trade, and on its currents, beneath the surface of his ability to predict them, things like peace, love, and music were about to be washed away in the undertow.

In many ways, Long's arrival in Miami was like Mick Jagger's arrival at Altamont — Long had no way of knowing it yet, but Woodstock Nation was dead.

"We have your marijuana," Virgil said, "but you owe us a hundred dollars a pound for Tony bringing it in."

Tony had prevailed upon Virgil and Lonnie to free up the entire load on the promise of a second payment from Long after the pot was sold, informing his partners that the Colombians had given their personal assurance of Long's honesty.

"Okay," said Long. "Let's go pick it up."

"Well, where's the money?"

"I'll give you the money," said Long, "let's get the pot."

"No offense," said Virgil, "but we don't know you. Now, we have the pot, and we can keep it, nothing you can do about that, so if you want it back, give us the money first."

Three strangers — none of whom, Long was guessing, knew the words to "Purple Haze," all of whom, just by the look of them, were a good bet to be gun owners — insisting that he hand over a briefcaseful of cash. And no guarantee that he would get the pot.

Long had to think it over.

Hell . . .

"Here are the keys to my car," he said. "The money's in the trunk."

Virgil did not bother to check. Sliding an ignition key across the table, he said, "It's in the truck outside." He described a cab-over camper parked behind the crab house. "We want the truck back tomorrow."

Long did not bother to check either. He drove away with the load. When finally he opened the back of the truck, the marijuana was there. But the marijuana was not his. It was Tony's commercial Colombian.

Virgil just laughed in his face when Long confronted him on it.

"You didn't really think you were going to get the good stuff back, did you? That's gone," he said. "You're not going to see it again. This is what you get, that's it."

The news came as no surprise in Ann Arbor.

"Yeah, well, I guess that was to be expected," said Myerson. "Just go back and see if you can buy more. Tell them we want another two thousand pounds at the same price to make up for it. See what they say." This, of course, was where the discussion with Tony was headed anyway. "What's important is to see how many more pounds we can buy," Myerson told Long. "Here's the message . . ."

Tony, of course, played dumb when Long complained of the switch.

"Is that what happened?" he said, shaking his head. "Oh, that's too bad, I didn't know that."

Long said, "This is not right, Tony."

Tony laughed. "You think this is a game? You think I'm going to get sideways with my partners over this? Forget it."

Long, in fact, was prepared to forget it. "Let's go somewhere from here," he said. "Let's make this thing work better for both of us."

"If you want more, you'll have to talk to my partners," said Tony. "They'll want a certain price for it."

"We don't want more," said Long, and now it was his turn to laugh. "We don't want more, Tony, we want it all."

Long had spent no more than a few hours with these guys, and he knew exactly what they were doing. First, they were dealing with each other, so naturally they were getting ripped

off, and getting ripped off on a regular basis. They were probably paying the Colombians $25 a pound and selling the pot for $150. And they were moving the product piece-meal, fronting out a few hundred pounds at a time and waiting for the money to come back. Every load was full of problems, real, imagined, often invented, and there were always disputes. Given the quality-control vacuum on both ends of the line, they were probably collecting about two thirds of the money due them, and they were likely to be paying the Colombians about three fifths of the money they owed. No matter what was said on the beach at Perico, the Colombians could be sure that they would never be paid in full: "Oh, it was full of seeds," they would be told, or something like that. They could be sure to end up with a minimum of 20 percent less than agreed on.

In Miami, with numerous people involved, none of whom trusted the others, every man was operating separately, each keeping his share of the load, searching for reliable customers, fronting to a brother, a cousin, sitting on the load forever, exposed on numerous fronts. Each of them was trying to develop a distribution network in South Florida, where the DEA and Customs had concentrated most of their resources. These guys were not going to last. Somebody was going to get busted and lead the government to everybody else.

"Here's what I can do for you," Long said, and laid it out for Tony.

"You can buy twenty thousand pounds?"

"Yes."

"At one time," Tony said, just to be sure he had heard Long correctly.

"I'll take the whole load. That's right. You bring me twenty thousand pounds, I'll take it all. And I'll pay for it all within a week."

Since the flights to Colombia had begun, Myerson's market had grown. With the quality he was getting, at the price at which he was getting it, he was in a position to sell not simply to his usual distributors, but to other wholesalers at his level. His reaction to the crash of the DC-3, the crew's escape, and the rescue of the load by Tony — his immediate response to hearing the story, lifted straight from the pages of a novel — had been: "How many pounds did you say he had on that boat?"

Long offered to pay Tony $200 a pound, $50 more than he was getting, for delivery in Miami of 20,000 pounds. He would pay $1 million on delivery, and another $3 million once the load was sold. Tony could rely on something like a seven-day turnover.

Tony, who had watched the DC-3 crash, said, "If you can do that, man, you'll never have to fly an airplane again. We will bring you more marijuana than you can sell."

"I dare you to do that," said Long, adding, however, that there was one very important condition. "The marijuana has to be good."

Long had reached this point in the pot business by treating it like any other marketing enterprise. It could be avocados or automobiles. What he knew was this: Quality drives the product. Jake Myerson could turn over 20,000 pounds of *good* pot in a week.

Myerson, when he met Long, was selling the best pot he could get his hands on, but as often as not it was the same pot that somebody else was selling. Taking a third of a load of grade-A dope, the balance of which might be going to two other Michigan wholesalers, he was typically competing for market share against the very same product. Pricing was a major concern. The further he was from the source, the more people between him and the merchandise, the less room

he had to maneuver. The average wholesaler found himself several transactions removed from the Colombians — a guy in Miami, a guy in New York, maybe two guys in each of those places. Allen Long occupied an enviable threshold in being a direct link between Colombia and the market. Working in partnership with him, Myerson was in a position to dominate it, he and the one or two others in Ann Arbor who had similar connections, because few could beat his price for a product the quality of which was always assured.

When Long, on his first flight to Colombia, started rejecting bales on the runway, saying, "I'm not taking this," it was the first time the Colombians had heard someone say it. No pilot had ever said it, no boat captain had ever said it. "It has to be this color. This color or that. Gold or red. Nothing else." It was a psalm Long had sung from the shores of the Guajira to the hills of Aracataca. To the growers there, he had carried the word. "The reason you're getting only eight dollars a pound," he told them, "is because you're selling marijuana *this* color with marijuana *that* color in the same bag. Why not separate it. Sell that to everybody else, sell this to me, and I'll take it at fifteen dollars."

And now, after his trip through Sabana Rubia, he knew it was possible to get the quality he sought in volume. His first move was to put Tony together with Colombians who understood quality. Both he and Tony were working with the same loosely affiliated group of people in Colombia. Whoever was behind Tony's loads was hooked into Ernesto. Long reached out through Miguel.

"Go to Ernesto," he told Miguel, "and tell him from now on that Tony is to be loaded with the good marijuana only."

The Colombians were quick to oblige. Working with Long, they had been working with one of the very few smugglers

who came back to Colombia and paid them exactly what he had said he would pay. He was paying them more per pound than anyone, and he was paying them in full. There was never a dispute.

The deal Long made with Tony and his crew was born of a simple reality. Tony's people, CIA operatives and cops, had the expertise, the connections, and the muscle to get marijuana into Miami. Maritime transport, landing the contraband, and securing it — they had these things locked up. They owned South Florida that way. Indeed, while they might have been exposed on the distribution side — and as hopelessly disorganized as they might have been there — the smuggling operation itself, as Long would later discover, was run with flawless proficiency. And more than that. They ran it with absolute impunity.

Organized and scrupulously supervised by Tony's handler, Jack, the entire operation was being run out of the Miami police department. With a mandate from Washington to see that CIA clandestine ops ran uninterrupted, Jack had access to the movements of the Coast Guard and other federal agencies; his access to criminal intelligence and his ability as a police lieutenant to misdirect the resources of those agencies immunized everyone involved.

Long was introduced to Jack on a visit to Tony's house. Stepping outside, carrying cognac and a Cuban coffee, he walked with Tony past the swimming pool and through the aviary to the back of his property, and passing through the rear gate, followed Tony across the neighboring yard to the police official's house.

Jack, tall, maybe five years older than Tony, greeted Long enthusiastically.

"Hey, there's somebody here you should meet," he said, and introduced Long to another guest, a county sheriff

visiting from Georgia. Presenting Long to the man in uniform, he said, "This is the guy with the airplanes."

A nervous grin set up camp on the lower perimeter of Long's face. Suppressing a shudder, he shook hands with the sheriff, a kind of whimsical odium maneuvering within him as the lawman assured him that the airplanes in question would be welcome in his jurisdiction. Long, when it was polite to do so, took Tony aside for a talk.

"Tony," he said, "I can't do business with guys in black shoes."

"What are you talking about, man?"

"I just can't work with someone wearing a uniform and a gun." Not in the United States anyway. "I can't work with cops."

Tony said, "I got news for you."

Protected, thanks to Jack, not simply from arrest but from actual scrutiny, the Miami smugglers could move as many tons of marijuana as they could sell. Their problem was they had no market, certainly not one sufficiently large or secure to reward their potential. Long, with access to some of the larger and more reliable marijuana outlets in the country, was the solution to their problem. He could make them all rich overnight. And he stood to gain just as much as they.

He would pay them $200 a pound to deliver to Miami, $50 more than he was paying after factoring in the airplane costs and the pilots' share of the take. The plane was gone, the pilots had been eliminated, and gone as well was the crapshoot of putting together a ground crew, not to mention the constellation of risks that came with flying in and out of Colombia. On a 20,000-pound load, if he split fifty-fifty with Myerson, Long would make $2 million before expenses. And he did not have to go anywhere.

It did not take spreadsheets or time and motion studies

to figure this one out. It did not even take an abacus to get a reading on the deal. He could do it on his fingers.

"Let's see if these guys can deliver," he said, laying it out for Lee Carlyle.

Long needed someone in Florida. You could not do this stuff alone. You had to have a partner. You had to have somebody just to watch your back. Lee Carlyle had been living in South Florida since 1972. He had been moving Jamaican pot, and though yet to turn his dime into a million bucks, he was doing pretty well. He was also pretty good at arithmetic. When Long called and told him he needed someone to cover his play, and was willing to cut him in for half, Carlyle said, "Cool," and he said it with no hesitation.

It was Carlyle who pulled all the local logistics together. He knew where to look for a safe house, knew a trucking company willing to do business. In Davie, a rural community featuring numerous cattle and truck farms about twelve miles southwest of Fort Lauderdale, Carlyle found a farm, 120 acres, with the house situated right in the middle of the property at the end of a half-mile driveway. From the house, the length of the driveway was visible all the way to the front gate, which cut off access from the highway.

In Davie, pickup trucks were ubiquitous, and it was not unusual to see tractor-trailers pulling in and out of farmsteads hauling hay, horses, cattle, feed, produce, and other agricultural freight. In a single semi-trailer rig, 20,000 pounds of pot could easily be concealed among crates of oranges, artichokes, or cucumbers, or whatever the current crop happened to be, coming out of somewhere like Homestead. Using a working farm that had been in operation for years — where such activity was not likely to draw scrutiny — and

an established long-haul trucking company, Long avoided having to lease, buy, or sign his name to anything.

The owner of the farm was paid $5 a pound; the truckers received $10.

The price that Long paid Tony, $200 a pound, was for delivery of the pot to Davie. Up to that point all the expenses were Tony's; beyond that they were Long's. Tony would pick up the pot in Colombia and deliver it offshore in Florida. (Eventually the Miami smugglers would pick up the pot closer to home, turning maritime transport over to their suppliers, the Colombians, whose freighters delivered the pot off the Bahamas. At the time, Colombian captains and crews, unlike U.S. nationals, were deported rather than imprisoned when arrested by American authorities.) Tony's people would land the pot in a small fleet of sport-fishing boats operating out of the Keys.

There would be at least four men involved in landing the typical haul. Tony's partner Lonnie would operate one boat. Virgil would operate a second. Long had yet to meet the other two men. One was a well-known Islamorada charter captain. The other was a guy named Frank, "Frank A.," as Tony A. referred to him. No relation. Frank A. was a former Miami police sergeant who sported the last name of a legendary (and violently late) New York crime family boss — which anyone could be expected to do if the (late) crime boss were his uncle.

These men were at the center of a smuggling enterprise that over the next two years would land over half a million pounds of marijuana in South Florida. The majority of the dope would be distributed by Jake Myerson in Ann Arbor. (As the numbers escalated, the Miami smugglers would develop additional outlets of their own.) In the middle, orchestrating the flow of traffic between Miami and Ann

Arbor — between Miami and wherever it went, the traffic becoming so heavy that Myerson could not handle it all — in the middle, taking their dime, stood Allen Long and Lee Carlyle.

It was the beginning of a new era for Long, an era in which he just went to Miami every month or so and waited. All he had to do was be there when the phone call came in.

By 1977 boat builders in Florida had ascended to the cultural status of movie stars. This was the age of the "go-fast." Go-fast was the smuggler's term for those production power boats, first manufactured by Miami's legendary Don Aronow, famous for their deep-V hull design, and marketed under various brand names, including Formula, Donzi, Magnum Marine, and Cigarette. The last fell into generic use as a term for all similar offshore speedboats. Featuring twin inboard V-8 engines, or up to four high-performance outboards, the oceangoing racers were typically thirty to forty feet long and cost in the neighborhood of $100,000. They were capable of traveling over 75 knots through choppy seas (only slightly slower carrying a thousand pounds of marijuana or cocaine) and could outrun anything the Coast Guard had.

Bertram and Hatteras, the big sport-fishing boat manufacturers, were well established at the time. Bertram had dominated speedboat racing until Aronow came along. A fifty-foot Bertram or Hatteras sport fisherman, every weekend sailor's wet dream, could cost $450,000. And could carry a lot of pot: between 6,000 and 12,000 pounds of it. The advantage of a Cigarette or similar muscle-boat was speed. The disadvantages included not only the go-fast's limited capacity, but the fact that every one of them drew

the scrutiny of the U.S. Coast Guard. A Bertram or Hatteras, or any other reliable sport fisherman, beyond its cargo capacity, benefited greatly from its ubiquity in the waters off South Florida. Late in the afternoon, on any given day, there were probably 350 charter boats out fishing the Gulf Stream between Fort Lauderdale and the Keys. There were so many of them, owned by so many legitimate people, that their very visibility made them invisible.

Steaming from the Guajira to, say, Orange Cay in the Bahamas, a Colombian coastal freighter could take anywhere from three and a half to seven days. To Orange Cay from the Keys was about five hours in a Hatteras. The typical off-loader would take his boat out fishing in the Straits all day, just waiting for the signal that his freighter was lying off Great Bahama Bank. On some nights, there might have been four freighters there unloading. Boats would be all over the place:

"Are you from Raúl?"

"No, I am from Rafael. Raúl is over there."

The setup invited the occasional rip-off: a guy with a death wish and a Cigarette, say, sneaking into the confusion, taking on some smuggler's dope, and speeding away. Or an off-loader who had business out there might simply succumb to greed. But such boat captains, while bold, rarely grew old. There was a price to pay. Various techniques — beyond retributive murder — were employed to prevent such losses. One was to provide the captain and off-loader with halves of the same hundred-dollar bill. If the serial numbers did not match up, the off-loader did not get the pot.

Tony's people would take on pot in the Bahamas at night, then fish the Gulf Stream, fully loaded, all the following day, coming in early that evening with all the other fishing boats returning to the Keys. Much of Tony's time was devoted to

the purchase of real estate, to finding and buying up what the CIA called "holes" — safe houses situated on the various canals that snaked through the Keys at which the pot could be unloaded. The boat would tie up to the dock at the rear of the house, and sometime after dark, once activity died down, with no more boats coming up the canal, the unloading would begin.

Long was on hand one day when the two A.'s, Tony and Frank, were overseeing an off-load, and was struck by the proficiency with which they handled the job.

Frank A., until he became a cop, was completely legit, having moved to Florida with his father, a Miami business-man, whose brothers back in Brooklyn were pursuing more newsworthy careers ascending to stardom in the New York rackets. Frank owned a five-acre compound on the ocean in Key Largo. It had a high fence, a heavy gate, and a long pier, tied up to which he kept a fifty-foot sport fisherman. The day Long showed up at the compound there were eight guys sitting around. On a canal about four miles away, tied up at the dock of a pink stucco house — a "hole" procured by Tony — were three boats and 12,000 pounds of dope waiting to be unloaded.

At four in the afternoon, the county sheriff's office called the compound. Reports had been received of suspicious activity in the vicinity of the safe house.

"A heads-up from the locals," said Frank, hanging up the phone.

Tony said, "Call Angie."

Frank put in the call.

At the compound two hours later, a policeman came through the door. He came in by way of the kitchen wearing the uniform of a Miami sergeant. Beyond him, as he entered, Long could see a squad car idling in the driveway. Long,

looking the cop over, figuring he could outrun him, was backing his way out of the kitchen when Frank started talking to the guy.

"Angie," Frank said to the sergeant, "we need to cool that neighborhood off. Go tell all the residents there to vacate their houses. Tell them there's an investigation, a drug operation going down at the pink house. Tell them vacate the premises or stay indoors, and stay away from the windows."

Angie left to take care of things, but at nine P.M., when it was time to move, all the off-loaders waiting at Frank's were nervous nonetheless.

"Come on, let's go, it's cool," said Frank, moving them toward the door. "Come on," he finally told them, "watch, I'll lead the way."

The off-loaders followed him out. A minute later Frank was back.

"They just needed somebody to open the door," he said, and everybody laughed.

The pot went into pickups fitted with cab-over campers, all equipped with air shocks, road-levelers like those installed in the limousines Long had used in Marin. At eight the next morning, with all the rush-hour traffic into Miami, the trucks headed for the parking lot of a strip mall near the farmhouse in Davie.

Letting the numerous truck drivers know where the stash house was located would have been a real security risk. That they might reveal its whereabouts to authorities, should they ever be arrested, was not the sole liability — a rip-off team coming in with guns, taking the load and leaving bodies behind, was another problem that came to mind. Long, to take delivery of a load, had set up a system of double cutouts. When he received a call that a boat was in, he would send

people to sit on the house, people he knew he could trust, people from out of town. People like Little Eddie and his crew.

The driver of the pickup knew only that he was to drop the truck in the designated parking lot. He was to leave the keys in the ashtray, and disappear for an hour, maybe in the bar across the street from the strip mall. Seeing the truck arrive, Long would pick it up, drive it to the house, log it in — plate number, number of bales — and unload it. He would sweep it out, deodorize it, and have it back in the parking lot well within the hour. When the driver returned to the lot, the keys to the truck would be in the ashtray, and the pickup would be empty. And that was all the driver needed to know. Twenty thousand pounds of pot amounted to maybe ten pickup loads, and Long could count on seeing the same driver two or three times.

The quality of the pot Long was moving, all gold and red and stacked in abundance, made a stunning impression on the guys from New Jersey sitting on the safe house. There was no air conditioner in the house, and all the windows were kept closed. The smell of pot permeated the place, and Long did not want it escaping. He did not want the pungent aroma picked up by some serviceman reading a meter. Walking into the house, he was not surprised to find Little Eddie ripped on the fumes.

"Man this is . . ."

"Yeah."

". . . the best stuff . . ."

"Uh-huh."

". . . I've . . ."

"See . . . ?"

". . . ever seen."

". . . I told you."

Later that night a Peterbilt tractor pulling a forty-four-foot refrigeration van turned onto the property. It was filled with crates of avocados, sidewall to sidewall, from the reefer unit to the rear door, from the upper side-rail to the deck. When the smugglers set to work, all the cargo from the side door forward was removed from the truck. The marijuana bales were then loaded in and stacked against the front wall. A plywood bulkhead was erected behind it, the edges sealed with duct tape. A layer of plastic was taped over that. The produce was reloaded, as much as was needed to refill the space, and the truck was dispatched to Ann Arbor.

(It was only one of the methods used. No more than 14,000 pounds could be hauled that way — two trucks would be needed to move a 20,000-pound load — because the bales had to be kept one foot forward of the side door to avoid detection by police. Florida state troopers searched for dope by forcing a hollow pipe through the load, from the door to the opposite sidewall, extracting the pipe to check its contents for contraband.)

As soon as the pot arrived in Davie, Long paid Tony and his friends. A million in cash, sent down from Michigan. He flew to Ann Arbor to pick up the rest. In less than a week everyone had his money.

VIOLETS FOR YOUR FURS

"That stuff is bad for you," Constance said, cleaning up around the cocaine.

All the time he was operating in Florida, Long maintained residence in New York. His housekeeper, Constance, from Belize, came twice a week to clean the apartment, and if when she arrived there was no blow out on the living room coffee table, she could find it there within a few hours.

Long did not rise until one P.M., and by late afternoon, as often as not, the apartment was crawling with an assortment of coke-snorting troublemakers around whom Constance found herself navigating.

At just after four there would be several limousines parked on the street below, each having deposited on 68th Street a stockbroker who had punched out of his Wall Street office at precisely 3:48. Long's playmates treated the place as if it were theirs, and just like working stiffs everywhere they had fallen into a routine. There was no limit on the liquor and cocaine, but girls from the outcall service had to be paid and gone from the apartment by no later than six-thirty,

when the boys got down to the business of colluding to churn stock. Selecting an issue to start pumping at, say, nine-thirty the following morning for a sell-off at two P.M., the crowd would then head home, leaving Long and the one unmarried broker among them to go running in Central Park.

There was no shortage of philosophies around the coffee table, and none better served to illuminate the world that Long and his friends were on top of than the following deconstruction of mankind's habits, which was ventured by one sage to the memorable music of rocks of cocaine being crushed:

"There are jewelry guys, and there are coat guys," he said.

"I'm a jewelry guy," responded one of the others.

"Most guys are jewelry guys. I'm a jewelry guy, you're a jewelry guy. Allen, he's a coat guy."

Long did not deny it, but he was justified in taking issue with the categorical nature of the assertion. Mink coats as sexual bribery were typically associated with older men. What made him stand out among his contemporaries, he insisted, was the fact that he was *also* a coat guy.

"I'd have to say I'm both," he admitted.

And he paid for his habits in ways that went beyond the expenditure of cash. One evening at Mary Lou's, a Ninth Street restaurant he favored, he was having a drink with a young record company employee he had romanced some months before, having surprised her back then with the black mink she was wearing at the moment. Now she had a surprise for him. The surprise arrived in the person of an ex-girlfriend of Long's who joined them at their table wearing a gray fox coat Long had bought her on the same day. ("You should wear your fur coat," he had told the

latter, inviting her to lunch. "I don't have one," she had said. "Let's fix that," Long had replied.) She in turn was now followed into the restaurant by Cherie, wearing a diabolical smile and the white custom-made mink she had received from Long at the time he was fooling around with the other two. Long, contemplating the fix he was in, yearned for the Guajira and the chattering of submachine guns.

While Long and Cherie were clearly a couple, Long had readily seen to it, once they were settled in New York, that Cherie had her own apartment. While Long was smuggling pot, and investing his time and money in various legitimate projects as well — his own, chiefly in the music business, and those of various entrepreneurial friends in need of working capital — Cherie studied acting at the Neighborhood Playhouse. For a while she ran a small business of her own, designing children's knitted wear. In 1977 she put together a portfolio to seek out modeling work. Long hired the most expensive fashion photographer available, and Cherie eventually signed with the Wilhelmina agency.

Like women in the lives of most dope smugglers, Cherie had little impact on Long's business activities, and because those activities ate up so much of his life, very little call on his time. What made her different from the other people to whom he devoted attention was that it was she to whom he did the really significant lying and, in spreading himself around sexually, upon her that he was officially cheating. She would do her best to protect him, from his friends and from himself, and like others in similar circumstances she would inevitably fail.

As relationships went, theirs was dysfunctional even by the standards of the dope business, and probably would have been even in its absence. Both the children of absentee fathers (and, as it happened, schoolteacher mothers), neither

was blessed with a stable frame of reference when it came to affairs of the heart. Long's father had left his wife and run off with an airline stewardess — at a time when the culture viewed flight attendants, stereotypically, as sexual trophies — and Cherie's dad, a high school coach, had managed to come up with an act that put that move in the shade. Cherie learned that her father, while living at home, before finally running out on her mother, was simultaneously raising another family across town.

Growing up in conjugal Disneyland, both would bring to their love affair an emotional history that was questionable at best. Nonetheless, for a good part of his career as a smuggler, Long's personal life, if you could call it that, would pretty much be seen by friends as the Allen and Cherie show. And for all the *Sturm und Drang,* his romance with Cherie was the one against which all of his other infatuations were measured.

With Long, Cherie would travel to Aruba, Jamaica, St. Croix, and the Dominican Republic, and to numerous places around the country. And, of course, she would travel regularly to Studio 54.

The disco on West 54th Street was the hottest ticket in town, and its operators, Steve Rubell and Ian Schrager, had yet to be danced to jail by their felonies, when Long, with Cherie and some friends visiting from Virginia, first showed up at the door in 1977, only to be turned away. Made guys from Brooklyn, similarly snubbed, got right in the doorman's face, muttering, "You don't know who you're fucking with." Which was patently ridiculous — a joint like Studio 54, in order to stay in business, was dealing with wiseguys every day. Long, who did know who he was fucking with, knew better than to waste his time.

The following morning he was on the phone to the office

of lawyer Roy Cohn, the notorious former counsel to the subcommittee of red-baiting Senator Joseph McCarthy in the 1950s. Now, some twenty years after nailing down his ignominious place in history, Cohn was celebrated by the New York media as the toughest lawyer in town. Among other things, he was a big-time mob lawyer. But Long was not looking for legal muscle. Long happened to know that Cohn was attorney for Studio 54. Getting a partner of Cohn's on the phone, Long explained that in trying to crack the door at the club he had been told he was "not on the list." Informed that "five thousand dollars will fix that," Long effectively "hired" the law firm, sending the money by messenger in cash. That night he showed up at the disco with Cherie and his friends, whispered to the doorman, "I'm on the list," and walked them in. There and at Xenon — same jive, different address — Long and Cherie remained regulars until both clubs ceased to be hip.

Studio 54 was neither the first nor the only public establishment in the country with a policy of ignoring the open use of illicit drugs on its premises. But the club, in the way it promoted itself, even in its decor, celebrated and effectively encouraged their use, and was by virtue of its visibility at the epicenter for their explosion out of the counterculture and into the mainstream. *High Times* magazine, whose Christmas card one year featured a photograph and the season's greetings of Andy Warhol and Truman Capote, threw private parties at the club at which one was likely to find himself standing with either or both of those celebrated Americans while waiting in line to avail himself of the large nitrous oxide tanks provided for the use of guests.

Studio 54, during the brief period in which it was the place to be seen, provided the backdrop for one of Long's

more gratifying performances as a pot smuggler. It was a moment the likes of which came around rarely for Long: a chance to luxuriate publicly in his illegal accomplishments. He and Cherie were dining one night with one of his record business associates at the upmarket Maxwell's Plum, an East Side saloon of some social significance at the time. His associate had invited a friend, a wealthy investment banker, who, having acquired his wealth legitimately, was unafraid to brag, albeit discreetly, about his success.

"Real estate speculation and equity financing. That's my specialty," he told Long.

As it happened, he and Long would grow to be very close friends, but that night Long resented the supposition that there was a big shot at the table bigger than he. Long had a limousine waiting out front, and after dinner suggested that the two men and their wives hop in with him and Cherie, and head across town "to 54." There, to the throbbing music and the flashing of colored lights, God blessed the smuggler with the sublime opportunity to assert bragging rights of his own.

"This is really great pot," the banker volunteered, shouting to be heard over the deafening thud of the sound system, as he sucked on a joint that Long had passed around.

"You like that?" asked Long.

"I don't think I've ever smoked anything better."

Long nodded his head, gave it a second, and leaned in to speak into the banker's ear.

"That's *my* specialty," he said.

Smuggling pot was high-risk work and promoted bonds of sincere friendship between Long and the people he worked with. When Pablo Cepeda paid him a visit in New York, there were two memories the high-strung *costeño* wanted to take home from the trip. He wanted to dance at Studio 54,

and he wanted to meet Raquel Welch. The trip was El Demonio's first to the United States, and Long did everything he could to oblige. The first request he handled immediately upon Pablo's arrival. And Pablo cut quite a figure on the dance floor at the club. In blue blazer, gray slacks, and black lace-up shoes, it was almost as if he were in costume, but the weird impression he made on the disco's jaded patrons did not measure up to the impression they made on him.

"I cannot believe it!" he said, rushing up to Long at one point, his incredulity having rendered him breathless.

"What is it, buddy?" said Long.

"No one in my country will believe it!"

"What happened, Pablo?" asked Cherie.

He pointed through the crowd. And there, just off the dance floor, stood the source of his dismay. El Demonio had been pushed to the point of near insensibility by the sight of two cowboys kissing. Both were six feet tall, blond and cut like bodybuilders. Draped in Western roundup gear, right down to the rawhide riding chaps, shirtless, muscles rippling beneath matching leather vests, they were also draped around each other, swaying to the music, doing those kinds of things that Lawrence of Arabia left out of his official reports to the Crown.

"My people won't believe this," said Pablo. "John Wayne is *maricón?*"

"Pablo," Cherie was quick to assure him, "not all cowboys kiss."

And the same was true, Long wanted to say, of construction workers and cops, even if one could not prove it by the evidence of the dance floor. But Pablo, he figured, probably knew that already.

Pablo's rendezvous with Raquel Welch was equally

memorable, but alas, it was memorable to everyone but Pablo. So drunk did he get at her show at Caesars Palace in Las Vegas that he would be unable to recall screaming "I love you, Raquel, I love you," just before passing out. Easy Matthews, who was along on the junket, caught him as he fell. The big redhead, laughing, hoisted the unconscious Colombian onto his shoulder and carried him out of the joint, transporting him in that fashion back to the Aladdin, where the smugglers were staying.

In Allen Long's New York, where the greatest sin, indeed, the only crime of any consequence, was being out of style, the money he made smuggling marijuana put him on everyone's A-list. But the acceptance he sought would never be complete, or at least be entirely trustworthy, until a year or so after he arrived.

Long was driving to Florida, making his way to Miami with a million in cash in his car. The money was in two Samsonite "two-suiters," a half a million dollars in each, in tens, twenties, and fifties. Passing through Virginia, he stopped in to see his grandfather. They were sitting in the den of his grandfather's house, and the elder Long, as always, was paying periodic visits to the bathroom, where he had his whiskey stashed in the toilet tank no more than an arm's length from the medicine cabinet, where he kept a bottle of mouthwash. His wife did not approve of his drinking, and like every alcoholic the old man had it worked out.

"This is what I made last month," Long said, unlocking the suitcases.

Long wanted nothing more than he wanted the approval of the man who had taught him to hunt and fish. He wanted his grandfather to be proud of him.

"How you makin' this money?"

"I'm a pot smuggler," said Long.

"What's that?"

"Marijuana."

"Marijuana?"

The old man laughed. He shook his head and laughed so hard that tears ran down his cheeks. They filled the furrows of his flesh. His hands were big, his wrists were thick, and his fingers, the size of sausages, all but obscured his face when he removed his glasses to dry his eyes.

"That's how I bought my first car," he confessed.

Using his handkerchief to dry his spectacles, he shook his head and reflected. He had run bootleg liquor, he said.

"Tennessee to Ohio."

He talked about moonshine and revenue agents. Long told him about the airplanes.

"Just one word of advice," the elder man said.

"What's that?

He gave his grandson three.

"Don't get caught."

It was shortly thereafter that Long was offered leadership of the family lock-manufacturing business. Long always saw it as his grandfather's acknowledgment of him as an achiever. And that was enough for the young scammer. Benefiting from the sad example set by his father, and seeing the offer for what it was — a promise of independence that would never be honored — Long declined the position, and not graciously. It was a negotiation whose low point came when his grandfather, in front of him, dismissed his father from the room. Long had challenged them to hand over control of the company to him in advance, telling them he was running a multimillion-dollar drug-smuggling enterprise — he had a Learjet waiting, he boasted — and was not about to give it up for $40,000 a year.

(Tom, his younger brother, ended up stepping into the

job. And after almost twenty years with the firm, he still never received any stock. As general manager Tom returned the business to profitability, but was not allowed to reverse the company's long-term slide, which was precipitated by the profit-taking of his father and aunt, who together withheld the stock from him, their mistreatment of his brother being something for which Long would never forgive them. The corporation was eventually liquidated.)

In Florida, Long's business was rolling, propelled by its own momentum, the conspirators' appetite for money expanding with the nation's appetite for dope. Everything tasted like "more."

Moving 20,000 pounds on their first load, the smugglers moved 40,000 on their second. They went from twenty to forty right away. Doing a dozen boats over the next year and a half, they never did less than twenty, and sometimes they did eighty. They began moving so much pot that Myerson's people in Michigan could not sell it all. Long and Carlyle, in control of the flow, had to search out other buyers. In Washington, Easy Matthews started receiving significant weight. Carlyle opened a new market with whole-salers in Northern California.

Finding themselves at the center of a spreading network, outgrowing the stash house in Davie, Long and Carlyle moved their operation to Jupiter, Florida, to a bigger farm with a capacious barn on the property. They started moving so much pot, they hit a point of diminishing returns. A buyer, a distributor, with two months to sell 20,000 pounds, could move the weight through his own channels. But to sell 100,000 pounds in that time, if the smugglers wanted the money right away, he would have to sell it to other

distributors, wholesalers with channels of their own, and he would have to sell it for a lot less.

Tony, after the initial deal had been struck, took Long aside for a chat.

"I don't want you to tell my partners," he said, "but you know, you wouldn't have made this deal without me."

Tony wanted an extra $5 a pound from Long's end on every load. Which amounted to a minimum of $100,000 on every boat that came in. Long subsequently discovered that Tony, God bless him, had gone to all of the others involved and made a similar pitch.

"Hey, I don't want you to think I'm greedy," he told them, "but I want an extra nickel from each of you for making you rich with this guy."

This was the "Cuban way" that Tony had been talking about. Everyone said okay, and everyone remembered not to say anything about Tony's nickel to anyone else. It was a measure of his charm. Everybody loved Tony.

Long figured Tony was making an extra $400,000 per trip. Or something in that vicinity. He was never quite sure how the Miami partnerships were set up. They seemed to be kind of fluid. Lonnie was definitely a partner — he was to Tony what Carlyle was to Long. Virgil and the others operated at a level of participation that probably changed after the first transaction.

With the operation up and running, Tony called Long in New York and asked him to attend a meeting.

"I want you to come down to Florida," he said. "Somebody wants to meet you."

Long flew to Miami and met Tony at Victoria Station, a restaurant not far from the airport. He found Tony and Lonnie there, seated with a Colombian gent. The man's name was Gilberto, he was somewhere in his fifties, and his outfit

was a giveaway. The boots, the solid gold belt buckle, the ten-gallon hat — he was straight off the Guajira. Gilberto was the man behind the man Tony did business with in Colombia. And he had come to Miami to meet the American who was sending him all the money.

It was a social call more than anything: a General Motors executive in a show of courtesy to the sales manager of Chevrolet's highest-performing dealership. The meeting was conducted in that spirit, an exercise in camaraderie, but the two men did not part company without paying passing attention to business.

"How much merchandise can you sell?" Gilberto was curious to know.

Long let his ego answer.

"If the quality remains the same," he said, "I can handle one hundred thousand pounds at a time."

"Good," said Gilberto, all energy and corporate enthusiasm. "I will send it to Tony."

And he did. And Long moved it. He and Carlyle, it seemed, could move anything.

Carlyle was living north of Fort Lauderdale, renting a house with a swimming pool on a canal off the Intracoastal Waterway. Tied to the dock behind the house was his thirty-eight-foot Magnum sedan, midnight blue on black, with twin 400 horsepower inboard V-8s. In it he and Long would cruise the clubs along the Intracoastal, the hippest of which all had docks. At any one of them on a good night, Cigarettes were tied three deep.

In the way that Studio 54 presented the new look of drug consumption, Miami nightlife was the contemporary expression of drug dealing in the United States. Gone was the tie-dyed-good-vibrations-cop-a-lid standard of cool. There was nothing laid back about the scene. Guys like Long and

Carlyle were no more a part of the counterculture than the typical movie star.

There was nothing particularly political about marijuana anymore. And from the point of view of the dealer, there probably never had been. For him, even on campus, it had always been about business. For the dealer, even as a dedicated pot smoker, it had always been less about revolution than it was about conspicuous consumption. The latter was the real organizing principle, and Miami was the movement's Jerusalem.

None of the scammers in Miami could have found his way to a college campus. Had he done so, he would have been about as comfortable there as one of the bootleggers in *Guys and Dolls*. And thus it was not surprising that Lee Carlyle, in the forefront of the movement, had his problems with Jake Myerson. Not only was Myerson fairly well educated, but the Ann Arbor resident was active, by way of other interests, in the academic life of the university. As were many businesspeople in the city. What Carlyle saw in Myerson was a guy who preached the old pot-smoking principles and values, and promoted the political rectitude of the cause, but who was always very religious about the dough.

He saw Myerson as a guy with "a bad attitude." Myerson just rubbed him the wrong way. And the hostility was reciprocal. The two did not like each other at all, and their mutual aversion was manifest right from the outset of the deal.

"What do we need him for?" Myerson demanded, when Long brought Carlyle aboard.

"Hey, Lee's my friend," said Long. "I'm cutting him in."

When Long and Carlyle branched out to supply other distributors, Carlyle naturally asked the same question about Myerson, developing an understandable myopia as he and

Long took in more money per pound from other buyers than Myerson was paying.

"What do we need him for?" Carlyle said "Why sell to him for two-twenty-five when we can sell it for two-seventy-five?"

Long grew weary of trying to impress upon his partner the advantages of the fast nickel over the slow dime. "No waiting, instant turnaround . . ."

"Allen, he's lying to you," Carlyle said. "He's not selling it for three hundred. It's going for three-fifty up there."

The beef intensified and took on more serious overtones when it became apparent to Myerson that Carlyle's prodigious intake of dope went far beyond the recreational. Carlyle was stoned, coked up, and drunk, it seemed, twenty-four hours a day. His tolerance for methaqualone was staggering. He was eating Quaaludes like they were candy, gobbling the pills by the handful. The popular hypnotic, marketed by more than one pharmaceutical house and bootlegged nationwide, had what Myerson saw as the distinct disadvantage of knocking Carlyle silly without knocking him out.

"This guy's trouble," said Myerson. "He's a liability."

Long was willing to concede that Carlyle lacked certain social graces.

"He's a complete fuck-up," Myerson said. "He's unreliable."

Carlyle *was* a fuck-up. Long knew that. But Carlyle was his friend. And Carlyle was his partner. And furthermore, in the end . . . well . . . Carlyle was no bigger a fuck-up than he, most of the time. Admittedly, Carlyle might have been slightly more dangerous. But Long was doing so much cocaine by now that he bore watching himself. As time passed and the money, flowing ashore with the predictability

of the tide, began rising to the level at which it threatened to take up living space, Long, to put it in Myerson's words, was growing "more detached." (The characterization being a measure of Myerson's social graces.) He was throwing more and more parties at which he was the only guest.

It was a month after the meeting with Gilberto that Tony said he had a problem.

"The feds were at my house."

He informed Long that his old bay shrimper had come back up out of the water. The Coast Guard had found it drifting upside down off Miami. There were still a few bales in the hull. The boat was in Tony's name. Tony had reported the boat stolen — legally he was in the clear — but there would be some heat on him for a while. Therefore, he would no longer be dealing hands-on.

"I'm sending someone else," he said.

Tony had, in fact, been visited by the feds, but that had happened sometime earlier. And it was not why he was stepping aside. If you could call it stepping aside. The truth was that Jack in Miami, sniffing the bureaucratic wind, had decided to sever the direct link between his operatives and the dope. Word had come down from Washington, where dope was beginning to draw a lot of political attention. The time had come for Tony and the others to distance themselves from the traffic, not to close down the operation, or even end their participation, but to insert a cutout that would put them beyond the reach of any criminal investigation.

Tony A. was a pioneer. On his own, like Long, he had traveled to Colombia and scared up a marijuana connection. One of the first smugglers to tap the Colombian pipeline, he transported the dope himself. As much as

anything, it was an adventure for Tony, an outlet for his specialized talents, the kind of thing the government had trained him to do. Tony did not need the money. Doing contract work for the CIA, and simultaneously pursuing lucrative cover careers secured for them by the agency, he and others like him had already amassed legitimate wealth. They worked for agency front companies, and in some cases controlled them, establishing their own corporations with ever available CIA financing. Jack invested their money for them and over the years it grew. They owned real estate, held interests in local businesses, and they had substantial holdings of cash. Tony was rich before he ever sailed to the Guajira. He started smuggling marijuana pretty much because it was there. And he had done it for the collective good of his Cuban brothers-in-arms. It was lucrative, it was fun, and the government looked the other way.

Tony was a worker. He was downright cavalier about the money. Jack's job was to handle the money, Tony's job was to handle the job. One of the standing rules Tony observed was never to smuggle cocaine. So serious was he about it, and so nonchalant was he about the money, that once, rather than haul it, he threw a hundred kilos of coke overboard. Somebody else's coke. He just threw it into the drink. The coke had been secreted by Colombian traffickers within a load of pot Tony was transporting. It was destined for a dealer in Miami. Tony's habit, after hitting the Florida Straits, was to cruise the coast, off-loading the pot to numerous boats as he made his way to Key Largo. The coke dealer could have been associated with any of the guys on that end of the line. Tony suspected the guy was tied into Frank A.

(Tony eventually met the dealer himself. Heaving the cocaine over the side resulted in an ongoing relationship in

which the dealer made repeated attempts to kill him. Finally Jack squared things away, bringing all the various forces of corruption in the Miami police department to bear on the solution.)

Now it was time for Tony to sever his connection to the dope. He would no longer be dealing with the Colombians. He was turning the operation over to someone else, a guy by the name of Jimmy, a Cuban exile who had worked for him, and who knew his way around boats. Tony was stepping aside, but he would still be making his money. He was going to retire "a little bit." Jimmy, who had trained with a different CIA cell, was the operation's cutout.

But Long would not learn this until much later. Long's assumption at the time was that Tony's wife was pressuring him to quit. Events would lead him to assume, also, that Jimmy — ruthless where Tony was charming, hungry where Tony was not — had effectively pushed Tony aside. Only later did Tony cop to the setup. All Long knew, or needed to know, was that he would be dealing with Jimmy from then on.

As he would later come to describe it: "This was a step in the wrong direction."

15

CEILING ZERO

Jimmy Alvarez was in his late thirties. He stood about five-feet-seven. His hair was black and wavy, and he wore it combed straight back, revealing the pale complexion and sharp patrician features that announced a highborn European ancestry. He had a broad face, a weightlifter's body, and a heart as cold as a New York bank lobby. He had been active at the Bay of Pigs, was protected by the CIA, was driven by ambition, paranoia, and greed, and had no wife or children. His family consisted entirely of a young girlfriend who was scared to death of him and 5,000 fighting roosters that he kept on a farm in Homestead.

In the fall of 1977 Long was in Miami, at the Coconut Grove with Cherie, when Tony showed up at the hotel unannounced, invited him outside, and, as a professional courtesy, explained that Long was about to be murdered.

"What are you talking about, Tony?"

"Jimmy says that someone stole two thousand pounds of his pot."

"And you believe it was me?"

"I told him that he must be mistaken," said Tony. "I said I would talk to you."

"So?"

"Before I go back," he said, "I just got to ask."

And look Long in the eye when he did.

"I just have to know," Tony said.

Long's blue eyes held fast, as though shot through with embalming fluid.

"Tony, I don't need to steal anything from anybody."

"Well, you know," said Tony, shrugging.

"No," said Long. "Don't give me that. You remember when you wanted me to steal that pot from Lonnie?"

"Hey . . ."

"And I said no? You remember that?"

"Man, that wasn't stealing."

Not according to Tony.

It had happened earlier that year. Lonnie, dispatching pickup trucks from Key Largo to the farm in Davie, had miscalculated the number of bales aboard. He had merely counted the trucks and multiplied. One truck was a bit bigger than the others, and Long had ended up with 2,000 pounds of pot he had not been charged for. Long had called Tony to straighten it out.

"Did you tell Lonnie yet?" Tony had asked.

"You're his partner. I'm telling you," said Long.

"But you didn't tell him?"

"No."

"Okay, let's keep it to ourselves," said Tony.

Long knew where he was going.

"I can't do that, Tony. Forget it."

Tony saw the screw-up as a free 2,000 pounds, a ton of pot that only he and Long knew anything about. Tony

figured that rather than split whatever he and Lonnie were making, he would split $600,000 with Long.

"I can't do it, Tony," Long said.

Tony said he would take care of the Colombians, he would make something up. Lonnie would not have to make good.

"Forget it," said Long. "It's not gonna happen, Tony. It's not how I do things."

"Hey, don't you think he would do the same thing if he had the chance?" Tony said.

"Listen to what you're saying, man. Right now, you trust me completely. If I did this, how could you ever trust me again?"

"Hey, that's how it works."

Long said, "It's not how I work."

And now, on the street outside the Coconut Grove, he said it to Tony again.

"You know that's not how I operate. If Jimmy is missing some pot," he said, "I had nothing to do with it."

"Okay," said Tony, "we know who it was."

Long had no idea who it was. Numerous people had handled the shipment in question. One of them, whom Long had met, a young Miami restaurateur named Andreas — a hardworking Cuban family man just getting started in business — was later found tied to a chair in his restaurant with a bullet hole in his head. Long figured maybe it was him.

Jimmy adhered to a homicide schedule the way other businessmen booked golf. Several months later, Long was in New York kicking back between shipments when Jimmy called from Miami.

"I want you to know that I am not going to kill you," he said.

Jimmy in a sentimental mood.

"Well, thanks, Jimmy," Long replied. "To what do I —"

"I am not mad at you," Jimmy said. "I know it is not your fault."

How nice, thought Long. "Okay," he said. He felt lucky.

"But I am going to kill Lee."

Shit.

"The money," said Jimmy, "is not important. It is the respect."

According to Jimmy, not only had Carlyle not paid him — to the tune of $420,000 — but Carlyle had insulted him. Long said he would fly to Miami and straighten it out. He asked Jimmy to hold off doing anything until he could get there.

"I'm sure it's just a misunderstanding," he said.

And then he called Carlyle.

"Fuck you . . . ! Fuck you and your Cuban friends . . . ! And fuck . . . !"

Right away Long had a feeling Carlyle was in trouble.

"Motherfucker . . . !" screamed Carlyle. "I'm not paying them shit . . . ! If they kill me, Allen, I guarantee I'm gonna fuckin' kill you!"

Yeah, he was in trouble.

Long flew to Miami, went directly to Jimmy's house, and explained the situation.

"Lee says he respects you tremendously, Jimmy. He told me he meant no insult. Lee would *never* insult you. It was just a mistake, a misunderstanding. I'm going to see him now."

"Excellent," said Jimmy.

He introduced Long to a Cuban gent, a recent arrival to the nation's shores, or so Long had to assume, for the young man spoke no English.

"This is the man who is going to kill him," said Jimmy. "He will go with you."

And kill Carlyle if he did not show the proper respect.

Long called Carlyle and arranged to meet him not far from his house in a parking lot off the Interstate. Long and Jimmy's hired assassin cruised to the meeting in a Cadillac Seville. Conversing in Spanish — on Long's part a very labored version thereof — they talked about the business at hand.

"Who is this man Lee?"

"He's my partner," Long explained. "He's a good guy. You'll like him. He just drinks a little too much."

It was about ten on a Saturday morning. Carlyle pulled into the lot in his black BMW coupé, stepped out of the car, and approached the yellow Seville in which Long and the Cuban were waiting. He wore cutoff jeans and a T-shirt, no more, and Long could see that he had been up all night. Carlyle stopped four feet from the driver's side window, folded at the waist, and rocked forward like a flamingo, craning his neck to eyeball the pair.

Long essayed a quick chemical analysis: cocaine, Quaaludes, alcohol . . .

As Carlyle extended his index finger to stick in the assassin's face, Long put his left hand over the assassin's right, which rested on the seat between them gripping a .38 caliber revolver.

"You Cuban motherfuckers . . ."

Oh, and he had had his coffee, too, it appeared.

"You Cuban motherfuckers . . ." he drawled, his eyelids holding at half-mast.

And that was just the beginning.

Carlyle from where he stood could not see the revolver, and Long from where he sat would not let go of the twitching hand that was holding it.

"What did he say?" asked the Cuban, turning to Long.

"He is telling you of the respect he has for the Cuban people."

"I don't think that is what he is saying."

Carlyle continued vomiting up verbiage, and Long continued to translate.

"He understands Jimmy's position, and he fully intends to pay . . ."

Carlyle growled out the last of his abuse, lowered his finger, and barked: "Did you tell him what I said?"

"Word for word," said Long.

Carlyle stalked off. Long smiled, nodded his head, and put his hand on the Cuban's shoulder.

"*Bueno!*" he said.

They returned to Coral Gables, where Long was pleased to report to Jimmy that everything was fine. He got Carlyle on the phone later that day.

"A gun?" said Carlyle.

"You are the biggest —"

Carlyle, suddenly sober, assured Long that he would phone Jimmy and make things right. He put in the call immediately. Apologizing to Jimmy, he was quick to affirm his abiding respect. He said that he had gotten the message and that he was grateful to Jimmy for giving him the opportunity to straighten things out.

He concluded by saying, "But, Jimmy, I don't owe you any money."

Carlyle was in Curaçao on an extracurricular sexual holiday, and his girlfriend was staying at his house, when two men wearing ski masks — professionals, good old-fashioned American gangsters — circumvented his $25,000 alarm system, killed his two Dobermans, and kidnapped his girlfriend at gunpoint, holding her for a week until Carlyle finally paid up.

* * *

So heavy was Carlyle into Quaaludes now, that one could hardly understand him when he spoke. Verbal congress with him was riddled with uncertainty, subject to immediate deterioration, vulnerable to the same critical vicissitudes that governed radioactive decay and things like collapse of the wave function. He was washing the quackers down with enough liquor to slur his speech in their absence. That he remained conscious at all was astounding, a tribute, no doubt, to the quality and vast quantity of cocaine he was doing. The first few hours of every morning Carlyle spent looking for his car. He could never remember where he had parked it before things went to black.

Things soon reached the point where Myerson insisted that Long introduce him to Jimmy that he might deal directly with the Cuban in the event of an emergency, like some complete, unexpected cocaine meltdown on Long's part. Long, Carlyle, and Myerson were returning from that meeting, heading to Fort Lauderdale, having just delivered $8 million to Jimmy, when Myerson and Carlyle got into it. All three men were high on coke. Carlyle had been dropping ludes and the pills were just kicking in. He was slurring his words so badly that they bordered on the inaudible. He was bellyaching about the price of pot in Ann Arbor, muttering at Myerson, going on to Long like Hamlet griping about his uncle. Myerson was giving it back to him. They started shouting each other down.

"Guys, guys . . ." said Long.

"Fuck you," responded Carlyle.

"Okay, fuck me," said Long. "Can you guys put an end to it?"

"Fuck you, fuck this guy, fuck you both, I'm leaving . . ."

Carlyle threw open the limousine door — at which point the driver deemed it prudent to pull over — staggered out

of the car, and walked right into a boxwood hedge, screaming, "Fuck you both," as he tumbled, disappearing into the foliage, presumably to spend the night.

Myerson could not abide the guy.

The following day Long and Carlyle returned to Jimmy's house in Coral Gables to deliver another $4 million, the balance of what they owed. The cash was contained in sixteen cardboard boxes. Jimmy met them at the door with a submachine gun in his hands.

"You cannot bring that money in here," he said. "Take it away." Jimmy's paranoia was visible. His trigger finger was twitching. "If my friends find out I have all this money here, they will come and they will kill me. Take it away, turn around, go."

Backing Jimmy up were two other armed men. One was a guy named Dennis, an all-American type — never said much, always there, Jimmy's right hand. Long had never met the other guy. Both carried automatic weapons.

In the dope trade the day had arrived of the multimission submachine gun — the industry standard was the Ingram MAC-10 — and you could have removed the selective-fire switch from any of those used in Miami. It was like the movies now. The weapons in town were always on auto.

Beyond the doorway, on the living room couch, unarmed and out of range of any ejected cartridges that might start flying, sat a grim-visaged Jake Myerson — no doubt thinking twice right now about getting to know Jimmy. Long said he would hold the $4 million until Jimmy made arrangements, but before leaving with the money, they would have to count the $8 million they had delivered the day before.

"No way we are counting this fucking money," said Jimmy. "Forget that shit."

There was no way Long was leaving until Jimmy corroborated the amount.

There are certain conventions observed in the dope business. Some of them are intuitively obvious. Smugglers, for example, do not take checks. (Hell, they do not even take pesos. In the Western Hemisphere, and in much of the rest of the world, the dope business is conducted in United States currency.) Others make eminent sense after you think about them for a minute. For instance, standard procedure demands that the books always be balanced immediately. In the absence of canceled checks, counterfoils, and signed receipts — as in any cash business, especially one in which the ledgers are balanced by the barrel of a gun — money must be counted in the presence of both buyer and seller as soon as it changes hands. No phone calls the next day.

"No way we're counting it now," said Jimmy.

Doing so would take hours.

"Okay," conceded Long.

Jimmy's paranoia was positively radiant.

"We'll just weigh it," Long said.

Which was agreeable to everyone. The money was packaged and boxed by denomination for just such a purpose. One of the many gratifying aspects of doing business with Jake Myerson and professionals like Easy Matthews was their on-the-job courtesy. Both men made every effort to pay for at least half of their pot in hundreds. They even employed staff to help accomplish it — personnel whose job was to make the rounds of numerous banks converting to hundreds currency of smaller denominations.

Major distributors of pot, given the number of people with whom they were dealing, were already exposed on numerous fronts. Employing drivers and money handlers — large operations moved singles and fives by the truckload

— put them that much closer to the heat. In the pot business, at the level at which Long and his associates were operating, the money, like the marijuana itself, had come to be viewed as cargo. (When the cocaine trade picked up a few years later, the money would represent the larger transportation problem for traffickers, the volume of cash exceeding the volume of the cocaine, every kilo of coke generating about three kilos of currency in singles, fives, tens, and twenties.) A quarter of a million dollars in hundreds, Allen Long discovered, fit nicely in fifty No. 10 envelopes containing $5,000 each. Five million dollars in hundreds, in a single stack, stood two stories high — just about twenty feet up — and weighed 110 pounds.

Like any respectable South Florida host, Jimmy had a precision scale in the house readily available to guests. The smugglers, emptying one of the cardboard boxes, placed it on the scale and came up with a tare weight. They reloaded the box, weighed it and all the other boxes, and then did the arithmetic, calculating a U.S. banknote at precisely a gram. They came up $100,000 short, which, out of $8 million-plus, fell well within the margin of error. Perhaps they overestimated the weight of the rubber bands. A hundred thousand was small change at the level at which everyone was operating. Long was spending around half that much every week in expenses. As Long was leaving the house that day, Jimmy, the way another man might hand him a cigar, gave him a Ferrari. A 308GTB.

"Looks new," Carlyle said, when Long stepped out in Fort Lauderdale.

"It's got about six hundred miles on the clock."

"Not a bad rig."

"You know, they're really pretty tight," said Long. "They're hard to move around in."

"They take some getting used to."

"I don't know. You want it?"

"It's not my kind of ride," said Carlyle.

Long gave it back a week later.

A hundred-thousand-dollar automobile Jimmy Alvarez would give away without breathing hard. Hide a nickel from him and he wanted to talk.

What Carlyle had pulled with Jimmy that had almost gotten him killed was what the Miami smugglers had been pulling on each other from day one. Jimmy himself was no exception. It explains why Allen Long was able to do so well in Miami — he was the first person with whom these crooks had ever done business they could actually trust to be honest. Virgil, Tony's pal, who had done the talking that day at the crab house, setting the tone for Long's initial South Florida transaction, was a good old boy in whom Long saw a sense of decency lacking in some of the others. Proving to be far more easygoing than had been apparent the day they met, Virgil, an honorable fellow, was quick to grow weary of doing business with Jimmy. And it was Virgil, working independently, who engineered the move that Lee Carlyle believed finally vindicated his position vis-à-vis Myerson.

"You won't believe this," Carlyle said, calling Long in New York and telling him to get down to Miami. "I made money for *you* for a change."

Carlyle, taking a load that Virgil had moved on his own, had sold 38,000 pounds of pot through his buyers in California.

"And instead of twelve dollars a pound, man, we made forty-seven."

They had made twice as much money as on the latest

Ann Arbor load, and on half the amount of pot. Long cleared $780,000. One deal. That day.

"There's only one thing I ask," Carlyle said.

"Go ahead, ask."

"Now can we get rid of Jake?"

"Are you out of your mind?"

"Give me one good reason to do business with the guy."

"Turnover," said Long. "Just think for a minute."

"You think for a minute. Take a look at this deal."

"This deal took a month. With Jake it's a couple of days. And this deal was three different deals. Which is three times the exposure."

"It's four times the money. I'm telling you," Carlyle said, "we don't have to work with the guy."

One guy Carlyle was determined to work with, however, was Virgil. And Virgil was ready to go. Eager to strike out on his own, he saw Carlyle and Long as the guys who could help him do it.

"You can't tell Jimmy," he said. "And don't tell Tony."

The three of them, Virgil, Long, and Carlyle, were sitting in the "Florida room" of Virgil's prefabricated tract house. The room, about ten feet square, had known life as a screened-in porch before Virgil installed the jalousie windows that made the new designation official. In the concrete pad on which the room sat, Virgil had chipped out a hole in which he had laid down some 4 mil polyethylene. When the excavation failed as a fishpond, he had thrown into the hole a plastic fountain, which gurgled now as the three men spoke. The rest of the floor was covered in Astroturf. A year later, when Virgil was living in a custombuilt place with water on three sides — a mansion complete with aviary and a sixty-foot power boat tied up to the dock on the bayside of Upper Matecumbe Key — the entire joint

would be decorated in the style of the room in which Long was presently sitting.

"I won't stand in your way," Long said. "But I'm not going to jeopardize my relationship with these guys."

"Fair enough," Virgil said.

Virgil was moving on, and in doing so, moving up. The trip he was putting together was four times the size of his first, and he was not bringing the load into Miami.

Carlyle said, "I'm gonna *do* it."

Long said he would back Carlyle's play.

Long's own disenchantment with Jimmy and the Miami operation, in general, coagulated around a series of events in early 1978. Jimmy was taking a piece of a 25,000-pound load that belonged to a local businessman, a Calle Ocho retailer by the name of Enrique who insisted upon being called Don Enrique. Jimmy was taking $10 a pound for hooking the guy up with Long.

"I will get my share from Don Enrique," Long was informed by Jimmy. "You can pay *him* the money."

When Enrique flew to New York to pick up the cash, Long paid him for all but a thousand pounds of the load, holding back $200,000, explaining to him that the bales were no good. "They got wet. They're moldy," Long said. The last twenty bales were sitting in a warehouse in Virginia. "I went down to look at them. I can't sell them," he told Enrique.

"When are you going to pay me for them?"

"The pot's wet. It's no good, Enrique. It got wet in the hold of the ship."

"There was nothing wet in my load."

"Look, Enrique, you can ask anybody," said Long.

"Ripping people off is not something I do." He was rich, and growing richer every day, he said. He did not need to steal anyone's money. But neither was he giving money away. "I'm not going to pay two hundred thousand for wet marijuana."

On a legal pad, over the dining room table in his apartment, Long laid out the numbers, providing Don Enrique with an itemized account of every dollar earned on the load.

"I understand the problem you have," he said, "but you can see the marijuana yourself. If you want, you can go pick it up. Or I will pick it up for you."

"Pick it up?" said Don Enrique, astonished.

"What I will do," said Long, "is I will pick it up myself, and bring it back to you in Miami."

"No. No. Don't bring it back to me. That won't be necessary. I believe you. I trust you," said Don Enrique.

They agreed to write off the twenty bales.

Two weeks later, Long received a call from Jimmy.

"Allen, you must come to Miami."

Jimmy picked him up at the airport.

In the back of the car when Long stepped in, sitting with Jimmy's man Dennis, was a guy introduced as Dwayne. Long had not met him before. He was pushing forty, he had dark hair and eyes, and was about the size of a mature Kodiak bear. You could probably bring him down, Long figured, if you loaded, say, .460 Weatherby Magnum. You definitely want to get him off his feet first, then you move in close, he told himself, using some decent power tools . . . Seeing Dennis was no surprise, Dennis was always there. But Long wondered why this guy was on hand. The .45 semiauto protruding from Jimmy's waistband added to Long's consternation.

Long thought of Jimmy as his friend, but he had to be

careful, he realized, not to forget who he was actually dealing with. Take Tony A., for example. Tony was a man who owned plenty of guns, but never to Long's knowledge was Tony seen cruising the streets of Miami with one of them stuck in his belt. In Miami that made Tony a gentleman. Jimmy, on the other hand, Long was now quick to remind himself, was something else altogether. Jimmy, yes, was rich, he called himself Don Jimmy, he dressed in Brioni suits, he drove Ferraris, but he was still — What was the expression Long was looking for? Oh, yeah — he was still a fucking gangster.

Long stepped into the car.

"We have a problem, Allen."

"You know, Jimmy," Long mused aloud, "if I ever do a Greatest Hits album, that's gonna be the title."

Long turned to smile at the boys in the back. Jimmy explained the problem. The problem was that Don Enrique was not paying Don Jimmy.

"He says it is because you, Allen, owe him money."

Long said, "That's not true."

And he told Jimmy what had happened.

"Okay," Jimmy responded, after hearing the story, "that is all you have to remember. When I ask you to tell your side of things, when I say go ahead, speak, that is what you have to say."

"What do you mean, Jimmy? Where are we going?"

"We're going to meet Don Enrique."

They met him at an Eighth Street restaurant. It was about one in the afternoon. Don Enrique, clearly uptight, arrived with two associates, the three of them joining Jimmy and the others at a semicircular banquette in the rear.

The joint was packed.

"Hello, Enrique," said Long.

"Oh, it is you," Enrique said. "It is your fault."

"Wait a minute . . ." said Long.

Jimmy said, "Nobody talk."

It was going to be an interesting lunch.

At the table, getting a fix on the talent, Long was hard pressed to identify anyone in his immediate vicinity whose membership in the Farmington Country Club he would unequivocally sponsor. He was reminded of every gangster movie he had seen in a lifetime, and he envisioned himself, in CinemaScope, lying face-down in motor oil on a garage floor in Chicago, leaking vital fluids through the threads of a double-breasted suit, hemorrhaging in honor of Saint Valentine. You could have cut the tension with any of the knives with which the table was set. Or anybody at the table could have shot it. Jimmy was carrying a gun, Dennis was carrying a gun, Dwayne was carrying a gun, Enrique's two henchmen were carrying guns, Enrique was carrying a gun. At the table, Long alone was unarmed. Not that he wanted a gun. But right now, clearly, it was the wrong table to be at.

Waiter, excuse me, I'm at the wrong table.

Everybody ordered iced tea.

"Enrique, tell Allen what you told me," said Jimmy. "Enrique says you did not pay him, Allen."

"That is right," said Don Enrique. "He did not pay me for part of the shipment." Enrique turned to Long, and said, "That is Jimmy's part. You have to pay him."

"Listen," Long said. He turned to Jimmy. "I'm going to say this one more time, and that is going to be it. You, Enrique, came to my *house*. We went over the bookwork together. I told you the remainder of the shipment was no good. I said I'd bring it back to Miami. You said you didn't want it back, that you believed me, and that was it. And, Jimmy, that's the truth."

"No, that is not true," Enrique replied. "You owe me. *You* are going to pay Jimmy. I am not going to pay him."

At issue was 4 percent of the load, a thousand pounds of wet marijuana. Enrique still owed Jimmy his dime on the other 96 percent. He had not even paid Jimmy *that*. By Enrique's reckoning the $200,000 Long had held back was coming out of Jimmy's two-fifty. He was going to pay Jimmy fifty grand and call it a day.

Long said, "I'm not staying here."

As Long was getting to his feet, he felt Dwayne take hold of his arm, gripping him under the shoulder, like a Boy Scout about to usher him across an unusually busy street.

"Stay here," he groaned, pulling Long back into his chair.

Jimmy is the one who stood. He jumped up, reached under his *guayabera,* and pulled the .45 out of his waist-band.

"I'm going to kill somebody at this table," he shouted, waving the pistol from one side of the table to the other.

It was Miami, it was Calle Ocho, no surprises here. The restaurant patrons kind of lowered their heads, but nobody in the crowd stopped eating.

"Somebody at this table is going to pay me," yelled Jimmy, "or somebody at this table is going to die."

It was not until he cocked the pistol that activity in the restaurant came to a halt. You could hear the silence fall. The only thing moving now was the barrel of the gun, swinging back and forth between Don Enrique and Long.

"I will pay," said Don Enrique. "But you," he said to Long, "you make a big mistake when you try to fuck me."

"You are going to pay, Enrique, correct?" said Jimmy.

"Yes."

"Very good. Now we will have lunch."

These were the kinds of people Long was dealing with

as a matter of routine. Enrique, who had just threatened to kill him, had tried to rip Jimmy off, and had been prepared to let Long die for it if he could induce Jimmy to believe he had been shorted. This is what it had come to after a year and a half.

"It is nothing, my friend," said Jimmy.

If he and Jimmy were in fact friends, Long asked, why would Jimmy need to restrain him? Why the muscle? Why have Dwayne holding him down in the booth?

"Oh, I had to know the truth," Jimmy said.

"I *told* you the truth," said Long.

And he wondered if Andreas had died saying the same thing. He wondered if after the young restaurant owner had taken the bullet, one of the fifteen other guys involved in the load, some guy like Don Enrique, or even a "gentleman" like Tony, had shaken his head and said, "I didn't know they were going to kill him . . . That's too bad . . . Hey, don't you think he would have done the same thing if he had the chance?"

"You don't have to be a marijuana smuggler," Nat Weiss advised. "You'd be a terrific record promotions man."

In the record business Nat Weiss was more than a major presence, he was something of a legend. Developing and representing talent as the manager of numerous acts and one of the industry's more powerful lawyers, he had been instrumental in the success of some of the more famous names in music. Weiss had his own label at CBS, and he and Long had been friends since Long's days as an aspiring filmmaker in New York, when Long had approached him seeking to promote concerts. In 1976 Weiss had signed song-writer Robbin Thompson, whom Long was managing at the time. Remaining a source of advice and support to Long,

Weiss never gave up on the younger man, whose energy and enthusiasm he admired. He was one of very few people Allen Long never thought he knew more than.

"Give record promotions a try," Weiss said, and offered Long a job doing it.

Long, fast on the heels of his lunch with the Dons Enrique and Jimmy, accepted Nat Weiss's job offer in the spring of 1978. He went to work in Special Projects and Promotions at Weiss's label, Nemperor Records. It had been years since Long had adhered to a work schedule, years since he had exercised the self-discipline required of a legitimate job, but he committed himself to trying, and he discovered that he actually enjoyed it. Not only did he like the job, but he found that he was good at it. For the first time in a long time he proved successful at something other than the dope business.

"I hear you did a great job in Dallas," he was told, when he returned from the Radio and Records Convention, at which he had represented the label. According to Weiss his success was reverberating through the corridors of CBS. He had "made a lot of noise," surprising many people with an outstanding performance in what was known to be an extremely tough business.

"Well, they weren't carrying submachine guns, Nat. You want to see a hard sell? Try negotiating with a guy named Ernesto."

"Yetnikoff and Lundvall want to meet you."

Walter Yetnikoff, president of CBS Records, and Bruce Lundvall, president of Epic, were among the more powerful executives in the entertainment business. They invited Long and Weiss to lunch at San Marco. It was the industry equivalent of an anointment.

Long did not show up.

When he walked into Weiss's office the next day, Weiss cut him off before he could speak. "Whatever you do, don't tell me the truth. Tell me anything," pleaded Weiss, "tell me your mother died. Tell me you were in an accident."

With the right story Weiss could probably smooth things out, he could probably salvage the job. But Weiss was not going to lie. If Long gave him the wrong story, if he gave him what Weiss supposed was the truth, Weiss would be hard pressed to save him.

But in the face of the problem before them, the slack that Weiss was prepared to cut him proved to be the problem itself. In the end, it was Weiss's faith in him that inevitably terrified Long. Fearing that one day he might fail to live up to it, Long left nothing to chance.

"Nat, I can't do this, I'll just let you down. Just like I did yesterday."

"Well, that's really sad," said Weiss.

Long had managed to go legit for a few months, and then, with the help of a quarter-ounce of cocaine, he chickened out of his future.

Long and Weiss remained friends. Weiss, who had never lied to him, never taken advantage of him, and had always responded when asked, continued as a source of encouragement and counsel, and like many who invested their belief in him, waited for his belief to be justified.

If you listened carefully, you could hear the sound of hearts breaking all over the place.

Cherie would have taken issue with the suggestion that her boyfriend was probably a drug addict. Cherie was not blind to reality, but even had she not been dragged so deeply into the strangeness of it all, enlightenment would have remained beyond reach. Cocaine, undergoing glorification at the time, was considered not only chic but relatively

harmless. And upon many people its impact was mild. But these were people who were measuring their intake by the line, buying it by the gram, maybe doing it on the weekend. Few were the people of Cherie's acquaintance who were *not* doing coke, but the severe psychological free fall that was sweeping her up in its wake was not yet a common affliction. Long was measuring his intake not by the gram, but by multiples thereof, doing cocaine every day, and worse, laying it on every night. Cherie viewed it as simple over-indulgence, much the way she viewed his random antics with other women.

But even as she remained naive to the ramifications of his drug use, Cherie had long since reached the point where she was no longer cavalier about the drug business. It had far outgrown the escapade, the small statement of personal freedom — the blow against the Empire — initially articulated by Long. He had left the counterculture way behind him. If the man she loved was not already a gangster, he was fast approaching the point at which he would do until one came along.

Long's unwillingness to confide in her, his insistence upon leaving his troubles at the office, as it were, was a source of constant fighting between them. The rule, as he saw it, was clear, a proscription promoted, if not always observed, by professional outlaws of all kinds: You did not share information with the women in your life beyond what you were unable to hide. Silence was the strongest safeguard — for you, for them, and just as importantly, for your friends.

"They won't trust me," he told Cherie, "if you know what's going on."

Knowledge was culpability. Giving Cherie deniability went a long way toward protecting her, and in doing so protected him and any of those associates, those co-conspirators of his,

against whom she might be forced to testify. You did not have to pass the bar exam to know that wives and girlfriends were a liability. Their innocence was not enough to prevent ambitious prosecutors from going after them, using them against you, threatening to lock them up if you refused to cooperate:

The drugs were in the trunk of your car when you picked her up for dinner. That makes her part of the conspiracy. She's facing forty years.

Which explained, in part, why drug smugglers were so generous in supporting the careers of prostitutes, not one of whom ever was known to ask, "How did things go today, honey?"

Long had used the drug business as leverage to get Cherie out of his apartment — he had rented her a place on Houston Street — but still, she spent much of her time there. Long was away a lot, and in his absence Cherie started using cocaine a lot to keep herself entertained. She found herself, now and then, picking the lock of his apartment to hit his stash when she ran out. Shortly before his failure at Nemperor Records, Long returned from a trip to Miami to find that, searching for cocaine, she had accidentally destroyed a treasured possession of his. An inlaid puzzle box, hand-carved of tropical woods, in which cocaine was occasionally hidden, the valuable piece of craftsmanship had been commissioned by Long from one of the many artists he supported. Cherie had splintered it beyond repair trying to get it open. The fight that followed the incident was as destructive as her assault on the artwork. Reckless, spiteful, and pointedly malicious, it ended with Long's leaving the bedroom to find JD Reed on the living room floor, kneeling on one of the Afghani prayer rugs he routinely gave away after using them to smuggle hash oil.

"What are you doing?" said Long.

"I'm praying for you, man."

Long and Cherie routinely rifled each other's stashes of cocaine, and it was nothing to get excited about. Long bought cocaine for both of them — he might be doing it in one room while she was doing it in another, it was like putting on a pot of coffee, an adjunct to other activities — and when his stash ran out, it was natural for him to hit hers. Long bought blow in volume, but rarely did he do all that he bought. He always found someone to share it with, if only until whoever it was gave up and said good night.

While Cherie was breaking into the puzzle box, Myerson was flying to Miami carrying $2 million in cash, all hundreds, in a suitcase, the back end of a payment on a 20,000-pound load. He and Long were to meet and deliver the money to Jimmy together. Long was late by several hours — sell him enough cocaine, the way things were going, and he could be late by several days — and when finally he did show up, he had a young woman with him in the limousine. A stranger. Maybe she was a prostitute, maybe just a young coke freak he picked up in a bar. When Myerson pressed him on it, Long was unable to recall. And as if that in itself were not dangerous enough, Long had the limousine driver cruise the dark streets of downtown Miami, dragging Myerson and the forty-four pounds of money along, as he and his date looked for a connection.

A clinical fog had begun to roll in behind the squall line of cocaine, that brume of psychological uncertainty in which cause and effect are slowly obscured, where what at first appeared to be a symptom of spiritual chaos becomes the agent of the chaos itself.

Cherie, studying to be an actress, was "too stoned to do anything emotionally," she confided to a friend, having come

to believe that the night before a scheduled class, Long always made sure to get her high, and in so doing insure her failure. She started spending more time at Houston Street. She started seeing other men casually. Long gave her a ring. He took it back.

Their days together were numbered.

"You know, man," Carlyle said, as though informing Long he had mail, "you need to come down here and pick up your money."

"Yeah, okay, I'll be there," said Long.

Virgil's load had come in, and Long and Carlyle, taking half of it, had moved 80,000 pounds of red through the system. Their share of the take was in cardboard boxes, stashed in the spare bedroom of Carlyle's house in Fort Lauderdale. Long flew from New York on the company jet — they had one under lease now — to collect his cut of the cash.

"Half of that's yours, brother," Carlyle announced, leaning against the door frame, as Long entered the bedroom to confront the tableau.

"You're kidding."

The cash filled a stack of boxes that covered an entire wall.

"Whenever you're ready," Carlyle said.

Dividing it took the rest of the day.

". . . One stack for you, one stack for me . . . five thousand for you . . ."

By nightfall the two smugglers were effectively corraled, sitting on the wall-to-wall carpet with a narrow walkway between them and eight inches of money covering the floor. They had split over $3 million.

"You know," Long said, as they counted the last of it, "maybe it's time to quit."

"Oh, man," declared Carlyle, "don't say that. Not yet. Let's not quit yet."

"We have to walk away sometime."

"Buddy, I'm in it for the gold watch."

"We didn't get into this to do it forever. How much money do we need?"

Carlyle started laughing.

"Yeah," he said.

"What?"

"That's funny."

"What's funny?"

"Huh?" Carlyle gave him a look of bewilderment. "Are you serious?"

"What do you mean?"

"Man, we don't do it for the money."

And now Long found himself laughing. "Say that again, I don't think I heard you right."

"We do it. It's what we do. It's what we're good at," said Carlyle. "We're like everybody else. We do it because . . . It's what we fuckin' *do*."

"What the hell are you smoking?"

Carlyle just smiled and shook his head.

"Smuggling pot," said Long, "is not something we're destined to spend our lives at. JD, maybe, but not us. JD's a guy who loves what he does. He would never think of doing anything else. Probably couldn't do anything else. He believes in pot. He's the next best thing to a missionary."

"Allen, being in it for the pot is no less ridiculous than being in it for the money. JD does it for the same reasons we do it."

"Wrong," said Long. "JD is a crusader. Pot, as far as he's

concerned, is the one thing on earth that's legit. Pot's his job, it's what he does best. It's his destiny. You and I, we could do anything."

"Pot's the only thing you and I have been good at in our lives," said Carlyle. "We've never done anything but suck at everything else. And we probably never will do anything but suck."

"I don't buy that."

"Pot's the only thing you and I haven't been losers at since the day we were born, Allen. That's why we do it. That's why we're going to be doing it tomorrow, and the next day and the day after that. Face it. Pot's what we do. When the ship goes down, we're going to be on it."

They had come some distance from Guadalajara and that table at La Copa de Leche. Carlyle's dime had carried them far. A little bit too far, perhaps. To Long's way of thinking, the terrain in which they found themselves was beginning to look downright exotic. The lives of both had been threatened. Carlyle was driving around Miami with a gun in his car. There had been the matter-of-fact murder of Andreas, the kidnapping of Carlyle's girlfriend, the business with Don Enrique. And the money. There was just so much of it.

This was *real* criminal activity now.

In a year and a half, over the course of maybe a dozen boats, Long had made $8 million. In cash. No taxes. Granted, he was spending over $5,000 a day whether the boat came in or not. Fifteen hundred a day on hotel rooms. Limo on call twenty-four hours at something like $400 a day. An executive jet, a pilot and co-pilot ready to go, call it $3,000 a day. These were the necessities of life. With what he was spending on women and coke, he was looking at a total outgo of a quarter of a million a month — minimum — maybe $350,000 a month without buying anything of real value.

The airplane, of course, was a legitimate business expense. A six-seat Rockwell Jet Commander, with a little more headroom than a Lear, the plane, in addition to everything else, was essential to the transport of money. One could not fly commercial carrying $10 million in cash, nor on a scheduled airline could one hope to move that kind of money in the necessary three to four days. On call around the clock — plane, pilot, and co-pilot — the twin-engine jet offered speed, security, and efficiency. Long had leased the plane for a year at a cost of $150,00, paying another $75,000 to extend the lease for an extra six months. It cost additional money to take the plane up. Round-trip between Miami and San Francisco cost roughly $10,000.

The typical flight for Long started at Fort Lauderdale Executive Airport, and went from there to Washington, New York, and Ann Arbor, making stops as far west as San Francisco or Lake Tahoe, before heading back to South Florida, where limousines would be waiting for the money. The plane and the limos were leased in the name of a front company established by Carlyle, Real-to-Reel Productions, its ostensible mission being to pick up dailies and fly them to the company's film lab in Miami. Long generally tipped the pilots $10,000 in cash.

With cash representing the headache it did, the flight usually included a stop in Las Vegas, not to collect money but to exchange it, to convert the currency to the hundreds and fifties necessary for international payoff. At one of the city's larger hotels, through connections provided by Luther Reed, Long would launder the money through the casino, paying a one percent commission to the establishment. Depositing cash at the teller's cage in singles, fives, tens, and twenties, he would buy one hundred chips in thousand-dollar denominations, proceed to the roulette table, place a

single thousand-dollar bet, lose it, then return to the cage and cash in the remaining ninety-nine chips for hundreds and fifties. Holding forth from a suite at the hotel, he would do this five or six times a day over a period of three or four days, before taking the jet back to Florida.

Occasionally Long and Carlyle used the jet simply for recreation.

"Let's fly to the Bahamas for breakfast," they decided, closing a disco one night, flying off with a couple of willing young women who had managed to stray into their orbit.

It was in that same spirit that Carlyle now, surrounded by $3 million, and sensing that his friend was glum, suggested flying out to the Coast.

"You know what? Miami sucks," he said. "Let's just take our entire scene and move it to San Francisco."

It was a $40,000 trip, with no reason behind it other than the fact that Long was in a grumpy mood, and Carlyle, who wanted to cheer him up, was nostalgic for the West Coast anyway.

Long said, "What the hell."

They stashed the money, grabbed a case of champagne, and flew to San Francisco. They checked into the Stanford Court for four days, putting the pilots up with a car and expenses for the duration of their stay.

And still Long could not shake the blues.

The guns, the Quaaludes, the coke. This was not the journey he had embarked upon six years earlier. This was not the same business he had drifted into back then. Once an illegal business is good to you, as you get better at it, as it gets bigger, other illegal things, Long discovered, become easier to do. Where do you draw the line? If it is okay to sell marijuana, is it not okay to sell cocaine? If it is okay to carry dope in your car, is it okay to carry a gun? Where

do you say no? If people are out to rip you off, you probably *should* carry a gun. If they try, will you kill them? he asked himself. If they do rip you off, will you *find* them and kill them? Where, he wondered, do you stop?

This was not the marijuana business he knew. The coordinates of the enterprise had shifted observably. He was dealing with pot scammers who took people's lives, they had been shooting people for years. Before he showed up in Miami, all the smugglers he had known had been pot smokers. These characters did not smoke pot, they were in it for the money, nothing more. And now, as he looked at it, so was he.

He was not an outlaw, he was a racketeer.

He bought thousand-dollar suits and five-hundred-dollar shoes and traveled by limousine wherever he went. He traveled first-class when he was flying commercial and only when not traveling by executive jet. Crippled by a cocaine habit, he did not, as they say, get out much. All he saw were the insides of limos, the insides of airplanes, and the insides of luxury hotel suites. The only people he spent time with were drug dealers, or people who worked for drug dealers, or people who liked being with him because he was a drug dealer himself.

Allen Long's dreams of smuggler's glory, his quest for gold, his magnificent vision of El Dorado — all of his dreams had come true.

16

MUCH HAVE I TRAVELED IN
THE REALMS OF GOLD

"Are you kidding?"

"If *you* want to," said Long, "go ahead. Do it. It's fine with me."

"We'll probably do five hundred thousand pounds with him," said Myerson, reminding Long that they had made $22 million working with Jimmy. "You'll make yours just being in the middle."

"No. But go ahead," said Long. "You guys do it without me."

When Long told Carlyle he was quitting, Carlyle told him he was insane.

"These are not my kind of people," Long said.

"It's crazy," mumbled Carlyle.

"You can say that again."

Carlyle would have said it again, but he could not remember it.

*   *   *

It would be natural to think that Allen Long had acquired a kind of dilatory wisdom, that he had seen the error of his ways and decided to go straight. But Long, for all his enlightenment, for all the retirement money at his disposal, was just not that kind of guy. Finding himself without spiritual coordinates, having somehow lost his position, Long decided that what he needed to do was — as they say in the music business — reinvent himself, he needed to get back to his roots.

He decided he needed to be a smuggler again.

Long was nothing more than a middleman now, a broker. He was just going through the motions. He was just another businessman, he might as well have been selling cars. It had been six years since he had smuggled his first load of pot and almost two since he had smuggled his last. Coming up on his thirtieth birthday, he was at an entrepreneurial standstill. In his journey along the contraband trail, he had stumbled into some bad terrain, a geography of the imagination in which the wilderness was closed. It was time to get back to the border. He missed the scamming, the adventure, he missed the creative thinking. He missed the thrill of going up against the prohibitive odds to deliver the goods. He missed the weirdness. He needed some action.

Allen Long had the soul of a smuggler. A smuggler, not a dealer. The two were not simply different, they were chromosomally distinct. Long was suffering the outlaw equivalent of classic gender dysphoria: He was a smuggler trapped in a dealer's body. It was time for reassignment surgery.

Carlyle would continue working with Virgil, selling to his people out west. He and Myerson, happy to be rid of each other, would do no business together. Long would strike out on his own. But trying to move large loads of marijuana without a guy like Jimmy Alvarez posed a challenge that

was growing more difficult. Jimmy's operation offered more than financial security, it offered safety, a comforting layer of insulation against arrest. Long wanted to get free of Jimmy, but he did not want to get caught.

The government, concentrating its resources in Miami, had turned up the temperature in South Florida. Jimmy was one of few smugglers there who could move weight with any success. Since 1974 marijuana consumption had quadrupled. By 1978, according to the DEA, more than a third of the nation's adults, and one in five of its teenagers, were frequent drug users. And they consumed about twice as much pot every day as they consumed in cocaine all year. Some 42 million Americans smoked pot. Dope, by far the biggest business in Colombia, generating greater revenue than coffee, had by now surpassed the tourist industry as the largest employer in South Florida. It was the largest retail business in the state.

More than 70 percent of the marijuana coming into the country was now coming from Colombia. In late December 1977, a few months before Long made his decision, the government had initiated a six-week-long enforcement effort called Operation Stopgap. The DEA conducted an average of two flights a day over the Guajira and offshore waters, monitoring mother ship traffic, identifying clandestine airstrips, picking up aircraft tail numbers, and forwarding the information by radio to Miami. The U.S. Coast Guard had blockaded the Yucatan Channel and the Windward and Mona Passages. Happy with their numbers, federal agencies had followed up the initiative with a similar effort in April.

Within two years the feds would virtually shut down the Caribbean. With Customs, the Coast Guard, and the DEA augmented by U.S. armed forces, government interdiction efforts would grow so intense that large shipments of pot

from Colombia would pretty much come to an end. It was due in great part to the government's success that Colombian marijuana traffickers switched to moving cocaine, a product far easier to conceal, expanding a market in the United States that had been relatively small up to then. The government campaign against importation of pot would eventually give rise to a domestic marijuana industry of great agricultural significance. But more than that, it would be instrumental in creation of the market for cocaine, a market that would change the cultural landscape of the country, inevitably darkening its domestic politics and the geopolitics of the hemisphere. Bureaucracies would grow up around it. Preoccupation with cocaine would drive careers, in and out of government. Soon the prospect of a drug-free society would become economically unthinkable; in the absence of a war on dope, at $30 billion a year, a large chunk of the nation's gainfully employed population would be out looking for work.

Long saw what he perceived to be the future of Colombian pot in the 160,000-pound load of *punta roja* that Virgil had moved. The feds, growing fat on interdiction in the Caribbean and the Gulf, were not looking for loads farther north. Virgil, bringing it into Chesapeake Bay, had landed his load in Baltimore. And the pot had come right into the harbor. No mother ships, no go-fasts — it came right into town on a barge towed by an oceangoing tug from Colombia.

What, in the eyes of the government, could be as unlikely as that, Long wondered. How about moving Colombian pot, specifically Santa Marta Gold — all of which grew on the country's northeastern coast — a thousand miles west before shipping it north? How about moving the pot off the Guajira to, say, the port of Buenaventura on the country's Pacific

coast, avoiding the Caribbean altogether, and shipping the pot north from there, smuggling it into California?

For the next year and a half, Long worked on a single move. It would come to be known as "the Pacific trip," and in many ways the Pacific trip would come to define him as a smuggler. For sheer ambition and logistical complexity, it showed off all his talents. If the trip did not sound the overture to the future of Colombian pot, it did play as something of a crescendo, and in it were echoed all the sentiments that had driven Long's pursuit of his dream.

As a statement of artistic purpose, the move found its parallel in the annals of rock and roll, in a remark attributed to the late Jim Morrison, legendary lead singer of the Doors. Early in the band's career, playing a small club before a near-empty house, Morrison had closed the act with a physical, characteristically theatrical, signature assault on the microphone stand. Falling to the floor with it, writhing and screaming the set to a conclusion, he took the show over the top, as histrionic and dangerously energetic as if playing before a sold-out stadium. Or so the story goes. Asked what inspired him to do so in the face of such obvious indifference — there was no audience present to speak of — Morrison replied: "You never know when it's going to be your last performance."

The midtown Holiday Inn, situated on the outer reaches of civilization in Manhattan, within loud-hailing distance of the Hudson, within shotgun range of the New York headquarters of the Drug Enforcement Administration, served always to highlight Allen Long's deficiencies as a tour guide. Its position in the hierarchy of New York hoteldom was best illustrated by the confusion it suffered, in his and the

minds of many, with the Howard Johnson Motor Lodge six blocks south, where the FBI in 1970 had arrested fugitive Angela Davis, the gifted social philosopher and theoretical Communist who after her acquittal on murder and kidnapping charges sought spiritual refuge, it was rumored, on an ample parcel of improved real estate in Northern California, there to distribute her wealth, America liked to believe, among various dealers in imported automobiles, each according to his needs, and miscellaneous day help with nothing to lose but their chains.

Long's choosing the Holiday Inn in which to contravene the federal conspiracy statutes had nothing to do with the hotel's proximity to DEA headquarters and little to do with the FBI. It suggested not that Long possessed a refined sense of that which was fitting and just. There were a couple of conventions in town. Everything else was booked. It was Miguel's first visit to New York, and agreeing that "it would not be a good idea" for the Colombian to stay at the apartment — why supply potential prosecutors with that kind of ammunition — Long, who had intended to put his friend up at the Plaza, had reserved the only room in the city he could find.

"Isn't this where they popped Angela Davis?" he said, looking around the lobby, as the assistant manager working the desk was putting him through to the room.

"Howard Johnson's," the young woman said, handing him the phone. "They control the means of production on the Connecticut Turnpike."

At five P.M. Long was standing at the window of Miguel's room, looking down on West 57th Street. The sidewalks were acrawl with pedestrians. The vehicular traffic in both directions was choked by the afternoon rush. On the far side of the street, a uniformed cop with his hat pushed back

was asking a bearded man in a business suit if he could possibly cool the reefer. Gesturing patiently with his nightstick, pointing north by northeast, in the general direction of Newfoundland, the patrolman appeared to be telling the young exec, "Pal, the park's just over there."

"Ernesto can do only half," Miguel said. "The other half we will get from the people in Valledupar."

"It has to be good," said Long, turning away from the window.

"Only the gold and the red," Miguel replied. "We will pay them now. For next year's harvest. They will grow the marijuana just for you."

Miguel poured Scotch for both of them. He handed a glass to Long.

"And," said Long, "you are looking for a ship."

"There is a man in Cali. You will meet him when you come."

"Okay," said Long, raising his glass. "Now we will talk about the important things."

"Sir?" asked Miguel, raising his own.

Long downed the Scotch in one hit, set the glass down, and clapped his hands.

"Where would you like to eat tonight, and how many women do you want?"

The trip, in order to pay for itself, had to be worth at least $15 million. It had to be a 60,000-pound move. An investor asked to put up $500,000 had to receive ten to one on his money. At a meeting at the Trident hotel in Port Antonio, Jamaica, to which Miguel, Myerson, and Easy Matthews traveled with their wives, and Long traveled with Cherie — lunch every day was the same, lobster salad and Dom Pérignon — Myerson and Matthews agreed to invest a half a million each in the load. At a minimum

sale price of $300, they and Long stood to make $5 million apiece.

The logistics of the move were head-spinning. The plan was to move the pot to Buenaventura by air, and from there by Colombian freighter to the Northern California coast. The move required the purchase of a cargo plane, a freighter, and the lease of a helicopter. Necessary personnel included three pilots, a ship's captain and crew, and several off-loaders both in Colombia and in the United States.

It was like a pot-smuggling WPA project.

Long would be bringing some old friends together. And they needed a good place to talk. He set up a meeting in Las Vegas.

A city engorged with gamblers, hustlers of every stripe, and citizens from all over the country with nothing but time on their hands, Las Vegas, Nevada, was a short-odds favorite on any day to be playing host to a complement of wiseguys in collusion to violate the criminal statutes. The town was a national boardroom, of sorts, in which the underworld was free to convene, a dead end not only to the American Dream, but to the federal conspiracy investigation as well. As circumstantial evidence presented before a grand jury, a trip to the desert metropolis was about as persuasive as a trip to the lavatory. It was Vegas. A man never had to explain what he had been doing there.

Long arrived on the FBI breakfast flight, and when he exited the terminal at McCarran, JD Reed was waiting outside, leaning on the fender of his car, the brim of his Stetson cocked forward about 40 degrees off the horizontal. He grabbed Long's luggage, threw it in the car, handed him a twenty-eight-ounce Mason jar filled with bootleg 300 mg Quaaludes — "a gift from my dad" — and drove him to the Aladdin.

Reed was on probation. In the years leading up to the Colombian loads, while flying pot out of Sonora and selling it to Long in Richmond, Reed had also been moving boats out of Jalisco. In 1976, just before the first flight to Perico, he was arrested off-loading some 800 pounds of Mexican weed at a dock in Newport Beach, California. He made bail, and continued to postpone his court date, succeeding with the help of a lawyer paid for by Jake Myerson. Not until two years after his arrest did he go before a judge.

Three *days* after his arrest Reed was aboard the maiden flight of the DC-3 to Colombia. When the plane hit the trees on takeoff, and he jumped out with his survival gear, he naturally figured "I'm livin' here." As it was, he missed a date with his parole officer. He told him he "went fishin'." When the DC-3 was abandoned, and Long started middling pot in Miami, Reed returned to moving his own loads. In 1978 he finally appeared in court to answer the charges out of Newport Beach. Facing a maximum of five years in prison, he was sentenced to ninety days in jail and put on three years' probation, for the duration of which he was determined to behave himself. He would not be part of the Pacific trip. He had just been released from custody when Long arrived in Las Vegas.

When Long flew into town, followed in short order by Will McBride, his own arrival immediately followed by that of Frank Hatfield, Reed was on hand to welcome the boys to Las Vegas like a member of the Chamber of Commerce. He was there just to say hi. And just maybe to get high. And party a little. With Long in town, he knew there would be plenty of that. After ninety days in jail, he allowed, "I could use me some of that under yonder." Within an hour of their getting together, what *none* of the four men could use was a driver's license.

"So the guy tells me," Hatfield was saying, "'I like to look to my left and see nothing but engines. I like to look to my right and see nothing but co-pilots. Now that's a safe airplane. You take off in a jet, you're already in an emergency. Look behind you. You're on fire . . . !'"

"Allen," said McBride, holding up a joint.

Long was standing at the window with his head against the pane, talking to a pigeon roosting on the ledge outside the hotel room.

"Hey, buddy, how's it look up there?" Long whispered, tapping the glass. "You catch that breeze out of Barbados?"

". . . He tells me, 'If God wanted us to fly jets, son, he wouldn't have given us the sound barrier.'"

"Allen."

Long walked over to where the others were sitting, took the joint from McBride, and threw a thumb back in the direction of the window.

"Pilot talk," he said.

It had been almost two years since Long had worked with Hatfield and McBride. During that time, the pilots, doing business with Miguel, had made four flights to the Guajira in Hatfield's twin-engine Titan, but had met with little success. For what it was worth, McBride informed Long, they had found a 4,000-foot runway of hard-packed dirt about ten miles west of Perico.

"Which," he pointed out, "would have been kind of nice to know about when we were flying the 3."

Hatfield, smiling, turned to Reed.

"Let's not set sail on *that* sea of heartbreak," he said.

Reed raised a beer bottle to salute the notion.

Long, in Las Vegas, hired the pilots to find, purchase, and outfit a cargo plane at least as large as the DC-3 to handle cross-country transport of the marijuana within

Colombia. Because buying such an airplane in the States would draw the immediate scrutiny of several agencies, bureaucracies extending from the FAA to the Department of Defense, it was agreed that McBride and Hatfield would do their shopping elsewhere. They left Las Vegas with expense money and an eye on Central America.

"Action, action, action. That's the answer to your question. We do it for the action."

Long and Reed were taking the sun on the stern of Reed's thirty-two-foot Sea Ray, anchored off the Valley of Fire on the edge of Lake Meade.

"Yeah, you and me and Belle Starr," said Long, "before she lost her looks. The money never sucked either."

"She sucked for the money, as I remember."

"The old girl was never much of a tournament player."

"Strictly C.O.D."

"Hooking for the James gang, she never made as much as we did."

"She should have sold them weed."

"Sorry you can't help me on this one," said Long.

"Tell Ernesto I said *hola.*"

A few months later, in Costa Rica, the pilots picked up a DC-4. With new avionics, the plane came in at about $250,000. In February 1979, six months after the Vegas meeting, Long set out for Colombia.

"You must be careful," Miguel told him.

"What's the problem?"

"Raúl Gaviria is looking for you."

Oh, yeah. María.

On the trip through Sabana Rubia, Long and María had shared their dreams, mostly María's dreams, for Long's dreams changed dramatically once he had entertained hers. María wanted to see the world. She hoped one day to fly

her own plane. She wanted to see New York, Hong Kong, London, Paris, and Rome. She was *different* from traditional Colombian girls, she wanted Long to know. "I am not going to be like that," she insisted, of the timeworn values embraced by her friends and other Latin American women. The very feminine values, as luck would have it, that made her attractive to the Neanderthal in Long. No, she was a modern girl, she said. She wanted — and Long did not need to hear it to run from it — to be just like *American* girls.

"How bad is it, Miguel?" he asked.

"I believe it is serious, sir."

"As bad as a bullet with my name on it?"

"Worse, I am afraid. A tuxedo."

Just like American girls.

"I will be careful," said the fugitive bridegroom.

Long flew to Colombia, avoided María and her uncle, and spent several days traveling the country, setting out from the Guajira with Miguel and Pablo, visiting Buenaventura, Cali, Bogotá, and Valledupar. Looking at pot, laying out bribes, securing working relationships with numerous strangers, he stayed two weeks in South America.

Through Chase Manhattan, N.A., in Panama, Long bought a 170-foot Colombian freighter, the *Pituro Uno,* docked in Buenaventura. The ship, making regular runs between Peru and Colombia carrying ceramic tiles, was simultaneously being used by Colombian smugglers to bring coca leaves into the country for processing in the labs around Cali. The $480,000 Long paid for the freighter bought with it the compliance of the Colombian authorities who had been cooperating with the Cali traffickers.

Through Matthews, Long found a smuggler in California who would help orchestrate the off-load. The plan was to have the *Pituro Uno* lie seventy-five miles offshore, and to

remove the pot by air. Long secured a lease on a helicopter, a Sikorsky S-64 Skycrane, available from Georgia-Pacific for $60,000 a month in the summer. Capable of lifting over 20,000 pounds of cargo slung from its long fuselage boom, the helicopter had an operational range of 230 miles. Long bought a 5,000-gallon fuel truck to support the five trips necessary to off-load the freighter in 12,000-pound increments.

The pot would be brought ashore in the King Mountain Range on the north coast of Mendocino County, lowered from the Sikorsky into open-top tractor-trailer rigs running on logging roads.

The marijuana, purchased from two sources in Colombia, would be moved from separate locations. Ernesto would provide 30,000 pounds on the Guajira, and a second trafficker engaged by Miguel would provide another 30,000 in Valledupar, capital of César department, on the southern slope of the Sierra Nevada. The bales, triple-wrapped in 12 mil heat-sealed plastic and wound with heavy-gauge web netting, were to be transported in a total of four trips, air-dropped from the cargo bay of the DC-4 into a lagoon about a hundred miles north of Buenaventura. From there local villagers would move them by motor launch to the *Pituro Uno*. Successful test drops were conducted from 800 feet over the lagoon near Perico. The necessary Colombian coast guard commander cost $20,000.

Everything came together in the summer of 1979. The marijuana was cured and baled, all the money had been spent, and Long had a two-month window of opportunity in which the helicopter would be available, when Miguel called him in New York.

"Sir, we have a problem."

Without one, it would not be smuggling.

Ernesto's pot was ready to go, but in Valledupar, according to Miguel, police had received information that a shipment was about to be moved. Of the 30,000 destined for the airstrip there, the first 10,000 pounds were loaded aboard a tank truck that had been converted to carry dope, but with the heat coming down, the traffickers were afraid to move it. Long flew to Colombia, where he and Miguel, as time slipped away and their options rapidly diminished, made the decision to send the load, having little choice but to rely on the effectiveness of the scam, the bogus tank truck, itself. To thwart suspicion that the tanker was carrying anything other than bulk fuel, the truck had been rigged to pump gasoline from fuel drums hidden inside, one installed beneath the overhead tank hatch and the other behind the rear outlet.

With Long and Miguel preceding it through, the truck was detained at the first roadblock it hit. The police were obviously ready. They climbed all over the tanker, they pumped out gallons of fuel, they were certain there was dope aboard. Inevitably left scratching their heads, they reluctantly let the truck pass, but they were so sure that the truck was dirty, and so indignant in the face of defeat, that they radioed ahead, alerting officers at the next checkpoint. There the truck underwent the same scrutiny. The inspection yielded a similar result, but the truck was nevertheless refused passage. The smugglers were told they could not proceed, and their protestations of innocence were ignored. "We know you have marijuana," they were told. The truck was staying put.

Citing their rights got them absolutely nowhere. A smuggling arrest was never at issue. It was bribe money the cops were after. After the truck had been held for an hour, Long gave Miguel the last of his cash and instructed him to make the payoff. It took another hour for Miguel to convince the

officer in charge that the $8,000 he had given him was all the money he had. The officer let the truck pass, but he clearly was not happy with the story. He radioed his cousin, an army colonel, who met the smugglers at yet a third road-block fifteen miles down the road.

Negotiations with the colonel began at the roadblock and ended an hour later over beers in a nearby café. Long explained that he had no more money. The colonel explained that more money, and nothing short of more money, would activate the barrier gate behind which the truck was stalled. The conversation ended in a standoff, the deal was hope-lessly deadlocked, and it seemed the marijuana would never make the airstrip when Miguel made an inquiry of the colonel.

"Would you accept a check?"

The colonel said he would do so gladly.

Miguel wrote the colonel a postdated check in the amount of $10,000. The colonel, after thanking the smugglers, urged them to alert him in advance next time. In doing so, he advised them, they would avoid such inconvenience as they had experienced today and reduce their expenses to a single payoff.

Which is precisely what Ernesto on the Guajira had done in preparing to move his share of the load. And Ernesto did not rely on transactional bribery — he did not buy the service per se, he had bought and long since owned its provider. The payoff, covering a wide range of conditions and require-ments, secured him the working equivalent of a blanket policy, the kind made available by insurance companies and promoted in much the same spirit.

With the colonel's help, moving the pot to the airstrip in Valledupar was accomplished in a matter of three days. But by then enough time had slipped away to queer things

on the Guajira. There, thanks to a U.S.-sponsored drug-interdiction offensive, the bribery so assiduously applied by Ernesto was destined to go unrewarded. He would not be allowed to ship his pot, he was informed, until a respectable amount of time had passed. Long did not have time. There was only a month left in the operational window within which he was required to move.

He had 30,000 pounds ready to go, and 30,000 pounds would not do it. Moving half the load would pay for the trip, and he and his partners would walk away with a million dollars each, but Long, who was obsessed by now with the trip's being a serious crowd pleaser, wanted to move it all. Rather than move the 30,000, he gave up on the Sikorsky, and hustled to make other arrangements in California. Myerson led him to some Bay Area smugglers with a lease on an old Navy dry dock, who were preparing to bring loads of their own up from Colombia using a small fleet of fifty-foot trawlers, sailing them through the Golden Gate and right into San Francisco Bay. For a usurious 30 percent of the load, they agreed to meet the *Pituro Uno* and bring Long's pot ashore.

He would wish he had taken the million.

By the time he made it back to Colombia, Ernesto's marijuana had been busted, sacrificed to appease the DEA, and the smugglers in Valledupar, to secure their investment, had sold off the 30,000 pounds they were holding. "Not until next year," Miguel said, would he and Pablo be able to amass another 60,000 pounds of quality pot.

Six months later the *Pituro Uno* was busted. Eventually, by way of the DC-4 and a single San Francisco trawler — traveling directly to Buenaventura to make pickups in the lagoon — three loads of pot belonging to Miguel, a total of 45,000 pounds, ended up in Ann Arbor. But Long did not

learn that until later. By then he had been cut out of the deal.

The failure of the Pacific trip had cost him the trust of his partners, more than a year of his time, and about $3.5 million in cash. What he had seen as an opening to the future closed with the unmistakable sound of a door slamming on the past. Out of work and without a plan, Long called Tony A. in Miami. And it was Tony who showed him the future. It was Tony who helped him see where the dope business was *really* going.

He said: "Jimmy wants to talk to you."

Since Long had last done business with him, Jimmy had taken up residence in a three-million-dollar house he had built on a vast expanse of ranch land in the shadow of a Costa Rican volcano. He had been spending as much time there as in Miami, and it was there that Long reached him by phone.

"This man Santiago is killing me," said Jimmy.

Santiago was the Colombian middleman from whom Jimmy was now buying his pot. And Santiago, Jimmy alleged, was overcharging him for the product.

"He has grown too greedy," Jimmy complained.

Long understood this to mean that cheating him had grown too difficult.

Jimmy wanted Long to supply him with a new connection in Colombia. Long did not even bother to ask, "Whither Gilberto?" the original Colombian connection, with whom he had lunched at Victoria Station. That setup had been doomed to go south the instant Long stepped out of the deal. He had been the glue that held it together. In his absence, there would have been a host of "problems" —

discrepancies, alleged "contingencies," a "misunderstanding" here and there. Simply put, Gilberto would not be getting his money. No doubt, he had cut Jimmy off, refusing to do business with him. If "this man Santiago" were in fact guilty of overcharging Jimmy — and on that, the jury was still out — he was, as they say in California traffic court, "guilty with an explanation, Your Honor."

Long's professed misgivings about doing business with Jimmy had diminished in the course of a year and a half, and what remained of them he was able to set aside in the face of his failure to land a load on his own. Jimmy was a worker, you had to give him that. There would always be money in doing business with him. Long, seeking a new connection for him, reached out to Miguel in Barranquilla, who came back with the name of Samuel Calderón Sanchez. This was the man, Miguel said, to whom he would introduce Jimmy.

"That is his name!" shouted Jimmy when Long conveyed the news. "Calderón, that is the one!"

And Long just had to laugh. Thanks to Miguel, Jimmy had just accomplished the otherwise impossible. Jimmy had, without trying to, succeeded in jumping Santiago, in going around him to his supplier. Had Jimmy intended to do so, it never would have happened. Neither Jimmy nor Calderón could have made themselves known to each other. Santiago, who brokered their business, would always remain between them, he would always be entitled to a piece of their deal.

Positively blissful at the prospect of dealing directly with Calderón, Jimmy instructed Long to meet him in Miami. In the Everglades just west of Miami, Jimmy owned a ranch, the centerpiece of which was neither the lavish house nor small hotel situated on the property. Its focal point was the cockfighting ring to which breeders and high rollers from

all over the Caribbean were drawn to bet on fighting roosters like the thousands Jimmy owned.

"Let's go dig up some money," he said.

He and Long headed for the ranch. There Jimmy unearthed a trunk containing $850,000 in cash. Returning to Coral Gables, he transferred the money to briefcases, and the following morning set off to Bertram, where he bought two fifty-eight-foot power boats. Long shook hands with Jimmy on a fifty-fifty split. With an 80,000-pound load in the offing, he was looking at a $4 million payday.

The partners flew to Costa Rica.

La Finca de Don Jaime— or as others called it, Jimmy's place — as an ode to conspicuous consumption was state-of-the-poetic-art. The money he had spent to build the house, with indoor pool and a gymnasium, was a third of what he had spent on the barn. With ceramic tile floors, its numerous stalls were appointed each in the manner of a first-class hotel room, and accommodated what some considered the finest Andalusian horses in the Western Hemisphere. Jimmy had flown in the breeding stock from Austria and Spain. The stable was monitored by video camera twenty-four hours a day, except on those occasions when Jimmy threw a party, when he turned the horses out and equipped the stalls to house his guests. The ranch was also home to a congregation of fighting cocks, which were put up in individual cages. The sun did not rise quietly over the Finca de Don Jaime. The day after Long's arrival, and every day thereafter, he was awakened at dawn by the crowing of some 2,000 roosters, not blind (or deaf) to the piercing reality that he had helped generate the money that Jimmy had spent to accumulate them.

In residence at the ranch, anticipating the arrival of the vaunted Calderón, in addition to Long and Jimmy — and the ever-present Dennis — was a Miami Cuban named

Hector, the same CIA contract employee who had blown up that PT boat in Havana Harbor. Hector, employed by Jimmy, was related to Tony A. by marriage. Tony, let it be sufficient to say, had a nickel on everything that went down — from everybody.

When Calderón arrived at the airport, traveling with Miguel, Long and Jimmy were there to meet him. When Miguel introduced Calderón and Long, a look of recognition passed between them, but neither could place the other. It was on the ride back to the ranch that Long remembered where he had met the dark, heavyset Colombian who was seated with him in the car. It had been on the Guajira one night, the night Miguel told him about the burros.

Long remembered the night very well, a quiet night in Riohacha in 1976. He had been in Colombia selecting pot between flights of the DC-3. Returning from the fields with Miguel, walking through the jungle, he had seen two young boys jumping quickly through the brush, chasing a small donkey. Miguel, catching sight of them, provoked laughter in his fellow Colombians with an observation in Spanish that Long did not manage to catch.

Long asked about it that evening.

Because it would be unwise for a gringo to be seen spending the night in town, Long was camped with the Colombians in a compound near Riohacha, an outdoor encampment used by the local *contrabandistas* as a staging area, and for the storage and repair of equipment: trucks, guns, and other tools of the trade.

Sitting around the campfire that night, drinking *aguardiente,* Long asked Miguel what everyone had found so funny earlier in the day.

"Oh," said Miguel, "the little boys, they were trying to fuck the burro."

"Come on."

"You have never fucked a burro?"

"Are you serious?" said Long.

Miguel seemed genuinely surprised.

"Oh, yes, sir, it is done all the time."

Long laughed, certain that his friend was putting him on, convinced that this was some sort of time-honored gag the Colombians enjoyed at the expense of every visiting gringo.

"Oh, yes, sir," Miguel insisted, "they were trying to fuck the burro. You have never done this?"

"No."

"Oh, it is very good. Very sweet," Miguel said, kissing his fingertips, spreading them open like a bouquet. "Good pussy."

Long was incredulous now.

"Miguel, you fucked a donkey?"

"Not only me, sir," answered Miguel. "I bet you that every man here, around this fire, when he was a little boy, fucked a burro."

And with that he began polling his countrymen . . .

"*Sí* . . ."

"Oh, yes . . ."

"Very good . . ."

"*Muy buena* . . ."

. . . each man, in turn, answering in the affirmative.

"In my country, Allen," Miguel explained, "you learn when you are a boy that there are two kinds of women, the *señoritas* and the *putas*. The *señoritas,* they do not fuck. The *putas,* the whores, these are the ones who fuck. But we are only boys, we don't have any money to pay them. And so, when you reach the age where the desire to fuck is so

great, it is a tradition, you fuck the burros. The burros have no disease like the dogs. My father, when I was a little boy, he told me: 'Don't fuck the dog!' And you cannot fuck the chickens, because later they will die. It is only the burros you can fuck. Every man, when he is a child in Colombia, fucks a burro. And it can be very good."

As Miguel explained this to Long, the smugglers around the campfire nodded their agreement, ventured amplification, and injected words of wisdom. One man among them did not speak. He was larger than the others, darker, his skin tone a deep mahogany, mulatto where they were mestizo. His hair was black and thick, his features almost simian. Standing outside the conversation, he was working at a makeshift table over which he had thrown a dropcloth, cleaning automatic weapons by the light of the fire. He had pulled them out of a sack . . . Uzis, Ingrams . . . a half-dozen submachine guns, and his attention to them was proprietary. All were loaded and ready to go, and all of them were his. Snapping in their magazines as he finished oiling the weapons, he added audible punctuation to the conversation taking place, the intermittent click of steel on steel mimicking the crackling of the fire. Other than that he was silent.

"This is a very dangerous man," Miguel had said, pointing him out to Long, "very famous here in the Guajira."

This was Samuel Calderón Sanchez.

A rising power in the marijuana business, Calderón, according to Miguel, had already killed twelve men. His most recent murder was of a witness to another murder he had committed. As the witness was about to give evidence, Calderón had run up and shot him dead right on the steps of the courthouse.

Calderón's reputation for ruthlessness and the fear he inspired among his countrymen had not yet been matched

by wealth. Only recently had the killer turned his prodigious criminal talents to smuggling. Calderón, that night on the Guajira, did not make himself known to Long. He merely said hello. To attempt to effect a connection with the American was forbidden by the rules of the trade. Any business they did would be conducted by way of Miguel.

The night on which he had met Calderón was a memorable one for Long, if for nothing else than for being so instructive. There he sat before the campfire, the flames casting shadows across the brown, weathered faces of the armed *contrabandistas* of Colombia. All had 5,000 to 10,000 pounds of pot stashed somewhere in the jungle. Sitting there on boxes and rickety chairs in their cowboy hats and boots, on the dirt floor of a lean-to under a shed roof of corrugated tin, they were drinking *aguardiente* and discussing sexual congress with animals to the sound of submachine guns being cleaned. And Long would never forget being reminded of how far he was from home.

The events of the evening came back to him now, traveling to Jimmy's ranch from the airport in San Jose.

In the two years since that night in Riohacha, Samuel Calderón had ascended to a position of preeminent wealth and power as a smuggler. He now owned a significant interest in Colombia's Aerocondor Airlines, a commercial carrier recently subverted by traffickers, and turned to the purpose of smuggling large shipments of cocaine. His reputation for mercilessness, which put that of Jimmy Alvarez in the shade, foreshadowed the emergence later of the cocaine cartels in Colombia and the tide of violence upon which they rose.

"There is a time in Colombia," Long understood, unburdening himself of the understanding in a conversation he

had with Carlyle after the Pacific trip went bad, "a time when if you don't kill someone, you don't get the job done. That's how things are handled. You pull the trigger. And everything gets taken care of."

The time was rapidly approaching when no one who did business in Colombia did so without blood on his hands.

Jimmy turned the horses out and put his guests up in the stable, checking each man into a stall. He made reservations at his favorite restaurant, a local dining establishment that he owned.

"Down by the river," he said.

By the river on his ranch.

Jimmy's wealth and the distance it placed between him and the indigenous population had engendered in the drug kingpin severe paranoia. He believed that the locals were trying to poison his roosters and slaughter his horses, and were just waiting to murder him. It had driven him to desperate measures. That he might dine out whenever the fancy struck him, without fear of assassination, Jimmy had built his own restaurant. It sat on a verdant spit of land at a bend in the river traversing his property. Supporting a roof of thatch, featuring an indoor-outdoor barbecue pit and handmade tables and chairs, it was open to the air and not open to the public. The restaurant served Jimmy exclusively. When Jimmy felt like dining out, he picked up the phone, called his cook, and instructed him to slaughter a pig and break out a couple of bottles of Château Lafite. He then called the maintenance man and told him to turn on the lights, the brightest of which was the neon sign installed on the roof that read: "Jimmy's."

At the door of the restaurant, Long and the others were greeted by a pair of white-jacketed waiters. A pig was roasting, rice and beans were cooking, and the table was set

with several bottles of seventy-year-old Bordeaux. It was there, that night, in front of his other guests and putative business partners, that Jimmy, with a "by the way," informed Long that his cut of the load had been reduced from a half to a third. He had taken on another partner, he said, the man who would be handling the Florida off-load, using Jimmy's Bertrams to meet Calderón's freighter offshore.

There was little Long could do but accede to the new terms, however incensed he might be by their unilateral adoption. At a third of $8 million, he was still looking at a nice piece of change. He was in for $2.6 million, and all he had to do was go to Colombia and pick out the best pot he could find.

Conversation over dinner proceeded from that particular slap in the face to an orgy of whining and self-justification, with Jimmy and Calderón, two of the wealthier men in the dope industry, complaining about the exorbitant amount each of them had been losing to Santiago. The undisguised rapacity with which they cut out the middleman who had helped to make each of them so rich failed to make more than a passing impression upon Long, whose achievement, after all, had been to bring together these two creatures of God.

Calderón's digs in Barranquilla were the city-mouse equivalent of country-mouse Jimmy's Costa Rica crib. The extravagance of its forty-grand shower stalls, outfitted in marble and gold, was cast into vivid relief by the city's intermittent provision of municipal services. The morning after his arrival, Long, at Calderón's insistence, availed himself of the use of one, spending as much time therein as he deemed gracious under the circumstances — under no running water, hot or

cold — to be greeted upon his exit by an ain't-I-livin'-good smile from his host.

"The next thing I do," Calderón announced, "I will build a power plant."

From Barranquilla, with Hector in tow, Long set out for the Guajira, stopping in Santa Marta to check into the Irotama. Prized for its location, amenities, and service — for a long time it had been the city's only first-class hotel — the Irotama, quite innocently, had become a way station for every smuggler in the Western Hemisphere. Checking in was like genuflecting at Mass.

Out near Maicao, beyond Riohacha, in the dust of the high Guajira, Long got down to business, looking at truckload after truckload of marijuana, none of which was any good. He rejected about 400,000 pounds, finally amassing a shipment of some 80,000, maybe half of which was acceptable. The pot was not great, but four weeks had already passed — Long had picked up a terrible sunburn — and the time had come to move.

"What do you say?" asked Hector.

"It makes me high," said Long.

Period. End of evaluation. It was garden-variety, low-octane loco weed. It was not something the Rastas would ever want to write songs about.

"But there's no pot in the U.S.," said Long. "I guess we ought to send it."

"Good."

Using Ernesto's people, they loaded the pot aboard Calderón's freighter, a thousand pounds at a time, five trips each in sixteen *cayucas*. From the beach, in the dark, on a moonless night, Long watched the ship's mast light bobbing above the swells. Looking at a take of some $2.6 million, he hopped aboard the last *cayuca,* motored out, boarded

the freighter, and saw that the pot was stashed securely below. From the bow of the dugout, as he stepped back aboard to return to the beach, he kissed the stern of the freighter, sending it on its way.

They celebrated that night on the Guajira.

Calderón moved boats through the Caribbean where other smugglers could not, busting right through a U.S. task force that looked like the flotilla deployed at the Battle of Midway. Long was unsure how Calderón did it, but the pot arrived off the Marquesas Keys eight days after leaving the beach.

When Long arrived in Florida, Jimmy told him, "I need more Bertrams." They drove to the Everglades to dig up cash, and on the way Jimmy explained that to recoup his added expenses, he would be cutting Long's share down to 20 percent.

"Jimmy, we're partners, remember? It's getting ridiculous, it's gone far enough. I don't want to hear any more of it."

The pot came ashore, and Jimmy was too busy to meet.

"You cannot come here now," he told Long.

"Jimmy, I have a truck here in Florida, I'm ready to pick up my share."

"If you come here now, Allen, I will kill you."

Long let a couple of days go by, called Jimmy and said, "I'm coming over."

"Okay, my friend, it is not a good time, but okay," Jimmy said.

Evening had fallen. The house was in darkness but for the light of a few lamps. Jimmy sat alone at the dining room table. He motioned Long to a chair. Weapons covered the table, from end to end, from side to side, like a lawn. The weapons were new, many still packed in shipping grease. There were submachine guns, automatic rifles, and shoulder-fired grenade and rocket launchers.

"They got go-fasts now," Jimmy said.

Jimmy was talking about the U.S. Coast Guard. It was no secret that Jimmy now, in addition to pot, was moving large shipments of cocaine. And he did not intend to be stopped. His Bertrams, fully loaded, did maybe 27 knots. Unable to outrun the Coast Guard crews, he would blow their Cigarettes out of the water.

M-72s and M-79s. Rockets and grenades. This is where Long's adventure had brought him. This is where he had been led by the escapade he had decided to undertake almost ten years before, sitting there over a couple of joints in El Coyote's penthouse apartment.

"I'm ready to pick up my share of the load," he said.

"Yes, I know, I understand," said Jimmy, making room on the table in front of him. "But there are some things we need to talk about."

Jimmy flipped the page on a legal pad, and started playing with numbers. First of all, the load had been sold, he said. Long would not receive a share of the product to sell, he would be paid a share of the profit. Jimmy multiplied the weight of the load by a dollar figure significantly lower than reasonable, and started subtracting from there.

". . . Two new Bertrams, that is nine hundred thousand, and then, you see, I have a partner who does the off-load, he gets thirty-three percent, so we have to subtract that, and then I had to pay for the marijuana, we subtract that, then all the expenses . . ." Take this off, take this off and this off . . . "and your share is one hundred and fifty thousand dollars."

Long's payday, last seen at 20 percent, went from an already unacceptable $1.6 million to $150,000 in maybe a minute and a half.

He said, "You know what, Jimmy, this is no good, and

I'll tell you what I'm gonna do. I'm gonna have someone else come down and collect my money for me."

Jimmy drew a pistol, and placed the muzzle against Long's head.

"I like you, Allen," he said, "but I will kill you right now unless you take the money and agree to walk out the door."

Long's sunburned face surrendered its color. Something awful happened inside of him, something in Long of cellular origin. It seemed to rise in the germ plasm, a kind of genetic dread that had survived evolution, inflecting man's history as he ascended the food chain.

"Jimmy," he said, "I can't do it."

"Take the money."

Long stood up and turned around. Standing behind him was Dennis — inches away, in suspension, it seemed, like a barracuda at feeding time — holding an AR-15 aimed at his chest.

"Allen," said Dennis, extending a briefcase, "take the money."

The room was strung with invisible tension. Opposing vectors of excitement traversed it like the lines of force on a chessboard. The room, in low light, lugubrious at best, had assumed all the charm of a meat locker.

"Jimmy," said Long, "this wallpaper is new."

The wallpaper was silk. A pale silver silk moire. Jimmy's girlfriend had spent $3,700 for the job.

"Came out nice," Long said.

Jimmy narrowed his eyes. He shook his head.

"What the fuck, man, are you talking about?"

"It would be a shame to mess it up with my blood."

Jimmy smiled, said, "Allen, I like you. You are a good man, and you make me laugh. So, please, take the money. I do not want to, but I will kill you if I have to."

There was a very subtle point at issue. If Long took the money, he was accepting the deal. It was saying that Jimmy owed him nothing. He would not come back at Jimmy, or send someone else to do so. While Jimmy knew that Long was no gunman, he could not let him leave empty-handed and be sure that Long would not someday send someone to collect his money, or in some fashion close the books. And why, reasoned Jimmy, wait for a showdown? If Long did not take the money, better to kill him now.

Not so subtle was the coldness that came over Long in the echo of his own words, hearing himself advise Jimmy that he would send someone else to collect, a coldness that told him he was now one of them, in that instant, with that threat, a gangster himself. As he stood there, with weapons targeting him from opposite sides, it was his own behavior that startled him most.

"Allen, take this money, and we will talk about a percentage for you on the loads I do from now on."

"Jimmy, I don't think you're going to be doing any more loads. If you treat me like this, you're treating everybody like this. Nobody's going to work with you."

"Allen, please take the money."

"I don't want to die, so I'll take the money, but I'll never do business with you again."

"As you choose," Jimmy said.

He took the money, walked out of the house, and when the door closed behind him, it was over. In every real way it was finished.

Walking into the game a pioneer, Allen Long was now an anachronism.

The adventure was complete. He had seen it to a conclusion.

"Something funny?" said Jimmy, as he was showing him out.

"Me," said Long, unable to shake the absurd smile from his face. "It's me. It's what I was thinking. You wouldn't understand."

But he told Jimmy anyway, and he left the house laughing.

"I was just thinking," he said, "this would make a great movie."

EPILOGUE

There are three ways out of the dope business, the most dramatic of which will always be dying on the job. Of the other two, quitting while you are ahead or going to jail, the second is by far the more common. Those who have chosen the former — you have eaten in their restaurants, worn their sportswear, listened to music on their record labels, or maybe you have rented their real estate — are admittedly difficult to count. Those who have suffered the latter, they, and their customers, have provided 50 percent of the population of the nation's prisons over the last decade. Walking alive out of Jimmy's house that night, and faced with a choice between the two, Allen Long inevitably did both.

A little more than a year later, to use the words of JD Reed, "the dominoes started to fall." Of the North Americans involved in what the government would ultimately claim to be one of the larger marijuana-smuggling conspiracies of its time, virtually all wound up in prison.

*   *   *

Jake Myerson went down first. In 1982 his Ann Arbor operation was busted, and Myerson started cooperating. He was required to name names. Released from prison after serving three and a half years, he is the owner of a legitimate business and is a pillar of his community today.

Will McBride was doing business with Myerson when the feds closed Myerson down. Working with Canadian smugglers, he was landing boats in North Carolina and shipping the pot to Ann Arbor. Busted, McBride cooperated, and was required to name others. He served four years of a twelve-year sentence. McBride, who had "never wanted to be a farmer," said, "I always thought I'd be a rock and roll star, an astronaut, a movie star, a lawyer, or politician. I never expected to be an international criminal." Upon release from federal prison, accepting the opportunity presented by a friend, he went to work in advertising. He owns his own company today.

Frank Hatfield's participation in their enterprise was a few years behind him when he was arrested in 1984 on information provided by Myerson and McBride. He served three years of a five-year sentence. He fought to retain his pilot's license, but the license has done him no good, the necessary medical certificate being impossible to come by because his conviction is drug-related. "It was more beautiful than any woman I'd ever met," he recalled of the DC-3. "It was such a scammer's airplane. It saved our lives," he said. Acknowledged to be an extraordinary flyer by professionals who have heard of his exploits, today he drives a truck for a living.

Buddy Blanchard, in exchange for his cooperation, was allowed to plead guilty in U.S. Court to two counts of tax

fraud, on which he served reduced jail time, and was required to surrender his license to practice law in Virginia.

JD Reed was arrested in 1984 on marijuana charges unrelated to his work with Long and the others. Busted on a Virginia indictment, convicted on the testimony of co-conspirators, he was sentenced to thirty years in prison, all but eleven of which were suspended. Unlike most with whom he had worked over the years, Reed refused to cooperate. While serving his state time, he was picked up and tried on federal charges, and sentenced under the government's racketeering statutes for engaging in a continuing criminal enterprise. After doing three years on his state conviction, he did nine years' federal time. Asked what he could have offered authorities in exchange for a lighter sentence, he answered with a look of bemusement. "I never got that far with them. I don't think that way," he said. Noting that he was never arrested for anything he did by himself, he hastened to add that nobody else was ever arrested because of him: "If it was a cop, I wouldn't give him up." He saw his capture as inevitable. The business got so big, he said, and there were so many amateurs working, that it was only a matter of time. Reed, who served hard time because he stood up, never held it against those who did not. Today he is self-employed, earning his living as a cabinetmaker. Reed's father, Luther, died of heart complications in 1985 after completing a five-year sentence on his federal conviction for manufacturing bootleg Quaaludes. He was fifty-nine years old.

Abe succumbed to cancer in 2000 at the age of sixty-five.

Miguel and his friend Dr. Pablo Cepeda today earn their money legitimately. Neither was ever arrested.

Gilberto, the Colombian behind all the marijuana Long distributed out of Miami, was murdered on the Guajira sometime in the 1980s. His prominence and his estimated $100 million in cash, according to what Long was told, made him the target of leftist guerrillas, and refusing to pay their protection money, he was killed in a shoot-out with their forces during an assault they made on his farm.

Samuel Calderón Sanchez was gunned down outside his house in Barranquilla.

Raúl Gaviria escaped prosecution when the Black Tuna Gang was busted in Miami. He lives in Colombia, a prominent member of a politically influential family with lucrative commercial interests.

María, escaping marriage to an American dope smuggler, went on to marry the Colombian version. Today she is the mother of five children. To Long's knowledge she has never seen Paris.

Tony A., who had retired from the dope business, was arrested in 1982 on charges arising out of his reluctant response to a call for aid from his relative Hector, who had not. Tony served seven years of a twelve-year sentence. Hector escaped to Spain, where he lives today. Tony remains the only man Allen Long knows ever arrested for cattle rustling. Deer hunting on Florida panhandle property owned by his partner Lonnie's family, Tony and his pals shot a cow that had found its way into the woods, or an "Italian deer!"

as Frank A. exclaimed, being the first to draw a bead on the creature. Testing new ordnance for the CIA — they were hunting with automatic weapons — they managed only to wound the cow. By the time they caught up with the animal, it had walked as far as a local church, outside of which it finally collapsed dead. The local sheriff, who had always had it in for these troublemakers, one of whom, according to Tony, had been sleeping with the lawman's wife, threw them all in jail. It was a nuisance arrest more than anything. Nobody was surprised when the government showed up and squared things away. Today Tony is a successful real estate developer in Miami.

Lonnie, a former Miami police officer, was arrested on un-related drug trafficking charges while Tony was in prison. He drew a sixty-year sentence, and is still incarcerated.

Frank A., arrested in 1982 on tax-evasion charges, is believed to have turned state's evidence. He disappeared from the minimum security lockup at Eglin Air Force Base in Florida, presumably entering the federal Witness Security Program under an identity provided by the government. Only the U.S. marshals know where he is.

Jack, Tony's CIA handler, suffered a heart attack at his law office in 1989, just as the DEA was moving in on him, and died a few months thereafter, never having regained consciousness. He was fifty-five.

Virgil was never arrested. Having quit while he was ahead, he is a wealthy man today, with substantial holdings in South Florida.

Jimmy Alvarez is still in business.

El Coyote was never seen by Long after their trip to Guadalajara.

Ives, erstwhile saloon owner and documentary film producer, whom Long had not seen in more than twenty years, was, in Long's words, "still clipping coupons" — living on the proceeds of his stock portfolio — when Long in 1998 ran into him walking on West 57th Street in Manhattan.

Pomeroy was last seen by Long at the helm of a sailboat off Sausalito in 1988. He had just launched a business bottling and distributing a new brand of spring water.

Easy Matthews was convicted in 1990 on tax and drug charges unrelated to his work with Long, and served two years of a four-year federal sentence. A successful family man, and the owner of an equally successful, legitimate business today, he still drives the same car he was driving when Long first met him in Richmond in 1974, a four-door sedan that was eight years old even then.

Myles, Matthews's partner, sentenced in 1990 on charges of pot distribution and tax evasion, served 27 months at Eglin, where he enjoyed himself immensely. "If I had kids, any one of these guys, I'd let them baby-sit," he said of the people he did time with. This he said to his mother in a phone call from the facility. "On the outside," he told the parole board, just prior to his release, "I was working eighty hours a week. In here I'm working thirty." Today he distributes T-shirts to the tune of $30 million a year.

Lee Carlyle in 1983 took up alligator farming in Sebring, Florida. In 1999 he was arrested, having found his way back into the marijuana business, and is currently serving a federal sentence.

Cherie Harris, after she and Long split up, enjoyed a brief career as a model, discovering that she could "be successful without being a star." As a client of Wilhelmina and subsequently Ford, she did well on the commercial side of the business. "I put braces on my sister, a fence around my momma's house." In 1990 she returned to Richmond. Today she is married and the mother of a ten-year-old son.

The trajectory of Long's career was a predictable one. It followed pretty faithfully the breaking curve of pot smuggling's passage through the culture as an indulgence of the aficionado. Long was one of numerous gringos who all walked away at about the same time to leave dope trafficking to the professional felonry. No less predictable was the retirement package with which Long departed the business.

Jimmy's 80,000 pounds had arrived in Miami a week before Christmas 1980. Earlier that year Long and Cherie had finally put an end to things, and Long had since taken up with a young Fort Lauderdale businesswoman, a former girlfriend of Carlyle's. She and Long had been sharing a house for about a month when Long walked out of Jimmy's. Of the $150,000 that Jimmy gave him that night, Long owed half to Miguel, who was waiting for him in Aruba. With Miguel's $75,000 in a briefcase, Long left home the following day, flew to Aruba, delivered the money, stayed a couple of nights on the island, and when he returned to Fort Lauderdale

the house was empty, the safe was empty, and the young businesswoman had stolen his half of the one-fifty.

With that, Long returned to New York, knowing little more at the time than what he did *not* want to do with the rest his life, but before he departed South Florida, he took a shot at earning some necessary seed money.

He had been approached by a guy named Vargas, a Miami Cuban who had been directed to him through Gilberto's people on the Guajira. Vargas had a load in. He had 15,000 pounds that he needed to off. Long, in need of cash, and agreeing now to move the load, reached out to Carlyle, who arranged for delivery of the marijuana to a warehouse in Pompano Beach. The warehouse was one of a series of storage bays and other businesses, auto repair places and the like, set back from the road surrounding a parking area on the edge of a palmetto swamp. Long and Carlyle took delivery at night, and the following morning, Long, with JD Reed in the car — it was the day Reed's probation ended on his Newport Beach conviction — drove into the facility surprised to find that none of the businesses was open. The parking area was empty but for the presence of a refreshment cart at which two men in sunglasses were drinking coffee.

"There's definitely something wrong here."

"It don't look right," muttered Reed.

Long, circling the car, left the place without stopping.

The police report told the story:

The night before, unknown to Long and Carlyle as they were inside weighing the pot, a pair of homeless, yet nonetheless civic-minded, alcoholics were camped out with a bottle up against the rear wall of the storage bay. Like most of the nation's citizens, especially those registered voters within the municipal orbit of Miami, these two American taxpayers appreciated the meaning of expressions like "really good

shit," and overhearing the smugglers' conversation, they reported it to the police, who that morning set up a command center in the diner across the street.

Once it became clear that no one was going to claim the marijuana, the cops moved in and seized it.

Long called Vargas.

Vargas said, "Somebody has to come to Miami and explain this."

When Long showed up for the meeting, he was thrown into a car by Vargas's men, driven to a house on the edge of the Everglades, and dumped on the floor.

Vargas put a revolver on him.

"Where is my money, you motherfucker?"

"Kill him!" urged the others present, brandishing weapons of their own.

"Motherfucker, you stole my money!"

"Hey!" shouted Long. "I didn't steal anything."

"I am going to blow your fucking brains out!"

Vargas put a foot on Long's face, placed the barrel of the revolver behind Long's ear and cocked the hammer.

"Go ahead, blow my brains out. Kiss my ass. If you're gonna kill me, kill me. I didn't steal anything."

He handed Vargas the police report. He had hired a lawyer to obtain the report when a warrant was issued for the owner of the storage bay.

"You see it?" he asked Vargas.

Vargas saw it. He threw it aside.

"Fuck that," he said, "we are going to kill you."

But the twitch in Vargas's trigger finger lost some of its urgency as he pondered murdering for no reason now the only buyer he knew for any future shipments of pot.

Long said, "Why don't you get the Colombians over here. They own the pot. You guys haven't lost anything. It's the

Colombians who lost the load. It's their say whether somebody gets killed."

Vargas said okay.

Long had no idea who they were, but two Colombians eventually showed up, and the pair of them were straight off the Guajira: cowboy hats, no English, and neither of them capable of reading the police report Long was offering in support of his innocence. But Long walked them through the numbers, explained that it was an official document, and more than that, after that, he said, "Do you know Gilberto?"

Oh, yes. They knew Gilberto. Everybody knew Gilberto.

"Well, my name is Allen. Call Gilberto, and ask him about me."

No, Gilberto's name was enough. Calling him would not be necessary. The pot was not stolen, it was seized by the police. No problem, Long owed nothing. And the Colombians said so to Vargas.

Vargas and his associates apologized.

"Sorry, man . . ."

"Yeah . . ."

"Hey . . ."

"You know . . ."

Long was free to go.

The Colombians departed immediately, followed by Vargas's henchmen, one of whom, before leaving the house, tossed Long the keys to his car. The anthracite gray BMW sedan had been driven there by his kidnappers and was parked on the street out front. Long, left sitting there with Vargas after everyone else had gone, stood up and walked to the door. So quickly had everyone vanished that Vargas still had the gun in his hand. Vargas got to his feet, stuck the revolver back in his waistband, and then slowly he sat

back down, staring into the middle distance, his hands draped over the arms of an easy chair.

"Allen," he said, when Long opened the door.

"Yeah," said Long, before stepping outside.

"Allen, I don't have a ride home."

Long had the only car.

"Can you give me a ride?" Vargas asked.

Long drove Vargas home.

And Long was now out of the game.

But what happened that night in the Everglades, serving or not to enlighten him, was loaded with the freight of a parable. Examined even casually, it illustrates all you need to know about the dope business.

At the time, in Colombia, Pablo Escobar was in meteoric ascendancy. Escobar, the legendary architect of the Medellín cartel, was shot to death some twelve years later, and in the five years leading up to his eradication the streets of Colombia ran with the blood of the cocaine-financed murder of more than 60,000 people. The dead included more than a thousand police officers, sixty judges, seventy journalists, a governor, an attorney general, two cabinet ministers, and four of the six presidential candidates running in the campaign leading up to the 1990 national election. How many civil servants and public officials chose the *plata* (silver) over the *plomo* (lead) one could only speculate. Add to those naked statistics the fact that Allen Long on the floor of an Everglades house, with a foot on his face and a gun to his head, was waiting for salvation in the form of two strangers who, when they arrived, brought with them the comforting air of the Guajira. And all you need to know about the dope business is that the Colombians were the good guys.

*   *   *

With the arrest of Myerson and McBride, Allen Long became a federal fugitive, indicted on charges stemming from the original conspiracy and all the subsequent business he did with Myerson moving loads out of Miami. Long had moved back to New York by then, having made the decision to go straight.

In 1984 Long ceased to exist. For the next seven years he remained at large, a fugitive from justice, living under false identification. He supported himself by way of various legitimate jobs and the occasional small-time pot deal. A botched attempt to secure a passport — the papers held up, but Long did not; he bolted from the passport office in fear that he had drawn suspicion — led to a second identity change, and an outstanding arrest warrant on a charge of passport fraud. In 1987 he married a twenty-six-year-old German national he had met in the Caribbean. In December of that year his first son was born. In 1991, a year after his second son was born, the government finally caught up with him. He was arrested in Tampa, Florida.

The crimes that Long was wanted for were so far in the bureaucratic past that the prosecutors who inherited him saw very little political sunshine in the prospect of building a major case against him. There was no one for him to give up. Long was the last man standing. A plea agreement was in everyone's interest. In exchange for his pleading guilty to a federal marijuana trafficking conspiracy in the Middle District of Florida and passport fraud in the Virgin Islands, all other charges were dropped, and he was sentenced to five years in prison.

Officially considered a flight risk on the basis of his fugitive status, Long commenced his sentence in the maximum-security facility in Atlanta, one of the nation's tougher joints. Transferred eventually to medium-, then minimum-security

facilities, he was released from federal custody in 1995 after spending a year in pretrial detention and serving thirty months in prison. Having worked his way back into the music business, he lives today behind what he describes as "that white picket fence I always dreamed of," and attributes the current success he enjoys to the encouragement and support of his wife, to the second chance she gave him. "If it hadn't been for Simone, I would never have gotten where I am now." She and their children, Matthew and Sean, are "the real reward of my life," he says. The family lives in Virginia.

ACKNOWLEDGMENTS

The author first ran across this story as it was happening. The project, as proposed to him then, was a book very much of its time. Had it been written then, as a report from the front, it would have been in some ways ahead of its time, its journalistic value amplified by a wealth of inside infor-mation. The story would have been newsworthy, possessed inherently of an instructive edge, enlightening as a result of its immediacy. Now, any shock value the material holds, if any at all, derives from simple historical throw weight. That a loaded, top-of-the-line BMW could once be had brand-new for $17,000 is a good bet, one supposes, to liven up, however briefly, the national conversation.

Allen Long, over the course of his career, in addition to the Mexican pot, the Jamaican ganja, and the Thai weed he managed to smuggle, moved 972,000 pounds of pot out of Colombia. That is a lot of dope by any standard. The $8 million he made doing it, to be fully appreciated, must be measured against a standard that existed when you could put yourself in the leather and walnut interior of a

high-performance German sedan for a fifth of what it costs today.

The book presents a story from out of a time and place fogged in not only by the passage of years, but by an atmospheric shift in the political and cultural spirit of a generation. The effort to illuminate that time and place absorbed most of the research muscle applied to the book, and was made more challenging by circumstances inherent in the material. First, the people whose story it is, when not trying to reinterpret it, have spent the ensuing years trying to forget that time in their lives, and second, even at their most willing, have had to admit to being completely stoned while much of it was going down.

Unlike other, more famous American fortunes, Allen Long's was made illegally. Certain participants in the crimes reported cooperated in the writing of the book on the condition that their real names not be used. Those who sought such cover did so not to avoid incriminating themselves — they have been prosecuted for their crimes, and their convictions are a matter of record — but to spare themselves and their families the negative personal and professional consequences of what they consider to be ancient history. Accordingly, some names have been changed. Allen Long's is not one of them.

Because the need to protect their identities makes it impossible to thank them individually, the author wishes to thank collectively all those people who shared their stories. In the absence of their trust and generosity the story could not have been told. The author is particularly grateful to Cherie Harris, whose faith in the project was exceeded by no one's, and who, as the first to believe, was responsible in large part for originally bringing the author and the material together.

For their help in the preparation of the manuscript, for the research material they provided, or for other personal and professional efforts in support of the project, the author wishes to thank: Vincent Amicosante; Marjorie Braman; Arlene Burchell; Rosalba Butler; Patrick Cavanaugh; Bruce Fishelman; Michael Gochenour; Ryan Harbage; Myra Hicks; Joe Lewis; Russ Maguire; Jay Mandel; Marianne McCaffery; Ross McDonald; David Riley; Dianne Ripley; Richard Rosenthal; Jamie Saul; Andy Valvur; and Amy Weinberg. Specific acknowledgment is due Mary Ryan, particularly for her guidance; no one lived with this project through more changes than she.

Were it not for Jennifer Rudolph Walsh, this book would have remained nothing more than a notion, an idea for a book, forever. She made it real by decree. The force of her magic is absolute. It is hard to imagine anything she cannot do, and one of the more terrifying manifestations of her sorcery is that once you surrender to her power, it is hard to imagine anything you cannot do. Were it not for Michael Pietsch, who invigorated and constantly dignified the process that led to its completion, the enterprise would have been unworthy of the effort. His contribution to this book is immeasurable; in the absence of his participation its vision would never have been realized.

The story itself should demonstrate that whatever Allen Long has to prove in this life, it is not his courage. But nothing he has done up to now proves it better than his agreement to do this book. Given the opportunity to hide behind a pseudonym, he declined. He is not naive to any of the implications of his decision, or to the consequences it holds for his family. The author wishes to thank him for his faith, his patience, and for the hours he sacrificed in the struggle to get the story right, and to thank his wife, Simone,

and his sons, Matthew and Sean, for so graciously indulging the chronic interruption of their lives that writing the book forced upon them.

Special thanks is owed the following people, in default of whose assistance the author would still be sending up flares. On a different field of combat they would be awarded medals for valor; in action on another planet — call it Hollywood — they would be suing for production credits: Walter Bastian, whose lighting the way into Latin America was merely the most visible of his contributions. His encouragement and enthusiasm, mobilized here as behind every enterprise, no matter how slight, make showing up for work worthwhile even on the worst of days; because he is paying attention, you want to look good *all* the time. Thomas Butler, whose place in the scheme of things is inexpressible in all but the dead languages. *Semper honos nomenque tuum laudesque manebunt.* Sara Nelson, whose untiring friendship has occupied the horizon like a hospital ship, unqualified year after year. No man has ever had a greater ally, a surer source of aid and comfort, or more reliable source of intelligent counsel. Her generosity and that of her husband, Akira Yoshimura, can never be amply rewarded. Philip Richardson, who managed to insinuate himself into the project in so many different ways that his contribution to its success, difficult enough to quantify, is that much more difficult to qualify. His talents are kaleidoscopic. Watching his mind at work is like walking through the Renaissance with a fever. The first phone call was always to him. Stephen Sullivan, that rare friend who can articulate the first-person pleasures of flying at twice the speed of sound; rarer still, a friend whose idea of fun, when flying that fast, is to do it upside down. The author and a grateful nation wish to thank him for not doing it stoned. To him and his wife,

Rebecca, for their confidence in him and their encouragement of him not to give up and seek honest work, the author
is deeply in debt; without them, this book would not have
been written. And finally, preeminently, for that which defies
the power of all alphabets to specify, Patricia Riley. She is
the music you hear in the background.

INDEX

Abe, 92–93, 113, 381
  and Reed, 118
abrazo, 42, 203
Aerocondor Airlines, 370
Aeschylus, 254
aistrip, in Colombia *see* Perico
Alejandro, 51, 53, 56
ALL Air, Inc., 129, 130
almuerzo, 236–37
Altamont, 287
Alvarez, Jimmy, 318–19, 321–22, 348, 364, 366, 371, 372, 374, 384
  disenchantment with, 331–36
Andreas, 321, 344
Andrés Pérez, Carlos, 164
Angie (Miami police sargeant), 298
Ann Arbor, Michigan, 93, 109–10

marijuana market in, 113, 230, 288
Ann Arbor Sun, 110, 115
Aracataca, Colombia, 237, 239–40, 291
Aristotle, 254
Armando, 238, 261, 268, 270
Aronow, Don, 296
Aruba, 168, 169, 385
Aspen, Colorado, 87, 108–109
Atlantic Records, 106
Augusto, 271–72, 280

Bahía Profundo, 155, 242
Baranquilla, Colombia, 135–36, 236, 372
Bassett, Leslie, 23
Bassett, Steve, 106
Bay of Pigs, 282, 319
Benito (cabdriver), 136, 138

Bertram boats, 296, 366, 372, 374, 375
Big Jim, 72, 84
Billboard, 106
Billy (off-loader), 221, 224
Black Tuna Gang, 155, 382
Blanchard, Buddy, 129–30, 227, 380
Blonde on Blonde (Dylan), 23
Bogotá, Colombia, 266, 268
Braniff Airways, 197
brotherhood, birth of, 207
The Byrds, 24

C-47 Skytrain, 20, 128
   see also DC-3
cachaca, 268
Cactus Jack, 101
Caesars Palace, 309
Calderón Sanchez, Samuel, 365, 367, 369, 372, 382
caleta, 147, 182
California
   logistics of load to, 354–55
   off-loading in, 360, 363
   opening market in, 311
Camarones, Colombia, 146
Capone, Al, 17
Capote, Truman, 306
Carlyle, Lee, 294, 311–12, 329–30, 348, 385
   and coke, 233, 234
   drug habit of, 315, 323
   in Mexican pot trade, 46–48, 48–49, 63
   and Myerson, 314–15, 329–30

start as smuggler, 45
cash
   as cargo, 327–28
   problems with, 326, 327–28, 341–42, 344–45
Castro, Fidel, 282
CBS Records, 104, 106, 336, 337
Central Intelligence Agency (CIA), 170, 298, 317, 318–19, 367
   clandestine operations of, 292
   and Cuban exiles, 282
   role in dope trade, 282
Cepeda, Pablo (El Demonio), 140, 143, 149, 155, 265–67, 382
   in United States, 307
Chase Manhattan Bank, Panama, 359
Chateau Lafite-Rothschild, 45, 371
checkpoints, security, 140
   see also roadblocks
Chicago distributors, 46–47, 64
cigarette boat, 296
coastal freighters, Colombian, 295, 296
cocaine, 264, 317, 375
   see also Long, Allen
   cartels, mercilessness of, 370
   cultivation in Colombia, 169
   development of

Colombian trade in, 350
money in, 328
negative karma of, 85, 233–34
at Perico, 209
and pot, incompatibility of, 233
price of, 232
small market for in seventies, 234
cockfighting, 365
code of silence, 89
coffee, Colombian, as contraband, 168
Cohn, Roy, 306
Colombia
cocaine trade in, 169, 350, 389
drug interdiction in, 253, 263, 363
drug use in, 185
internal customs system in, 140
marital fidelity in, 238
narcoeconomy of, 153, 168–69, 171, 350
quality of marijuana from, 112, 236, 291
value of marijuana from, 115
Colombian Coffee Federation, 169
Columbia Records, 106
Concorde, 267
connections, protection of, 88, 164–65

conspicuous consumption, significance of, 314
conspiracy laws, 160, 355
Constance (housekeeper), 302
contraband, branding of, 205
costeños, 169, 268
Counts Four, 24
course of smuggling flight, 6, 196–97, 212–22
courtesy, among smugglers, 327
covering losses, conventions for, 202
El Coyote, 29–31, 32–40, 42–43, 47, 384
crooks, culture of, 42, 165, 228, 327, 329
Crosby, 30–31, 35–36, 38
Cuban Americans, in South Florida dope trade, 111, 282
Cuban exiles, and CIA, 282
"Cuban way", 281, 312
Culiacán, Mexico, 46
Dante Alighieri, 260
Darlington International Raceway, South Carolina, 211, 215, 217, 220
Davie, Florida, 294–95, 299, 311, 320
Davis, Angela, 353
Davis-Monthan Air Force Base, 128, 181
DC-3, 20, 128, 157, 173
auxiliary fuel tanks of, 181

durability of, 195–96
fuel requirements for, 141
identification marks of,
246
Long's purchase of, 128
operation of, 197–98
use of parts of in
Colombia, 171
DC-4, 358
Del Prado Hotel,
Baranquilla, 136
Del Río, 270, 271, 275,
278–80
deniability, function of, 339
Dennis, 326, 332, 376
Department of Defense, 358
deus ex machina, defined,
254
Don Enrique, 331, 333–36
Don Julio, 150–52, 266
Donzi boat, 296
The Doors, 352
dope business
conventions in, 202, 327
US currency in, 327
double cutouts, system of, 299
Douglas Aircraft Company,
20, 181, 195–96
Drug Enforcement
Administration (DEA),
127, 350
and Colombian drug inter-
diction, 263
in Florida, 289
New York headquarters
of, 352
drug interdiction, 7, 140,
296, 350, 375

Colombian, 253, 263, 363
costs of, 350
drug trade
attractions of, 209,
210–11, 343–44
as business, 100–102, 283
logistics of in South
Florida, 294–95
and music industry, 106
risks of, 174, 259, 344
turnover in, 102–103
volume in, 100
Dwayne, 332
Dylan, Bob, 23, 24

Eclair camera, 51, 52, 60
Eglin Air Force Base, 383,
384
emeralds, 168
Epic Records, 337
Ernesto, 10, 20, 146, 149,
152, 174, 178, 183, 185,
186, 204, 207, 209, 337,
358
and cocaine, 233
Escobar, Pablo, 389
Euripides, 254
Eurotrash, 108
executive jet, Long's use of,
344–46

F-4 Phantom jets, 218–19
FAA investigators, 246, 358
Falstaff, 228
FBO operator, 243–44, 247
Federal Bureau of
Investigation (FBI), 353
federal drug profile, 87

Filipe (cousin of Benito), 136
finca
  of Jimmy Alvarez, 366, 371
  of Pablo Cepeda, 261
La Finca de Don Jaime (Jimmy's Place), 366, 371
firearms, absence of in pot culture, 16
five-dollar herb law, Ann Arbor, 110
Fleurette, 72, 83
flight operation
  briefing for, 173
  logistics of, 157–58
Forcade, Tom, 234
Ford Agency, 385
Formula boat, 296
Fort Lauderdale Executive Airport, 345
Francisco (uncle of Tomás), 57–58, 73
Frank A., 295, 298, 317, 383
Fuchs, Howie, 89, 90, 95
fuel gaskets, 181

gangster tactics, 332, 335
ganja, 117
García Márquez, Gabriel, 239
Gaviria, Raúl, 155, 242–43, 270, 280, 358–59, 382
gifts, to Colombians, 170–71, 246, 260
Gilberto, 312, 316, 382, 388
go-fast boats, 296, 375

The Godfather, 83
greed and self-preservation, primacy of, 228
gringos, doing business with, 138
ground operations manual, 158, 171–72
ground-to-air radio, 175
Guadalajara, Mexico, 32, 33, 35
Guajira, 5, 167
  drug interdiction on, 7, 253, 363
  gun culture of, 10, 17, 174, 184–85, 277
Río Guasare, 272, 280

Hammond, John, 106
Harris, Cherie, 95–97, 126, 230, 245, 304, 307, 385
  and Long's cocaine addiction, 338–39, 340–41
  relationship with Long, 304–305, 339–41, 385
hash oil, 117–18, 230
Hatfield, Frank, 5, 7–13, 17–21, 123–25, 130, 243, 356–57, 380
  escape from Colombia of, 256–67
Hathaway, 158, 172, 193
Hatteras boat, 296
Hawthorne School, 23–24
Hector (relative of Tony A.), 285, 367, 373, 382
helicopter, lease of, 360
Hell's Angels Motorcycle Club, 68

High Times magazine, 234, 263, 306

"holes", 298

Holiday Inn, midtown Manhattan, 352

honor, among crooks, 89, 228, 320, 329

hot list, FAA, 247

Howard Johnson Motor Lodge, New York, 353

hypoxia and night vision, 197

Indian Springs, nuclear test site at, 107

Inferno, 260

Ingram MAC-10 submachine gun, 326

International System of Units, 45

Irotama Hotel, Santa Marta, 140, 242, 373

Ives, 32, 62, 66, 86, 384

Jack, 283, 292–93, 316, 318, 383

Jagger, Mick, 287

jail, attitude about, 127, 232

Jeff, 90–91, 103–104, 109, 113
   see also Myerson, Jake

Jeppesen Airport and Information Directory (J-AID), 157

Jesús, 47–49

Johnson, Hillary, 108

Jupiter, Florida, 311

Kennedy, John F., assassination of, 285

Key Largo, 298, 320

kidnapping, 324

Knoxville Metropolitan Airport, 247

Lake of Wells, Nevada, 107

Las Vegas, Nevada, 355
   money laundering in, 345

Little Eddie, 88, 95, 136, 300

Long, Allen
   career in filmmaking, 29, 48–49, 50, 62–63, 62–65, 69–70
   childhood of, 27
   cocaine addiction of, 60–61, 215, 216, 232–33, 302, 325, 338–41
   as deal maker, 209, 256–57, 289
   death threat to, 319–20, 376–77
   disillusionment of, 331–36, 346–47, 347
   earnings of, 245
   enters marijuana trade, 73–80, 349
   escape from Colombia, 265–80
   as fugitive, 390
   grandfather of, 27, 309
   legitimate career of, 104–105, 106–107, 336–37
   lifestyle of, 344–45, 347, 390

personality of, 216–17, 309

plea bargain, 390

relationship with Cherie Harris, 304–305, 339–41, 385

in Richmond, 95

as Spanish speaker, 137, 264

threat on life of, 206–207

youth of, 23–27

Long, John, 28, 304

Long, Tom, 231–32, 310–11

Long Manufacturing Company, 28, 310

Long T46, 28

Lonnie, 312, 320–21, 382–83

Lundvall, Bruce, 337

McBride, Will, 5, 101, 107, 123, 124–25, 126, 156, 243, 356–57, 380

arrest of, 390

escape from Colombia of, 256–67

McCarthy, Joseph, 306

MacDill Air Force Base, 216

McGuinn, Jim, 24

machismo

in drug trade, 81

on the Guajira, 14, 183–84

Magdalena River, Colombia, 135

Magnum Marine boat, 296

Maracaibo, Venezuela, 162, 200, 270, 280

Long and Myerson in, 162–63

María, 146, 154–55, 237, 242, 265–80, 358–59, 382

mariachis, 36–38

marijuana

Colombian economic dependence on, 171

cultivation of, 57–59, 169

distribution of, 93–94, 100–101, 300–301

forest of in Sabana Rubia, 277–78

harvest of, 51

increase in trade of, 286, 350

law in Ypsilanti, Michigan, 110–11

off-loading of, 73–80

packaging of, 225, 237

price of, 289, 290, 295

processing of, 147–48

profits from, 312

quality of Colombian, 112, 236, 290

subculture of, 16, 48

symbolic nature of, 25

from Thailand, 112

types of Colombian, 112

"marimba", 151

marimberos, 151

Marin County, California, 69, 82–83

marital fidelity in Colombia, 238

Martínez, Joey, 54–56, 59, 62–63

Mary Lou's, 303

Matthews, Easy, 100, 102,
114, 309, 311, 327, 354,
384
Maxwell's Plum, 307
Medellín cartel, 389
metric system *see*
International System of
Units
Miami
gun culture in, 16–17,
326, 332, 334
nightlife in, 313
police department, 283,
292–93
Miguel, 140, 145, 149, 165,
204, 207, 234, 264, 353,
382
Miguel, Sr., 167
military, Venezuelan, 164
military patrols, Colombian,
258, 261, 274, 276–77
mink coats as sexual bribes,
303
mochila, 277
Moisés, 139–40, 145, 167
mona, 112, 143
Mona Passage, 284
Morrison, Jim, 352
Motion Associates, 29, 66,
104
music industry and drugs,
106
Myerson, Jake, 193–94, 224,
225–26, 227–28, 230,
288, 290, 295–96, 349,
354, 380
see also Jeff
arrest of, 390

and Carlyle, 314–15, 325,
329–30
courtesy of, 327
as financier of Colombian
trip, 119–22, 131
and Jimmy, 325, 326
to Maracaibo meeting,
163
Myles (partner of Easy
Matthews), 100, 384

Narco Avionics, 175
Neighborhood Playhouse,
304
Nemperor Records, 337, 340
Newton, Wayne, 230
night, flying at, 197
N-number, 246–47
North Carolina, spring
climate of, 196
Northern California, pot
market in, 311

off-loading
after second trip, 221,
222, 225
basic rule of, 172–73,
186
in California, 360, 363
failure of, 188–89,
201–202
logistics of, 157–58,
172–73, 211–12
of Mexican marijuana,
73–80
payoff for, 225–26, 228
in South Florida, 297
One Hundred Years of

Solitude – Cien Años de Soledad (García Márquez), 239
Operation Stopgap, 350
oxygen, use of in flight, 197

"the Pacific trip", 352–63
Río Palomino, 5, 146, 253, 261
Pan Am conversion, 181
passport fraud, 263, 390
Patton, George S., 209
pay phones, 92–93, 156, 161–62
  security protocol for, 159–60, 160–61
Perico, 148, 167, 171, 174, 182, 186, 209, 356, 307
perico, 186
pilots
  brotherhood among, 244–45, 248
  dress of, 196–97
Piper Navajo Chieftain airplane, 101
Pituro Uno, bust of, 363
  purchase of, 359
Plazuela de los Mariachis, Guadalajara, 35–36, 44
police
  department, Miami, 283, 292–93, 298–99
  former officers of in dope trade, 283, 286
Pomeroy, 68–69, 69–71, 82, 233, 384
Port Antonio, Jamaica, 354
Portete Bay, 253

pot and cocaine, incompatibility of, 233
pot smokers, number of in Seventies, 5, 84
power boats, production, 296, 366, 372
Puerto Galeón Hotel, Santa Marta, 153
punta roja, 112, 153, 351

Quaaludes, 65, 224, 315, 323, 325, 346, 355
Quicksilver Messenger Service, 71–72

Radio and Records Convention, Dallas, 337
Real-to-Reel Productions, 345
Reed, JD, 97–99, 107, 108, 112, 116, 179–82, 191, 340, 355, 379, 380–81
  and Abe, 118
  and coke, 232–33, 233
  in Colombia, 136–45
  as off-loading expert, 211, 262
Reed, Luther, 212, 222–24, 382
Ricardo (cousin of Pablo Cepeda), 270, 280
Richmond Times-Dispatch, 205
Riohacha, Colombia, 140, 162, 253, 367, 373
rip-offs, in marijuana trade, 287, 288–89, 299, 347
Rita, 49, 63

roadblocks, 261, 271, 361
rock concerts, filming, 104
Rockwell Jet Commander
    airplane, 345–46
ruana (poncho), 271, 277
Rubell, Steve, 305
rubia, 112, 143
rubia de la costa, 143

Sabana Rubia, 269, 277–79,
    280, 291
Santa Marta, Colombia, 135,
    140
Santa Marta Gold, 5, 112,
    115, 143, 152
    price of, 153
Santiago (Colombian
    middleman), 364, 373
Schrager, Ian, 305
Sierra de Perija, 271
Sierra Nevada de Santa
    Marta, 5, 112, 152, 200,
    239, 272
Sikorsky S-64 Skycrane, 360
sixties, marijuana culture of,
    16, 25–2, 114, 314
smuggling
    brotherhood in, 307
    channels of affiliation in,
        88
    increased volume of,
        311–14
    risks of, 174, 259, 344
    situation ethics in, 228–29
    thrill of, 209, 210–11,
        343–44
    volume in 1976 of, 253
    and waiting, 76–78

smuggling trip, first to
    Colombia, 175–90
    mistakes of, 192–94
Sony Trinitron, 171
Sophocles, 254
South Florida
    dope trade, 282
    logistics of drug trade in,
        294–95
    off-loading in, 297
    volume of traffic in,
        295–96
South Hill, Virginia, 2728
souvenir T-shirts, 263
sport-fishing boats, ubiquity
    of, 297
stash house, 295, 299–300
state troopers, Florida, 301
Studio 54, 305–306, 313
Summer of Love, 25, 71
"Sweet Virginia Breeze", 106

T-6 trainer, 73, 76, 80
telephone records, prosecu-
    tors' use of, 160
Tepic, Mexico, 57–59, 73
Teterboro Airport, New
    Jersey, 92
Tex, 73, 76, 80
Thailand, marijuana from,
    112
"the man", 137–38
Thompson, Robbin, 106,
    336
El Tigre (Del Río's man),
    278
Tomás (street hustler,
    Mazatlán), 57

Tony A., 255, 281, 288, 316, 382
boat trip from Colombia, 284
Tourneau, 246
Trade-A-Plane, 124, 128
transmigration, of souls, 117
Trident, Sausalito, 72, 83
Truman, Harry S., 23

Upper Matecumbe key, 330
U.S. Coast Guard, 297, 350, 375
U.S. currency
in Colombia, 136–37
in dope business, 327
as wallpaper, 240
U.S. Customary System of measurement, 45
U.S. Customs, 350

Valledupar, Colombia, 354, 359, 360, 362, 363
Vargas, 386–89
Variations for Orchestra (Bassett), 23
Victoria Station restaurant, 312
Villa, Pancho, 58
Villanueva, Colombia, 270, 272–73

Virgil, 286, 287, 295, 312, 329–30, 342, 349, 383
Virginia Commonwealth University, 95
Virginia Youth for Goldwater, 27
Volvo engines, 203

Wadleigh, Michael, 51
Warhol, Andy, 306
Watergate burglary, 282
Wayne, John, 308
weather interference, 215–16
Weiss, Nat, 336
Welch, Raquel, 308
Wexler, Jerry, 106
Wilhelmina Agency, 304, 385
Winterland, 72, 83
Witness Security Program, 383
Woodstock, 25
Woodstock (film), 51

Xenon, 306

Yetnikoff, Walter, 337
youth vote, in Ann Arbor, 110
Ypsilanti, Michigan, marijuana law, 111